CW00794042

# Jaguar/Daimler 12-cylinder Owners Workshop Manual

Peter G Strasman

**Models covered**
Jaguar XJ12 and Sovereign
Jaguar XJS, including XJSC (Cabriolet)
Daimler Double Six, including Vanden Plas
Series 1, 2 & 3 with 5343 cc V12 engine

*Does not cover E-type or XJS Convertible*

**ISBN 1 85010 437 9**

© Haynes Publishing Group 1992

All rights reserved. No part of this book may be reproduced or transmitted in any form or by any means, electronic or mechanical, including photocopying, recording or by any information storage or retrieval system, without permission in writing from the copyright holder.

Printed in England *(478-1U3)*

ABCDE
FGHIJ
KLMN

2

Haynes THE BOOK ®

**Haynes Publishing**
Sparkford Nr Yeovil
Somerset BA22 7JJ England

**Haynes Publications, Inc**
861 Lawrence Drive
Newbury Park
California 91320 USA

**British Library Cataloguing in Publication Data**

Strasman, Peter G, *1923–*
Jaguar/Daimler 12-cylinder models owners workshop manual.
1. Cars. Maintenance & repair – Amateurs' manuals
I. Title II. Series
629.28'722
ISBN 1-85010-437-9

# Acknowledgements

Thanks are due to Jaguar Cars for the provision of technical information and for the use of certain illustrations. The Champion Sparking Plug Company supplied the illustrations showing the various spark plug conditions. Duckhams Oils supplied the lubrication data.

Thanks are also due to all of those people at Sparkford who helped in the production of this manual.


# About this manual

### *Its aim*

The aim of this manual is to help you get the best value from your car. It can do so in several ways. It can help you decide what work must be done (even should you choose to get it done by a garage), provide information on routine maintenance and servicing, and give a logical course of action and diagnosis when random faults occur. However, it is hoped that you will use the manual by tackling the work yourself. On simpler jobs it may even be quicker than booking the car into a garage and going there twice to leave and collect it. Perhaps most important, a lot of money can be saved by avoiding the costs the garage must charge to cover its labour and overheads.

The manual has drawings and descriptions to show the function of the various components so that their layout can be understood. Then the tasks are described and photographed in a step-by-step sequence so that even a novice can do the work.

### *Its arrangement*

The manual is divided into thirteen Chapters, each covering a logical sub-division of the vehicle. The Chapters are each divided into Sections, numbered with single figures, eg 5; and the Sections into paragraphs (or sub-sections), with decimal numbers following on from the Section they are in, eg 5.1, 5.2, 5.3 etc.

It is freely illustrated, especially in those parts where there is a detailed sequence of operations to be carried out. There are two forms of illustration: figures and photographs. The figures are numbered in sequence with decimal numbers, according to their position in the Chapter – eg Fig. 6.4 is the fourth drawing/illustration in Chapter 6. Photographs carry the same number (either individually or in related groups) as the Section or sub-section to which they relate.

There is an alphabetical index at the back of the manual as well as a contents list at the front. Each Chapter is also preceded by its own individual contents list.

References to the 'left' or 'right' of the vehicle are in the sense of a person in the driver's seat facing forwards.

Unless otherwise stated, nuts and bolts are removed by turning anti-clockwise, and tightened by turning clockwise.

Vehicle manufacturers continually make changes to specifications and recommendations, and these, when notified, are incorporated into our manuals at the earliest opportunity.

**Whilst every care is taken to ensure that the information in this manual is correct, no liability can be accepted by the authors or publishers for loss, damage or injury caused by any errors in, or omissions from the information given.**

# Introduction to the Jaguar/Daimler V12

Without a doubt, these cars are designed for the connoisseur and enthusiast, and the maintenance and repair of them will require rather more than a basic knowledge of 'do it yourself' techniques.

The cars are conventional in every respect but due to their sheer size, and high standard of specification, most operations will require more time to carry out than would be the case with a more moderately sized vehicle. The inclusion of automatic transmission and power steering as standard on all models (manual transmission option on XJS only) increases the complication of major overhaul.

On the credit side, the fact that many mechanical and body parts are common to the XJ6/Sovereign range increases the chances of obtaining good secondhand components.

These cars have a certain something which gives a pride of ownership rarely found in other makes. Provided maintenance and tuning are meticulously carried out, the vehicles will not exhibit temperamental behaviour or unreliability in operation but will provide exhilarating performance as economically as their engine capacity allows.

The following production dates will prove useful if contemplating a used model.

### *Jaguar XJ12*

| | |
|---|---|
| July 1972 | Introduced, automatic transmission and power-assisted steering standard |
| October 1972 | Long wheelbase four-door saloon available |
| September 1973 | Series 2 long wheelbase saloon and new 2-door Coupe launched. Coupe has air conditioning as standard |
| April 1975 | Fuel injection supersedes carburettor fuel system on all models |
| November 1977 | Coupe discontinued |
| March 1979 | Series 3 saloon introduced. GM400 automatic transmission supersedes Borg Warner type |

### *Daimler Double Six*

The production dates follow very closely those for the Jaguar XJ12 except that in September 1972, the Vanden Plas version was introduced.

### *Jaguar XJS*

| | |
|---|---|
| September 1975 | Introduced with Coupe styling. Fuel injection, automatic transmission and air conditioning standard. Four-speed manual gearbox optionally available. |
| March 1979 | GM400 automatic transmission supersedes Borg Warner type |

# Contents

Daimler Double Six Vanden Plas Series 2 saloon

Jaguar XJ12 Series 3 saloon

Jaguar XJ12 saloon – N. American specification

Jaguar XJS Coupé

# General dimensions, weights and capacities

## Overall dimensions

### *Jaguar XJ12/Daimler Double Six (excluding N America)*

**4-door models (Series 1 and 2)**

| | |
|---|---|
| Length | 194.7 in (494.5 cm) |
| Width | 69.7 in (177.0 cm) |
| Height | 54.1 in (137.4 cm) |
| Wheelbase | 113.1 in (287.3 cm) |
| Track (front) | 58.0 in (147.3 cm) |
| Track (rear) | 58.6 in (148.8 cm) |
| Ground clearance | 7.0 in (17.8 cm) |

**4-door models (Series 3)**

| | |
|---|---|
| Length | 195.3 in (496.1 cm) |
| Width | 69.7 in (177.0 cm) |
| Height | 54.1 in (137.4 cm) |
| Wheelbase | 112.8 in (286.5 cm) |
| Track (front) | 58.3 in (148.0 cm) |
| Track (rear) | 58.9 in (149.6 cm) |
| Ground clearance | 7.0 in (17.8 cm) |

**2-door models (1973 to 1977)**

| | |
|---|---|
| Length | 190.7 in (484.4 cm) |
| Width | 69.7 in (177.0 cm) |
| Height | 54.1 in (137.4 cm) |
| Wheelbase | 109.1 in (277.1 cm) |
| Track (front) | 58.0 in (147. 3 cm) |
| Track (rear) | 58.6 in (148.8 cm) |
| Ground clearance | 7.0 in (17.8 cm) |

### *Jaguar XJ12 (N America)*

**4-door models (1972)**

| | |
|---|---|
| Length | 189.5 in (481.3 cm) |
| Width | 69.7 in (177.0 cm) |
| Height | 56.8 in (144.3 cm) |
| Wheelbase | 108.8 in (276.4 cm) |
| Track (front) | 58.0 in (147.3 cm) |
| Track (rear) | 58.3 in (148.0 cm) |
| Ground clearance | 6.0 in (15.2 cm) |

**4-door models (1973 to 1978)**

| | |
|---|---|
| Length | 194.7 in (494.5 cm) |
| Width | 69.7 in (177.0 cm) |
| Height | 54.1 in (137.4 cm) |
| Wheelbase | 112.8 in (286.5 cm) |
| Track (front) | 58.0 in (147.3 cm) |
| Track (rear) | 58.6 in (148.8 cm) |
| Ground clearance | 6.0 in (15.2 cm) |

**4-door models (1979 on)**

| | |
|---|---|
| Length | 200.5 in (509.3 cm) |
| Width | 69.7 in (177.0 cm) |
| Height | 54.1 in (137.4 cm) |
| Wheelbase | 112.8 in (286.5 cm) |
| Track (front) | 58.0 in (147.3 cm) |
| Track (rear) | 58.6 in (148.8 cm) |
| Ground clearance | 6.0 in (15.2 cm) |

**2-door models (1973 to 1977)**

| | |
|---|---|
| Length | 195.0 in (495.3 cm) |
| Width | 69.7 in (177.0 cm) |
| Height | 54.1 in (137.4 cm) |
| Wheelbase | 108.8 in (276.4 cm) |
| Track (front) | 58.0 in (147.3 cm) |
| Track (rear) | 58.6 in (148.8 cm) |
| Ground clearance | 6.0 in (15.2 cm) |

*Jaguar XJS*

**1975 to 1978**

| | |
|---|---|
| Length | 190.5 in (483.9 cm) |
| Width | 70.6 in (179.3 cm) |
| Height | 49.0 in (124.5 cm) |
| Wheelbase | 102.0 in (259.1 cm) |
| Track (front) | 58.0 in (147.3 cm) |
| Track (rear) | 58.6 in (148.8 cm) |
| Ground clearance | 5.5 in (14.0 cm) |

**1978 to 1984**

As for earlier models except:

| | |
|---|---|
| Length (except N America) | 191.7 in (486.9 cm) |
| Length (N America) | 192.3 in (488.4 cm) |
| Height | 49.6 in (126.0 cm) |

**1984 on**

As for earlier models except:

| | |
|---|---|
| Length | 187.6 in (476.4 cm) |
| Track (front) | 58.6 in (148.8 cm) |
| Track (rear) | 59.2 in (150.4 cm) |
| Height | 49.7 in (126.1 cm) |

## Kerb weights (approx) (Fuel tanks full, car equipped with automatic transmission and air conditioning)

*Jaguar XJ12/Daimler Double Six*

**4-door models**

| | |
|---|---|
| 1972 (excluding N America) | 3947 lb (1791 kg) |
| 1972 (N America) | 4000 lb (1816 kg) |
| 1973 to 1978 (excluding N America) | 4123 lb (1872 kg) |
| 1973 to 1978 (N America) | 4179 lb (1897 kg) |
| 1979 on (excluding N America) | 4246 lb (1928 kg) |
| 1979 on (N America) | 4300 lb (1952 kg) |

**2-door models**

| | |
|---|---|
| 1973 to 1975 (excluding N America) | 4045 lb (1836 kg) |
| 1976 to 1977 (excluding N America) | 4100 lb (1861 kg) |
| N America (all models) and others 1978 on | 4270 lb (1939 kg) |

*Jaguar XJS**

| | |
|---|---|
| All except N America | 3795 lb (1723 kg) |
| N America (1975 to 1977) | 4085 lb (1855 kg) |
| N America (1978 on) | 4656 lb (2114 kg) |

**For versions with manual transmission, deduct 106 lb (48 kg) from the kerb weights shown*

## Maximum roof rack load ........ 176 lb (80 kg)

## Capacities

| | Imp | US | Metric |
|---|---|---|---|
| *Engine oil (including filter change)* | | | |
| XJ12, Double Six: | | | |
| Series 1 | 16 pints | 19.2 pints | 9.1 litres |
| Series 2 on | 19 pints | 23.0 pints | 10.7 litres |
| XJS: | | | |
| Up to 1981 | 20 pints | 24.0 pints | 11.4 litres |
| 1982 on | 19 pints | 23.0 pints | 10.7 litres |
| *Cooling systems (all models)* | 37 pints | 44.4 pints | 21.0 litres |
| *Fuel* | | | |
| XJ12, Double Six (carburettor models): | | | |
| Except N America (each tank) | 12 gals | – | 54.6 litres |
| N America (each tank) | 10 gals | 12 gals | 45.5 litres |
| XJ12, Double Six (fuel injection models, each tank) | 10.5 gals | 12.6 gals | 47.75 litres |
| XJS: | | | |
| Coupe | 20 gals | 24.0 gals | 90.0 litres |
| Cabrio | 18 gals | 21.7 gals | 82.0 litres |
| *Transmission* | | | |
| Manual transmission (XJS) | 3.0 pints | 3.6 pints | 1.7 litres |
| Type 12 automatic transmission: | | | |
| Service drain and refill | 11 pints | 13.2 pints | 6.3 litres |
| Refill from dry | 16 pints | 19.2 pints | 9.1 litres |
| GM400 automatic transmission: | | | |
| Service drain and refill | 16.5 pints | 19.8 pints | 9.4 litres |
| Refill from dry | 22.5 pints | 27.0 pints | 12.75 litres |
| *Final drive (all models)* | 2.75 pints | 3.3 pints | 1.6 litres |

# Use of English

*As this book has been written in England, it uses the appropriate English component names, phrases, and spelling. Some of these differ from those used in America. Normally, these cause no difficulty, but to make sure, a glossary is printed below. In ordering spare parts remember the parts list may use some of these words:*

| English | American | English | American |
|---|---|---|---|
| Accelerator | Gas pedal | Locks | Latches |
| Aerial | Antenna | Methylated spirit | Denatured alcohol |
| Anti-roll bar | Stabiliser or sway bar | Motorway | Freeway, turnpike etc |
| Big-end bearing | Rod bearing | Number plate | License plate |
| Bonnet (engine cover) | Hood | Paraffin | Kerosene |
| Boot (luggage compartment) | Trunk | Petrol | Gasoline (gas) |
| Bulkhead | Firewall | Petrol tank | Gas tank |
| Bush | Bushing | 'Pinking' | 'Pinging' |
| Cam follower or tappet | Valve lifter or tappet | Prise (force apart) | Pry |
| Carburettor | Carburetor | Propeller shaft | Driveshaft |
| Catch | Latch | Quarterlight | Quarter window |
| Choke/venturi | Barrel | Retread | Recap |
| Circlip | Snap-ring | Reverse | Back-up |
| Clearance | Lash | Rocker cover | Valve cover |
| Crownwheel | Ring gear (of differential) | Saloon | Sedan |
| Damper | Shock absorber, shock | Seized | Frozen |
| Disc (brake) | Rotor/disk | Sidelight | Parking light |
| Distance piece | Spacer | Silencer | Muffler |
| Drop arm | Pitman arm | Sill panel (beneath doors) | Rocker panel |
| Drop head coupe | Convertible | Small end, little end | Piston pin or wrist pin |
| Dynamo | Generator (DC) | Spanner | Wrench |
| Earth (electrical) | Ground | Split cotter (for valve spring cap) | Lock (for valve spring retainer) |
| Engineer's blue | Prussian blue | Split pin | Cotter pin |
| Estate car | Station wagon | Steering arm | Spindle arm |
| Exhaust manifold | Header | Sump | Oil pan |
| Fault finding/diagnosis | Troubleshooting | Swarf | Metal chips or debris |
| Float chamber | Float bowl | Tab washer | Tang or lock |
| Free-play | Lash | Tappet | Valve lifter |
| Freewheel | Coast | Thrust bearing | Throw-out bearing |
| Gearbox | Transmission | Top gear | High |
| Gearchange | Shift | Torch | Flashlight |
| Grub screw | Setscrew, Allen screw | Trackrod (of steering) | Tie-rod (or connecting rod) |
| Gudgeon pin | Piston pin or wrist pin | Trailing shoe (of brake) | Secondary shoe |
| Halfshaft | Axleshaft | Transmission | Whole drive line |
| Handbrake | Parking brake | Tyre | Tire |
| Hood | Soft top | Van | Panel wagon/van |
| Hot spot | Heat riser | Vice | Vise |
| Indicator | Turn signal | Wheel nut | Lug nut |
| Interior light | Dome lamp | Windscreen | Windshield |
| Layshaft (of gearbox) | Countershaft | Wing/mudguard | Fender |
| Leading shoe (of brake) | Primary shoe | | |

# Buying spare parts and vehicle identification numbers

## *Buying spare parts*

Spare parts are available from many sources, for example: BL garages, other garages and accessory shops, and motor factors. Our advice regarding spare parts is as follows:

*Officially appointed BL garages* – This is the best source of parts which are peculiar to your car and otherwise not generally available (eg complete cylinder heads, internal gearbox components, badges, interior trim etc). It is also the only place at which you should buy parts if your car is still under warranty; non-BL components may invalidate the warranty. To be sure of obtaining the correct parts it will always be necessary to give the storeman your car's engine and chassis number, and if possible, to take the old part along for positive identification. Remember that many parts are available on a factory exchange scheme – any parts returned should always be clean! It obviously makes good sense to go to the specialists on your car for this type of part for they are best equipped to supply you.

*Other garages and accessory shops* – These are often very good places to buy material and components needed for the maintenance of your car (eg oil filters, spark plugs, bulbs, fan belts, oils and grease, touch-up paint, filler paste etc). They also sell general accessories, usually have convenient opening hours, charge lower prices and can often be found not far from home.

*Motor factors* – Good factors will stock all of the more important components which wear out relatively quickly (eg clutch components, pistons, valves, exhaust systems, brake cylinders/pipes/hoses/seals/shoes and pads etc). Motor factors will often provide new or reconditioned components on a part exchange basis – this can save a considerable amount of money.

## *Vehicle identification numbers*

When buying spare parts, always quote the car model, chassis or engine number, as necessary, to the partsman. This will ensure that the correctly fitting item is supplied for your particular car.

*The chassis number* is stamped on the right-hand tie-bar bracket on top of the wing valance and is repeated on the plate within the engine compartment. On XJS models, a suffix BW to the chassis number indicates automatic transmission. After 1979 this suffix is changed to GM.

*The engine number* is stamped on the rear of the cylinder block (photo) and on the commission plate within the engine compartment. Suffix L to engine number indicates low compression. Suffix S to engine number indicates standard compression.

*The gearbox number* is stamped on a label attached to the left-hand side of the gearbox and on the commission plate.

North American vehicles bear additional identification as described below.

*Federal Safety Standard Plate.* Attached to the driver's door pillar, this plate contains the date of manufacture and the vehicle identification number.

*Tyre recommendation plate.* Attached to the glovebox lid beneath the vanity mirror, it shows weight, seating capacity, seating distribution, specified tyre pressures and specified tyre size.

*Timing label.* Fitted under the bonnet lid, this gives basic adjustment data such as spark plug gaps and ignition timing.

*Unleaded fuel label.* Located on the dash panel, this warns against the use of any other type of fuel.

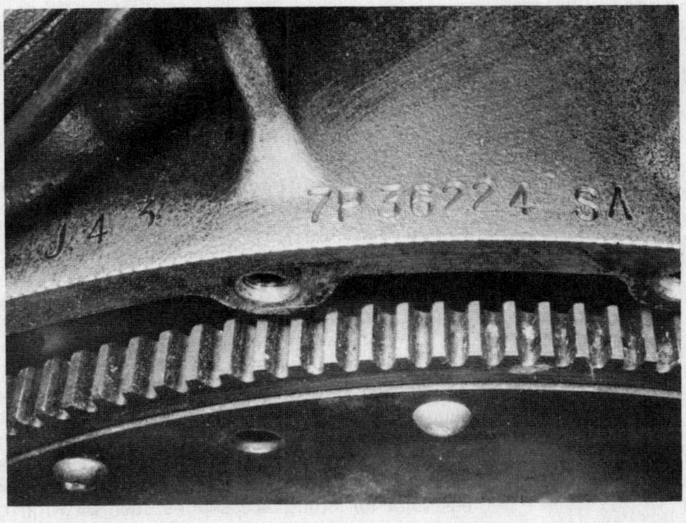

**Location of engine number**

# Tools and working facilities

## *Introduction*

A selection of good tools is a fundamental requirement for anyone contemplating the maintenance and repair of a motor vehicle. For the owner who does not possess any, their purchase will prove a considerable expense, offsetting some of the savings made by doing-it-yourself. However, provided that the tools purchased meet the relevant national safety standards and are of good quality, they will last for many years and prove an extremely worthwhile investment.

To help the average owner to decide which tools are needed to carry out the various tasks detailed in this manual, we have compiled three lists of tools under the following headings: *Maintenance and minor repair, Repair and overhaul,* and *Special.* The newcomer to practical mechanics should start off with the *Maintenance and minor repair* tool kit and confine himself to the simpler jobs around the vehicle. Then, as his confidence and experience grow, he can undertake more difficult tasks, buying extra tools as, and when, they are needed. In this way, a *Maintenance and minor repair* tool kit can be built-up into a *Repair and overhaul* tool kit over a considerable period of time without any major cash outlays. The experienced do-it-yourselfer will have a tool kit good enough for most repair and overhaul procedures and will add tools from the *Special* category when he feels the expense is justified by the amount of use these tools will be put to.

It is obviously not possible to cover the subject of tools fully here. For those who wish to learn more about tools and their use there is a book entitled *How to Choose and Use Car Tools* available from the publishers of this manual.

## *Threads*

The majority of bolts and nuts used in the cars covered by this manual are to UNF standards. A few metric sizes may be encountered however on certain proprietary components.

Partial metrication of the brake hydraulic system has been carried out and in the interest of safety reference should be made to Chapter 9, Section 2 for location and thread compatability of hydraulic components.

Hydraulic fittings on the power-assisted steering circuit are to UNF standards.

## *Maintenance and minor repair tool kit*

The tools given in this list should be considered as a minimum requirement if routine maintenance, servicing and minor repair operations are to be undertaken. We recommend the purchase of combination spanners (ring one end, open-ended the other); although more expensive than open-ended ones, they do give the advantages of both types of spanner.

*Combination spanners to cover the range $\frac{7}{16}$ in to 1 in AF*
*Adjustable wrench - 9 inch*
*Spark plug spanner (with rubber insert)*
*Spark plug gap adjustment tool*
*Set of feeler gauges*
*Brake bleed nipple spanner*
*Screwdriver - 4 in long x $\frac{1}{4}$ in dia (flat blade)*
*Screwdriver - 4 in long x $\frac{1}{4}$ in dia (cross blade)*
*Combination pliers - 6 inch*
*Hacksaw, (junior)*
*Tyre pump*
*Tyre pressure gauge*
*Grease gun*
*Oil can*
*Fine emery cloth (1 sheet)*
*Wire brush (small)*
*Funnel (medium size)*

## *Repair and overhaul tool kit*

These tools are virtually essential for anyone undertaking any major repairs to a motor vehicle, and are additional to those given in the *Maintenance and minor repair* list. Included in this list is a comprehensive set of sockets. Although these are expensive they will be found invaluable as they are so versatile - particularly if various drives are included in the set. We recommend the $\frac{1}{2}$ in square-drive type, as this can be used with most proprietary torque wrenches. If you cannot afford a socket set, even bought piecemeal, then inexpensive tubular box spanners are a useful alternative.

The tools in this list will occasionally need to be supplemented by tools from the *Special* list.

## *Care and maintenance of tools*

Having purchased a reasonable tool kit, it is necessary to keep the tools in a clean serviceable condition. After use, always wipe off any dirt, grease and metal particles using a clean, dry cloth, before putting the tools away. Never leave them lying around after they have been used. A simple tool rack on the garage or workshop wall, for items such as screwdrivers and pliers is a good idea. Store all normal spanners and sockets in a metal box. Any measuring instruments, gauges, meters, etc, must be carefully stored where they cannot be damaged or become rusty.

Take a little care when tools are used. Hammer heads inevitably become marked and screwdrivers lose the keen edge on their blades from time to time. A little timely attention with emery cloth or a file will soon restore items like this to a good serviceable finish.

## *Working facilities*

Not to be forgotten when discussing tools, is the workshop itself. If anything more than routine maintenance is to be carried out, some form of suitable working area becomes essential.

It is appreciated that many an owner mechanic is forced by circumstances to remove an engine or similar item, without the benefit of a garage or workshop. Having done this, any repairs should always be done under the cover of a roof.

Wherever possible, any dismantling should be done on a clean flat workbench or table at a suitable working height.

Any workbench needs a vice: one with a jaw opening of 4 in (100 mm) is suitable for most jobs. As mentioned previously, some clean dry storage space is also required for tools, as well as for lubricants, cleaning fluids, touch-up paints and so on which become necessary.

Another item which may be required, and which has a much more general usage, is an electric drill with a chuck capacity of at least $\frac{5}{16}$ in (8 mm). This, together with a good range of twist drills, is virtually essential for fitting accessories such as wing mirrors and reversing lights.

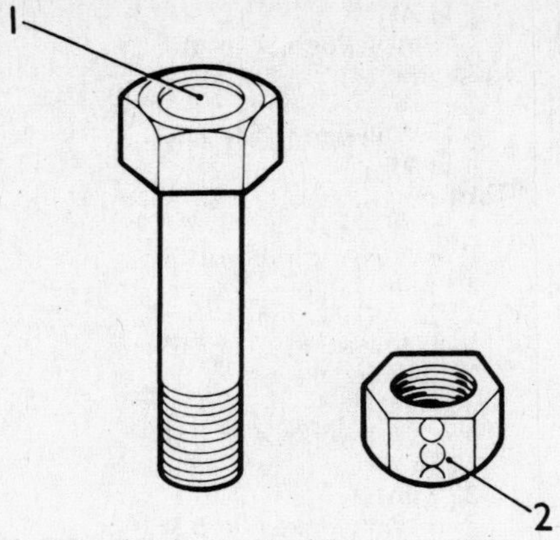


**UNF bolt and nut identification**

1 *Recess in bolt head*
2 *Circles stamped onto flat of nut*

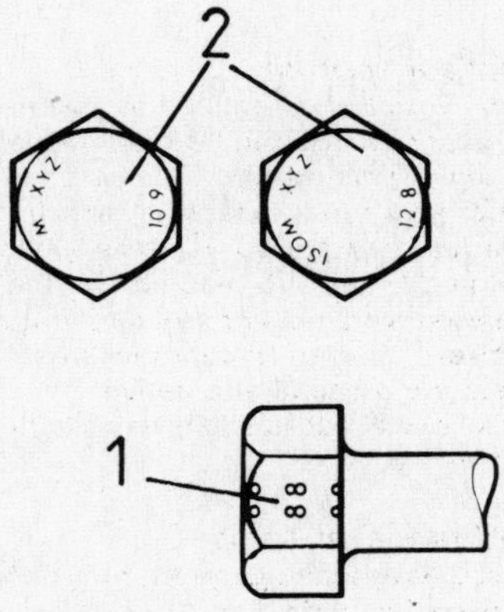


**Metric bolt identification**

1 *Strength grade on flat of bolt head*
2 *Alternative markings on top of bolt head*

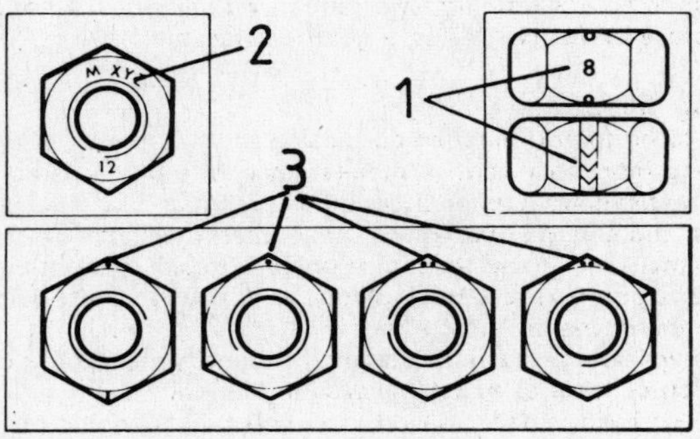


**Metric nut identification**

1 *Strength grade on flat of nut*
2 *Top face marking with strength indicated numerically*
3 *Top face marking with dots (clock face system) used to indicate strength*

Last, but not least, always keep a supply of old newspapers and clean, lint-free rags available, and try to keep any working area as clean as possible.

*Sockets (or box spanners) to cover range in previous list*
*Reversible ratchet drive (for use with sockets)*
*Extension piece, 10 inch (for use with sockets)*
*Universal joint (for use with sockets)*
*Torque wrench (for use with sockets)*
*'Mole' wrench - 8 inch*
*Ball pein hammer*
*Soft-faced hammer, plastic or rubber*
*Screwdriver - 6 in long x $\frac{5}{16}$ in dia (flat blade)*
*Screwdriver - 2 in long x $\frac{5}{16}$ in square (flat blade)*
*Screwdriver - $1\frac{1}{2}$ in long x $\frac{1}{4}$ in dia (cross blade)*
*Screwdriver - 3 in long x $\frac{1}{8}$ in dia (electricians)*
*Pliers - electricians side cutters*
*Pliers - needle nosed*
*Pliers - circlip (internal and external)*
*Cold chisel - $\frac{1}{2}$ inch*
*Scriber*
*Scraper*
*Centre punch*
*Pin punch*
*Hacksaw*
*Valve grinding tool*
*Steel rule/straight edge*
*Allen keys*
*Selection of files*
*Wire brush (large)*
*Axle-stands*
*Jack (strong scissor or hydraulic type)*

## *Special tools*

The tools in this list are those which are not used regularly, are expensive to buy, or which need to be used in accordance with their manufacturers' instructions. Unless relatively difficult mechanical jobs are undertaken frequently, it will not be economic to buy many of these tools. Where this is the case, you could consider clubbing together with friends (or a motorists' club) to make a joint purchase, or borrowing the tools against a deposit from a local garage or tool hire specialist.

The following list contains only those tools and instruments freely available to the public, and not those special tools produced by the vehicle manufacturer specifically for its dealer network. You will find occasional references to these manufacturers' special tools in the text of this manual. Generally, an alternative method of doing the job without the vehicle manufacturers' special tool is given. However, sometimes, there is no alternative to using them. Where this is the case and the relevant tool cannot be bought or borrowed you will have to entrust the work to a franchised garage.

*Valve spring compressor*
*Piston ring compressor*
*Balljoint separator*
*Universal hub/bearing puller*
*Impact screwdriver*
*Micrometer and/or vernier gauge*
*Dial gauge*
*Stroboscopic timing light*
*Dwell angle meter/tachometer*
*Universal electrical multi-meter*
*Cylinder compression gauge*
*Lifting tackle*
*Trolley jack*
*Light with extension lead*

## *Buying tools*

For practically all tools, a tool factor is the best source since he will have a very comprehensive range compared with the average garage or accessory shop. Having said that, accessory shops often offer excellent quality tools at discount prices, so it pays to shop around.

There are plenty of good tools around at reasonable prices, but always aim to purchase items which meet the relevant national safety standards. If in doubt, ask the proprietor or manager of the shop for advice before making a purchase.

*Spanner jaw gap comparison table*

| Jaw gap (in) | Spanner size |
|---|---|
| 0.250 | $\frac{1}{4}$ in AF |
| 0.275 | 7 mm |
| 0.313 | $\frac{5}{16}$ in AF |
| 0.315 | 8 mm |
| 0.344 | $\frac{11}{32}$ in AF; $\frac{1}{8}$ in Whitworth |
| 0.354 | 9 mm |
| 0.375 | $\frac{3}{8}$ in AF |
| 0.394 | 10 mm |
| 0.433 | 11 mm |
| 0.438 | $\frac{7}{16}$ in AF |
| 0.445 | $\frac{3}{16}$ in Whitworth; $\frac{1}{4}$ in BSF |
| 0.472 | 12 mm |
| 0.500 | $\frac{1}{2}$ in AF |
| 0.512 | 13 mm |
| 0.525 | $\frac{1}{4}$ in Whitworth; $\frac{5}{16}$ in BSF |
| 0.551 | 14 mm |
| 0.562 | $\frac{9}{16}$ in AF |
| 0.590 | 15 mm |
| 0.600 | $\frac{5}{16}$ in Whitworth; $\frac{3}{8}$ in BSF |
| 0.625 | $\frac{5}{8}$ in AF |
| 0.629 | 16 mm |
| 0.669 | 17 mm |
| 0.687 | $\frac{11}{16}$ in AF |
| 0.708 | 18 mm |
| 0.710 | $\frac{3}{8}$ in Whitworth, $\frac{7}{16}$ in BSF |
| 0.748 | 19 mm |
| 0.750 | $\frac{3}{4}$ in AF |
| 0.812 | $\frac{13}{16}$ in AF |
| 0.820 | $\frac{7}{16}$ in Whitworth; $\frac{1}{2}$ in BSF |
| 0.866 | 22 mm |
| 0.875 | $\frac{7}{8}$ in AF |
| 0.920 | $\frac{1}{2}$ in Whitworth; $\frac{9}{16}$ in BSF |
| 0.937 | $\frac{15}{16}$ in AF |
| 0.944 | 24 mm |
| 1.000 | 1 in AF |
| 1.010 | $\frac{9}{16}$ in Whitworth; $\frac{5}{8}$ in BSF |
| 1.023 | 26 mm |
| 1.062 | $1\frac{1}{16}$ in AF, 27 mm |
| 1.100 | $\frac{5}{8}$ in Whitworth; $\frac{11}{16}$ in BSF |
| 1.125 | $1\frac{1}{8}$ in AF |
| 1.181 | 30 mm |
| 1.200 | $\frac{11}{16}$ in Whitworth; $\frac{3}{4}$ in BSF |
| 1.250 | $1\frac{1}{4}$ in AF |
| 1.259 | 32 mm |
| 1.300 | $\frac{3}{4}$ in Whitworth; $\frac{7}{8}$ in BSF |
| 1.312 | $1\frac{5}{16}$ in AF |
| 1.390 | $\frac{13}{16}$ in Whitworth; $\frac{15}{16}$ in BSF |
| 1.417 | 36 mm |
| 1.437 | $1\frac{7}{16}$ in AF |
| 1.480 | $\frac{7}{8}$ in Whitworth; 1 in BSF |
| 1.500 | $1\frac{1}{2}$ in AF |
| 1.574 | 40 mm; $\frac{15}{16}$ in Whitworth |
| 1.614 | 41 mm |
| 1.625 | $1\frac{5}{8}$ in AF |
| 1.670 | 1 in Whitworth; $1\frac{1}{8}$ in BSF |
| 1.687 | $1\frac{11}{16}$ in AF |
| 1.811 | 46 mm |
| 1.812 | 163 in AF |
| 1.860 | $1\frac{1}{8}$ in Whitworth; $1\frac{1}{4}$ in BSF |
| 1.875 | $1\frac{7}{8}$ in AF |
| 1.968 | 50 mm |
| 2.000 | 2 in AF |
| 2.050 | $1\frac{1}{4}$ in Whitworth; $1\frac{3}{8}$ in BSF |
| 2.165 | 55 mm |
| 2.362 | 60 mm |

# Jacking and towing

## *Jacking*

Use the jack supplied with the car only for wheel changing during roadside emergencies. The jack engages with spigots situated below the body side members.

To remove a roadwheel, release the wheel nuts but do not remove them before raising the car. Fully tighten the wheel nuts after the car has been lowered to the ground.

For under-car repair or maintenance, use a hydraulic or screw jack, preferably of the trolley type. Place the jack as indicated in the following paragraphs and always supplement it with axle stands before working under the car.

*To raise one front wheel,* place the jack under the spring lower support pan.

*To raise one rear wheel* place the jack under the outer fork of the suspension wishbone. Avoid damage to the alloy hub carrier and grease nipple.

*To raise both front wheels,* position the jack centrally under the front suspension crossmember. Use a block of wood as an insulator on the jack head.

*To raise both rear wheels,* position the jack under the tie plate immediately below the differential unit. Cut a piece of wood to shape as shown and use it as an insulator to avoid the head of the jack applying pressure to the lips of the tie plate.

## *Towing*

The car may be towed by means of the two hooks located under the front bumper. The two hooks at the rear of the car are for lashing down the vehicle during transportation and must *not* be used to tow another vehicle.

When it is necessary to be towed behind another vehicle, remember that the power steering system and the brake servo system will not be operational. Allowances must therefore be made for the extra steering effort and pedal pressure required.

As is usual with all vehicles equipped with automatic transmission, special precautions must be observed when being towed. Add 3.6 pints (2 litres) of extra automatic transmission fluid and position the speed selector lever in 'N'. Do not tow the car for more than 30 miles (48 km) and restrict the speed to 30 mph (48 kph).

On all models, when being towed, make sure that the ignition key is in the ACC position so that the steering column will be unlocked.

With automatic transmission vehicles, remember to reduce the fluid level again before resuming normal operation. As a drain plug is not fitted, the oil pan will have to be unbolted and lowered or the union nut at the base of the fluid filler/dipstick guide tube released and sufficient fluid allowed to drain out.

**Wheel changing jack**

**Spare wheel and anchor bolt**

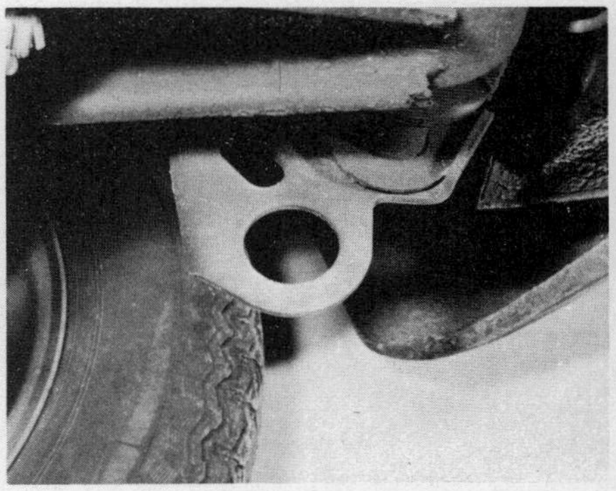

**Front towing hook**

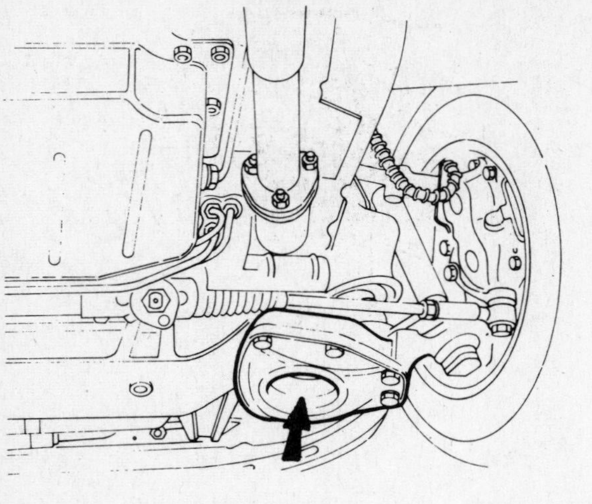

Front wheel jacking point

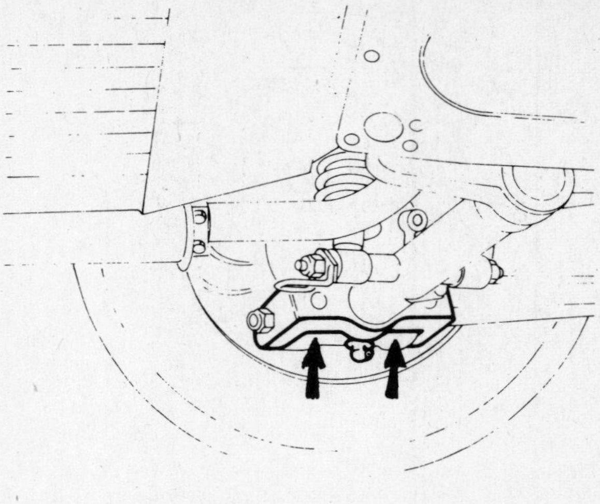

Rear wheel jacking point

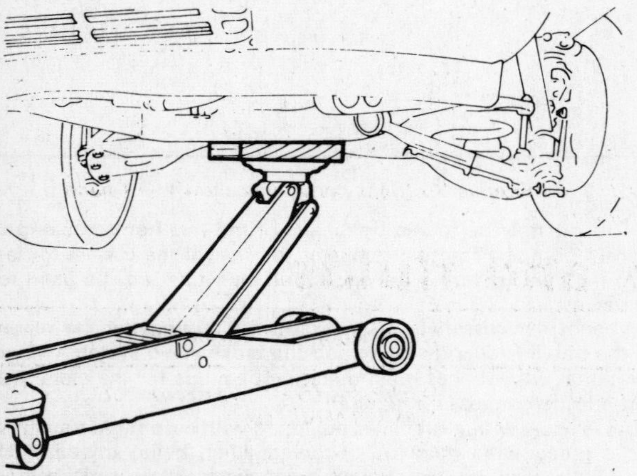

Front end (both wheels) jacking point

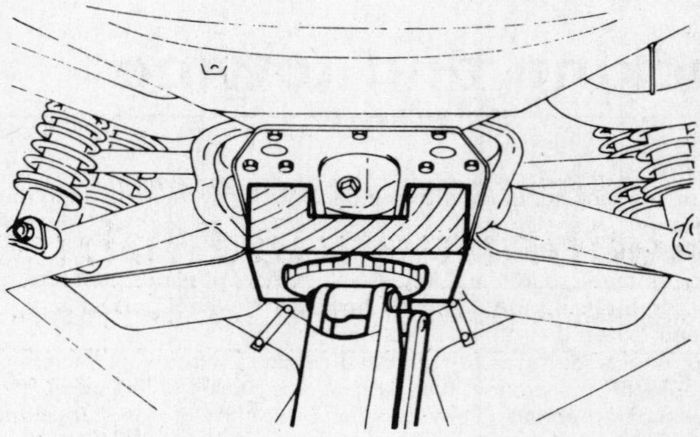

Rear end (both wheels) jacking point –
note shaped block of wood

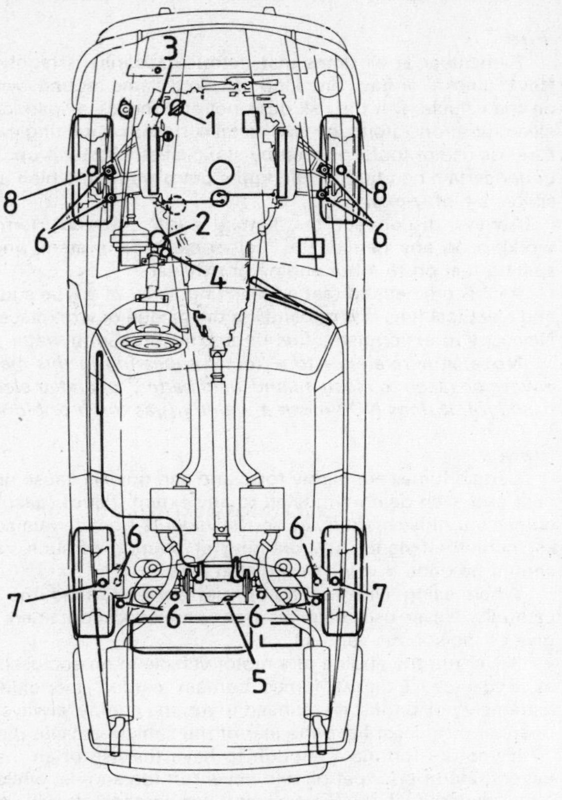


*XJS (left-hand drive shown, right-hand similar)*

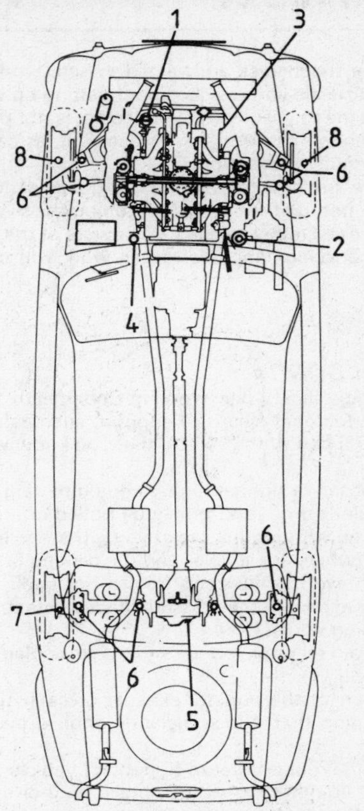


*XJ12 and Double Six (right-hand drive shown left-hand similar)*

# Recommended lubricants and fluids

| Component or system | Lubricant type/specification | Duckhams recommendation |
|---|---|---|
| **1 Engine** | Multigrade engine oil, viscosity range SAE 10W/30 to 20W/50, to BLSO 0L.02, MIL-L-2104B or API SE* | Duckhams QXR, Hypergrade, or 10W/40 Motor Oil |
| **2 Brake hydraulic system** | Hydraulic fluid to SAE J1703/D | Duckhams Universal Brake and Clutch Fluid |
| **3 Power-assisted steering** | ATF type F (to M2C 33F), type G (to M2C 33G), or Dexron IID | Duckhams D-Matic or Q-Matic |
| **4 Automatic transmission** | | |
| Borg Warner | ATF type F, to M2C 33F | Duckhams Q-Matic |
| GM 400 | Dexron IID type ATF | Duckhams D-Matic |
| **Manual gearbox** | Hypoid gear oil, viscosity SAE EP90, to MIL-L-2105B | Duckhams Hypoid 90 |
| **5 Final drive** | | |
| Refill | Special limited slip differential oil | Duckhams Hypoid 90DL |
| Top up only | Hypoid gear oil, viscosity SAE EP90, to MIL-L-2105B | Duckhams Hypoid 90DL, or Hypoid 90S |
| **6 Grease nipples** | Multi-purpose lithium-based grease, to NLGI No 2 | Duckhams LB 10 |
| **7 Rear hubs** | Multi-purpose lithium-based grease, to NLGI No 2 | Duckhams LB 10 |
| **8 Front hubs** | Multi-purpose lithium-based grease, to NLGI No 2 | Duckhams LB 10 |
| **Cooling system** | Ethylene glycol based antifreeze, to BS 3151, 3152 or 6580 | Duckhams Universal Antifreeze and Summer Coolant |
| **Clutch hydraulic system** | Hydraulic fluid to SAE J1703/D | Duckhams Universal Brake and Clutch Fluid |

** The vehicle manufacturers do not recommend the use of oils with viscosity SAE 10W/30 or 10W/40 when the ambient temperature is above 59°F (15°C)*

# Safety first!

Professional motor mechanics are trained in safe working procedures. However enthusiastic you may be about getting on with the job in hand, do take the time to ensure that your safety is not put at risk. A moment's lack of attention can result in an accident, as can failure to observe certain elementary precautions.

There will always be new ways of having accidents, and the following points do not pretend to be a comprehensive list of all dangers; they are intended rather to make you aware of the risks and to encourage a safety-conscious approach to all work you carry out on your vehicle.

### *Essential DOs and DON'Ts*

**DON'T** rely on a single jack when working underneath the vehicle. Always use reliable additional means of support, such as axle stands, securely placed under a part of the vehicle that you know will not give way.

**DON'T** attempt to loosen or tighten high-torque nuts (e.g. wheel hub nuts) while the vehicle is on a jack; it may be pulled off.

**DON'T** start the engine without first ascertaining that the transmission is in neutral (or 'Park' where applicable) and the parking brake applied.

**DON'T** suddenly remove the filler cap from a hot cooling system – cover it with a cloth and release the pressure gradually first, or you may get scalded by escaping coolant.

**DON'T** attempt to drain oil until you are sure it has cooled sufficiently to avoid scalding you.

**DON'T** grasp any part of the engine, exhaust or catalytic converter without first ascertaining that it is sufficiently cool to avoid burning you.

**DON'T** allow brake fluid or antifreeze to contact vehicle paintwork.

**DON'T** syphon toxic liquids such as fuel, brake fluid or antifreeze by mouth, or allow them to remain on your skin.

**DON'T** inhale dust – it may be injurious to health (see *Asbestos* below).

**DON'T** allow any spilt oil or grease to remain on the floor – wipe it up straight away, before someone slips on it.

**DON'T** use ill-fitting spanners or other tools which may slip and cause injury.

**DON'T** attempt to lift a heavy component which may be beyond your capability – get assistance.

**DON'T** rush to finish a job, or take unverified short cuts.

**DON'T** allow children or animals in or around an unattended vehicle.

**DO** wear eye protection when using power tools such as drill, sander, bench grinder etc, and when working under the vehicle.

**DO** use a barrier cream on your hands prior to undertaking dirty jobs – it will protect your skin from infection as well as making the dirt easier to remove afterwards; but make sure your hands aren't left slippery. Note that long-term contact with used engine oil can be a health hazard.

**DO** keep loose clothing (cuffs, tie etc) and long hair well out of the way of moving mechanical parts.

**DO** remove rings, wristwatch etc, before working on the vehicle – especially the electrical system.

**DO** ensure that any lifting tackle used has a safe working load rating adequate for the job.

**DO** keep your work area tidy – it is only too easy to fall over articles left lying around.

**DO** get someone to check periodically that all is well, when working alone on the vehicle.

**DO** carry out work in a logical sequence and check that everything is correctly assembled and tightened afterwards.

**DO** remember that your vehicle's safety affects that of yourself and others. If in doubt on any point, get specialist advice.

**IF,** in spite of following these precautions, you are unfortunate enough to injure yourself, seek medical attention as soon as possible.

### *Asbestos*

Certain friction, insulating, sealing, and other products – such as brake linings, brake bands, clutch linings, torque converters, gaskets, etc – contain asbestos. *Extreme care must be taken to avoid inhalation of dust from such products since it is hazardous to health.* If in doubt, assume that they *do* contain asbestos.

### *Fire*

Remember at all times that petrol (gasoline) is highly flammable. Never smoke, or have any kind of naked flame around, when working on the vehicle. But the risk does not end there – a spark caused by an electrical short-circuit, by two metal surfaces contacting each other, by careless use of tools, or even by static electricity built up in your body under certain conditions, can ignite petrol vapour, which in a confined space is highly explosive.

Always disconnect the battery earth (ground) terminal before working on any part of the fuel or electrical system, and never risk spilling fuel on to a hot engine or exhaust.

It is recommended that a fire extinguisher of a type suitable for fuel and electrical fires is kept handy in the garage or workplace at all times. Never try to extinguish a fuel or electrical fire with water.

**Note:** *Any reference to a 'torch' appearing in this manual should always be taken to mean a hand-held battery-operated electric lamp or flashlight. It does NOT mean a welding/gas torch or blowlamp.*

### *Fumes*

Certain fumes are highly toxic and can quickly cause unconsciousness and even death if inhaled to any extent. Petrol (gasoline) vapour comes into this category, as do the vapours from certain solvents such as trichloroethylene. Any draining or pouring of such volatile fluids should be done in a well ventilated area.

When using cleaning fluids and solvents, read the instructions carefully. Never use materials from unmarked containers – they may give off poisonous vapours.

Never run the engine of a motor vehicle in an enclosed space such as a garage. Exhaust fumes contain carbon monoxide which is extremely poisonous; if you need to run the engine, always do so in the open air or at least have the rear of the vehicle outside the workplace.

If you are fortunate enough to have the use of an inspection pit, never drain or pour petrol, and never run the engine, while the vehicle is standing over it; the fumes, being heavier than air, will concentrate in the pit with possibly lethal results.

### *The battery*

Never cause a spark, or allow a naked light, near the vehicle's battery. It will normally be giving off a certain amount of hydrogen gas, which is highly explosive.

Always disconnect the battery earth (ground) terminal before working on the fuel or electrical systems.

If possible, loosen the filler plugs or cover when charging the battery from an external source. Do not charge at an excessive rate or the battery may burst.

Take care when topping up and when carrying the battery. The acid electrolyte, even when diluted, is very corrosive and should not be allowed to contact the eyes or skin.

If you ever need to prepare electrolyte yourself, always add the acid slowly to the water, and never the other way round. Protect against splashes by wearing rubber gloves and goggles.

When jump starting a car using a booster battery, for negative earth (ground) vehicles, connect the jump leads in the following sequence: First connect one jump lead between the positive (+) terminals of the two batteries. Then connect the other jump lead first to the negative (–) terminal of the booster battery, and then to a good earthing (ground) point on the vehicle to be started, at least 18 in (45 cm) from the battery if possible. Ensure that hands and jump leads are clear of any moving parts, and that the two vehicles do not touch. Disconnect the leads in the reverse order.

### *Mains electricity and electrical equipment*

When using an electric power tool, inspection light etc, always ensure that the appliance is correctly connected to its plug and that, where necessary, it is properly earthed (grounded). Do not use such appliances in damp conditions and, again, beware of creating a spark or applying excessive heat in the vicinity of fuel or fuel vapour. Also ensure that the appliances meet the relevant national safety standards.

### *Ignition HT voltage*

A severe electric shock can result from touching certain parts of the ignition system, such as the HT leads, when the engine is running or being cranked, particularly if components are damp or the insulation is defective. Where an electronic ignition system is fitted, the HT voltage is much higher and could prove fatal.

# Routine maintenance – early models

*For information applicable to later models, see Supplementary section at end of manual*

Maintenance is essential for ensuring safety and desirable for the purpose of getting the best in terms of performance and economy from the car. Over the years the need for periodic lubrication – oiling, greasing and so on – has been drastically reduced if not totally eliminated. This has unfortunately tended to lead some owners to think that because no such action is required the items either no longer exist or will last for ever. This is a serious delusion. It follows therefore that the largest initial element of maintenance is visual examination. This may lead to repairs or renewals.

### *Special note*

Spark plug leads, fuel injector leads and certain other components will have identification sleeves fitted to them. The letter and number shown will conform to the following arrangement:

A – right-hand cylinder bank.
B – left-hand cylinder bank.

No 1 cylinder is nearest the crankshaft pulley/damper end of the engine; left and right-hand are as viewed from the driver's seat.

The identity sleeves may become discoloured or obliterated over a period of time. If confusion is to be avoided when disconnecting electrical leads, also vacuum, coolant or fuel pipes, always mark the ends before disconnection. The simplest way to do this is to use a piece of masking tape on each end with matching numbers or letters written on the tape with a ballpoint pen.

**Every 250 miles (400 km) or weekly, whichever comes first**

### *Brakes*

Check reservoir fluid level (photo)
Check foot and handbrake movement for increased travel or falling off in efficiency

### *Engine*

Check oil level and top up if necessary (photos)
Check coolant level (photo)
Check battery electrolyte level

### *Lights*

Check for operation
Clean lenses

### *Steering*

Check tyres for pressure ana wear characteristics

### *General*

Clean windscreen
Top up washer reservoir (photo)

**Every 3000 miles (4800 km) or three months, whichever comes first**

### *Engine*

Check security of all hoses
Check fuel system for leaks
Check exhaust system for corrosion or leaks

### *Steering*

Check power steering fluid level and top up if necessary (photo)

### *Transmission*

Check oil level in final drive unit (photo)
Check fluid level in automatic transmission (photo) or oil level in manual gearbox (XJS option)

### *Braking system*

Check disc pads for wear

**Every 6000 miles (9600 km) or six months, whichever comes first**

### *Engine*

Check ignition timing
Clean and gap spark plugs
Renew engine oil and filter (photo)
Check operation of ignition retard control valve
Check idle speed
Check exhaust CO content
Check choke and fast idle setting (carburettors)
Top up piston dampers (carburettors)

### *Steering/suspension*

Check for wear in all steering joints and condition of gaiters, then lubricate all nipples including steering housing (photos)
Adjust front hub bearings

### *Braking system*

Check condition of all hydraulic hoses and pipes
Check and adjust handbrake

Topping up the brake fluid

Engine oil dipstick markings

Withdrawing engine oil dipstick

Topping up engine oil

Topping up the coolant

Windscreen washer fluid reservoir

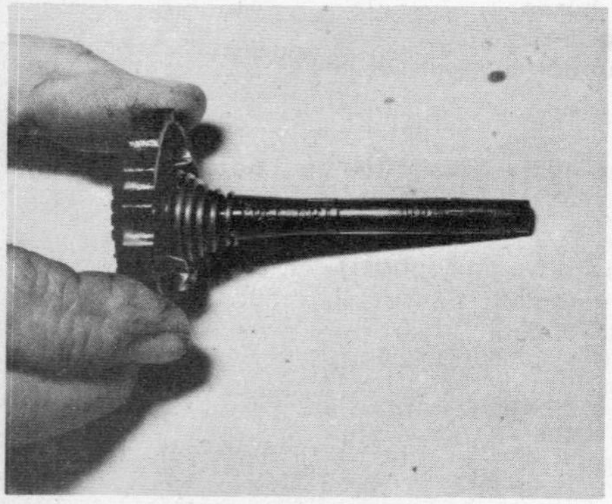

Power steering fluid dipstick

Final drive unit oil level/filler plug (arrowed)

Withdrawing the automatic transmission fluid dipstick

Engine sump drain plug (arrowed)

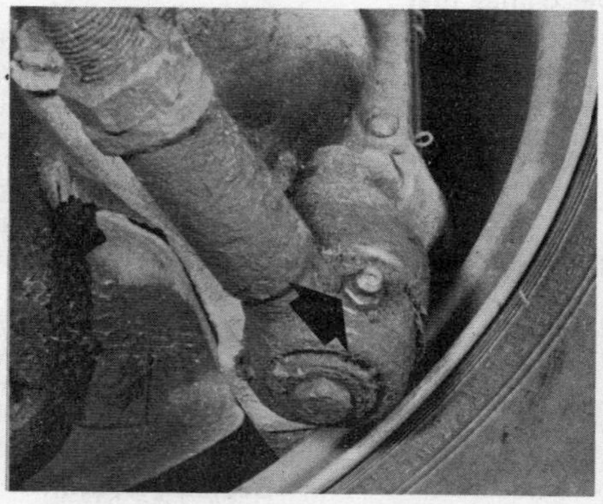

Tie-rod grease nipple (arrowed)

Front suspension upper balljoint grease nipple

Front suspension lower balljoint grease nipple

Rear suspension lower wishbone outboard grease nipple

Rear suspension lower wishbone inboard grease nipple

Steering rack grease nipple (arrowed)

Rear hub grease nipple

Final drive oil drain plug

*General*
Lubricate all controls

**Every 12 000 miles (19 300 km) or twelve months, whichever comes first**

*Engine*
Check operation of EGR valve (emission control)
Clean throttle housing bore
Clean crankcase breather pipes and filter
Renew air cleaner elements, test air intake valve
Test operation of diverter and check valves and gulp valve (emission control)
Renew fuel filter
Check security of all vacuum pipes
Clean and inspect ignition HT leads
Check distributor cap for cracks
Renew spark plugs
Check ignition timing
Check idle speed
Check exhaust CO content at idle speed
Check tension of drivebelts, renew where necessary

*Steering and suspension*
Check front wheel alignment
Lubricate rear wheel hubs

*Cooling system*
Drain coolant and renew with fresh antifreeze mixture (annually, regardless of mileage)

*Transmission*
Drain and refill final drive unit (photo)

*General*
Check rubber seal in fuel filler cap

**Every 24 000 miles (38 600 km) or two years, whichever comes first**

*Engine*
Clean EGR valve (emission control)
Renew all drivebelts
Renew charcoal canister (fuel evaporative emission control)
Lubricate distributor

*Braking system*
Bleed out hydraulic fluid and refill with fresh

*Transmission*
Adjust rear brake band on Borg Warner Type 12 automatic transmission
Drain and refill the automatic transmission if operating under particularly arduous conditions giving rise to discoloration of the fluid. (Under normal operating conditions, renewal of the automatic transmission fluid is not specified as a routine service operation)

*General*
Inspect the windscreen wiper blades and renew if necessary

**Every 48 000 miles (77 200 km) or four years, whichever comes first**

*Engine*
Renew EGR valve (emission control)
Renew catalytic converters (emission control)

*Suspension and steering*
Check the shock absorbers and renew if necessary

*Braking system*
Renew all hydraulic system seals

# Chapter 1 Engine

*For modifications, and information applicable to later models, see Supplement at end of manual*

## Contents



## Specifications

### Engine – general

| | |
|---|---|
| No of cylinders | 12 |
| Bore | 3.543 in (90.0 mm) |
| Stroke | 2.756 in (70.0 mm) |
| Cubic capacity | 326.0 cu in (5343 cc) 5.3 litre |
| Compression ratio | 9:1 (S), 7.8:1 (L) |
| Firing order | 1A, 6B, 5A, 2B, 3A, 4B, 6A, 1B, 2A, 5B, 4A, 3B (A – right bank, B – left bank, No 1 at front) |
| Maximum power (DIN) | 284 hp at 5750 rpm |
| Maximum torque (DIN) | 294 lbf ft at 4500 rpm |

### Cylinder block

| | |
|---|---|
| Material | Aluminium alloy |
| Cylinder angle | 60° vee |
| Liners | Wet, cast iron |
| Outside diameter of liners | 3.858 in +0.001 in (97.99 mm +0.02 mm) |

### Cylinder heads

| | |
|---|---|
| Material | Aluminium alloy |
| Valve seat angle | $44\frac{1}{2}$° |

## Crankshaft

| | |
|---|---|
| No of main bearings | 7 |
| Journal diameter | 3.0007 to 3.0012 in (76.218 to 76.231 mm) |
| Journal length: | |
| Front | 1.170 to 1.180 in (29.72 to 29.97 mm) |
| Centre and rear | 1.425 to 1.426 in (36.21 to 36.22 mm) |
| Intermediate | 1.198 to 1.202 in (30.43 to 30.53 mm) |
| Endfloat control | Centre bearing thrust washers |
| Thrust washer thickness | 0.010 in (0.25 mm), 0.020 in (0.51 mm) |
| Endfloat | 0.004 to 0.006 in (0.10 to 0.15 mm) |
| Main bearing widths: | |
| Front and intermediate | 0.963 to 0.973 in (24.40 to 24.65 mm) |
| Centre and rear | 1.190 to 1.200 in (30.2 to 30.5 mm) |
| Running clearance | 0.0015 to 0.003 in (0.04 to 0.07 mm) |
| Crankpin diameter | 2.2994 to 2.3000 in (58.40 to 58.42 mm) |
| Crankpin length | 1.699 to 1.701 in (43.15 to 43.20 mm) |
| *Regrind undersizes | 0.010 in (0.25 mm), 0.020 in (0.51 mm), 0.030 in (0.76 mm), 0.040 in (1.02 mm) |

**Due to the extreme hardness of the crankshaft material, regrinding is not possible on normal grinding equipment*

## Connecting rods

| | |
|---|---|
| Big-end bearing width | 0.720 to 0.730 in (18.3 to 18.5 mm) |
| Running clearance | 0.0015 to 0.0034 in (0.04 to 0.09 mm) |
| Big-end side clearance | 0.007 to 0.013 in (0.17 to 0.33 mm) |
| Small-end bush width | 1.03 to 1.05 in (26.2 to 26.7 mm) |
| Small-end bush bore | 0.9375 to 0.9377 in (23.813 to 23.818 mm) |

## Pistons

| | |
|---|---|
| Skirt clearance | 0.0012 to 0.0017 in (0.03 to 0.04 mm) |

## Piston rings

| | |
|---|---|
| Number | 2 compression, 1 oil control (self-expanding, 2 rails) |
| Compression ring width | 0.150 to 0.160 in (3.81 to 4.06 mm) |
| Compression ring thickness: | |
| Top | 0.062 to 0.063 in (1.58 to 1.60 mm) |
| Second | 0.077 to 0.078 in (1.96 to 1.98 mm) |
| Compression ring clearance in groove: | |
| Top | 0.0029 in (0.07 mm) |
| Second | 0.0034 in (0.09 mm) |
| Oil control ring clearance in groove | 0.0055 to 0.0065 in (0.14 to 0.17 mm) |
| Piston ring end gap: | |
| Top compression | 0.014 to 0.020 in (0.36 to 0.51 mm) |
| Second compression | 0.010 to 0.015 in (0.25 to 0.38 mm) |
| Oil control rails | 0.015 to 0.045 in (0.38 to 1.14 mm) |

## Gudgeon pins

| | |
|---|---|
| Type | Fully floating |
| Length | 3.120 to 3.125 in (79.25 to 79.38 mm) |
| Outside diameter: | |
| Red (Grade A) | 0.9375 in (23.81 mm) |
| Green (Grade B) | 0.9373 in (23.76 mm) |

## Camshafts

| | |
|---|---|
| No of journals | 7 on each shaft |
| No of bearings | 7 on each shaft (machined direct in caps) |
| Journal diameter | 1.0615 in + 0.0005 in (26.95 mm + 0.013 mm) |
| Running clearance | 0.001 to 0.003 in (0.03 to 0.07 mm) |
| Thrust | Taken on front ends of shaft |

## Jackshaft

| | |
|---|---|
| No of bearings | 3 |
| Running clearance | 0.0005 to 0.003 in (0.013 to 0.076 mm) |
| Thrust | Taken on front end of shaft |
| Endfloat | 0.005 in (0.13 mm) |

## Valve timing

| | |
|---|---|
| Inlet valve opens | 17° BTDC |
| Inlet valve closes | 59° ABDC |
| Exhaust valve opens | 59° BBDC |
| Exhaust valve closes | 17° ATDC |

## Valves and valve springs

| | |
|---|---|
| Valve clearance (inlet and exhaust, cold) | 0.012 to 0.014 in (0.305 to 0.356 mm) |

| | |
|---|---|
| Inlet valve head diameter: | |
| XJ12 and Double Six | 1.623 to 1.627 in (41.22 to 41.32 mm) |
| XJS models | 1.620 to 1.630 in (41.15 to 41.40 mm) |
| Exhaust valve head diameter: | |
| XJ12 and Double Six | 1.358 to 1.362 in (34.5 to 34.6 mm) |
| XJS models | 1.355 to 1.365 in (34.42 to 34.67 mm) |
| Valve stem diameter | 0.3092 to 0.3093 in (7.854 to 7.866 mm) |
| Valve lift | 0.375 in (9.5 mm) |
| Valve spring free length: | |
| Outer | 2.103 in (53.4 mm) |
| Inner | 1.734 in (44.0 mm) |

## Valve guides and seats

| | |
|---|---|
| Valve guide length: | |
| Inlet | 1.910 in (48.5 mm) |
| Exhaust | 2.125 in (54.0 mm) |
| Valve guide outside diameter: | |
| Standard | 0.502 to 0.501 in (12.75 to 12.72 mm) |
| 1st oversize (2 grooves) | 0.507 to 0.506 in (12.88 to 12.85 mm) |
| 2nd oversize (3 grooves) | 0.512 to 0.511 in (13.01 to 12.98 mm) |
| Valve guide finished bore | 0.311 to 0.312 in (7.90 to 7.92 mm) |
| Minimum clearance, valve stem to guide | 0.0020 to 0.0023 in (0.05 to 0.06 mm) |
| Interference fit in head | 0.002 to 0.006 in (0.05 to 0.15 mm) |

## Tappets

| | |
|---|---|
| Outside diameter | 1.373 to 1.374 in (34.87 to 34.90 mm) |
| Running clearance | 0.001 to 0.002 in (0.02 to 0.04 mm) |

## Timing gear

| | |
|---|---|
| Chain | Duplex endless |
| Pitch | 0.375 in (9.5 mm) |
| No of pitches | 180 |
| Camshaft sprocket teeth | 42 |
| Crankshaft sprocket teeth | 21 |
| Jackshaft sprocket teeth | 21 |

## Lubrication system

| | |
|---|---|
| Oil pump type | Epicyclic gear |
| Gear clearances: | |
| Driving gear to housing | 0.005 to 0.012 in (0.127 to 0.305 mm) |
| Driving gear to crescent | 0.0025 to 0.006 in (0.065 to 0.152 mm) |
| Driven gear to housing | 0.007 to 0.010 in (0.178 to 0.254 mm) |
| Driven gear to crescent | 0.011 to 0.018 in (0.28 to 0.46 mm) |
| Driving and driven gear endfloat | 0.0045 to 0.0065 in (0.115 to 0.165 mm) |
| Oil filter type | Full flow, externally mounted. Early models – renewable element; later models – disposable cartridge |
| Oil type/specification | Multigrade engine oil, viscosity range SAE 10W/30 to 20W/50, to BLSO OL.02, MIL-L-2104B or API SE* (Duckhams QXR, Hypergrade, or 10W/40 Motor Oil) |
| Engine oil capacity (including filter change) | |
| XJ12, Double Six: | |
| Series 1 | 16 Imp pts (19.2 US pts, 9.1 litres) |
| Series 2 on | 19 Imp pts (23.0 US pts, 10.7 litres) |
| XJS | 20 Imp pts (24.0 US pts, 11.4 litres) |

** The vehicle manufacturers do not recommend the use of oils with viscosity SAE 10W/30 or 10W/40 when the ambient temperature is above 59°F (15°C)*

## Torque wrench settings

| | lbf ft | Nm |
|---|---|---|
| Cylinder head nuts ($\frac{7}{16}$ in): | | |
| Stage 1 | 25 | 34 |
| Stage 2 | 40 | 54 |
| Stage 3 | 52 | 71 |
| Cylinder head nuts ($\frac{3}{8}$ in): | | |
| Stage 1 | 20 | 27 |
| Stage 2 | 28 | 38 |
| Main bearing nuts ($\frac{3}{8}$ in) | 28 | 38 |
| Main bearing nuts ($\frac{1}{2}$ in) | 62 | 84 |
| Big-end nuts | 37 | 50 |
| Flywheel bolts | 66 | 90 |
| Crankshaft pulley bolt | 150 | 204 |
| Camshaft bearing cap nuts | 9 | 12 |
| Camshaft cover screws | 8 | 11 |
| Driveplate to torque converter bolts | 35 | 48 |
| Oil filter centre bolt | 20 | 27 |
| Rear mounting to bodyframe bolts ($\frac{5}{16}$ in) | 18 | 25 |
| Rear mounting to bodyframe bolts ($\frac{3}{8}$ in) | 32 | 44 |
| Front mounting to crossmember | 18 | 25 |
| Rear mounting to engine | 30 | 41 |
| Flexible mounting nuts | 30 | 41 |
| Exhaust manifolds to downpipes | 25 | 34 |

## 1 General description

1 The engine fitted to all models is of twelve cylinder V type with a single overhead camshaft on each bank of cylinders.
2 The crankshaft runs in seven main bearings and from a sprocket mounted on its front end drives the camshafts and a centrally mounted jackshaft by means of a self-adjusting endless duplex chain.
3 The jackshaft drives the distributor.
4 The cylinder block is of light alloy construction with wet liners.
5 Aluminium alloy pistons are used with shallow combustion chamber depressions in their heads.
6 Two compression piston rings and one oil control ring are fitted to each piston. The gudgeon pins are of the fully floating type, retained by circlips.
7 The cylinder heads are also of light alloy construction, incorporating the valves with double valve springs.
8 The camshafts run directly in bores machined in the tappet blocks, which can be detached separately from the cylinder heads. A complete cylinder head and tappet block can be removed from its cylinder block without the need to disturb the valve timing.
9 The lubrication system comprises a crankshaft driven oil pump, an externally mounted oil filter and a bypass oil cooler (connected to the cooling system).
10 Earlier models use carburettor fuel systems (with emission control for N America). Later versions are equipped with a fuel injection system.
11 The ignition system is of Lucas Opus electronic type and incorporates a magnetic impulse type distributor which does away with the conventional mechanical contact breaker.

## 2 Major operations possible with engine in car

1 The following components or assemblies can be removed and refitted without removing the engine from the car:

*Ancillaries:*
- *Alternator (Chapter 10)*
- *Distributor (Chapter 4)*
- *Manifolds (Chapter 3)*
- *Fuel injection system components (Chapter 3)*
- *Carburettors (Chapter 3)*

*Covered in later Sections of this Chapter:*
- *Camshaft covers (Section 8 or 9)*
- *Camshaft (Section 10)*
- *Tappet block (Section 11)*
- *Crankshaft front oil seal (Section 12)*
- *Oil sump pan (Section 13)*
- *Sandwich plate (Section 14)*
- *Oil pressure relief valve (Section 15)*

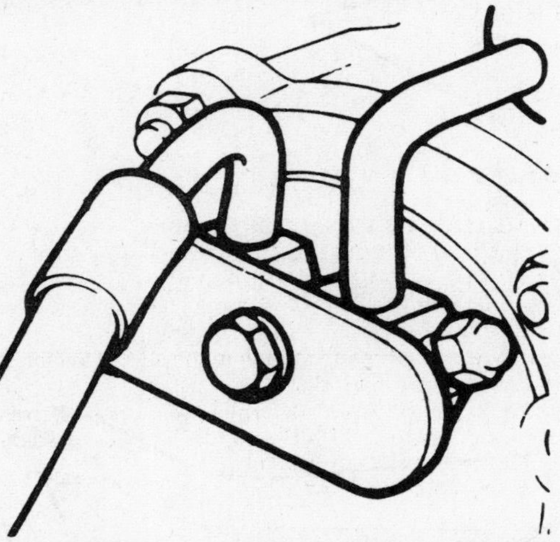

**Fig. 1.1 Suction and pressure hose connections to air conditioner compressor (Sec 3)**

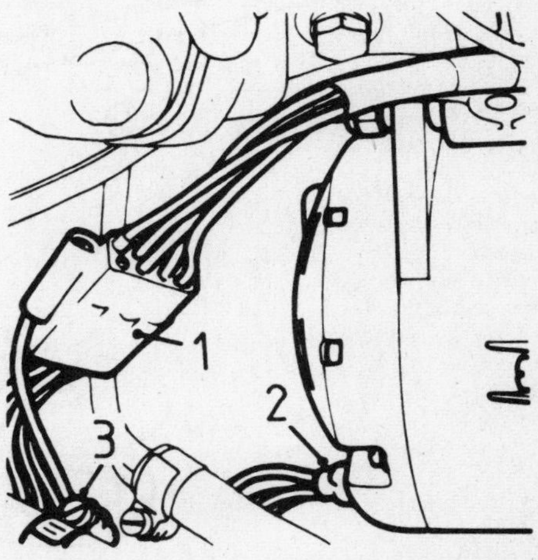


**Fig. 1.2 Engine harness connector plug (1), alternator connector (2) and brake servo pipe (3) (Sec 3)**

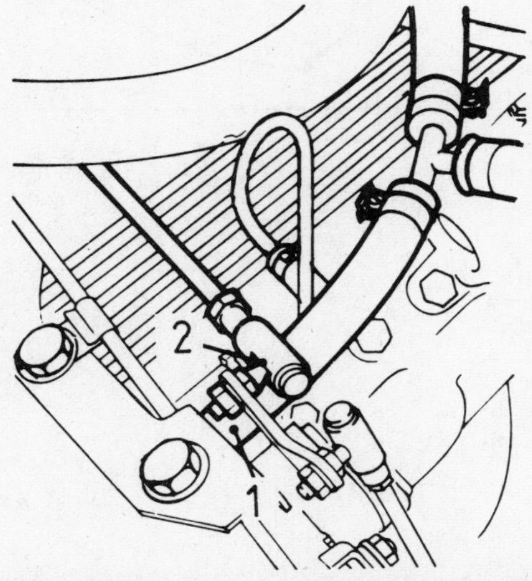


**Fig. 1.3 Heater system vacuum pipe (1) and throttle cross-rod (2) (Sec 3)**

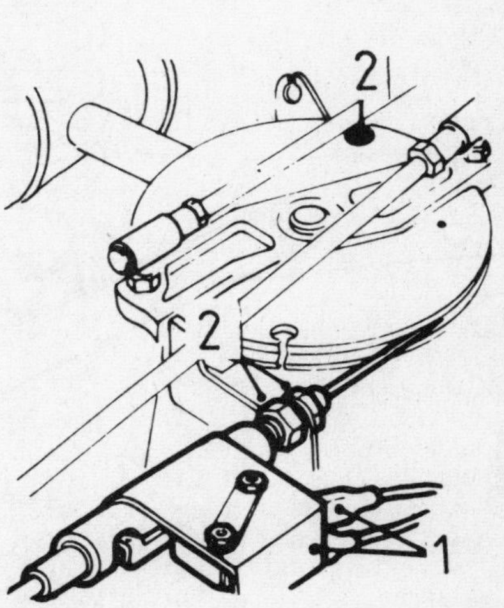


**Fig. 1.4 Kickdown switch electrical connector (1) and throttle cables (2) (Sec 3)**

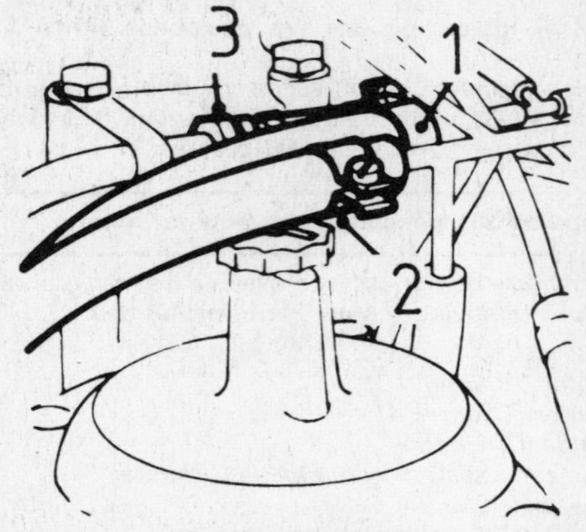


Fig. 1.5 Hose to carburettor balance pipe (1), float chamber breather balance pipe (2) and petrol feed pipe (3) (Sec 3)

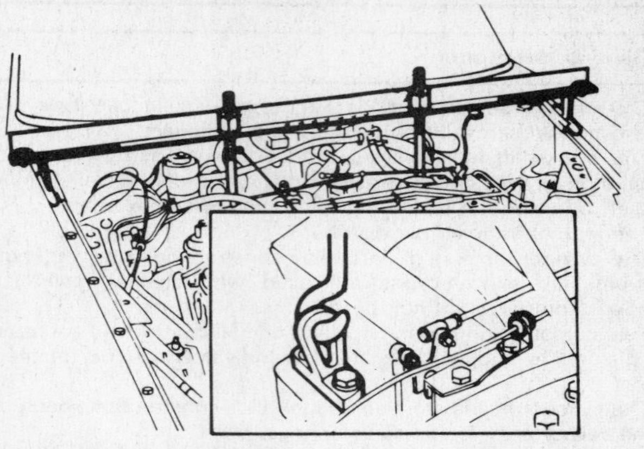

Fig. 1.6 Typical engine support crossbar (Sec 3)

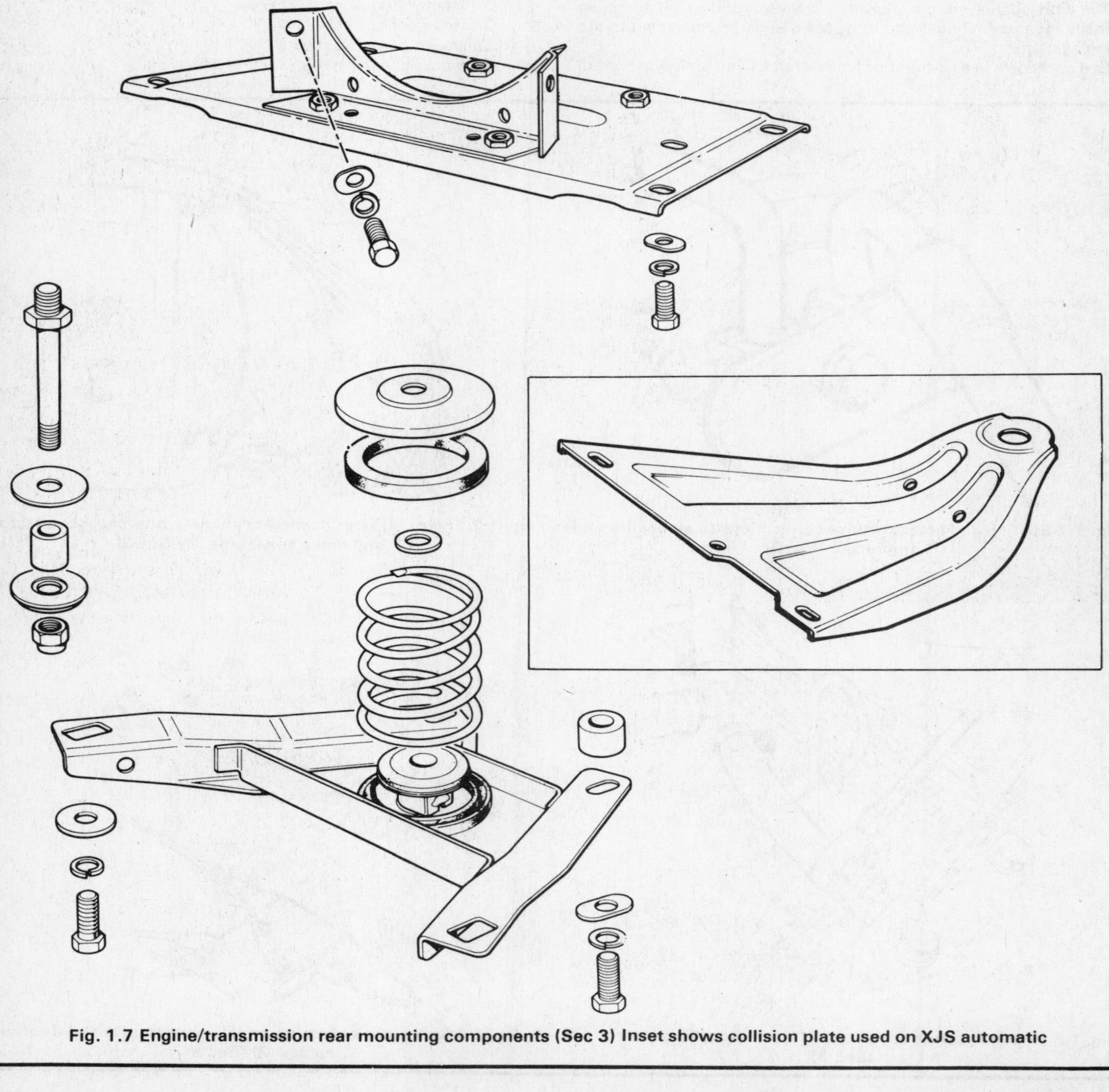

Fig. 1.7 Engine/transmission rear mounting components (Sec 3) Inset shows collision plate used on XJS automatic

3.9A Disconnecting the refrigerant pipe ahead of the condenser

3.9B Disconnecting the refrigerant pipe at the right-hand side of the engine compartment

3.11 Air conditioning compressor removed to the side of the engine compartment

3.15A Power steering pump pipe connection (arrowed)

3.15B Power steering fluid cooler

3.27 Starter motor cable bulkhead terminal (arrowed)

3.28A Engine front shield

3.28B Engine front shield bolt and bracket

3.33 Speedometer drive cable connection to transmission

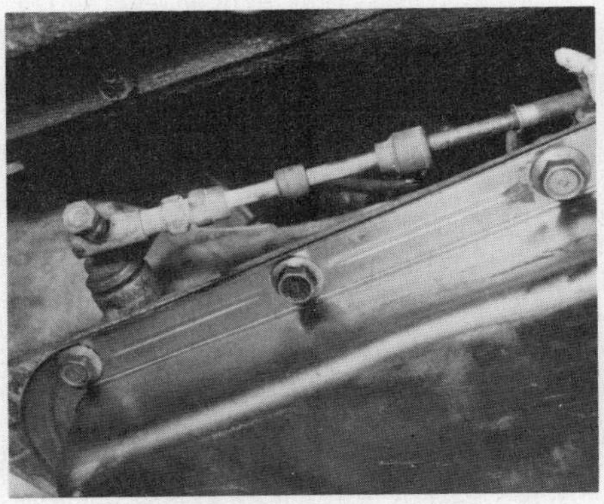

3.34 Front end attachment of speed selector cable

3.35 Transmission-to-body earth strap

*Oil pick up strainer (Section 16)*
*Engine oil cooler (Section 17)*
*Cylinder heads (Section 18, 19 or 20)*
*Crankshaft main bearing shells (Section 22)*
*Big-end bearing shells (Section 23)*
*Engine mountings (Section 24, 25 or 26)*
*Oil filter (Section 27 or 29)*

2 For all other major overhaul operations, the engine/transmission should be removed and the transmission then separated from the engine.
3 Remember that most of the engine castings are of light alloy construction. Do not lever against them or strike them with a heavy hammer or they may distort or fracture.

## 3 Engine/transmission (XJ12 and Double Six with carburettors) – removal

### *Cars equipped with air conditioning*

1 Have the system discharged by your dealer or a professional refrigeration engineer. *On no account release any of the refrigerated circuit pipe unions before discharging the system,* otherwise dangerous refrigerant gas will escape.

### *All cars*

2 Position the car over an inspection pit or place it on ramps to give working space under the engine/transmission.
3 Mark the bonnet hinge and restraining link positions and with the help of an assistant, unbolt and remove the bonnet. Store it in a safe place where it will not get scratched.
4 Disconnect and remove the battery. If the car is to be left outside whilst the overhaul takes place, remember to raise the power-operated windows before removing the battery.
5 Unbolt and remove the wing valance stays (angled corners nearest the engine compartment rear bulkhead).
6 Drain the cooling system, retaining the antifreeze if it is suitable for further use.
7 Remove the air cleaners (Chapter 3).
8 Remove the radiator and engine oil cooler as described in Chapter 2. As the radiator top rail is unbolted, disconnect the minimum number of electrical relay connections and swing the top rail onto the top of the right-hand front wing.

### *Cars with air conditioning*

9 Disconnect the air conditioner (system previously discharged) by releasing the union nut at the flexible-to-rigid pipe connection located just before the condenser (photo). Disconnect the remaining hose from the condenser (photo). Plug or cap all refrigerant circuit openings immediately to prevent the entry of moist air. Unbolt and remove the condenser.
10 Unbolt the amplifier from the forward end of the jackshaft cover plate located between the two cylinder banks. Lift the amplifier and unbolt the compressor rear mounting. Unbolt the compressor and release the hoses from the right-hand wing valance stay. Slacken the compressor drivebelt idler pulley adjuster and slip the belt from the compressor pulley.
11 Unbolt the compressor front mounting and having disconnected the electrical leads, lift the compressor from the engine and secure it on the left-hand wing upper surface (photo).

### *All cars*

12 Identify and disconnect the coolant expansion tank hoses at the engine end.
13 Reaching down on either side of the engine, remove the nuts which hold the engine mountings to their brackets.
14 Drain the fluid from the power-assisted steering pump reservoir and cooler (see Chapter 11).
15 Disconnect the fluid supply and return pipes from the power steering pump. Move the pipes complete with cooling fins (photos).
16 Disconnect the leads from the rear of the alternator and separate the engine harness connector plug.
17 Disconnect the brake servo vacuum hose.
18 Disconnect the fuel supply pipe at the crossover pipe stub (see Fig.

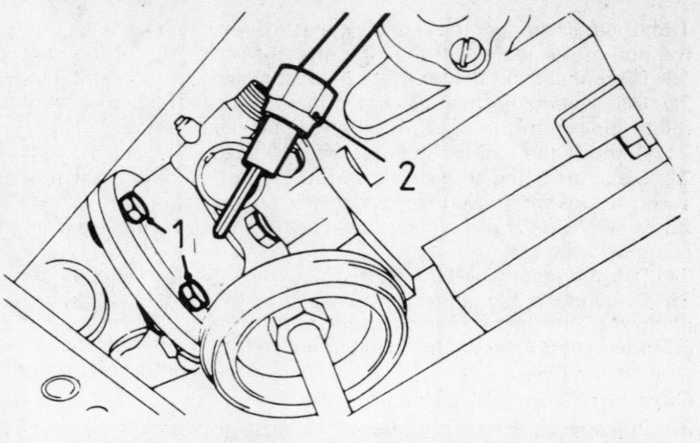


**Fig. 1.8 Propeller shaft front flange bolts (1) and speedometer drive cable (2) (Sec 3)**

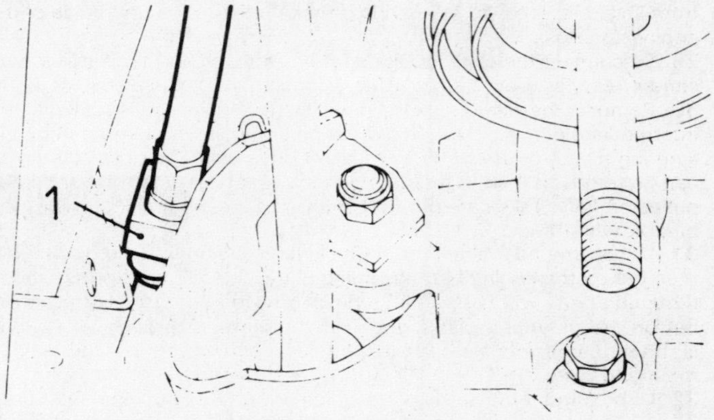


**Fig. 1.9 Gearshift selector abutment (1) (Sec 3)**

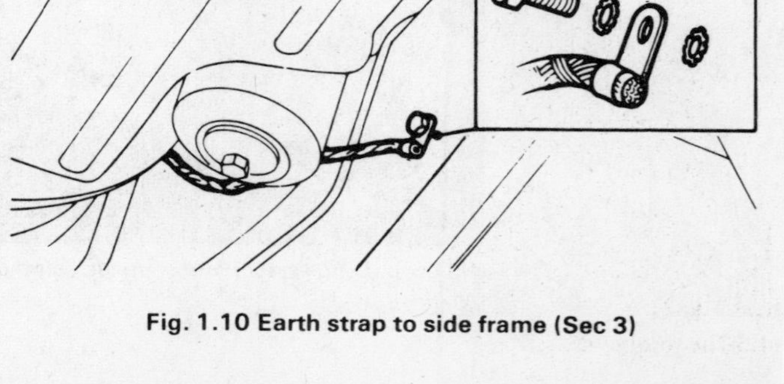

**Fig. 1.10 Earth strap to side frame (Sec 3)**

1.5), then disconnect the return pipe at the flexible hose which runs to the non-return valve. Tie the pipe and hose back out of the way.
19 Disconnect the heater system vacuum pipe at its manifold stub.
20 Disconnect the heater system coolant valve feed pipe, also the return pipe from the coolant rail at the bulkhead union.
21 Remove the ignition coil and ballast resistor.
22 Disconnect the throttle cross-rod at the left-hand bellcrank and swing it forward so that it rests on the engine.
23 Where fitted, disconnect the choke operating cables from the carburettors.
24 Pull the electrical connectors from the kickdown switch.
25 Disconnect the throttle cables from the pedestal plate and platform. On right-hand drive models, remove the throttle cable grommet bracket from the manifold bolt.

### *Cars with fuel emission control*

26 Pull the pipe (carbon canister connecting) from the carburettor balance pipe, also the one from the carburettor float chamber breather balance pipe.

### *All models*

27 Disconnect the starter motor supply cable from the bulkhead terminal (photo).
28 A crossbar engine support fitted with a hook will now be required similar to the one shown in Fig. 1.6. It should engage in the drip channel on either side of the engine compartment and be positioned directly above the engine rear lifting eyes. Rotate the raising or lowering screws on the support bar to take the weight of the engine off its mountings. At this stage, it is recommended that the engine front shield is removed to provide better access to the underside of the engine (photos).
29 Disconnect the exhaust pipes from the manifold flanges. The nuts can be reached from below using a long socket extension.
30 Remove the exhaust front pipe flanges which connect with the intermediate pipes and withdraw the pipe that is not obstructed by the steering pinion housing. On right-hand drive cars, the obstructed pipe can be removed if full right steering lock is applied and the handbrake pulled on fully. Take care not to damage the steering rack gaiter as the pipe is withdrawn.
31 Unbolt the heat shield on both sides of the engine rear mounting, then unbolt the engine rear mounting plate. Support the spring-loaded mounting plate with a jack and a block of wood and release the centre nut on the mounting plate. Unbolt the stengthening plate where one is fitted (later models). Lower the jack and withdraw the engine mounting plate.
32 Unbolt and remove the plate which covers the propeller shaft front flange. The two setscrews above the plate, which are accessible from the forward edge, should not be overlooked. Mark the relative alignment of the propeller shaft and transmission output flanges and unbolt them.
33 Disconnect the speedometer drive cable from the transmission (photo).
34 Disconnect the front end of the speed selector cable from the transmission and then release the outer cable pinch-bolt at the cable trunnion bracket on the side of the transmission casing. If the centre console is now removed (see Chapter 12), the speed selector cable assembly can be withdrawn towards the rear of the car by gripping the cable loop adjacent to the speed selector quadrant on the transmission tunnel. The cables will then be drawn out of the trunnion bracket and disconnected from the transmission (photo).
35 Disconnect the earth strap from the side subframe by unscrewing the setscrew (photo).
36 Support the transmission oil pan on a trolley jack using a block of wood as an insulator. Once the weight is taken on the jack, remove the engine crossbar support and lifting hooks.
37 A substantial hoist will now be required to be able to lift out the engine/transmission. Make sure that the chains attached to the engine lifting eyes meet the following length requirements:

*Front engine lifting eyes to hook of hoist – 34.5 in (876 mm)*
*Rear engine lifting eyes to hook of hoist – 41.0 in (1041 mm)*

38 Take the weight of the engine on the hoist, at the same time raising the trolley jack to keep the engine level. Raise 2 to 3 in (50 to 70 mm) initially, then commence sideways pressure on the engine to keep it clear of the steering pinion housing and power steering gear pipework. Continue to lift, keeping the engine/transmission level so that damage does not occur to the air conditioner expansion valve or the evaporator unions.
39 Hoist the engine/transmission from the engine compartment, increasing its tilt angle until the transmission output flange clears the bulkhead.

## 4 Engine/transmission (XJ12 and Double Six with fuel injection) – removal

1 The operations are very similar to those described in Section 3 for carburettor engines, except that all reference to carburettor and fuel system operations should be ignored and the following work substituted.
2 With the air conditioning system discharged, depressurise the fuel system as described in Chapter 3 and then remove the fuel cooler. Plug all open hoses.
3 Disconnect the leads from the ambient and coolant temperature sensors.
4 Release the cold start relay wiring harness from its relay.
5 Disconnect the cable from the throttle switch and trigger unit (photo).

4.5 The throttle switch

4.10 The modulator (GM400 automatic transmission)

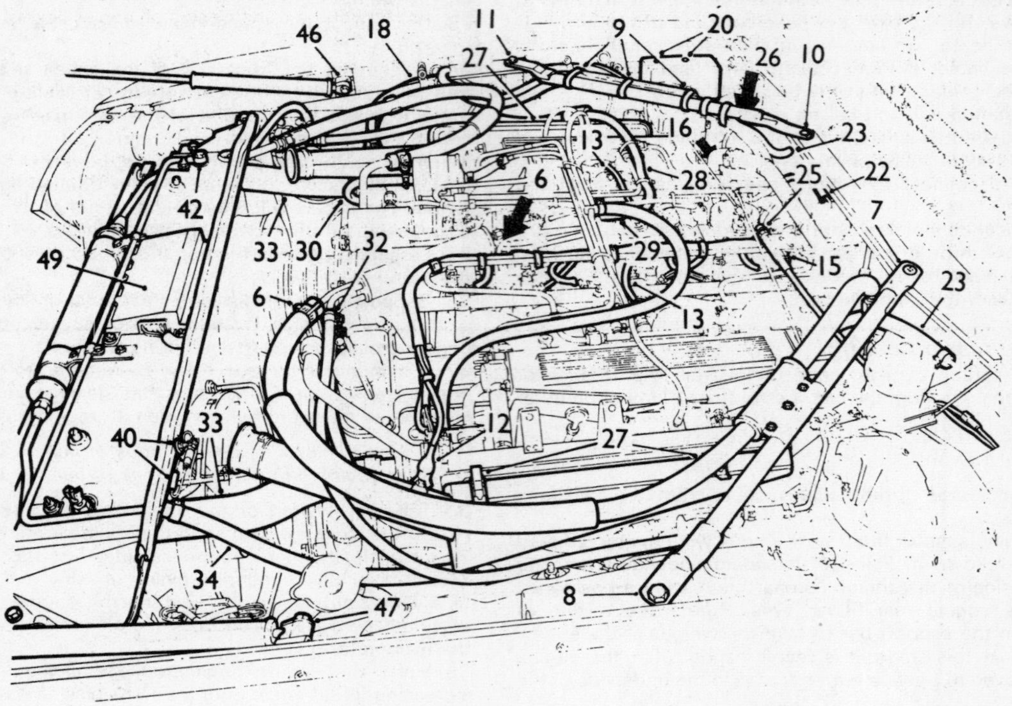


Fig. 1.11 XJS engine disconnection points (Sec 5)

*6 Fuel cooler refrigerant pipe*
*7 Wing valance stay screw*
*8 Wing valance stay bolt*
*9 Wiring harness clips*
*10 Right-hand stay screw*
*11 Right-hand stay bolt*
*12 Temperature sensors*
*13 Cold start relay wiring harness*
*15 Kickdown switch wires*
*16 Earth leads to induction manifold*
*18 Engine main harness*
*20 Cold start relay cover screws*
*22 Coolant rail to heater valve connection*
*23 Brake servo pipe*
*25 Throttle cable at pedestal*
*26 Starter leads at bulkhead connector*
*27 Air cleaners*
*28 Fuel pressure sensor feed pipe*
*29 Fuel pressure sensor feed pipe tee piece*
*30 Fuel pipes to filter*
*32 Fuel pipe to fuel cooler*
*33 Hose connections to thermostat housing*
*34 Expansion tank hose*
*40 Fan motor fuse clips*
*42 Radiator expansion pipe banjo connector*
*46 Bonnet stay bracket*
*47 Bonnet stay bracket*
*49 Radiator top rail assembly*

6 Remove (two screws) the cover from the cold start relay. Refer to Chapter 3 for details of the relay. Note the positions of the connecting wires, disconnect them and manoeuvre them through the valance bracket.
7 Remove the air cleaner covers and elements.
8 Release the clips which secure the pressure sensor feed pipe, then disconnect the pipe from the T-piece and plug all open connections.
9 Disconnect the lead from the low coolant sensor on the right-hand side of the radiator.
10 On cars which are equipped with GM400 automatic transmission (1978 on), disconnect the kickdown solenoid supply wire and unclip the wire from the transmission. Disconnect the vacuum tube from the modulator capsule (photo). Unbolt the modulator and withdraw it, but make sure that a suitably large container is placed underneath to catch the transmission fluid which will drain out. Discard the O-ring seal.

## 5 Engine/transmission (XJS with manual or automatic transmission) – removal

### *Cars with air conditioning*

1 Have the air conditioning system discharged by your dealer or a qualified refrigeration engineer. *Do not disconnect any part of the system yourself* or dangerous refrigerant gas may escape.

### *All cars*

2 Place the car over an inspection pit or on ramps to provide adequate working clearance underneath.
3 Remove the bonnet with the help of an assistant and then the radiator lower grille. Store them in a safe place.
4 Disconnect the battery.
5 Drain the cooling system (Chapter 2).
6 Depressurise the fuel system (Chapter 3).

### *Cars with air conditioning*

7 Disconnect and remove the fuel hoses from the fuel cooler. Plug all open hoses. Unclip the condenser pipe from the radiator top rail.
8 Disconnect the outlet pipe from the receiver dryer.

### *All cars*

9 Remove the left-hand wing valance stay, releasing the wiring harness or hose from it as it is withdrawn.
10 Disconnect the wires from the air temperature and coolant temperature sensors (fuel injection system).
11 Release the cold start relay wiring harness from the left-hand fuel rail and crossover pipe.
12 Disconnect the operating cable from the throttle switch and trigger unit (fuel injection system).
13 Disconnect the earth leads from the right-hand induction manifold, and the cables from the kickdown switch (automatic transmission).
14 Unclip the engine main wiring harness and swing it clear, then uncouple the harness multi-plug connector.
15 Remove the cover from the cold start relay on the right-hand wing valance. Mark the wiring connections, disconnect them from the relay and pull the harness through the valance bracket.
16 Disconnect the right-hand coolant rail feed pipe from the heater valve.

17 Disconnect the brake vacuum servo hoses from the left and right induction manifolds and the heater vacuum pipe from the right-hand induction manifold.
18 Disconnect the throttle cable from the throttle bracket.
19 Disconnect the starter motor and solenoid cables from their bulkhead connector.
20 Remove the air cleaner covers and filter elements.
21 Release the pressure sensor pipe securing clips (fuel injection system). Disconnect the pipe from the T-piece and plug all openings.
22 Release and disconnect the fuel pipes from the fuel filter and plug all openings. Also disconnect the fuel pipe from the cooler.
23 Disconnect the radiator top hoses from the thermostat housings.
24 Disconnect the hose from the remote expansion tank, also the heater return hose from the T-piece.

*Cars with automatic transmission*

25 Disconnect the transmission oil cooler flexible hoses from the rigid pipes. Plug the pipes.

*All cars*

26 Disconnect the alternator wiring harness at the snap connectors.
27 Disconnect the thermostatic switch two pin connector, then release the harness clips.
28 Remove and disconnect the fan motor line fuse.
29 Disconnect the smaller of the two block connectors at the front end of the right-hand wing valance.
30 Disconnect the expansion pipe (banjo union) from the radiator.
31 Unbolt the radiator top rail, noting the positions of the earth lead and wiring harness clip.
32 Unbolt the fan cowl from the radiator top rail.

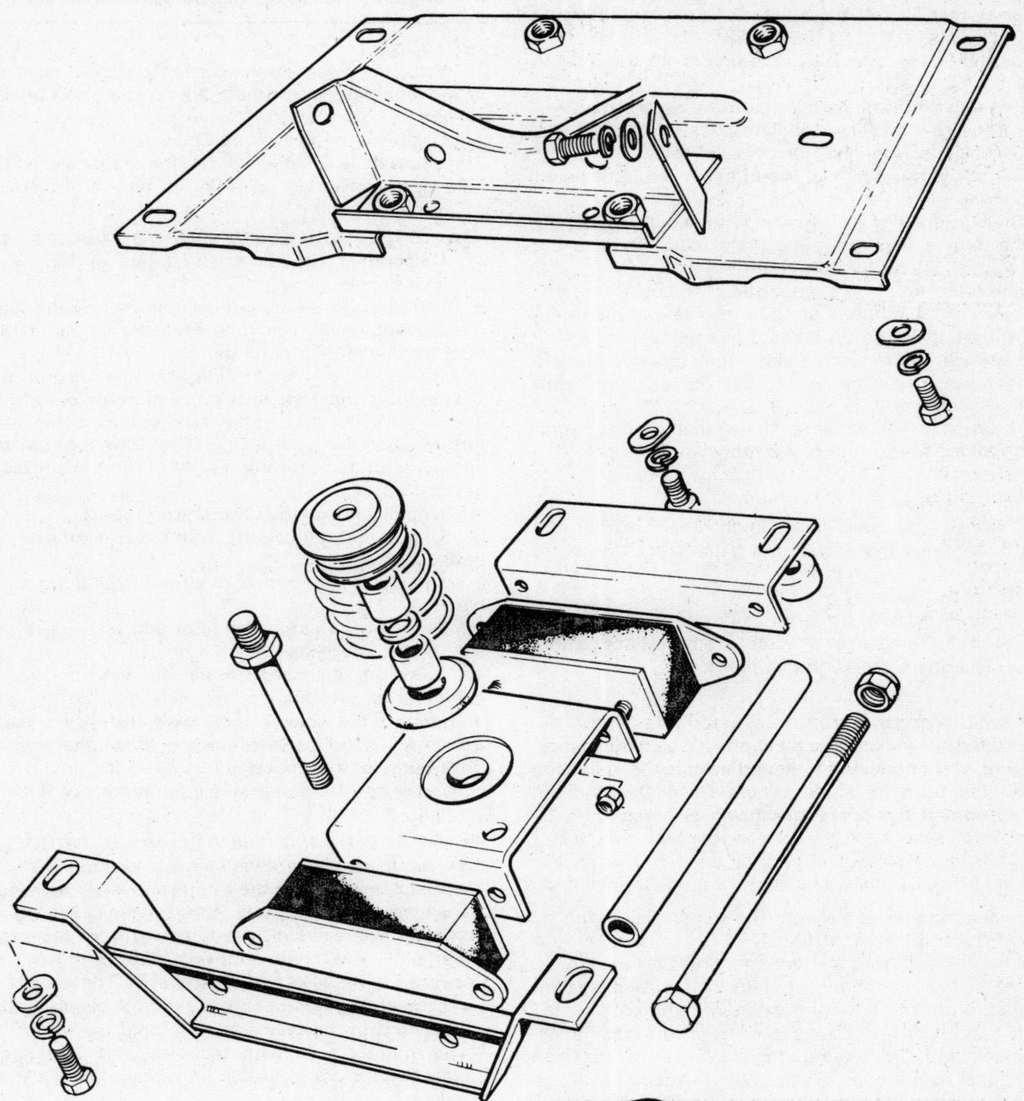

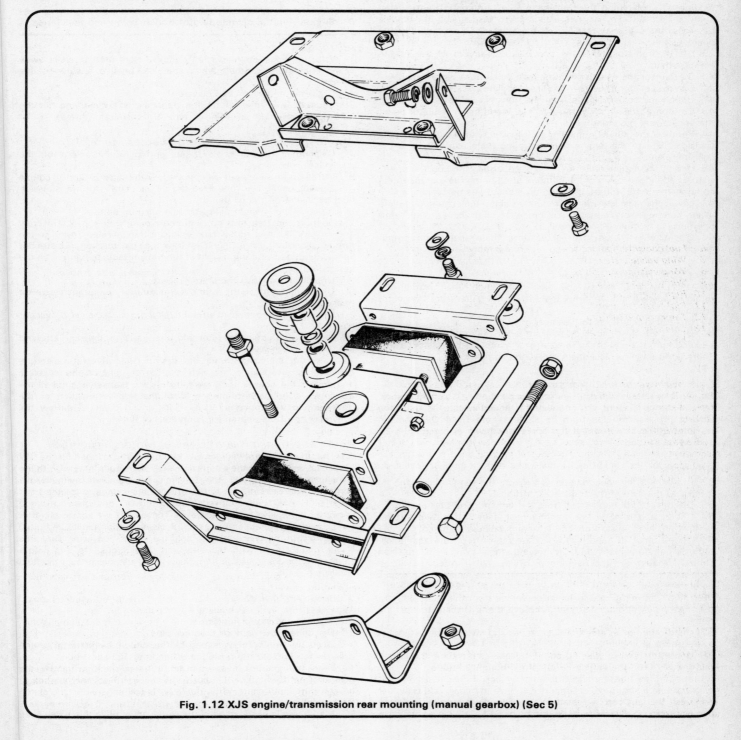

Fig. 1.12 XJS engine/transmission rear mounting (manual gearbox) (Sec 5)

33 Unbolt the stays from the left and right-hand brackets.
34 Remove the radiator top rail (complete with evaporator and receiver dryer on air conditioned cars). Note the copper washers and spacer located over the tapped hole into which the expansion pipe banjo bolt screws.
35 An engine support crossbar should now be fitted to engage in the drip channel on either side of the engine compartment. Position it directly over the engine rear lifting eyes, connect the lifting hooks and adjust to take the weight of the engine.
36 Disconnect the wire from the low coolant sensor which is located in the right-hand side of the radiator.
37 Unbolt the fan cowl from the bottom of the radiator.
38 Disconnect the radiator bottom hose and then lift the radiator enough to be able to disconnect the oil cooler pipes from the base (engine oil cooler) and the right-hand side (automatic transmission fluid cooler). Always use two spanners to disconnect the unions, otherwise the seat may tear out of the radiator coolant tank. Plug all openings.
39 Lift the radiator, fan cowl and electric fan out of the engine compartment.
40 Disconnect the exhaust intermediate pipes from the downpipes.
41 Disconnect the front, rear and intermediate heat shields.
42 Unbolt the collision plate from the transmission unit.
43 Position a trolley jack with a block of wood as an insulator under the engine rear mounting plate.
44 Remove the single remaining self-locking nut which holds the collision plate to the engine rear mounting plate stud. Remove the collision plate.
45 Unbolt the engine rear mounting plate, noting the position of any spacers and the location of the different sized bolts. The rear mounting components are of different design on manual gearbox versions.
46 Lower the jack, remove the mounting plate, the seating plate and allied components. Remove the propeller shaft cover plate after reference to Section 3, Paragraph 32.
47 Disconnect the propeller shaft from the transmission output flange, marking the flanges for correct reassembly.

### *Cars with manual gearbox*

48 Unscrew and remove the gear lever knob, then extract the retaining screws and withdraw the gasket and gaiter from the centre console.
49 Move the gear lever to first gear position.
50 Unbolt the clutch slave cylinder from the bellhousing. Release the pushrod from the end of the release lever and push the cylinder aside. There is no need to disconnect the hydraulic pipes.

### *Cars with automatic transmission*

51 Disconnect the gearshift selector cable from its trunnion block, remove the self-locking nut and slide the speed selector lever on the side of the transmission from its shaft. Where GM400 automatic transmission is fitted, repeat the operations given in paragraphs 24 and 34 of Section 3.

### *All cars*

52 Disconnect the speedometer cable from the transmission and tie it back to the side of the transmission tunnel.
53 Disconnect the earth strap from the transmission bellhousing.
54 Unbolt and remove the steering gear gaiter heat shields, then remove the heat shield from the left-hand exhaust manifold.
55 Unbolt the left-hand exhaust downpipes from the manifolds, remove the downpipes and the sealing rings. Where an emission control exhaust gas recirculation (EGR) system is fitted, it will be necessary to disconnect the EGR pipes from the exhaust downpipes before removal.
56 Unbolt the right-hand exhaust downpipe from the manifold, turn the downpipes through 180° and remove them. Discard the sealing rings.
57 Unbolt the power steering fluid cooler and swing it on its bracket away from the engine.
58 Unbolt the power steering pump, release its drivebelt and tie the pump away from the engine in its normal upright attitude.
59 Support the transmission with a trolley jack. If the car is over a pit or on ramps, a strong cross support will have to be laid under the car on which the jack can be rested. Where possible it is to be preferred if the car can be pushed from the ramps or pit to provide a solid base for the jack. On cars with automatic transmission, place the jack under the rear extension housing, *not* the oil pan.
60 Remove the engine support crossbar (see paragraph 35) and attach lifting chains to the engine lifting eyes. The rear chains should be 6.0 in (154 mm) longer than the front ones. Use a hoist of adequate lifting capacity.
61 Lift the engine/transmission carefully from the car (photo). Adjust the jack under the transmission as necessary so that the engine/transmission finally takes on a steeply inclined angle as it is withdrawn from the engine compartment. On cars with manual gearbox, take care that the gear control lever is below the console and transmission tunnel during removal. Ensure that the steering gear and hydraulic pipework are not damaged during engine removal.

## 6 Engine – initial dismantling of transmission and ancillaries

### *All models*

1 With the engine/transmission removed from the car, clean away all external dirt using either paraffin and a stiff brush or a water-soluble solvent.
2 Drain the engine oil and discard it.
3 Separate the engine from the transmission by carrying out the following operations according to type of transmission fitted.

### *Automatic transmission (Borg Warner Model 12)*

4 Disconnect the oil cooler pipes and plug the unions on the transmission housing.
5 Withdraw the breather pipe, withdraw the dipstick and uncouple the dipstick guide/filler tube from the oil pan. Drain the transmission fluid by taking off the oil pan.
6 Remove the vacuum pipe from the vacuum unit.
7 Support the transmission, preferably on a trolley jack. Unscrew and remove the four nuts which hold the transmission casing to the torque converter bellhousing. Withdraw the transmission in a straight line, without allowing the weight of the transmission to hang upon the input shaft.
8 Unbolt and remove the starter motor.
9 Unbolt and remove the front cover plate from the torque converter housing.
10 Unbolt the torque converter housing from the engine cylinder block.
11 Remove the engine oil filter and the plug from the rear left-hand side of the crankcase.
12 Turn the crankshaft until the first of the driveplate-to-torque converter screws comes into view. Flatten the tabs on the lockplate and extract the screw. Continue to rotate the crankshaft until all the setscrews have been removed. Mark the relative position of the driveplate to the converter using quick-drying paint. Withdraw the converter and be prepared for some loss of fluid.

### *Automatic transmission (General Motors Type 400)*

13 The operations are very similar to those just described for the BW Model 12, except that the torque converter housing is integral with the transmission casing and the transmission complete with torque converter will therefore be removed from the engine, once the front cover plate has been removed (photo) and the driveplate-to-torque converter bolts have been withdrawn. These bolts are accessible after the rubber plug has been extracted. A clamping bar should be bolted to the front of the bellhousing to hold the torque converter rearwards in full engagement with the oil pump drive tangs. Do this before separating the transmission from the engine, also disconnect the fluid cooler pipes (photos).

### *Manual transmission*

14 Unbolt the flywheel housing cover plate.
15 Remove the starter motor.
16 Disconnect the gearbox breather pipe.
17 Unscrew the bolts which hold the clutch bellhousing to the cylinder block. Note the positions of the long and short bolts.
18 With the gearbox supported on a trolley jack, withdraw the gearbox from the engine. Do not allow the weight of the gearbox to hang on the input shaft whilst the latter is still engaged in the clutch driven plate.
19 Mark the relative position of the clutch cover plate to the flywheel.

5.61 Removing the engine/transmission

6.13A Front plate (GM400 transmission)

6.13B Side view of engine and GM400 automatic transmission

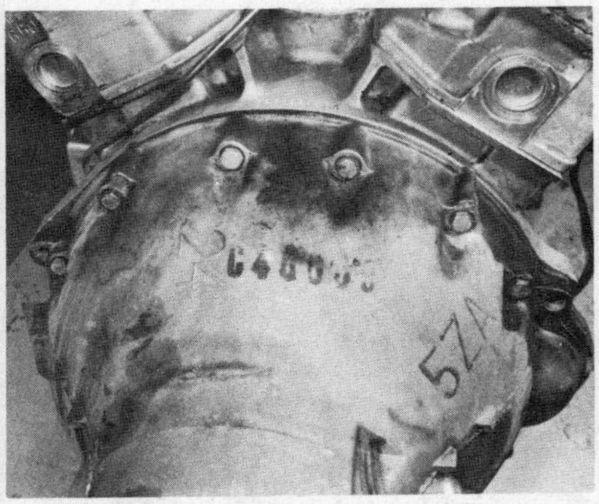

6.13C Torque converter housing upper bolts (GM 400)

6.13D Removing the driveplate bolt access plug (GM 400)

6.13E Unscrewing a driveplate/converter bolt (GM 400)

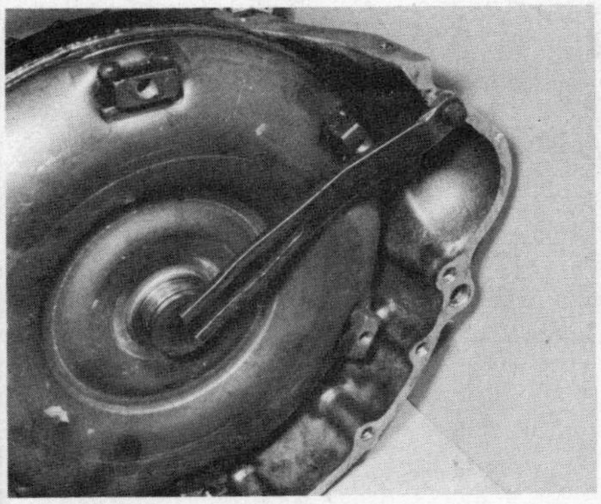

6.13F Torque converter temporary clamp

6.24 Idler assembly (fanbelt and fan removed)

7.3 Crankshaft front pulley fixing

7.4 Crankshaft front pulley/damper and centre bolt

7.5 Crankshaft damper cone

7.8A Coolant transfer pipe (arrowed)

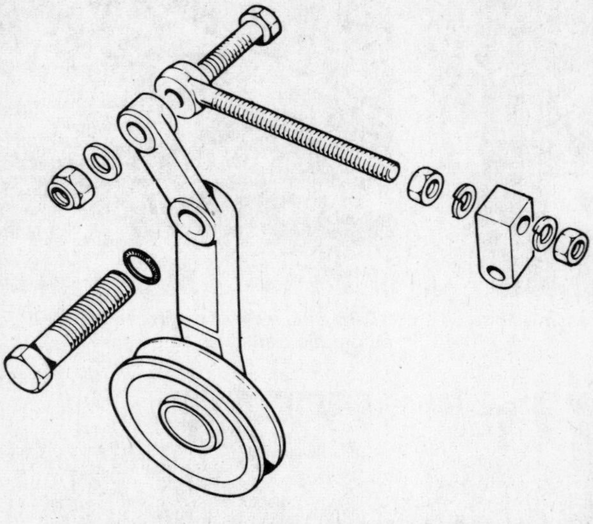

Fig. 1.13 Fanbelt idler (jockey) pulley assembly (Sec 6)

Fig. 1.14 Crankshaft damper and pulley (Sec 7)

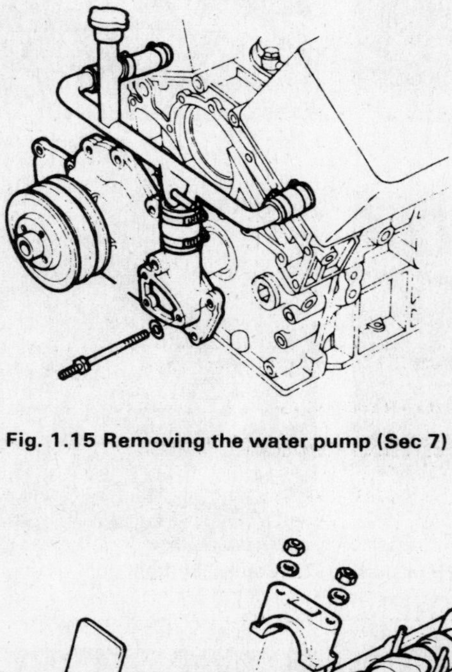

Fig. 1.15 Removing the water pump (Sec 7)

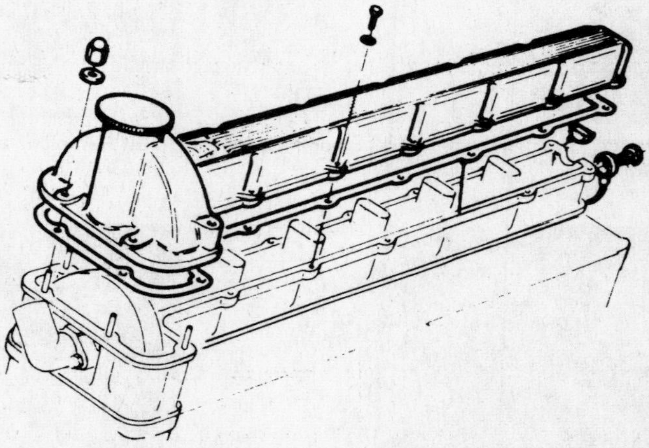

Fig. 1.16 Removing the camshaft cover (Sec 7)

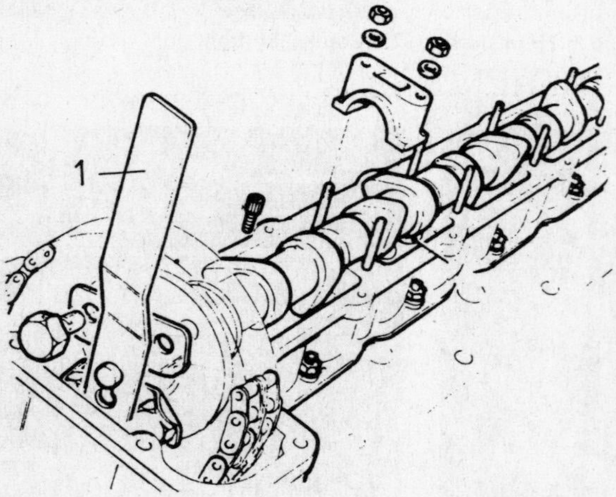


Fig. 1.17 Camshaft sprocket retaining tool (1) (Sec 7)

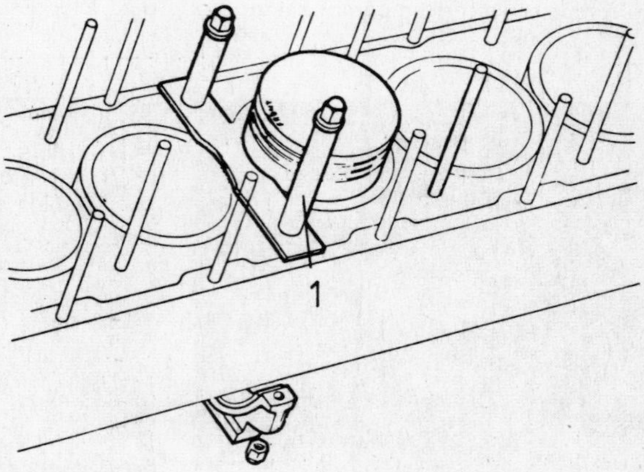


Fig. 1.18 Cylinder liner clamp (1) in position (Sec 7)

# Are your plugs trying to tell you something?

**Normal.**
Grey-brown deposits, lightly coated core nose. Plugs ideally suited to engine, and engine in good condition.

**Heavy Deposits.**
A build up of crusty deposits, light-grey sandy colour in appearance.
Fault: Often caused by worn valve guides, excessive use of upper cylinder lubricant, or idling for long periods.

**Lead Glazing.**
Plug insulator firing tip appears yellow or green/yellow and shiny in appearance.
Fault: Often caused by incorrect carburation, excessive idling followed by sharp acceleration. Also check ignition timing.

**Carbon fouling.**
Dry, black, sooty deposits.
Fault: over-rich fuel mixture.
Check: carburettor mixture settings, float level, choke operation, air filter.

**Oil fouling.**
Wet, oily deposits. Fault: worn bores/piston rings or valve guides; sometimes occurs (temporarily) during running-in period.

**Overheating.**
Electrodes have glazed appearance, core nose very white – few deposits. Fault: plug overheating. Check: plug value, ignition timing, fuel octane rating (too low) and fuel mixture (too weak).

**Electrode damage.**
Electrodes burned away; core nose has burned, glazed appearance. Fault: pre-ignition. Check: for correct heat range and as for 'overheating'.

**Split core nose.**
(May appear initially as a crack). Fault: detonation or wrong gap-setting technique. Check: ignition timing, cooling system, fuel mixture (too weak).

# WHY DOUBLE COPPER IS BETTER FOR YOUR ENGINE.

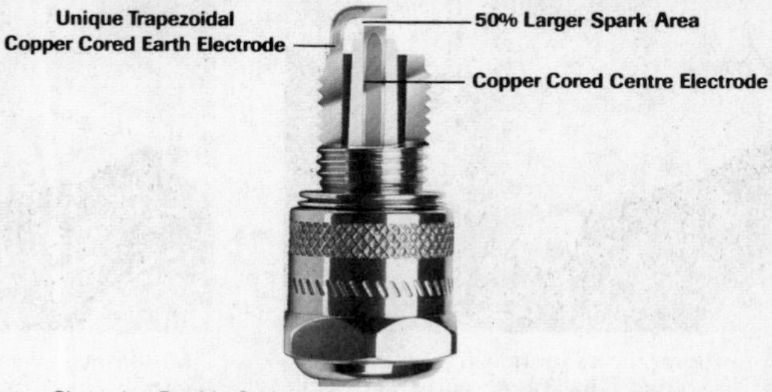


Champion Double Copper plugs are the first in the world to have copper core in both centre and earth electrode. This innovative design means that they run cooler by up to 100°C – giving greater efficiency and longer life. These double copper cores transfer heat away from the tip of the plug faster and more efficiently. Therefore, Double Copper runs at cooler temperatures than conventional plugs giving improved acceleration response and high speed performance with no fear of pre-ignition.

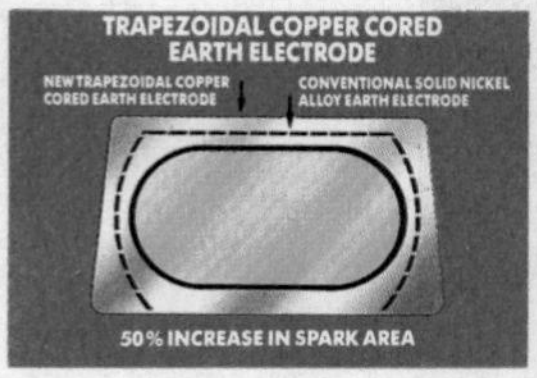


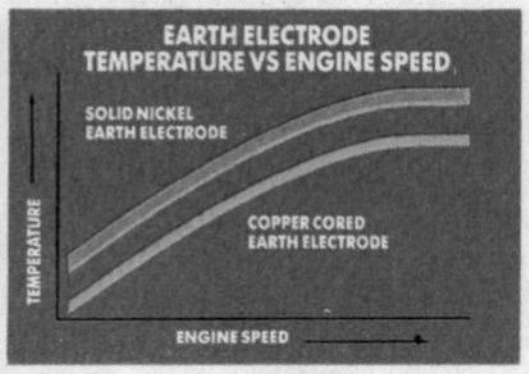


Champion Double Copper plugs also feature a unique trapezoidal earth electrode giving a 50% increase in spark area. This, together with the double copper cores, offers greatly reduced electrode wear, so the spark stays stronger for longer.

- FASTER COLD STARTING
- FOR UNLEADED OR LEADED FUEL
- ELECTRODES UP TO 100°C COOLER
- BETTER ACCELERATION RESPONSE
- LOWER EMISSIONS
- 50% BIGGER SPARK AREA
- THE LONGER LIFE PLUG

**Plug Tips/Hot and Cold.**
Spark plugs must operate within well-defined temperature limits to avoid cold fouling at one extreme and overheating at the other.
Champion and the car manufacturers work out the best plugs for an engine to give optimum performance under all conditions, from freezing cold starts to sustained high speed motorway cruising.
Plugs are often referred to as hot or cold. With Champion, the higher the number on its body, the hotter the plug, and the lower the number the cooler the plug.

**Plug Cleaning**
Modern plug design and materials mean that Champion no longer recommends periodic plug cleaning. Certainly don't clean your plugs with a wire brush as this can cause metal conductive paths across the nose of the insulator so impairing its performance and resulting in loss of acceleration and reduced m.p.g.
However, if plugs are removed, always carefully clean the area where the plug seats in the cylinder head as grit and dirt can sometimes cause gas leakage.
Also wipe any traces of oil or grease from plug leads as this may lead to arcing.

CHAMPION
DOUBLE COPPER

1

This photographic sequence shows the steps taken to repair the dent and paintwork damage shown above. In general, the procedure for repairing a hole will be similar; where there are substantial differences, the procedure is clearly described and shown in a separate photograph.

2

First remove any trim around the dent, then hammer out the dent where access is possible. This will minimise filling. Here, after the large dent has been hammered out, the damaged area is being made slightly concave.

3

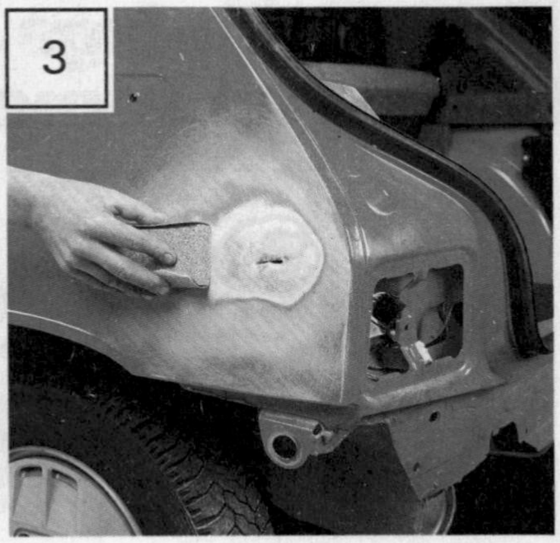

Next, remove all paint from the damaged area by rubbing with coarse abrasive paper or using a power drill fitted with a wire brush or abrasive pad. 'Feather' the edge of the boundary with good paintwork using a finer grade of abrasive paper.

4

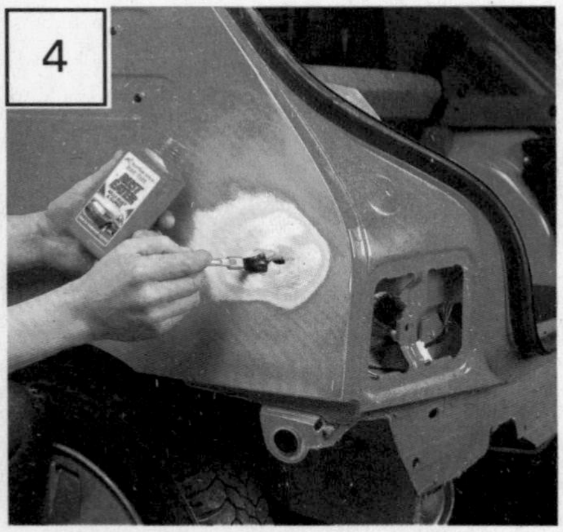

Where there are holes or other damage, the sheet metal should be cut away before proceeding further. The damaged area and any signs of rust should be treated with Turtle Wax Hi-Tech Rust Eater, which will also inhibit further rust formation.

5

*For a large dent or hole* mix Holts Body Plus Resin and Hardener according to the manufacturer's instructions and apply around the edge of the repair. Press Glass Fibre Matting over the repair area and leave for 20-30 minutes to harden. Then ...

5A

... brush more Holts Body Plus Resin and Hardener onto the matting and leave to harden. Repeat the sequence with two or three layers of matting, checking that the final layer is lower than the surrounding area. Apply Holts Body Plus Filler Paste as shown in Step 5B.

5B

*For a medium dent,* mix Holts Body Plus Filler Paste and Hardener according to the manufacturer's instructions and apply it with a flexible applicator. Apply thin layers of filler at 20-minute intervals, until the filler surface is slightly proud of the surrounding bodywork.

5C

*For small dents and scratches* use Holts No Mix Filler Paste straight from the tube. Apply it according to the instructions in thin layers, using the spatula provided. It will harden in minutes if applied outdoors and may then be used as its own knifing putty.

6

Use a plane or file for initial shaping. Then, using progressively finer grades of wet-and-dry paper, wrapped round a sanding block, and copious amounts of clean water, rub down the filler until glass smooth. 'Feather' the edges of adjoining paintwork.

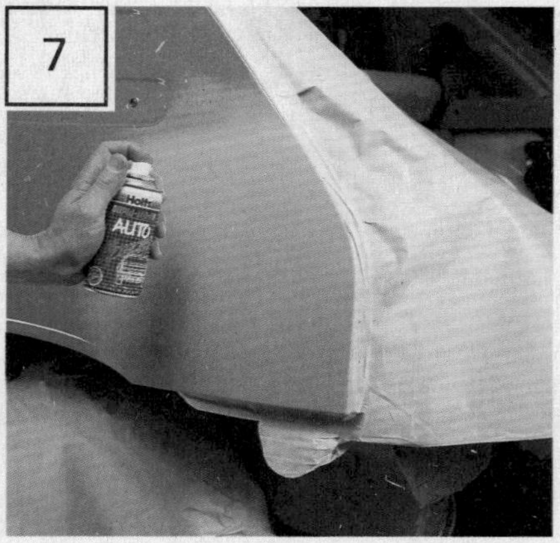


Protect adjoining areas before spraying the whole repair area and at least one inch of the surrounding sound paintwork with Holts Dupli-Color primer.

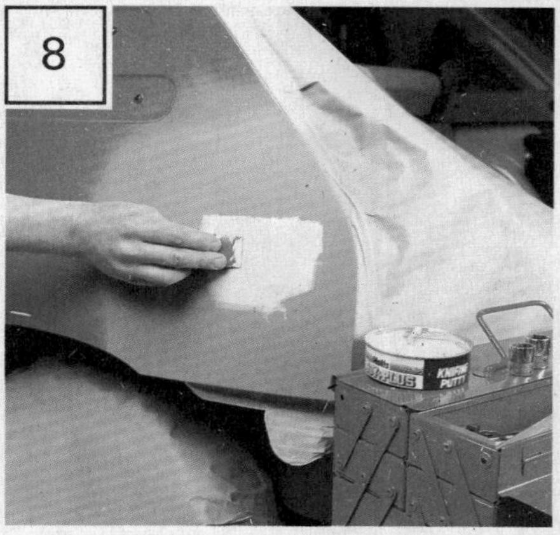


Fill any imperfections in the filler surface with a small amount of Holts Body Plus Knifing Putty. Using plenty of clean water, rub down the surface with a fine grade wet-and-dry paper – 400 grade is recommended – until it is really smooth.

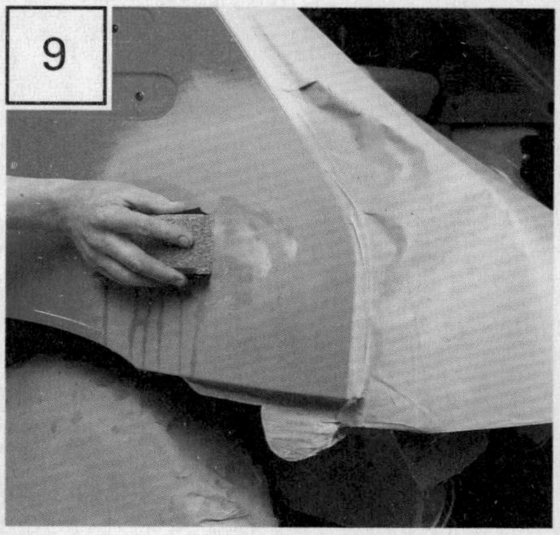


Carefully fill any remaining imperfections with knifing putty before applying the last coat of primer. Then rub down the surface with Holts Body Plus Rubbing Compound to ensure a really smooth surface.

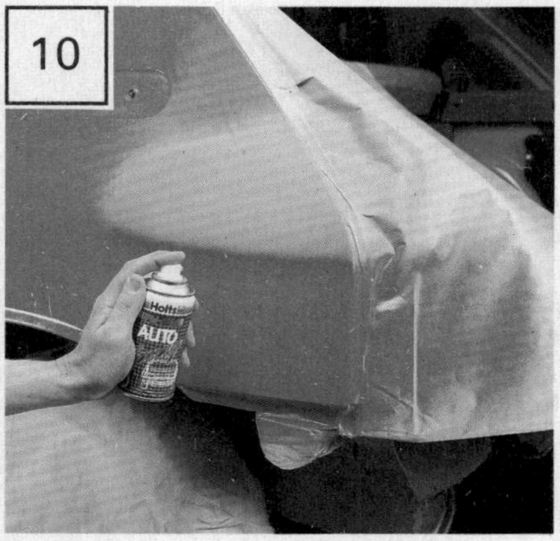


Protect surrounding areas from overspray before applying the topcoat in several thin layers. Agitate Holts Dupli-Color aerosol thoroughly. Start at the repair centre, spraying outwards with a side-to-side motion.

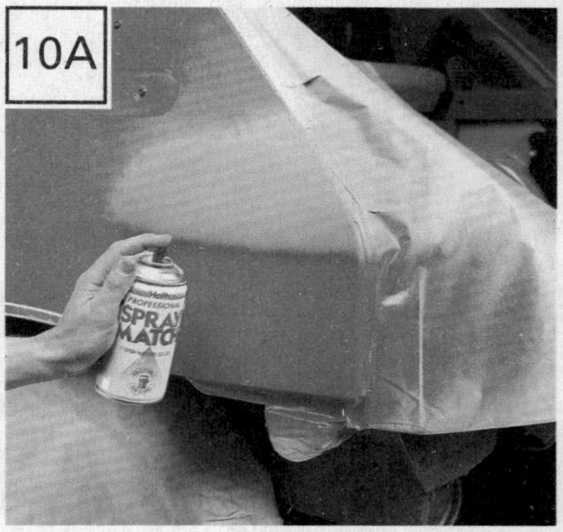


If the exact colour is not available off the shelf, local Holts Professional Spraymatch Centres will custom fill an aerosol to match perfectly.

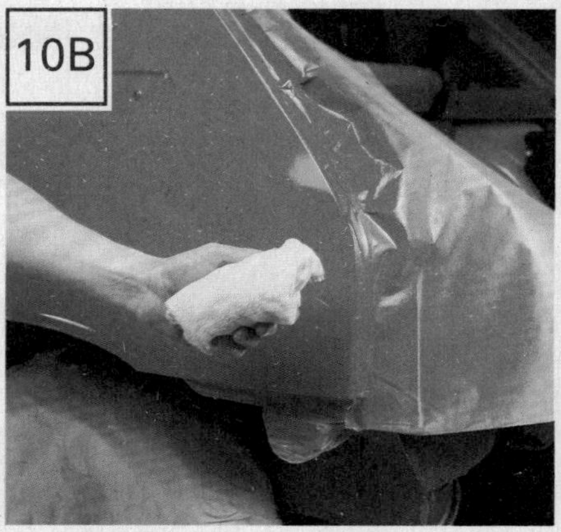


To identify whether a lacquer finish is required, rub a painted unrepaired part of the body with wax and a clean cloth.

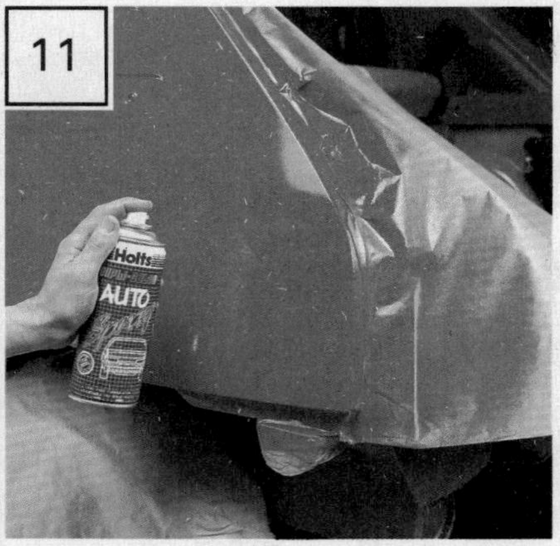


If *no* traces of paint appear on the cloth, spray Holts Dupli-Color clear lacquer over the repaired area to achieve the correct gloss level.

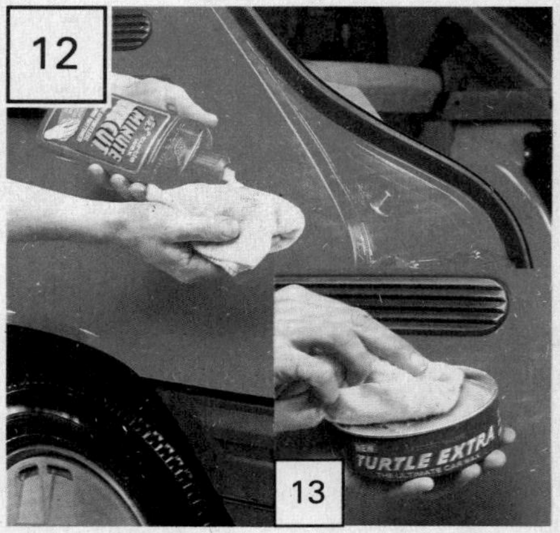


The paint will take about two weeks to harden fully. After this time it can be 'cut' with a mild cutting compound such as Turtle Wax Minute Cut prior to polishing with a final coating of Turtle Wax Extra.

When carrying out bodywork repairs, remember that the quality of the finished job is proportional to the time and effort expended.

# HAYNES No1 for DIY

Haynes publish a wide variety of books besides the world famous range of ***Haynes Owners Workshop Manuals***. They cover all sorts of DIY jobs. Specialist books such as the ***Improve and Modify*** series and the ***Purchase and DIY Restoration Guides*** give you all the information you require to carry out everything from minor modifications to complete restoration on a number of popular cars. In addition there are the publications dealing with specific tasks, such as the ***Car Bodywork Repair Manual*** and the ***In-Car Entertainment Manual***. The ***Household DIY*** series gives clear step-by-step instructions on how to repair everyday household objects ranging from toasters to washing machines.

Whether it is under the bonnet or around the home there is a Haynes Manual that can help you save money. Available from motor accessory stores and bookshops or direct from the publisher.

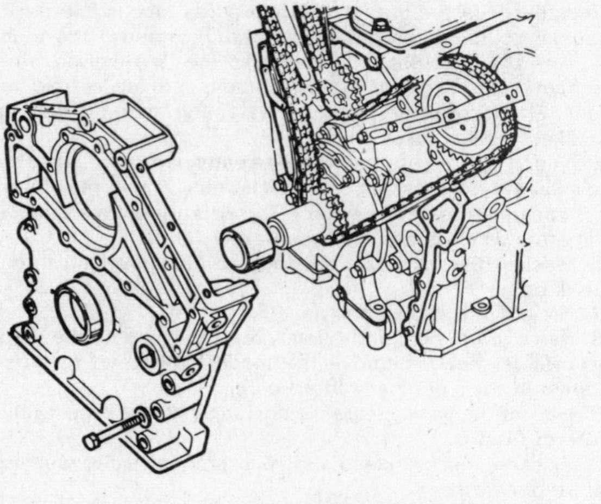

Fig. 1.19 Timing cover removed (Sec 7)

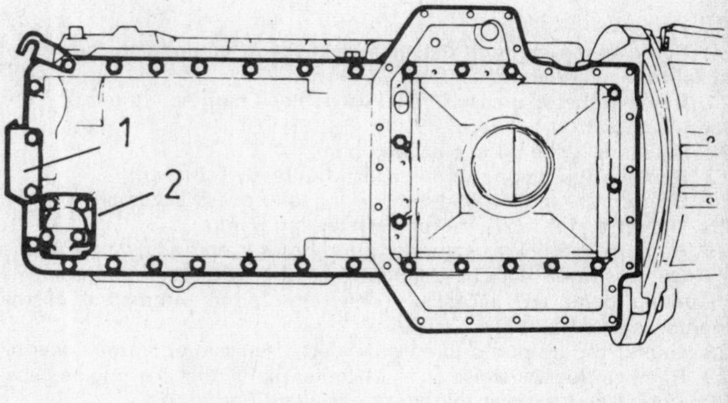


Fig. 1.20 Sandwich plate and baffle screws (Sec 7)

1 *Timing scale* 2 *Suction union*

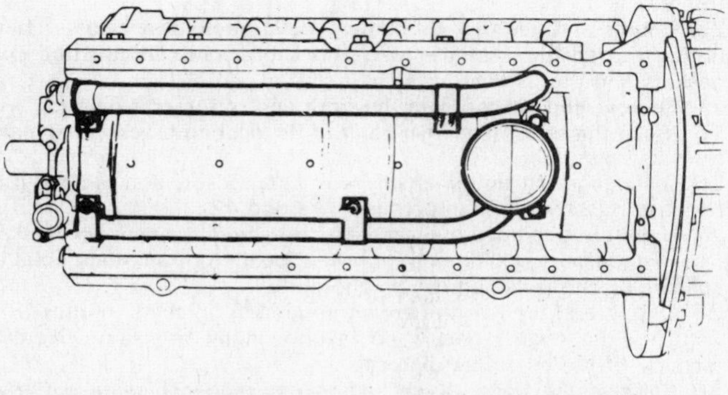

Fig. 1.21 Crankshaft undershield and delivery pipe clips (Sec 7)

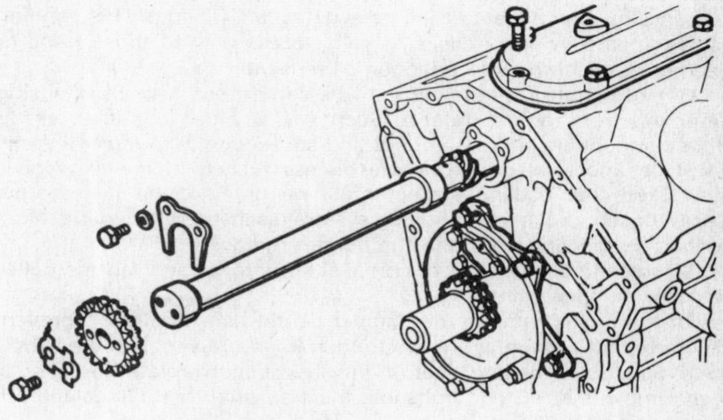

Fig. 1.22 Removing the jackshaft (Sec 7)

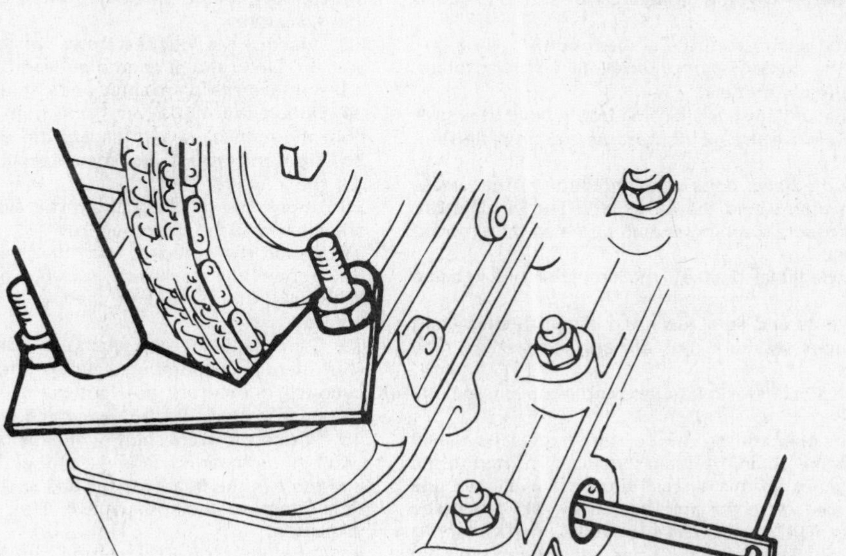

Fig. 1.23 Timing chain tensioner tools installed (XJ12 and Double Six) (Sec 7)

cylinder head' and number the compartments 1 to 12, number 1 being at the timing chain end of the cylinder head.
6 Repeat the operations on all remaining valves.
7 Remove and discard the valve stem oil seals which are fitted to the inlet valve guides.
8 Identification of the valves is no problem as the inlet valve heads are larger than the exhaust (photo).
9 Refer to Section 43 for cylinder head examination and renovation procedures.
10 Reassembly is a reversal of dismantling. Smear each valve stem with clean engine oil before fitting and fit new valve stem oil seals. Make sure that all components are returned to their original positions. If new components have been fitted or the valves have been ground in (see Section 38) then the valve clearances will require checking and adjusting as described in Section 50.

## 22 Crankshaft main bearing shells – renewal (engine in car)

1 Renewal of the main bearing shells is possible without removing the engine, but it is unlikely to be required unless it is positively known that main bearing failure alone has occurred as the result of high mileage or a lubrication fault. Normally, the crankshaft will also have worn and will be renewed at the same time as the bearings during major overhaul.
2 To obtain access to the main bearings, first remove the sandwich plate as described in Section 14.
3 Unbolt and withdraw the suction pipe from the O-ring at the elbow.
4 Unbolt the crankshaft undershield and draw it clear.
5 Unbolt and remove the oil delivery pipe elbow from the oil pump casting. Leave the bolt at the outboard hole in the oil pump casting. If it must be removed, make sure that it is refitted in its original position. Note also the position of the pillar nuts.
6 Unbolt and remove the front main bearing cap. Renew the cap shell bearing and the upper shell from the crankcase web. The upper shells can often be pushed out using a probe, if not, insert a split pin into the oil hole in the crankshaft journal and slowly turn the crankshaft so that the head of the split pin pushes the shell around and out of its seat. Fit the new shell in a similar manner.
7 Oil the journal and refit the cap, tightening the nuts to the specified torque.
8 Renew the remaining main bearing shells in a similar way, but only release one bearing cap at a time. Note that the rear main bearing shell incorporates an oil groove whilst the centre shell is plain.
9 Clean the suction pipe strainer and renew all O-ring seals before refitting the dismantled components.

## 23 Connecting rod big-end bearings – renewal (engine in car)

1 Refer to Section 22, paragraphs 1 to 5, which apply equally to the big-end bearings.
2 Turn the crankshaft until two crankpins are at the lowest position.
3 Unbolt and remove the big-end bearing caps. Do not mix them up. Do not rotate the crankshaft with the caps off.
4 Renew the bearing shells. The piston/rod may be pushed up the bore just enough to provide access to the rod shell but do not push it further than necessary.
5 Oil the crankpins, fit the caps and tighten the nuts to the specified torque.
6 Rotate the crankshaft until two more crankpins are at their lowest point and renew the shells.
7 Repeat the foregoing operations until all big-end shell bearings have been renewed.

## 24 Engine front mountings – removal and refitting (engine in car, XJ12 and Double Six)

1 Disconnect the battery.
2 Remove the wing valance stays and the air cleaners.
3 Remove the horn from the engine left-hand mounting bracket.

21.4A Using a valve spring compressor

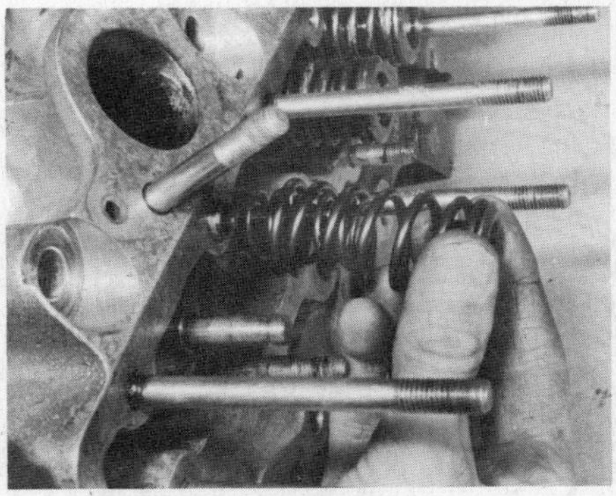

21.4B Removing valve springs

21.4C Valve stem oil seal and spring lower seat

21.8 Inlet and exhaust valve heads. The exhaust valve is the smaller

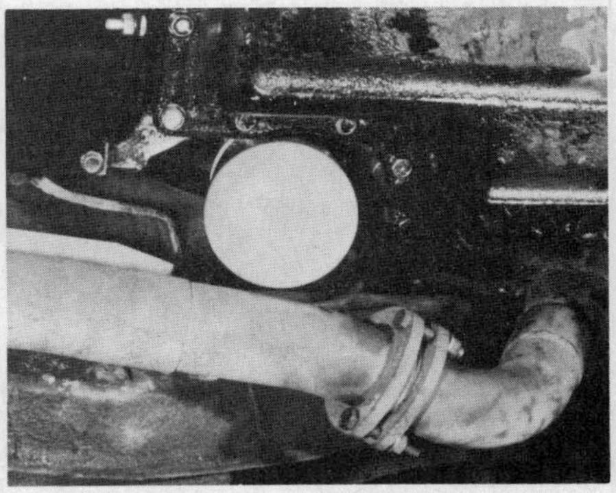

29.2 Cartridge type oil filter viewed from below

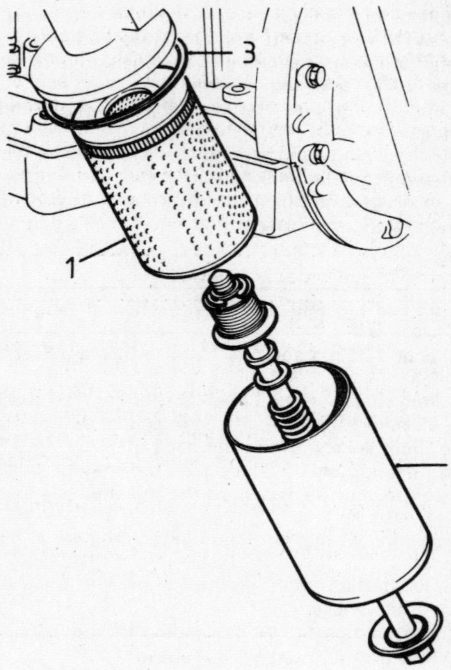


**Fig. 1.33 Early type engine oil filter (Sec 27)**

*1 Renewable element*
*2 Filter casing*
*3 Sealing ring*

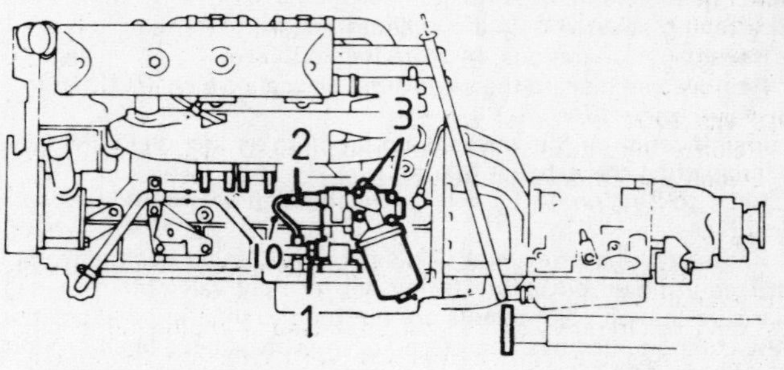


**Fig. 1.34 Oil filter assembly connections (early models) (Sec 28)**

*1 Oil cooler supply pipe*
*2 Pressure relief valve vent hose*
*3 Oil filter head retaining bolts*

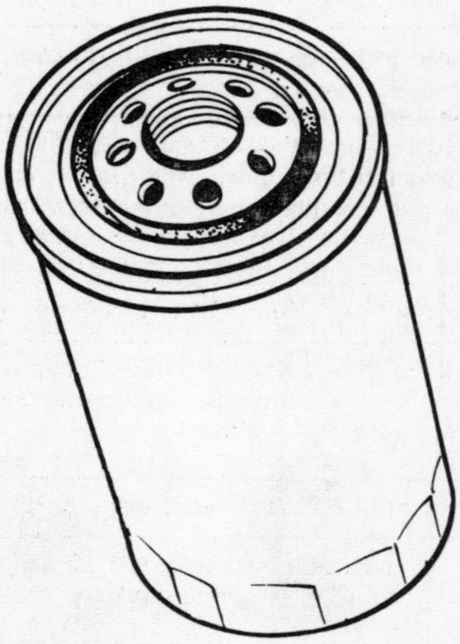

**Fig. 1.35 Cartridge type oil filter (Sec 29)**

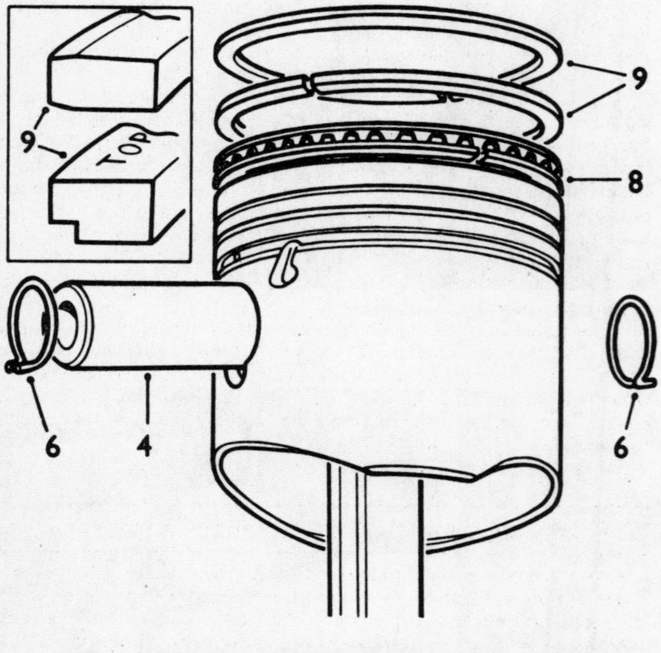


**Fig. 1.36 Piston/connecting rod assembly (Sec 32)**

*4 Gudgeon pin*
*6 Circlips*
*8 Oil control piston ring*
*9 Compression rings – inset shows details*

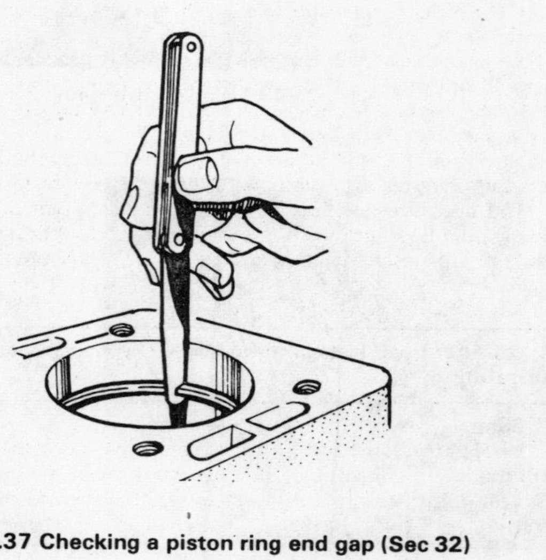

**Fig. 1.37 Checking a piston ring end gap (Sec 32)**

*Cars with air conditioning*

4 Unbolt the fan and fluid coupling unit and rest it carefully against the radiator.

*Cars without air conditioning*

5 Release the fan relay from the radiator top rail.
6 Unbolt and remove the fan shield.

*All cars*

7 Unscrew and remove the nuts from the tops and the bottoms of both engine mountings.
8 Using a suitable hoist and chains, raise the engine just enough to be able to free the front mountings. Take care not to damage the expansion valve on air conditioned cars. Do not lose the fibre washers.
9 Fit the new engine mountings so that the fibre washer is on top of the front suspension crossmember brackets.
10 Fit the plain nut and washer to hold each mounting to its crossmember bracket.
11 Lower the engine gently to locate it on its mountings. Fit the nuts to secure the engine to its mountings.
12 Remove the chains and hoist and refit all the remaining components.

## 25 Engine front mountings – removal and refitting (engine in car, XJS)

1 For access to the engine mountings, remove the air cleaners.
2 The removal and refitting operations are then as described in Section 24.

## 26 Engine rear mounting – removal and refitting (engine in car)

1 The operations are as described in earlier Sections of this Chapter. (XJ12 and Double Six – Section 3, paragraphs 28 to 31; XJS – Section 5, paragraphs 35 and 40 to 46).

## 27 Oil filter (renewable element type, early cars) – renewal

1 The oil filter is accessible from under the car and should be renewed at the same time as the engine oil.
2 Drain the engine oil (hot).
3 Unscrew the centre bolt from the oil filter canister. Withdraw the canister complete with bolt, sealing ring and the filter element. It will be full of oil so try not to spill it.
4 Discard the filter element and the sealing ring. If the sealing ring is still in the groove in the filter head, pick it out with a sharply pointed tool.
5 Clean out the canister and wash the filter bypass valve in clean petrol.
6 Press the new canister sealing ring into its groove, fit the new filter element and offer up the canister to the sealing ring.
7 Keep pressure applied to the canister and tighten the centre bolt to the specified torque only – no tighter.
8 Having refilled the engine with clean oil, start the engine and run for a few minutes at a fast idle. Check for leaks from the filter.
9 The new filter element will absorb about a pint of oil and the oil level should be checked on the dipstick and topped up as necessary after the engine has been switched off for a few minutes.

## 28 Oil filter head (renewable element type, early cars) – removal and refitting

1 Remove the left-hand air cleaner.
2 Unbolt the left-hand exhaust downpipe from the manifold and from the intermediate pipe. Remove the downpipe. On left-hand drive cars, full left steering lock must be applied before the pipe can be removed.
3 Disconnect the union on the oil cooler supply pipe.
4 Cut off the clip from the pressure relief vent hose at the nearest point to the valve.
5 Remove the oil filter canister and element.
6 Unbolt and remove the left-hand front heat shield.
7 Extract the four setscrews which secure the filter head.
8 Tap the filter head carefully to break the gasket seal and push the head upwards until the bypass valve stub pipe clears the housing.
9 Separate the vent pipe from the relief valve and withdraw the filter head assembly.
10 Refitting is a reversal of removal, but renew the O-ring seal on the bypass valve stub pipe and fit a new filter head-to-block gasket.

## 29 Oil filter (cartridge type) – renewal

1 Drain the engine oil (hot).
2 Use a chain, strap or special oil filter wrench to unscrew the oil filter, which is accessible from under the car (photo).
3 The new filter will be supplied with captive sealing ring.
4 Wipe the sealing surface of the filter head clean and then smear the filter cartridge seal with a little engine oil or light grease.
5 Screw the new filter into position as tightly as possible *using hand pressure only.*
6 With the engine filled with fresh oil, start it and run at a fast idle. Check the filter for leaks.
7 The new filter will absorb about one pint of oil so check and top up the engine oil after the engine is switched off.

## 30 Examination and renovation – general

1 With the engine stripped, all components should be thoroughly cleaned and examined for wear, as described in the following Sections. Where a high mileage has been covered, consideration should be given to renewing an assembly on an exchange basis rather than renewing an individual component in a well worn unit.

## 31 Crankshaft and bearings – examination and renovation

1 Examine the surfaces of the crankshaft journals and crankpins. If there is evidence of scoring, then the crankshaft will have to be renewed as the material is so hard that the regrinding facilities to be found locally will not be suitable.
2 If the bearing surfaces are good, always take the opportunity of renewing the shell bearings as a matter of routine.
3 On XJS manual gearbox models, examine the pilot bush which is installed in the centre of the crankshaft rear flange onto which the flywheel is mounted. If it is worn, it must be renewed. To do this, either tap a thread into it and screw in a bolt to extract the bush or fill the bush with grease and drive in a close fitting mandrel. The hydraulic pressure created by the latter method will eject the bush. The new bush should be soaked in engine oil for 24 hours before pressing it into position.
4 Clean out the crankshaft oil passages with wire and blow them out with compressed air if available.
5 The thrust washers which fit either side of the centre main bearing should normally be renewed at the time of major overhaul. However, when the crankshaft is installed, its endfloat must be checked, as described in Section 47, and new thrust washers of different thicknesses may be required to bring the endfloat within the specified tolerance.

## 32 Pistons and connecting rods – examination and renovation

1 New pistons and gudgeon pins are supplied as matched sets.
2 Worn pistons can be removed from the connecting rod simply by extracting the circlips and pushing the gudgeon pin from the piston and small end bush. The ambient temperature should not be less than 68°F (20°C) when doing this work.
3 Each piston has three rings, two upper compression and a lower oil control. Remove the rings by sliding two or three old feeler blades behind the top ring and locating the blades at equidistant points. Slide the ring upwards and off using a twisting motion.
4 Repeat the removal operations on the remaining rings.

5 If the connecting rod small-end bush is worn, exchange the rod for a factory reconditioned one as it is not possible to renew the bushes without special equipment.
6 When connecting a piston to its connecting rod, make sure that with the word 'FRONT' on the piston crown towards the timing cover end of the engine, the chamfer on the big-end rod eye is adjacent to the radius which is to be found at one end of each crankpin.
7 Use new circlips to retain the gudgeon pin.
8 Fit the new piston rings into their respective cylinder bores one at a time, push each ring half way down the bore and check the ring end gap. Any slight variation from that specified may be corrected by grinding the end squarely.
9 Test each ring in its piston groove for side clearance, which should be as specified. It is unlikely that the clearance will be incorrect if new pistons and rings are being fitted. Use a feeler blade for checking.
10 Fit the piston rings to the pistons. Start with the oil control ring assembly, making sure that the expander ends do not overlap.
11 Fit the second compression ring, which has the word 'TOP' stamped on its upper face.
12 Fit the top compression ring, which has a chromium plated periphery and is coated red. The ring may be fitted either way up. Do not remove the red coating.

## 33 Cylinder liners – examination and renovation

1 The cylinder bores must be examined for taper, ovality, scoring and scratches. Start by carefully examining the top of the cylinder bores. If they are at all worn a very slight ridge will be found on the thrust side. This marks the top of the piston ring travel. The owner will have a good indication of the bore wear prior to dismantling the engine, or removing the cylinder head. Excessive oil consumption accompanied by blue smoke from the exhaust is a sure sign of worn cylinder bores and piston rings.
2 Measure the bore diameter just under the ridge with a micrometer and compare it with the diameter at the bottom of the bore, which is not subject to wear. If the difference between the two measurements is more than 0.006 in (0.15 mm) then it will be necessary to fit special pistons and rings or to have the cylinder liners renewed.
3 Sometimes specially designed proprietary piston rings can be fitted to overcome bore wear for a further mileage but in the long term, new liners and pistons are the only effective cure.
4 When fitting new liners, apply jointing compound to their lower shoulders before pushing them into the cylinder block. Remove excess sealant and immediately fit retaining clamps (Tool JD41).

## 34 Crankshaft pulley and damper – examination and renovation

1 Check that the rubber of the damper has not deteriorated; if it has, renew the damper.
2 The drivebelt should not bottom in the Vee of the pulley; if it does, try renewing the belt but if this new belt still bottoms, then the pulley will have to be renewed as well.

## 35 Flywheel and starter ring gear (XJS with manual gearbox) – examination and renovation

1 If the starter ring gear is worn or the teeth are chipped, then the flywheel should be renewed complete.
2 If the surface of the flywheel is badly scored or small cracks are visible, it should be renewed; machining or surface grinding is not recommended.
3 The flywheel and clutch are balanced and if a new flywheel is fitted, then before installation, have the components re-balanced by your Jaguar dealer.

## 36 Driveplate – examination and renovation

1 *On cars equipped with automatic transmission,* examine the bolt holes of the driveplate for cracks and the starter ring gear for wear. If these conditions are evident, renew the driveplate complete.

## 37 Camshafts and bearings – examination and renovation

1 Check the camshaft bearing surfaces and lobes of the cams for wear, scoring or corrosion.
2 Check the bearing caps and the bearing surfaces on the tappet blocks in the same way.
3 If the inspection brings to light such conditions the camshaft and the tappet block must be renewed as the camshaft runs directly in the tappet block without the use of separate bearing shells.

## 38 Valves and seats – examination and renovation

1 Examine the heads of the valves for pitting and burning, especially the exhaust valves.
2 If the valves appear serviceable, scrape all the carbon away and carefully clean the stem of the valve. Clean the valve guide in the cylinder head and fit the valve to its guide.
3 With the valve about threequarters of its way in the guide, check it for sideways movement. If the movement appears to be excessive, remove the valve and measure the diameter of the stem, this should be not less than specified. If the stem diameter is satisfactory it means that the valve guide is worn and remedial action as indicated in Section 40 will have to be taken.
4 If no wear is present, check the valve stem for distortion by moving the valve up and down in its guide and at the same time rotating it, no restriction to movement should be felt.
5 Grinding the valves to their seats is easily carried out. First place the cylinder head upside down on the bench resting on a block of wood at each end to give clearance for the valve stems.
6 Smear a trace of course carborundum paste on the seat face and apply a suction grinding tool to the head of the valve. With a semi-rotary action, grind the valve to its seat, lifting the valve occasionally to re-distribute the paste. When a continuous ring of dull matt even finish is produced on both the valve seat and the valve, then wipe off the coarse paste and repeat the process with a fine paste, lifting and turning the valve as before. A light spring placed under the head of the valve will assist in the lifting operation. When a smooth unbroken ring of light grey matt is produced on both valve and valve seat faces, the grinding operation is complete. Be very careful during the grinding operation not to get the abrasive paste on the stem of the valve, do not handle the valve stem once you have started to use the paste because it will be transferred from the fingers to the stem and the result will be rapid wear of the valve guide. Trouble is often experienced with the suction tool not gripping the valve head, this can be overcome if the valve head and the tool are kept free of oil and grease at all times.
7 When grinding is completed, thoroughly clean the cylinder head to remove any trace of carborundum paste as this can cause a lot of damage after first start up of the engine.
8 If a valve seat is too badly burned to be renovated by grinding, it should be re-cut or renewed by your dealer.

## 39 Valve springs – examination and renewal

1 The valve springs should be renewed as a matter of course if they have been in use for 25 000 miles (40 000 km) or more.
2 If they have been in use for a shorter period, check their free lengths against Specification. If they have been compressed excessively when compared with a new spring, renew them.

## 40 Valve guides – renewal

1 If the valve guides are found to be worn as a result of the checks carried out in Section 38, first immerse the cylinder head in boiling water for half an hour.
2 Using a suitably stepped drift, drive the valve guide from the cylinder head. Attack the guide from the combustion chamber side.
3 Ream the guide bore in the head to the correct oversize (see below).
4 Coat the new valve guide with graphite grease and fit the circlip.
5 Bring the cylinder head back to temperature in boiling water and drive the guide into position until the circlip seats.

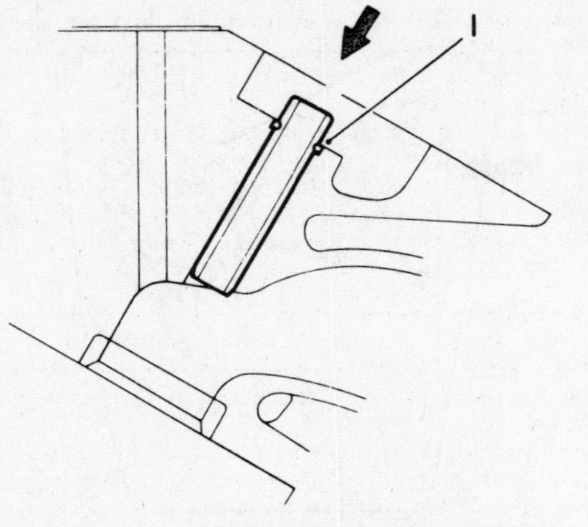


**Fig. 1.38 Valve guide installation (Sec 40)**

*1 Circlip*

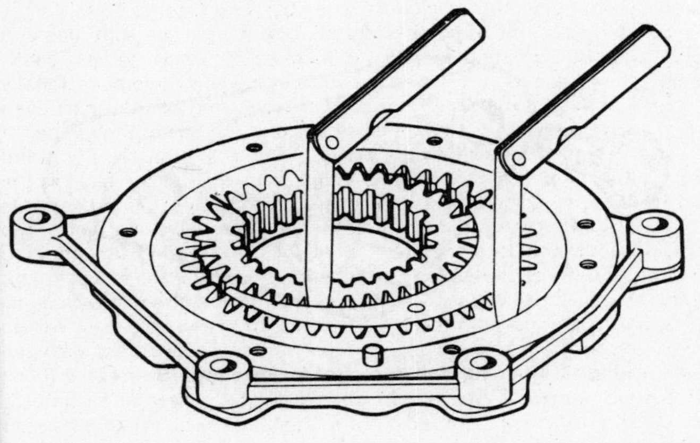

**Fig. 1.39 Checking the oil pump gear radial clearance (Sec 45)**

**Fig. 1.40 Checking the oil pump gear endfloat (Sec 45)**

6 Replacement valve guides are available in two oversizes as given in the Specifications.
7 When fitting new guides always fit one which is one oversize larger than the original. The valve guide bores in the cylinder head will require reaming to accept the oversize guides as follows:

*1st oversize (2 grooves) – ream to*
*0.505 in (12.83 mm) + 0.0005 in (0.012 mm) – 0.0002 in (0.005 mm)*
*2nd oversize (3 grooves) – ream to*
*0.510 in (12.95 mm) + 0.0005 in (0.012 mm) – 0.0002 in (0.005 mm)*

## 41 Tappet and shims – examination and renovation

1 Examine the bearing surface of the tappet on which the camshaft bears. Any indentation on this surface or any cracks indicate serious wear and the tappet must be renewed.
2 It is unlikely that the sides of the tappet will be worn, but if the tappet can be rocked in its guide in the tappet block it should be established by measurement which item is at fault; details of dimensions are given under Specifications at the beginning of this Chapter.
3 The tappet should also be checked to see that it moves freely in its guide, the most likely cause of restriction is dirt but rectify as necessary.
4 Clean and examine the valve adjusting shims. After a considerable mileage the valve stem will probably have made an indentation on the shim face. In this case the shim should be renewed but where the valves have been ground in, shims of alternative thickness will probably be required (refer to Section 50).

## 42 Timing gear and chain – examination and renovation

1 Clean the sprockets and chain in a paraffin bath and dry them on a non-fluffy rag.
2 Examine the teeth of the sprockets for wear. Each tooth forms an inverted 'V' with the periphery of the sprocket and, if worn, the side of the tooth under tension will be slightly concave in shape when compared with the other side of the tooth. If any wear is present the sprocket should be renewed.
3 Examine the links of the chain for side slackness and renew the chain if any slackness is noticeable when compared to a new chain. It is sensible to replace the chain if the engine is stripped for overhaul and when the cylinder heads are removed for decarbonisation or some other purpose, if it is known that the chain has been in use for a considerable time.
4 The chain tension slipper and the rubbing surfaces of the dampers should be examined for grooves or deterioration and renewed, if necessary.
5 If the dampers must be removed or renewed, first mark the exact positions of the camshaft sprocket hangers and the chain dampers before unbolting them. Do this using quick-drying paint or by scribing their outline on the front face of the cylinder block. If the dampers are disturbed without having marked their position then a special damper setting jig will be required as described in Section 47, paragraph 50.
6 Check the teeth of the jackshaft sprocket for wear. If there is any rocking movement when the sprocket is gripped, this is probably due to worn jackshaft bearings in the cylinder block. Closer inspection can be had by removing the top cover. Once the top cover screws are extracted do not try to tap the cover sideways if it is stuck as it is located to the block by hollow dowel pins.
7 Renewal of the jackshaft bearings is best left to your dealer unless the appropriate removal and refitting tools are available.

## 43 Cylinder head – decarbonising and examination

1 With the cylinder head removed, use a blunt scraper to remove all trace of carbon and deposits from the combustion spaces and ports. Remember that the cylinder head is made of aluminium alloy and can be damaged easily during the decarbonising operations. Scrape the cylinder head free from scale or old pieces of gasket or jointing compound. Clean the cylinder head by washing it in paraffin and take

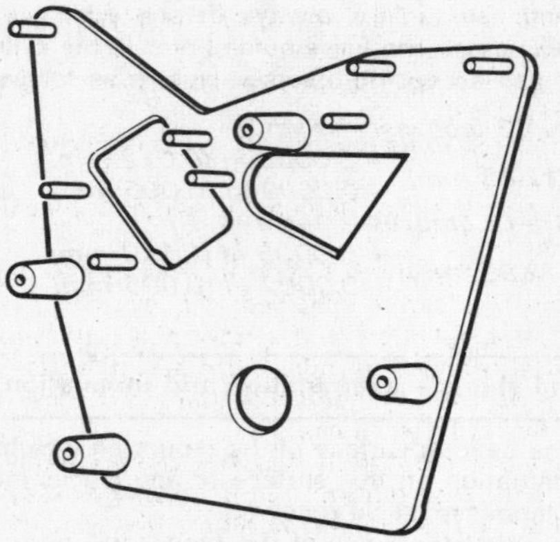

Fig. 1.41 Timing chain damper setting jig (JD38) (Sec 47)

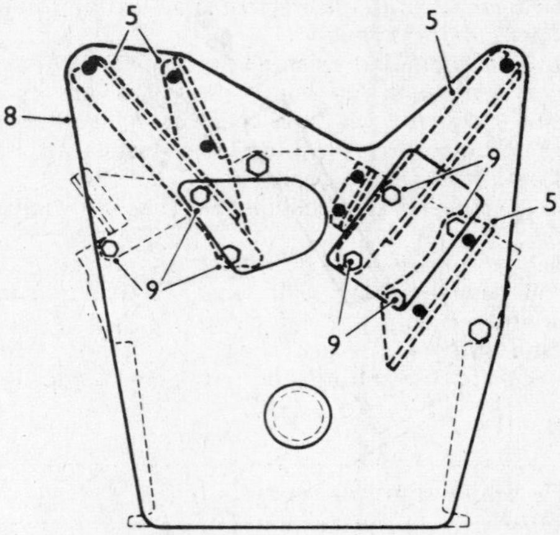


Fig. 1.42 Timing chain damper setting diagram (Sec 47)

*5 Camshaft sprocket hangers*
*8 Setting jig*
*9 Damper/hanger securing bolts*

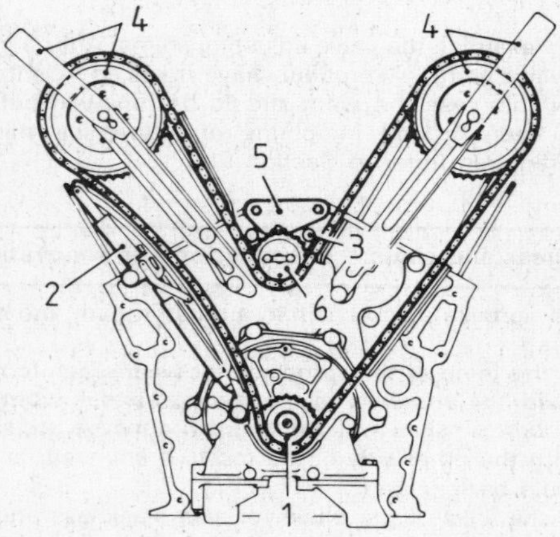


Fig. 1.43 Timing chain and gears (Sec 47)

*1 Camshaft sprocket*
*2 Timing chain tensioner*
*3 Jackshaft locking plate*
*4 Camshaft sprockets and retaining tools*
*5 Jackshaft sprocket locking tool*
*6 Jackshaft sprocket*

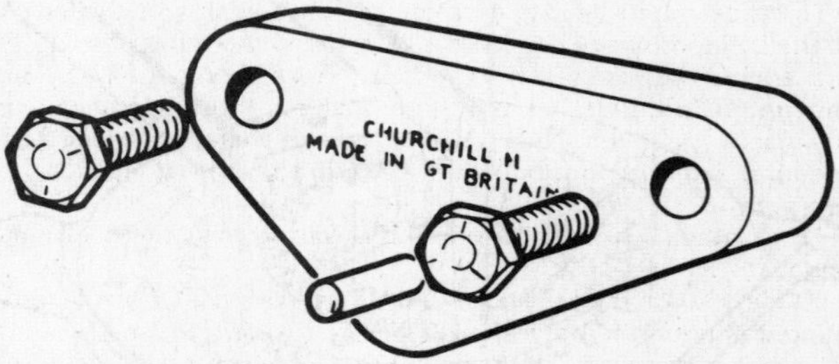


Fig. 1.44 Jackshaft sprocket locking tool (Sec 47)

particular care to pull a piece of rag through the ports and cylinder head bolt holes. Any dirt remaining in these recesses may well drop onto the gasket or cylinder block mating surface as the cylinder head is lowered into position and could lead to a gasket leak after reassembly is complete.

2 With the cylinder head clean, test for distortion if a history of coolant leakage has been apparent. Carry out this test using a straight-edge and feeler gauges or a piece of plate glass. If the surface shows any warping in excess of 0.0039 in (0.1015 mm) then the cylinder head will have to be resurfaced which is a job for a specialist engineering company.

3 Clean the pistons and top of the cylinder bores. If the pistons are still in the block then it is essential that great care is taken to ensure that no carbon gets into the cylinder bores as this could scratch the cylinder walls or cause damage to the piston and rings. To ensure this does not happen, first clamp the liners and turn the crankshaft so that two of the pistons are at the top of their bores. Stuff rag into the other four bores or seal them off with paper and masking tape to prevent particles of carbon entering the cooling system and damaging the water pump.

4 Rotate the crankshaft and repeat the carbon removal operations on the remaining pistons and cylinder bores.

5 Thoroughly clean all particles of carbon from the bores and then inject a little light oil round the edges of the pistons to lubricate the piston rings.

6 Stripped spark plug threads can be reinstated by having inserts fitted or Helicoil spring threads wound in. Either of these jobs is best left to your dealer or to a suitably equipped engineering works.

## 44 Oil seals – renewal

1 At time of major overhaul always renew engine oil seals even if they appear in good condition.

2 Renew the crankshaft front and rear oil seals and the O-rings on the oil pump suction and return pipes.

## 45 Oil pump – overhaul

1 With the oil pump removed as described in Section 7, unbolt the pump cover from the gear housing.

2 Mark the gear faces to ensure that they will be returned to their original positions on reassembly.
3 Remove both gears and wash all parts in clean fuel.
4 Check the gear teeth for wear or damage. If they are in good condition, refit the driven gear and check the clearance between the gear and the oil pump housing using feeler blades. Do not make the checks at the six flats on the gear.
5 Refit the drive gear and check the clearance between the gear and the crescent.
6 Now check the endfloat of both gears by placing a straight-edge across the oil pump housing joint face and inserting feeler blades between the straight-edge and the gears.
7 All the measurements taken should conform to the clearances given in the Specifications. If they do not, the oil pump will have to be renewed.

## 46 Engine – preparation for reassembly

1 To ensure maximum life with reliability from a rebuilt engine, not only must everything be correctly assembled but all components must be spotlessly clean and the correct spring or plain washers used where originally located. Always lubricate bearing and working surfaces with clean engine oil during reassembly of engine parts.
2 Before reassembly commences, renew any bolts or studs the threads of which are damaged or corroded.
3 As well as your normal tool kit, gather together clean rags, oil can, a torque wrench and a complete (overhaul) set of gaskets and oil seals.

## 47 Engine – reassembly

1 To reassemble the engine after complete dismantling first check that the cylinder liners are correctly seated with clamps fitted. If new liners are to be installed, smear their lower shoulders with jointing compound before pressing them into position. If the original liners are being used again but have been removed, then again use jointing compound and align the marks made prior to removal (see Section 7, paragraph 48).
2 Fit new sealing strips into the grooves in the rear main bearing casting.
3 Fit new crankshaft rear oil seal halves. Place a single drop of jointing compound in each groove before fitting the seals.
4 Fit the rear main bearing casting to the cylinder block and tighten the nuts. The oil seal should now be pre-sized by passing a piece of tubing into it of similar outside dimension to the rear journal diameter of the crankshaft. With this done, remove the main bearing casting and apply colloidal graphite to the seal.
5 Wipe out all the crankcase bearing shell recesses, fit the seven shells and oil them. Do not confuse the centre and rear main bearing shells. The rear shell incorporates a groove, the centre one does not.
6 Lower the crankshaft into position.
7 Fit the main bearing caps complete with shells having oiled the journals ready to accept them.
8 Refit the pillar nuts to their original positions.
9 Tighten all the nuts to the specified torque.
10 Now check the crankshaft endfloat using feeler blades, prising it first one way and then the other. The endfloat will be excessive as no thrust washers have yet been fitted. Select thrust washers of sufficient thickness to reduce the endfloat to that specified.
11 Remove the centre main bearing cap and slide the selected thrust washer halves into the grooves on either side of the crankcase web. Note that the oil grooves must face outwards.
12 Refit the centre main bearing cap, then tighten all cap bolts and check the crankshaft for ease of rotation.
13 Smear the bore of number 1A cylinder liner (RH front) with engine oil. Also oil the piston rings of the appropriate piston/connecting rod assembly.
14 Check that the piston ring end gaps are located at equidistant points around the piston in order to prevent gas blow-by.
15 Fix a piston ring compressor to the piston rings and compress them fully.
16 Enter the connecting rod into the cylinder bore so that the 'FRONT' mark on the piston crown is towards the timing cover end of the engine. Let the piston rest squarely on the surface of the cylinder block.
17 Place the end of a wooden handle of a hammer on the centre of the piston crown and give the head of the hammer a sharp blow with the palm of the hand. This will drive the piston assembly into the cylinder. Remove the compressor.
18 Draw the connecting rod down without scratching the bore and fit the rod bearing shell.
19 Set the crankpin to its lowest point and then draw the connecting rod big-end onto it.
20 Fit the bearing shell to the cap, making sure that the locktabs are correctly engaged.
21 Squirt oil onto the crankpin and fit the big-end cap.
22 Tighten the nuts to the specified torque.
23 Repeat the installation and reassembly operations on all the remaining piston/connecting rods. Make sure that the assemblies are returned to their correct cylinders and that the piston crown marks are all facing the front of the engine.
24 Check that the crankshaft can be rotated freely using a lever between two bolts inserted into the crankshaft rear flange.
25 Fit the oil pump to its drivegear on the front end of the crankshaft.
26 Fit new O-ring seals at both ends of the oil delivery pipe, then fit the crankshaft undershield on its pillar nuts and install the oil delivery pipe. Loosely secure the undershield and oil delivery pipe with two setscrews.
27 Fit the suction pipe using a new O-ring seal at the suction elbow. Fix the suction pipe clips and bracket using four setscrews and then tighten all six setscrews to secure the undershield.
28 Refit the flywheel (manual gearbox) or driveplate (automatic transmission) to the rear end of the crankshaft. Use new lockplates, tighten the bolts to the specified torque and bend up the lockplate tabs.
29 Fit the sprocket to the front end of the crankshaft, together with the Woodruff key.
30 If a timing chain damper has been removed or renewed, then it must be refitted in its original position (see Section 42, paragraph 5), otherwise a special setting jig will be required and the following resetting work carried out. Fit the camshaft sprocket hangers and timing chain dampers to the cylinder block, but with all bolts only finger-tight. Install the damper setting jig on the front of the cylinder block and lightly tighten the fixing bolts. Position the camshaft sprocket hangers and timing chain dampers so that they make even contact with the jig locating dowels. Tighten the hanger and damper bolts. Remove the jig.
31 Fit the timing chain tensioner, making sure that it is fully retracted.
32 Fit the jackshaft, having first oiled its journals, then install the jackshaft locking plate.
33 Fit the camshaft sprockets and retain them with the special tools (JD40) or equivalent.
34 Engage the timing chain with the teeth of the camshaft and crankshaft sprockets. Now engage the jackshaft sprocket with the chain and temporarily bolt the sprocket to the jackshaft.
35 Turn the crankshaft until No 1 piston on the right-hand (A) bank is at TDC. Check this by temporarily refitting the crankshaft pulley so that it engages with its key and observing that the 'A' mark is aligned with the 'O' mark on the timing scale (photo).
36 Check that the punch marks on the jackshaft and the jackshaft sprocket are at 180° to each other with the jackshaft mark at its highest point. If this is not so, unbolt and reposition the sprocket without moving the crankshaft.
37 In order that the jackshaft sprocket bolts can be tightened fully, the sprocket must be locked to prevent it rotating. A special tool is available for this purpose (JD39) but a rod passed between two sprocket teeth and locked in position will usually prove a good substitute. Bend up the lockplate tab.
38 Remove the sprocket locking tool but do not disturb the position of the crankshaft until the camshaft sprockets have been coupled to their respective camshafts, see paragraphs 50 to 55.
39 Fit the timing cover using a new oil seal and gaskets. Tighten the bolts in a diagonal pattern.
40 Fit the spacer to the front end of the crankshaft.
41 Fit the crankcase sandwich plate using a new gasket and remembering to secure the timing scale at the front end.
42 Fit the baffle plate to the sandwich plate.
43 Fit the sump, returning the oil cooler pipe bracket to its originally marked position.
44 Connect the suction union elbow to the sandwich plate using a new seal.

47.35 'A' mark aligns with 'O' mark when No 1A piston is at TDC

47.45 Cylinder liner top rims burnished

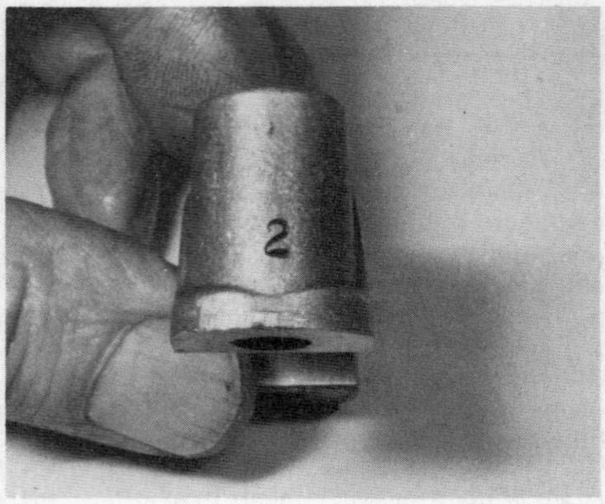


47.48 Camshaft bearing cap number

47.50 Cylinder head gasket in position

47.51 Camshaft setting gauge

47.52 Using a crowfoot wrench to tighten the cylinder head nuts

47.53A Installing a cylinder head without the tappet block

47.53B Tightening a cylinder head nut without the tappet block fitted

47.54A Fitting a tappet block

47.54B Tightening a tappet block socket headed screw

47.54C Installing the tappet blocks and shims

47.56 Tightening a camshaft bearing cap

47.60A Camshaft coupling circlip

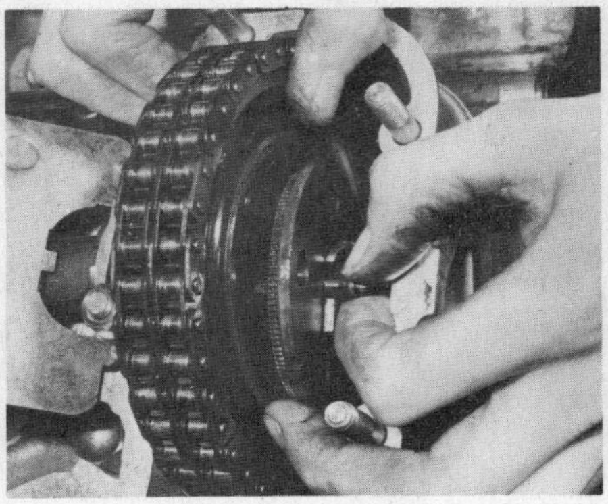

47.60B Camshaft coupling splines

47.65A Fitting a plug to the tappet block

47.65B Camshaft cover gasket in position

47.67 Coolant pump and mounting bolts 1 – Studs with nuts; 2 – Long bolts. All remaining bolts are of the same standard length

49.2A One of four engine lifting hooks (arrowed)

49.2B Installing engine over front mountings

49.5A Aluminium spigot bolted to transmission

49.5B Rear mounting plates, spigot and collision plate

49.5C Transmission lowered onto mounting plate

49.5D Collision plate and spigot self-locking nut being fitted

49.6A Right-hand exhaust heat shields

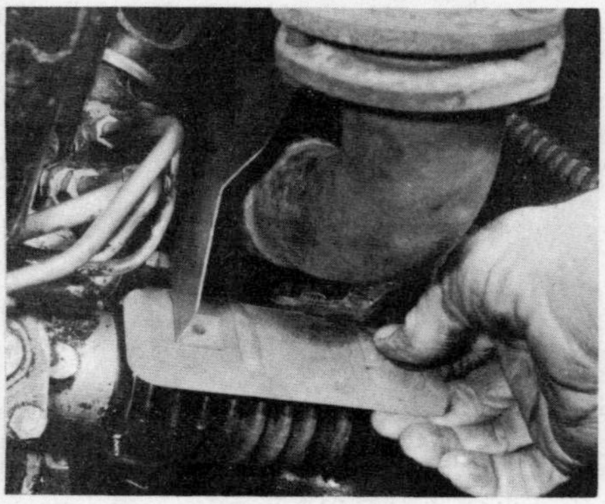
49.6B Right-hand steering gaiter heat shield

49.6C Left-hand steering gaiter heat shield

49.6D Starter solenoid heat shield

49.8 Exhaust downpipe sealing rings

49.9 Tightening the left-hand exhaust manifold flange nuts

49.10A Installing the right-hand exhaust downpipe

49.10B Right-hand exhaust downpipe in position

49.12A Fitting the fluid coupling centre bolt

49.12B Using two spanners to tighten the fluid coupling bolt

49.13 Cowl/electric fan assembly

49.14 Radiator being installed

49.15A Radiator hose connections

45 Remove the cylinder liner retaining tools and clean all rust and corrosion from the top rims of the liners (photo).
46 If a crowfoot type wrench is available to reach the domed cylinder head nuts, carry out the operations in paragraphs up to 52. If such a tool is not available, move onto paragraph 53.
47 Fit the tappet blocks to their respective cylinder heads, having first smeared jointing compound to their mating faces. Tighten the socket headed screws and then the nuts to the specified torque, working from the centre towards each end. Fit the shims and tappets (cam followers) in their originally installed sequence.
48 Refit the camshafts, tightening the bearing caps (from the centre towards each end) to the specified torque. The bearing caps are numbered (photo).
49 Adjust the valve clearances as described in Section 50.
50 Locate a new cylinder head gasket, with the word 'TOP' uppermost, on scrupulously clean block surfaces without the use of jointing compound or grease (photo).
51 Rotate each camshaft until a setting gauge (C.3993, photo) can be engaged in the camshaft front flange slots.
52 Refit the cylinder heads and tighten the securing nuts in the sequence shown in Fig. 1.31 to the specified torque and in the specified stages (photo). Now proceed from paragraph 58.
53 Where a crowfoot type wrench is not available to reach the cylinder head domed nuts, fit the cylinder heads without their tappet blocks and tighten the nuts (in stages and in sequence) to the specified torque (photo).
54 Fit the tappet blocks, having smeared their cylinder head face with jointing compound. Screw in the socket headed securing screws, then the nuts. Fit the shims and the tappets in their originally fitted order (photos).
55 Before fitting the camshafts, check that the crankshaft has not moved from its TDC alignment.
56 Oil the camshaft bearing caps. Install them in their correct positions from the front of the engine onto the camshafts. The camshafts must be set as near as possible so that the notches in their front flanges are vertical and at the highest point. Some of the cam lobes will depress the valve springs as they are bolted down, so tighten the bearing caps in a very even and progressive manner to avoid distortion of the camshafts (photo).
57 Rotate each camshaft fractionally so that a setting gauge can be fitted and engaged in the front flange notches.
58 Reconnect the camshaft oil feed pipe, pressure sender and warning switch.
59 Remove the camshaft sprocket retaining tools.
60 Extract the circlip which retains the camshaft sprocket couplings. Press the sprocket onto the camshaft shoulder and then turn the coupling until the sprocket bolt holes align with those in the camshaft (photos).
61 Reconnect the couplings to the camshaft sprockets, refit the circlips and then withdraw the setting tools. Bolt the couplings to the camshafts and bend up the lockwasher tabs, using two bolts.
62 Insert the screwdriver member of the chain tensioner tool into the hole in the timing cover and release the chain tensioner locking catch. Refit the rubber plug to the hole.
63 Turn the crankshaft until the camshaft sprocket takes up a position suitable to be able to insert the remaining two bolts and lockplate. Fit and tighten the bolts and bend up the lockplate tabs.
64 Check the valve clearances (Section 50) if this was not done at paragraph 49.
65 Refit the camshaft covers, using new gaskets and neoprene plugs. The left-hand cover has the oil filler at the front (photos).
66 Refit the jackshaft cover, noting that the throttle pedestal and ignition coil mounting bracket is to the rear.
67 Reverse the dismantling operations described in paragraphs 3 to 10 inclusive of Section 7. Note the location of the coolant pump mounting bolts identified in the photograph (photo).

## 48 Engine – reconnecting transmission and refitting ancillaries

1 The work is a reversal of the removal operations described in Section 6. If the car is fitted with a manual gearbox then the clutch must be centralised as described in Chapter 5 before attempting to reconnect the gearbox to the engine.
2 When reconnecting the GM 400 automatic transmission to the engine, it is imperative that just before it is mated, the holes in the driveplate are aligned with the tapped holes in the torque converter. This is achieved by aligning the torque converter/driveplate paint spots. Failure to carry out this alignment before mating prevents insertion of the bolts as the rivet heads on the driveplate prevent rotation of the plate in relation to the torque converter once they are closely coupled.
3 Tension the drivebelts as described in Section 51.

## 49 Engine – refitting

1 The engine/transmission is refitted by reversing the removal operations described in either Section 3, 4 or 5 according to model. The following special points must however be noted.
2 Have the engine/transmission supported on the hoist so that the rear end is inclined slightly downward. As it is lowered into position, watch that components on the sides of the engine compartment are not damaged and that the engine sump drain plug does not foul the engine front mounting studs as the unit is lowered into position (photos).
3 Lower the engine/transmission until the front mounting brackets engage with the studs on the flexible mountings. Screw the nuts onto the studs.
4 Raise the rear of the transmission using a jack and a block of wood as an insulator.
5 Fit the rear mounting components according to model and type of transmission. With XJ12 or Double Six versions, the sequence is as follows:

*(a) Fit the longer plate to the underside of the floor pan. Note the two internal securing bolts*
*(b) Bolt the cast aluminium spigot to the transmission casing (photo)*
*(c) Bolt the smaller plate to the underside of the floor pan. Note the spacers between this plate and the previously fitted larger one, also the coil spring and damper rings (photo)*
*(d) Lower the transmission gently when the spigot will project through the hole in the lower plate (photo)*
*(e) Screw on the self-locking nut complete with the collision plate. Note the spacers on the collision plate and the two other self-locking nuts (photo)*
*(f) Tighten all nuts and bolts and remove the jack*

6 Fit the exhaust heat shields (photos).
7 Connect the speedometer cable to the transmission.
8 Cut off the sealing rings from the tops of the exhaust downpipes. Wire brush the ring seats to remove rust and corrosion. Tap new sealing rings into position, except for the front ring on the right-hand downpipe which should be fitted later (photo).
9 Fit the left-hand exhaust downpipe from below, using new securing nuts. These nuts can be tightened using a socket spanner and a long extension operated from below the car (photo).
10 Fit the right-hand exhaust downpipe from above (photos). An assistant moving the steering wheel slightly from one lock to another will facilitate the passage of this downpipe. Once the front rim of the downpipe has cleared the forward mounting stud on the manifold, tap the remaining sealing ring (paragraph 8) into position. Fit the securing nuts and tighten evenly. Refit the downpipes to the intermediate pipes.
11 Once the engine is securely mounted, locate the engine oil cooler in position and tighten the connecting pipe unions.
12 Fit the belt-driven fan to its hub, making sure that the roll pin engages in its hole. Restrain the fan by using a backing spanner on the flats of the fan shaft (photos).
13 Fit the cowl with electric fan (photo).
14 Fit the radiator by engaging its lower spigots in their cut-outs. Position the engine oil cooler on the brackets at the base of the radiator (photo).
15 Pull the top of the radiator forward, together with the fan cowl assembly, so that the hoses on the left-hand side of the radiator can be connected and the transmission fluid cooler hoses connected to the right-hand side of the radiator (photos).
16 Secure the engine oil cooler by inserting the mounting bracket bolts upwards through the holes in the lower front panel (photo). Once they are tight, fit the rubber plugs into the holes.
17 Locate the radiator top rail and the upper and lower cowl brackets, but do not fix them at this stage.
18 When refitting the air conditioner compressor, tighten the bolts on

49.15B Tightening a radiator hose clip

49.15C Tightening a transmission fluid cooler hose on the right-hand side of the radiator

49.16 Tightening the engine oil cooler mounting bolts

49.18A Compressor rear mounting bracket

49.18B Compressor front mounting bracket (1) and coolant cross-pipe (2)

49.19 Ignition amplifier bracket

50.4 Checking a valve clearance

50.7A Thickness mark engraved on valve clearance shim

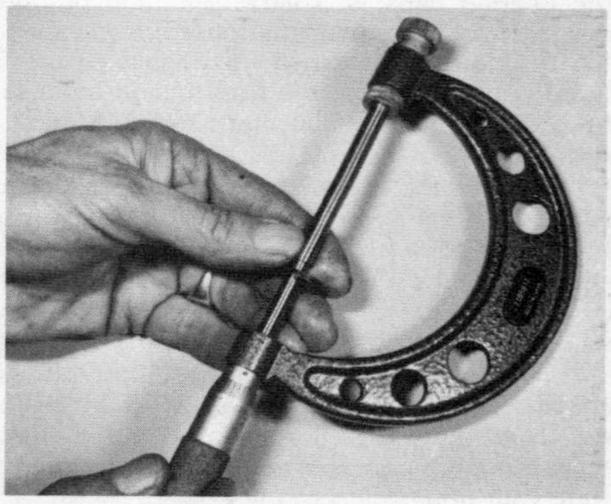

50.7B Checking the thickness of a valve clearance shim

51.3 The alternator drivebelt adjuster is accessible from below

the front mounting bracket but leave the ones on the rear bracket loose. Fit the compressor tight against the rear face of the front mounting bracket and then slide the rear bracket forward until it touches the rear mounting plate on the compressor. Lift the compressor away again and tighten the rear bracket bolts. Fit the compressor and drivebelt (photos).
19 When fitting the amplifier, note the spacers located under the bolt holes to prevent fracture of the baseplate when tightening the mounting nuts (photo).
20 The air conditioning condenser should be offered into position before bolting down the radiator top rail as the two connecting pipe stubs at the right-hand top corner must pass under the top rail.
21 Note that the brake servo hose to the induction manifolds runs (together with the air conditioner hose) at the rear quarter of the engine compartment.

### *Cars with automatic transmission*

22 Adjust the kickdown switch and the speed selector cable as described in Chapter 6.

### *Cars with manual transmission*

23 Bleed the clutch hydraulic system as described in Chapter 5.

### *Cars with air conditioning*

24 Reconnect all system pipes and components.

### *All models*

25 Refill the cooling system, refill and bleed the power steering system and refill the engine with oil.
26 Check and top up the transmission oil level. (In the case of automatic transmission, the level must be checked again when the fluid is hot – see Chapter 6.)

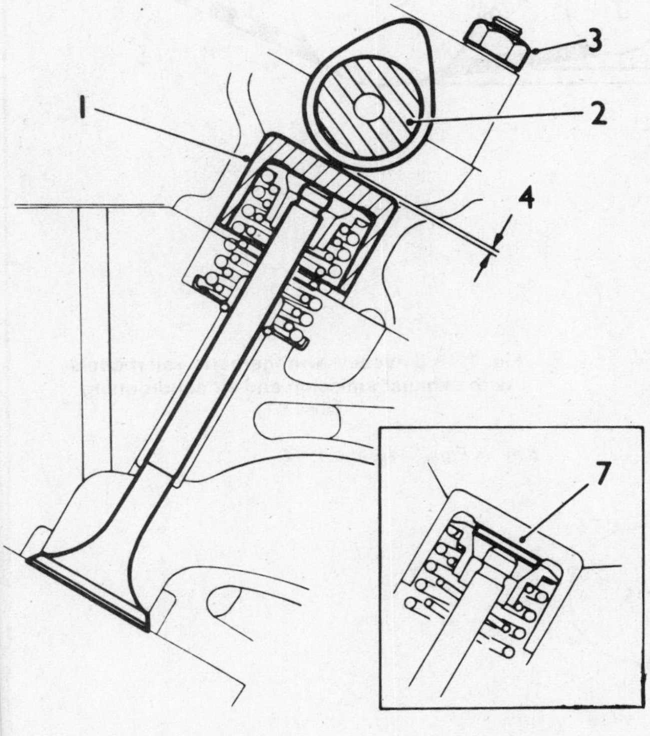


**Fig. 1.45 Sectional view of valve and cam (Sec 50)**

1 *Tappet*
2 *Cam*
3 *Camshaft bearing cap nut*
4 *Clearance*
7 *Adjustment shim*

## 50 Valve clearance – adjustment

1 This work can be carried out at the time of engine overhaul or as a maintenance operation at the specified service intervals. The valve clearances are measured with the engine cold.
2 *If the engine is in the car,* remove the camshaft covers (Section 8 or 9) and turn the crankshaft (by means of a socket spanner applied to the crankshaft damper centre bolt) until the first tappet is opposite the heel of the cam.
3 *If the cylinder head or tappet block is away from the engine,* the camshaft should be rotated carefully by its front flange to achieve the correct cam heel to tappet block relationship.
4 Using feeler blades, measure and record the clearance between the heel of the cam and the surface of the tappet (photo).
5 Turn the crankshaft or camshaft until each clearance on the remaining 23 tappets has been checked and recorded. Record the clearances separately for the two cylinder heads and count from the timing cover end.
6 The correct valve clearance is given in the Specifications. Where the recorded clearance differs from that specified, then by simple subtraction, establish the difference in thickness of the tappet shim required to reduce or increase the clearance as the case may be.
7 Shims are available in increments of 0.001 in (0.03 mm) from a thickness of 0.085 in to 0.110 in (2.16 to 2.79 mm). The shims are etched with a letter of the alphabet to indicate thickness, A indicating the thinnest and each succeeding letter denoting an increase in thickness of 0.001 in (0.03 mm). Obviously the possession of a micrometer will make life easier, particularly if the etched letters are indistinct or have worn off in service. In many cases, some of the original shims can be interchanged to achieve the correct clearances and it is worthwhile calculating whether this can be done before purchasing new shims (photos).
8 The shims can be changed after removing the camshafts, lifting out the tappets and extracting the shims from the tappet interiors.
9 With the camshafts refitted, recheck the valve clearances before refitting the camshaft covers.

## 51 Drivebelts – adjustment or renewal

1 The drivebelt configuration depends upon the equipment fitted.
2 The deflection of all drivebelts, measured under firm thumb pressure at the centre point of the longest run of the belt, should be $\frac{5}{32}$ in (4.0 mm), except for the air pump/compressor belt which should have a deflection of $\frac{1}{4}$ in (6.4 mm).
3 All drivebelts can be adjusted from above except the one for the alternator which is accessible from underneath the car (photo).
4 Adjustment is made in all cases by first releasing the jockey pulley or accessory mounting bolt and then releasing the locknut on the threaded adjuster link trunnion and turning the adjusting nut in or out to vary the effective length of the link.
5 A drivebelt may be renewed by releasing the accessory mounting bolts and by turning the adjuster nut. Move the accessory as far as possible until the belt can be slipped off the driving and driven pulleys. Never use a lever to remove or fit a belt.
6 Renewal of any but the front belt will necessitate the removal of the belts in front of it in all drivebelt arrangements.
7 Recheck the tension of a new drivebelt after the first hundred miles or so.

## 52 Initial start-up after major overhaul

1 Double check all hoses, wiring and battery connections. Check also that engine and cooling system drain plugs have been refitted tightly with the correct quantities of oil and coolant poured in.
2 Make sure that the battery is fully charged and that all lubricants and fuels are replenished.
3 Switch on the ignition and allow the petrol pump time to fill the carburettor float chambers or to pressurise the fuel injection system.
4 Start the engine; as soon as it fires and runs, keep it going at a fast tickover only (no faster). Watch the oil pressure gauge, after a very short wait, whilst the oil filter is being filled, it should register around 40 $lbf/in^2$. If, after 30 seconds, no oil pressure is registered, switch off

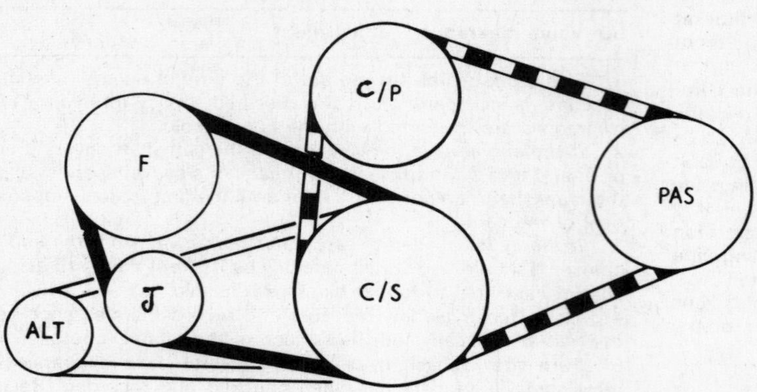


**Fig. 1.46 Drivebelt arrangement – all models without exhaust emission control or air conditioning (Sec 51)**

| | |
|---|---|
| *Alt* | *Alternator* |
| *C/S* | *Crankshaft* |
| *F* | *Fan* |
| *PAS* | *Power-assisted steering* |
| *C/P* | *Coolant pump* |
| *J* | *Jockey pulley* |

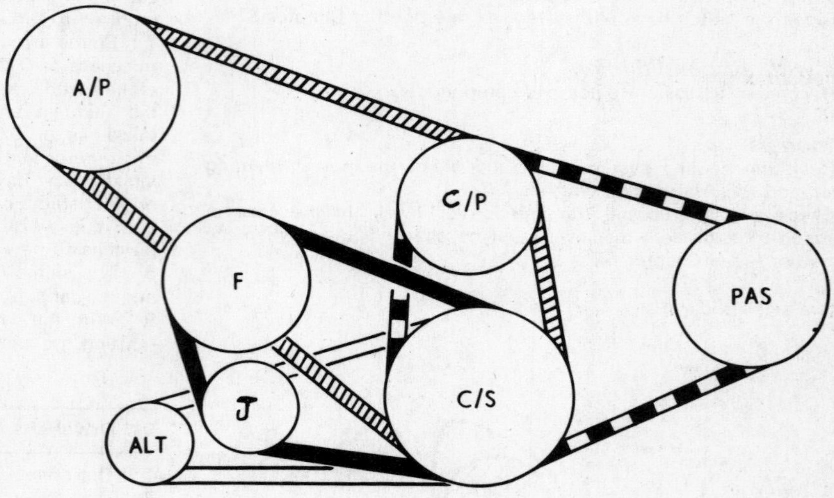


**Fig. 1.47 Drivebelt arrangement – all models with exhaust emission control but without air conditioning (Sec 51)**

*Key as Fig. 1.46 plus:*
*A/P* *Air pump*

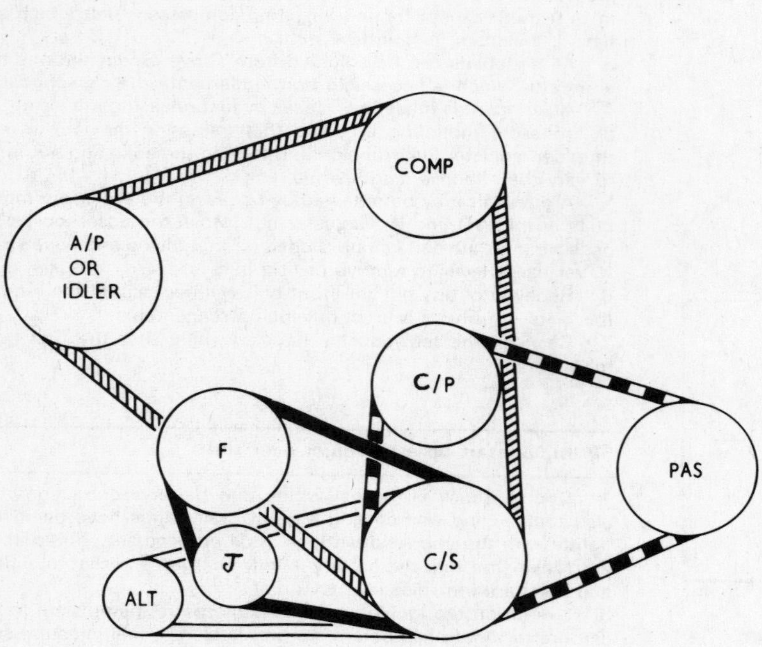


**Fig. 1.48 Drivebelt arrangement – all models with exhaust emission and air conditioning (Sec 51)**

*Key as Figs. 1.46 and 1.47*

the engine and investigate the cause; it may be that you have not fully tightened a union or the filter canister is not correctly seated on the rubber sealing ring in the head of the filter.

5 Bring the engine up to its normal working temperature. As it warms up there will be odd smells and some smoke from parts getting hot and burning off oil deposits. Look round carefully for water and oil leaks.

6 When the engine running temperature has been reached, adjust the fuel injection system or carburettors as described in Chapter 3.

7 Stop the engine and wait a few minutes to see if there are any water or oil leaks.

8 Before road testing the car it is advisable to have an assistant listening to the brake servo, run the engine for a few minutes and then operate the footbrake. If the brake servo connections are satisfactory the exhaust from the servo will be plainly heard.

9 Road test the car to check that the timing is correct and is giving the necessary smoothness and power. Do not race the engine. If new bearings or pistons or rings have been fitted, it should be treated as a new engine and run in at reduced revolutions for the first 500 miles (800 km).

10 When you are satisfied that the overhaul is completely successful, have the air conditioning system recharged by your dealer.

## 53 Fault diagnosis – engine

| Symptom | Reason(s) |
|---|---|
| Engine fails to turn over when starter switch operated | Flat or defective battery<br>Loose battery leads<br>Defective starter solenoid or switch or broken wiring<br>Engine earth strap disconnected<br>Defective starter motor |
| Engine turns over but will not start | Ignition system damp or wet<br>Ignition leads to spark plugs loose<br>Shorted or disconnected low tension leads<br>Disconnected or faulty component in electronic ignition system<br>No petrol in petrol tank<br>Vapour lock in fuel line (in hot conditions or at high altitude)<br>Fuel pump filter blocked<br>Faulty fuel pump<br>Carburettor or fuel injection system fault |
| Engine stalls and will not start | Ignition failure<br>No petrol in petrol tank<br>Petrol tank breather choked<br>Sudden obstruction in carburettors or fuel injection system<br>Water in fuel system<br>Ignition leads loose<br>Battery leads loose on terminals<br>Battery earth strap loose on body of attachment point |
| Engine misfired or idles unevenly | Engine earth lead loose<br>Low tension leads loose<br>Dirty or incorrectly gapped plugs<br>Tracking across inside of distributor cover<br>Ignition too retarded<br>Faulty electronic ignition component<br>Mixture too weak<br>Air leak at inlet manifold<br>Incorrect valve clearances<br>Burnt out exhaust valves<br>Sticking or leaking valves<br>Weak or broken valve springs<br>Worn valve guides or stems<br>Worn pistons and piston rings |
| Lack of power | Burnt out exhaust valves<br>Sticking or leaking valves<br>Worn valve guides and stems<br>Weak or broken valve springs<br>Blown cylinder head gasket (accompanied by increase in noise)<br>Worn pistons and piston rings<br>Worn or scored cylinder bores<br>Ignition timing wrongly set<br>Incorrect valve clearances<br>Incorrectly set spark plugs<br>Mixture too rich or too weak<br>Fuel filters blocked causing fuel starvation<br>Distributor automatic balance weights or vacuum advance and retard mechanisms not functioning correctly<br>Faulty fuel pump giving top end fuel starvation |
| Excessive oil consumption | Badly worn, perished or missing inlet valve stem oil seals<br>Excessively worn valve stems and valve guides |

| Symptom | Reason(s) |
|---|---|
| | Worn piston rings |
| | Worn pistons and cylinder bores |
| | Excessive piston ring gap allowing blow-by |
| | Piston oil return holes choked |
| | Leaking oil filter gasket |
| | Leaking camshaft cover gasket |
| | Leaking timing case gasket |
| | Leaking sump gasket |
| | Loose sump plug |
| | Worn crankshaft oil seals |
| | Leaking external oil pipes or union O-ring seals |
| Unusual noises from engine | Worn valve gear (noisy tapping from top cover) |
| | Worn big-end bearing (regular heavy knocking) |
| | Worn main bearings (rumbling) |
| | Worn camshaft chain |

# Chapter 2 Cooling system

*For modifications, and information applicable to later models, see Supplement at end of manual*

**Contents**



**Specifications**

| | | |
|---|---|---|
| **System type** | Thermo-syphon with front mounted radiator, expansion tank and coolant pump. Two cooling fans, one belt-driven and one electric | |
| **Coolant type/specification** | Ethylene glycol based antifreeze, to BS 3151, 3152 or 6580 (Duckhams Universal Antifreeze and Summer Coolant) | |
| **Thermostat** | | |
| Starts to open: | | |
| Early cars | 174° to 181°F (79° to 83°C) | |
| Later cars | 190°F (88°C) | |
| Fully open | 200° to 205°F (93° to 96°C) | |
| **Pressure cap rating** | | |
| XJ12 and Double Six | 13 lbf/in² (0.91 kgf/cm²) | |
| XJS | 15 lbf/in² (1.05 kgf/cm²) | |
| **System capacity** | 37 Imp pints (44.4 US pints, 21.0 litre) | |
| **Torque wrench settings** | **lbf ft** | **Nm** |
| Radiator to front crossmember | 25 | 34 |
| Fan cowl nuts and bolts | 6 | 8 |
| Fan motor to mounting bracket | 7 | 10 |
| Engine oil cooler pipe unions | 45 | 61 |
| Expansion tank mounting bolts | 10 | 14 |
| Fan guard | 5 | 7 |

## 1 General description

1 The cooling system comprises a radiator, a belt-driven coolant pump and a remotely sited expansion tank. Two thermostatic valves are incorporated to assist in rapid warm-up. The radiator is cooled by an electric fan, thermostatically controlled from the coolant pump inlet, a belt-driven fan incorporating a fluid coupling.

2 The heating system is connected into the engine cooling system.

3 Bleeding of the system after drain and refill is automatic by means of induction housing bleed tubes.

4 A cooler for the automatic transmission fluid is built into the tank at the radiator right-hand end.

5 There are certain differences between the cooling systems used on cars with carburettor fuel systems and those with fuel injection systems, as shown in the illustrations.

6 On cars with fuel injection, the thermotime switch, the coolant temperature sensor and the auxiliary air valve (see Chapter 3) function as an automatic choke during cold start conditions.

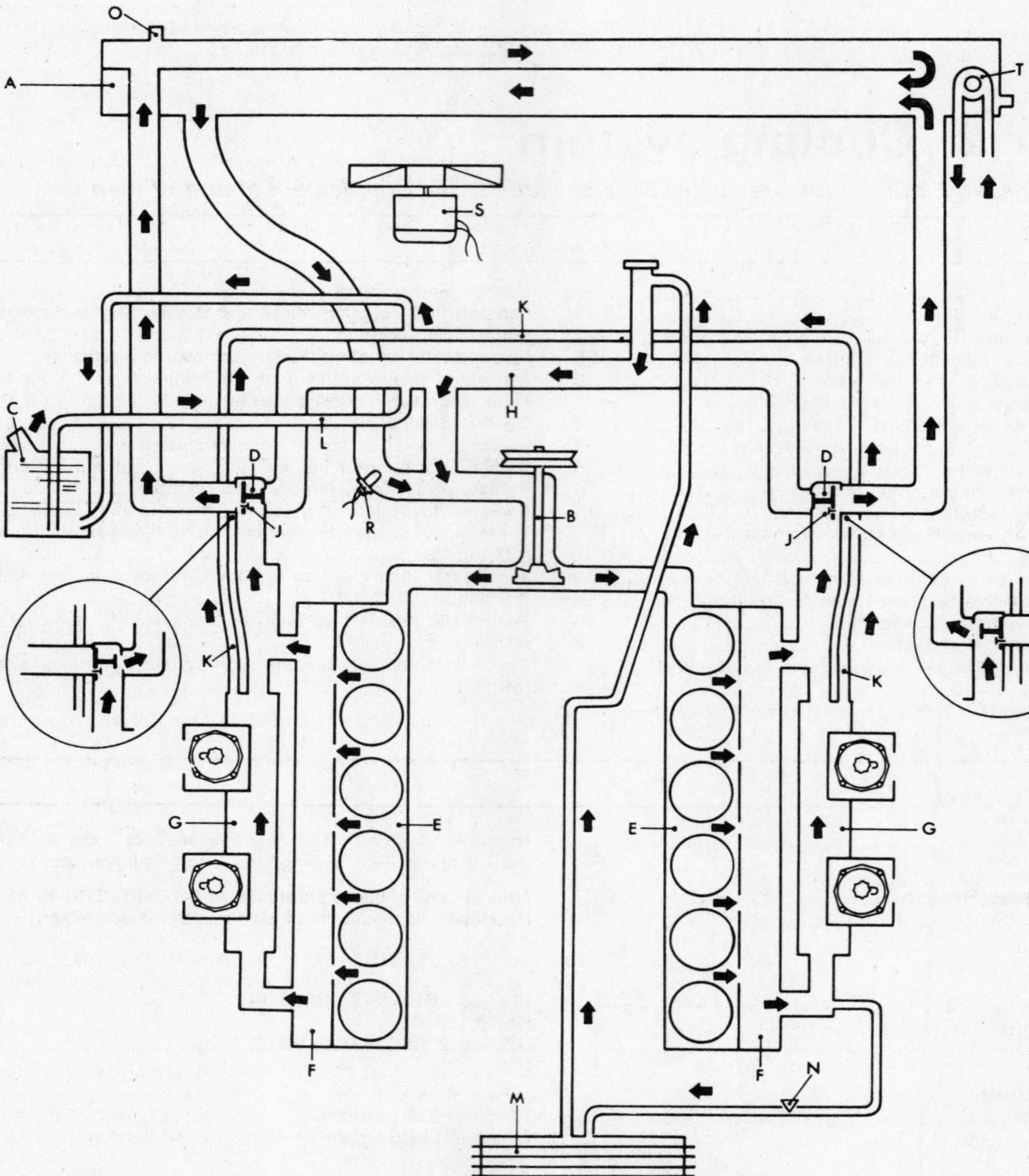


**Fig. 2.1 Cooling system (carburettor engines) (Sec 1)**

| | | | |
|---|---|---|---|
| *A* | *Radiator* | *K* | *Bleed pipes* |
| *B* | *Coolant pump* | *L* | *Coolant supply pipe* |
| *C* | *Expansion tank* | *M* | *Heater matrix* |
| *D* | *Thermostats (insets show cold positions)* | *N* | *Heater coolant control valve* |
| *E* | *Cylinder block* | *O* | *Radiator bleed tap* |
| *F* | *Cylinder head* | *R* | *Electric fan thermostatic switch* |
| *G* | *Induction housing* | *S* | *Electric fan* |
| *H* | *Engine cross-pipe* | *T* | *Transmission fluid cooler* |
| *J* | *Thermostat jiggle pins* | | |

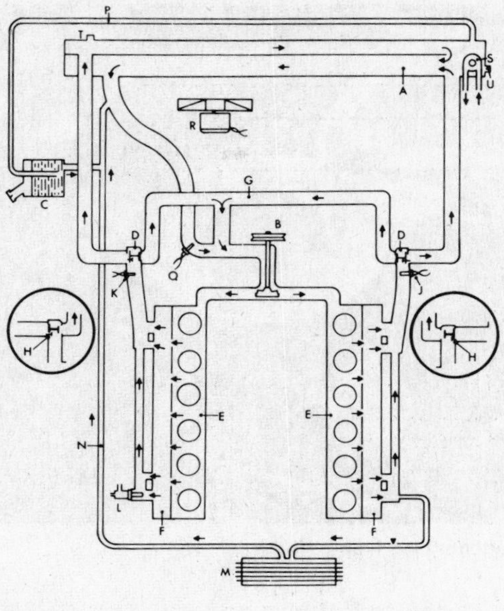

**Fig. 2.2 Cooling system (fuel injection engines) (Sec 1)**

| | |
|---|---|
| *A* | *Radiator* |
| *B* | *Coolant pump* |
| *C* | *Expansion tank* |
| *D* | *Thermostats* |
| *E* | *Cylinder block* |
| *F* | *Cylinder head* |
| *G* | *Engine cross-pipe* |
| *H* | *Thermostat jiggle pins (thermostats in cold position)* |
| *J* | *Thermotime switch* |
| *K* | *Coolant temperature sensor* |
| *L* | *Auxiliary air valve* |
| *M* | *Heater matrix* |
| *N* | *Purge pipe* |
| *P* | *Purge pipe* |
| *Q* | *Electric fan thermostatic switch* |
| *R* | *Electric cooling fan* |
| *S* | *Automatic transmission fluid cooler* |
| *T* | *Bleed tap* |
| *U* | *Radiator drain tap* |

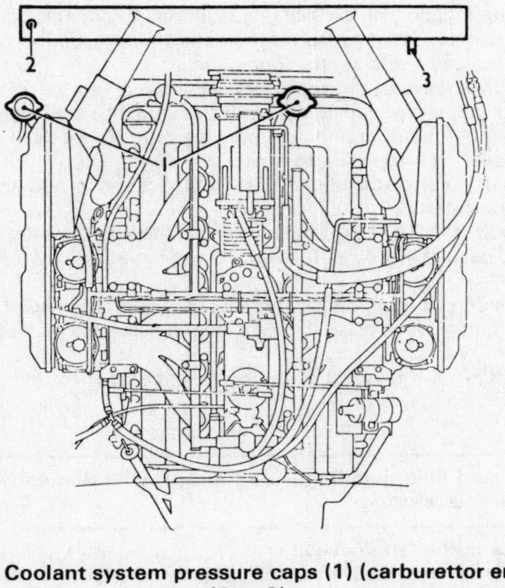

**Fig. 2.3 Coolant system pressure caps (1) (carburettor engines) (Sec 2)**

*2 Bleed tap* — *3 Drain tap*

## 2 Cooling system (carburettor models) – draining

1 With the engine cold, remove the pressure caps from the remote expansion tank and the engine cross-pipe.
2 Open the bleed tap on the left-hand side of the radiator top rail.
3 Place a container of adequate capacity under the radiator and open the drain tap. If the coolant is less than a year old and in good condition it can be saved for re-use.
4 The expansion tank can be drained by releasing the clip and pulling the pipe from the lower stub connection.
5 If the coolant appears rusty or dark in colour, insert a hose in the expansion tank and flush the system until clear water emerges from the drain tap. If the contamination is severe it may be necessary to remove the radiator and reverse flush it.

## 3 Cooling system (fuel injection models) – draining

1 The operations are similar to those described in Section 2 except that there is only one cap which can be removed, the one from the expansion tank (photo).

## 4 Cooling system (carburettor models) – refilling

1 Make sure that both pressure caps are removed and the radiator bleed tap is open.
2 Move the right-hand heater control to 'DEF', or 'HI' on models without air conditioning.
3 Using the correct coolant mixture (see Section 7), pour it slowly into the filler neck on the engine cross-pipe until the expansion tank is full and then fit the cap to the expansion tank. Make sure that the correct cap is being refitted and that its rubber seal is in good condition.
4 Now observe the radiator bleed tap. As soon as a continuous flow of coolant runs from it, close the tap.
5 Continue to pour coolant into the cross-pipe filler until the level is within 2 in (51 mm) of the rim. Fit the cap.
6 Start the engine and run at idling speed for about three minutes. Switch off and wait for one minute, then open the radiator bleed tap and remove the cross-pipe pressure cap.
7 Add more coolant slowly into the cross-pipe filler neck until coolant again flows from the bleed tap. Close the tap.
8 Continue to pour in coolant until the level is again within 2 in (51 mm) of the top of the cross-pipe filler. Refit the pressure cap.
9 This somewhat laborious refilling method must not be shortened as air pockets remaining in the cooling system may cause local hotspots with consequent engine damage.

## 5 Cooling system (fuel injection models) – refilling

1 Close the radiator drain tap and then check that the pressure cap is removed from the expansion tank and the radiator bleed tap is open (photo).
2 Slowly fill the expansion tank to the brim with correct coolant (see Section 7). Wait for one or two minutes and if the level has dropped, add more coolant.
3 Close the bleed tap and fit the pressure cap to the expansion tank, having made sure that the sealing ring is in good order.
4 On cars equipped with air conditioning, set the controls to '80' and 'DEF'.
5 Start the engine and let it idle (1000 rpm approx) for about three minutes, then switch off.
6 Open the bleed tap and wait until a continuous flow of coolant is seen to be ejected, then close the tap.
7 Remove the pressure cap from the expansion tank and slowly pour in more coolant until it is full to the brim. Refit the cap.
8 This somewhat laborious refilling method must not be shortened as air pockets remaining in the cooling system may cause local hotspots with engine damage.

## 6 Cooling system – level checking and topping up

1 Coolant level checking should be carried out regularly as described

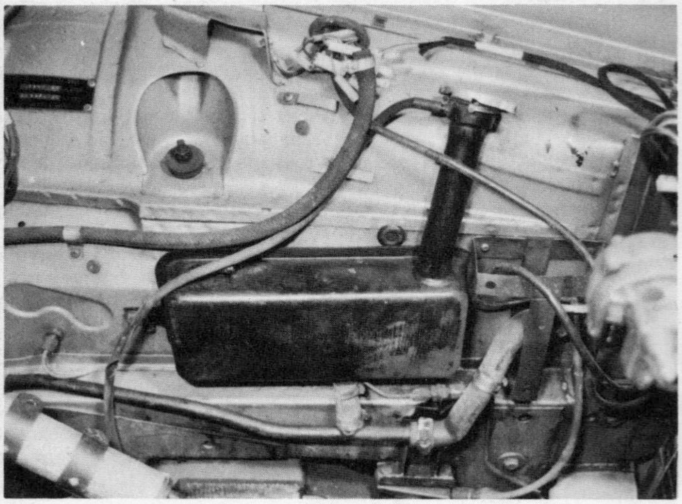

3.1 The expansion tank (fuel injection models)

5.1 The radiator bleed tap

in Routine Maintenance. If topping up is required frequently, then a leak in the system should be suspected.

2 To check the coolant level on carburettor models, make sure that the engine is cold and remove the pressure cap from the engine cross-pipe. If the coolant level is within 2 in (51 mm) of the rim, the system does not require topping up. If the level is lower, open the radiator bleed tap and pour coolant into the cross-pipe filler neck until coolant flows from the bleed tap. Close the tap and refit the pressure cap.

3 To check the coolant level on fuel injection models, make sure that the engine is cold and remove the expansion tank cap. If no more coolant can be added the system evidently does not require topping up and the cap can be refitted. If coolant is needed, fill the tank to the brim and then refit the cap.

## 7 Antifreeze mixture

1 Plain water should never be used in the cooling system as apart from not providing protection against adverse climatic conditions, the internal metal surfaces of the water passages will also corrode. The inhibitors found in good quality antifreeze mixtures protect iron and aluminium against corrosion for periods not exceeding twelve months.

2 In climatic conditions where antifreeze is not required make sure that a suitable corrosion inhibitor is used in the coolant.

3 The following table gives a guide to the proportion of antifreeze required for various levels of protection:

| Antifreeze volume | Protection to |
|---|---|
| *25%* | *-15°F (-26°C)* |
| *35%* | *-38°F (-39°C)* |
| *40%* | *-42°F (-41°C)* |
| *50%* | *-53°F (-47°C)* |

4 When carrying out routine topping up of the cooling system, always use coolant which has been mixed in the same proportion as the original coolant.

## 8 Expansion tank – removal and refitting

1 Remove the left-hand air cleaner.

2 Unclip and disconnect the pipe on the top of the expansion tank and tie it up as high as possible.

3 Disconnect and tie the pipe at the base of the expansion tank in a similar way. Drain the tank and then pull the vent pipe from the filler neck.

4 Turn the steering to full left-hand lock.

5 Working under the front left-hand wheel arch, unbolt the tank and lift it clear.

6 Refit the tank by reversing the removal operations and then refill with coolant, referring to Section 4 or 5 as applicable.

## 9 Fan and coolant pump drivebelt – adjustment, removal and refitting

1 The procedure for all belt configurations is covered in Chapter 1, Section 51.

## 10 Electric fan cowl (XJ12 and Double Six) – removal and refitting

1 Disconnect the battery and drain the cooling system.

2 *On cars equipped with air conditioning*, remove the fan and the fluid coupling unit as described in Section 12, also the right-hand air intake ram tube. Unbolt the relays from the radiator top rail and lay them with their wiring harness across the engine.

3 *On all models*, remove the left-hand air intake ram tube.

4 Detach the headlamp relay.

5 Remove the four self-locking nuts from the rear of the top rail, noting the location of the clips, washers and connectors.

6 Disconnect the lead from the coolant pump suction pipe and the cooling fan red leads at the connectors.

7 *On cars without air conditioning*, slacken the fan relay securing nuts and detach the fan shield from the studs. Unclip (one screw) the float chamber breather and vent pipe (carburettor models) and pull the pipe through the top rail grommet.

8 *On all cars*, disconnect the radiator top hose and the fan cowl lower brackets.

9 Unbolt the radiator top rail and without straining the wiring harness, ease the top rail forward to clear the fan cowl. Remove the cowl.

10 On some air conditioned models, the electric fan cowl is attached to the belt-driven cowl by self-tapping screws which must be extracted.

11 Refitting is a reversal of removal. Remember to refill the cooling system on completion.

## 11 Fan and fluid coupling (XJ12 and Double Six, early models) – removal and refitting

1 Slacken the fan drivebelt.

2 Unscrew and remove the four nuts which hold the fan to the fluid coupling.

3 Unscrew and remove the four nuts which hold the fluid coupling to the pulley.

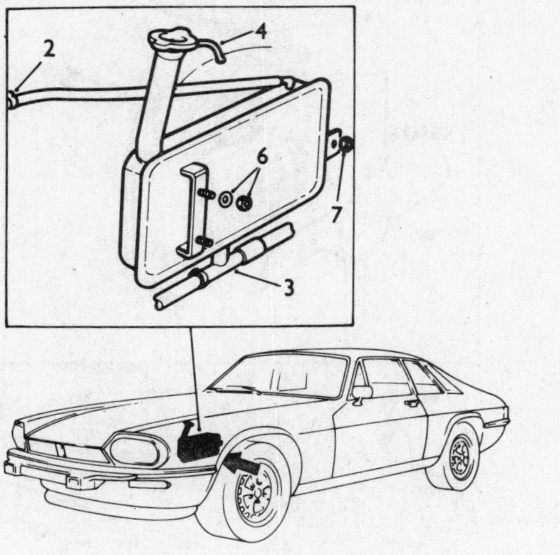


**Fig. 2.4 Expansion tank fixing details (Sec 8)**

2 *Hose clip*
3 *Base pipe*
4 *Vent pipe*
6 *Mounting nut and washer*
7 *Mounting nut*

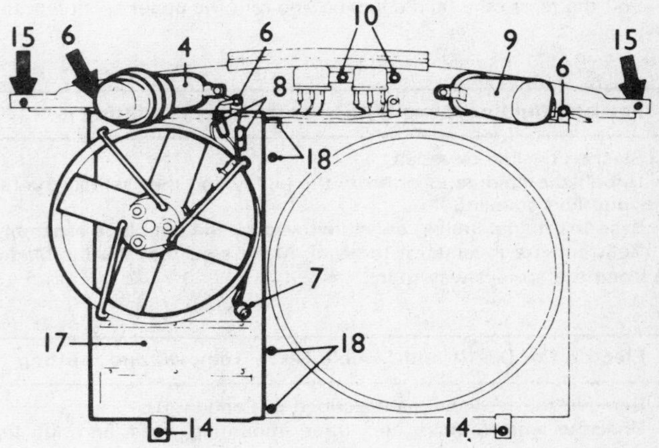


**Fig. 2.5 Electric fan cowl (XJ12, Double Six) removal (Sec 10)**

4 *Left-hand intake ram tube*
6 *Top rail nuts*
7 *Thermostatic switch*
8 *Fan wires*
9 *Right-hand intake ram tube (air conditioned models)*
10 *Relay mounting screws (air conditioned models)*
14 *Fan cowl bracket screws*
15 *Top rail securing screws*
17 *Fan cowl*
18 *Screws (electric fan cowl to belt-driven fan cowl)*

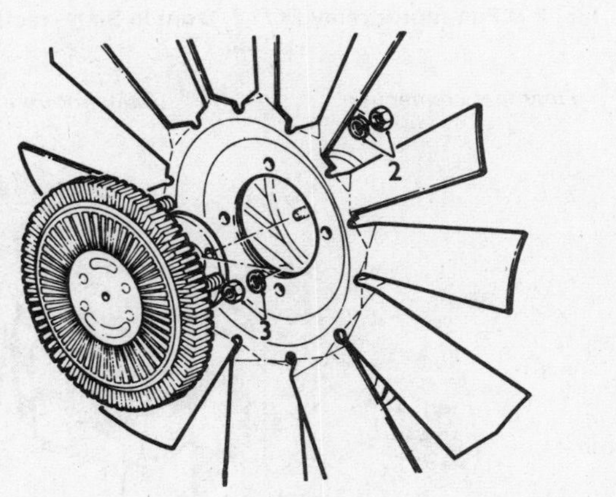


**Fig. 2.6 Fan and fluid coupling (XJ12 and Double Six, early models, and XJS) (Sec 11)**

2 *Fan to fluid coupling nuts*
3 *Fluid coupling to coolant pump nuts*

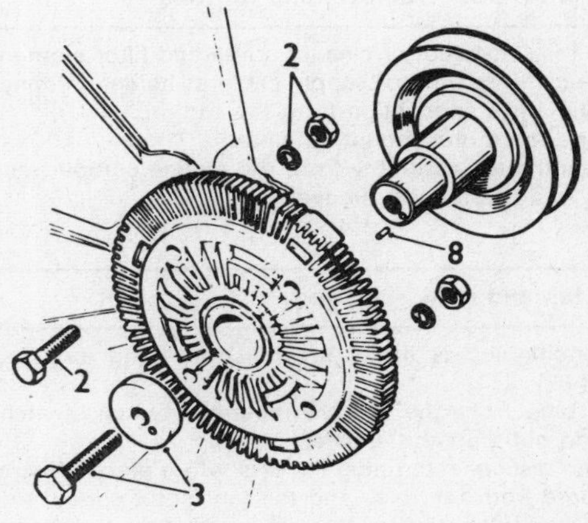


**Fig. 2.7 Fan and fluid coupling (XJ12 and Double Six, later models) (Sec 12)**

2 *Fan to fluid coupling nuts and bolts*
3 *Fluid coupling centre bolt and special washer*
8 *Locating pin*

4 Remove the fan and fluid coupling.
5 Refitting is a reversal of removal.

## 12 Fan and fluid coupling (XJ12 and Double Six, later models) – removal and refitting

1 Unscrew and remove the setscrews which hold the top section of the fan cowl.
2 Unbolt the fan from the fluid coupling.
3 Hold the pulley against rotation (flats are provided on the shaft for this purpose) and then unscrew the fluid coupling centre bolt. Do not lose the special washer.
4 Using a plastic faced mallet, gently tap the fluid coupling from the pulley spigot.
5 Remove the fan from the cowl.
6 To refit, first locate the four bolts in the fluid coupling and then place the fan over the pulley spindle.
7 Check that the locating pin is in position in the pulley spigot and smear the spigot with grease.
8 Position the fluid coupling on the pulley and then fit the coupling with the special bolt and washer. Ensure that the special washer engages correctly with the pin in the pulley spigot before tightening the bolt. Hold the shaft flats with an open-ended spanner.
9 Bolt the fan to the fluid coupling and refit the upper section of the cowl.

## 13 Fan and fluid coupling (XJS) – removal and refitting

1 Slacken the fan drivebelt.
2 Unbolt the fluid coupling from the pulley and then unbolt the fan from the fluid coupling.
3 Ease the fluid coupling away followed by the fan blade assembly.
4 Refitting is a reversal of removal. Make sure that the fan blades are fitted the correct way round.

## 14 Electric fan (XJ12 and Double Six) – removal and refitting

1 Remove the fan cowl as described in Section 10.
2 Unscrew and remove the three mounting nuts and lift the fan/motor assembly from the engine compartment.
3 Refitting is a reversal of removal.

## 15 Electric fan (XJS) – removal and refitting

1 Remove the left-hand air cleaner cover and filter element.
2 Disconnect the fan motor supply cable at its snap connector.
3 Unbolt the earth connection from the top rail.
4 Unbolt the fan motor mounting plate.
5 Lift the fan/motor assembly from the engine compartment.
6 Refitting is a reversal of removal.

## 16 Electric fan and relay – testing

1 If air conditioning is fitted, set the right-hand air conditioning switch to 'OFF'.
2 Pull the plug from the fan thermostatic switch, switch on the ignition but do not start the engine.
3 Bridge the disconnected plug sockets wth a piece of wire. A click should be heard from the relay and the fan motor should rotate.
4 Remove the bridge wire, switch off the ignition and reconnect the plug.

### *Cars with air conditioning*

5 Again switch on the ignition and set the left-hand air conditioning control to '65' and the right-hand one to 'AUTO'. The air conditioner relay should be heard to operate, the cooling fan should start and the compressor clutch should engage.
6 Switch off the ignition and set the right-hand air conditioning system control to the 'OFF' position.

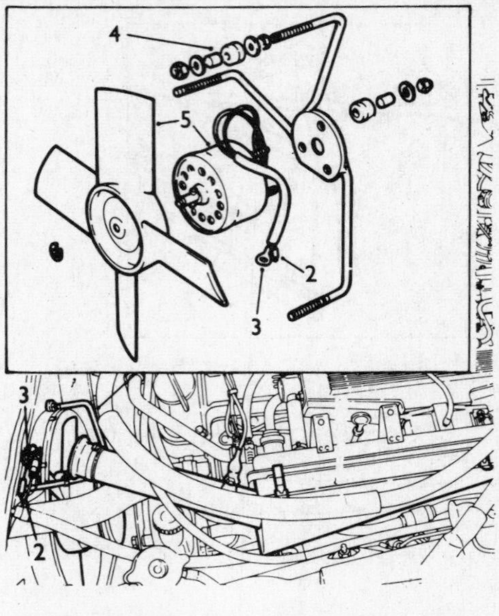


**Fig. 2.8 Electrican fan (XJS) (Sec 15)**

*2 Motor supply wire*
*3 Earth lead*
*4 Motor mounting plate nuts*
*5 Fan/motor*

**Fig. 2.9 Fan motor relay (XJ12, Double Six) – rectangular type (Sec 17)**

*1 Electrical connection*
*2 Relay mounting nuts*

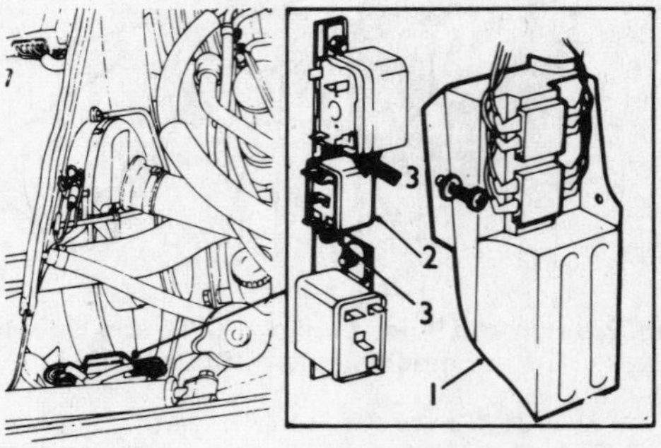


**Fig. 2.10 Fan motor relay (XJS) (Sec 17)**

*1 Cover*
*2 Relay*
*3 Mounting nuts*

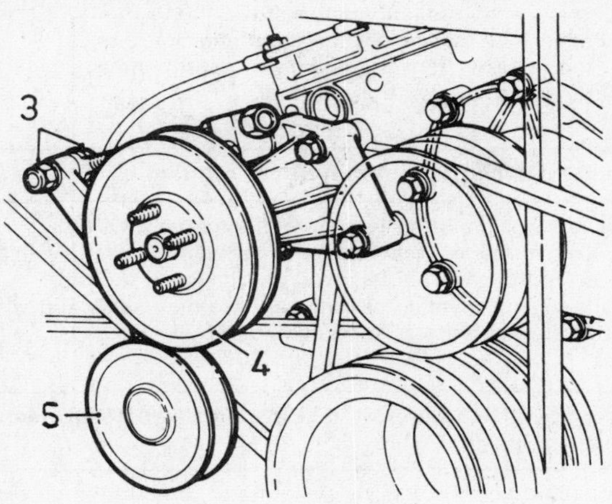


**Fig. 2.11 Idler and jockey pulleys (Sec 18)**

*3 Adjuster bolt securing nut*
*4 Idler pulley*
*5 Jockey pulley*

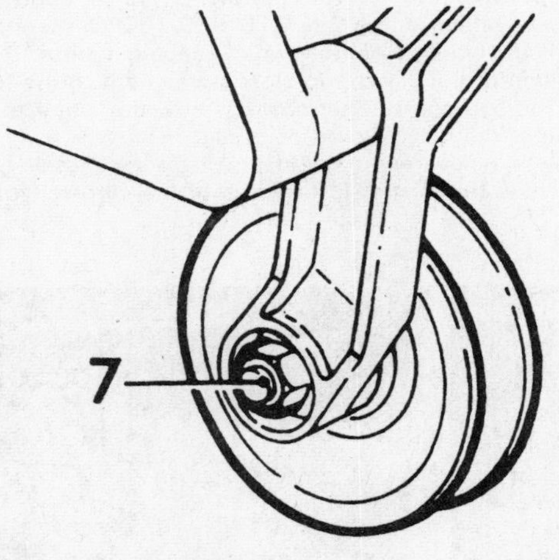


**Fig. 2.12 Jockey pulley retaining nut (7) (Sec 18)**

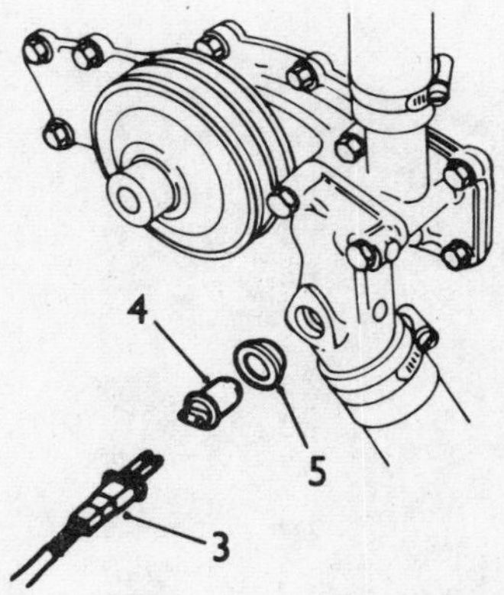


**Fig. 2.13 Electric fan thermostatic switch (4), seal (5) and connector (3) (Sec 19)**

## 17 Fan motor relay – removal and refitting

1 *On XJ12 and Double Six models,* the relay (see Chapter 10) is mounted on the right-hand side of the radiator top rail. It may be of round or rectangular design, according to model.
2 *On XJS models* the relay is mounted on a block on the left-hand side of the engine compartment.
3 Identify the connecting leads to their terminals, disconnect them and then unbolt and remove the relay.
4 Refitting is a reversal of removal.

## 18 Idler and jockey pulleys – removal and refitting

1 To remove the idler pulley, first take off the drivebelt and remove the fan and fluid coupling.
2 Remove the bolt which holds the adjuster bolt eye to the pulley arm.
3 Unbolt the idler pulley housing from the engine and remove it complete with jockey pulley.
4 To remove the jockey pulley from the engine independently, first withdraw the right-hand air cleaner.
5 Screw back the locknut on the fanbelt adjustment bolt and then slacken the locknut on the adjuster bolt trunnion.
6 Slacken the jockey pulley arm pivot bolt and then remove the bolt which holds the adjustment bolt eye to the pulley arm.
7 On early XJ12, Double Six and all XJS models, unscrew the nut and special washer which hold the jockey pulley spindle in the arm.
8 Refitting is a reversal of removal.

## 19 Electric fan thermostatic switch – removal and refitting

1 Disconnect the battery and drain the cooling system.
2 Disconnect the electrical plug from the thermostatic switch (photo).
3 Grip the switch with a pair of pliers and pull it from its rubber seal in the coolant pump bottom connector (photo).
4 Prise the rubber seal from its housing.
5 Always use a new seal when fitting the switch.
6 Fit the new seal to the housing. **Do not** apply any grease or lubricant to the seal.
7 Press the switch into the seal.
8 Reconnect the switch plug and the battery and refill the cooling system. Check the switch and seal for coolant leaks when the engine is first run.

## 20 Radiator (carburettor fuel system) – removal and refitting

1 Disconnect the battery, drain the cooling system and remove the bonnet.
2 Remove the left-hand air intake ram tube.
3 Disconnect the leads and remove the headlamp relay.
4 Identify the leads and pull them from the headlamp fuse boxes. Pull the leads through the radiator top rail grommet.
5 Unscrew and remove the self-locking nuts from the rear of the top rail noting the location of clips and connectors.
6 Disconnect the lead from the thermostatic switch.
7 Disconnect the fan supply cable (red) at the snap connector.
8 Unbolt the fan relay from the top rail.
9 Unbolt the top rail.
10 *On cars equipped with air conditioning,* lift up the top rail complete with receiver/drier and condenser, and lay the assembly across the top of the engine. **Do not** disconnect any of the air conditioning system hoses, but move the components as far as the flexible connecting hoses will permit.
11 *On cars without air conditioning,* remove the top rail.
12 Disconnect the top hoses from the radiator.
13 Disconnect the automatic transmission oil cooler lines from the radiator and plug all openings.
14 Remove (two self-tapping screws) the radiator lower grille.
15 Using two spanners to avoid tearing the stubs out, disconnect the hoses from the engine oil cooler.
16 Unbolt the engine oil cooler from its brackets and remove it, noting the spacers between the oil cooler and the brackets.

17 Working underneath the car, disconnect the bottom hose from the radiator.
18 Withdraw the radiator from the engine compartment.
19 Refitting is a reversal of removal. Renew any damaged grommets.

## 21 Radiator (fuel injection system) – removal and refitting

1 If the car is equipped with air conditioning, have the system discharged by your dealer.
2 Disconnect the battery, remove the bonnet and drain the cooling system.
3 On XJS and early XJ12 models, remove the lower grille.
4 Detach relays and sensors (but do not disconnect the leads) from the radiator assembly.
5 Disconnect the amplifier block connector (see Chapter 3).
6 Unbolt the fan cowl from the radiator top rail, noting the locations of the earth lead and the line fuse.
7 Disconnect the expansion pipe (banjo bolt) from the radiator.
8 Unbolt the radiator top rail and disconnect the earth leads from the left and right-hand harnesses.
9 Unbolt the right-hand front stay.
10 Unbolt the left-hand wing valance stay.
11 On cars equipped with air conditioning, disconnect and plug the hoses from the receiver/drier. Unclip the condenser hose from the right-hand wing valance.
12 Remove the radiator top rail (complete with receiver/drier on air conditioned models).
13 Disconnect the lead from the low coolant level sensor.
14 Disconnect the radiator right-hand top hose.
15 On cars fitted with automatic transmission, disconnect the hoses from the transmission oil cooler and plug the openings.
16 Disconnect the left-hand top hose from the radiator, also the hose from the expansion tank T-piece.
17 Disconnect the hoses from the engine oil cooler. Use two spanners to avoid tearing the stub out of the cooler.
18 Disconnect the radiator bottom hose.
19 Unbolt the fan cowl from the mounting brackets.
20 Lift the radiator from the engine compartment.
21 Refitting is the reverse of removal.

## 22 Radiator drain tap – removal and refitting

1 The radiator drain tap is remotely operated by a rod.
2 To remove the tap, drain the cooling system, pull the split pin from the lower end of the operating rod and unscrew the tap.
3 Refitting is a reversal of removal. Use new seals and smear the threads of the tap with jointing compound.

## 23 Thermostat (carburettor fuel system) – removal, testing and refitting

1 Partially drain the cooling system and remove the air cleaner to obtain access to a thermostat.
2 Disconnect the hose from the thermostat housing cover.
3 Unbolt and remove the thermostat housing cover.
4 Lift out the thermostat. If it is stuck in its seat, cut round it with a sharp knife.
5 Clean the thermostat and ensure that the small hole on the valve is clear. If the valve is open it indicates that the thermostat is unserviceable and should be renewed with one of similar operating temperature, this figure will be seen on the top side of the thermostat.
6 If correct operation of the thermostat is in doubt test it by immersing it together with a 0 to 212°F (0-100°C) thermometer in a container of cold water. Heat the water, keeping it stirred, and observe if the operation of the valve is in close agreement to the temperature marked on the body of the thermostat. Allow the water to cool down and check that the valve closes correctly.
7 Refitting is a reversal of removal. Use a new gasket, and make sure that a new thermostat (if fitted) is of the correct type.

19.2 Fan thermostatic switch connecting plug (arrowed)

19.3 Fan thermostatic switch removed

24.1A Thermostat housing

24.1B Removing the thermostat from the right-hand side of the engine

24.1C Thermostat removed

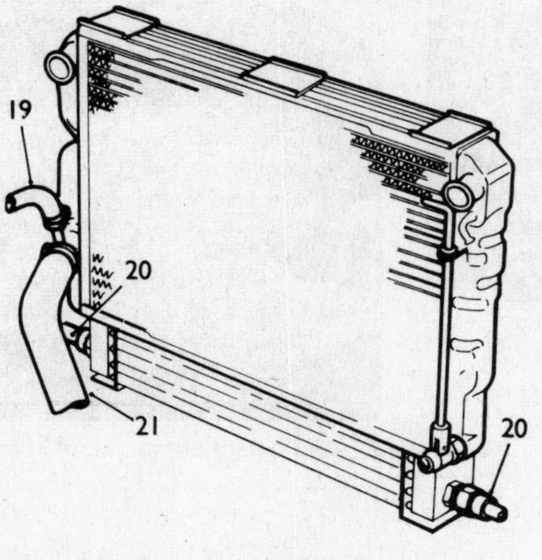


**Fig. 2.14 Radiator connections (Sec 21)**

*19 Expansion tank T-piece hose*
*20 Engine oil cooler hose connections*
*21 Radiator bottom hose*

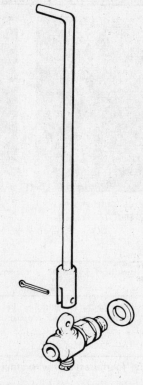

**Fig. 2.15 Radiator drain tap (Sec 22)**

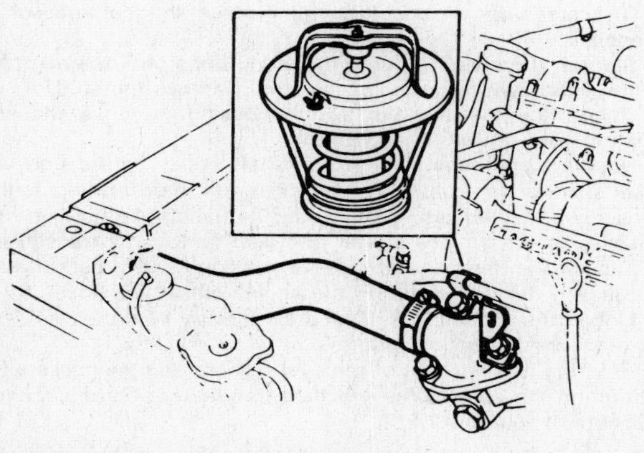

**Fig. 2.16 Left-hand thermostat and housing (carburettor engines) (Sec 23)**

**Fig. 2.17 Removing the coolant pump pulley (Sec 29)**

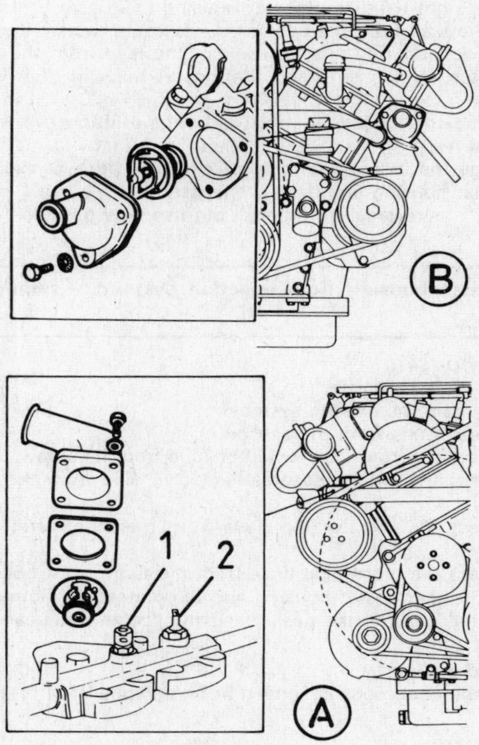


**Fig. 2.18 Thermostats (fuel injection engines) (Sec 24)**

*A Right-hand*
*B Left-hand*
*1 Thermotime switch*
*2 Coolant temperature switch*

27.10 Removing the thermostatic switch housing from the coolant pump

27.14 Removing the coolant pump

27.15 Coolant pump gasket in position

## 24 Thermostat (fuel injection system) – removal, testing and refitting

1 The operations are similar to those described in Section 23 except that it is not necessary to remove the air cleaner for access to the thermostat (photos).

## 25 Thermostat housing (carburettor fuel system) – removal and refitting

1 Partially drain the cooling system and remove the air cleaner.
2 Release the clips from the three hoses attached to the thermostat housing.
3 From the right-hand thermostat housing (if it is to be removed) disconnect the lead from the coolant temperature transmitter.
4 On emission control cars, disconnect the lead from the thermal override switch on the left-hand thermostat housing (if it is to be removed).
5 Unbolt the thermostat housing and engine lifting eye from the cylinder head.
6 Disengage the induction housing bleed pipe from its clip. Lift off the thermostat housing and discard the gaskets.
7 Refitting is a reversal of removal, but use new gaskets.

## 26 Thermostat housing (fuel injection system) – removal and refitting

### *Left-hand housing*

1 Remove the air cleaner.
2 Partially drain the cooling system.
3 Disconnect leads from the sensors.
4 Disconnect the crankcase breather tube from its elbow.
5 Disconnect the crankcase breather valve pipe from the coolant pipe.
6 Disconnect the radiator top hose from the thermostat housing cover.
7 Disconnect the cross-pipe hose from the thermostat housing.
8 Unbolt the thermostat housing and disconnect the housing from the coolant rail. Discard the gasket and the coolant rail sealing ring.

### *Right-hand housing*

9 Repeat the operations described in paragraphs 2, 3, 6, 7 and 8.

### *Both housings*

10 Refitting of both housings is a reversal of removal. Use new gaskets and coolant rail sealing rings.

## 27 Coolant pump (XJ12 and Double Six) – removal and refitting

1 Remove the radiator as described earlier in this Chapter.
2 Unbolt the radiator cowl lower brackets and move the cowl to one side.
3 Remove the fan and fluid coupling.
4 Remove the fanbelt.
5 Remove the fanbelt adjuster trunnion bolt and unbolt the idler pulley housing.
6 Extract the two studs so that the power steering pump belt can be removed.
7 On emission control cars, remove the air pump belt.
8 On cars with air conditioning, remove the compressor pump drivebelt.
9 Slacken the steering pump mounting bolts until the adjuster bolt can be withdrawn from its special stud. Remove the stud.
10 Unbolt the thermostatic switch housing. Remove the housing complete with bottom hose (photo).
11 Unscrew and remove the crankshaft pulley centre bolt using a socket spanner. In order to prevent the crankshaft rotating as the bolt is unscrewed try engaging gear with the handbrake fully on (manual transmission) or jam the starter ring gear (automatic transmission).
12 Tap off the damper and retrieve the cone and Woodruff key.
13 Slacken the upper clip on the engine cross-pipe hose.
14 Unbolt the coolant pump and draw it away from the cylinder block in a downward direction (photo).
15 Refitting is a reversal of removal but use all new gaskets (photo) and tighten the bolts to the specified torque. (For bolt locations, refer to Chapter 1, photo 47.86).

## 28 Coolant pump (XJS) – removal and refitting

1 The operations do not require prior removal of the radiator and disconnection of cowl brackets, otherwise they are as described in Section 27, paragraphs 2 to 15.

## 29 Coolant pump – overhaul

1 It is recommended that when a fault develops in the coolant pump, the pump is renewed or exchanged for a factory rebuilt unit.
2 Where overhaul of the original unit is preferred and the necessary repair kit is available, carry out the following operations.
3 With the coolant pump removed from the engine, clean away external dirt.
4 Using a puller with two $\frac{5}{16}$ in UNF x 2 in long bolts screwed into the tapped holes provided, draw off the pulley.
5 Using the same tool and bolts, draw off the impeller.
6 Release the locknut and using an Allen key, extract the screw from the water pump body.
7 Support the pump body and press out the bearing/shaft assembly, applying pressure at the impeller end.
8 Tap the seal assembly from the pump body.
9 Support the coolant pump sandwich plate front face and tap the pump body through the impeller orifice. On no account prise the coolant pump body and sandwich apart.

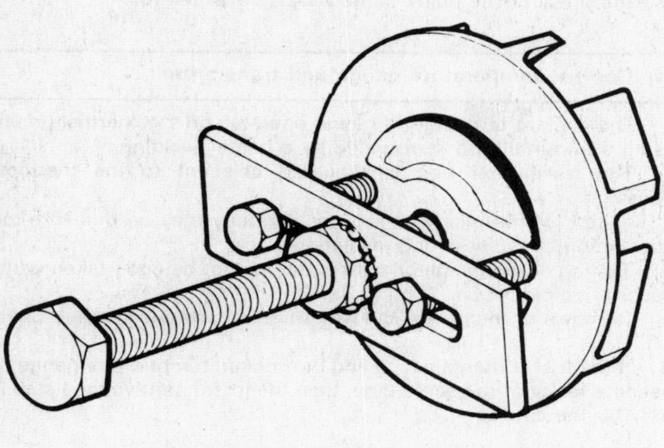

**Fig. 2.19 Removing the coolant pump impeller (Sec 29)**

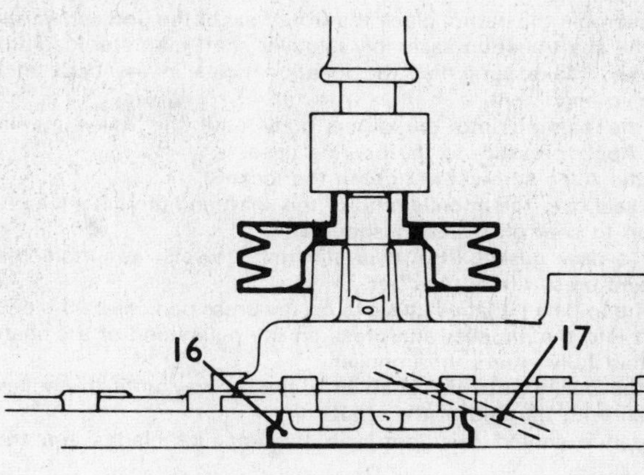


**Fig. 2.20 Coolant pump impeller clearance (Sec 29)**

*16 Impeller* *17 Clearance (impeller to sandwich)*

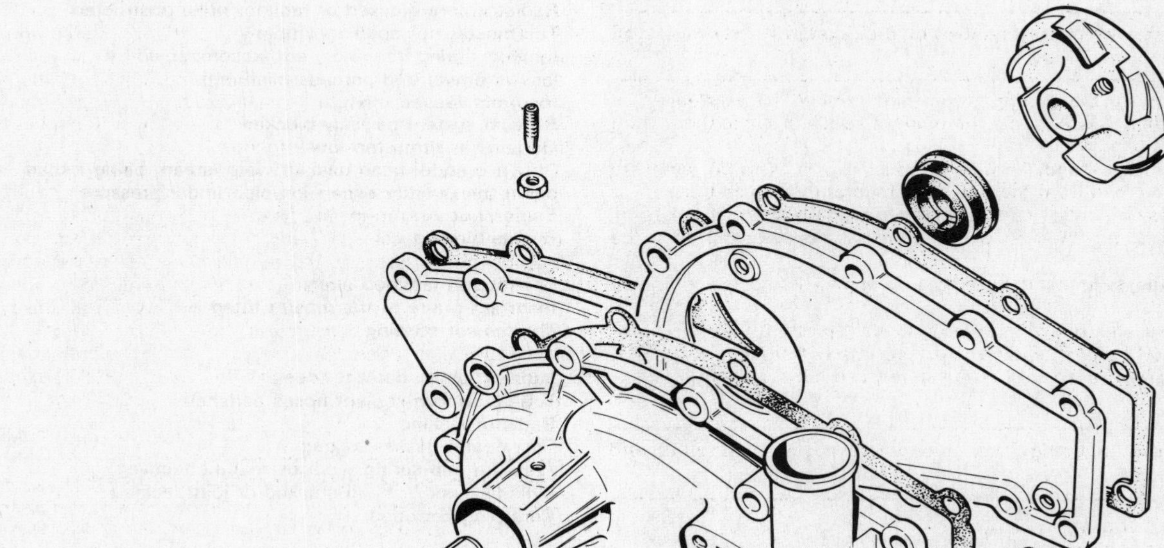

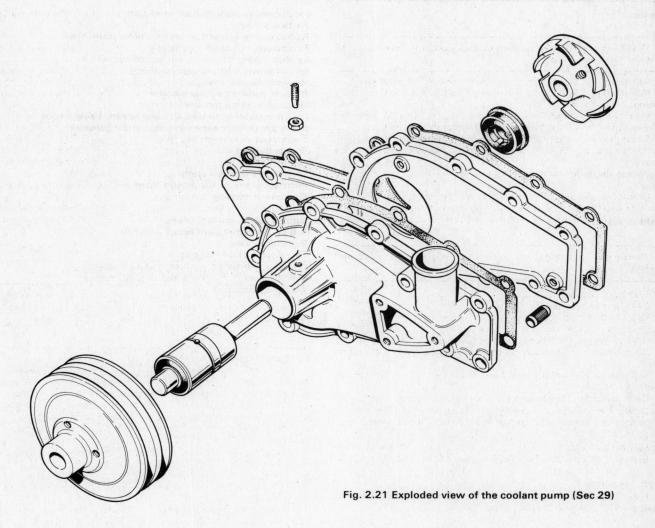

**Fig. 2.21 Exploded view of the coolant pump (Sec 29)**

10 Clean out the coolant pump body and scrape away old gasket from the mating flanges.
11 To reassemble the pump, place the front face of the body upwards and enter the shaft/bearing assembly (smaller shaft diameter leading) into the body. Make sure that the location holes in the body and bearing are in alignment.
12 Press the bearing into the pump body until the holes are in alignment. Apply pressure to the bearing case.
13 Insert the Allen screw and tighten the locknut.
14 Fit the seal over the impeller end of the shaft and drive it squarely into position to seat on the body shoulder.
15 Locate a new gasket (dry) over the ring dowels, assemble the sandwich and press firmly together.
16 Place the impeller, blades upward, on the press bed, insert the end of the shaft into the impeller and press on the pulley end of the shaft until the shaft fully enters the impeller.
17 Press the pulley onto the shaft in a similar way until the pulley boss is flush with the end of the shaft.
18 A clearance should exist between the impeller blades and the sandwich face of 0.025 in (0.635 mm). If this clearance is incorrect, use the press or the puller as necessary to adjust it.

## 30 Coolant temperature gauge and transmitter

1 The coolant temperature gauge operates on the thermal principle using a bi-metal strip surrounded by a heater winding.
2 The transmitter unit is mounted adjacent to the thermostat housing.
3 Failure of the gauge to register correctly may be due to a loose connection or faulty wiring insulation.
4 Testing of the gauge or transmitter cannot be undertaken without special equipment.
5 Removal of the gauge can be carried out, as described in Chapter 10.
6 If the fuel contents gauge and the coolant temperature gauge both become faulty at the same time, then the instrument voltage stabilizer may be the cause.

## 31 Fault diagnosis – cooling system

| Symptom | Reason(s) |
|---|---|
| Overheating | Insufficient coolant in cooling system<br>Fanbelt slipping<br>Radiator core blocked or radiator grille obstructed<br>Thermostat not opening properly<br>Ignition timing incorrecty set (accompanied by loss of power and perhaps misfiring)<br>Incorrect fuel/air mixture<br>Exhaust system partially blocked<br>Oil level in sump too low<br>Blown cylinder head gasket (water/steam being forced down the radiator expansion pipe under pressure)<br>Engine not yet run-in<br>Brakes binding |
| Engine running cold | Thermostat jammed open<br>Incorrect grade of thermostat fitted<br>Thermostat missing |
| Leaks in system | Loose clips on coolant hoses<br>Top or bottom coolant hoses perished<br>Radiator leaking<br>Thermostat gasket leaking<br>Pressure cap spring worn or seal ineffective<br>Cylinder liner or head cracked or joint leaking<br>Core plug corroded |

# Chapter 3
# Fuel, exhaust and emission control systems

*For modifications, and information applicable to later models, see Supplement at end of manual*

**Contents**

**Specifications**

*Carburettor systems*

## Fuel pumps

| | |
|---|---|
| Make and type | Electric, SU AUF 411 (two twin assemblies) |

## Carburettors

| | |
|---|---|
| Make and number | Zenith Stromberg, two on each cylinder head |
| Type: | |
| 1972/73 (all models) | 175 CD2SE |
| 1973/74 (except N America): | |
| RH | 3551 A1 and A2 |
| LH | 3552 B1 and B2 |
| 1973/74 (N America): | |
| RH | 3656 A1 and A2 |
| LH | 3657 B1 and B2 |
| Needle: | |
| Except N America | BICE |
| N America 1972/73 | BICF |
| N America 1973/74 | BICK |
| Spring colour (all models) | Red |
| Idle speed (all models) | 640 to 750 rpm |
| Fast idle speed | 1600 to 1700 rpm |
| Exhaust CO content: | |
| Without emission control | 4 to 6% |
| With emission control | 3 to 4.5% |

## Fuel tanks

| | |
|---|---|
| Number and situation | Two, rear mounted |
| Capacity (each tank): | |
| Except N America | 12 Imp gals (54.6 litres) |
| N America | 12 US gals (45.5 litres) |

*Fuel Injection Systems*

| | |
|---|---|
| **System type** | Bosch-Lucas electronic (D-Jetronic) |

## Fuel pump

| | |
|---|---|
| Type | Lucas electric |
| System pressure (regulated) | 28.5 to 31.3 lbf/in$^2$ (2.0 to 2.2 kgf/cm$^2$) |

| | |
|---|---|
| **Exhaust CO content** | 1 to 2% |

## Fuel tanks

| | |
|---|---|
| Number and situation: | |
| XJ12 and Double Six | Two, rear mounted |
| XJS | One, rear mounted |
| Capacity (each tank): | |
| XJ12 and Double Six | 10.5 Imp gals (12.6 US gals, 47.75 litres) |
| XJS | 20.0 Imp gals (24.0 US gals, 90.0 litres) |

## Fuel octane requirement

| | |
|---|---|
| S compression engines | 97 octane (UK 4-star) |
| L compression engines | 94 octane (UK 3-star) |
| N American with catalytic converter | 91 RON (unleaded) |

## Torque wrench settings

| | lbf ft | Nm |
|---|---|---|
| Fuel tank mounting bolts | 18 | 25 |
| Fuel tank drain plug (small) | 26 | 35 |
| Fuel tank drain plug (large) | 28 | 38 |
| Fuel pipe unions | 14 | 19 |
| Fuel pipe banjo union bolts | 25 | 34 |
| Exhaust manifolds to downpipes | 25 | 34 |
| Exhaust mounting ring to crossmember | 18 | 25 |
| Exhaust tailpipe to body | 18 | 25 |

### 1 General description

1 Cars built up until 1974/75 were equipped with twin carburettors on each cylinder bank.

2 Dual rear mounted fuel tanks and two (twin unit) electrically-operated fuel pumps were fitted.

3 From 1974/75 on, all models including the newly introduced XJS were equipped with the Jetronic 'D', Bosch-Lucas electronic fuel injection system.

4 XJS models have a single rear mounted fuel tank.
5 All models are equipped with some emission control devices, but the complexity and design of the system depends upon the particular model, date of production and intended operating territory.

## PART A – CARBURETTOR, FUEL AND EMISSION CONTROL SYSTEMS

### 2 Air cleaner element – renewal

1 Open the bonnet and remove the special bolts which hold the air cleaner cover to the backplate.
2 Release the air cleaner toggle clips and remove the cover.
3 Extract the air cleaner element.
4 Wipe out the casings and fit the new element with its rectangular openings facing inward. Engage the bottom lugs of the cover, prise the top edge together and fit the toggle clips.

### 3 Air cleaner – removal and refitting

*Left-hand*
1 Disconnect the battery.
2 Unbolt the air cleaner cover from the backplate, release the clips and extract the filter element.
3 Disconnect the gulp valve inlet pipe from the air cleaner backplate.
4 Disconnect the float chamber vent pipe from the air cleaner backplate.
5 *On N American vehicles,* disconnect the canister purge pipe from the plenum chamber.
6 Disconnect the flexible air pipe from the air cleaner backplate.
7 Unbolt the backplate (five setscrews) and disconnect the vacuum pipe which runs between the manifold and temperature sensor.
8 Remove the backplate from the ram pipe flexible hose. Discard the gaskets.

*Right-hand*
9 The operations are similar to those described for the left-hand air cleaner except that reference to the gulp valve inlet pipe should be ignored.

*Both sides*
10 Refitting is a reversal of removal. Use new gaskets between the air cleaner and carburettors.

### 4 Air cleaner – overhaul

1 The temperature sensor unit on the air cleaner can be renewed if the retaining tabs are prised up.
2 When fitting the new sensor, use new seals.
3 The air flap vacuum motor cannot be renewed and in the event of a fault developing, the backplate must be renewed complete.

### 5 Ram tube – removal and refitting

1 Unbolt the ram tube brackets from the radiator top rail.
2 Disengage the flexible sleeve and withdraw the ram tube through the top rail.
3 Refit by reversing the removal operations.

### 6 Fuel supply system – description

1 The fuel supply system is of the full recirculation type and comprises the fuel tanks, two fuel pumps, two solenoid valves, a fuel filter and a non-return valve.
2 An instrument panel switch selects the particular tank from which fuel is to be drawn.
3 Later models have a slightly modified layout in that the system solenoid valves are normally open instead of closed as in earlier arrangements. This means that the valve adjacent to a pump operates to close the fuel return line not required instead of the opposite valve opening to provide a fuel return line to the tank. This later system prevents float chamber flooding.

### 7 Fuel pressure limiting (non-return) valve – removal and refitting

1 Disconnect the battery.
2 Release the clips and remove the valve from the fuel pipeline.
3 Unscrew the two sections of the valve and withdraw the ball and spring.
4 Clean the components and reassemble.
5 Refitting is a reversal of removal, but make sure that the arrow points away from the cross-pipe.

### 8 Fuel solenoid valve – removal and refitting

1 Disconnect the battery, remove the spare wheel and unscrew the cover from over the fuel pump. Do not extract the screw from the centre of the edge of the cover.

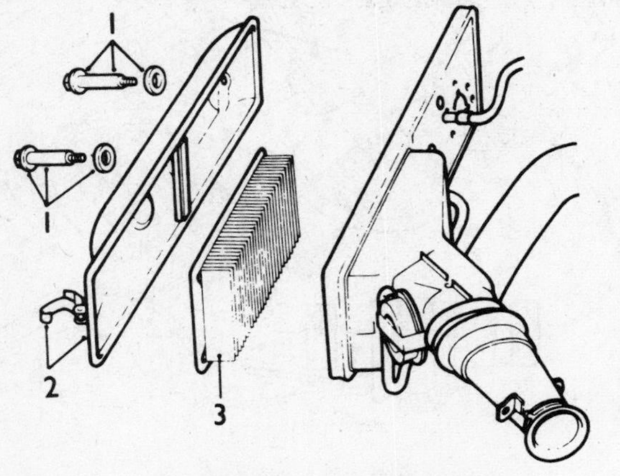


**Fig. 3.1 The air cleaner (Sec 1)**

*1 Cover bolts*
*2 Toggle clips and cover*
*3 Filter element*

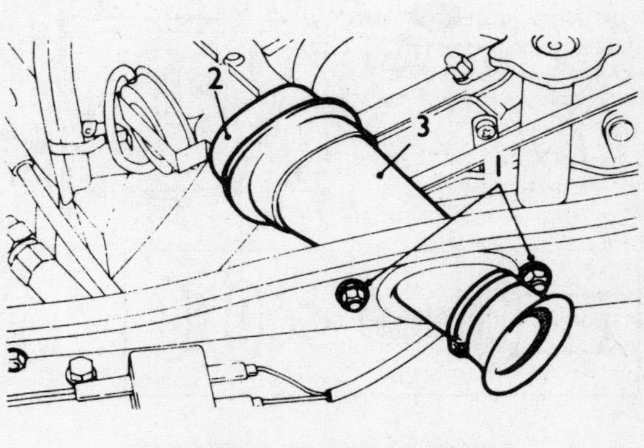


**Fig.3.2 The air ram tube (Sec 5)**

*1 Securing bolts*
*2 Rubber sleeve*
*3 Ram tube*

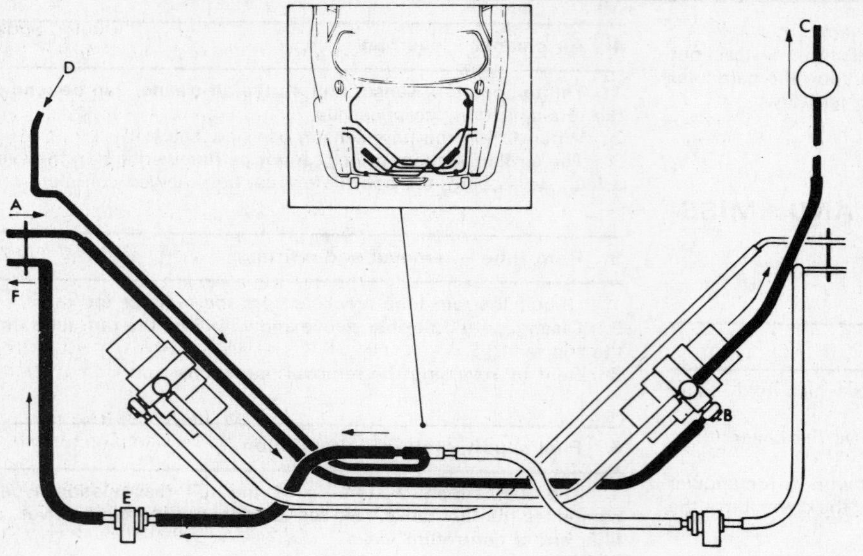


Fig. 3.3 Fuel supply system (early cars) (Sec 6)

*A* *Tank union*
*B* *Fuel pump*
*C* *Bulkhead connector*
*D* *Bulkhead union*
*E* *Solenoid valve*
*F* *Tank union*

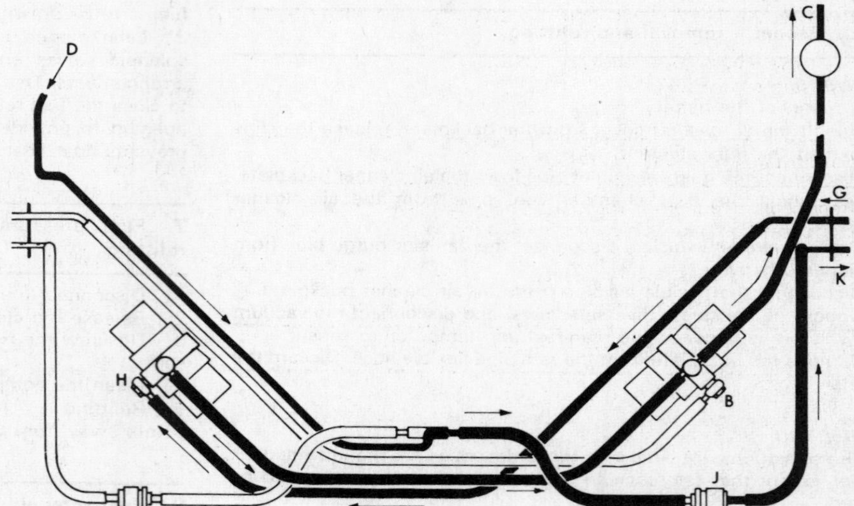


Fig. 3.4 Fuel supply system (later cars) (Sec 6)

*B* *Fuel pump*
*C* *Bulkhead connector*
*D* *Bulkhead union*
*G* *Tank union*
*H* *Fuel pump*
*J* *Solenoid valve*
*K* *Tank union*

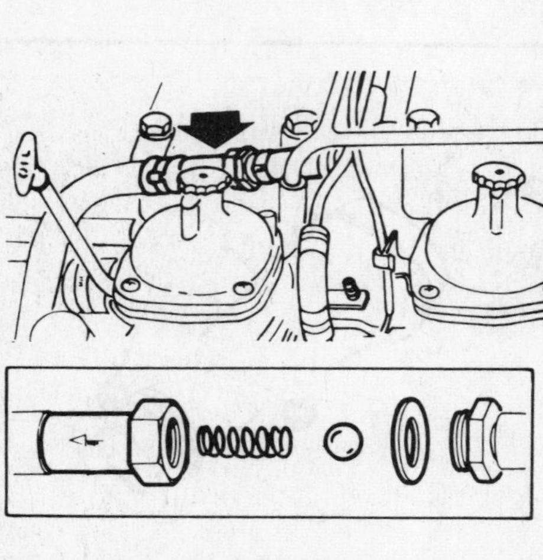

Fig. 3.5 Fuel pressure limiting valve – inset shows component parts (Sec 7)

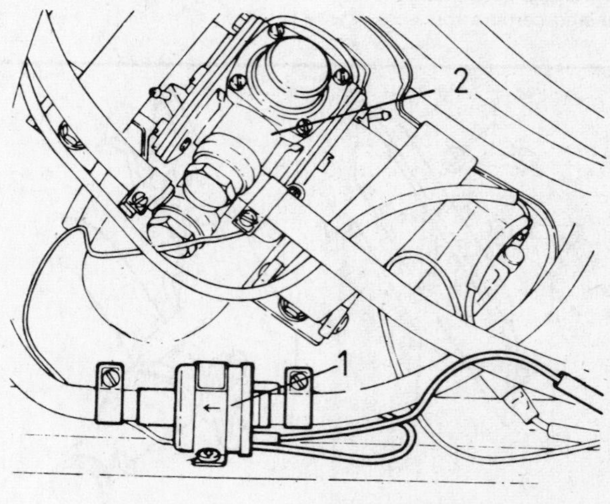


Fig. 3.6 Location of a solenoid valve (Sec 8)

*1* *Solenoid valve*
*2* *Fuel pump*

2 Clamp the inlet and outlet hoses to the valve to prevent loss of fuel.
3 Disconnect the hoses and separate the electrical connector.
4 Extract the securing screws and withdraw the valve.
5 The valve on earlier models can be tested after removal by connecting a 12V supply across it when it should be observed to open.
6 On later models when this test is carried out, the valve will be observed to close.
7 Refitting is a reversal of removal but make sure that the arrow on the valve points away from the centre line of the car.
8 Check that the earth leads from the valve and the fuel pump are secured beneath the lower fixing screw.

## 9 Fuel filter – renewal of element

1 Disconnect the battery and remove the spare wheel.
2 Clamp the fuel filter inlet hose to prevent loss of fuel.
3 Place a small container under the fuel filter bowl and unscrew and remove the centre bolt.
4 Extract and discard the filter element.
5 Clean out the filter bowl, fit the new element with the larger hole at the top and use the new seals supplied.
6 Do not overtighten the centre bolt.
7 Remove the hose clamp and the container and reconnect the battery.
8 Start the engine and check for leaks.
9 Refit the spare wheel.

## 10 Fuel filter – removal and refitting

1 Repeat the operations described in Section 9, paragraphs 1 and 2.
2 Disconnect both fuel pipes from the filter body and then unbolt the filter bracket.
3 Refitting is a reversal of removal.

## 11 Fuel cut-off inertia switch – removal and refitting

1 As an aid to safety in the event of a collision, an inertia fuel cut-off switch is located under the instrument panel on the passenger side (photo) or adjacent to the driver's door pillar (XJS models).
2 To remove the switch, first disconnect the battery. Unscrew the switch cover, disconnect the leads and pull the switch from its securing clips.
3 Refit the switch so that the terminals are at the bottom and the moulded ribs towards the rear of the car. Push the switch upwards until it abuts the bracket.
4 Reconnect the lead, polarity being unimportant.
5 If a new switch is being fitted, or if the switch fitted has been tripped, depress the plunger to reset it.
6 Fit the switch cover and reconnect the battery.

## 12 Fuel pumps – removal and refitting

1 Before removing either fuel pump, first disconnect the battery. Remove the spare wheel and the fuel pump cover from both pump assemblies.
2 Clamp the fuel inlet hoses at both pumps to prevent loss of fuel.
3 On the pump which is being removed, disconnect the two banjo bolts.
4 Disconnect the pump mounting strap from the anchor hooks.
5 Remove the pump after identifying the leads and disconnecting them.
6 Disconnect the earth lead.
7 Refitting is a reversal of removal, but renew the banjo bolt seals where necessary.

## 13 Fuel pump – overhaul

1 With the fuel pump removed, note the location of the wiring harness and then clean away all external dirt.
2 Mark the relationship of the coil housing to the pump body.
3 Extract the flange screws and withdraw the coil housing from the pump body. Discard the gasket.
4 Unwind the sealing tape and remove the ring from the cover.
5 Remove the polythene sleeve from the terminal stud on the cover.
6 Remove the terminal nut, tag and lockwasher and lift off the cover.
7 Release the diaphram assembly and withdraw the coil housing. Do not separate the diaphragm/spindle as they are a combined assembly.
8 Remove the spring and rubber washer from the spindle.
9 Remove the nylon centralising guide.
10 Extract the screw which holds the terminals and contact blade to the pedestal and remove the contact blade.
11 Extract the screw which holds the condenser and earth terminals and the pedestal to the coil housing.
12 Extract the remaining screw and lift the pedestal away from the coil housing. Unless the pedestal is being renewed, do not remove the terminal from its stud.
13 Withdraw the rocker pivot pin, then the rocker assembly.
14 Extract the screws and remove the valve clamping plate from the body.
15 Note which way the valves face and then remove the valve caps and withdraw the valves. Discard the neoprene sealing rings.
16 Extract the filter gauze from the inlet valve seat and discard the neoprene sealing ring.
17 Repeat the foregoing operations on the twin section of the pump assembly.
18 Unbolt the air bottle cover from the pump body and discard the cork seal.
19 Extract the screws and remove the cover from the flow smoothing valve. Discard the O-ring.
20 Remove the diaphragm and discard the sealing washer.
21 With the pump assembly completely dismantled, clean and inspect all components. Obtain a repair kit.
22 Check that each valve lift is approximately 0.062 in (1.6 mm). If not, bend the valve cage tongues to achieve this.
23 Check the diaphragm of the flow smoothing valve and renew if necessary.
24 Check the contact breaker points for burning or pitting. If necessary, renew the rocker assembly and contact blade.
25 Make sure that the ball in the non-return vent is free to move.
26 Check the pedestal for cracks, also the ridge on which the contact blade rests. If this is damaged, renew the pedestal.
27 Commence reassembling by fitting a new sealing washer in the pump body. Observe absolute cleanliness during the following operations.
28 Fit the diaphragm to the body, concave side facing inwards.
29 Fit the flow smoothing valve cover with a new O-ring. Tighten the securing screws diagonally and evenly.
30 Fit the air bottle cover with a new cork seal, do not overtighten the centre bolt.

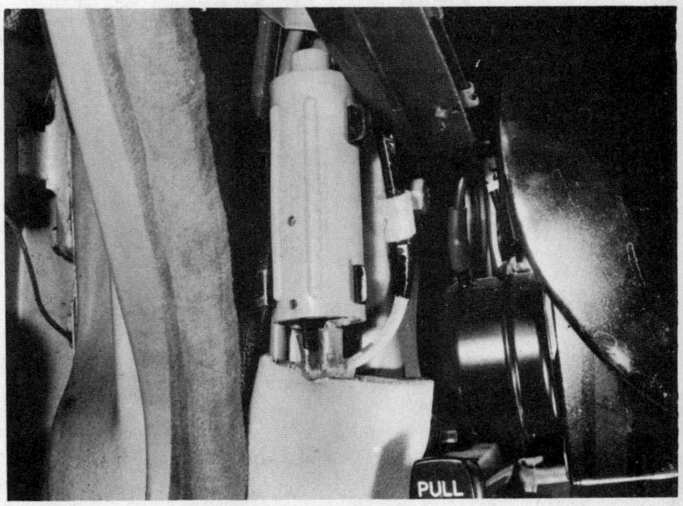

11.1 Fuel cut-off switch (Saloon models)

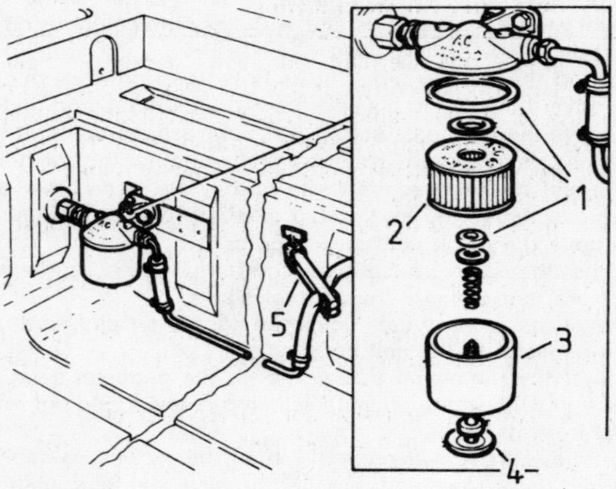


**Fig. 3.7 The fuel filter (Sec 9)**

*1 Seals*
*2 Element*
*3 Bowl*
*4 Centre bolt*
*5 Fuel pipe clamp*

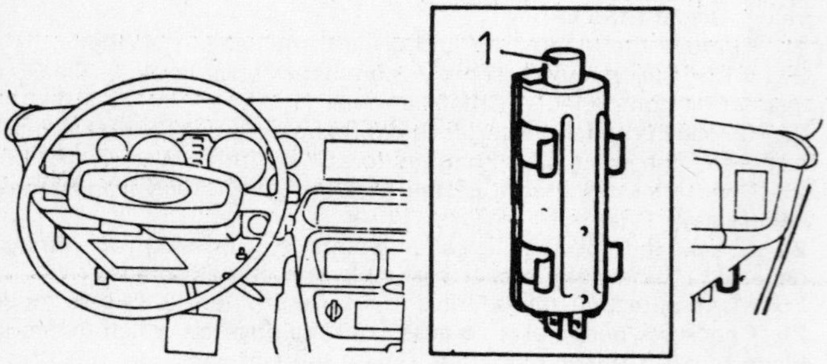


**Fig. 3.8 Fuel cut-off inertia switch (Sec 11)**

*1 Plunger*

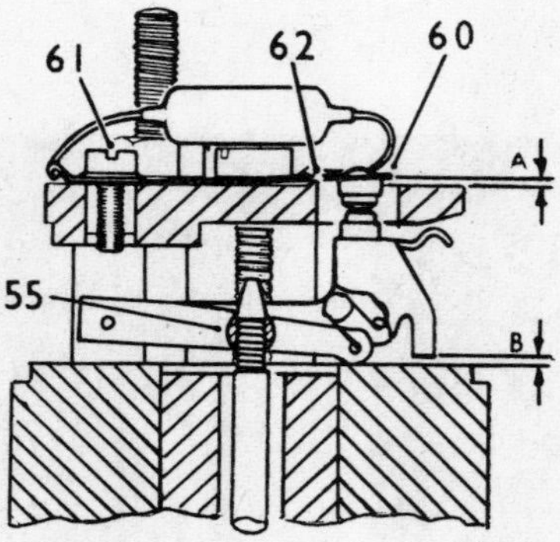


**Fig. 3.10 Fuel pump contact points adjusting diagram (Sec 13)**

*55 Spindle/rocker trunnion*
*60 Securing screw for contact blade and condenser and coil leads*
*61 Blade securing screw*
*62 Pedestal ridge*
*A = 0.035 in (0.9 mm)*
*B = 0.070 in (1.8 mm)*

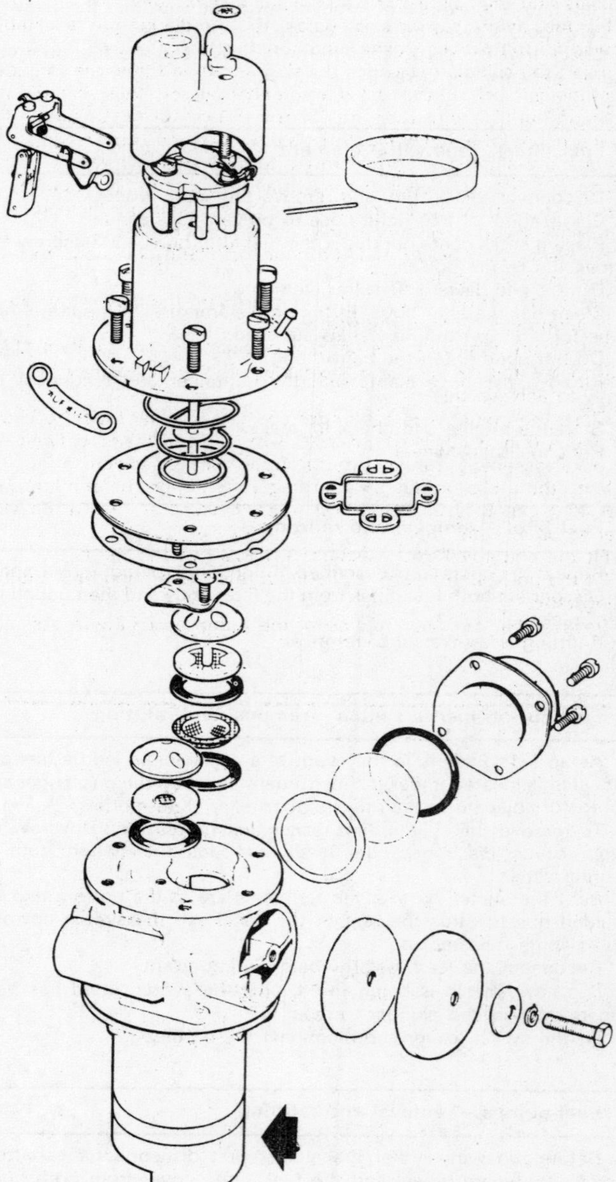

**Fig. 3.9 Exploded view of a fuel pump. Twin section is arrowed (Sec 13)**

7 Pull the vacuum pipes from the manifold and then manoeuvre the manifold from the engine. Discard the gaskets and plug all openings to prevent the entry of dirt.
8 If a new manifold is being fitted, transfer the original brake servo vacuum non-return valve and stub pipe blanking caps.
9 Refitting is a reversal of removal; use new gaskets.

## 29 Induction manifold (rear) – removal and refitting

1 Disconnect the battery.
2 On emission control cars, unscrew the setscrews which hold the air rail.
3 Release the throttle pushrod from the bellcrank.
4 Disconnect the throttle cable. (On left-hand drive cars this is necessary only if the left-hand rear manifold is being removed, or on right-hand drive cars if the right-hand manifold is being removed).
5 If the left-hand manifold is being removed, pull the vacuum pipes from the manifold stubs.
6 On emission control cars, if the left-hand manifold is being removed, disconnect the tube from the throttle edge tapping.
7 Unscrew and remove the four bolts which hold the induction manifold to the induction housing.
8 On emission control cars, remove the three nuts which hold the air rail feet to the front manifold.
9 Unscrew and remove the six nuts which hold the manifold to the cylinder head.
10 On emission control cars, pull the vacuum pipes from the manifold.
11 Manoeuvre the manifold from the engine. Discard the gaskets and plug all openings to prevent the entry of dirt.
12 If a new manifold is being fitted, transfer the brake servo vacuum non-return valve from the original manifold, also the stub blanking caps.
13 Refitting is a reversal of removal; use new gaskets.

## 30 Induction housing (left-hand) – removal and refitting

1 Remove the carburettors as described in Section 18.
2 Drain the cooling system (Chapter 2).
3 Disconnect the manifold balance pipe.
4 Disconnect the top hose from the thermostat housing cover, then pull the hose from the engine cross-pipe clip. Also disconnect the hose on the front end of the induction housing.
5 Unbolt the thermostat housing and engine lifting eye from the cylinder head.
6 Disconnect the bleed pipe.
7 Pull the thermostat housing and hose from the induction housing.
8 Unscrew the setscrew which holds the transmission dipstick guide tube clip.
9 Release the hose from its clip at the rear end of the induction housing.
10 Unscrew and remove the eight bolts which hold the induction manifolds to the induction housing.
11 On USA emission control cars, release the union and swing the EGR pipe clear of the induction housing.
12 Draw the induction housing from the branch pipe.
13 Refitting is a reversal of removal; use new gaskets.

## 31 Induction housing (right-hand) – removal and refitting

1 Repeat the operations described in paragraphs 1 to 3 of Section 30.
2 Disconnect the top hose from the thermostat housing cover. Release the hose from the heater return pipe and the engine cross-pipe, also the clip on the front end of the induction housing.
3 Repeat the operations in paragraphs 5, 6 and 7 of Section 30, then follow with the remaining work detailed in paragraphs 9 to 13 of that Section.

## 32 Exhaust manifold (left-hand) – removal and refitting

1 Working under the car, remove the eight nuts and washers from the manifold/front downpipe studs.
2 Remove the three nuts and bolts which hold the front exhaust downpipe to the intermediate pipe.
3 Free the downpipe and let it rest on the suspension crossmember.
4 Disconnect the battery; remove it also if the exhaust manifold is being removed from the battery side.
5 Remove the complete carburettor/induction manifold/housing assembly (Section 19).
6 On USA emission control cars, slacken the EGR pipe union nut and remove the adaptor. Do not lose the restrictor.
7 Unbolt and remove the exhaust manifold heat shield.
8 Unbolt the front exhaust manifold from the cylinder head and lift the manifold from the engine compartment.
9 Remove the rear exhaust manifold in a similar way.
10 Refitting is the reverse of removal. Use new gaskets and fit the rear manifold first.

## 33 Exhaust manifold (right-hand) – removal and refitting

1 Carry out the operations described in Section 30, paragraphs 1 to 5.

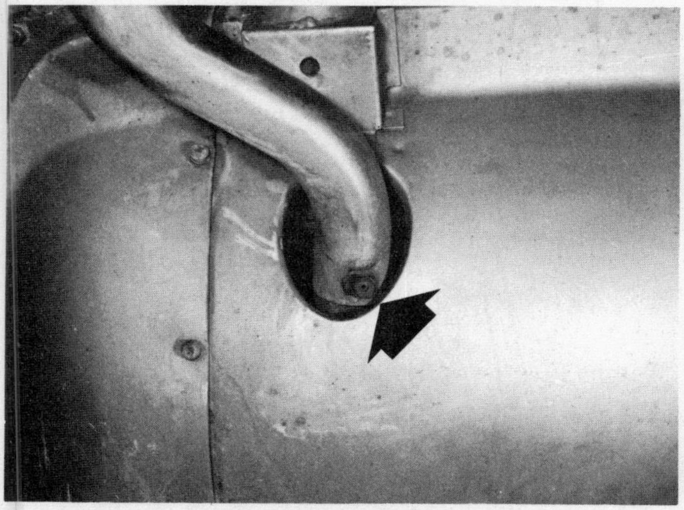
34.10 Exhaust tailpipe trim screw (arrowed)

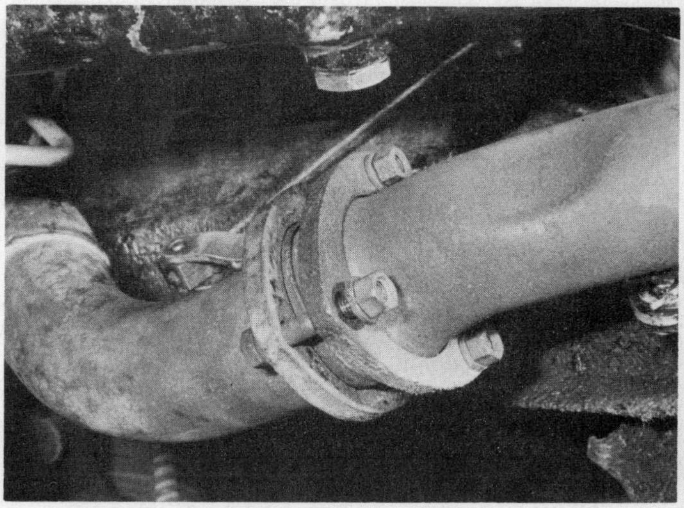
35.3 Exhaust joint (downpipe to front intermediate pipe)

2 Detach (two screws) the starter solenoid heat shield from the main heat shield.
3 Repeat the operations described in paragraphs 6 to 10 in Section 30.

## 34 Exhaust system (complete) – removal and refitting

1 If one or both of the dual exhaust systems is badly corroded, it is recommended that the complete system is withdrawn and a new system installed.
2 Where only one section of the system is in need of renewal then the section can be removed independently as described in Section 35.
3 Remove the air cleaner.
4 Working within the luggage boot, unscrew the two self-locking nuts which hold the rear silencer mounting.
5 Disconnect the front to front intermediate exhaust pipe flange.
6 Release the clamp at the front end of the silencer nearer the front of the car.
7 Separate the front intermediate pipe and front silencer from the rear intermediate pipe.
8 Release the rear silencer/tailpipe clamp and separate the rear silencer/tailpipe from the rear intermediate pipe.
9 Draw the rear intermediate pipe towards the rear of the car from its mounting rubber and suspension unit.
10 Use an Allen key to remove the tailpipe trim grub screw, pull off the trim and then withdraw the tailpipe/silencer forwards from the body (photo).
11 Unbolt the exhaust downpipe from the manifold and draw the pipe downward.
12 If the right-hand downpipe is being removed from a right-hand drive car, then apply full right steering lock. Conversely, if the left-hand pipe is being removed from a left-hand drive car, apply full left steering lock.
13 Do not damage the steering rack gaiter during removal.
14 Renew all clamps, mountings and other components as necessary.
15 Commence reassembly by offering the rear intermediate pipe into the rear suspension unit.
16 Attach the rear mounting bracket.
17 Fit the tailpipe and silencer into the mounting, apply exhaust jointing paste to the joint and clamp up.
18 The refitting operations for the remaining sections of the exhaust system are a reversal of removal.

## 35 Exhaust system – removal and refitting of individual sections

### *Front downpipe*

1 Remove the air cleaner from the side concerned.
2 Unbolt the downpipe from the exhaust manifold.
3 Working under the car unbolt the front pipe from the front intermediate pipe (photo). On right-hand drive cars, if removing a right-hand pipe, apply full right steering lock before removal. Conversely, apply full left lock if a left-hand pipe is being removed from a left-hand drive car.

### *Intermediate pipe (front)*

4 Unbolt the flange which connects with the front downpipe.
5 Release the clamp at the forward end of the front silencer.
6 Remove the intermediate pipe.

### *Front silencer*

7 Remove the intermediate pipe as previously described.
8 Slacken the clamp and draw the silencer from the rear intermediate pipe.

### *Tailpipe and rear silencer*

9 Extract the grub screw with an Allen key and pull off the trim from the tailpipe.
10 Release the clamp which holds the rear silencer to the rear intermediate pipe.
11 Draw the rear silencer and tailpipe towards the front of the car and downwards to clear the mounting rubber.

### *All sections*

12 Refitting is a reversal of removal, but smear joints with exhaust

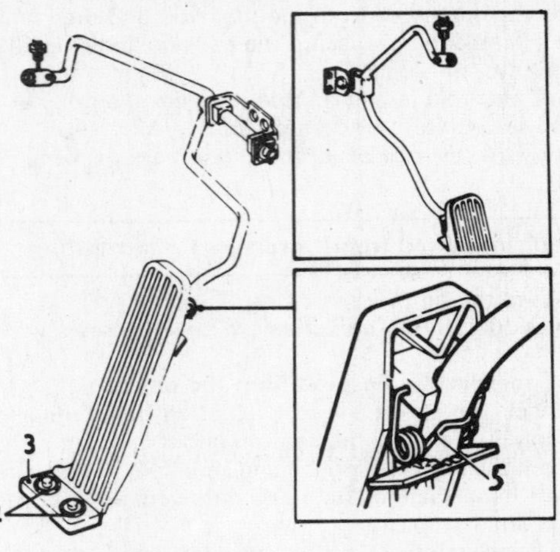


**Fig. 3.39 Accelerator pedal (Sec 36)**

*2 Pedal mounting nuts*
*3 Pedal*
*5 Spring*

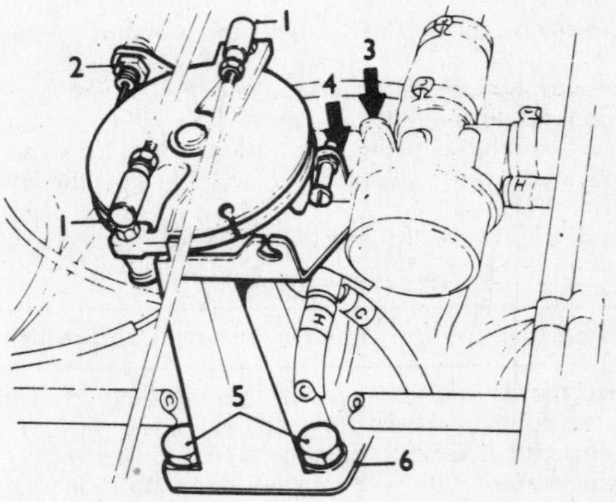


**Fig. 3.40 Throttle pedestal (Sec 36)**

*1 Throttle pushrod*
*2 Cable locknut*
*3 Gulp valve (emission control cars only)*
*4 Solenoid valve (emission control cars only)*
*5 Mounting bolts*
*6 Jackshaft cover gasket*

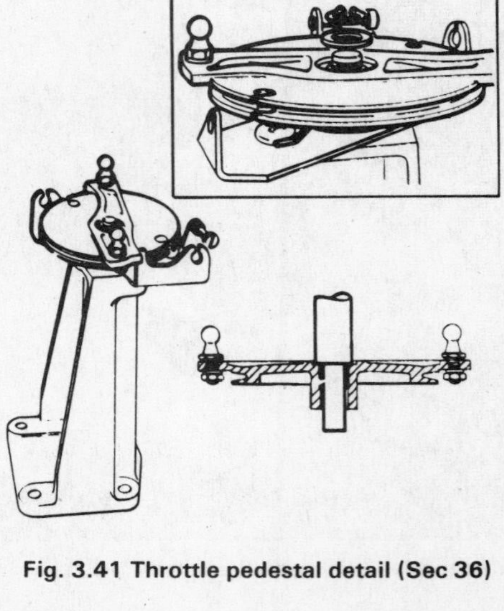

**Fig. 3.41 Throttle pedestal detail (Sec 36)**

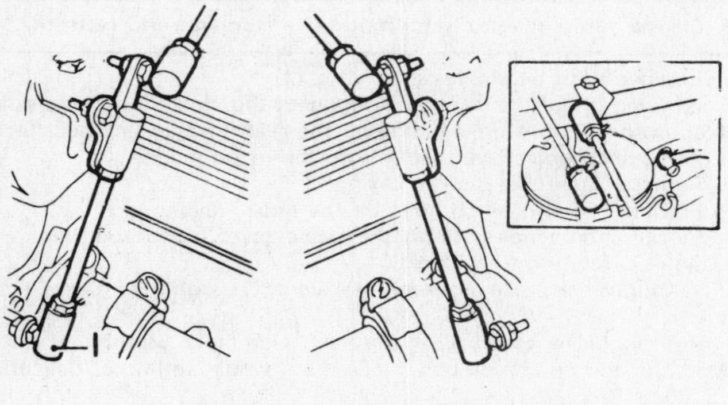


Fig. 3.42 Throttle linkage detail (Sec 37)

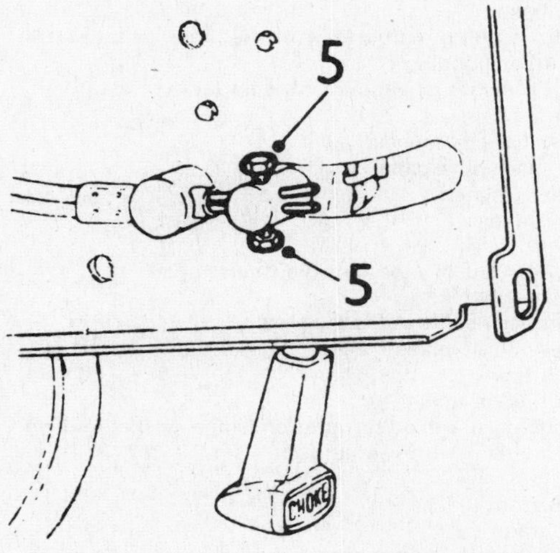


Fig. 3.43 Choke cable pinch-bolts (5) (Sec 38)

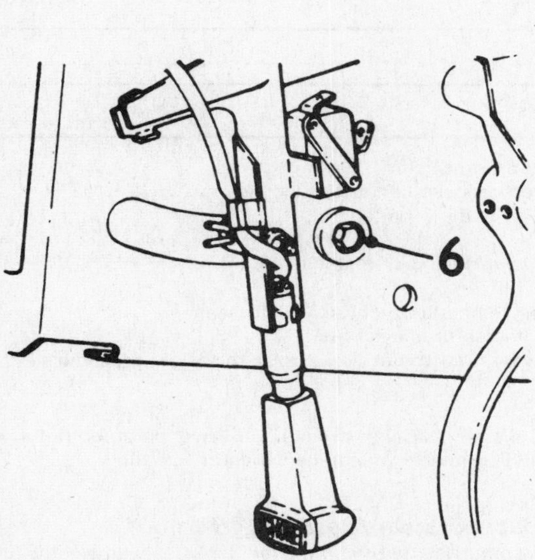


Fig. 3.44 Choke cable pivot block pinch-bolt (6) (Sec 39)

pipe jointing paste before connecting, renew seals, mountings and clamps as necessary.

13 On USA Federal Specification cars, there must be a clearance between the top surface of the exhaust trim and the lower surface of the energy absorbing beam of 1.5 in (38.0 mm).

## 36 Accelerator pedal and throttle linkage – removal and refitting

### *Accelerator pedal*

1 Pull the carpet away from the base of the pedal and unscrew and remove the two securing nuts.

2 Withdraw the bottom of the pedal and disengage the spring and the rod from the pedal.

### *Throttle pedestal*

3 Disengage the throttle pushrods from the platform on top of the pedestal.

4 Release the locknuts and disconnect the throttle cable.

5 On cars equipped with emission control, unscrew the three screws which secure the gulp valve and unbolt the solenoid valve from the pedestal top plate.

6 Remove the four setscrews which hold the oil pressure transducer mounting and the throttle pedestal. Lift the pedestal away.

7 Clean off the old gasket from the jackshaft cover.

8 The throttle pedestal can be overhauled once the circlip has been prised off.

### *Throttle cable*

9 Disconnect the battery and pull the leads from the kickdown switch.

10 Release the locknuts and disconnect the throttle cable.

11 Working under the bonnet, slacken the locknut on the upper surface of the footwell.

12 Extract the split pin from the top end of the operating rod, then disengage the sleeve and nipple from the rod.

13 Remove the nut from the cable sheath and draw the throttle cable assembly into the engine compartment.

### *Throttle rod bushes*

14 Remove the accelerator pedal as previously described.

15 Remove the under scuttle casing. On LHD cars, prise the spring clips from the cover on the steering column universal joint.

16 Extract the split pin from the top end of the operating rod, then disengage the sleeve and nipple from the rod.

17 Extract the split pin from the operating rod pivot, then pull the rod from the pivot and take off the washer.

18 Remove the bushes.

### *All components*

19 Refitting of all components is a reversal of removal, but lubricate all pivots and bushes. Seal round the footwell locknut with suitable mastic.

20 On completion check the throttle linkage adjustment as described below, also the kickdown switch adjustment as described in Chapter 6.

## 37 Throttle linkage – adjustment

1 This work should be carried out after overhaul or the fitting of new components, or when wear has occurred.

2 Disconnect the throttle linkage from the throttle levers.

3 Check that the angle across the top of the left-hand bellcrank is exactly the same as that across the top of the right-hand one. If it is not, slacken the locknuts and while holding the platform in the 'throttle closed' position, turn the rod clockwise to increase the angle or anti-clockwise to decrease it.

4 When the correct angle has been obtained tighten the locknuts, making sure that the rod balljoints are at the centre of their areas of travel.

5 Now slacken the locknuts and adjust the lengths of the vertical links until they can be connected to the throttle levers without having to move the position of the levers. Tighten the locknuts, holding the balljoints in the centres of their areas of travel.

6 Release the throttle stop locknut. Open the throttle fully and screw

in the throttle stop until it just contacts the platform. Close the throttle and tighten the throttle stop locknut.

**38 Choke operating inner cable – renewal**

1 Remove the air cleaner from the appropriate side.
2 Working under the bonnet, disconnect the choke inner and outer cables from the carburettor.
3 If the crossover cable is being renewed, remove the outer cable from the nylon guides.
4 Remove the under scuttle casing.
5 Slacken the pinch-bolt on the choke cable and draw the cable from its sheath into the engine compartment.
6 Refitting is a reversal of removal, but enter the cable from the engine compartment. Check the fast idle setting (Section 17) on completion.

**39 Choke cable assembly (complete) – removal and refitting**

1 Remove both air cleaners.
2 Working under the bonnet, disconnect the choke inner and outer cables from the front right-hand and the rear left-hand carburettor.
3 Remove the crossover cable from the nylon guides.
4 Remove the under scuttle casing.
5 Slacken the two pinch-bolts on the choke lever.
6 Slacken the pinch-bolt on the cable pivot block abutment and press the cable from the block.
7 Withdraw the cable assembly rearwards through the bulkhead into the car.
8 Refitting is a reversal of removal. Use new grommets where necessary, and on completion check the fast idle setting as described in Section 17.

**40 Fault diagnosis – carburettor fuel system**

| Symptom | Reason(s) |
|---|---|
| Excessive fuel consumption | Air filter choked<br>Leakage from pump, carburettor or fuel lines or fuel tank<br>Float chamber flooding<br>Distributor weights or vacuum capsule faulty<br>Mixture too rich<br>Incorrect valve clearances<br>Incorrect spark plug gaps<br>Tyres under inflated<br>Dragging brakes |
| Insufficient fuel delivery or weak mixture | Fuel tank air vent or pipe blocked or flattened<br>Clogged fuel filter<br>Float chamber needle valve clogged<br>Faulty fuel pump valves<br>Fuel pump faulty<br>Fuel pipe unions loose<br>Inlet manifold gasket or carburettor flange gasket leaking<br>Incorrect adjustment of carburettor |
| Rough idling, hesitation or flat spot | Sticking piston<br>Split diaphragm<br>Faulty temperature compensator<br>Perforated vacuum pipes<br>Fuel level in float chamber too high<br>Air filter choked<br>Broken piston return spring |

**41 Fault diagnosis – carburettor emission control system**

| Symptom | Reason(s) |
|---|---|
| Fault in air injection system | Slack pump drivebelt<br>Perforated or loose connecting hoses<br>Choked air pump air filter |
| Fault in EGR system | Choked inlet drilling or restrictor |
| High CO content in exhaust gas | Faulty air temperature control in air cleaner<br>Choked engine breather filter<br>Faulty system switch or valve (refer to testing procedure in text) |

## PART B – FUEL INJECTION AND EMISSION CONTROL SYSTEMS

**42 Description and operating principles**

1 The electronic fuel injection system fitted to all models between 1975 and 1979 is of the Bosch-Lucas D-Jetronic type.
2 The system can be divided into two parts both for ease of understanding and for maintenance and overhaul.

*Fuel supply system (Sections 48 to 63)*
3 This comprises rear mounted fuel tanks, and an electric fuel pump to keep a constant pressurised flow of fuel always available at the injectors.

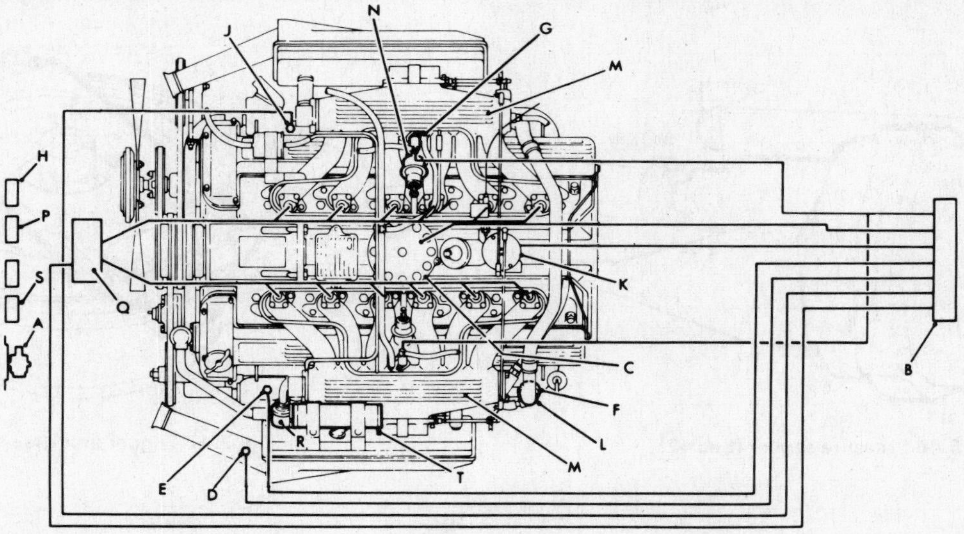


**Fig. 3.45 Typical fuel injection system (Sec 42)**

| | | | |
|---|---|---|---|
| *A* *Manifold pressure sensor* | *F* *Auxiliary air valve* | *L* *Idle speed adjusting screw* | *Q* *Power amplifier* |
| *B* *Electronic control unit (ECU)* | *G* *Cold start injector* | *M* *Induction manifolds* | *R* *Overrun valve* |
| *C* *Trigger unit* | *H* *Cold start relay* | *N* *Fuel pressure regulator* | *S* *Main relay* |
| *D* *Air temperature sensor* | *J* *Thermotime switch* | *P* *Fuel pump relay* | *T* *Fuel cooler* |
| *E* *Coolant temperature sensor* | *K* *Throttle switch* | | |

### *Sensing and control system (Sections 64 to 74)*

4 This monitors the engine operating conditions of load, speed, temperature (coolant and intake air) and throttle movement, and by means of electrical pulses causes the injector solenoid valves to open for the exact time required to deliver the quantity of fuel which is required for any engine cycle.

5 The injectors are operated by an electrical control unit (ECU) in two groups of six, each group following the engine firing order.

6 The induction system is very similar to that used on an engine with carburettors.

7 The main components of the sensing and control part of the fuel injection system are explained below.

### *Pressure sensor*

8 The position of the throttle pedal and the airflow into the engine determine the pressure within the plenum chamber. This pressure is converted by a pressure sensor into an electrical signal passed to the electronic control unit (ECU). The signal varies the duration of the injector operating pulse as necessary.

### *Trigger unit*

9 This is fitted within the ignition distributor and utilises two switches 180° apart which close alternately at each revolution of the crankshaft. Each switch triggers the ECU to begin the timed pulse to a group of six fuel injectors.

10 The trigger pulse itself has no influence on the duration of the injection pulse, but the frequency of the trigger pulses modifies the duration of injection determined by the ECU.

### *Air temperature sensor*

11 This is located in the air cleaner ram pipe and has a small effect to make sure that according to the temperature of the intake air (and in consequence its density), so the volume of fuel is varied to maintain the optimum fuel/air ratio.

### *Coolant temperature sensor*

12 This operates in conjunction with the cold start system and the auxiliary air valve to form what is the equivalent of an automatic choke on a carburettor.

### *Cold start system (thermotime switch and cold start relay)*

13 This is a system for injecting additional fuel into the induction manifolds. The cold start injectors are controlled by a cold start relay and thermotime switch. The thermotime switch senses coolant temperature and above a certain temperature level interrupts the relay earth connection. When the starter motor is operated, the cold start relay is energised through the thermotime switch. This switch also limits the duration of energising of the relay according to prevailing climatic conditions. The enrichment provided by this arrangement is in addition to that provided by the coolant temperature sensor. If the coolant temperature is above 95°F (35°C), the switch does not actuate as no additional enrichment will be required over and above the normal cranking enrichment (see next paragraph).

14 The ECU provides an increased pulse duration during engine cranking in addition to any enrichment resulting from the coolant temperature sensor or the cold start injectors.

### *Throttle switch*

15 This is a rotary switch directly coupled to the throttle pulley. It signals the ECU as to the position and rate of movement of the throttle bufferfly valves.

### *Auxiliary air valve*

16 This valve is controlled by coolant temperature and opens to allow air to bypass the throttles and so increase engine speed at cold start. This prevents stalling at cold start and cold idling. The valve incorporates an adjusting screw to regulate the air flow for idle speed adjustment. The valve is located on the left-hand cylinder bank rear coolant pipe.

## 43 Precautions and maintenance

1 Never allow the engine to run without the battery connected.

2 Do not use a high-speed battery charger as an aid to starting the car.

3 Always disconnect the battery before charging it from a mains charger.

4 A fuel flooding protection system is built in. If the ignition is switched on but the starter motor is not cranking the engine, then the fuel pump will run for a second or two to pressurise the fuel in the fuel rail. The pump is then automatically switched off by the ECU. Once the engine is turned by the starter motor the pump is switched on again. This arrangement prevents flooding with fuel should a fault develop in

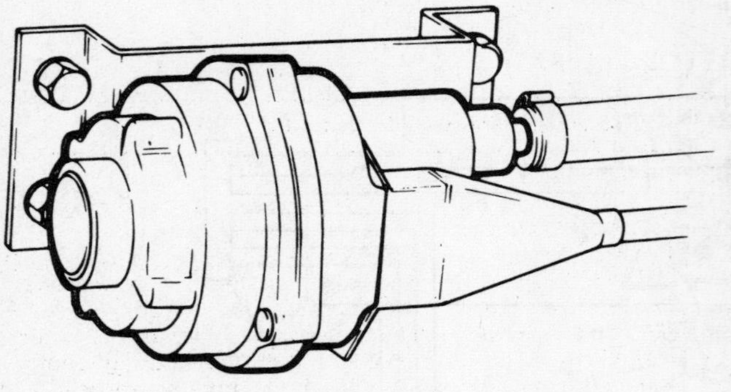

Fig. 3.46 Pressure sensor (Sec 42)

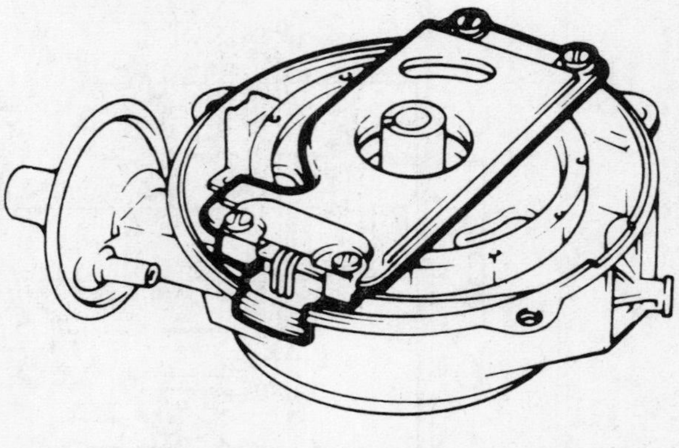

Fig. 3.47 Trigger unit (Sec 42)

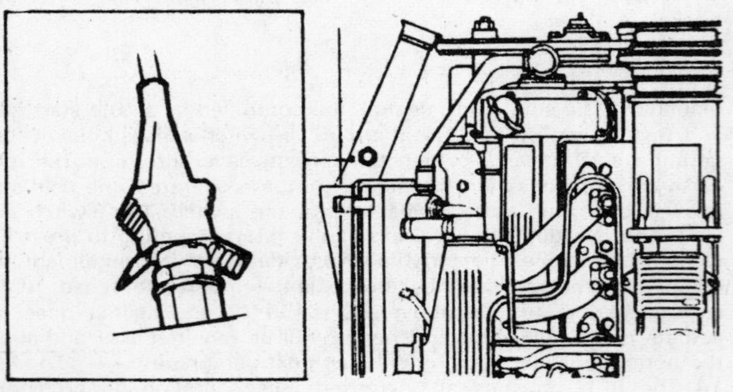

Fig. 3.48 Air temperature sensor (Sec 42)

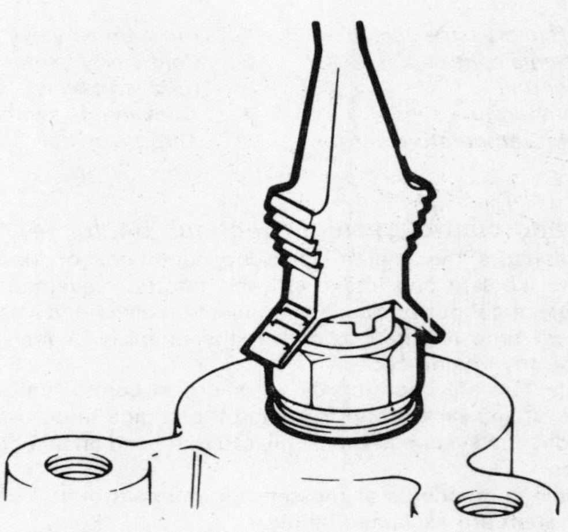

Fig. 3.49 Coolant temperature sensor (Sec 42)

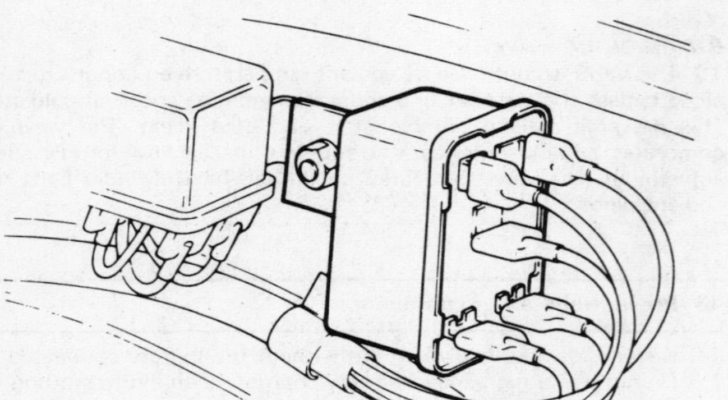

Fig. 3.50 Cold start relay (Sec 42)

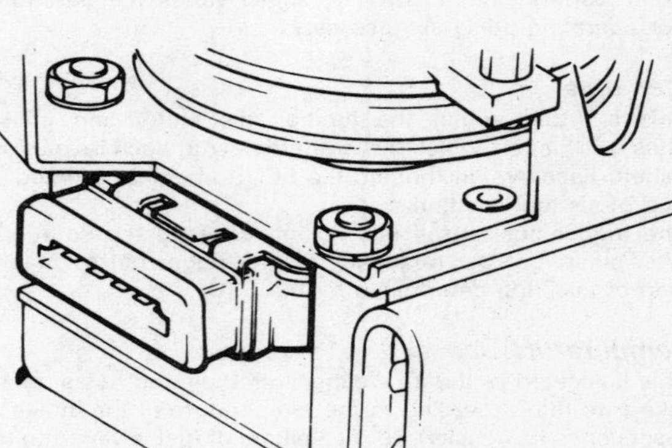

Fig. 3.51 Throttle switch (Sec 42)

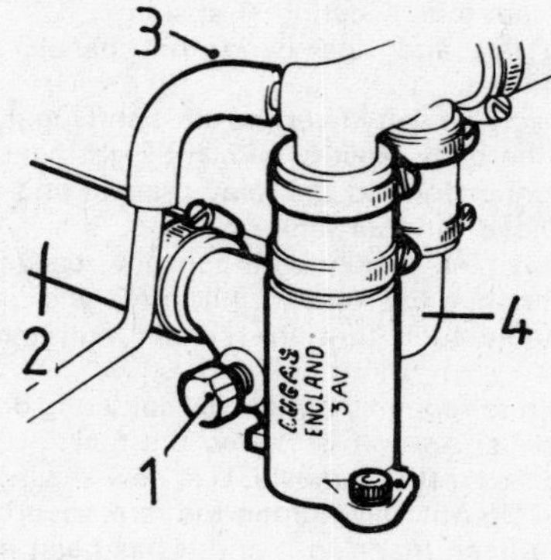


Fig. 3.52 Auxiliary air valve (Sec 42)

*1 Adjusting screw*
*2 Manifold bleed pipe*
*3 Air cleaner hose*
*4 Air balance pipe*

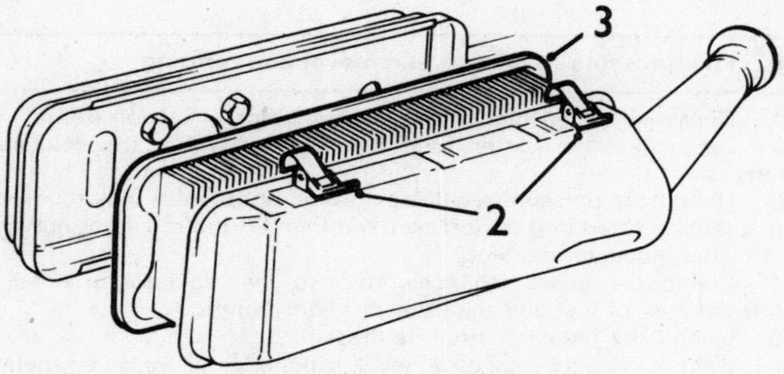


Fig. 3.53 Air cleaner (Sec 44)

*2 Toggle clips*
*3 Element*

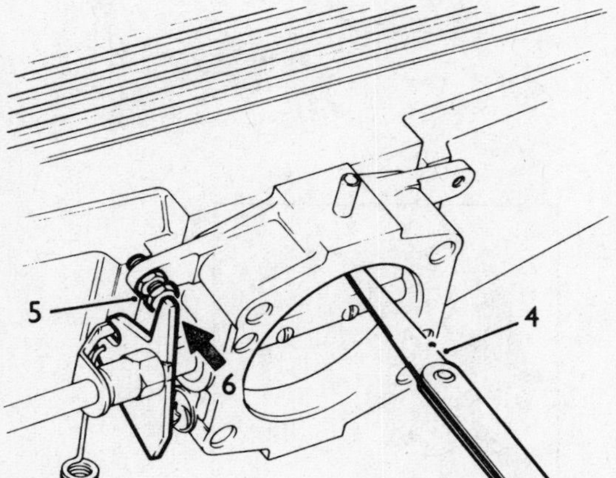


Fig. 3.54 Adjusting throttle butterfly valve (Sec 47)

*4 Feeler blade*
*5 Stop screw*
*6 Press arm against screw*

an injector whilst the ignition is on but the engine is not being cranked or running.

5 Maintenance consists of checking the security of all system hoses, pipes and electrical connections, and renewing the air and fuel filters at the specified service intervals.

## 44 Air cleaner – renewal of element

1 Disconnect the battery.
2 If the left-hand element is being renewed, disconnect the lead from the temperature sensor on the ram tube (photo).
3 Release the two toggle clips and remove the air cleaner cover.
4 Discard the filter element, wipe out the casing and check the condition of the seals.
5 Refit the new filter. Make sure that it is fitted the correct way round with the metal plate against the throttle housing (photo).
6 Refit the cover, reconnect the temperature sensor lead and the battery.

## 45 Air cleaner – removal and refitting

### *Left-hand*

1 Disconnect the battery and the lead from the air temperature sensor on the ram tube.
2 Remove the air cleaner cover and filter element.
3 Disconnect the auxiliary air valve hose from the air cleaner backplate.
4 Disconnect the feed pipe hose from the positive crankcase ventilation (PCV) valve, also the engine breather hose.
5 Unbolt the air cleaner backplate from the throttle housing, pull it away and disconnect the overrun valve hose. Discard the flange gasket.
6 Refitting is a reversal of removal.

### *Right-hand*

7 Repeat the operations described in paragraphs 2, 5 and 6 of this Section.

## 46 Idle speed – adjustment

1 Have the engine at normal operating temperature.
2 If the engine has been switched off after a run, re-start it and run it for two or three minutes.
3 Turn the idle speed screw (located on the auxiliary air valve) until the engine speed is 750 rpm.
4 If the idle speed fails to respond to turning the screw, check all manifold pipes and hoses for leakage, also the joint gaskets.
5 Check the security of the fuel injectors and cold start injectors.
6 Check the operation of the overrun valves (Section 62).
7 Check the auxiliary air valve (Section 61).
8 Check the adjustment of the throttle butterfly valves (Section 47).

## 47 Throttle butterfly valves – adjustment

1 Remove both air cleaners.
2 Slacken the locknut on the throttle butterfly stop screw and unscrew the screw.
3 Check that the throttle butterfly valve closes fully.
4 Insert a feeler blade (0.004 in (0.105 mm) for early models, 0.002 in (0.05 mm) for 1978 on) between the upper edge of the butterfly valve and the housing to hold the valve open.
5 Turn the stop screw until it just touches the stop arm, then tighten the locknut with the feeler in position. Pull out the feeler blade.
6 Press the stop arm against the stop screw and then carry out the foregoing operations on the opposite side of the engine.
7 Refit the air cleaners.
8 Check the throttle linkage adjustment (Section 37).
9 Check the operation of the throttle switch (Section 73).
10 Check the operation of the kickdown switch (Chapter 6).

## 48 Fuel system – depressurising

1 On XJS models remove the right-hand trim from within the luggage boot.
2 Pull the lead from terminal 85 of the fuel pump relay. Disconnect the ignition coil HT lead.
3 Switch on the ignition and operate the starter motor for a few seconds. The fuel system will now be depressurised.
4 After carrying out any work on the fuel system, reconnect the HT and relay leads.

## 49 Fuel tanks (XJ12 and Double Six) – removal and refitting

1 Refer to Section 14 after first depressurising the fuel system (Section 48).

## 50 Fuel tank (XJS) – removal and refitting

1 Remove the spare wheel and depressurise the fuel system (Section 48).
2 Disconnect and remove the battery.
3 Drain the fuel tank. To do this, remove the fuel pump cover from the battery tray and floor clips.
4 Clamp the fuel inlet hose at the pump to prevent loss of fuel and disconnect the hose from the pump.
5 Extract the grommet from the vent hole in the luggage boot floor. Connect a length of pipe to the inlet hose and pass the pipe through the hole in the floor.
6 Remove the fuel filler cap and after placing a container under the car, release the hose clamp and drain the tank.
7 Fold back the carpet from the fuel tank.
8 Clamp the fuel return hose to prevent loss of fuel and then disconnect the hose from the tank.
9 Disconnect the expansion tank supply hose from the rigid part of the pipeline and then disconnect the return pipe from the fuel tank.
10 Note the fuel tank vent pipe connections and disconnect them.
11 Disconnect the electrical leads from the fuel tank sender unit.
12 Disconnect the fuel filter assembly from the tank filler neck and then detach the assembly (three screws) from the body panel.
13 Release the fuel tank securing straps.
14 Remove the left and right-hand trim panels from inside the luggage compartment.
15 Remove the screws and lower the left-hand luggage compartment side panel from the body. Follow with the right-hand panel, but note the earth lead connections to the relay bracket and the pump relay.
16 Carefully remove the fuel tank.
17 The expansion tank supply pipe can now be detached, also the sender unit. To remove the sender unit, twist and unlock the locking ring with a suitable tool, turn the sender unit through 180° and withdraw it.
18 Never attempt to repair a fuel tank by soldering or welding. Always take it to a specialist repairer or renew the tank.
19 Refitting is a reversal of removal. Use new sealing rings and hoses where necessary. Do not fully tighten the tank securing straps until all connections have been made to it and it has been correctly located.

## 51 Fuel system filter – renewal

1 Depressurise the fuel system as described in Section 48.
2 Clamp the fuel inlet and outlet hoses either side of the filter to prevent loss of fuel.
3 Disconnect the hoses from the filter and then unbolt it from its bracket on the induction manifold (photo).
4 Remove the clamp from the filter and fit it to the new one. Discard the old filter.
5 Refitting is a reversal of removal.

## 52 Fuel pressure regulators – removal and refitting

1 Depressurise the fuel system as described in Section 48.
2 Disconnect the battery and then the lead from the cold start injector.
3 Unbolt the pressure regulator bracket, note which way round the regulator is fitted into the bracket and then lift the regulator upwards from the induction manifold.
4 Clamp the hoses which connect to the regulator in order to prevent loss of fuel and then detach them from it.
5 Unbolt the regulator from its bracket.
6 Refitting is a reversal of removal. If the original pressure regulator is being refitted, do not alter the setting of the adjuster screw and

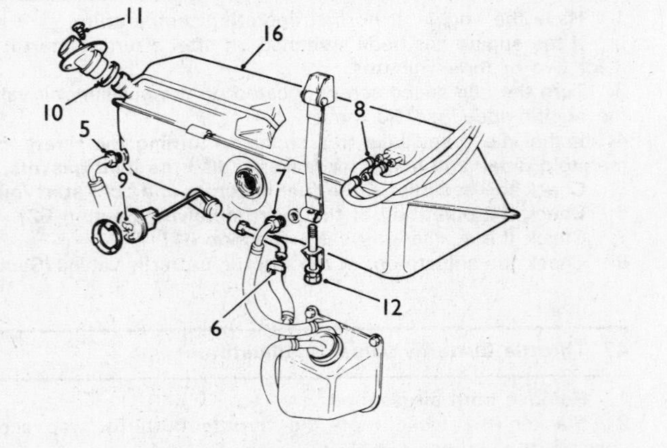


Fig. 3.55 Fuel tank (XJS) (Sec 50)

5 *Fuel return*
6 *Expansion tank supply hose*
7 *Expansion tank return hose*
8 *Vent hoses*
9 *Tank sender unit*
10 *Filler hose*
11 *Filler neck screws*
12 *Mounting strap bolts*
16 *Fuel tank*

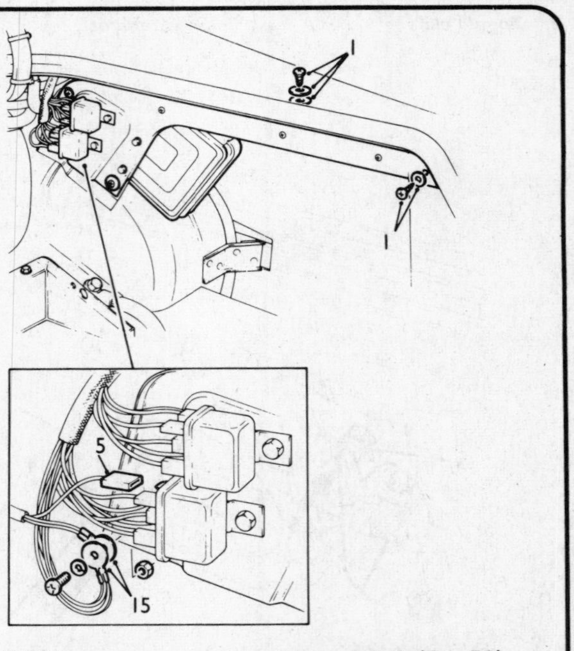


Fig. 3.56 Luggage compartment relay details (Sec 50)

1 *Side panel screws*
5 *Pump relay plug*
15 *Earth to relay bracket*

44.2 Left-hand air cleaner carries the temperature sensor

44.5 Air filter element

51.3 Fuel filter (1), fuel supply rail (2), right-hand (3) and left-hand (4) fuel rails

54.5 Fuel pump

58.1 Fuel cooler

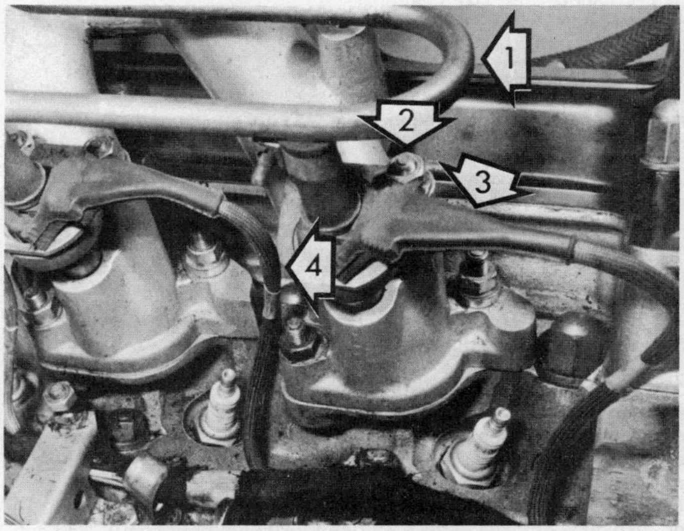


59.14 Fuel injector, showing fuel rail (1), injector clamp nut (2), electrical connector (3) and flexible fuel connecting hose (4)

locknut. If a new regulator is being fitted, it may require adjusting after checking as described in the next Section.

## 53 Fuel pressure regulators – checking and adjustment

1 Depressurise the fuel system as described in Section 48.
2 Disconnect the left-hand cold start injector supply pipe to the fuel rail and in its place connect a reliable pressure gauge.
3 Pull the negative LT lead from the ignition coil and switch the ignition on.
4 Earth terminal 85 of the fuel pump relay. The pressure gauge should indicate between 28.5 and 30.8 $lbf/in^2$ (2.0 and 2.2 $kgf/cm^2$).
5 The pressure indicated on the gauge may fall slowly, this is normal, but a rapid drop will indicate a fault in the system.
6 On the XJ12 and Double Six models only, operate the fuel changeover switch on the dash centre panel. Check the gauge pressure reading again as described in paragraph 4.
7 If the readings have proved satisfactory then both regulators are in good condition and the gauge can be removed and the original connections re-made.
8 Where one or both readings are outside the pressure specified then continue with the following adjustment procedure.
9 Unbolt both pressure regulators from the induction manifolds.
10 Clamp the fuel pipe between the left-hand pressure regulator inlet and the fuel rail.
11 Reconnect the negative LT lead to the ignition coil and start the engine.
12 Release the locknuts on both pressure regulators.
13 Turn the adjuster screw on the right-hand regulator until the reading on the pressure gauge is within the specified limits.
14 Release the clamp on the fuel pipe and transfer it to the right-hand fuel pipe. Turn the left-hand regulator adjuster screw until the pressure is within the specified limits.
15 Release the fuel pipe clamp and check that the pressure gauge still reads within the specified limits.
16 Without moving the adjuster screws, tighten the locknuts.
17 Switch off the ignition and again depressurise the fuel system so that the pressure gauge can be removed and the original connections re-made.

## 54 Fuel pump – removal and refitting

1 Depressurise the fuel system as described in Section 48.
2 Disconnect the battery.
3 Remove the spare wheel.
4 On XJS models, peel back the carpet and remove the fuel pump cover from within the luggage compartment.
5 Clamp the fuel inlet and outlet hoses at the pump and disconnect them (photo).
6 Disconnect the electrical plug.
7 Unbolt the pump mounting bracket, then release the pump from its clamping ring and remove it.
8 A faulty pump should not be overhauled but renewed complete.
9 Refit by reversing the removal operations. Make sure that the earth wire makes good metal-to-metal contact beneath one of the mounting screws.

## 55 Fuel pump relay – testing, removal and refitting

1 To test the relay, switch on the ignition. The pump should run for one or two seconds then stop. If the pump fails to operate or will not shut off, test by the following sequence.
2 Check that the inertia switch cut-out button is depressed (see Section 11) and that the connecting leads are secure. Check the switch for continuity when the button is depressed.
3 If the inertia switch is satisfactory, earth the pump relay terminal 85, switch on the ignition and check for battery voltage at terminal 86 of the main relay (see Section 56). If no reading is obtained, check the security of the electrical connections from the ignition switch through the inertia switch.
4 Now check for battery voltage at terminal 87 of the main relay. If no reading is obtained, check for battery voltage at the earth lead and connection from terminal 85 of the mains relay. If readings are obtained then the mains relay is faulty and should be renewed.
5 Check for battery voltage at terminal 86 of the fuel pump relay. If no reading is obtained, then an open circuit exists between terminal 87 of the main relay and 86 of the pump relay.
6 Check for battery voltage at terminal 87 of the pump relay. If no reading is obtained, check for battery voltage to earth and from terminal 85 of the pump relay. If these readings are satisfactory then the pump relay is faulty and must be renewed.
7 Finally, check all the supply and earth connections at the fuel pump.

### *Pump relay removal (XJ12 and Double Six)*

8 Disconnect the battery and pull the leads from the pump relay, which is located second from the right on the radiator top rail.
9 Unscrew and remove the relay securing screw.

### *Pump relay removal (XJS)*

10 Disconnect the battery and remove the right-hand trim panel from within the luggage compartment.
11 Identify the leads and disconnect the necessary ones from the main relay.
12 Extract the securing screw and remove the relay from the side panel of the luggage compartment.

### *Refitting*

13 Refitting on all models is a reversal of removal.

## 56 Fuel system main relay – removal and refitting

1 The main relay on XJ12 and Double Six models is fitted at the extreme left-hand side of the radiator top rail.
2 On XJS models, the main relay is located adjacent to the fuel pump relay.
3 Removal is by means of extracting a single mounting screw. Mark the connecting leads before pulling them from the relay.
4 Refitting is the reverse of the removal procedure.

## 57 Fuel tank changeover valves (XJ12 and Double Six) – testing, removal and refitting

1 These valves are located adjacent to the fuel pump in the luggage compartment. The right-hand valve is the supply valve and is energised when the right-hand fuel tank is selected.
2 The left-hand valve is the return one and ensures that fuel in excess of the requirements of the engine is returned to the same tank. On later models, two solenoid operated return valves are fitted under the rear wheel arches.
3 To test a valve, disconnect the battery and remove the spare wheel.
4 Clamp the inlet and outlet hoses at the valve and then disconnect them.
5 Disconnect the electrical leads from the valve.
6 Push a length of rubber tubing onto the stub on the valve which is at right angles to its body. Blow through the tubing; air should be ejected from the outlet port at the larger diameter end of the valve body.
7 Energise the solenoid valve by applying a 12V current to the supply lead and earthing the remaining lead.
8 Blow through the rubber tubing again: air should be ejected from the outlet port at the smaller diameter end of the valve body.
9 Failure to operate as indicated will mean that the valve is faulty and must be renewed.
10 To remove the valve with the hoses disconnected, simply disconnect its securing clamp.
11 Refitting is a reversal of removal. Make sure that the earth is located beneath one of the clamp screws.

## 58 Fuel cooler – removal and refitting

1 This is fitted to cars which are equipped with an air conditioning system. It is essential to identify correctly the fuel lines before carrying out any dismantling operations (photo).
2 Depressurise the fuel system (Section 48).

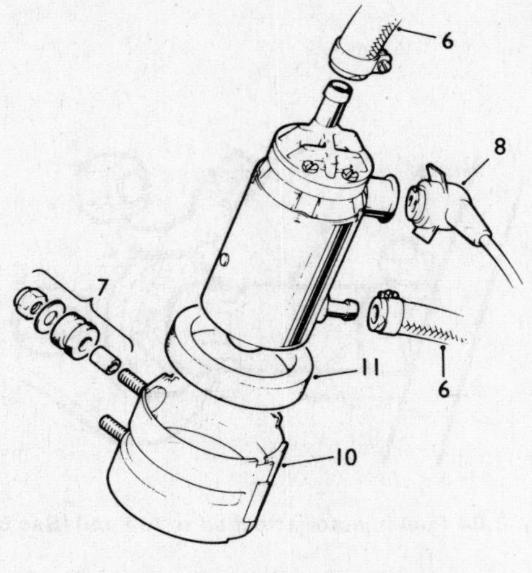


**Fig. 3.57 Fuel pump (Sec 54)**

*6 Fuel hoses*
*7 Mounting nuts and spacers*
*8 Electrical connector*
*10 Mounting clamp*
*11 Insulator*

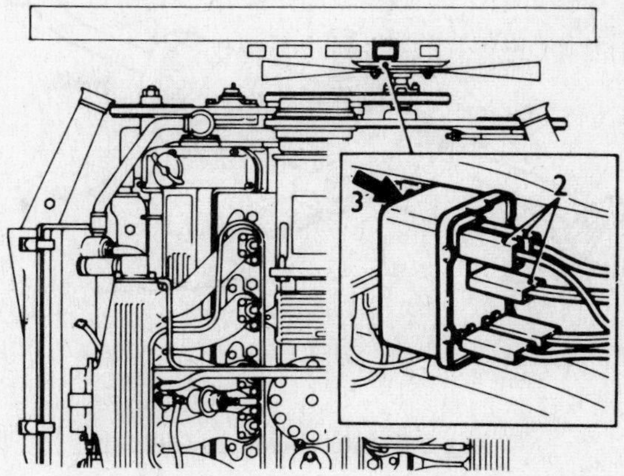


**Fig. 3.58 Fuel pump relay (XJ12 and Double Six) (Sec 55)**

*2 Lead connectors*
*3 Relay securing screw*

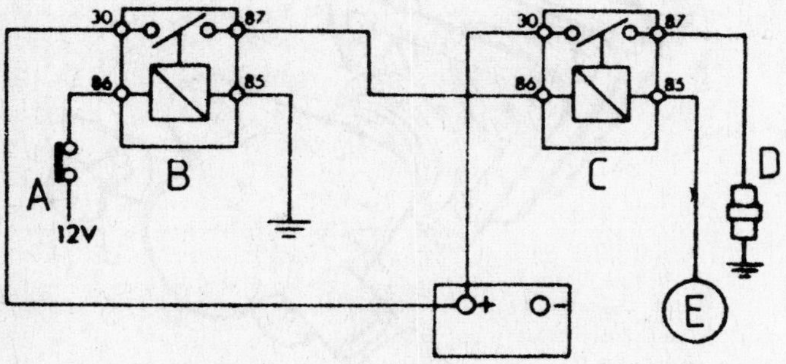


**Fig. 3.59 Fuel system relay circuit diagram (Sec 55)**

*A Inertia switch*
*B Main relay*
*C Pump relay*
*D Pump*
*E ECU*

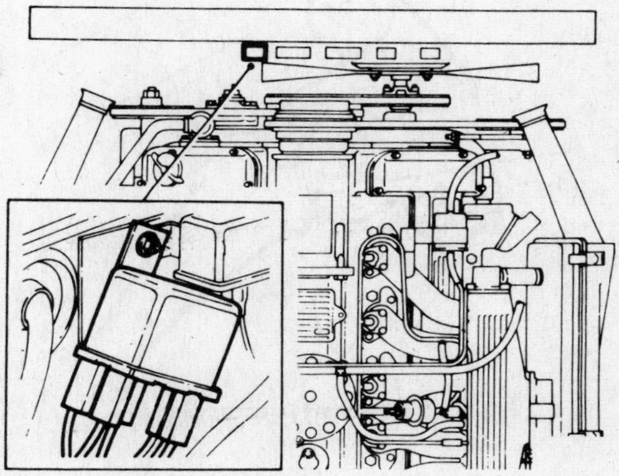

**Fig. 3.60 Fuel system main relay (XJ12, Double Six) (Sec 56)**

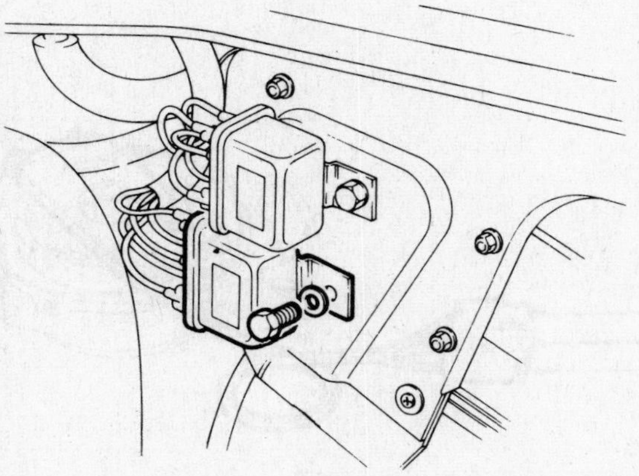

**Fig. 3.61 Fuel system main relay (XJS) (Sec 56)**

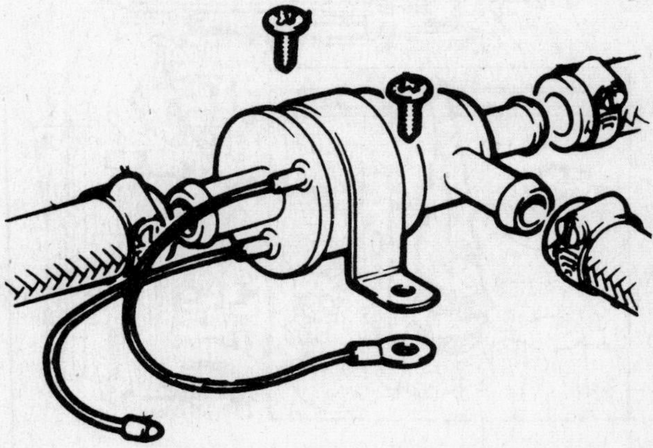

**Fig. 3.62 Fuel tank changeover valve (XJ12, Double Six) (Sec 57)**

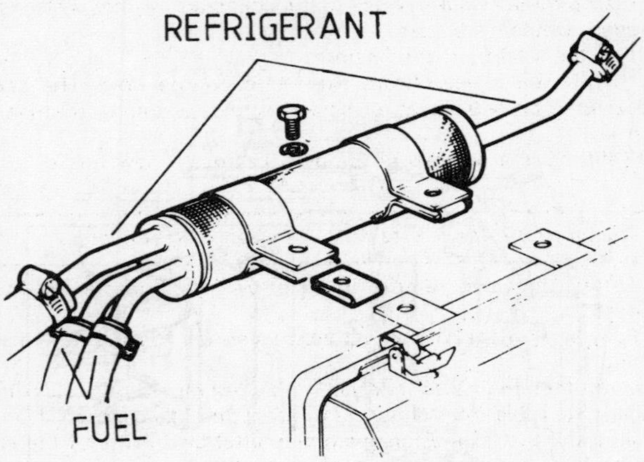


Fig. 3.63 Fuel cooler (Sec 58)

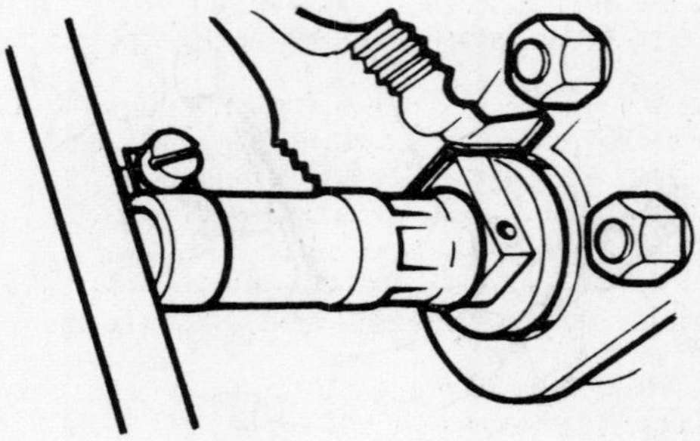

Fig. 3.64 Fuel injector attached to fuel rail (Sec 59)

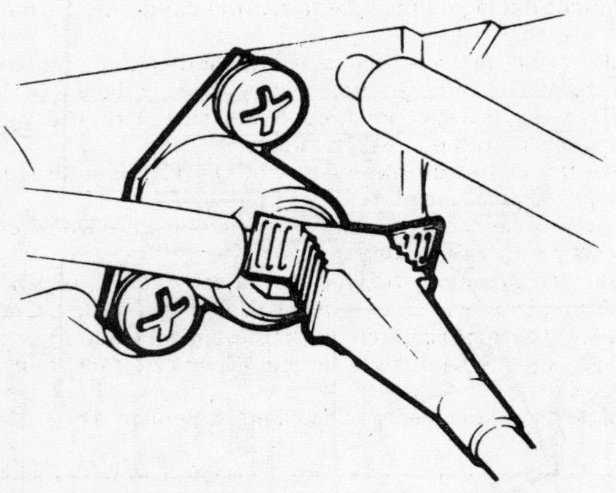

Fig. 3.65 Cold start injector (Sec 60)

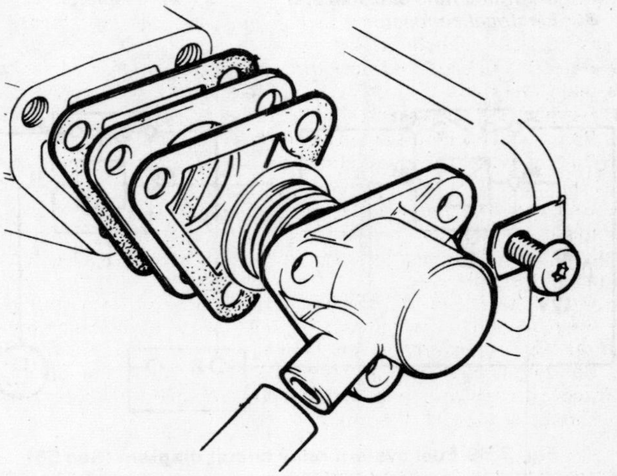

Fig. 3.66 Overrun valve (Sec 62)

Fig. 3.67 Thermotime switch (Sec 65)

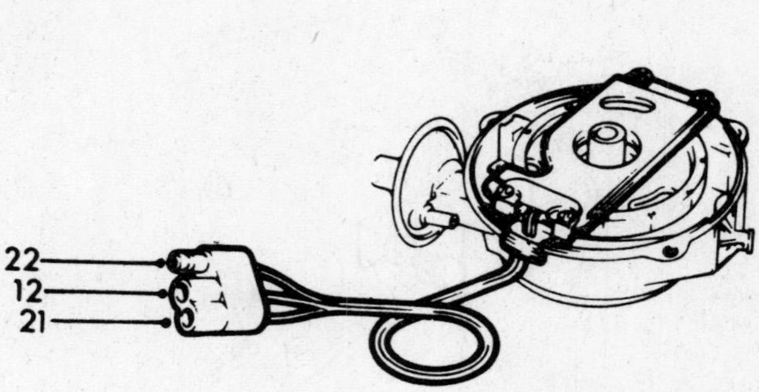


Fig. 3.68 Trigger unit plug terminals (Sec 67)

3 Clamp the fuel hoses on the end of the cooler to prevent loss of fuel and then disconnect them from the cooler.
4 If the refrigerant hoses must be disconnected then it is essential that the air conditioning system is discharged by your dealer beforehand. Refrigerant gas is very dangerous if allowed to escape into the atmosphere in an enclosed building.
5 The fuel cooler is attached to the air cleaner brackets by two setscrews.
6 Refitting is a reversal of removal. If the refrigerant was discharged by your dealer, have it recharged by him on completion of the work.

## 59 Fuel rail and injectors – removal and refitting

1 Depressurise the fuel system (Section 48) and then disconnect the battery.
2 Pull the manifold pressure pipe from the induction manifold.
3 Disconnect the throttle switch.
4 Disconnect the throttle cross-rods.
5 Clamp the fuel hose between the filter and the fuel supply rail.
6 Release the return fuel rail from the supply rail.
7 Extract the screws which hold the return fuel rail brackets to the induction manifolds. If the right-hand rail is being removed, note the longer spacer under the screw.
8 Release and pull the regulator to rail outlet hoses and the fuel return pipe from the fuel return rail.
9 Similarly release and pull the cold start injector and regulator inlet hoses from the fuel supply rail.
10 Release the clips that hold the fuel supply rail to the filter and to the main fuel rail.
11 Remove the supply and return fuel rails.
12 Release the wiring harness from the main fuel rail.
13 Pull the electrical connectors from the injectors, including the cold start injectors.
14 Unscrew and remove the twelve nuts which hold the injector clamps to the induction ram pipes. Lift the main fuel rail complete with injectors from the induction ram pipes. Mop up any spilled fuel with clean rag (photo).
15 Plug or tape over the injector holes to prevent dirt entering.
16 Release the clips which hold the injectors to the stubs on the main fuel rail. Pull the injectors from the rail and discard the O-ring seals.
17 Refitting is a reversal of removal. Make sure that the injectors are all fitted with new O-ring seals and their electrical connectors are fitted the correct way round (photo).

## 60 Cold start injector – removal and refitting

1 A cold start injector is mounted on each induction manifold.
2 Depressurise the fuel system (see Section 48).
3 Disconnect the battery.

59.17 Fuel injector O-ring seals (arrowed)

4 Clamp the fuel supply hose to the cold start injector which is to be removed. Detach the hose.
5 Pull the lead from the injector.
6 Unbolt the injector from the induction manifold. The securing screws may be setscrews, or socket screws requiring the use of an Allen key.
7 Refitting is a reversal of removal, but use a new gasket.

## 61 Auxiliary air valve – testing. removal and refitting

1 To test the valve, remove the filter element from the left-hand air cleaner.
2 Fully turn in the idle adjustment screw on the auxiliary air valve housing.
3 With the engine at normal running temperature, blocking the auxiliary air valve inlet should not affect the idling speed. If it does, continue the test in the following way after switching off the engine.
4 Carefully unscrew the expansion tank pressure cap, release any pressure and then refit the cap.
5 Disconnect the air balance pipe, the engine crankcase breather pipe and the manifold bleed pipe (XJS) from the valve.
6 Disconnect the air cleaner pipe from the auxiliary air valve.
7 Unbolt and remove the air valve from the coolant pipe and lift the valve clear.
8 Without damaging the seat, clean the old gasket from the coolant pipe.
9 Fully close the idle speed screw noting the number of turns needed to do so. Immerse the auxiliary air valve bulb in boiling water and watch the valve head through the side port. The valve should move smoothly to the closed position.
10 Take the valve from the water and quickly blow through the side port: no air should pass.
11 Let the valve cool and watch the valve head move smoothly back to open the main air passage.
12 If the movement of the valve is not satisfactory, renew the valve.
13 Refitting is a reversal of removal. Use a new gasket. Open the idle speed screw to approximately the same position as that originally set.
14 Check the coolant level in the expansion tank and top up if necessary.
15 Adjust the idle speed as described in Section 46.

## 62 Overrun valve – testing, removal and refitting

1 An overrun valve is fitted to each induction manifold. Each valve is designed to open and limit manifold depression under conditions of closed throttle overrun. This provides additional air to maintain a combustible fuel/air mixture under these conditions, so preventing an increase in exhaust emission levels.
2 To test the valve, remove the air cleaners, block the overrun valve pipes and start the engine.
3 If the idle speed is correct, stop the engine and unblock one valve inlet pipe only. Restart the engine. If the idle speed is correct, stop the engine again and unblock the second valve. Restart the engine. If the idle speed is now excessively fast, the last valve to be unblocked must be faulty and should be renewed.
4 To remove an overrun valve, extract the screws which hold it to the inlet manifold. Retrieve the spacer from the left-hand valve.
5 Disconnect the air cleaner hose and remove the valve complete with valve body.
6 Clean away all old pieces of gasket. Extract the valve from the valve body.
7 Refitting is a reversal of removal. Use a new gasket.

## 63 Fuel cut-off inertia switch

1 Refer to Section 11.

## 64 Coolant temperature sensor – testing, removal and refitting

1 Disconnect the battery.
2 Pull the lead from the coolant temperature sensor, which is located on the thermostat housing.

3 Connect an ohmmeter between the sensor terminals and note the resistance, which should correspond with those given in the following table according to the coolant temperature at the time of the test.

| Coolant temperature | Resistance across terminals (kilohms) |
|---|---|
| *14°F (-10°C)* | *9.2* |
| *32°F (0°C)* | *5.9* |
| *50°F (10°C)* | *3.7* |
| *68°F (20°C)* | *2.5* |
| *86°F (30°C)* | *1.7* |
| *104°F (40°C)* | *1.18* |
| *122°F (50°C)* | *0.84* |
| *140°F (60°C)* | *0.60* |
| *158°F (70°C)* | *0.435* |
| *176°F (80°C)* | *0.323* |
| *194°F (90°C)* | *0.250* |
| *212°F (100°C)* | *0.190* |

4 Disconnect the ohmmeter and then use it to check the resistance between each sensor terminal in turn and the sensor body. There should be a very high resistance shown on the ohmmeter. If not, renew the sensor as described in the following paragraphs.
5 Have the engine and coolant cold.
6 Disconnect the battery and pull the lead from the coolant temperature sensor.
7 Remove the expansion tank cap to release any residual pressure. Refit the cap.
8 Have the new sensor ready to hand with its threads smeared with jointing compound and a new sealing washer fitted.
9 Unscrew the original sensor and fit the new one as quickly as possible to avoid loss of coolant.
10 Reconnect the electrical leads and check and top up the coolant level.

## 65 Thermotime switch – testing, removal and refitting

1 Check the coolant temperature with a thermometer and record the reading. Note also the rating of the thermotime switch which is stamped on its body.
2 Disconnect the battery and the lead from the thermotime switch.
3 To test when the recorded coolant temperature is higher than that stamped on the switch, connect the ohmmeter between switch terminal W and earth. A very high resistance should be observed. If a low reading is observed, renew the switch.
4 To test when the recorded coolant temperature is lower than that stamped on the switch, connect the ohmmeter as previously described; a very low resistance should be observed.
5 If the switch is to be renewed, make sure that the engine is cold. Disconnect the battery and the lead from the switch. Have the new switch ready with a sealing washer fitted and its threads coated with jointing compound.
6 Remove the expansion tank cap and release any residual pressure. Unscrew and remove the switch from the thermostat housing. Quickly screw in the new switch.
7 Reconnect the electrical leads and top up the coolant level if necessary.

## 66 Air temperature sensor – testing, removal and refitting

1 This device is located in the left-hand air cleaner.
2 To test the sensor, disconnect the battery and pull the connector from the air temperature sensor.
3 Connect an ohmmeter between the sensor terminals and note the resistance, which should be very close to the readings in the following table according to the ambient air temperature at the time of the test.

| Ambient air temperature | Resistance (ohms) |
|---|---|
| *14°F (-10°C)* | *960* |
| *32°F (0°C)* | *640* |
| *50°F (10°C)* | *435* |
| *68°F (20°C)* | *300* |
| *86°F (30°C)* | *210* |
| *104°F (40°C)* | *150* |
| *122°F (50°C)* | *108* |
| *140°F (60°C)* | *80* |

4 Now check the resistance between each terminal and the body of the sensor. A very high resistance must be obtained, otherwise renew the sensor.
5 To renew the sensor, simply unscrew it from the air cleaner ram pipe.

## 67 Trigger unit – testing

1 An ohmmeter will be required for this work.
2 Disconnect the electrical lead from the fuel pump relay terminal 85.
3 Disconnect the negative LT lead from the ignition coil.
4 Separate the in-line connector which runs to the trigger unit.
5 Connect an ohmmeter between terminals 21 and 12 on the section of the in-line connector nearest the distributor.
6 Switch on the ignition and then operate the starter motor. The ohmmeter should indicate a regular even swing of its needle between low resistance and a very high resistance.
7 Reconnect the ohmmeter between terminals 22 and 12 and repeat the test. A similar reading must be obtained to the one previously described.
8 Any variation in the pattern of ohmmeter readings will mean that the trigger unit is faulty and must be renewed.

## 68 Trigger unit – removal and refitting

1 Disconnect the battery. Having identified the spark plug HT leads, disconnect them from all twelve spark plugs.
2 Disconnect the HT lead from the distributor.
3 On XJ12 and Double Six models, disconnect the manifold pressure sensor pipe at the T-piece and tie it away from the distributor cover.
4 Extract the three screws and lift the distributor cover away.
5 Remove the rotor arm.
6 Disconnect the trigger unit lead from the main wiring harness at the in-line connector.
7 Extract the four nylon screws and withdraw the trigger unit from the platform.
8 Remove the nylon clamp from the right-hand side of the unit. Release the trigger unit rubber seal and pull the unit from the distributor body.
9 Refitting is a reversal of removal.

## 69 Manifold pressure sensor – testing, removal and refitting

1 Disconnect the battery and pull the lead from the pressure sensor.
2 Connect an ohmmeter between the pressure sensor terminals and check that the indicated resistance is within the limits shown in the following table. If not, the sensor must be renewed.

| Sensor terminals (see wiring diagrams) | Resistance (ohms) |
|---|---|
| *7 and 15* | *85.5 to 94.5* |
| *8 and 10* | *346.5 to 353.5* |
| *7 or 15 and earth* | *Open circuit ∞* |
| *8 or 10 and earth* | *Open circuit ∞* |

3 To remove the pressure sensor, disconnect the electrical lead and hose and unbolt the sensor from its position, which is on the radiator top rail on XJ12 and Double Six models or on the wing valance on XJS models.
4 Refitting is a reversal of removal.

## 70 Cold start relay – removal and refitting

1 On XJ12 and Double Six models, the relay is mounted on the extreme right-hand side of the radiator top rail.
2 On XJS models, the relay is mounted on the front wing valance and the relay cover must first be removed.
3 Disconnect the battery, then identify the electrical leads and pull them from the cold start relay terminals.

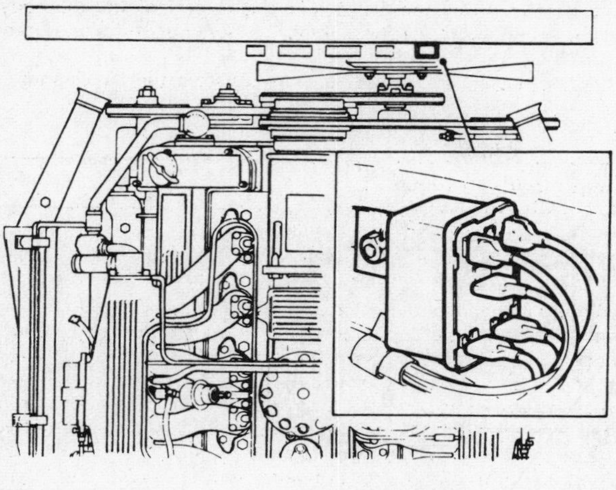

Fig. 3.69 Cold start relay (XJ12, Double Six) (Sec 70)

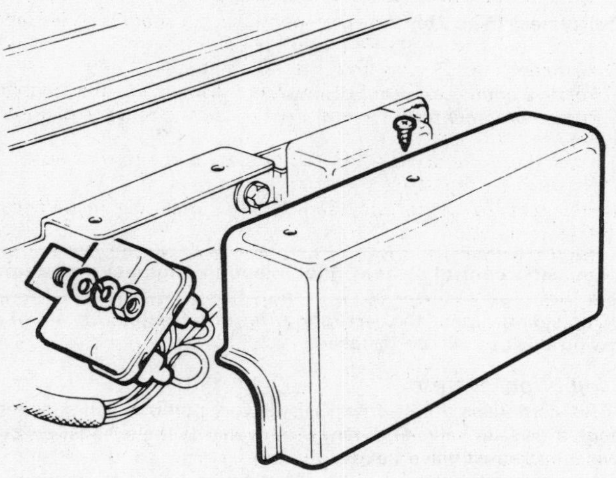

Fig. 3.70 Cold start relay (XJS) (Sec 70)

4 Unbolt and remove the relay. On right-hand drive XJS models, better access is obtained if the relay mounting bracket is unbolted and raised together with all the relays as one assembly.

## 71 Power amplifier – removal and refitting

1 The power amplifier is mounted on the radiator top rail (photo). Its purpose is to isolate the ECU from the large current draw which occurs when six fuel injectors are switched simultaneously.
2 Disconnect the battery and then separate the in-line connectors at the wiring harness.
3 Release the rubber grommet from the radiator top rail. Unbolt the amplifier and draw the wiring and plug through the hole in the rail.
4 Refitting is a reversal of the removal procedure.

## 72 Electronic control unit (ECU) – removal and refitting

1 The ECU is mounted within the luggage compartment and receives the input signals from the various fuel injection system sensors. The ECU then computes the period for which the injectors must open for each engine cycle.
2 Do not alter the setting of the idle fuelling potentiometer control knob on the amplifier unit or the idle CO level will be upset, see Section 82.
3 To remove the ECU, first disconnect the battery.
4 Remove the cover from the ECU which is located at the forward end of the luggage compartment (XJ12 and Double Six). On XJS models, remove the right-hand trim panel from the luggage compartment.
5 Release the clamp at the wiring harness entry, remove the clip and end cover and withdraw the harness plug.
6 Remove the ECU from its mounting bracket (photo).
7 Refitting is a reversal of removal. If a new unit has been fitted, check the CO level as described in Section 82.

## 73 Throttle switch – testing and adjusting

1 Check that the throttle linkage and throttle butterfly valve are correctly set (Sections 37 and 47).
2 Disconnect the battery and pull the electrical multi-connector from the throttle switch which is located underneath the throttle pulley.
3 Connect an ohmmeter between terminals 12 and 17 of the throttle switch. A very low resistance should be registered. If not, adjust in the following way.

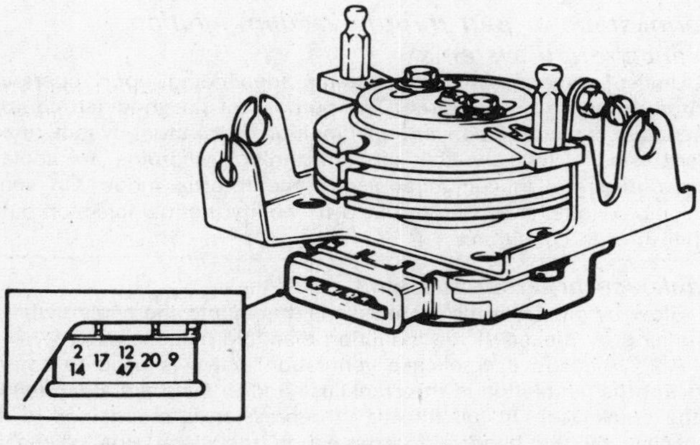


Fig. 3.71 Throttle switch terminal identification (Sec 73)

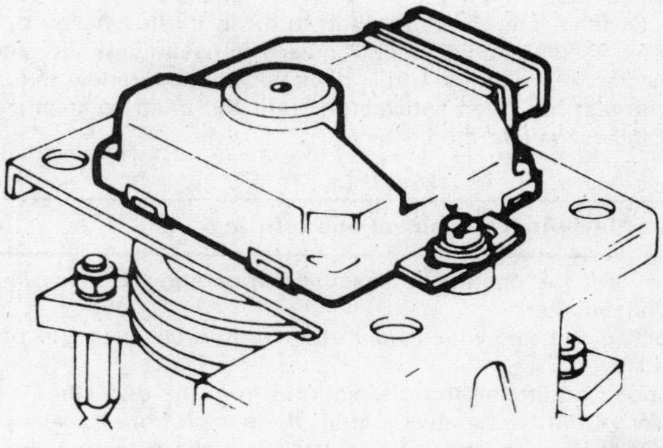

Fig. 3.72 Throttle switch correctly fitted (Sec 74)

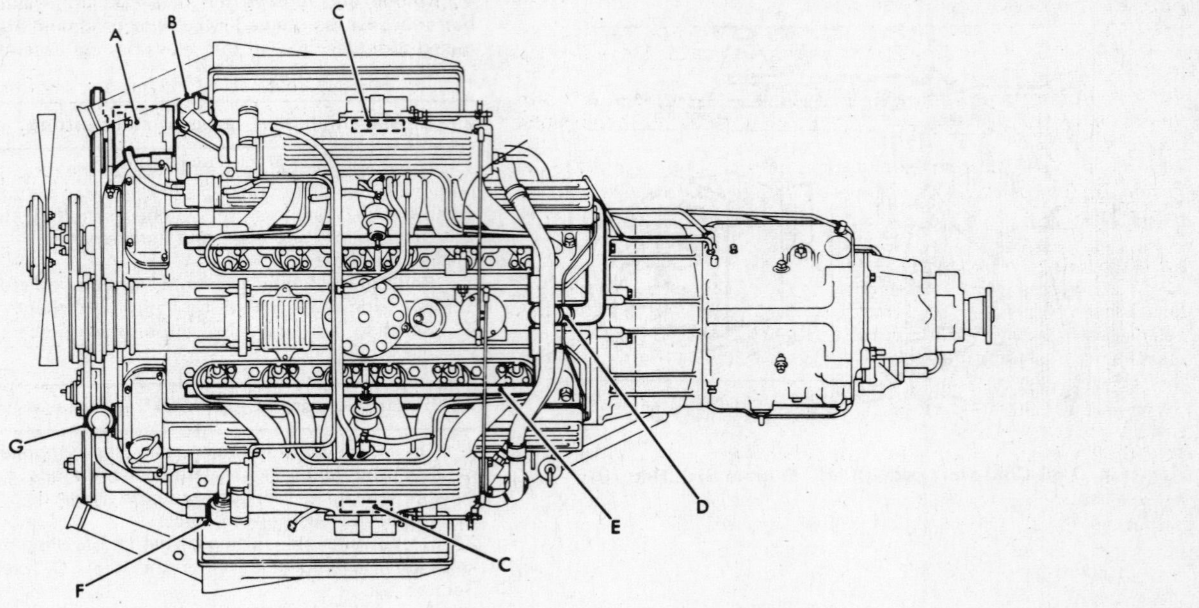


**Fig. 3.73 Typical emission control system (Sec 75)**

*A Air pump*
*B Diverter valve*
*C EGR valves*
*D Non-return valve*
*E Air rail*
*F Positive crankcase ventilation valve*
*G Engine breather filter*

4 Disconnect the pushrods from the throttle pulley (photo).
5 Unbolt and lift the throttle pulley from the pedestal. Disconnect the throttle switch plug.
6 Slacken the two throttle switch screws.
7 Insert a feeler blade (0.050 in (1.27 mm) thick for XJS or 0.030 in (0.76 mm) for XJ12 and Double Six) between the pulley and the closed throttle stop.
8 With the ohmmeter connected between terminals 12 and 17 of the throttle switch, turn the switch very slowly until the ohmmeter flicks to indicate a very low resistance. Tighten the two switch screws.
9 Remove the feeler blade and the ohmmeter should indicate a very high resistance when the pulley is closed against its stop. Remove the ohmmeter.
10 Reconnect the pushrods. If their balljoints will not connect to the bellcranks without displacing the latter, adjust the lengths of the rods. When tightening the rod locknuts, make sure that the balljoints are held at the centres of their arcs of travel.
11 With the throttle switch now correctly adjusted, continue the test in the following way.
12 Connect the ohmmeter between terminals 9 and 12/47 of the switch. Observe the ohmmeter and turn the throttle pulley by hand. The meter needle should swing regularly between very low and very high resistance ten times. If this does not happen, renew the switch.
13 If the test has been satisfactory, refit the multi-connector to the switch and reconnect the battery.

## 74 Throttle switch – removal and refitting

1 Carry out the operations described in paragraphs 2 and 4 of the preceding Section.
2 Slacken the nut which holds the throttle cable to the pedestal bracket.
3 Unbolt and lift the throttle platform from the pedestal.
4 Remove the two screws and lift the switch from its seat.
5 Refitting is a reversal of removal but make sure that the multi-connector socket faces towards the rear of the car (photo).

## 75 Emission control system (fuel injection engines) – description

1 Depending upon the operating territory, some or all of the following devices will be installed.

### *Air injection system*

2 This comprises a belt-driven air delivery pump which supplies air through a diverter valve and non-return valve to the exhaust ports just above the exhaust valve heads.
3 This injected air mixes with the exhaust gases to continue the oxidisation process within the exhaust system.
4 The non-return valve prevents reverse flow in the injection rails when the exhaust gas pressure exceeds the air supply pressure.
5 The diverter valve operates when there is a sudden drop in manifold pressure, such as occurs when the throttle is closed quickly. Secondary air is diverted to atmosphere for between 2 and 3 seconds. This reduces the fuel/air ratio which would otherwise be too rich to burn and would cause a backfire in the exhaust system.

### *Thermostatic or part throttle vacuum ignition advance/retard systems*

6 One of several different systems (depending upon operating territory) may be encountered. The purpose of the modified components as opposed to a conventional ignition distributor advance/retard mechanism is to vary the ignition timing according to coolant temperature and in conjunction with the throttle mode. On some versions, a signal is sent to the ECU to modify the fuel injection pulse at full throttle conditions.

### *Crankcase breather system*

7 Blow-by gas from the crankcase is drawn into the engine while it is running by means of the induction manifold balance pipe.
8 A PCV (positive crankcase ventilation) valve is used to control part-throttle ventilation in the crankcase and to maintain a depression in the crankcase. On full throttle, a depression is maintained in the crankcase by the depression created on the clean side of the air cleaner.

### *Fuel evaporative control system*

9 To prevent the emission of fuel vapour from the fuel tank to atmosphere, the vapour is stored in a carbon-filled canister when the engine is not running.
10 When the engine is running, the vapour in the canister is drawn into the induction manifold and burned during the normal combustion cycle.
11 The fuel tanks have an inbuilt expansion tank to accommodate the increase in fuel volume which occurs as the result of a rise in ambient temperature.

### *Exhaust Gas Recirculation (EGR)*

12 In this system, exhaust gas is tapped from the exhaust downpipe and injected into the induction system. The system incorporates solenoid-operated valves which are controlled by an EGR controller to prevent valve operation under idle or full throttle conditions or during the warm-up period and at high roadspeeds.

### *Catalytic converters*

13 These are fitted into the exhaust systems to further reduce CO or hydrocarbon emissions. Unleaded fuel only must be used on cars equipped with catalytic converters.
14 Under certain conditions, the temperature of the catalytic converter may be very high. To reduce the possibility of damage to the converter or the underside of the car generally, the following precautions should be observed.

- *(a) Do not continue to operate the car if the engine is misfiring or runs on after switching off*
- *(b) Do not park in areas of long grass or other combustible materials*
- *(c) Do not overload the car or pull excessively heavy trailer loads*
- *(d) Do not operate the car downhill with the engine switched off*
- *(e) Do not run the engine with a spark plug removed or HT lead disconnected*
- *(f) Do not use a type of tyre pump which can be screwed into a spark plug hole*
- *(g) Do not push or tow start the car, use only battery jumper leads connected to the battery of another vehicle*

## 76 Emission control systems – maintenance

1 Regularly inspect all hose and pipe connections. Check the air pump drivebelt tension as described in Chapter 1, Section 41.
2 At the intervals specified in Routine Maintenance, carry out the following operations.

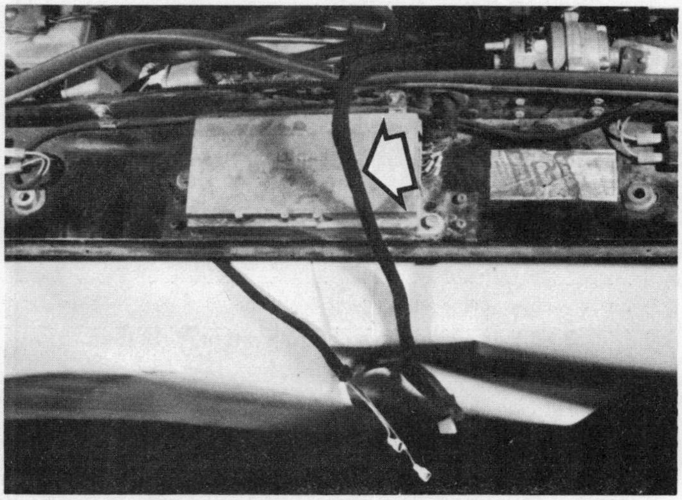
71.1 Power amplifier (arrowed)

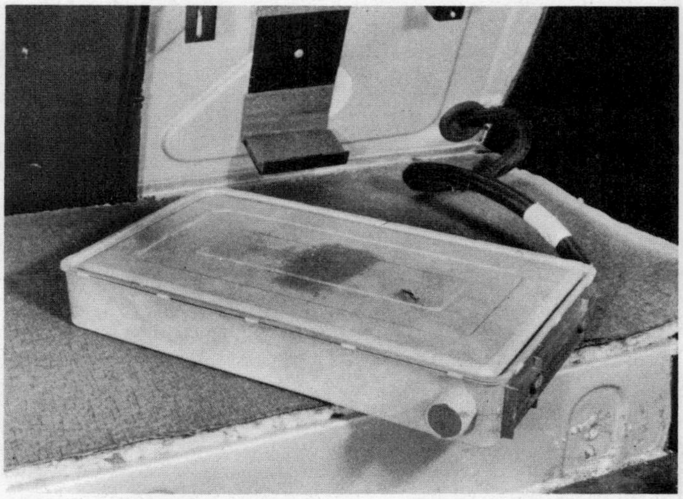
72.6 Close-up of ECU and bracket

73.4 Throttle pulley and pushrods

74.5 Throttle pedestal and multi-connector sockets (induction manifolds removed)

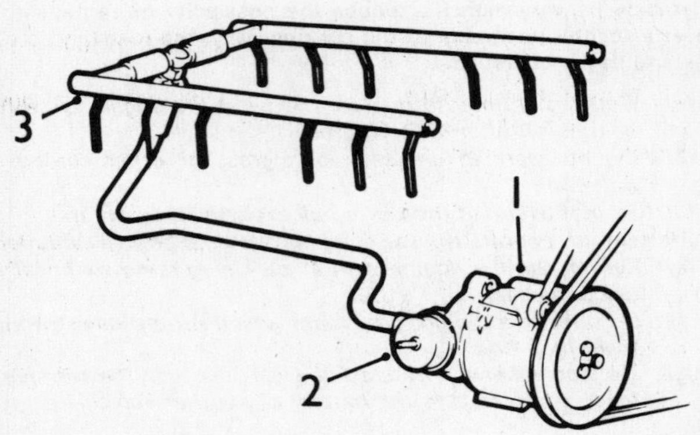


**Fig. 3.74 Air injection system (diagrammatic) (Sec 75)**

*1 Air pump*
*2 Diverter valve*
*3 Non-return valve*

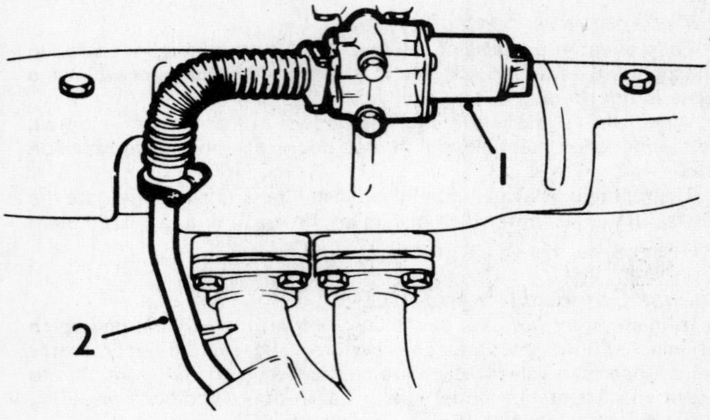


**Fig. 3.75 EGR valve (Sec 75)**

*1 Valve assembly*
*2 Exhaust downpipe tapping*

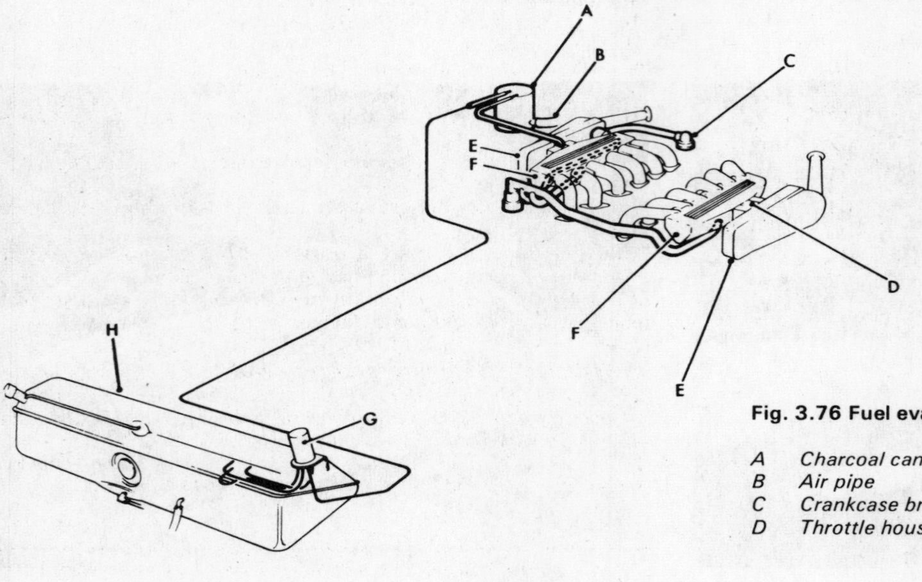


**Fig. 3.76 Fuel evaporative control system (XJS) (Sec 75)**

*A Charcoal canister*
*B Air pipe*
*C Crankcase breather*
*D Throttle housings*
*E Air cleaners*
*F Induction manifolds*
*G Vapour separator*
*H Fuel tank*

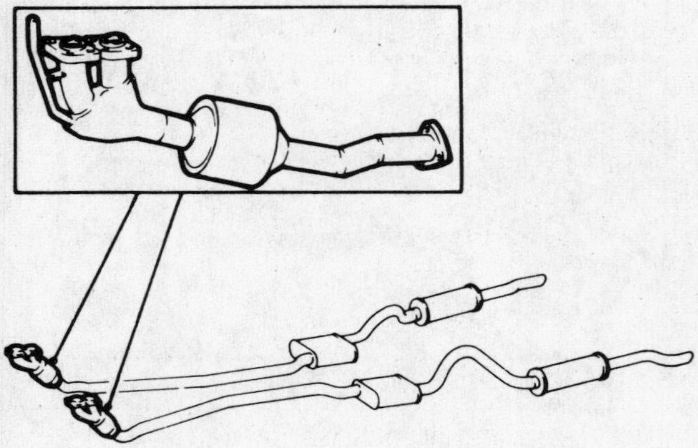

**Fig. 3.77 Catalytic converter (Sec 75)**

**Fig. 3.78 Engine breather (Sec 75)**

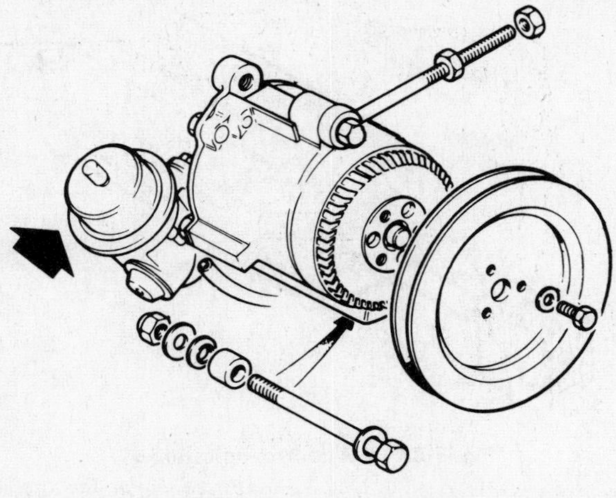

Fig. 3.79 Air pump and (arrowed) diverter valve (Sec 77)

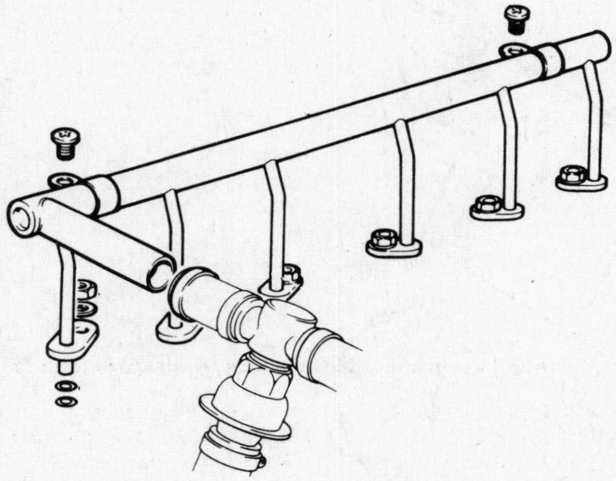

Fig. 3.80 Air rail (Sec 78)

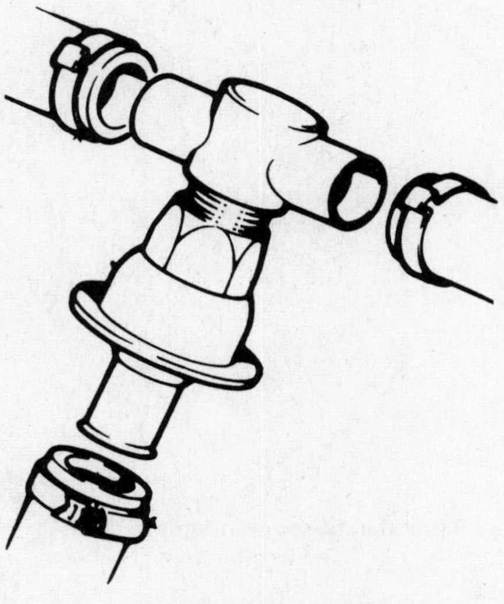

Fig. 3.81 Non-return valve (Sec 79)

*Engine breather filter – cleaning*

3 Release the clip and pull off the rubber cover from the breather housing.

4 Disconnect the pipe from the cover and clean away any sludge.

5 Lift out the filter, clean it in fuel, dry it and refit.

6 Reconnect the rubber cover.

*Carbon canister – renewal*

7 Raise the front of the car and remove the left-hand roadwheel.

8 On XJS models, unbolt and remove the access cover from the spoiler.

9 Identify the hoses and disconnect them from the canister.

10 Release the clamp and withdraw the canister.

11 Fit the new carbon canister by reversing the process just described.

*Catalytic converter – renewal*

12 On early models, the catalytic converter must be renewed at 25 000 mile (40 000 km) intervals. A service interval warning indicator is built into the centre switch panel and also indicates the service interval for the EGR system. A special key resets the indicator.

13 On later cars, a 50 000 mile (80 000 km) service interval is recommended and a reminder device is not installed.

14 To remove a catalytic converter, first withdraw the air cleaner element.

15 Release the EGR transfer pipe clamp at the take-off pipe and disconnect the transfer pipe.

16 Working under the car, remove the power steering rack bellows heatshield.

17 Support the front intermediate exhaust pipe and disconnect it from the downpipe.

18 Unbolt the downpipe and the heatshield from the exhaust manifold.

19 Remove the downpipe and catalytic converter. Removal will be made easier if the steering is turned as necessary.

20 Refitting is a reversal of removal, but use exhaust jointing compound at the joints and flanges.

*EGR valve – cleaning and renewal*

21 At 25 000 mile (40 000 km) intervals, the EGR valve, ports and transfer pipe should be removed as described later in this Chapter and all carbon deposits removed with a wire brush or scraper.

22 At 50 000 mile (80 000 km) intervals, the valve should be renewed.

## 77 Air pump and diverter valve (emission control) – removal and refitting

1 Remove the cover from the right-hand air cleaner.

2 Unbolt (three bolts) and remove the pulley from the pump. Do not prise the pulley off with a lever but pull it by hand only, otherwise the pump filter will be damaged.

3 Release the pump adjuster rod and swing the pump away from the engine.

4 Disconnect the vacuum pipe from the diverter valve, followed by the secondary air pipe. Discard the seal.

5 Unbolt the pump mountings and lift it from the engine.

6 Remove the elbow and diverter valve from the pump. Discard the gasket.

7 Refitting is a reversal of removal; use a new elbow gasket and secondary air pipe seal.

8 Tension the drivebelt as described in Chapter 1, Section 41.

## 78 Air rail (emission control) – removal and refitting

1 Depressurise the fuel system as described in Section 48.

2 Disconnect the battery.

3 Remove the fuel rail (Section 59).

4 Remove the fuel pressure regulators (Section 52).

5 Unbolt the air rail bracket from the induction manifold ram tubes.

6 If the right-hand air rail is being removed, disconnect the earth strap from the rear induction manifold ram tube.

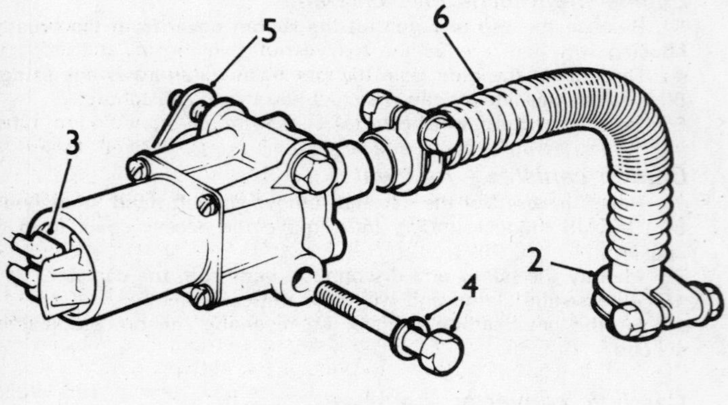


**Fig. 3.82 EGR valve (Sec 80)**

*2 Clamp*
*3 Electrical connectors*
*4 Mounting bolt and washer*
*5 Gasket*
*6 Transfer pipe*

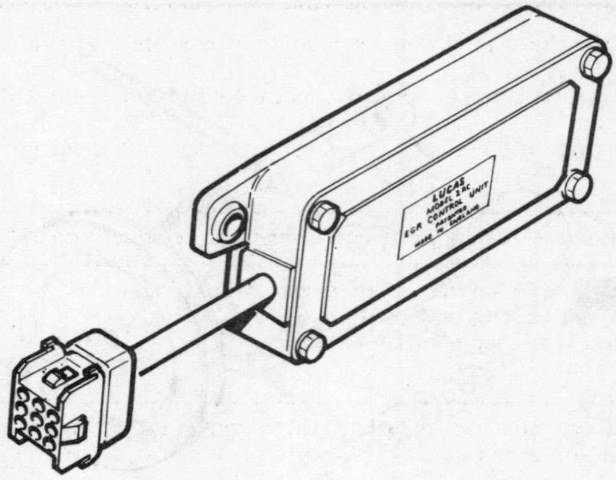


**Fig. 3.83 EGR control unit (Sec 81)**

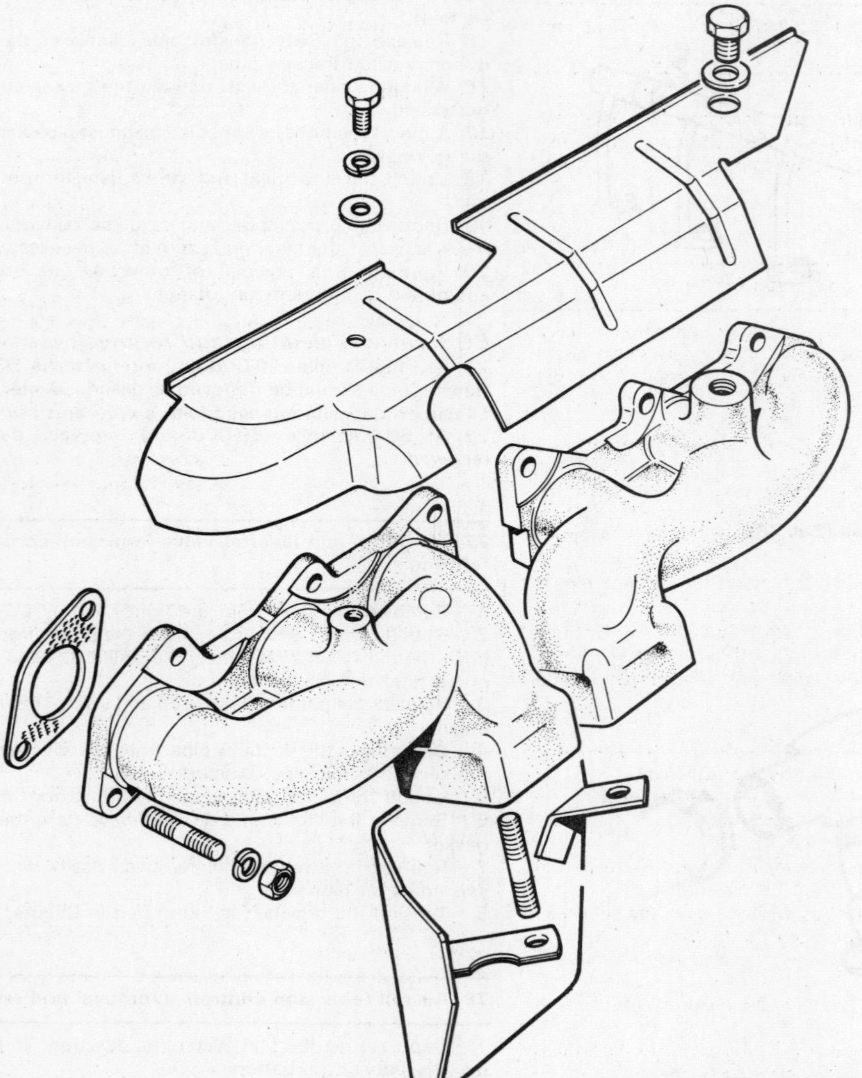

**Fig. 3.84 Typical exhaust manifolds (Sec 85)**

7 Unbolt the air rail and manifold stud spacers from the cylinder head.
8 Lift out the air rail and disconnect the non-return valve hose from it.
9 Refitting is a reversal of removal; use new rubber sealing rings.

## 79 Non-return valve (emission control) – removal and refitting

1 Note which way round the valve is fitted, release the hose clips and pull the hoses from the valve.
2 Refitting is a reversal of removal.

## 80 Exhaust gas recirculation (EGR) valve (emission control) – removal and refitting

1 Remove the cover from the air cleaner and disconnect the EGR valve transfer pipe.
2 Disconnect the electrical leads.
3 Unscrew and remove the valve mounting bolts.
4 Refitting is a reversal of removal, but use a new gasket.

## 81 Exhaust gas recirculation (EGR) control unit – removal and refitting

1 Disconnect the battery.
2 Remove the two nuts and washers which hold the rear right-hand lamp cluster. Disconnect the lamp earth lead and withdraw the cluster.
3 With the EGR control unit now accessible, pull off the multi-connector and remove the control unit.
4 Refitting is a reversal of removal.

## 82 CO level (mixture) – checking and adjusting

1 These operations will only be required if new components have been fitted to the fuel injection or emission control systems. It is essential to carry out this work immediately after renewal of the fuel injection electronic control unit (ECU).
2 Adjust the throttle butterfly valves (Section 47).
3 Adjust the idle speed (Section 46) with the engine at normal operating temperature.
4 Take off the cap from the air injection system diverter valve (Section 77) which will interrupt the air injection. Increase the engine speed to 2000 rpm for a period of 15 seconds, then allow it to return to idle speed.
5 Using an infra-red exhaust gas analyser, insert the probe into the sampling point at each end of the air injection rail. The CO reading should be within the specified limits. If necessary, adjust the idle potentiometer knob on the ECU until the correct reading is obtained.
6 Refit the diverter valve cap and reset the idle speed to the specified level.

## 83 Induction manifold (left-hand) – removal and refitting

1 Disconnect the battery and remove the air cleaner.
2 Depressurise the fuel system (Section 48).
3 Disconnect the fuel pipe from the overrun valves. Retrieve the spacer from the left-hand valve.
4 Disconnect the pressure regulator return hose from the fuel rail.
5 Disconnect the fuel crossover pipe from the fuel rail.
6 Disconnect the manifold pressure hose from the induction manifold.
7 Where fitted, disconnect the vacuum hose from the throttle housing.
8 On left-hand drive cars, disconnect the leads from the kickdown switch and the throttle cable from the throttle pedestal.
9 Disconnect the throttle pushrod from the bellcrank.
10 Unclip the wiring harness from the fuel rail.
11 Pull the electrical leads from the fuel and cold start injectors.
12 Disconnect the brake servo vacuum hose from the non-return valve.
13 Remove the throttle return spring.
14 Disconnect the manifold bleed pipe from the rubber elbow.
15 Unscrew and remove the twelve nuts which hold the induction manifold to the cylinder head. Under each outboard nut is fitted a spacer and washer, on inboard nuts, a washer only (photo).
16 Where fitted, detach the air rail clips from the manifold ram tubes, release the non-return valve hose, remove the air rail and discard the O-ring seals.
17 Where fitted, remove the EGR valve from the throttle housing.
18 Remove the six spacers from the manifold studs. Withdraw the manifold, at the same time easing aside the balance pipe and the fuel pipes.
19 Discard the manifold gaskets and obtain new ones. Note that the gaskets used originally are of composition type, while replacements are of sheet steal. These later type gaskets are handed left and right (photo). Plug the open ports to prevent the entry of dirt.
20 Refitting is a reversal of removal. Use new gaskets and injector sealing rings. Check the throttle linkage adjustment on completion (Section 37).

## 84 Induction manifold (right-hand) – removal and refitting

1 Disconnect the battery, remove the air cleaner and depressurise the fuel system (Section 48).
2 Disconnect the fuel filter and bracket from the manifold ram tube.
3 Repeat paragraph 3 of Section 83.
4 Disconnect the manifold pressure hose from the manifold and T-piece.
5 Repeat paragraph 5 of Section 83.
6 On RHD cars, disconnect the leads from the kickdown switch and the throttle cable from the throttle pedestal.
7 Release the throttle crossrod from the bellcrank and disconnect the vacuum hoses from the induction manifold (photo).
8 Disconnect the vacuum hoses from the throttle housing and the air balance pipe from the rubber elbow.
9 Unclip the wiring harness from the fuel rail and disconnect the electrical leads from the fuel and cold start injectors.
10 Release the earth strap from the manifold ram tube.
11 Disconnect the brake servo vacuum hose from the non-return valve.
12 Disconnect the heater vacuum hose from the manifold stub.
13 Where fitted, disconnect the diverter valve vacuum hose from its manifold stub.
14 Disconnect the automatic transmission vacuum hose from its rigid pipe section.
15 Repeat the operations described in paragraphs 13 and 15 to 20 of Section 83 (photo).

## 85 Exhaust manifold (left-hand) – removal and refitting

1 Disconnect the battery.
2 Remove the air cleaner.
3 Remove the exhaust front pipe by disconnecting it from the manifold and intermediate pipe flanges. The nuts are accessible from underneath the car using a socket and long extension.
4 Still working under the car, unbolt and remove the heatshields to give access to the manifold lower nuts. Unscrew and remove these nuts and their washers.
5 Working within the engine compartment, unbolt and remove the manifold heatshields.
6 Unscrew and remove the manifold upper securing nuts.
7 Withdraw the front section of the exhaust manifold first, followed by the rear section.
8 Discard the gaskets and clean the mating flanges.
9 Refitting is a reversal of removal, use new gaskets.

## 86 Exhaust manifold (right-hand) – removal and refitting

1 The operations are very similar to those described for the left-hand manifold in the preceding Section except that in addition, the starter motor heatshield must be removed before the rear manifold can be removed (photo).

83.15 Induction manifold washers (1) and spacers (2)

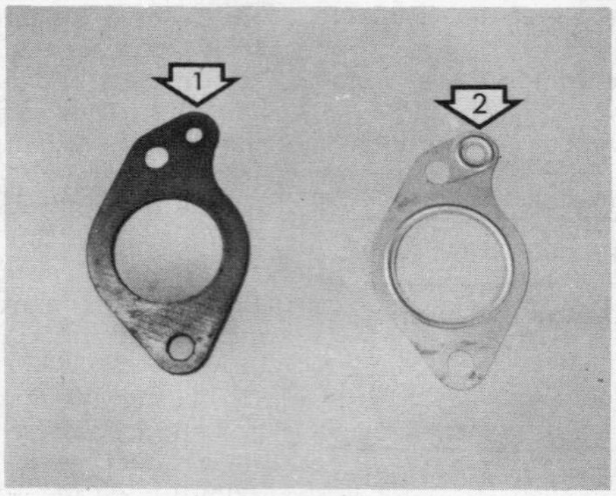

83.19 Induction manifold gaskets. 1 – Old type. 2 – New type

84.6 Vacuum hose connections to right-hand induction manifold

84.14 Tightening right-hand induction manifold nuts

86.1 Right-hand front exhaust manifold

## 87 Exhaust system – removal and refitting

1 Refer to Section 34 or 35.

## 88 Accelerator pedal and throttle linkage – removal and refitting

1 Extract the split pin and disconnect the cable from the pedal, after pulling off the sleeve.
2 Unbolt the pedal assembly from the bulkhead.
3 Remove the two circlips which secure the nylon bushes to the throttle pedal bracket. Turn the bushes through 45° and remove them. Remove the pedal from the bracket.

### *Throttle pedestal (all models)*

4 Disconnect the throttle rods from the throttle pulley, then unscrew and remove the nut which holds the throttle cable to the pedestal bracket.
5 Rotate the pulley and release the throttle cable nipple.
6 Pull the multi-pin connector from the throttle switch.
7 Unscrew the nuts and lift the platform from the throttle pedestal.
8 Release the two screws and remove the switch operating rod from the throttle pulley.
9 Extract the circlip and remove the pulley from the platform.
10 Extract the bushes and remove and discard the return spring. Unscrew and remove the ballpins.

### *Throttle cable (XJS)*

11 Release the cable from the accelerator pedal as previously described.
12 Unscrew the locknut and disconnect the cable from the pulley.
13 Disconnect the cable assembly from the bulkhead tube and then pull the cable through into the engine compartment. On RHD cars, the cable is secured to the bulkhead by a nut above the footwell on the driver's side.
14 Disconnect the leads from the kickdown switch.
15 Release the cable nipple from the pedestal and slacken the cable locknut at the pedestal bracket.
16 Remove the kickdown switch (two screws) from its mounting plate.

### *Accelerator pedal (XJ12 and Double Six)*

17 Fold back the carpet and remove the pedal base nuts.
18 Withdraw the pedal and disconnect the retaining spring.

### *Throttle cable (XJ12 and Double Six)*

19 Disconnect the battery and the kickdown switch plug.
20 Loosen the adjustment locknuts and the retaining locknut at the footwell, and detach the cable from the support bracket and pedestal.
21 Remove the operating rod split pin, disengage the sleeve and nipple, and withdraw the cable into the engine compartment after removing the nut from the sheath.

### *Refitting (all components)*

22 Refitting of all components is a reversal of removal, but lubricate all pivots and bushes. Seal round the footwell locknut with mastic.
23 On completion, check the throttle linkage adjustment as described in Section 37.

## 89 Cruise control system – description

1 This device is optionally available on Series 3 models.
2 Its purpose is to maintain a set roadspeed with the foot released from the accelerator pedal. This is a most useful facility for long distance travel.
3 Immediate reversion to normal control is obtained once the brake

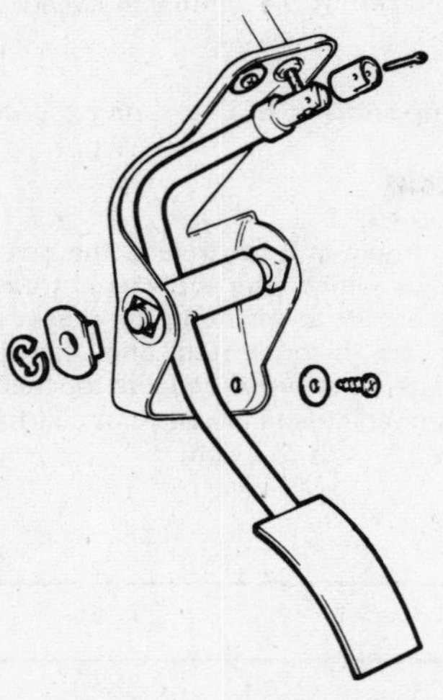

Fig. 3.85 Throttle pedal (LHD) (Sec 88)

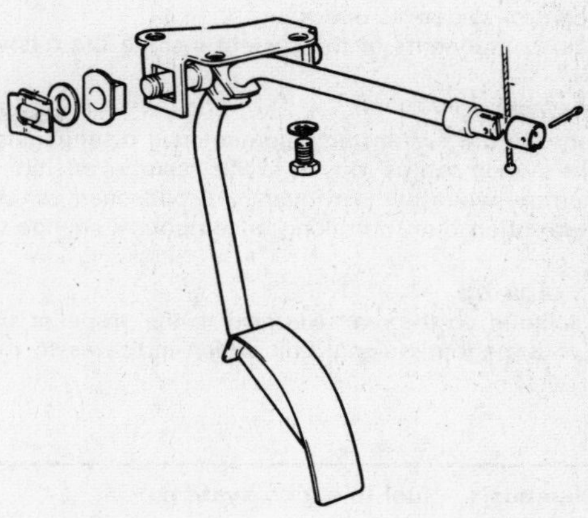

Fig. 3.86 Throttle pedal (RHD) (Sec 88)

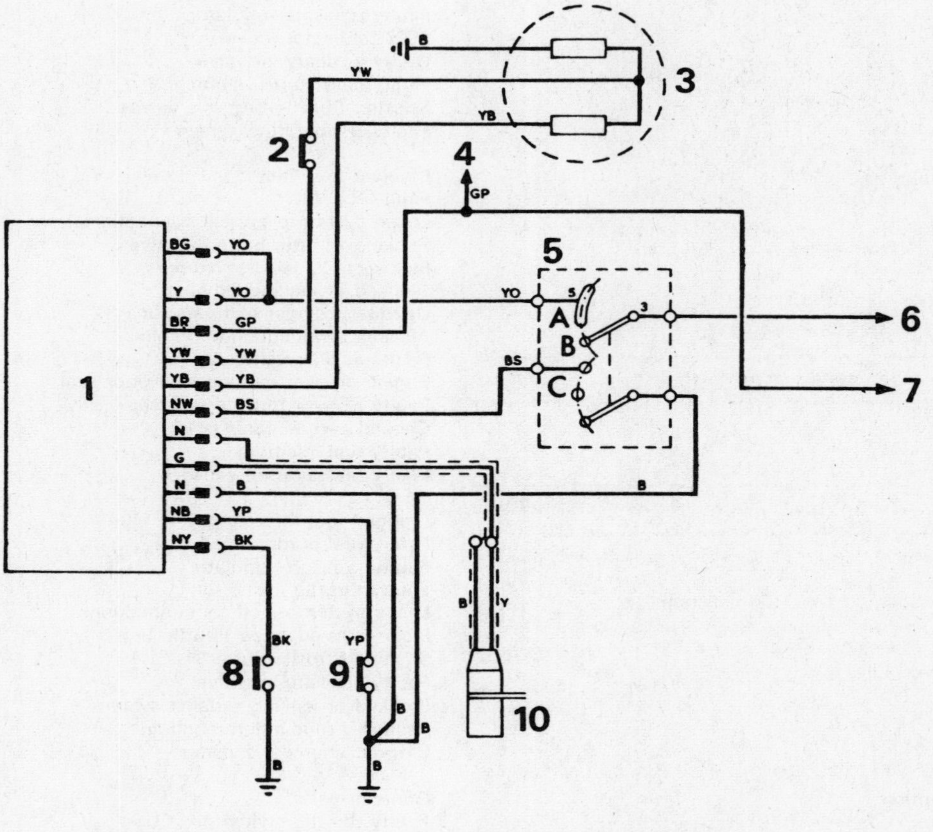


Fig. 3.87 Cruise control system wiring diagram (Sec 89)

*1 Speed control switch*
*2 Brake operated switch*
*3 Actuator*
*4 Stoplamp bulb failure unit*
*5 Control switch:*
*A On*
*B Off*
*C Resume*
*6 Fuse No 12*
*7 Stoplamp switch*
*8 Set switch*
*9 Inhibit switch*
*10 Magnetic pick-up*

pedal is operated and an inhibitor switch is incorporated to prevent the engine overrevving if the speed selector lever is moved to neutral while the cruise control system is operating.

4 The main components of the system include the following:

### Control switch

5 This controls the system engagement and disengagement. Once actuated, the switch can be moved to the 'resume' position to actuate the ECU memory when the previously set roadspeed can be regained after an interruption due to braking or temporary change of speed.

### Magnetic pick-up

6 This is located on the rear axle next to the propeller shaft flange. It consists of a magnetic signal unit which indicates to the ECU the roadspeed calculated from the rotational speed of the flange.

### Set switch

7 This switch triggers the ECU to bring the cruise control system into operation.

### Speed control unit

8 This is an electronic unit controlling the operation of the system. It operates solenoids which vary the vacuum used to open and close the throttle as necessary to maintain the preset roadspeed. 'Resume' and 'Off' modes are incorporated and the actuating vacuum is destroyed immediately the brake pedal is touched causing the throttle to close. The control unit also includes a circuit to prevent actuation of the system below 20 mph (32 kph).

## 90 Fault diagnosis – fuel injection system

| Symptom | Reason(s) |
|---|---|
| Engine will not start when warm | Fuel tank(s) empty<br>Clogged fuel filter<br>Faulty fuel pump<br>Faulty pressure regulator<br>ECU connector loose<br>Faulty auxiliary air valve<br>Faulty cold start system<br>Sticking throttle butterfly valves<br>Faulty temperature sensor |
| Rough idle (cold engine) | Clogged fuel filter<br>Faulty fuel filter<br>Loose system electrical connections<br>Sticking throttle butterfly valves<br>Incorrect CO level (mixture)<br>Blocked or leaking exhaust<br>Unequal cylinder compressions<br>Air leak at induction manifold<br>Faulty auxiliary air valve<br>Engine oil filler cap loose or poor seal<br>Faulty ECU or throttle switch<br>Choked carbon canister<br>Faulty fuel injectors<br>Faulty temperature sensors |
| Flat spot (hesitation) | Clogged fuel filter<br>Faulty fuel pump<br>Faulty pressure regulator<br>Faulty throttle switch or ECU<br>Loose system electrical connections<br>Incorrectly adjusted throttle butterfly<br>Sticking throttle butterfly<br>Faulty auxiliary air valve<br>Blocked or leaking exhaust system<br>Air leak at induction manifold<br>Blocked charcoal canister |
| Excessive fuel consumption | General leaks<br>Faulty throttle switch or ECU<br>Faulty cold start system<br>Air leak at induction manifold<br>Blocked exhaust system<br>Engine oil filler cap loose or poor seal<br>Charcoal canister blocked<br>Faulty fuel injectors or pressure sensor<br>Faulty temperature sensors |
| High idle speed and lack of engine braking | Air leak in induction manifold<br>Sticking throttle butterfly<br>Faulty auxiliary air valve<br>Incorrect CO level (mixture)<br>Leaks around throttle butterfly spindle<br>Faulty overrun valve |

| Symptom | Reason(s) |
|---|---|
| Engine stalls at idling speed | Leaks in fuel system<br>Clogged fuel filter<br>Faulty pressure regulator<br>Faulty fuel pump<br>Loose electrical connections<br>Faulty temperature sensors<br>Faulty cold start system<br>Clogged air cleaner element<br>Sticking throttle butterfly<br>Blocked or leaking exhaust<br>Air leak in induction manifold<br>Incorrect CO lever (mixture)<br>Engine oil filler cap loose or poor seal<br>Faulty ECU<br>Charcoal canister blocked |
| Running on or pre-ignition (pinking) | Incorrect fuel grade<br>Blocked hoses on crankcase or fuel vent systems<br>Leaking cylinder head gasket<br>Incorrect idle speed<br>Engine overheating due to cooling system fault<br>Over-advanced ignition |
| Backfire in exhaust | Fuel starvation due to faulty fuel pump, pressure regulator or blocked fuel filter<br>Loose electrical connections<br>Blocked air cleaner element<br>Blocked or leaking exhaust<br>Air leak in induction manifold<br>Loose engine oil filler cap or poor seal<br>Faulty diverter valve |

## 91 Fault diagnosis – fuel injection emission control system

| Symptom | Reason(s) |
|---|---|
| Fault in air injection system | Slack pump drivebelt<br>Perforated or loose connecting hoses<br>Choked air pump filter element |
| Fault in EGR system | Choked inlet drilling or restrictor |
| High CO content in exhaust gas | Faulty air temperature control in air cleaner<br>Choked engine breather filter<br>Faulty system switch or valve (refer to testing procedure in text) |

# Chapter 4 Ignition system

*For modifications, and information applicable to later models, see Supplement at end of manual*

**Contents**



**Specifications**

## Ignition system type

| | |
|---|---|
| Ignition system type | Lucas OPUS contactless electronic |

## Distributor

| | |
|---|---|
| Make and type | Lucas OPUS 36DE12 |
| Rotor rotation (viewed from above) | Anti-clockwise |
| Pick-up module to timing rotor gap | 0.020 to 0.022 in (0.50 to 0.55 mm) |
| Firing order | 1A-6B-5A-2B-3A-4B-6A-1B-2A-5B-4A-3B |

*(A = right-hand bank, B = left-hand bank, No 1 cylinders at timing chain end)*

## Ignition timing

| | |
|---|---|
| Australia and California (vacuum pipe connected) | 4° ATDC @ 750 rpm |
| Sweden (vacuum pipe disconnected) | 0° BTDC static or up to 750 rpm |
| All others (vacuum pipe disconnected) | 10° BTDC static or up to 750 rpm |
| Centrifugal advance (vacuum pipe disconnected, crankshaft degrees and rpm) | No advance below 900rpm |
| | 22° to 26° @ 2000 rpm |
| | 29° to 33° @ 4000 rpm |
| | 34° to 38° @ 6200 rpm |
| Vacuum advance or retard (crankshaft degrees): | |
| UK models (typical) | Maximum 8° advance at 10 in (254 mm) Hg |
| | No advance below 6 in (152 mm) Hg |
| N American models (typical) | Maximum 18° retard with rising vacuum from 7 in to 10 in (178 mm to 254 mm) Hg. No retard below 1 in (25.4 mm) Hg |

## Ignition coil

| | |
|---|---|
| Make and type | Lucas 13C12 or 22C12* |
| Primary resistance @ 20°C (68°F) | 0.9 to 1.1 ohms |
| Ballast resistance | 0.9 to 1.0 ohms |

** From engine No 7P8169 special 'High Load' coil and amplifier fitted. 'High Load' coil must not be fitted with earlier amplifier*

## Spark plugs

| | |
|---|---|
| Type | Champion N9YC or equivalent |
| Electrode gap: | |
| All models (excluding N America): | |
| Up to 1977 | 0.025 in (0.64 mm) |
| 1977 on | 0.035 in (0.89 mm) |
| N America | 0.035 in (0.89 mm) |

## 1 General description and maintenance

1 An electronic ignition system is fitted to all models. The main components include the distributor, an amplifer unit, ballast resistor and ignition coil.
2 The timing rotor and pick-up module, working in conjunction with the amplifier unit, are substitutes for the mechanical contact breaker on conventional distributors.
3 The timing rotor is a nylon disc with ferrite rods embedded in its outer edge corresponding with the number of cylinders.
4 The pick-up module is really a small transformer with input and output windings.
5 The timing rotor and pick-up coil generate a signal which is fed to the amplifier unit. The amplifier unit interprets the signal and feeds it to a power transistor in the printed circuit which functions as a switch in the ignition coil primary circuit.
6 A ballast resistor unit is wired in series with the ignition coil primary winding and is also associated with a function of one transistor in the amplifier unit.
7 When the engine is stationary, the timing rotor is in such a position that none of the ferrite rods are in alignment with the core of the pick-up module. Once the ignition is switched on, a transformer in the amplifier unit becomes conductive and the coil primary circuit is completed through electrodes of the power transistor. At the same time, a pulsating ac voltage is applied by the amplifier unit to the primary windings of the pick-up module. A small residual ac voltage is produced at the pick-up secondary windings, although at this time the pick-up is magnetically balanced. This voltage at the pick-up secondary terminals is applied to the amplifier unit, but is insufficient to affect the transistor circuits which control the switching off of the power transistor in the output stage of the amplifier unit.
8 Once the engine is cranked, one of the ferrite rods in the rotor which is in close proximity with the ferrite core of the pick-up module creates magnetic unbalance in the module core, so increasing the voltage at the module output terminals.
9 This voltage is then applied to the amplifier unit where it is rectified. The resulting direct current operates the transistor circuits which control the switching off of the power transistor in the output stage.
10 With the power transistor switched off, its electrodes no longer conduct and the ignition coil primary winding is disconnected. This causes a collapse of the primary winding magnetic field through the secondary windings of the ignition coil and as a result, high tension (HT) voltage is supplied at the HT terminal on the ignition coil.
11 On cars equipped with a fuel injection system, the distributor incorporates a trigger unit (refer to Chapter 3, Part B).
12 On cars equipped with a full emission control system, an additional ignition retard facility is built into the system (refer to Chapter 3, Section 21).
13 Routine maintenance has been virtually eliminated with this type of ignition system which does not have the conventional mechanical contact breaker. However, all connections should be checked, as should the ignition timing, at the intervals recommended in Routine Maintenance.

## 2 Distributor cap – removal and refitting

1 Check that the leads to the sparking plugs have a numbered sleeve on each of them. (A) denotes a lead running to the right-hand cylinder bank and (B) a lead to the left-hand cylinder bank (when viewed from the rear of the car).
2 Disconnect the leads from the spark plugs.
3 Disconnect the HT lead from the ignition coil.
4 Unscrew the three captive screws which hold the distributor cap and remove it.
5 With the cap removed, wipe the inside with a clean rag and check that the centre carbon brush is in good condition and moves freely on its spring.
6 Refit by reversing the removal operations.

## 3 Rotor arm and timing rotor – removal and refitting

1 Detach the distributor cap as described in the preceding Section and lay it to one side.
2 Pull off the rotor arm (photo). Take care not to damage the reed switch capsule or glass cover of the trigger unit.
3 On fuel injection models, withdraw the trigger unit (photo).
4 Extract the circlip and wave washer and withdraw the timing rotor (photo).
5 Refitting is a reversal of removal, but apply two or three drops of engine oil to the pad on top of the distributor shaft before pushing on the rotor arm. Make sure that the rotor arm is pressed fully home into its keyway.

## 4 Pick-up module – removal and refitting

1 Carry out the operations described in paragraphs 1 to 4 of the preceding Section.
2 Extract the two screws which hold the pick-up module to the pick-up arm.
3 Prise the cable grommet inwards out of its hole in the distributor body. Feed the cable through the hole and then remove the pick-up module.
4 To refit, pass the cable through the hole in the distributor body and fit the grommet.

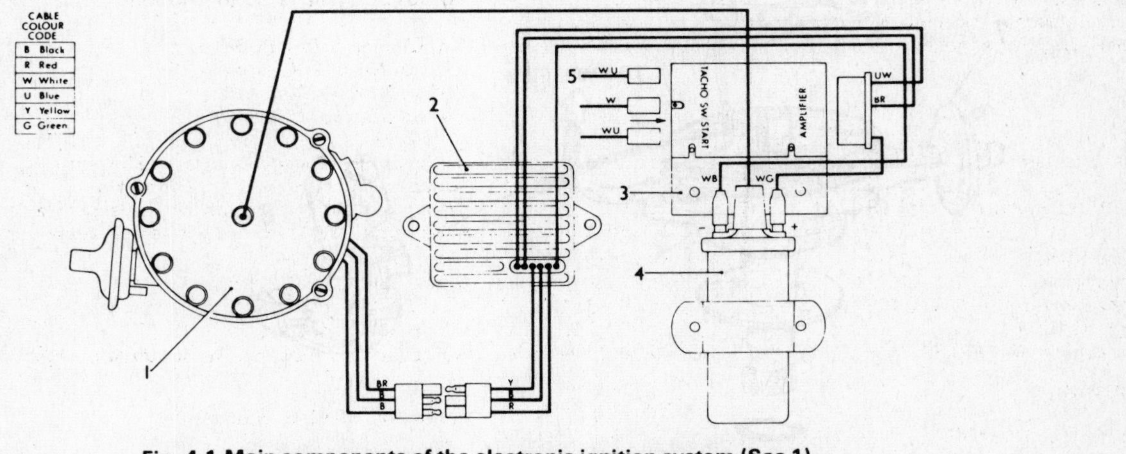


**Fig. 4.1 Main components of the electronic ignition system (Sec 1)**

*1 Distributor*
*2 Amplifier unit*
*3 Ballast resistor*
*4 Ignition coil*
*5 Lead to tachometer*

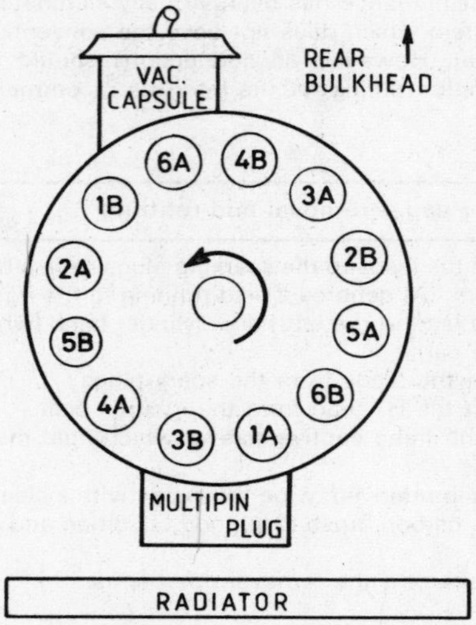


**Fig. 4.2 Distributor cap spark plug HT lead connections (Sec 2)**

*A = right-hand cylinder bank*
*B = left-hand cylinder bank*
*Spark plugs numbered from front of engine*

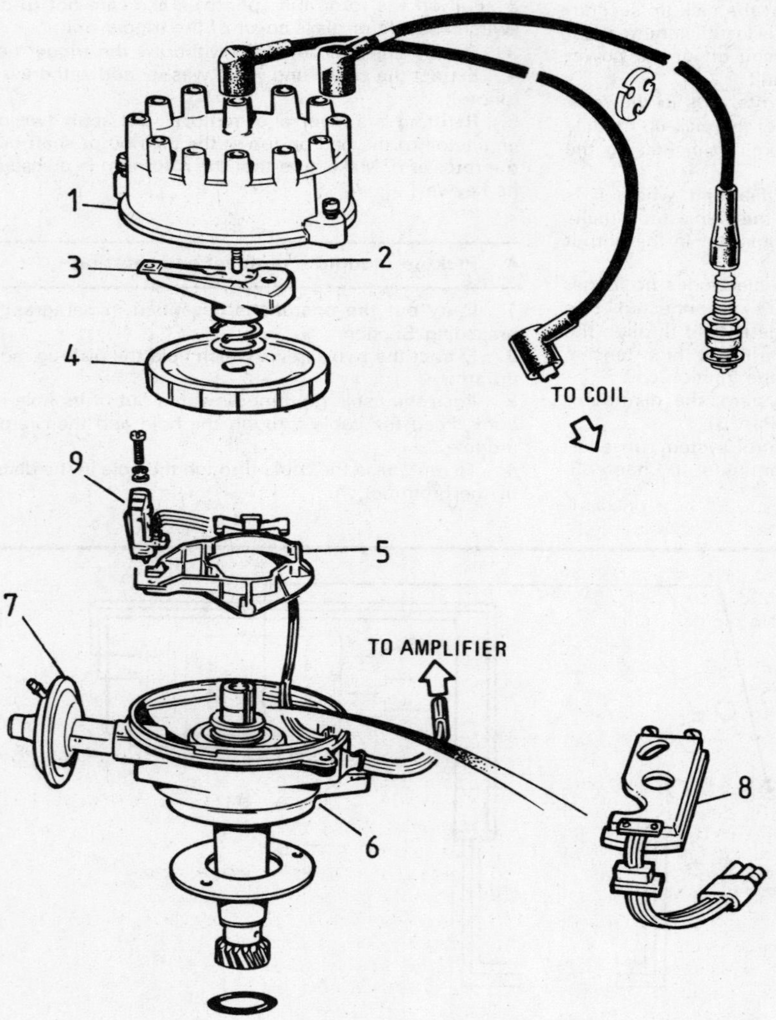


**Fig. 4.3 Main components of the distributor (Sec 3)**

*1 Cap*
*2 Carbon brush*
*3 Rotor arm*
*4 Electronic timing rotor*
*5 Pick-up arm*
*6 Distributor body*
*7 Vacuum unit*
*8 Trigger unit*
*9 Pick-up module*

5 The pick-up module should be fitted to the pick-up arm loosely with the core towards the distributor shaft.
6 Fit the electronic timing rotor, wave washer and circlip.
7 The gap between the pick-up module core faces and the edge of the electronic timing rotor must now be set. Use feeler blades to do this and when the gap is within the specified limits, tighten the module securing screws.
8 Fit the rotor arm and distributor cap.

## 5 Distributor – removal and refitting

1 Detach the distributor cover and lay it to one side.
2 Rotate the crankshaft until No 1 cylinder mark on the electronic timing rotor is in alignment with the mark on the pick-up module. The 'A' and 10° BTDC crankshaft timing marks should now be in alignment.
3 Disconnect the wiring to the distributor at the multi-pin plug.
4 Disconnect the vacuum pipe from the distributor.
5 Using an Allen key, insert it through the slots in the distributor electronic timing rotor and release the socket-headed screws. The distributor will have to be lifted at the same time as the screws are turned in order to fully release them (photo).
6 As soon as the screws are free, lift the distributor directly upward from the engine without restricting the rotation of the timing rotor with the fingers (photo).
7 Observe the timing mark on the periphery of the timing rotor and mark its position in relation to the distributor body. This work assumes that the timing rotor has not been moved from its 'withdrawn' setting.
8 Provided the position of the crankshaft has not been altered while the distributor has been out of the engine, then refitting can be carried out in the following way.
9 Hold the distributor over its hole in the jackshaft cover plate with the peripheral mark on the timing rotor in alignment with the distributor body mark made at removal. The distributor vacuum unit must be towards the rear of the engine and the timing mark on the pick-up module in alignment with the raised rib on the rear part of the jackshaft cover.
10 Without restricting the rotation of the timing rotor with the fingers, push the distributor directly downward, at the same time screwing in the three socket-headed screws evenly, so drawing the distributor gear into mesh with the one on the jackshaft. As the gears mesh, the timing rotor will turn (approximately 15°) and its peripheral mark will align with the one on the pick-up module.
11 If the crankshaft has been turned while the distributor has been out of the car, then re-position it by turning it until No 1 piston at the front end of the right-hand cylinder bank is rising on its compression stroke (verified by removing the spark plug and holding the finger over the hole), then continue to turn until the 'A' mark on the crankshaft damper is aligned with the 10° BTDC mark on the timing scale. Refit the distributor as previously described.
12 If a new distributor is being installed, or if the relative position of the mark on the timing rotor to the distributor body was not marked at time of removal, use the following method to fit the distributor. Set the crankshaft as previously described.
13 Remove the rotor arm. Unscrew the four nylon screws and withdraw the trigger unit (where fitted).
14 Extract the circlip and wave washer and remove the timing rotor.
15 Unscrew and remove the three spring-loaded screws and then withdraw the micro housing.
16 Hold the distributor body over its hole in the jackshaft coverplate so that the vernier adjuster projection on the body is parallel with the rib on the jackshaft cover on its forward section and the pick-up module is in alignment with the raised rib on the rearward section of the jackshaft cover plate. Temporarily push the timing rotor onto its shaft.
17 Turn the distributor timing rotor until the peripheral mark is 15° out of alignment with the mark on the pick-up module. Insert the distributor into its hole and as the gears mesh, the timing rotor will rotate to bring its mark into alignment with the one on the pick-up module. Insert and tighten the socket screws. Refit the micro housing but do not overtighten the spring-loaded screws (photos).
18 Refit the remaining components.
19 After installation of the distributor, always check the ignition timing as described in Section 7.

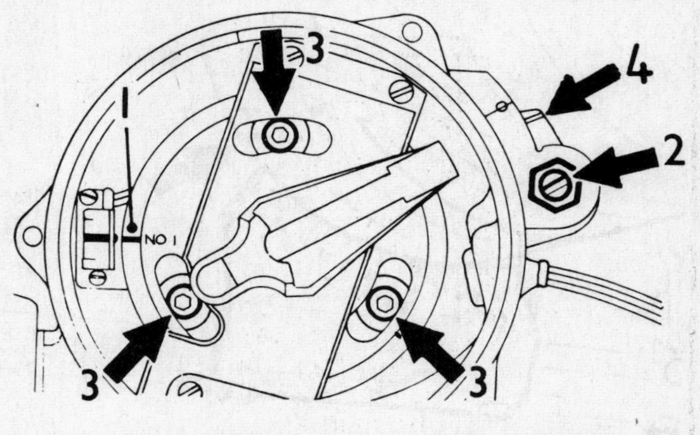


**Fig. 4.4 Distributor securing screws (3) arrowed (Sec 5)**

*1 Pick-up to timing rotor alignment marks*
*2 Vernier adjuster*
*4 Vernier scale*

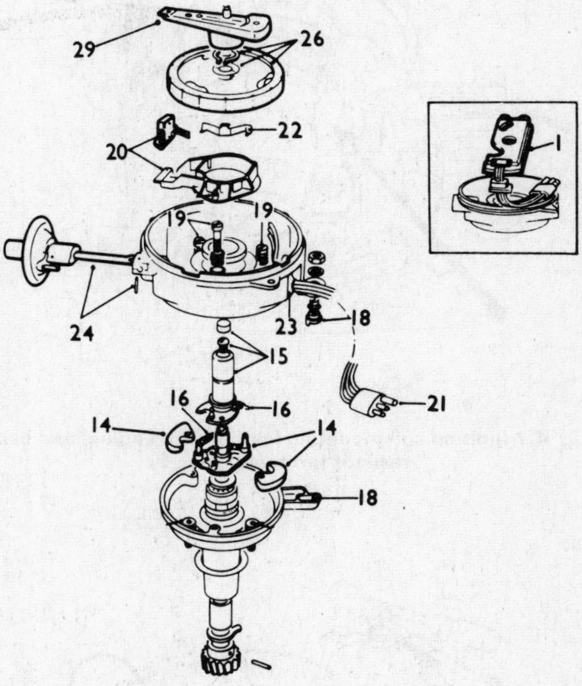


**Fig. 4.5 Exploded view of distributor (Sec 6)**

*1 Trigger unit located above electronic timing rotor (fuel injection models)*
*14 Counterweight*
*15 Shaft, screw and felt lubrication pad*
*16 Counterweight retaining springs*
*18 Micro housing and eccentric peg*
*19 Securing screws*
*20 Pick-up module and arm*
*21 Harness multi-pin plug*
*22 Bearing spring*
*23 Cable grommet*
*24 Vacuum unit and roll pin*
*26 Electronic timing rotor, wave washer and circlip*
*29 Rotor arm*

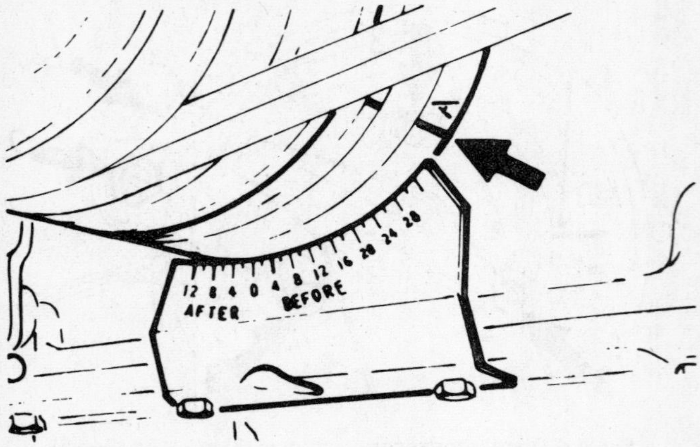


Fig. 4.6 Ignition timing scale and (arrowed) crankshaft timing mark (Sec 7)

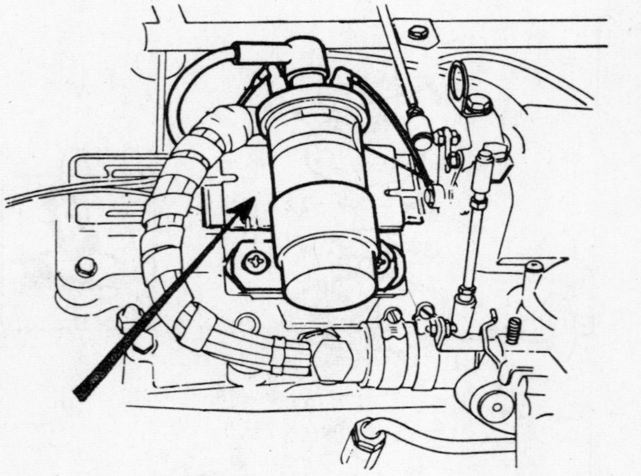

Fig. 4.7 Ignition coil mounting (carburettor engine) and ballast resistor (arrowed) (Sec 9)

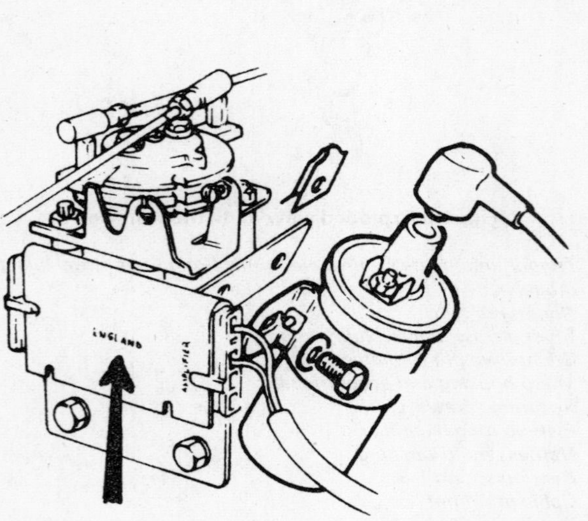

Fig. 4.8 Ignition coil mounting (fuel injection engine) and ballast resistor (arrowed) (Sec 10)

## 6 Distributor – overhaul

1 With the distributor removed from the car as previously described, clean away external dirt.
2 Remove the rotor arm.
3 On fuel injection models, remove the trigger unit.
4 Remove the electronic timing rotor.
5 Lift the vacuum operating rod from its peg on the pick-up arm (photo).
6 Prise the wiring grommet from the distributor body.
7 Remove the pick-up arm bearing spring, then slide the pick-up arm sideways to disengage it from its bearing. Lift the arm from the micro housing, drawing the wiring through the hole in the distributor body.
8 Detach the pick-up module.
9 Use a suitable punch to drive out the roll pin which secures the vacuum unit in the micro housing. Withdraw the vacuum unit.
10 Extract the three spring-loaded screws and lift the micro housing from the distributor body.
11 Prise the felt lubricating pad from the top of the distributor shaft and release the screw which is exposed.
12 Release the control springs from their fixing posts.
13 Lift the rotor carrier shaft from the distributor shaft and retrieve the centrifugal advance weights.
14 Inspect all components for wear. If the shaft or distributor body bushes are worn, a complete new distributor must be fitted.
15 Reassembly is a reversal of dismantling. Apply grease to the rotor carrier pivot posts before assembling the weights and smear the advance mechanism generally with grease.
16 When fitting the micro housing, make sure that the adjustment eccentric peg engages in its slot. Make sure also that the micro housing screws are really tight.
17 Adjust the pick-up module core gap as described in Section 4.

## 7 Ignition timing

1 Remove the distributor cap and rotor.
2 Rotate the crankshaft until the No 1 cylinder timing mark on the electronic timing rotor is about 0.25 in (6 mm) from the centre of the pick-up module housing (approaching in an anti-clockwise direction).
3 Slowly turn the crankshaft damper bolt until the timing mark on the damper is in alignment with the specified static mark on the timing scale (photo).
4 Release the adjuster screw locknut and turn the screw until the timing mark on the rotor is exactly opposite the centre of the pick-up module housing (photo). If there is insufficient adjustment the distributor must be repositioned after loosening the retaining screws as described in paragraph 7.
5 Tighten the vernier adjuster screw locknut and refit the distributor cap and rotor.
6 With the engine now started and brought to normal operating temperature, the ignition timing should be checked using a stroboscope connected in accordance with the maker's instructions.
7 Disconr ect the vacuum pipe from the distributor vacuum unit if necessary – see Specifications and have the idling speed set to between 600 and 750 rpm on XJS models, 500 and 600 rpm on XJ12 and Double Six models. When the light is pointed at the specified timing scale/damper marks, they should appear stationary and in alignment. If they are not in alignment, then the distributor will have to be turned one way or the other to correct the timing by bringing them into alignment. This is achieved by using the vernier adjuster screw. If the timing is so badly out that the vernier does not provide sufficient adjustment, then the distributor cap will have to be removed and the socket-headed distributor screws released by pressing an Allen key through the slots in the timing rotor. Where this is necessary, make sure that with the ignition timing correctly set, the vernier adjuster is left in its central position. This will provide more scope for adjustment by means of the vernier on future occasions. Retighten the distributor securing screws.
8 Reconnect the distributor vacuum pipe if it was disconnected.
9 Readjust the idling speed where necessary (see Chapter 3).

## 8 Amplifier unit – removal and refitting

1 Disconnect the battery.

3.2 Distributor rotor arm (1), fuel injection trigger unit (2) and timing rotor (3)

3.3 Extracting a trigger unit securing screw

3.4 Timing rotor showing circlip

5.5 Releasing the distributor securing screws

5.6 Distributor removed, showing securing screws

5.17A Distributor body and securing screws

5.17B Micro housing spring loaded screws

6.5 Vacuum unit operating rod

7.3 Ignition timing marks set to 10° BTDC

7.4 Distributor vernier adjuster screw

10.2 Ignition coil is at the rear of the throttle pedestal. Ballast resistor is arrowed

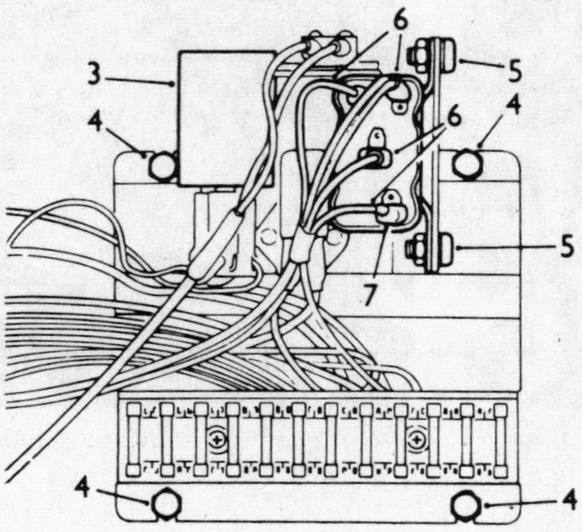


Fig. 4.9 Ignition protection relay (XJ12, Double Six) (Sec 11)

*3 Flasher unit*
*4 Fuse block mounting screws*
*5 Relay mounting bolts to bracket*
*6 Connecting leads*
*7 Connecting leads*

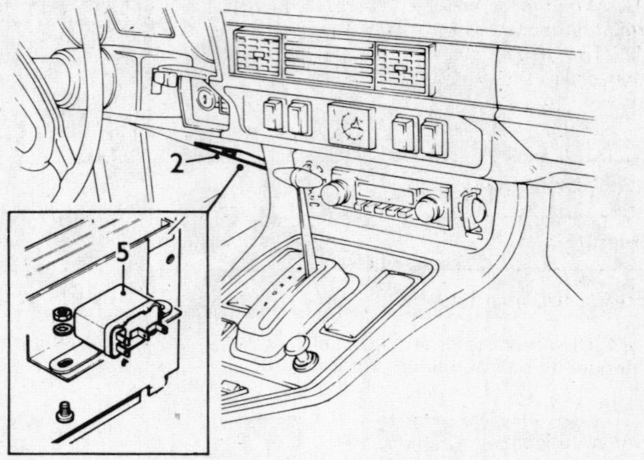


Fig. 4.10 Ignition/starter controlled relay (XJS) (Sec 12)

*2 Cover to fuse block*
*5 Relay*

2 Disconnect the wiring plug from the ballast resistor.
3 Disconnect the plug from the distributor/amplifier line.
4 Unscrew and remove the amplifier mounting screws and lift the unit from the top surface of the jackshaft cover plate on the engine.
5 It should be noted that commencing with engine number 7P8169, a revised type of coil and amplifier were fitted. If one component is being renewed, a late type amplifier is compatible with an early type coil, but if a new coil is being fitted then an old type amplifier will have to be renewed as well.
6 A fitting kit will be required for the later type amplifier which is mounted at 180° to the earlier type.
7 These later type components are identified by a label marked 'High Load'.

## 9 Ignition coil (carburettor engines) – removal and refitting

1 Disconnect the battery and the leads from the coil.
2 Unscrew and remove the two setscrews and lift the coil from its mounting bracket. Retrieve the ballast resistor distance pieces.
3 If a new coil is being fitted, refer to Section 8, paragraphs 5 to 7.
4 The ballast resistor can be removed from its location adjacent to the coil after extracting the mounting screws and disconnecting the wiring plugs.
5 Refitting is a reversal of removal.

## 10 Ignition coil (fuel injection engines) – removal and refitting

1 Disconnect the battery and the leads from the coil.
2 Unbolt the coil from the throttle pedestal (photo).
3 If the ballast resistor is to be removed from its location at the side of the coil, disconnect the electrical plugs from it, also the No 5 fuel injector lead for better access.
4 Disconnect the throttle rod at the bellcrank on the induction manifold and swing it to one side.
5 Extract the mounting screws and remove the resistor.
6 Refitting is a reversal of removal.

## 11 Ignition protection relay (XJ12, Double Six) – removal and refitting

1 Disconnect the battery and remove the under scuttle casing from the driver's side.
2 Remove the direction indicator/hazard warning flasher unit from the connector block.
3 Unscrew the four fuse box mounting nuts and ease the box down as far as it will go.
4 Unbolt the ignition protection relay from the mounting bracket, identify the cables and disconnect them.
5 Refitting is a reversal of removal.

## 12 Ignition/starter controlled relay (XJS) – removal and refitting

1 Disconnect the battery and remove the access cover from the fuse block on the driver's side under scuttle casing (see Chapter 12).
2 Remove the relay from its bracket above the fuse block, identify the leads and disconnect them.
3 Refitting is a reversal of removal.

## 13 Spark plugs and leads

1 The correct functioning of the spark plugs is vital for the correct running and efficiency of the engine. The plugs fitted as standard are listed on the Specifications page.
2 At intervals of 6000 miles (9600 km) the plugs should be removed, examined and cleaned. If worn excessively, renew the plugs at 12 000 miles (19 300 km). The condition of the spark plug will also tell much about the overall condition of the engine.
3 If the insulator nose of the spark plug is clean and white, with no deposits, this is indicative of a weak mixture, or too hot a plug. (A hot plug transfers heat away from the electrode slowly – a cold plug transfers it away quickly).
4 If the top and insulator nose is covered with hard black looking deposits, then this is indicative that the mixture is too rich. Should the plug be black and oily, then it is likely that the engine is fairly worn, as well as the mixture being too rich.
5 If the insulator nose is covered with light tan to greyish brown deposits, then the mixture is correct and it is likely that the engine is in good condition.
6 If there are any traces of long brown tapering stains on the outside of the white portion of the plug, then the plug will have to be renewed, as this shows that there is a faulty joint between the plug body and the insulator, and compression is being allowed to leak away.
7 Plugs should be cleaned by a sand blasting machine, which will free them from carbon more thoroughly than cleaning by hand. The machine will also test the condition of the plugs under compression. Any plug that fails to spark at the recommended pressure should be renewed.
8 The spark plug gap is of considerable importance, as, if it is too large or too small the size of the spark and its efficiency will be seriously impaired. The spark plug gap is given in the Specifications.
9 To set it, measure the gap with a feeler gauge, and then bend open, or close, the outer plug electrode until the correct gap is achieved. The centre electrode should never be bent as this may crack the insulation and cause plug failure, if nothing worse.

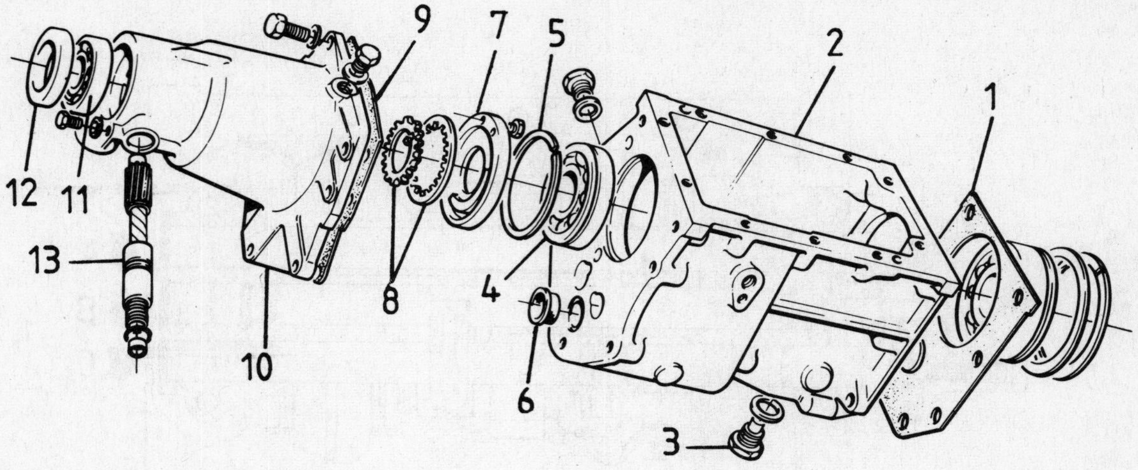


**Fig. 6.1 Gearcase and rear extension housing (Sec 3)**

1 *Gasket*
2 *Gearcase*
3 *Drain plug*
4 *Mainshaft rear bearing*
5 *Bearing circlip*
6 *Filter*
7 *Oil pump housing*
8 *Oil pump gears*
9 *Gasket*
10 *Rear extension housing*
11 *Bearing*
12 *Oil seal*
13 *Speedometer driven gear*

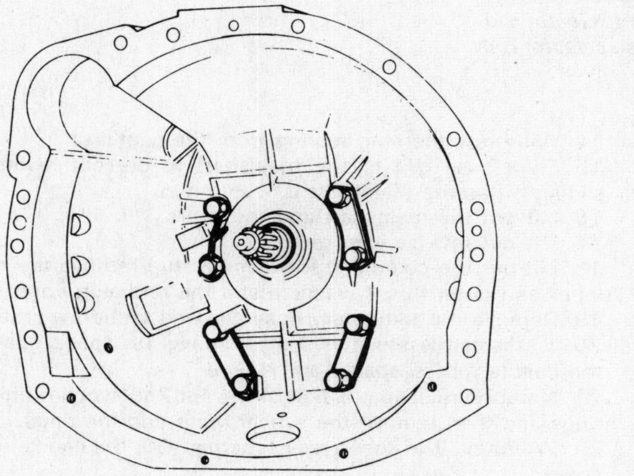

**Fig. 6.2 Setscrews and lockplate retaining clutch bellhousing to gearcase (Sec 4)**

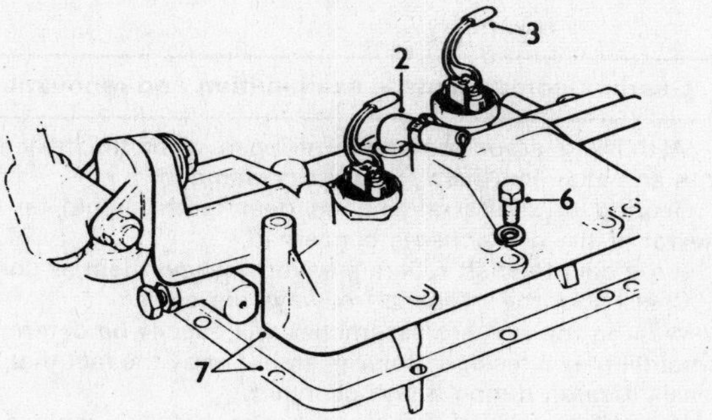


**Fig. 6.4 Gearbox top cover (Sec 5)**

2 *Breather hose*
3 *Reversing lamp switch*
6 *Securing bolt*
7 *Top cover and gasket*

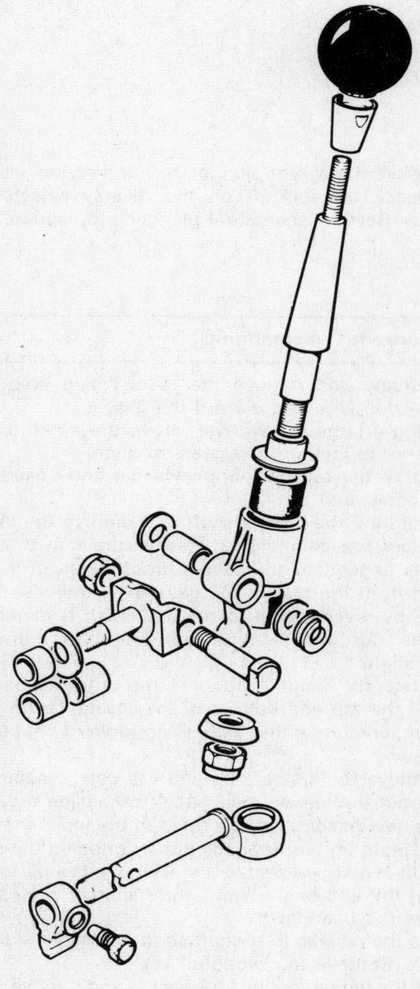

**Fig. 6.3 Gearshift lever detail (Sec 5)**

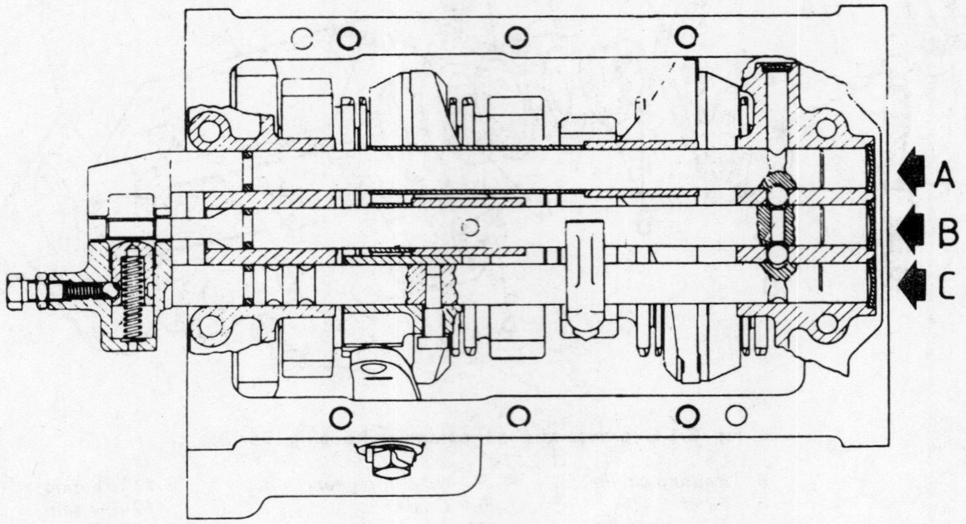


Fig. 6.5 Sectional view of selector mechanism (Sec 5)

*A 3rd/4th selector rod*
*B 1st/2nd selector rod*
*C Reverse selector rod*

and retrieve the detent plunger, ball and spring, also the interlock ball.
11 Release the locknut on the reverse selector and slacken the setscrew. Retrieve the detent plunger, stop spring, detent ball and the spring.

## 6 Geartrain – dismantling

1 Unscrew and remove the bolts which hold the adaptor plate. Remove the plate and discard the gasket.
2 Using a large screwdriver, move the synchro sleeves away from each other to lock up two gears at once.
3 Flatten the tab on the lockwasher and unscrew and remove the rear bearing nut.
4 Withdraw the countershaft and retrieve the Woodruff key. When pulling out the countershaft, make sure that the rear thrust washer which is pegged to the casing drops down in a clockwise direction (viewed from the rear of the gearbox), otherwise the washer may be trapped by reverse gear as the mainshaft is driven forward.
5 Prise out and discard the fibre plug from the front of the countershaft.
6 Rotate the input shaft until the cutaway parts of the gear are towards the top and bottom of the casing. Using two suitable levers, prise the input shaft and its bearing forward until the assembly can be withdrawn.
7 Retrieve the spacer ring and 4th gear synchro ring.
8 Extract the needle roller race from inside the input shaft.
9 If a new bearing is to be fitted to the input shaft, flatten the tab on the lockplate and remove the nut by gripping the shaft in a vice fitted with soft metal jaw protectors. Remove the oil thrower.
10 Tap the end of the input shaft sharply against a solid surface to dislodge the bearing.
11 Tap the reverse idler shaft so that it is ejected from the rear of the gearbox. Retrieve the Woodruff key.
12 Flatten the tab on the lockwasher and remove the bolt which holds reverse lever.
13 Turn the mainshaft until one of the large cutaway parts of the 3rd/4th synchro hub is in line with the countershaft gear and then tap the mainshaft forward through the rear bearing, making sure that reverse gear is kept pressed against 1st gear during the process.
14 Withdraw the rear bearing from the gearcase.
15 Fit a hose clip to the mainshaft to prevent reverse gear from sliding off as the mainshaft is withdrawn.
16 Lift out the mainshaft and the gears.
17 Lift out reverse idler gear.
18 Lift out the countergear assembly and retrieve the needle rollers, inner and outer thrust washers and the retaining rings.
19 Remove the temporary hose clip and withdraw reverse gear.
20 To dismantle the mainshaft, remove 1st speed gear and retrieve the needle rollers, spacer and sleeve.
21 Note the relative position of the 1st/2nd synchro unit to the baulk rings and then remove the synchro unit and the rings.
22 Withdraw 2nd speed gear together with the needle rollers and the spacer.
23 Flatten the tab on the lockwasher and unscrew and remove the nut which holds the 3rd/4th synchro. Note the relative position of the synchro unit to the baulk rings and remove the components including the thrust washer.
24 Withdraw 3rd speed gear, the needle rollers and the spacer.

## 7 Gearbox components – examination and renovation

1 With the gearbox completely stripped, clean the individual components and examine them for wear or damage.
2 Scoring of shafts or chipped gear teeth should be rectified by renewal of the components concerned.
3 If the countershaft rollers are worn, renew them as complete sets.
4 Check that the mainshaft oilways are clear.
5 Wear in the synchro assemblies will usually be determined before dismantling as a result of noisy gearshift or by the fact that the synchro is easily beaten during a fast gearshift.
6 It is recommended that a synchro assembly is renewed complete, but hubs and sleeves in good condition can be used again provided the springs, balls and plungers are renewed.
7 To dismantle a synchro unit, mark the relationship of hub to sleeve with quick-drying paint or a spirit marker. Cover the unit with a cloth to prevent the springs and balls flying out as the hub is pressed out of the sleeve.
8 To reassemble a synchro unit, locate the hub to the sleeve so that the longer projection on the hub is on the side opposite to the wider

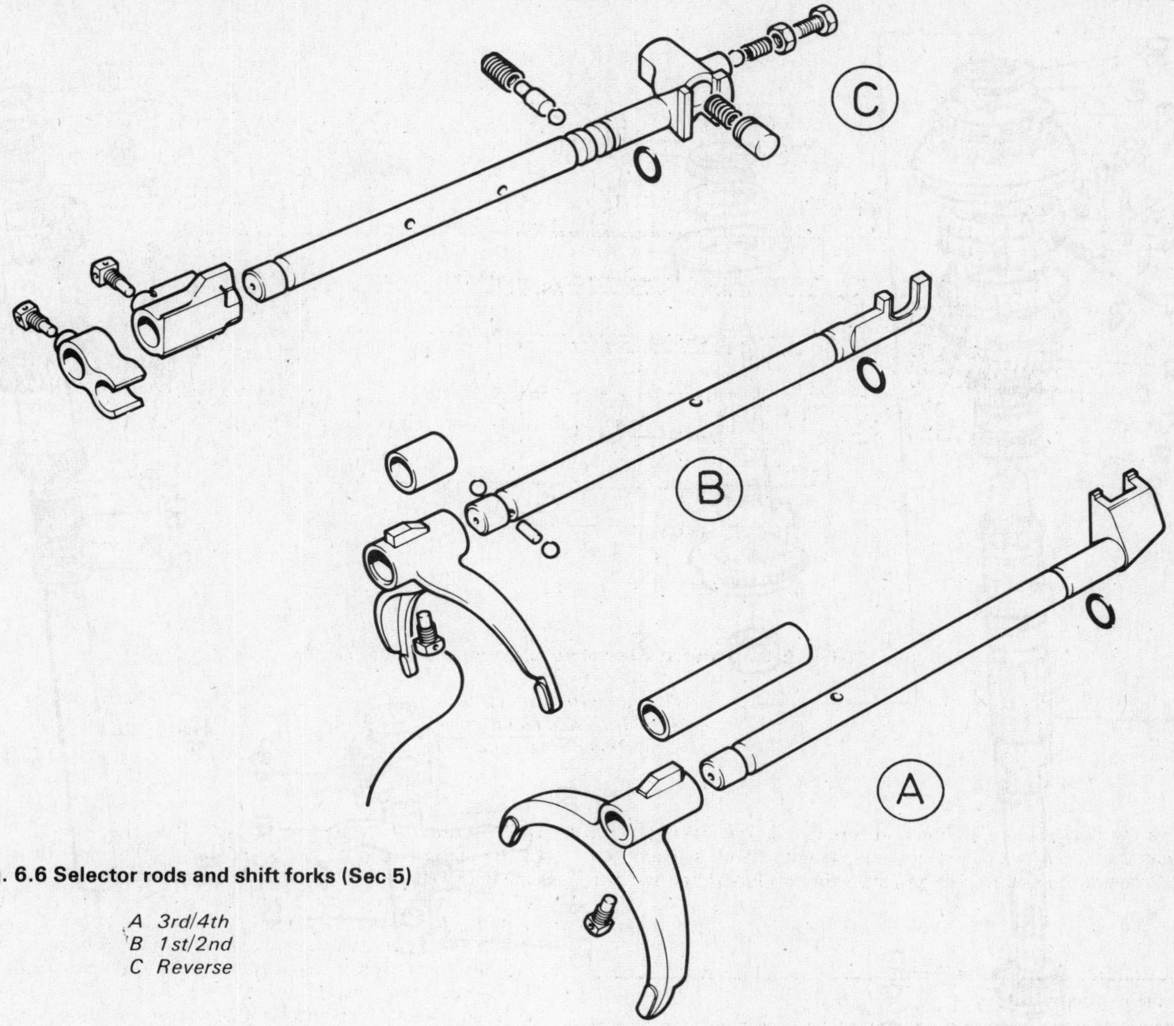


**Fig. 6.6 Selector rods and shift forks (Sec 5)**

*A 3rd/4th*
*B 1st/2nd*
*C Reverse*

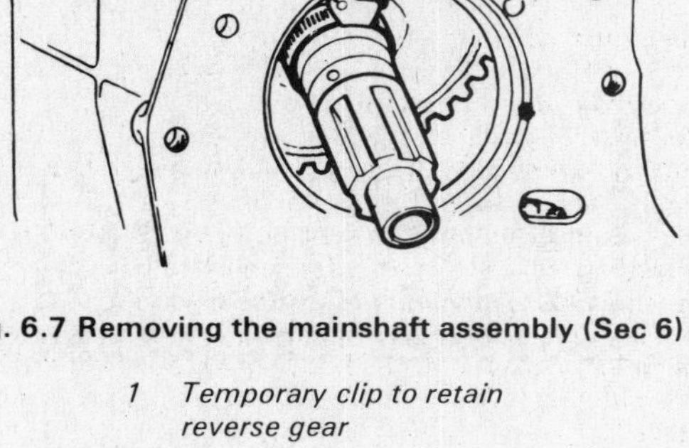

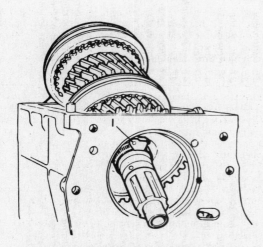

**Fig. 6.7 Removing the mainshaft assembly (Sec 6)**

*1 Temporary clip to retain reverse gear*

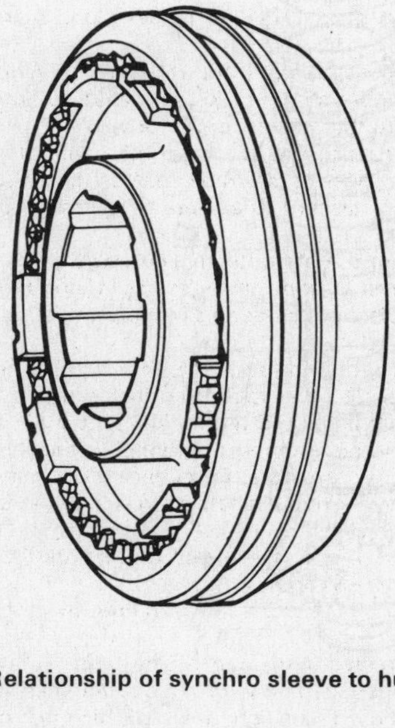

**Fig. 6.8 Relationship of synchro sleeve to hub (Sec 6)**

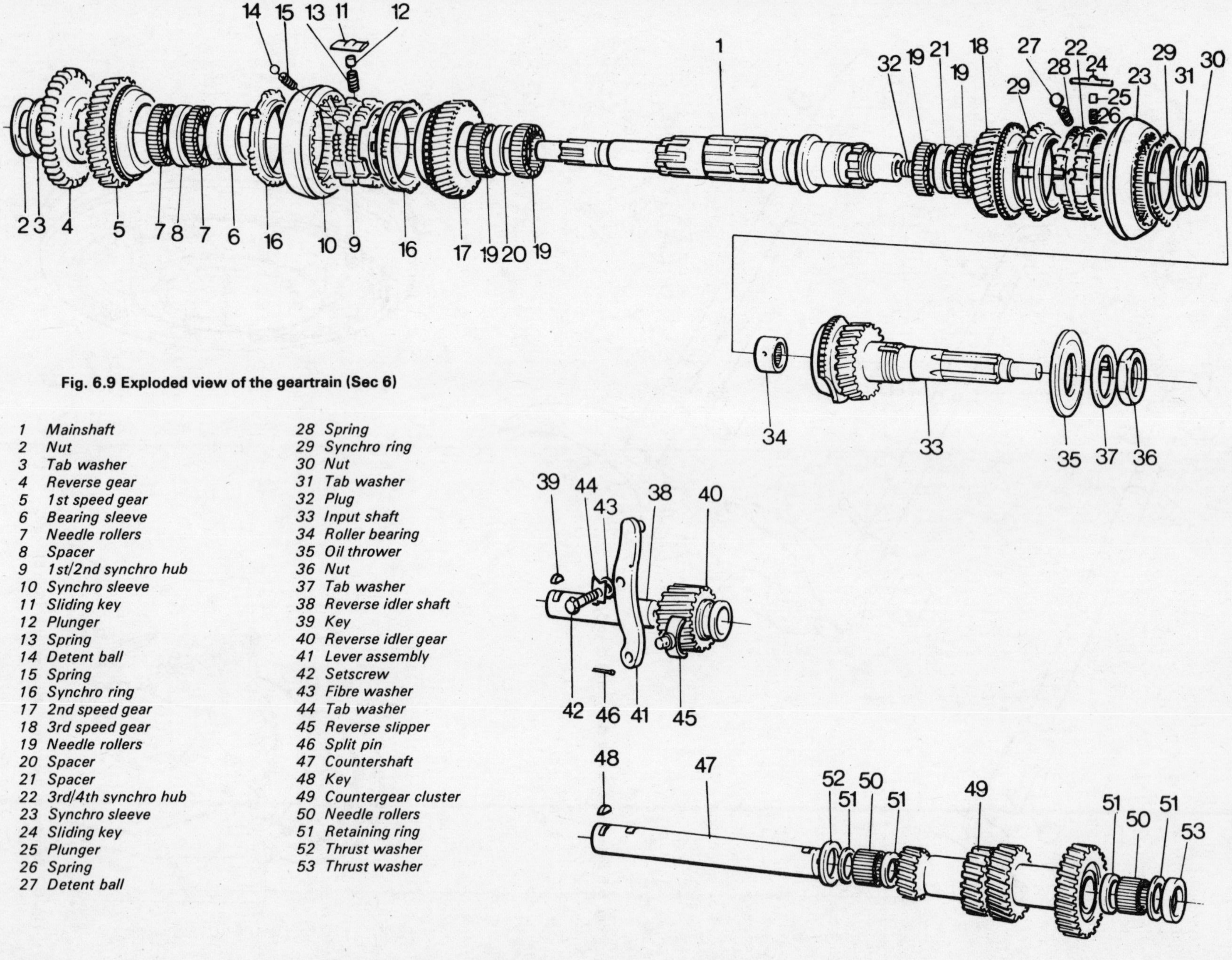

**Fig. 6.9 Exploded view of the geartrain (Sec 6)**

1 *Mainshaft*
2 *Nut*
3 *Tab washer*
4 *Reverse gear*
5 *1st speed gear*
6 *Bearing sleeve*
7 *Needle rollers*
8 *Spacer*
9 *1st/2nd synchro hub*
10 *Synchro sleeve*
11 *Sliding key*
12 *Plunger*
13 *Spring*
14 *Detent ball*
15 *Spring*
16 *Synchro ring*
17 *2nd speed gear*
18 *3rd speed gear*
19 *Needle rollers*
20 *Spacer*
21 *Spacer*
22 *3rd/4th synchro hub*
23 *Synchro sleeve*
24 *Sliding key*
25 *Plunger*
26 *Spring*
27 *Detent ball*
28 *Spring*
29 *Synchro ring*
30 *Nut*
31 *Tab washer*
32 *Plug*
33 *Input shaft*
34 *Roller bearing*
35 *Oil thrower*
36 *Nut*
37 *Tab washer*
38 *Reverse idler shaft*
39 *Key*
40 *Reverse idler gear*
41 *Lever assembly*
42 *Setscrew*
43 *Fibre washer*
44 *Tab washer*
45 *Reverse slipper*
46 *Split pin*
47 *Countershaft*
48 *Key*
49 *Countergear cluster*
50 *Needle rollers*
51 *Retaining ring*
52 *Thrust washer*
53 *Thrust washer*

chamfer on the sleeve. Check that the hub slides smoothly in the sleeve.
9 With the unit on a bench, raise the hub in the sleeve until the holes in the hub are visible above the sleeve and insert the three springs, plungers and sliding keys into the holes. These particular springs are coloured red. Make sure that the ridge on each sliding key is visible when fitted to the hub.
10 Now fit the three springs which are not colour marked and the balls in alignment with the teeth on the synchro sleeve which have three detent grooves.
11 Compress and retain the springs in the hub using a hose clip or piston ring compressor.
12 With the hub resting on the sleeve, depress it slightly and push the sliding keys down until they engage in the neutral groove of the sleeve.
13 Using a plastic-faced mallet, tap the hub down squarely until the balls can be heard and felt to engage in the neutral groove (the second click).

## 8 Gearbox reassembly

1 Make sure that the gearcase is clean, with all traces of old gasket removed.
2 Using thick grease as an adhesive, stick one needle retaining ring into the hole in the larger gear of the countergear. Fit the needle rollers and the inner thrust washer. Make sure that the peg on the washer engages in the groove in the countergear.
3 Fit the similar needle roller assembly into the hole in the rear end of the countergear.
4 Using grease, stick a new (pegged) rear thrust washer into position on its boss. Stick the front thrust washer to the front of the countergear in a similar way.
5 Carefully lower the countergear into position in the gearcase with the larger gear towards the front of the casing. A dummy countershaft should now be inserted through the casing and countergear (without disturbing the needle bearings) to retain the countergear in position.
6 Using a feeler blade, check the clearance between the countershaft rear thrust washer and the face of the countergear. The endfloat must be between 0.004 and 0.006 in (0.10 and 0.15 mm). If the endfloat is not within the specified tolerance, the thrust washer will have to be changed for an oversize one.
7 A thin rod should now be substituted for the countershaft. Insert the rod by pressing out the countershaft, always keeping the rod in contact with the end of the shaft and at the same time supporting the weight of the countergear.
8 Fit the Woodruff key to the reverse idler shaft and then fit the reverse idler gear, the lever and the reverse idler shaft to the gearcase. Do not fit the retaining bolt at this stage.
9 Fit the needle roller race into the end of the input shaft.
10 Locate the oil thrower on the input shaft so that its raised centre part will be towards the bearing.
11 Fit the snap-ring into the groove in the input shaft bearing outer track.
12 Press the bearing squarely up to the shoulder on the input shaft.
13 Fit a new lockplate and tighten the input shaft nut to the specified torque.
14 Reassemble the mainshaft by fitting 3rd speed gear, the needle rollers and the wide spacer.
15 Fit 3rd/4th synchro, the baulk rings and the thrust washer. Fit a new lockplate and screw on and tighten the nut to the specified torque.
16 Fit 2nd speed gear, the needle rollers and the narrow spacer.
17 Fit 1st/2nd synchro and the baulk rings.
18 Fit 1st speed gear, the needle rollers, spacer and sleeve.
19 Refit reverse gear and temporarily fit a hose clip to retain it.
20 Lower the assembled mainshaft down through the top of the casing and then pass the rear end of the shaft through the bearing aperture. Take off the temporary hose clip.
21 Using thick grease, stick a new gasket to the front face of the gearcase.
22 Place the baulk ring on the front face of the 3rd/4th synchro hub.
23 Insert the input shaft through the front of the gearcase so that the cutaway parts of its gear are at the highest and lowest points.
24 Using a plastic-faced mallet, tap the input shaft into position making sure that the front end of the mainshaft enters the input shaft needle bearing squarely.

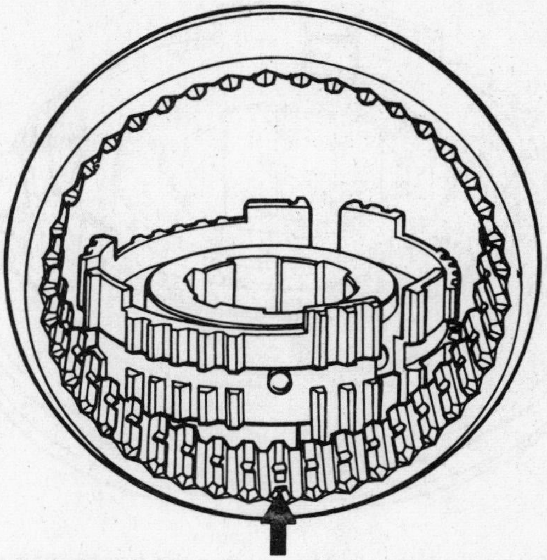

**Fig. 6.10 Synchro sleeve tooth with three grooves (arrowed) (Sec 6)**

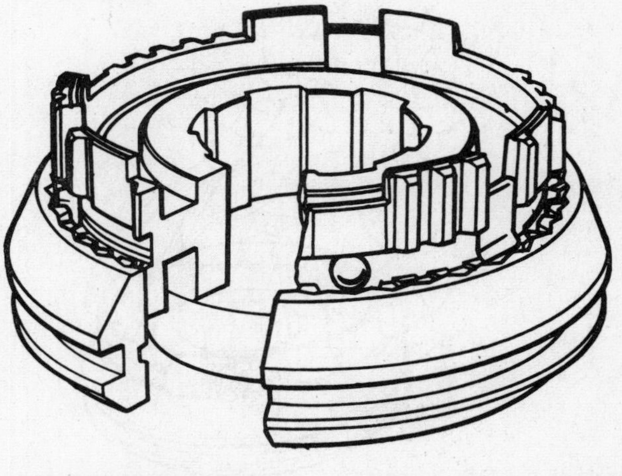

**Fig. 6.11 Setting synchro hub on sleeve ready for insertion of balls and springs (Sec 6)**

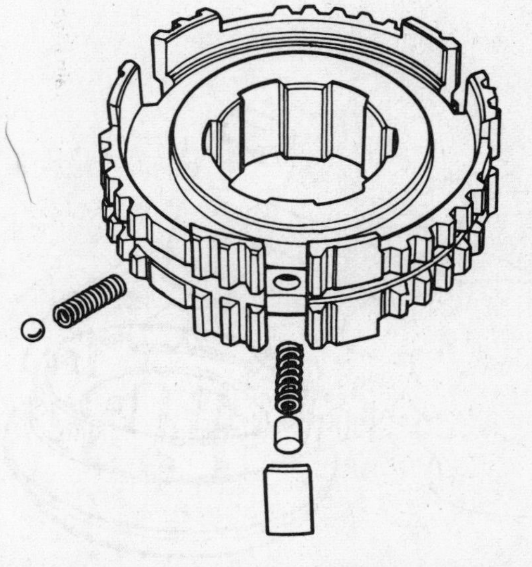

**Fig. 6.12 Synchro hub showing springs, ball, plunger and sliding key (Sec 6)**

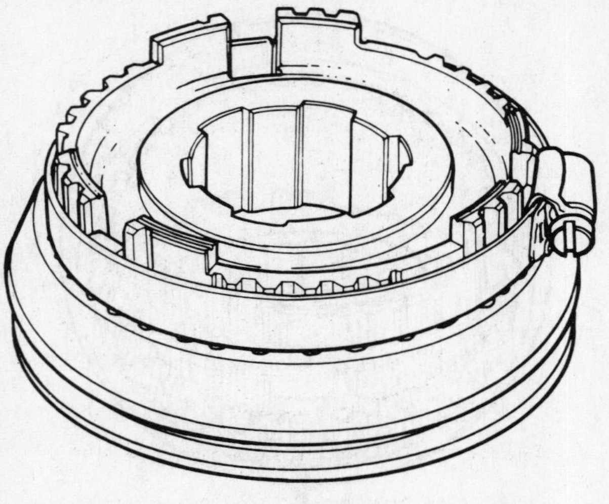

Fig. 6.13 Using a hose clip to compress the synchro coil springs (Sec 6)

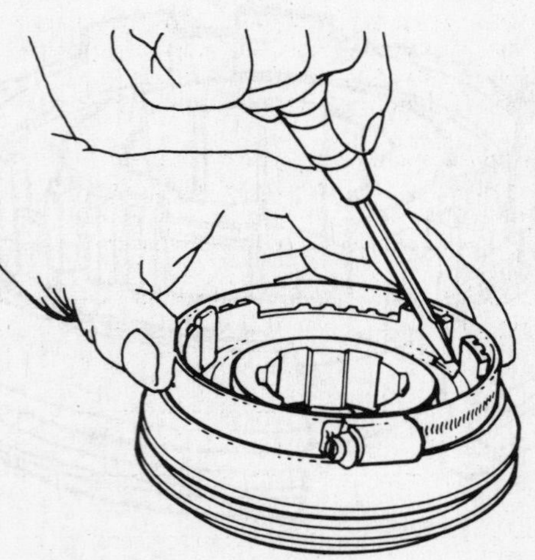

Fig. 6.14 Depressing the synchro sliding keys (Sec 6)

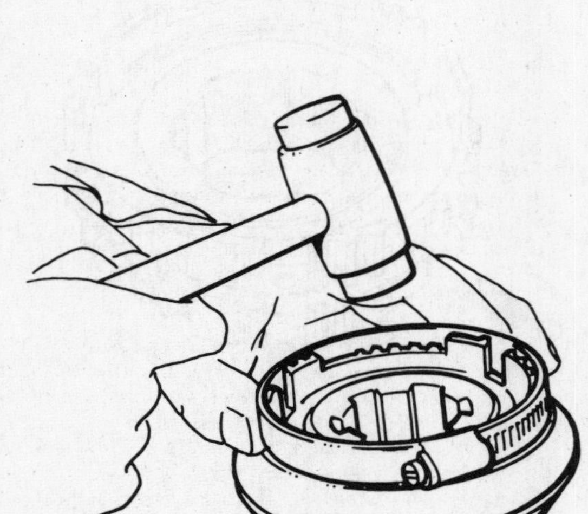

Fig. 6.15 Tapping the synchro hub fully into its sleeve (Sec 6)

25 Fit the snap-ring to the groove in the rear bearing.
26 Hold a block of hardwood against the front of the input shaft and carefully drive the mainshaft rear bearing forward onto the rear end of the mainshaft until it seats in the casing.
27 Insert the countershaft into the countergear, so displacing the thin rod. Keep the shaft and rod in end-to-end contact during this operation and slightly raise the countergear. Take care not to displace the needle roller assemblies.
28 Fit the Woodruff key to the countershaft and tap it fully home.
29 Fit a new fibre plug to the front of the countershaft.
30 Fit the reverse lever bolt, using a new lockplate.
31 Lock up two gears simultaneously by moving the synchro sleeves in opposite directions. Fit a new lockwasher and tighten the mainshaft rear bearing nut to the specified torque.
32 Refit the adaptor plate.
33 Complete the reassembly of the gearbox by refitting the top cover, the bellhousing and the rear extension as described in the following sections.

## 9 Gearbox top cover – reassembly and refitting

1 Fit the detent plunger and spring to the reverse selector rod.
2 Fit the detent ball, spring, setscrew and locknut.
3 Press the detent plunger fully home and tighten the setscrew to lock the plunger. Now slowly release the setscrew until the plunger is withdrawn far enough for the detent ball to engage in its groove. Tighten the locknut without allowing the setscrew to move.
4 Place the reverse selector rod detent spring, plunger and ball into their housing. Depress the plunger and fit the selector rod.
5 Fit the selector fork and locating arm to the reverse selector rod. Fit the retaining screws.
6 Fit the 1st/2nd selector rod into the top cover far enough to pick up the selector fork and spacer tube with the rod.
7 Position the top cover on its side, reverse selector rod at the bottom of the cover, and then push an interlock ball through the 1st/2nd selector rod hole at the front of the top cover. Manoeuvre the ball until it is against the groove in the reverse selector rod. Now push the 1st/2nd selector rod into its hole to retain the ball in its groove. Make sure that the ball is not displaced and is pushed ahead of the selector rod.
8 Fit the lockscrew to the 1st/2nd selector fork.
9 At this stage, check that if one selector rod is moved it will lock the other and that it is not possible to move the rods together at the same time.
10 Insert the interlock plunger through the 3rd/4th selector rod hole at the front of the top cover.
11 Gently manoeuvre the 1st/2nd selector rod until the plunger drops through.
12 Check that reverse and 1st/2nd selector rods are level and carefully push the 2nd interlock ball through the 3rd/4th hole to lie in the hole in the casting.
13 Pass the 3rd/4th selector rod through the hole in the top cover and fit the selector fork and spacer tube. Push the rod home to retain the ball in its groove. Fit the locking screw.
14 Check the interlock as described in paragraph 9.
15 Check the tightness of all the locking screws and fit a locking wire to them.
16 Fit a fibre washer to the gearshift lever pivot jaw pin. Locate the gearshift lever to the top cover.
17 Push the pivot pin through the bush in the top cover and then fit the second fibre washer, the plain washer, coil spring and self-locking nut.
18 Refit the top cover to the gear casing using a new gasket. Make sure that the synchro units are in the neutral mode and that the reverse idler gear is out of mesh. Check the latter by pushing the reverse lever towards the rear of the gearbox.

## 10 Clutch bellhousing – refitting

1 Refitting is a reversal of removal as described in Section 4, but observe the following points.
2 Make sure that the new oil seal is fitted with its lip towards the gearbox and then smear the lip with engine oil.
3 Tape over the input shaft splines to prevent them cutting into the

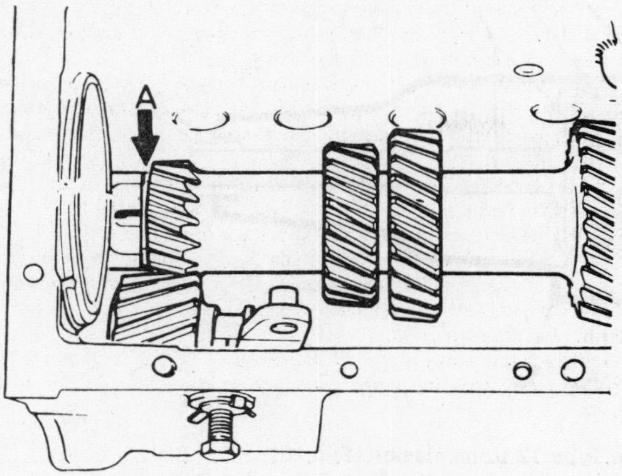


Fig. 6.16 Checking countergear endfloat (A) (Sec 8)

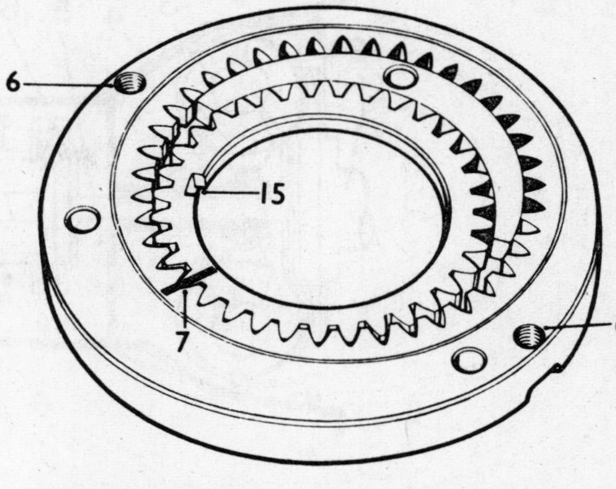


**Fig. 6.17 Oil pump drivegear assembly (Sec 11)**

*6 Tappet holes for withdrawing gear housing*
*7 Alignment marks*
*15 Notch for oil pump drive sleeve pin*

oil seal as the bellhousing is fitted.
4 Use new locking plates, tighten the setscrews to the specified torque and bend up the locktabs.

## 11 Gearbox rear extension - reassembly and refitting

1 Assemble the oil pump gears, making sure that the faces marked before dismantling are aligned.
2 Fit the oil pump housing to the gear casing using three countersunk-headed screws. Stake the screw heads.
3 Fit the oil pump drive sleeve to the oil pump gear so that the longer shoulder enters first.
4 Use a new paper gasket and fit the rear extension to the gear casing. During this operation, make sure that the oil pump drive sleeve pin engages with the gear.
5 Screw in and tighten the seven retaining setscrews.
6 Insert the spacer tube over the mainshaft through the rear end of the extension housing.
7 Tap the ball bearing race into the end of the rear extension housing.
8 Fit the speedometer drive gear to the end of the mainshaft.
9 Apply clean oil to the new oil seal and drive it squarely into the end of the extension housing.
10 Fit the speedometer driven gear assembly using the single setcrew.
11 Fit the output flange, tighten the nut to the specified torque and insert a new split pin.

## 12 Fault diagnosis – manual gearbox

| Symptom | Reason(s) |
|---|---|
| Ineffective synchromesh | Worn baulk rings or synchro hubs |
| Jumps out of one or more gears (on drive or overrun) | Weak detent springs, worn selector forks, rods or gears |
| Noisy, rough operation, whining or vibration | Worn bearings or thrust washers |
| Noisy or difficult engagement of gears | Clutch fault |

*Note: It is sometimes difficult to decide whether it is worthwhile removing and dismantling the gearbox for a fault which may be nothing more than a minor irritant. Gearboxes which howl, or where the synchromesh can be 'beaten' by a quick gearchange, may continue to perform for a long time in this state. A worn gearbox usually needs a complete rebuild to eliminate noise because the various gears, if re-aligned on new bearings, will continue to howl when different wearing surfaces are presented to each other. The decision to overhaul therefore, must be considered with regard to time and money available, relative to the degree of noise or malfunction that the driver has to suffer.*

# PART B – AUTOMATIC TRANSMISSION (BORG WARNER TYPE 12)

## 13 General description

1 The automatic transmission which is fitted as standard equipment to all models up until 1978 is the Borg Warner Model 12.
2 All forward ratios are automatically engaged in accordance with accelerator position and car speed. Overriding control is still maintained by manual selection and a kick-down facility is provided for rapid change down.
3 Servicing and overhaul operations should be restricted to those described. Due to the complexity of the transmission unit and the need for special tools it is not recommended that major overhauls are undertaken.
4 In the event of a fault developing, always diagnose the problem **before** removing the unit from the car. This fault finding can be carried out either by referring to the Fault Diagnosis Sections in this Chapter or by consulting your Jaguar/Daimler dealer.
5 Factory reconditioned units are normally available through your dealer on an exchange basis, and in the case of a major fault developing in the original unit, this method of rectification can usually show an advantage compared with overhaul charges.

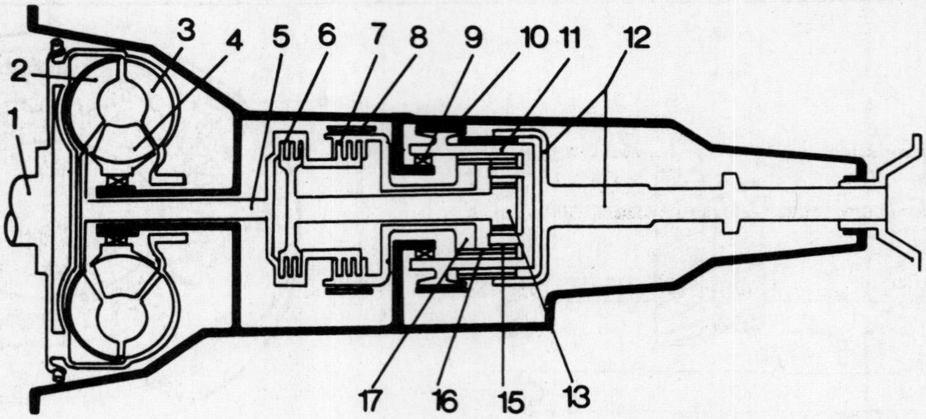


**Fig. 6.18 Diagrammatic view of Borg Warner Type 12 transmission (Sec 13)**

1 Engine crankshaft
2 Turbine
3 Impeller
4 Stator
5 Input shaft
6 Front clutch
7 Rear clutch
8 Front brake band
9 Uni-directional clutch
10 Rear brake band
11 Pinion carrier
12 Ring gear and output shaft
13 Sun gear and shaft
15 Planet pinion
16 Planet pinion
17 Reverse sun gear

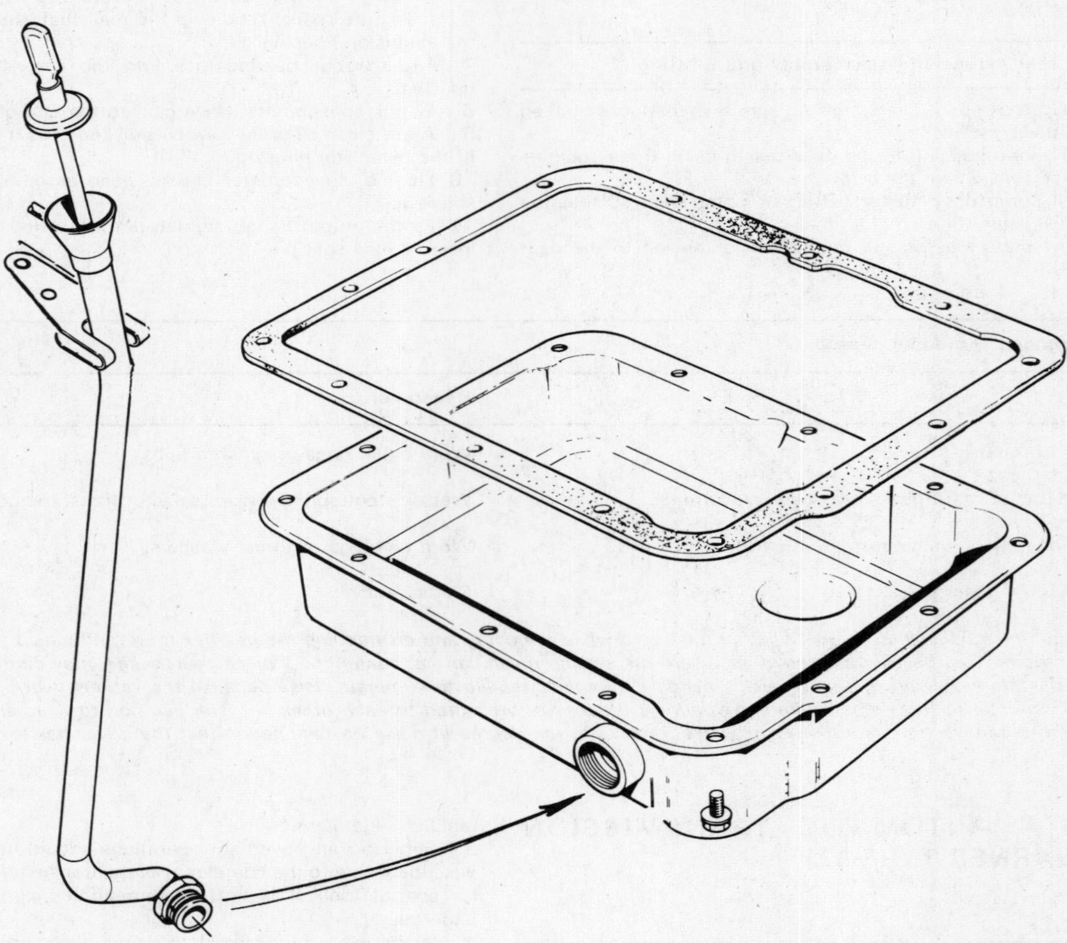

**Fig. 6.19 Oil pan and dipstick guide/filler tube (Sec 15)**

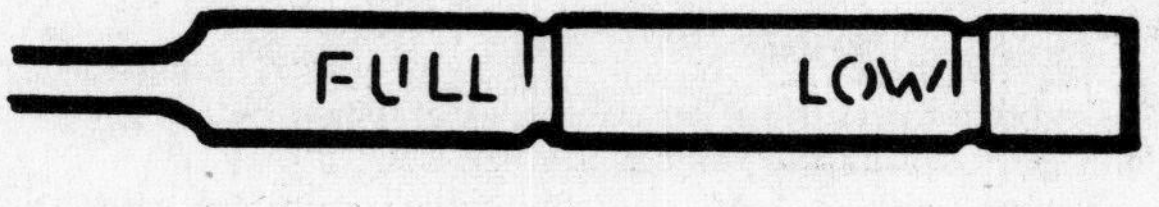


Fig. 6.20 Dipstick markings on Borg Warner transmission (Sec 14)

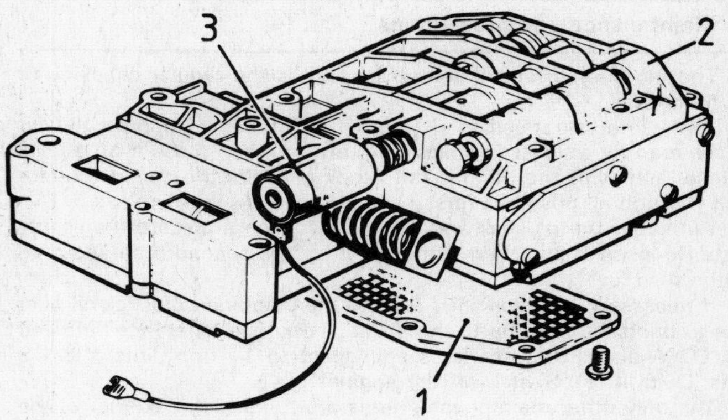


Fig. 6.21 Fluid strainer on valve block (Sec 15)

*1 Strainer*
*2 Valve block*
*3 Kickdown solenoid*

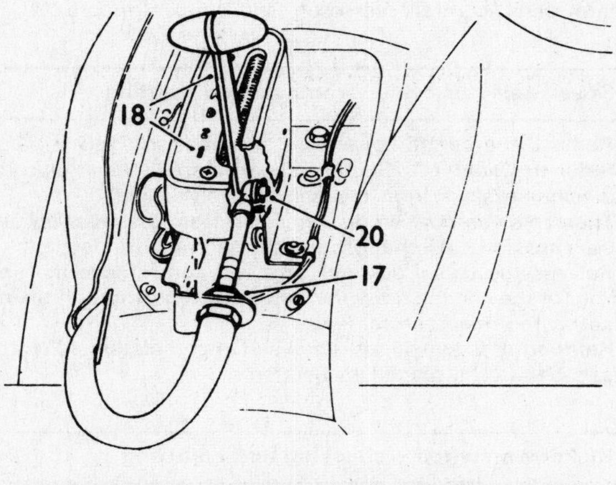


Fig. 6.22 Speed selector lever and cable (Sec 16)

*17 Cable locknuts*
*18 Indicator plate*
*20 Cable attachment (split pin)*

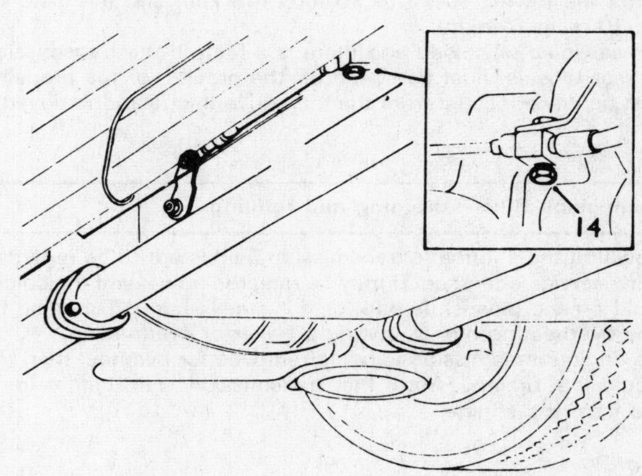


Fig. 6.23 Selector lever on transmission casing (Sec 16)

*14 Cable trunnion bolt*

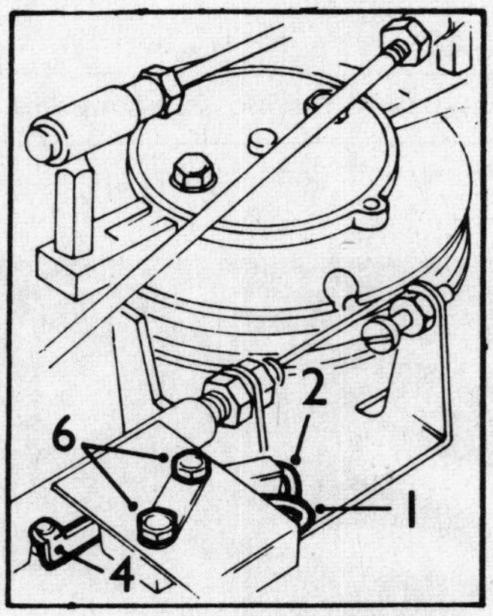


Fig. 6.24 Kickdown switch (Sec 18)

*1 Switch terminal*
*2 Switch terminal*
*4 Switch arm*
*6 Switch securing bolts*

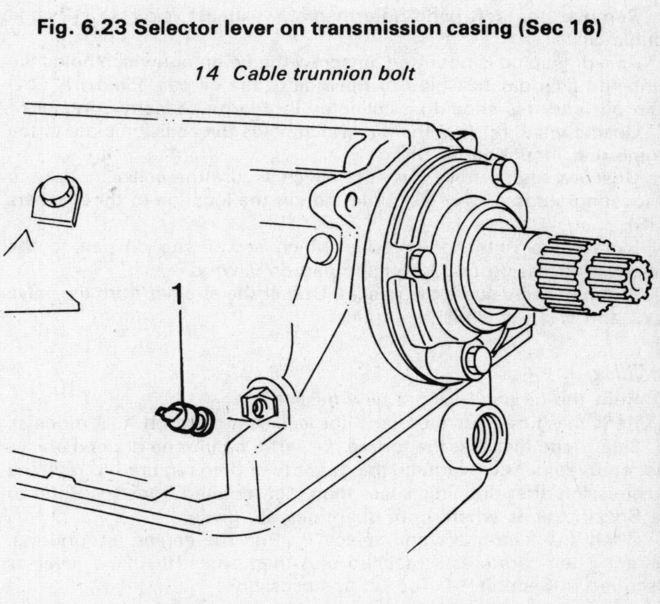


Fig. 6.25 Kickdown solenoid connector terminal (1) (Sec 19)

## 14 Maintenance and precautions

1 The most important maintenance task is the regular checking of the fluid level.
2 At the intervals specified in 'Routine Maintenance', operate the car on the road for at least 15 miles (24 km) and then place it on a level surface, and with the engine still running, move the speed selector lever through all positions finally placing the lever in 'P'.
3 Withdraw the dipstick and wipe it clean on a piece of non-fluffy cloth. Re-insert it and then withdraw it for the second time and read off the fluid level.
4 If necessary, add specified fluid to the combined dipstick/oil filler tube to bring the level up to the 'FULL' mark. The difference between the 'LOW' and 'FULL' marks is equivalent to $1\frac{1}{2}$ Imp pints (1.8 US pints, 0.75 litres). Switch off the engine.
5 The only other maintenance items are to keep the exterior of the transmission casing clean to prevent the unit overheating and periodically to check the condition and security of the fluid flow and return pipes to the cooler located on the right-hand tank of the cooling system radiator.
6 If the car must be towed due to a fault in the engine, then an extra 3 Imp pts (3.6 US pints, 1.7 litres) of fluid must be added to the transmission, the speed selector lever must be placed in 'N' and the ignition key turned to the ACC position.
7 Restrict the towing speed to 30 mph (48 kph) and the distance towed to 30 miles (48 km).
8 If the car must be towed and there is a fault in the transmission then the rear wheels must be raised off the ground, or the propeller shaft must be disconnected from the final drive flange and removed.

## 15 Transmission fluid – draining and refilling

1 Renewal of the automatic transmission fluid is not to be regarded as a routine service operation. It may be required however if the colour of the fluid on the dipstick is dark or if it smells burnt. This may be caused by overheating due to towing a trailer or overloading.
2 If the engine/transmission is being removed for overhaul then the fluid should be drained from the transmission unit before it is separated from the engine.

### *Draining*

3 Place the car on ramps or over a pit.
4 Remove the left-hand intermediate exhaust pipe (XJ12 and Double Six).
5 As a drain plug is not fitted, unscrew the union nut which holds the combined filler/dipstick tube to the side of the oil pan. Fluid will now drain out and this should be collected in a large capacity container.
6 Unscrew and remove the nut which holds the collision plate to the engine rear mounting (XJS).
7 Unscrew and remove the nuts which secure the collision plate to its locating studs. Lower the plate, noting the location of the washers (XJS).
8 Extract the nuts and/or bolts which secure the oil pan to the transmission casing and lower the pan downward.
9 Remove and discard the gasket. Unbolt the strainer from the valve block and clean it. Refit the strainer.

### *Refilling*

10 Refit the oil pan, using a new gasket.
11 Refit the fluid filler tube (and the collision plate on XJS models).
12 Due to the fact that the torque converter cannot be drained unless it is removed during overhaul, the quantity of fluid required to refill the transmission after draining is less than that required from dry. Refer to the Specifications where both quantities are given.
13 Apply the handbrake and select 'P'. Run the engine until normal operating temperature is reached and then check the fluid level as described in Section 14. Top up as necessary.

## 16 Speed selector cable – adjustment

1 Remove the centre console as described in Chapter 12.
2 Unscrew the two halves of the knob on the hand control lever (photo) and then set the lever to '1'.
3 Extract the screws and lift the speed selector indicator plate from the lever.
4 Extract the split pin which secures the cable to the base of the hand control lever and disconnect the cable.
5 Set the selector lever on the side of the transmission to '1'. The correct position of the lever can be established by pressing it as far as it will go towards the rear of the car.
6 Release the locknuts at the cable abutment and adjust their position until the selector cable can be connected to the hand control lever without having to disturb the previously set position of the hand control or transmission lever.
7 Tighten the locknuts and fit a new split pin.
8 Check for correct operation, particularly with regard to the operation of the reversing lamp and starter inhibitor switch. Refit the indicator plate, control lever knob, and the centre console.

## 17 Speed selector cable – removal and refitting

1 Remove the centre console as described in Chapter 12.
2 Refer to Chapter 1, Section 3, paragraph 34 and disconnect the cable trunnion block from the transmission casing.
3 The cable can now be disconnected from the lever on the side of the transmission casing and from the hand control lever.
4 Release the cable locknuts, unscrew and remove the one nearer the front of the car and draw the cable assembly through the mounting bracket at the hand control lever.
5 Refitting is a reversal of removal. On completion adjust the cable as described in the preceding Section.

## 18 Kickdown switch – checking and adjusting

1 Switch on the ignition and check that the input terminals on the switch are live. These terminals have the green coloured wires running to them.
2 Connect an earthed test lamp to the output terminal (green/white wire) and fully depress the throttle pedal. If the lamp does not light, release the pedal and gently depress the arm of the switch. If the lamp still does not light, renew the switch by unscrewing its mounting bolts.
3 If the lamp lights, loosen the retaining bolts and move the switch towards the cable so that the lamp lights by the switch action with the throttle pedal fully depressed.

## 19 Kickdown solenoid – testing, removal and refitting

1 The kickdown solenoid connector plug is screwed into the side of

16.2 Automatic transmission speed select control lever

the transmission casing. Pull the wire from the connector terminal.
2 Using a jumper lead, momentarily connect the battery positive terminal to the terminal on the connector. If a click is heard, then the kickdown solenoid is operating correctly. If a click is not heard then the solenoid is faulty and must be renewed.
3 To renew the solenoid, remove the oil pan as described in Section 15, disconnect the lead from the connector terminal on the wall of the transmission casing, rotate the solenoid through 180° and remove it.
4 Refitting is a reversal of removal.

## 20 Vacuum control unit – testing, removal and refitting

1 A fault in the vacuum control unit will be indicated by one or more of the following symptoms:

(a) *Smoky exhaust*
(b) *Low oil level in transmission requiring constant topping up*
(c) *Rough automatic gearshifts*

2 To test the unit, first remove it from the transmission by disconnecting the hose, then unscrewing it and withdrawing the pushrod. A small panel is fitted to the left-hand side of the transmission tunnel for access.
3 If the unit is now connected to a vacuum source, the indicated vacuum should not fall below 18 in (46 cm) Hg, otherwise it will indicate a perforated diaphragm and a new unit will have to be fitted.
4 Once a new vacuum unit has been fitted, it must be adjusted immediately. To do this, connect a vacuum gauge and the original vacuum pipe to the unit using a 'T' piece.
5 Remove the small plug (0.125 in – 3.2 mm dia.) from the left-hand side of the transmission casing towards the front and connect a fluid pressure gauge (Part No CBW 1A-642 and STN 6752).
6 Have the engine/transmission at normal operating temperature, select 'D' and apply the hand and foot brakes.
7 Increase the engine speed until the vacuum gauge reads between 9 and 10 in (23 to 25 cm) Hg at 1200 rpm. Do not maintain this condition for longer than necessary – see paragraph 11.
8 The reading on the pressure gauge should now be between 70 and 95 $lbf/in^2$ (4.92 and 6.67 $kgf/cm^2$).
9 A pressure reading lower than that specified will cause clutch slip and transmission damage.
10 To adjust the vacuum control unit, remove the vacuum hose, insert a screwdriver into the pipe stub. Turn the adjusting screw clockwise to increase pressure or anti-clockwise to decrease it. Two complete turns of the screw will vary the pressure by 10 $lbf/in^2$ (0.7 $kgf/cm^2$). If when the adjustment is being checked, a rapid knocking noise is heard between 600 and 800 rpm, then the adjusting screw has been turned too far and has lost contact with the servo actuating rod.
11 When carrying out the foregoing adjustment, do not hold the engine speed for the pressure check (stall speed) for longer than 10 seconds at a time. The total stall period should not exceed one minute in every half hour.

## 21 Front brake band – adjustment

1 Remove the oil pan as described in Section 15.
2 Release the brake band adjusting screw until it no longer contacts the piston pin. *Note that the screw has a left-hand thread.*
3 Pull the front servo lever back until a gauge block (part No CBW 34) can be inserted between the adjusting screw and the piston pin.
4 Adjust the screw to a torque of 10 lbf in (0.12 kgf m), making sure that the locking spring is located in its retaining slot.
5 Remove the gauge block, refit the oil pass and refill the transmission.

## 22 Rear brake band – adjustment

1 This operation should be carried out when a new transmission has been installed and at 24 000 miles (38 600 km) intervals thereafter.
2 The adjuster screw is located on the right-hand side of the transmission casing. Release the locknut and unscrew it two turns.
3 Lubricate the adjuster screw and check that it turns freely. Tighten the screw to a torque of 10 lbf ft (1.4 kgf m) and then loosen it exactly $1\frac{1}{4}$ turns. Retighten the locknut to a torque of 44 lbf ft (6 kgf m).

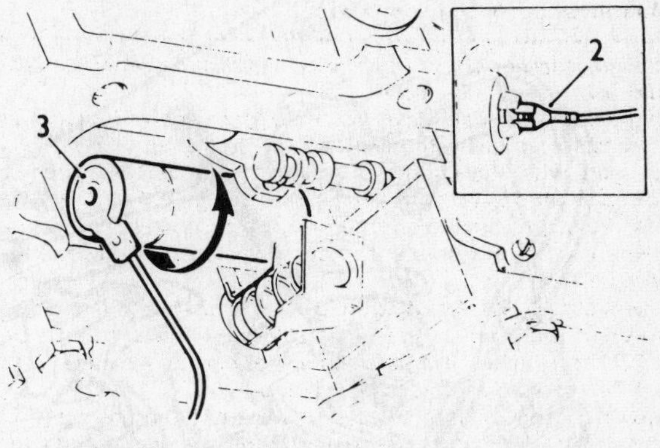


**Fig. 6.26 Kickdown solenoid (3) and internal connection to connectors terminal (2) (Sec 19)**

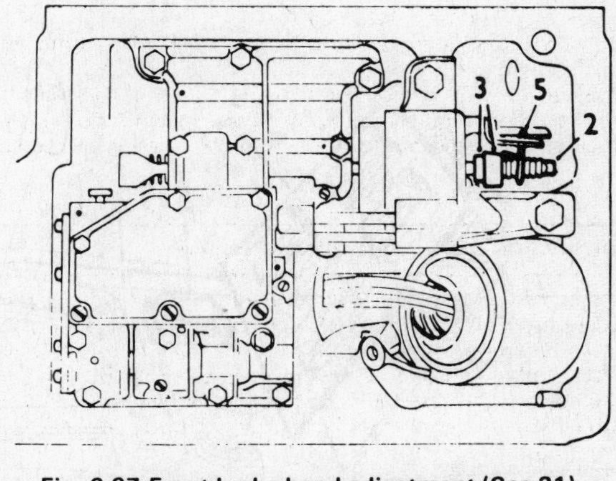


**Fig. 6.27 Front brake band adjustment (Sec 21)**

2 *Adjusting screw*
3 *Gauge block (CBW 34)*
5 *Locking spring*

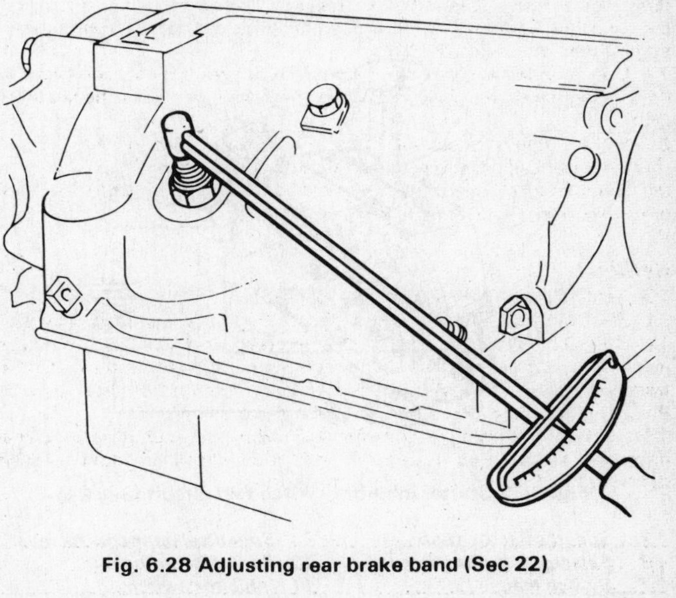

**Fig. 6.28 Adjusting rear brake band (Sec 22)**

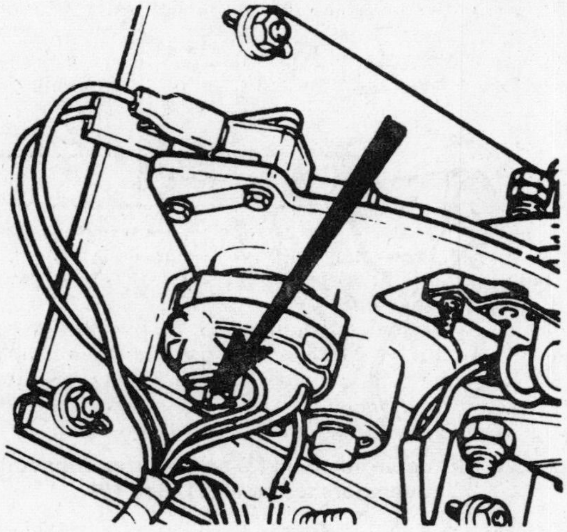

Fig. 6.29 Reversing lamp switch (arrowed) (Sec 23)

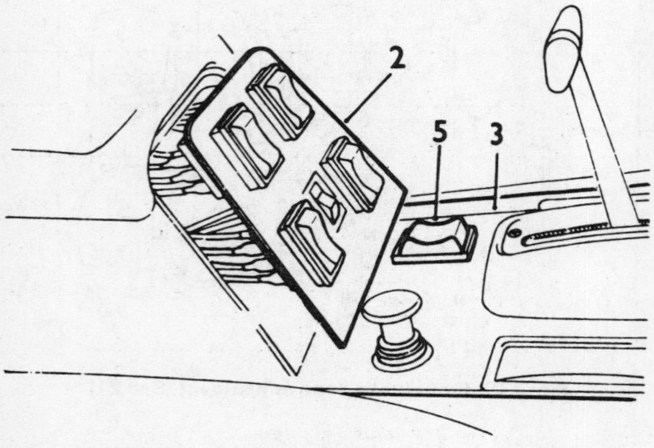


Fig. 6.30 Electric window switch panel (2), escutcheon (3) and door lock switch (5) (Sec 24)

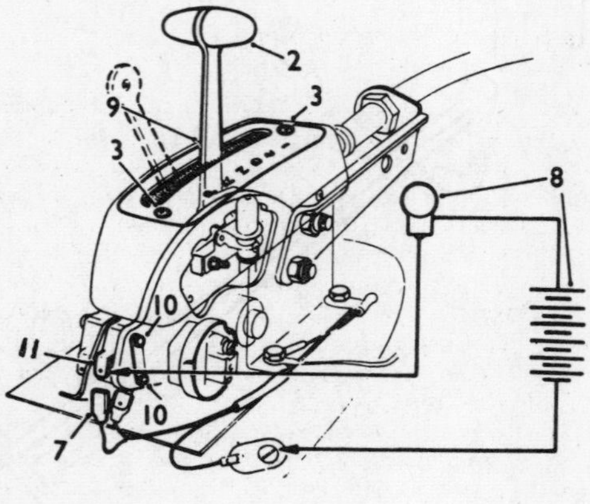


Fig. 6.31 Starter inhibitor switch test circuit (Sec 24)

*2 Speed selector knob*
*3 Selector indicator screws*
*7 Switch leads*
*8 Test lamp circuit*
*9 Speed selector control lever*
*10 Switch securing nuts*
*11 Inhibitor switch*

## 23 Reversing lamp switch – removal and refitting

1 Disconnect the battery.
2 Raise the lid on the centre console glove box and extract the console centre panel securing screw (XJS models only).
3 Remove the electric window lift control panel and the selector lever handgrip (XJ12 and Double Six models only).
4 Extract the centre panel screws and raise the panel until the leads to the various switches can be identified and disconnected. Remove the panel.
5 Unbolt and remove the selector indicator cover.
6 Identify the leads to the reverse switch terminals and disconnect them. Remove the switch, noting the washer and spacers.
7 Refitting is a reversal of removal.

## 24 Starter inhibitor switch – adjusting, removal and refitting

1 The starter motor should only operate if the ignition key is turned with the speed selector lever in 'N' or 'P'. If the starter operates with the selector lever in any other position, carry out the following adjustment.
2 Disconnect the battery.
3 Unscrew and remove the two halves of the selector control lever knob.
4 Extract the screws and draw the speed selector indicator off the hand control lever (XJS models only).
5 Prise the electric window switch panel away from the centre console without disconnecting the switches.
6 Extract the screws which hold the selector control escutcheon so that it can be slightly withdrawn to gain access to the cigar lighter and door lock switch terminals. Identify the wires and disconnect them. Remove the escutcheon.
7 Disconnect the supply cable from the starter inhibitor switch.
8 Connect a test lamp and battery in series with the switch and then move the selector lever to 'N'.
9 Slacken the switch locknuts and move the switch until the test lamp lights up. Tighten the locknuts.
10 Move the selector lever to 'P' and check that the test lamp is on but goes off when the lever is moved to any drive position.
11 Remove the battery and test lamp, re-make all the original connections and refit the components which were removed. Reconnect the battery.

## 25 Stall test

1 This test is only required if the performance of the transmission is suspect. The stall speed is the maximum engine rpm obtained whilst driving the impeller against the stationary turbine.
2 The engine must be in a correct state of tune and adjustment and the engine/transmission at normal operating temperature.
3 Fully apply the handbrake and the foot brake.
4 Start the engine, select 'D' and depress the accelerator pedal to the limit of its travel. Note the tachometer reading.
5 If the indicated rpm is under 1300 (XJS) or 1000 (XJ12 and Double Six) then the stator free wheel is slipping.
6 If the indicated rpm is between 1950 and 2050 (XJS) and 1600 and 1700 (XJ12 and Double Six) it can be assumed that the transmission is operating normally and is in good condition.
7 If the rpm is above 2400 (XJS) or 2100 (XJ12 and Double Six) then the transmission internal clutch is slipping.
8 To avoid overheating the transmission, *do not carry out the stall test for longer than ten seconds at a time.* The total stall period should not exceed one minute in every half hour.

## 26 Transmission unit – removal and refitting

1 The transmission is removed and refitted in conjunction with the engine as described in Chapter 1, Section 3, 4 or 5 as applicable.
2 The transmission should be separated from the engine as described in Section 6 of Chapter 1.

### 27 Torque converter housing and torque converter – removal and refitting

1 The operations described in this Section will normally only be required if a new or rebuilt transmission is to be installed. The original torque converter and converter housing can be fitted to the new transmission unit.
2 Remove the engine/transmission as described in Chapter 1.
3 Disconnect the oil cooler pipes.
4 Remove the breather pipe, dipstick and oil filler tube. Disconnect the pipe from the vacuum unit.
5 Drain the transmission fluid.
6 Unscrew and remove the four nuts which hold the transmission housing to the torque converter housing. Support the weight of the transmission and withdraw it.
7 Unbolt and remove the starter motor.
8 Unbolt and remove the cover plate from the lower half of the front of the torque converter housing.
9 Unbolt the converter housing from the engine cylinder block.
10 Remove the engine oil filter.
11 Extract the plug from the rear left-hand side of the crankcase to provide access to the driveplate-to-torque converter setscrews.
12 Turn the crankshaft until the first of the driveplate-to-torque converter setscrews comes into view.
13 Flatten the tabs on the lockplate and extract the setscrew. Continue to rotate the crankshaft until all the setscrews have been removed. Mark the driveplate-to-torque converter relationship and withdraw it.
14 Refitting is a reversal of removal, but make sure that the torque converter lugs engage with the cut-outs in the oil pump gear.

### 28 Rear oil seal – renewal

1 Leakage of fluid from the rear end of the transmission extension housing will almost certainly be from a worn output shaft oil seal.
2 Disconnect the front end of the propeller shaft (see Chapter 7) and place the shaft to one side.
3 Unscrew and remove the output shaft coupling flange nut. The nut may be secured by a split pin or a tab washer. The coupling flange will have to be held quite still while the nut is unscrewed. Make up a lever for this which can be bolted to the coupling flange using the original bolts which will still be in position in the flange.
4 Withdraw the coupling flange and washer.
5 Prise out the oil seal and then tap in a new one using a piece of tubing as a drift.
6 Apply grease to the coupling flange surfaces which will be in contact with the lips of the oil seal, install the coupling, tighten the nut to the specified torque and fit a new split pin or bend over the tab washer.
7 Reconnect the propeller shaft and then check and top up the fluid level in the automatic transmission unit.

### 29 Fault diagnosis – automatic transmission (BW type 12)

| Symptom | Reason(s) |
|---|---|
| Engine will not start in 'N' or 'P' | Faulty starter or ignition circuit<br>Incorrect speed selector linkage adjustment<br>Incorrectly adjusted inhibitor switch |
| Engine starts in selector positions other than 'N' or 'P' | Incorrect speed selector linkage adjustment<br>Incorrectly adjusted inhibitor switch |
| Severe bump when selecting 'D' or 'R' or excessive creep when handbrake released | Idling speed too high<br>Vacuum circuit fault<br>Solenoid fault |
| Poor acceleration and low maximum speed | Incorrect fluid level<br>Incorrect linkage adjustment |
| No movement when 'R' selected | Incorrect rear band adjustment<br>Low fluid level |
| Poor upshift quality | Front band requires adjustment |
| No movement in 'D' | Front brake band requires adjustment<br>Fault in one-way clutch |

## PART C – AUTOMATIC TRANSMISSION (GM 400)

### 30 General description

1 This type of transmission is fitted as standard to XJ12 and Double Six models on Series 3 versions and to XJS models from 1979 cars onwards.
2 The transmission is fully automatic and incorporates a vacuum modulator and pressure regulator to monitor the position of the throttle so that the transmission is always engaged in the correct speed ratio.
3 The transmission can be distinguished from earlier Borg Warner units by the fact that the speed selector control lever has a longer travel between P and R, and that the torque converter bellhousing is cast in one piece with the transmission casing and cannot be detached from the casing.

### 31 Transmission fluid – topping up and renewal

1 The fluid level should be checked in a similar way to that described for the Borg Warner unit in Section 14 (photos).
2 Renewing the transmission fluid is not a routine service operation and should only be needed if the fluid on the dipstick appears discoloured or smells burnt. These conditions can be caused by towing a trailer or by overloading.
3 To drain the fluid, the oil pan must be removed as described in Section 35, there being no drain plug.
4 As the torque converter will not drain unless it is removed during overhaul, the quantity of fluid required to fill the transmission will be less than that required to fill from dry. Pour in the specified quantity of fluid and then check the fluid level as previously described. Top up as necessary but do not overfill.

### 32 Speed selector cable – adjustment

1 Remove the centre console as described in Chapter 12.

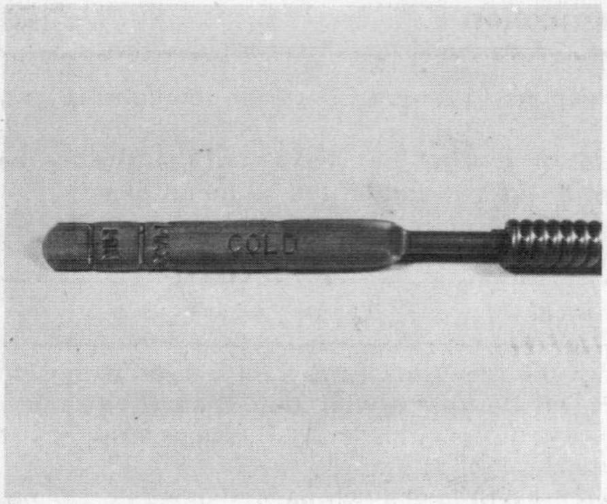


31.1A Dipstick marking (COLD side)

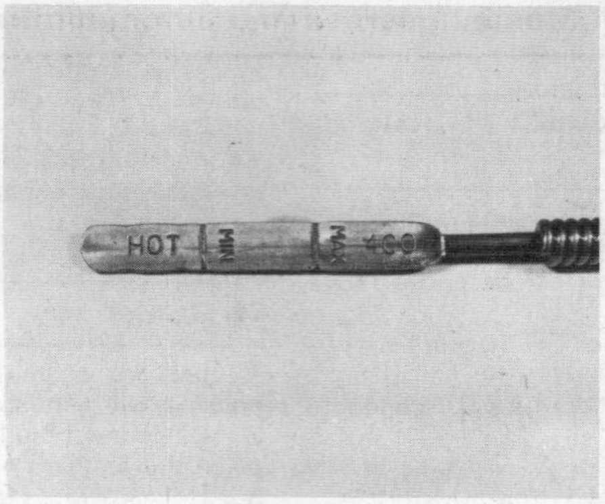


31.1B Dipstick marking (HOT side)

32.2 Selector quadrant details: 1 – Reversing lamp switch; 2 – Starter inhibitor switch; 3 – Index bulb; 4 – Operating cable locknuts

35.5 Removing the transmission oil pan – GM400 (transmission inverted on bench)

35.6A Unbolting the fluid filter – GM400 (transmission inverted on bench)

35.6B View of the GM 400 automatic transmission (filter removed)

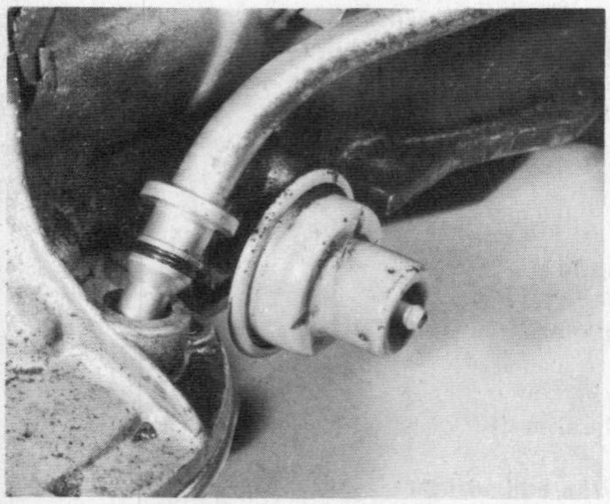

37.3 Removing the fluid dipstick guide tube

37.29 Rear mounting (GM 400 transmission)

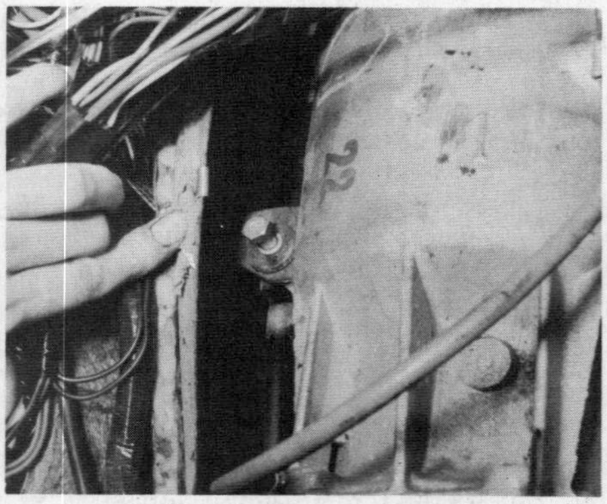

38.1 Speed selector cable trunnion bracket bolt

38.2A Trunnion bracket bolt removed (viewed from below)

38.2B Speed selector cable and trunnion bracket (transmission removed)

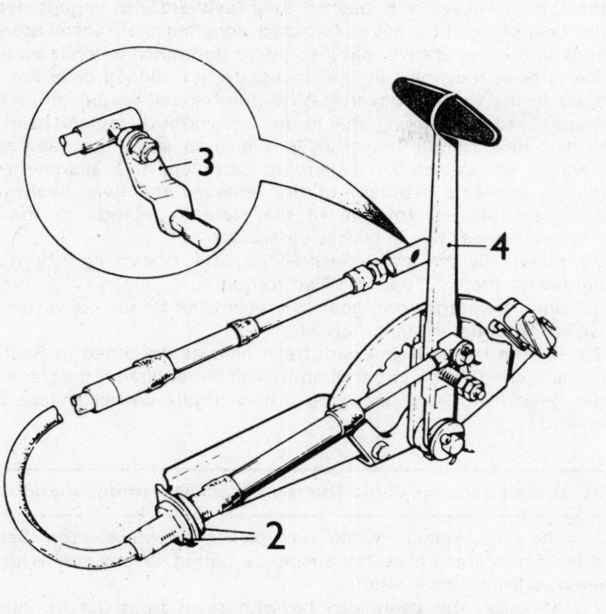


**Fig. 6.32 Speed selector control cable (Sec 32)**

2 *Locknut*
3 *Transmission lever*
4 *Selector control lever*

2 Slacken the locknuts at the cable abutment bracket just to the rear of the selector control lever (photo).
3 Set the control lever on the side of the transmission casing in the 'N' position. To do this, count the number of detents ('clicks') back from P or 1.
4 Now set the selector control lever in 'N'.
5 Without moving either lever from its centre of detent position, tighten the cable locknuts.
6 When correctly adjusted, a little free play should be evident at each selector position.

## 33 Kickdown switch – checking and adjusting

1 Refer to Section 18.

## 34 Starter inhibitor switch – adjusting, removal and refitting

1 Refer to Section 24.

## 35 Oil pan and filter – removal and refitting

1 Raise the car on ramps or place it over an inspection pit.
2 From the transmission casing unclamp the vacuum capsule, disconnect it and allow the fluid to drain into a container.
3 Reconnect and re-clamp the capsule.
4 Unscrew and remove all the oil pan bolts except for two at the front edge and one at the rear.
5 Place a container under the oil pan and press the oil pan upwards while the remaining bolts are removed and the oil pan tilted downward to allow the remaining fluid to drain. Discard the gasket (photo).
6 Unscrew and remove the oil filter securing bolt, remove the filter and discard it (photos).
7 Fit the new filter and tighten the securing screw.
8 Wipe out the oil pan with a non-fluffy rag, discard the old gasket and stick a new one to clean flanges using petroleum jelly as an adhesive.
9 Refit the oil pan and fill with fresh fluid as described in Section 31.

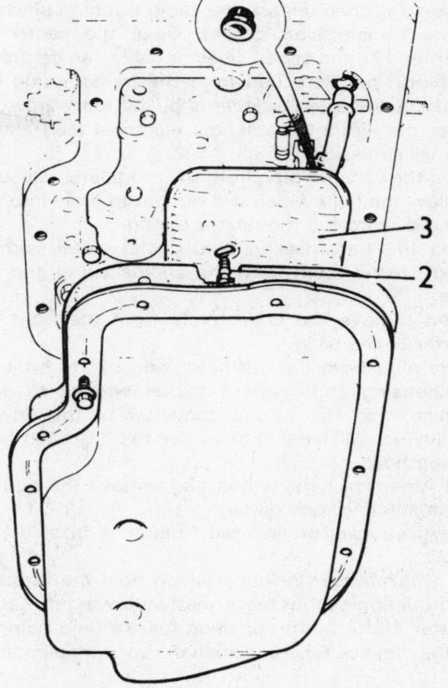


**Fig. 6.33 Oil pan and filter (Sec 35)**

2 *Filter retaining screw*
3 *Filter*

## 36 Stall test

1 Refer to Section 25. The information applies equally to the GM 400 transmission except that the stall speed for a transmission in good condition should be approximately 2400 rpm.

## 37 Transmission unit – removal and refitting

1 Place the car on ramps or over an inspection pit and disconnect the battery.
2 Withdraw the fluid dipstick from the transmission.
3 Unbolt the dipstick guide tube from the engine lifting eye and remove the upper tube (photo).
4 Unbolt the wing stays from the wings, release the pipe from one of the stays and then swing both stays away from the wings.
5 Using a suitable crossbeam (its ends located in the wing valance channels), and adjustable lifting hooks engaged in the rear lifting eyes, take the weight of the engine.
6 Disconnect the front exhaust pipes from the intermediate pipes by uncoupling the flanges.
7 Unbolt and remove the heat shields from the intermediate exhaust pipes. Remove the rear heat shield.
8 Pull the exhaust pipes outwards and tie them to the underframe.
9 Unbolt and remove the front heat shields.
10 Remove the centre nut from the transmission rear mounting. Remove the spacer.
11 Using a jack and a block of wood as an insulator, support the rear mounting plate of the transmission, then unscrew and remove the rear mounting bolts and spacers.
12 Lower the jack, remove the rear mounting and extract the crossmember bolts. Remove the crossmember.
13 Disconnect the front of the propeller shaft from the transmission output flange and tie the shaft to one side of the car.
14 Adjust the engine support hooks so that the engine is lowered by not more than one inch (25.4 mm).
15 Working under the car, disconnect the speedometer cable from the transmission.

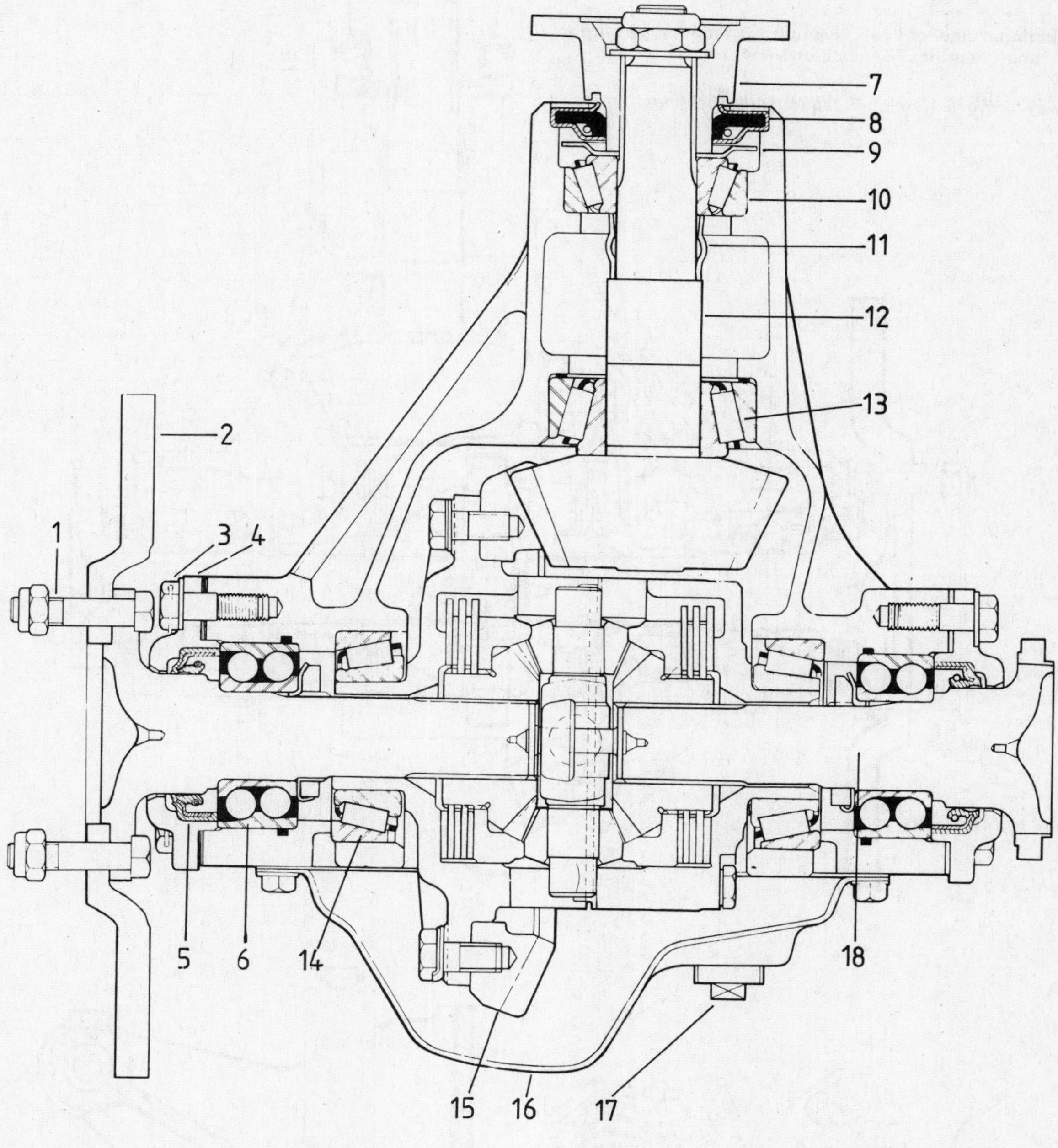


**Fig. 8.1 Sectional view of final drive unit with ball type output shaft bearings (Series 1) (Sec 1)**

*1 Driveshaft connecting bolts*
*2 Brake disc*
*3 Caliper mounting bracket bolt*
*4 Caliper mounting bracket*
*5 Oil seal*
*6 Ball bearing*
*7 Pinion drive flange*
*8 Oil seal*
*9 Oil thrower*
*10 Tapered roller bearing (outer)*
*11 Collapsible spacer*
*12 Pinion shaft*
*13 Tapered roller bearing (inner)*
*14 Differential side bearing*
*15 Crownwheel*
*16 Rear cover plate*
*17 Filler/level plug*
*18 Output shaft*

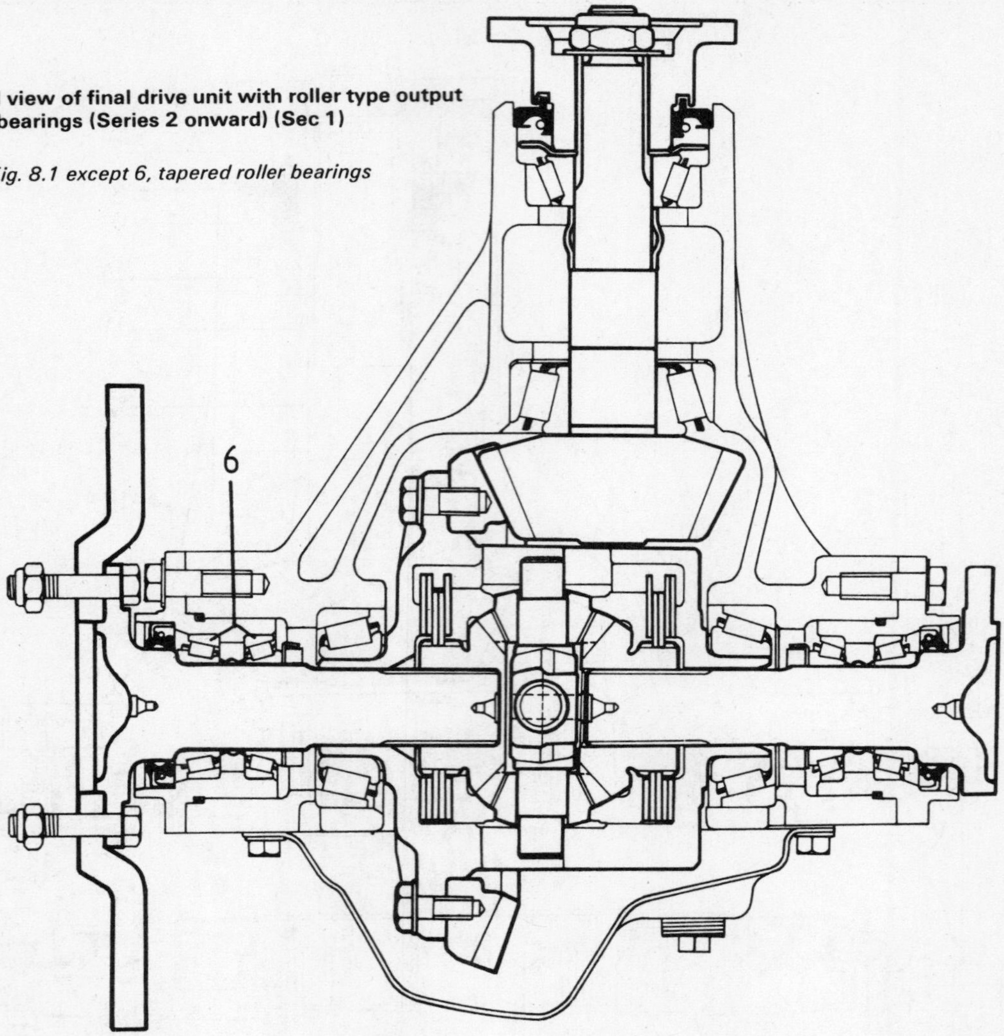


Fig. 8.2 Sectional view of final drive unit with roller type output shaft bearings (Series 2 onward) (Sec 1)

*Key as for Fig. 8.1 except 6, tapered roller bearings*

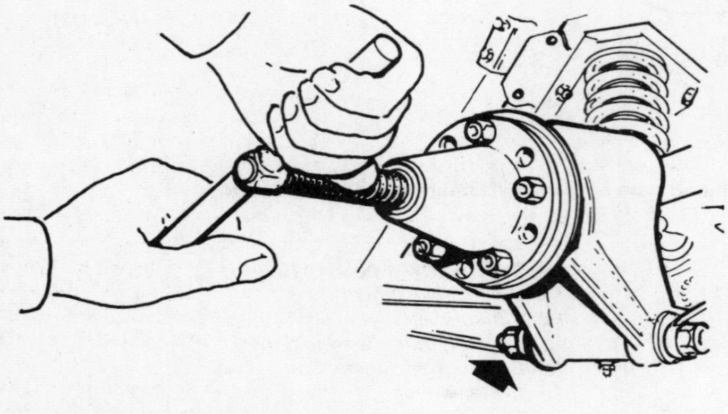

Fig. 8.3 Rear hub showing hub extractor and (arrowed) wishbone outboard pivot shaft (Sec 2)

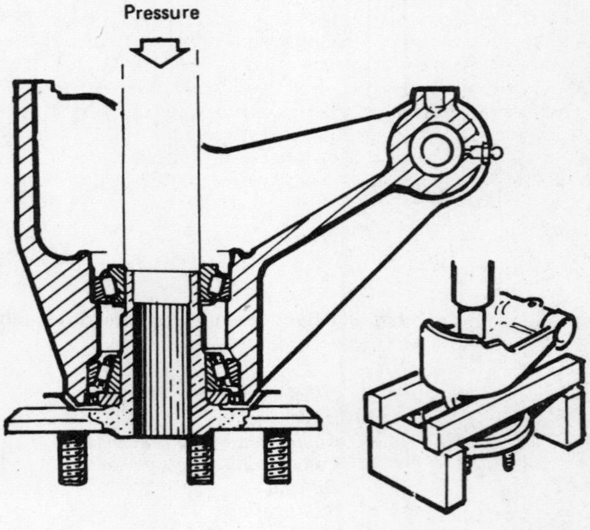


Fig. 8.4 Pressing the rear hub from the carrier (Sec 2)

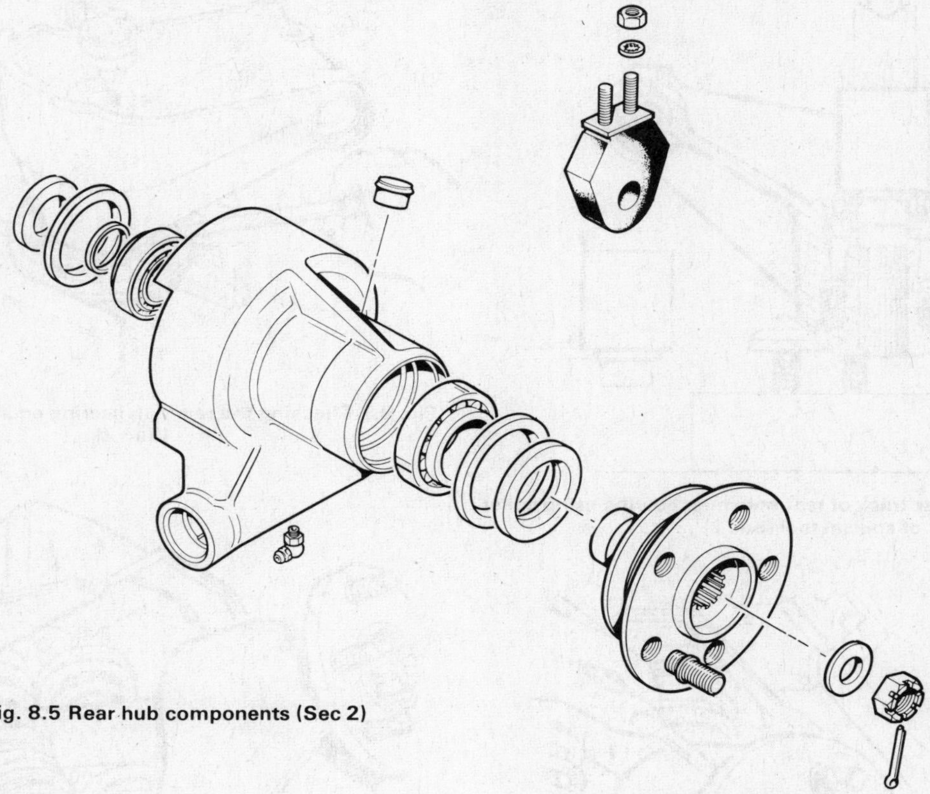

Fig. 8.5 Rear hub components (Sec 2)

track into the inner track of the outer bearing until the hub is fully home.

11 Hold the hub and hub carrier vertically so that the inner end of the hub is uppermost.

12 Locate the inner track of the inner bearing on the hub followed by the special collar of the official tool no. JD15. Press the track onto the hub until its inner face is flush with the special collar.

13 Mount a dial gauge as shown in Fig. 8.7. Tap the hub carrier downwards, zero the dial gauge and then use two levers inserted between the hub and hub carrier to move the carrier upwards. Record the maximum reading on the dial gauge.

14 Remove the special collar and then fit a spacer (if necessary) to give endfloat of between 0.001 and 0.003 in (0.025 and 0.076 mm). Spacers are supplied in thicknesses of 0.109 to 0.151 in steps of 0.003 in (0.076 mm) and are lettered 'A' (smallest) to 'R' (largest) omitting letters 'I', 'O' and 'N', as given in the following table:

| Letter | Thickness in | Thickness mm |
|---|---|---|
| *A* | *0.109* | *2.77* |
| *B* | *0.112* | *2.85* |
| *C* | *0.115* | *2.92* |
| *D* | *0.118* | *3.00* |
| *E* | *0.121* | *3.07* |
| *F* | *0.124* | *3.15* |
| *G* | *0.127* | *3.23* |
| *H* | *0.130* | *3.30* |
| *J* | *0.133* | *3.38* |
| *K* | *0.136* | *3.45* |
| *L* | *0.139* | *3.53* |
| *M* | *0.142* | *3.61* |
| *P* | *0.145* | *3.68* |
| *Q* | *0.148* | *3.75* |
| *R* | *0.151* | *3.84* |

15 For example, assume that the endfloat measured with the collar in position is 0.25 in (0.64 mm). Take the mean permissible endfloat as 0.002 in (0.05 mm) and subtract this from the measured endfloat, giving 0.023 in (0.59 mm). The special collar is 0.150 in (3.81 mm) thick so the thickness of the spacer to be fitted will be 0.150 - 0.023 in ie 0.126 in (3.22 mm). The nearest spacer in thickness to this is 0.127 in (3.23 mm) so fit a letter 'G' spacer in place of the special collar.

16 Fit the inner oil seal and its seating ring. This leather oil seal must be soaked in engine oil prior to fitting.

17 Locate the hub assembly between the jaws of the suspension wishbone, install the pivot shaft and nuts.

18 Clean the splines of the hub and shaft with a suitable solvent and then apply a thin coating of thread locking compound to the splines.

19 Engage the hub with the shaft splines, fit the washer and castellated nut and tighten to the specified torque.

20 Fit a new split pin to the castellated nut and refit the outer pivot grease nipple.

21 It is worth rechecking the hub bearing endfloat again at this stage by attaching the dial gauge as shown in Fig. 8.8 and levering the hub outwards.

22 Where possible, do not drive the car for a period of between 4 and 12 hours in order to allow the thread locking compound to harden.

23 Remove the hub bearing grease cap (photo) and inject wheel bearing grease until no more will go in. Do not pressurise the grease, or it will be forced past the oil seals. Refit the cap.

24 Refit the roadwheel and lower the car to the ground.

## 3 Driveshaft (XJ12, Double Six, Series 1) – removal and refitting

1 Remove the rear suspension assembly, as described in Chapter 11 and then remove the hub assembly as described in the preceding Section.

2 Remove the rear shock absorber which is nearest the front of the car. To do this, remove the upper and lower mounting pivot nuts and drive out the pivot pin until the shock absorber mounting is released.

3 Unscrew and remove the four self-locking nuts which secure the driveshaft inner universal joint to the output flange of the final drive unit and brake disc.

4 Withdraw the driveshaft. Extract and note the exact location of any shims which are used for camber purposes and are fitted between the shaft flange and the brake disc.

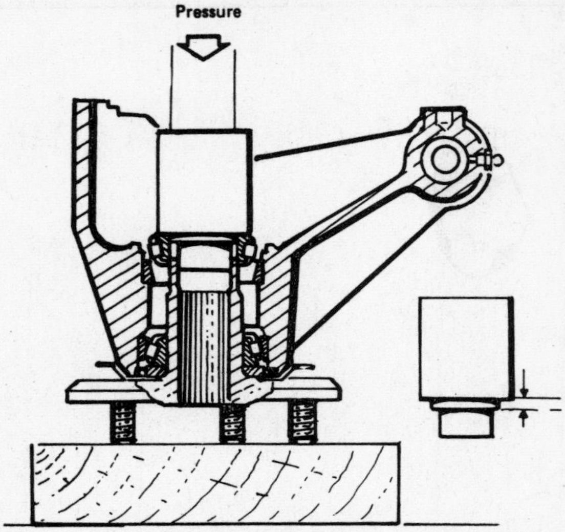


Fig. 8.6 Pressing inner track of rear hub inner bearing using collar of special tool (Sec 2)

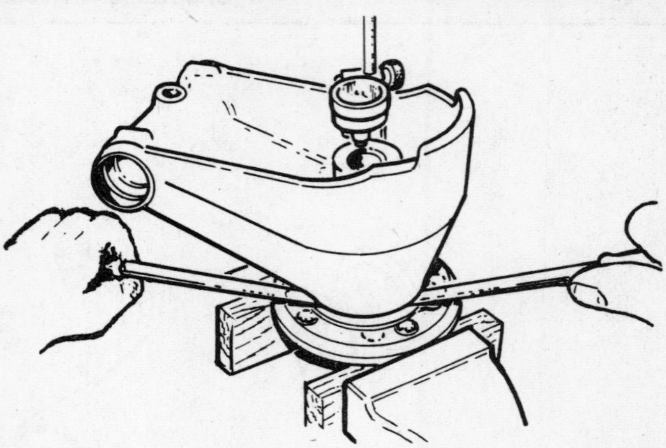

Fig. 8.7 Checking the rear hub bearing endfloat on the bench (Sec 2)

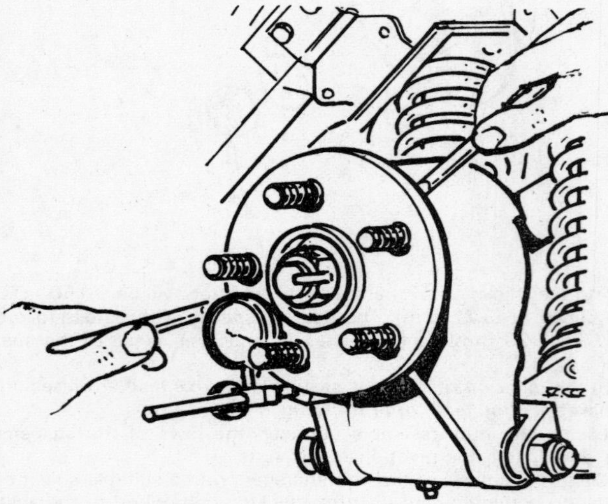

Fig. 8.8 Checking the rear hub bearing endfloat with hub installed on car (Sec 2)

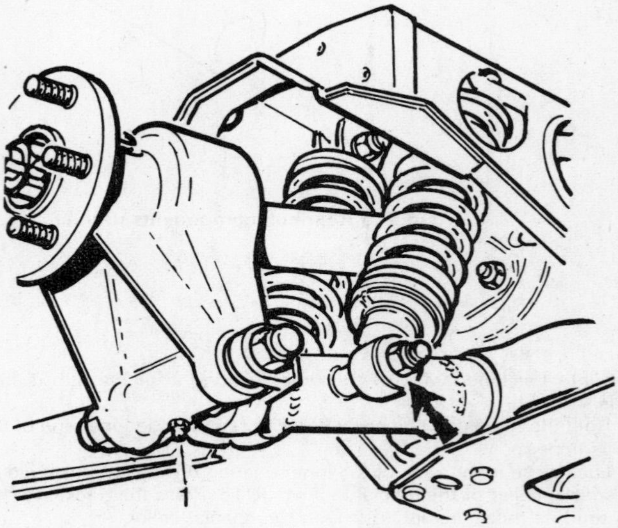


Fig. 8.9 Shock absorber lower mounting (arrowed) and pivot shaft grease nipple (1) (Sec 3)

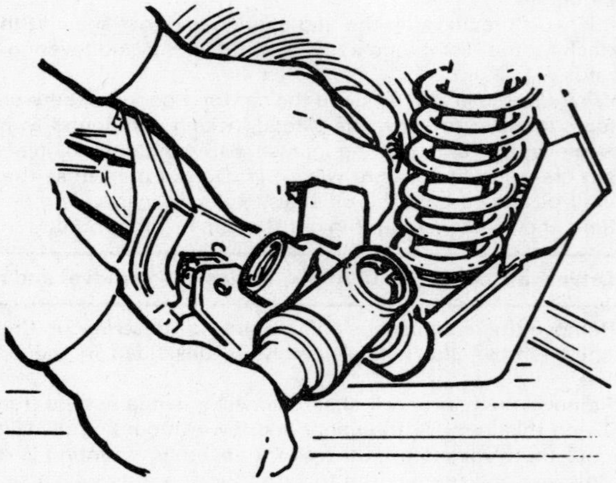

Fig. 8.10 Withdrawing a driveshaft (Sec 3)

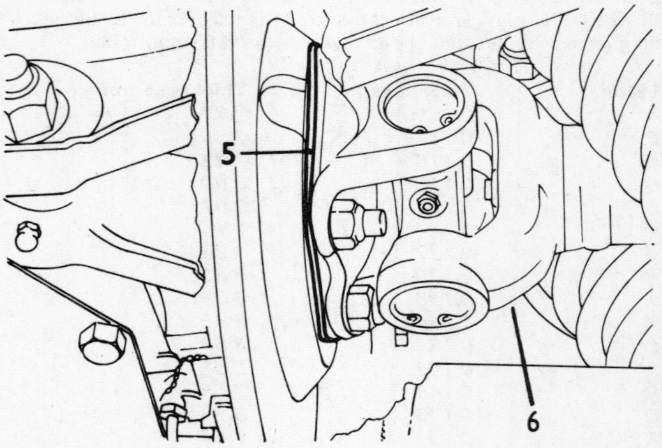


Fig. 8.11 Location of rear wheel camber shims (5) (Sec 3)

6 *Driveshaft*

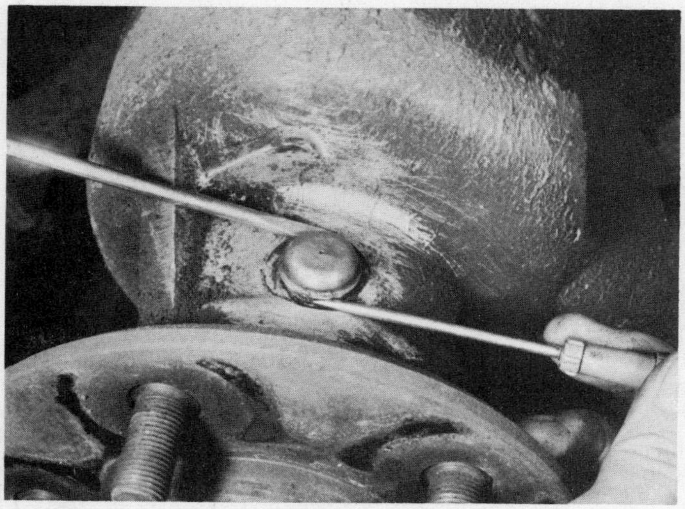

2.23 Removing a rear hub grease cap

4.3 Driveshaft inboard shroud and clip

5 Refitting is a reversal of removal, but make sure that the camber shims are returned to their original locations.

## 4 Driveshaft (XJ12, Double Six, Series 2 on and XJS) – removal and refitting

1 Jack up the rear of the car and support it securely on axle stands.
2 Remove the roadwheel.
3 Slacken the clip on the driveshaft inboard shroud (photo) and slide the shroud away from the flange.
4 Unscrew and remove the flange nuts.
5 Extract the split pin and unscrew and remove the castellated nut and washer from the end of the driveshaft at the hub.
6 Unscrew and remove the grease nipple from the hub carrier.
7 Fit a suitable extractor to the hub and draw the hub from the splined end of the driveshaft.
8 Pivot the hub assembly on its shaft.
9 Remove the nut from the shock absorber mounting. Detach the lash-down bracket, then drive the pin forward and release the lower end of the damper.
10 Withdraw the driveshaft, noting carefully the camber control shims which are located between the driveshaft inner flange and the brake disc.
11 If a new driveshaft is being fitted, then the original shrouds, oil seal track and spacer should be removed and fitted on the new shaft. The shrouds are secured with pop rivets and when fitted should have their seams sealed with suitable mastic. Make sure that the inner oil seal track chamfer clears the round edge on the driveshaft.
12 Refit the inboard end of the driveshaft, replacing the original camber shims onto clean surfaces. Do not fully tighten the nuts at this stage.
13 Reconnect the shock absorber and the lash-down bracket.
14 Apply thread locking compound to the splines of the driveshaft, raise the hub carrier and insert the end of the driveshaft into it.
15 Use a piece of tubing to drive the hub fully onto the shaft, fit the washer and tighten the castellated nut to the specified torque. Insert a new split pin.
16 Check the hub bearing endfloat as described in Section 2.
17 Screw in the hub carrier grease nipple.
18 Tighten the driveshaft nuts at the inboard flange to the specified torque.
19 Slide the inboard driveshaft shroud into position and tighten the clip.
20 Refit the roadwheel and lower the car to the ground.
21 Check the rear wheel camber at the earliest opportunity (see Chapter 11).

## 5 Driveshaft universal joints – overhaul

1 The procedure is very similar to that described in Chapter 7 for the overhaul of propeller shaft universal joints, to which reference should be made.

## 6 Output shaft, oil seal and ball bearing (earlier models) – removal and refitting

1 Remove the driveshaft as described in Section 3.
2 Cut the locking wire and unbolt the brake caliper from the final drive unit.
3 Remove the brake disc.
4 Cut the locking wire and unbolt the caliper mounting bracket.
5 Withdraw the output shaft together with the caliper mounting bracket shims, the bearing assembly and the square section oil seal from the final drive casing.
6 Flatten the tab of the lockwasher and unscrew and remove the nut from the output shaft.
7 Draw the ball bearing assembly and the caliper mounting bracket from the output shaft.
8 Commence reassembly by pressing a new square section oil seal into the groove in the final drive casing. Do not attempt to cut off the projecting part of the oil seal (Fig. 8.13).
9 Apply oil to the seal lips, the four special flange bolts and locate the caliper mounting bracket and the oil seal over the driveshaft.
10 Slide the ball bearing onto the output shaft, then fit a new lockplate and nut.
11 Tighten the nut to the specified torque and turn up the tab of the lockplate.
12 Smear oil on the splines and insert the output shaft into the final drive casing.
13 Screw in the five mounting bracket bolts finger-tight only at this stage.
14 Using feeler blades, measure between the inner face of the caliper mounting bracket and the differential housing. When finally assembled, there must be a compression (nip) of 0.003 in (0.076 mm) on the oil seal and ball bearing, so deduct this from the measured dimension and then select shims to suit from the following thicknesses available:

*0.003 in (0.076 mm)*
*0.005 in (0.127 mm)*
*0.010 in (0.254 mm)*
*0.030 in (0.762 mm)*

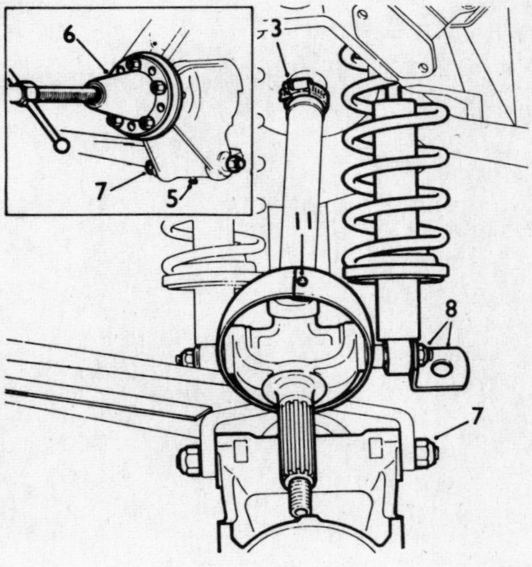


**Fig. 8.12 Driveshaft removal (Sec 4)**

3 *Shroud clip*
5 *Grease nipple*
6 *Hub puller*
7 *Pivot shaft*
8 *Shock absorber lower mounting and lash-down bracket*
11 *Shroud pop rivet*

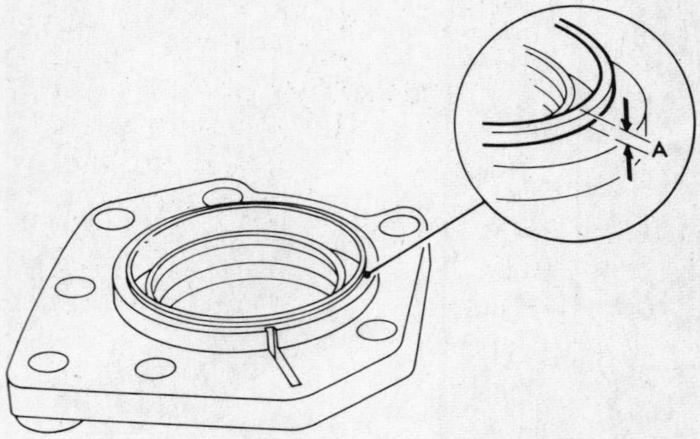


**Fig. 8.13 Output shaft oil seal (early type) (Sec 6)**

*A Projection of seal above casing*

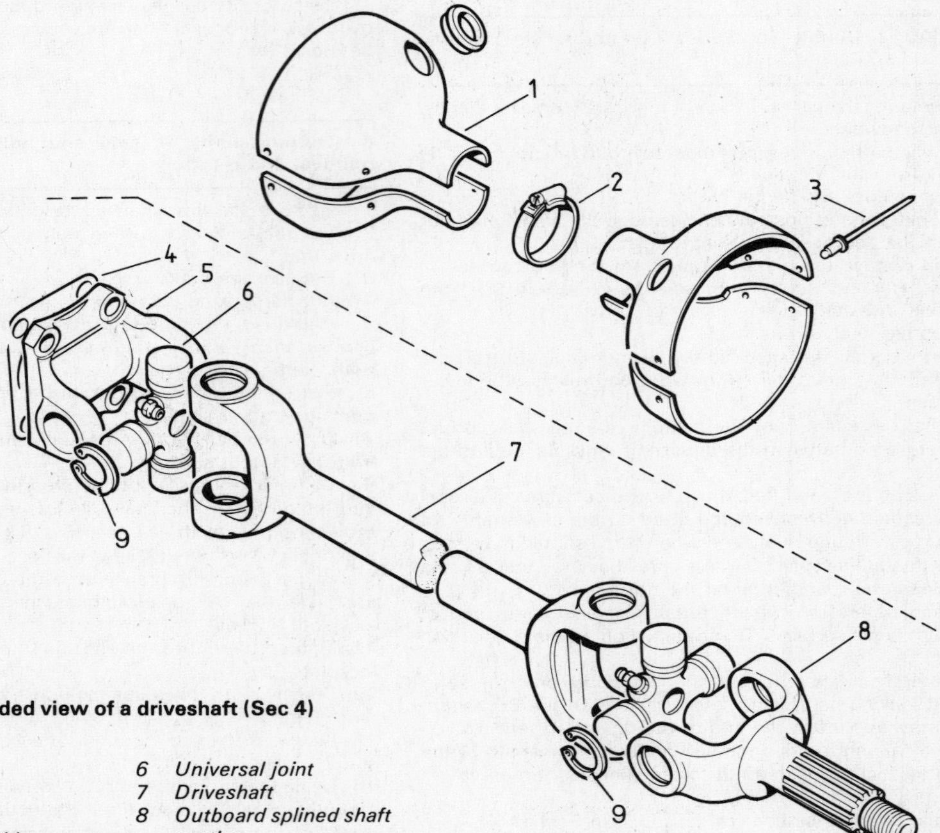


**Fig. 8.14 Exploded view of a driveshaft (Sec 4)**

1 *Shroud*
2 *Shroud clip*
3 *Pop rivet*
4 *Camber control shim*
5 *Inboard flange*
6 *Universal joint*
7 *Driveshaft*
8 *Outboard splined shaft section*
9 *Circlip*

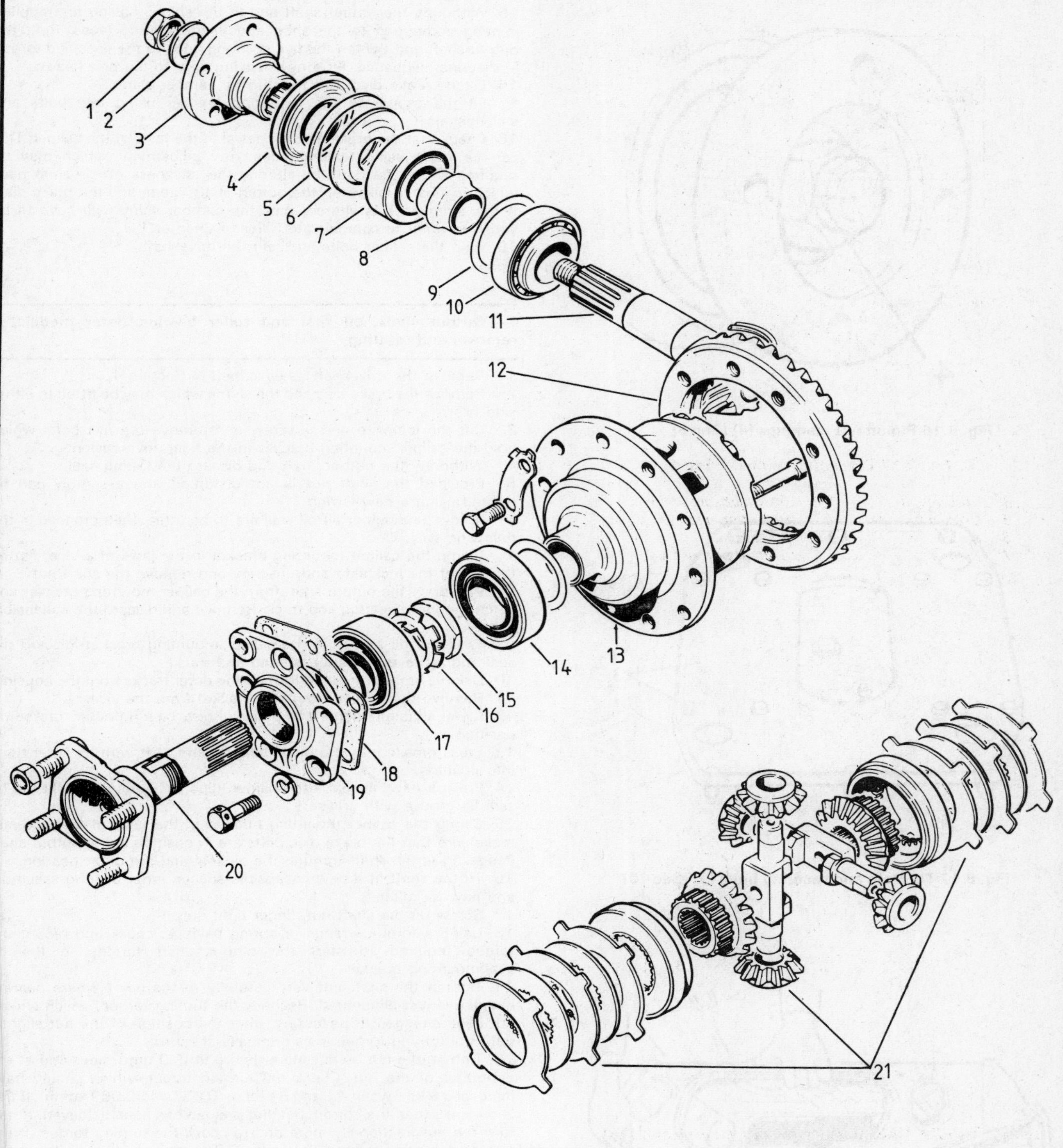


**Fig. 8.15 Exploded view of the final drive unit (Sec 7)**

1 *Pinion nut*
2 *Washer*
3 *Pinion drive flange*
4 *Oil seal*
5 *Spacer*
6 *Oil thrower*
7 *Outer pinion bearing*
8 *Collapsible spacer*
9 *Shim*
10 *Pinion inner bearing*
11 *Pinion shaft*
12 *Crownwheel*
13 *Differential case*
14 *Ouput shaft inner bearing*
15 *Output shaft nut*
16 *Nut lockplate*
17 *Output shaft outer bearing*
18 *Caliper centralising shim*
19 *Caliper mounting bracket*
20 *Output shaft*
21 *Differential assembly*

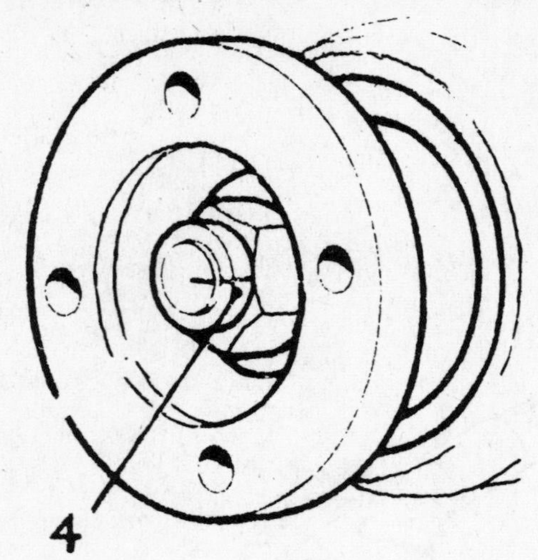


Fig. 8.16 Pinion nut markings (4) (Sec 8)

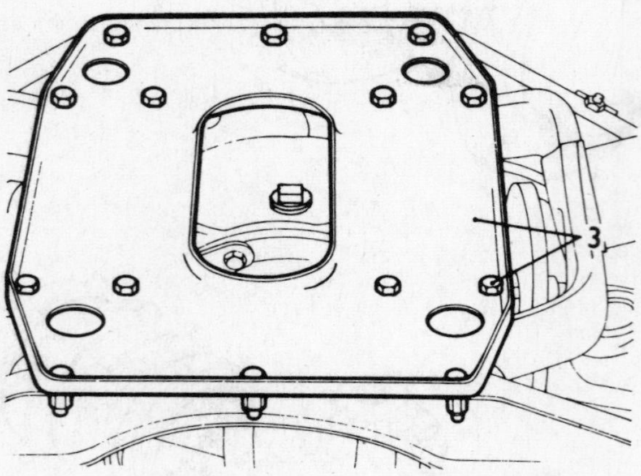


Fig. 8.17 Tie plate and securing bolts (3) (Sec 10)

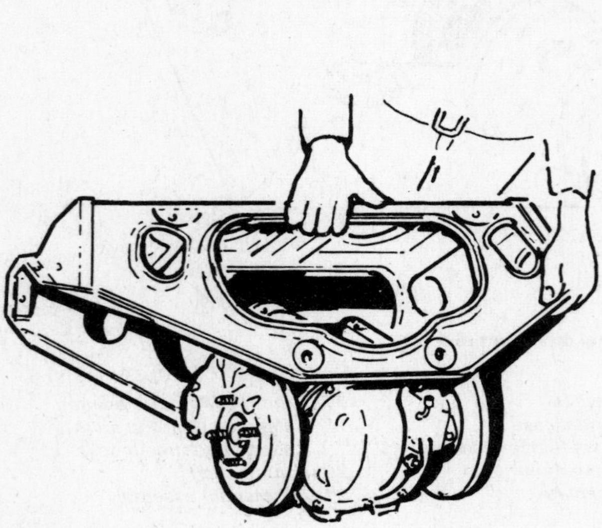

Fig. 8.18 Separating the crossmember from the final drive unit (Sec 10)

15 Withdraw the output shaft and fit the shims, having first applied jointing compound to the shim and flange mating faces. Refit the output shaft and tighten the five securing bolts to the specified torque in diagonal sequence. Fit a new locking wire to the bolt heads.
16 Fit the brake disc with the original camber shims.
17 Fit the caliper to the mounting bracket using two bolts and lockwashers.
18 Check that the brake disc is central in the jaws of the caliper. This can be done using feeler blades. Any adjustment which may be required should be done by altering the thickness of the shim pack which is located between the output shaft flange and the brake disc. If this shim pack is altered, then the camber shims will have to be varied in order to compensate (refer to Chapter 11).
19 Wire the caliper bolts and refit the driveshaft.

## 7 Output shaft, oil seal and roller bearing (later models) – removal and refitting

1 Remove the driveshaft as described in Section 4.
2 Remove the brake disc and the shims which may be fitted to either side of it.
3 Cut the lockwire and unscrew and remove the five bolts which hold the caliper mounting bracket to the final drive casing.
4 Withdraw the output shaft and discard the O-ring seal.
5 Provided the shaft nut is not disturbed, the assembly can be refitted using a new O-ring.
6 If new bearings or an oil seal are to be fitted, then proceed in the following way.
7 Clamp the caliper mounting bracket in the jaws of a vice, flatten the tab of the lockplate and unscrew and remove the shaft nut.
8 Withdraw the output shaft from the caliper mounting bracket and catch the inner bearing and track. Remove and discard the collapsible spacer.
9 Prise the oil seal from the caliper mounting bracket, discard the seal and retrieve the outer bearing and track.
10 Using a brass drift, drive the bearing outer tracks from the housing.
11 Remove the caliper mounting bracket from the vice.
12 Clean all components and press all new bearing outer tracks into position.
13 Press grease into the outer bearing and fit it with its inner track into position.
14 Press a new oil seal into position (lips to bearing) and fill the oil seal lip groove with grease.
15 Clamp the caliper mounting bracket in the jaws of the vice and make sure that the brake disc bolts are in position in the output shaft flange. Pass the shaft through the oil seal and the outer bearing.
16 To the shaft fit a new collapsible spacer, inner bearing assembly and new lockplate.
17 Screw on the shaft nut, finger tight only.
18 Using a torque wrench or spring balance, check and record the torque required to start the output shaft turning in the oil seal/mounting bracket.
19 Tighten the shaft nut very carefully to the point where bearing endplay is just eliminated. Recheck the turning torque, which should not have changed. If necessary, alter the position of the nut slightly until the turning torque is as originally checked.
20 Tighten the nut by not more than $\frac{3}{16}$ in (5.0 mm) measured at the perimeter of the nut. Check the turning torque which should have increased by between $4\frac{1}{2}$ and $5\frac{1}{2}$ lbf in (0.052 and 0.063 kgf m). If this is the case then the correct bearing preload has been achieved. If not, turn the nut fractionally more and re-check the turning torque. If the turning torque exceeds 6 lbf in (0.07 kgf m) then the nut has been overtightened and the assembly must be dismantled, a new collapsible spacer fitted and the setting operations started again. The collapsible spacer will not regain its original length if the shaft nut is backed off and when overcompressed, must be discarded and a new one fitted.
21 Once the correct preload has been set, bend down two tabs on the lockplate to lock the shaft nut
22 Refit the output shaft assembly as described in the following paragraphs.
23 Fit a new O-ring seal into the bearing housing groove.
24 Oil the shaft splines and insert the assembly into the final drive housing.
25 Using the five bolts, secure the caliper mounting bracket to the

final drive unit, tightening the bolts to the specified torque. Lock the bolt heads with wire.
26 Refit the brake disc and shims. Check the rear wheel camber angle (Chapter 11).

## 8 Pinion oil seal – renewal

1 A leaking oil seal can be renewed without the need to remove the final drive unit from the car.
2 Raise the rear of the car and disconnect the driveshaft inboard flanges from the final drive unit, noting the number and the location of any camber control shims.
3 Disconnect the rear end of the propeller shaft from the final drive pinion compression flange.
4 Use a suitable torque wrench (lbf in) or wind a cord round the companion flange of the pinion and attach it to a spring balance. Check and record the force required to start the flange moving. Take the average of several recordings.
5 Mark the relative position of the pinion nut to the end of the pinion shaft (Fig. 8.16).
6 Make up a suitable lever, 3 to 4 ft (0.9 to 1.2 m) in length and drilled so that by bolting it to the companion flange, the flange can be held still while the nut is unscrewed.
7 Unscrew and remove the pinion nut and washer and withdraw the companion flange. Use an extractor if necessary.
8 Prise out the faulty oil seal and install the new one.
9 Refit the companion flange (complete with propeller shaft flange bolts) and the washer and screw on the pinion nut. The pinion threads should be clean with thread locking compound applied to them.
10 Tighten the pinion nut very carefully until it takes up its previously marked position. Hold the flange still with the long restraining lever.
11 Check the rotating force required to turn the flange using the cord and spring balance. Tighten the pinion nut, *only a fraction of a turn at a time,* until the force recorded on the spring balance exceeds that recorded before dismantling by between 5 and 10 lbf in (0.06 and 0.12 kgf m).
12 The correct turning torque of the pinion flange should be between 25 and 30 lbf in (0.29 and 0.35 kgf m). If the required torque is lower than specified, tighten the nut slightly. If it is higher (above 45 lbf in, 0.52 kgf m maximum) then the collapsible spacer which is located between the pinion bearings will be overcompressed and a new spacer will have to be fitted. It is no good attempting to reduce the preload by backing off the nut. A new spacer can only be fitted after almost complete dismantling of the final drive unit.
13 Reconnect the propeller shaft and the driveshafts and lower the car. Check and top up the oil in the final drive.

## 9 Final drive casing rear cover gasket – renewal

1 A leaking rear cover gasket can be renewed in the following way.
2 Raise the rear of the car and support it on axle stands.
3 Unbolt the bottom tie plate from the crossmember and inner fulcrum brackets.
4 Drain the oil from the final drive unit.
5 Unscrew and remove the ten setscrews and detach the rear cover and gasket.
6 Refitting is a reversal of removal, but clean the mating flanges and smear the new gasket with grease.
7 Fit the drain plug and fill the final drive unit with specified oil to the level of the filler plug hole. Recheck the level when the car has been lowered to the ground.

## 10 Final drive unit – removal and refitting

1 Remove the rear suspension as described in Chapter 11. Drain the oil from the final drive unit.
2 Invert the suspension assembly on the bench and remove the 14 bolts which secure the tie plate.
3 Disconnect the four shock absorber/roadspring assemblies but do not dismantle them.
4 Remove the four self-locking nuts which secure the driveshaft

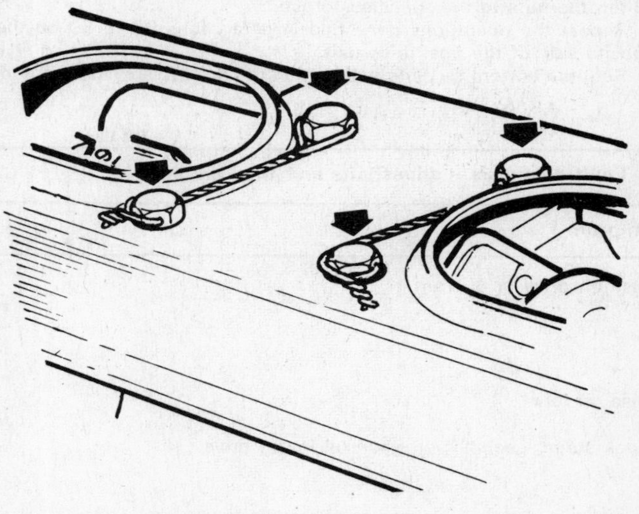

Fig. 8.19 Final drive to crossmember bolts (arrowed) and locking wire (Sec 10)

inner universal joint flange to the brake disc and final drive output flanges (remove the shrouds first on later models).
5 Pull the driveshafts aside, noting the number and location of the camber shims.
6 Remove a nut from one end of the suspension inner wishbone pivot shafts and drive out the shafts.
7 Withdraw the hubs, driveshafts and radius arm assemblies.
8 Disconnect the handbrake levers from the compensator.
9 Disconnect the brake lines from the caliper units.
10 Turn the final drive assembly over and cut the locking wire from the differential carrier bolts. Unscrew the bolts and remove the crossmember from the carrier by tilting the crossmember forward over the nose of the pinion.
11 Cut the lockwires and unbolt the wishbone pivot brackets from the final drive unit. Note the location and number of any shims.
12 Cut the caliper locking wire and unbolt and remove the calipers.
13 Remove the brake discs, noting the location and number of shims.
14 Commence refitting by placing the caliper centralising shims onto the face of the output flange of the final drive unit, followed by a brake disc. Secure with two nuts.
15 Fit a caliper, tighten the mounting bolts and check that the disc runs centrally in the caliper jaws. If it does not, transfer a shim from one side of the disc to the other.
16 Tighten the caliper bolts and lock them with wire.
17 Refit the opposite brake disc and caliper in a similar way.
18 Remove the nuts from both discs.
19 Place the crossmember over the final drive unit, refit the bolts and tighten to the specified torque. Lock the bolt heads with wire.
20 Refit the handbrake lever return springs.
21 Invert the complete assembly on the bench and offer the wishbone pivot brackets to the final drive unit. Secure each loosely with two setscrews.
22 Insert the shims removed at dismantling between the wishbone pivot brackets and the final drive unit.
23 Tighten the bracket setscrews to the specified torque and lock them with wire.
24 Refit the camber shims to one side onto the brake disc studs. Refit the driveshaft and tighten the nuts to the specified torque.
25 Fit the spacer tube between the lugs of the wishbone pivot bracket on one side of the final drive unit.
26 Lubricate the wishbone bearings. Offer up the wishbone to the pivot bracket and insert a dummy shaft to retain the bearing components.
27 Now drive the pivot shaft into position, keeping its end in close contact with the dummy shaft as the latter is displaced.
28 Tighten the pivot shaft nut to the specified torque.
29 Re-locate and fix the driveshaft shroud.
30 Refit the shock absorber with spacer and lash-down bracket.

Tighten the nuts to the specified torque.
31 Repeat the operations described in paragraphs 20 to 30 on the opposite side of the final drive unit.
32 Refit the bottom tie plate and tighten the bolts to specified torque.
33 Refit the rear suspension unit as described in Chapter 11.
34 On completion of installation, bleed the brakes (Chapter 9), check the rear wheel camber (Chapter 11) and check and top up the oil in the final drive unit.

## 11 Fault diagnosis – driveshafts and final drive

| Symptom | Reason(s) |
|---|---|
| Noise on drive or overrun | Low oil level<br>Loose crownwheel bolts<br>Loose bearing cap bolts<br>General wear in bearings or gear teeth |
| Noise on turn | Seized broken or damaged pinion or side gear or thrust washers |
| Knock during gearshift or when taking up drive | Excessive crownwheel to pinion backlash<br>Worn gears<br>Worn driveshaft splines<br>Drive pinion nut loose<br>Loose crownwheel bolts or bearing cap bolts<br>Worn side gear splines<br>Wear in driveshaft universal joints |

# Chapter 9 Braking system

*For modifications, and information applicable to later models, see Supplement at end of manual*

**Contents**



**Specifications**

### Front brakes

| | |
|---|---|
| Type | Girling ventilated disc, bridge type calipers |
| Disc diameter | 11.18 in (284.0 mm) |
| Disc thickness | 0.95 in (24.13 mm) |
| Minimum disc thickness (after regrind) | 0.9 in (22.86 mm) |

### Rear brakes

| | |
|---|---|
| Type | Girling inboard damped disc, bridge type calipers incorporating mechanically operated handbrake caliper |
| Disc diameter | 10.375 in (263.5 mm) |
| Disc thickness | 0.50 in (12.7 mm) |
| Minimum disc thickness (after regrind) | 0.45 in (11.43 mm) |

### Hydraulic system

| | |
|---|---|
| Master cylinder bore diameter: | |
| XJS: | |
| Up to 1983 | 0.938 in (23.83 mm) |
| 1984 on | 0.875 in (22.23 mm) |
| XJ12 and Double Six | 0.875 in (22.23 mm) |
| Fluid type/specification | Hydraulic fluid to SAE J1703/D (Duckhams Universal Brake and Clutch Fluid) |
| Servo unit | Girling Supervac 100 |

### Torque wrench settings

| Torque wrench settings | lbf ft | Nm |
|---|---|---|
| Brake pedal box to body | 13 | 18 |
| Master cylinder mounting nuts | 20 | 27 |
| Servo unit to pedal box | 10 | 14 |
| Rear flexible hose bracket to crossmember | 18 | 25 |
| Vacuum reserve tank to body nuts | 18 | 25 |
| Front disc to hub bolts | 35 | 48 |
| Front caliper mounting bolts | 55 | 75 |
| Tie plate bolts and nut | 18 | 25 |
| Rear caliper mounting bolts | 55 | 75 |
| Master cylinder banjo bolts | 23 | 31 |
| Master cylinder tipping valve nut (early models) | 40 | 54 |
| Handbrake mounting bolts: | | |
| XJS | 18 | 25 |
| XJ12 and Double Six | 7 | 10 |

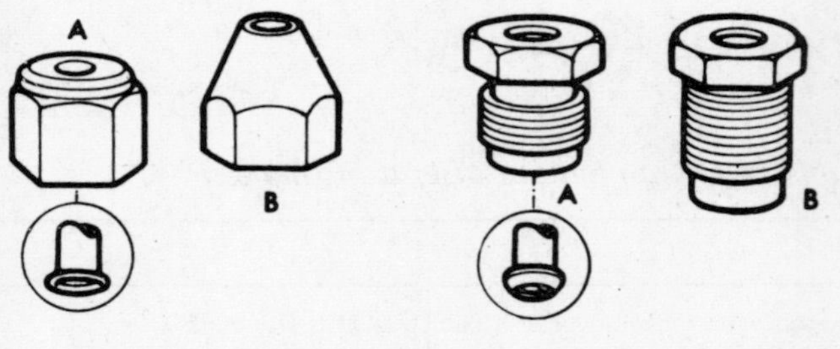


**Fig. 9.1 Brake pipe union nuts identification (Sec 2)**

*A Metric*
*B UNF*

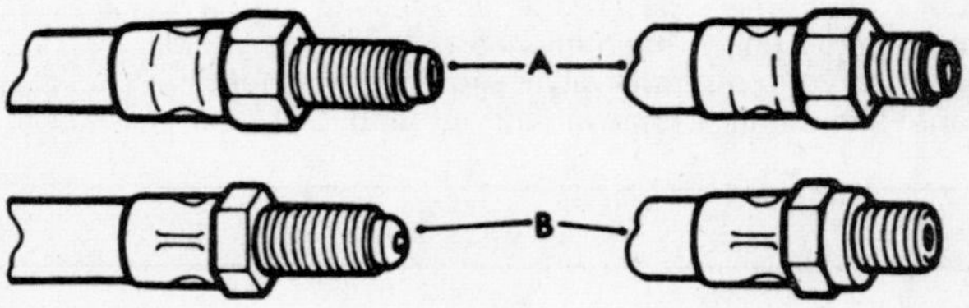


**Fig. 9.2 Flexible brake hose end fittings – identification (Sec 2)**

*A Metric*
*B UNF*

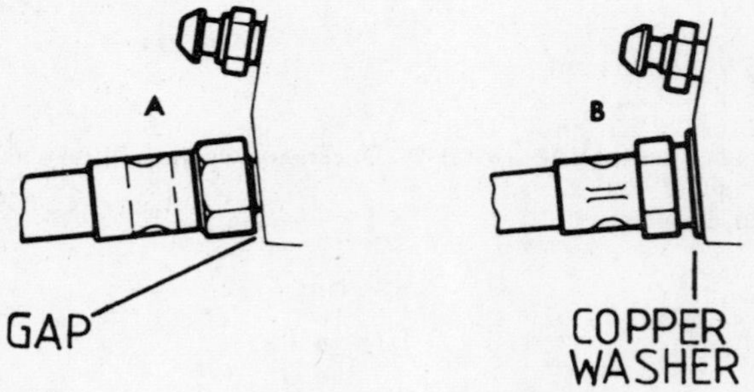


**Fig. 9.3 Flexible hoses installed – identification (Sec 2)**

*A Metric*
*B UNF*

## 1 General description

1 The braking system is of four-wheel disc type. The hydraulic system is of dual type with a tandem master cylinder. Servo assistance is provided.
2 The rear calipers and discs are mounted inboard on the differential housing and output flanges.
3 The handbrake operates through mechanical linkage to the rear calipers which incorporate automatically adjustable handbrake mechanism.
4 Later models differ from earlier cars in respect of the following:

*(a) Redesigned master cylinder*
*(b) Redesigned pressure differential warning actuator*
*(c) Four piston type front calipers*
*(d) Partial metrication of the system (see Section 2)*

5 Cars incorporating the new components can be identified by the plastic adaptors which connect the reservoir fluid lines to the master cylinder, or on very late versions by the reservoir being mounted directly on the master cylinder (photo).

## 2 Precautions

1 When topping up or bleeding the system, always use hydraulic fluid which meets SAE J1703/D specification.
2 When dismantling and cleaning internal components of the system, use only hydraulic fluid or brake cleaning fluid – nothing else, otherwise the seals will be ruined.
3 On later cars with partial metrication of the brake hydraulic system, the following components do not yet have metric threads or connections, but retain UNF threads:

*(a) Rear calipers*
*(b) Handbrake calipers*
*(c) Hydraulic pipes from the rear three-way connector to rear calipers and the rear three-way connector itself*

4 For safety reasons, always screw any component of the hydraulic system into position using the fingers only initially to test that the threads are compatible.
5 Identification of UNF and metric components can be made after reference to the accompanying illustrations.
6 Always discard fluid which has been bled from the system and top up the system with fluid which has been stored in an airtight container and has remained unshaken for the preceding 24 hours.

## 3 Disc pads – inspection and renewal

1 At the intervals specified in Routine Maintenance, examine the thickness of the friction material on the disc pads.
2 In the case of the front brakes, remove the roadwheels.
3 The pads are clearly visible through the aperture in the caliper units and if the friction material has worn down to $\frac{1}{8}$ in (3.2 mm) or less then they must be renewed.
4 Always renew the pads in axle sets.
5 Withdraw the spring clips and pull out the pad retaining pins (photo). Extract the anti-chatter springs (front pads).
6 Withdraw the pads from the caliper, gripping their edges with a pair of pliers if they are hard to remove (photo). Do not depress the brake pedal while the pads are out of the caliper or the pistons will be ejected.
7 Brush out any dust from the interior of the caliper and then depress the caliper pistons squarely into their bores in order to accommodate the new, thicker pads (photo). Depressing the pistons will cause the fluid level to rise in the master cylinder reservoir and eventually overflow, so it is advisable to draw off some of the hydraulic fluid from the reservoir before commencing operations. A poultry baster or an old hydrometer is useful for drawing off some fluid. Do not spill any hydraulic fluid on the paintwork as it acts as a paint stripper!
8 Install the new pads making sure that the friction lining is against the disc. Insert the retaining pins, the spring clips and the anti-chatter springs (front pads).
9 Apply the footbrake several times to bring the pads into contact with the discs and then top up the fluid reservoir to the indicated level.
10 For renewal of handbrake friction pads, see Section 18.

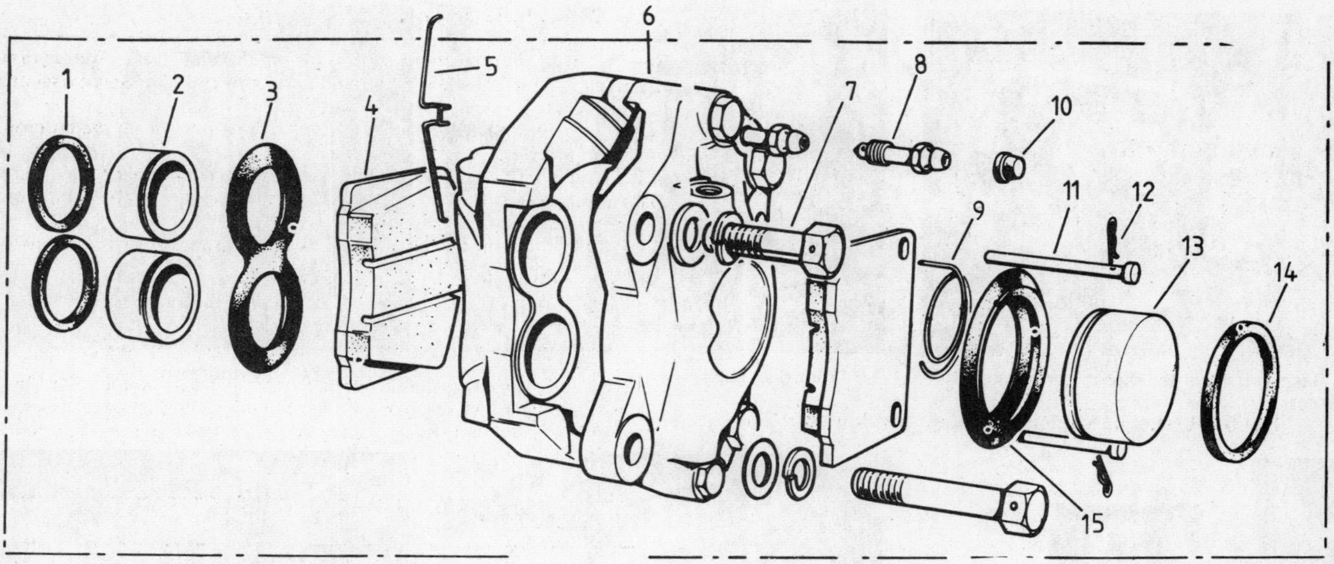


**Fig. 9.4 Three-piston type front caliper (Sec 4)**

1 Piston seal
2 Piston
3 Dust-excluding boot
4 Disc pad
5 Anti-chatter spring
6 Caliper
7 Caliper mounting bolt
8 Bleed nipple
9 Dust-excluding boot clip
10 Bleed nipple cap
11 Pad retaining pin
12 Pin clip
13 Piston
14 Piston seal
15 Dust-excluding boot

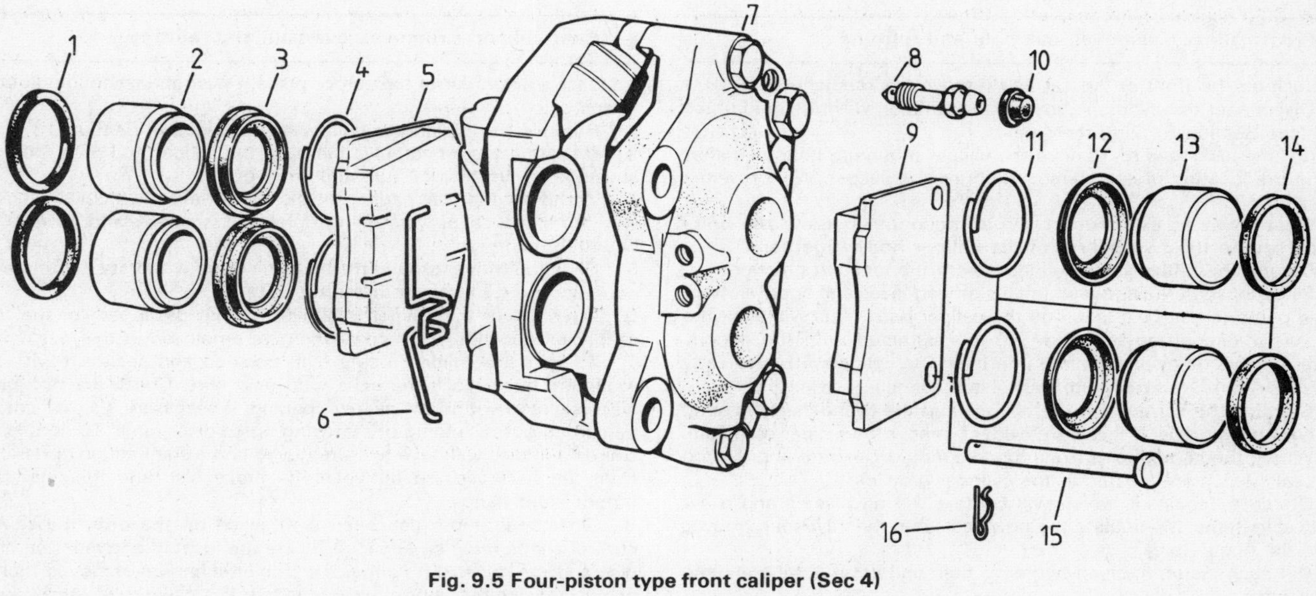


**Fig. 9.5 Four-piston type front caliper (Sec 4)**

1 Piston seal
2 Piston
3 Dust-excluding boot
4 Dust-excluding boot clip
5 Disc pad
6 Anti-chatter spring
7 Caliper
8 Bleed nipple
9 Disc pad
10 Bleed nipple cap
11 Dust-excluding boot clip
12 Dust-excluding boot
13 Piston
14 Piston seal
15 Pad retaining pin
16 Pin clip

1.5 Reservoir mounted directly onto master cylinder

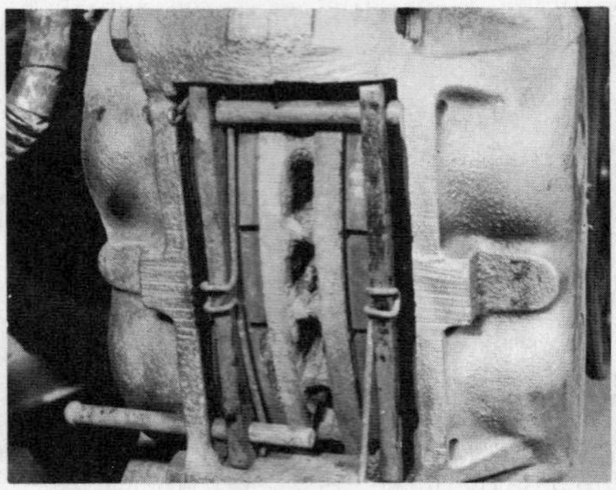

3.5 Front disc pads

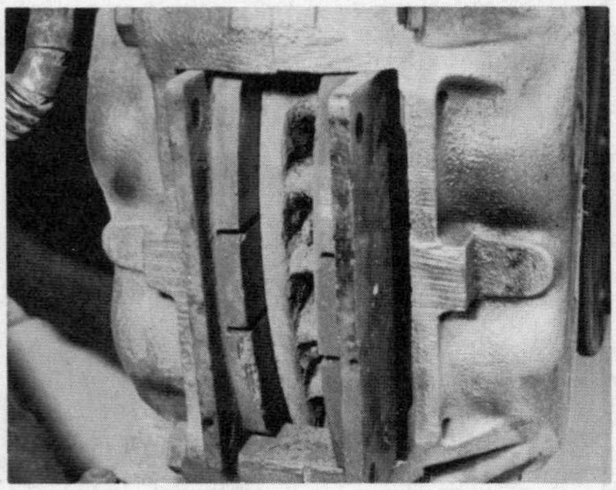

3.6 Pads being withdrawn

3.7 Pads removed

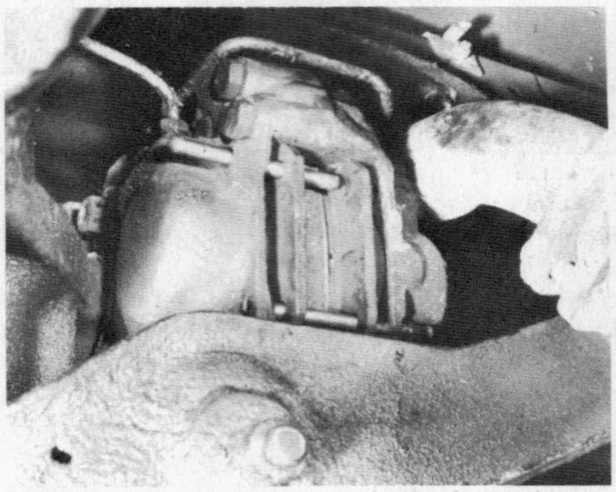

5.4A Rear disc caliper

5.4B Withdrawing rear disc pads

## 4 Front caliper – removal, overhaul and refitting

1 Jack-up the front of the car and remove the roadwheel.
2 Disconnect the hydraulic hose at the junction with the rigid brake pipe (see Section 8). Plug the pipes.
3 Cut the locking wire, remove the caliper mounting bolts and after noting the location of any shims, withdraw the caliper. Withdraw the disc pads.
4 Clean away all external dirt. **On no account unscrew the bolts which secure the two halves of the caliper body together.**
5 Detach the rubber dust excluders from the locating grooves.
6 Place a pad of rag between the piston end faces and apply air from a tyre pump to the fluid union on the caliper body. This will eject the pistons far enough so that they can be extracted with the fingers. There are two outer pistons and one inner, on calipers fitted to early cars; later cars are fitted with four-piston calipers.
7 Examine the surfaces of the pistons and the cylinders for scoring or bright wear areas. If these are evident, renew the caliper complete.
8 Where the components are in good condition, extract and discard the seals which are located in the cylinder grooves.
9 Obtain a repair kit which will contain the new seals and other renewable items. Manipulate the new seals into their cylinder grooves using the fingers only.
10 Dip each piston in clean hydraulic fluid and enter it squarely into its cylinder.
11 Refit the dust excluders and engage their lips in the cylinder grooves. Depress the pistons fully into their cylinders.
12 Refit the caliper to the stub axle carrier and refit the shims. Add or remove shims if necessary to centralise the caliper jaws on the disc. Tighten the bolts to the specified torque wrench setting. Lock the bolts with new wire.
13 Refit the disc pads.
14 Reconnect the hydraulic hose and bleed the front circuit, as described in Section 16.
15 Refit the roadwheel and lower the car to the ground.

## 5 Rear caliper – removal, overhaul and refitting

1 Jack up the rear of the car, or place it over an inspection pit or on ramps.
2 Remove the handbrake caliper as described in Section 18.
3 Disconnect the hydraulic line from the caliper and plug the open ends to prevent loss of fluid and entry of dirt.
4 Withdraw the disc pads from the caliper and then cut the locking wire from the caliper mounting bolts and unscrew and remove the bolts (photos).
5 Slide the caliper around the brake disc and withdraw it through the gap exposed by removal of the tie plate.
6 Overhaul of the caliper is similar to that described for the front caliper except that only two pistons are employed in the rear unit.
7 To refit the caliper, locate it in position and secure it with two mounting bolts. Lock the bolts with new wire. Check that the brake disc is central within the caliper opening. If necessary, adjustment can be carried out by adding or removing brake disc shims. To do this, the caliper and disc will have to be removed and a shim added or removed from the pack located between the brake disc and the final drive output shaft flange.
8 Once the caliper has been centralised on the disc, the camber control shims must be adjusted. These are located between the brake disc and the driveshaft flange. If a caliper shim was removed then an equivalent camber shim must be added. If a caliper shim was added then a camber shim of equivalent thickness must be removed.
9 Reverse the rest of the removal operations and when refitting is complete, bleed the rear brake circuit as described in Section 16.

## 6 Master cylinder (early type) – removal, overhaul and refitting

1 Remove the cap from the master cylinder reservoir and draw off as much fluid as possible by syphoning or using a poultry baster or old hydrometer.

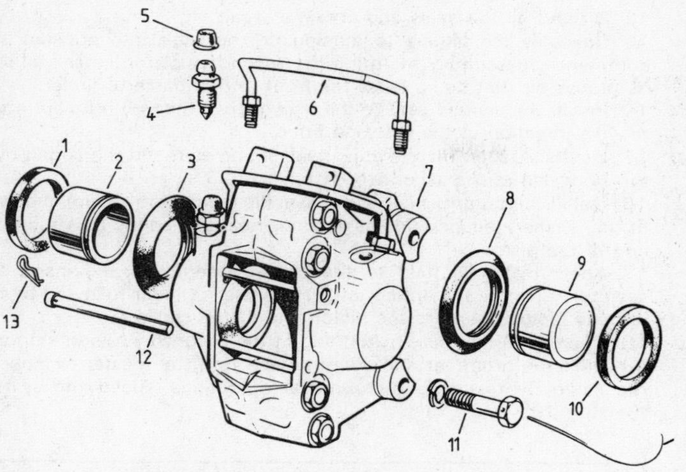


**Fig. 9.6 Rear caliper (typical) (Sec 5)**

*1 Piston seal*
*2 Piston*
*3 Dust-excluding boot*
*4 Bleed nipple*
*5 Bleed nipple cap*
*6 Bridge pipe*
*7 Caliper*
*8 Dust-excluding boot*
*9 Piston*
*10 Piston seal*
*11 Caliper mounting bolt*
*12 Pad retaining pin*
*13 Pin clip*

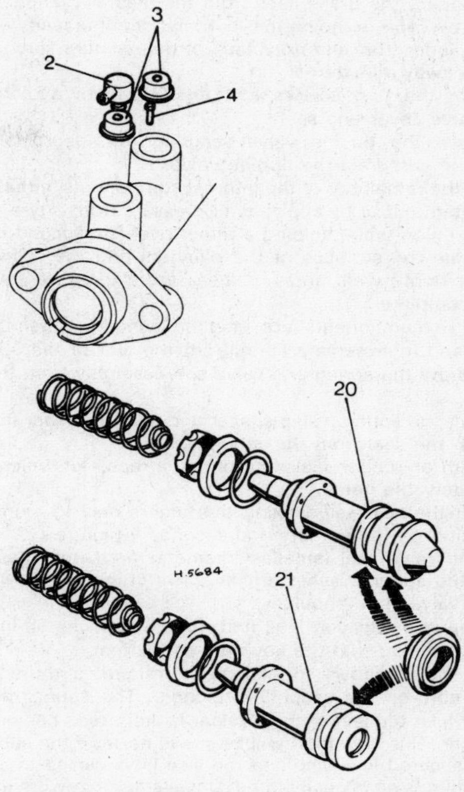


**Fig. 9.7 Exploded view of later type master cylinder (Sec 7)**

*2 Fluid pipe adaptor*
*3 Grommets*
*4 Lock pin*
*20 Secondary piston*
*21 Primary piston*

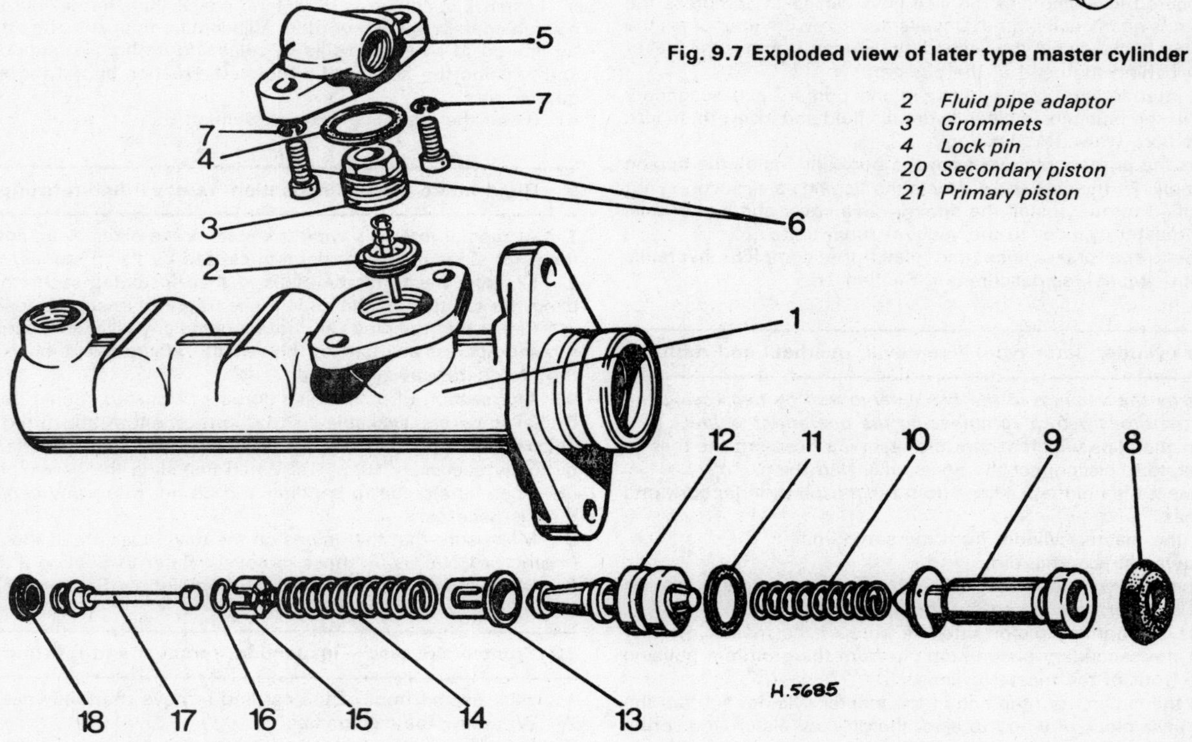


**Fig. 9.8 Exploded view of early type master cylinder (Sec 6)**

*1 Body*
*2 Tipping valve*
*3 Tipping valve securing nut*
*4 Tipping valve cover seal*
*5 Cover*
*6 Screws*
*7 Spring washers*
*8 Gland seal*
*9 Primary plunger*
*10 Intermediate spring*
*11 Ring seal*
*12 Secondary plunger*
*13 Thimble*
*14 Spring*
*15 Valve spacer*
*16 Spring washer*
*17 Valve stem*
*18 Valve seal*

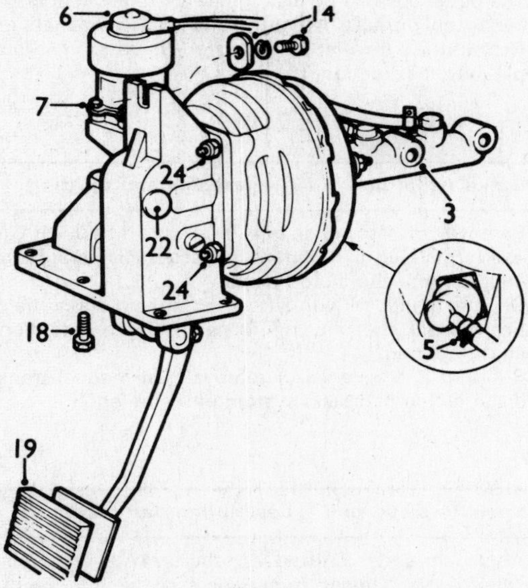


**Fig. 9.27 Brake pedal box assembly (XJ12, Double Six) (Sec 24)**

*3 Master cylinder*
*5 Vacuum hose to servo unit*
*6 Fluid reservoir cap*
*7 Reservoir mounting bolts*
*14 Pedal box upper mounting bolt*
*18 Pedal box base bolts*
*19 Brake pedal pad*
*22 Rubber sealing plug*
*24 Servo mounting nuts*

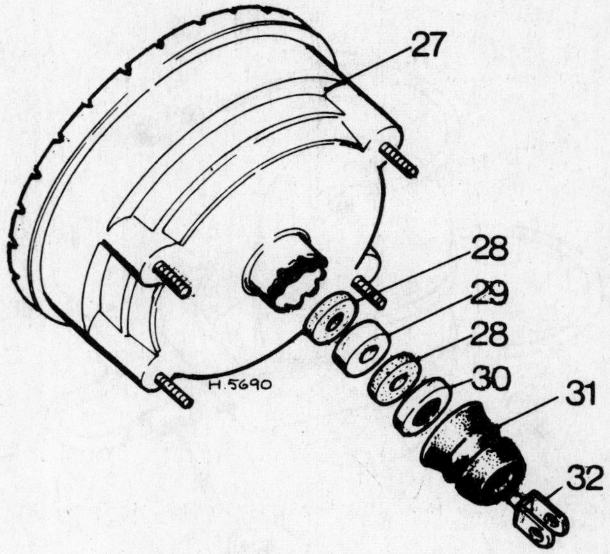


**Fig. 9.28 Typical brake servo air filter components (Sec 27)**

*27 Rear shell*
*28 Filter felts*
*29 Air filter*
*30 Filter retainer*
*31 Dust cover*
*32 Clevis fork*

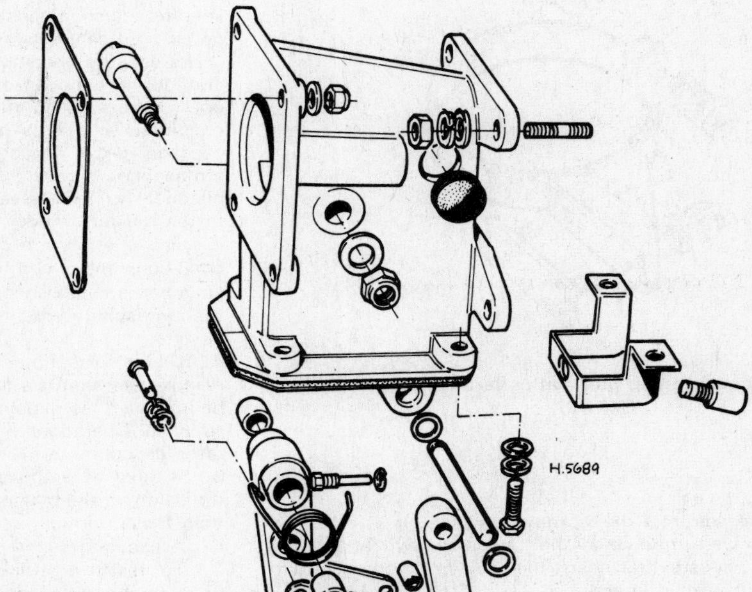

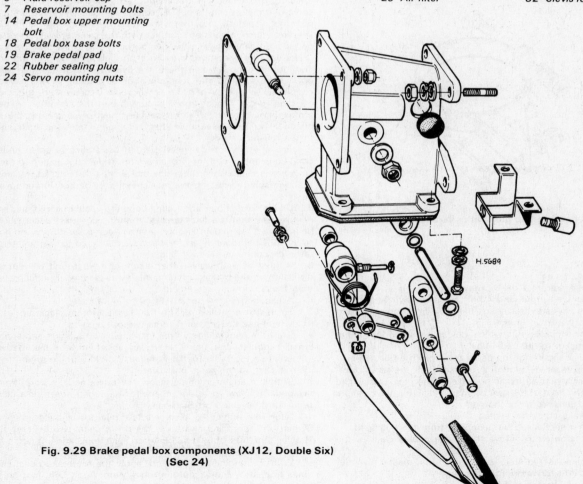

**Fig. 9.29 Brake pedal box components (XJ12, Double Six) (Sec 24)**

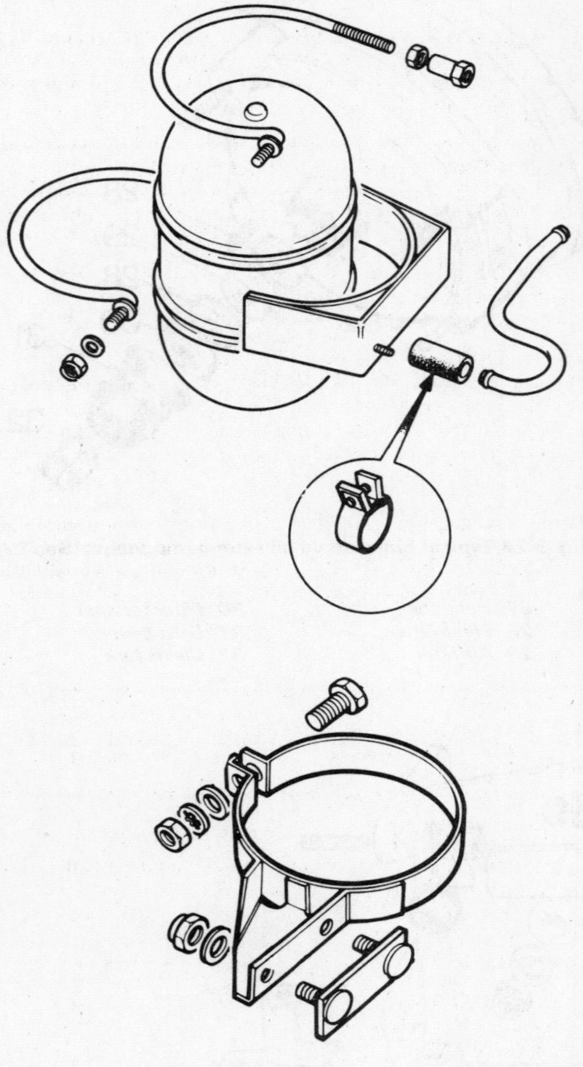

Fig. 9.30 Vacuum reservoir tank with alternative mountings (Sec 30)

8 Disconnect the leads from the kickdown switch.
9 Slacken the locknut that holds the kickdown switch and the throttle cable to the pedestal. Disengage the cable from the pulley and move it away from the servo unit.
10 Remove the self-locking nut which holds the steering column lower mounting bracket to the pedal box.
11 Unbolt the upper section of the pedal box from the bulkhead.
12 Unbolt the fluid reservoir mounting bracket from the servo unit.
13 Move the driver's seat as far as possible to the rear. Extract the single screw from the front of the seat cushion and lift out the cushion.
14 Remove the carpets from the footwell.
15 Remove the brake stoplamp switch.
16 Unbolt the lower section of the pedal box from the bulkhead.
17 On cars with carburettors, move the choke cables clear of the servo unit.
18 Lift the combined servo unit, pedal box and master cylinder upwards and remove it forwards from the car.
19 Extract the two rubber plugs from the sides of the pedal box.
20 Disconnect the servo operating rod from the brake pedal arm.
21 Unbolt the pedal box from the servo unit.
22 The pedal box can be dismantled for renewal of bushes and thrust washers. Apply grease to shafts, bushes and washers on reassembly.
23 Refitting is a reversal of removal. Bleed the hydraulic system on completion (see Section 16).

## 25 Brake pedal box (XJS) – removal and refitting

1 Removal of the pedal box from cars fitted with manual transmission is covered in Chapter 5, Section 3, paragraphs 1 to 14, in conjunction with the clutch pedal.
2 On cars equipped with automatic transmission, the operations are identical except that any reference to clutch actuating components should be ignored.
3 Refitting is a reversal of removal. On manual transmission cars, bleed the clutch hydraulic system on completion.

## 26 Vacuum servo unit – description and testing

1 A vacuum servo is fitted into the brake hydraulic circuit in series with the master cylinder, to provide assistance to the driver when the brake pedal is depressed. This reduces the effort required by the driver to operate the brakes under all braking conditions.
2 The unit operates by vacuum obtained from the induction manifold and comprises basically a booster diaphragm and non-return valve. The servo unit and hydraulic master cylinder are connected together so that the servo unit piston rod acts as the master cylinder pushrod. The driver's braking effort is transmitted through another pushrod to the servo unit piston and its built in control system. The servo unit piston does not fit tightly into the cylinder, but has a strong diaphragm to keep its edges in constant contact with the cylinder wall, so assuring an air tight seal between the two parts. The forward chamber is held under vacuum conditions created in the inlet manifold of the engine and, during periods when the brake pedal is not in use, the controls open a passage to the rear chamber so placing it under vacuum conditions as well. When the brake pedal is depressed, the vacuum passage to the rear chamber is cut off and the chamber opened to atmospheric pressure. The consequent rush of air pushes the servo piston forward in the vacuum chamber and operates the main pushrod to the master cylinder.
3 The controls are designed so that assistance is given under all conditions and, when the brakes are not required, vacuum in the rear chamber is established when the brake pedal is released. All air from the atmosphere entering the rear chamber is passed through a small air filter.
4 Under normal operation conditions the vacuum servo unit is very reliable, but should a fault develop then the complete assembly must be renewed as repair kits or internal components are no longer supplied. Operations must therefore be restricted to the maintenance tasks described in the next Section.
5 It must be emphasised that failure of a servo unit will not affect the safety of the braking system, merely cause higher pedal pressures than those normally required.
6 A vacuum reserve tank is fitted to all models.
7 To test the efficiency of the servo system, jack up a front roadwheel and check that it turns without binding.
8 Start the engine, allow time for vacuum to build up and apply the brake pedal several times. Have an assistant turn the roadwheel immediately the brake pedal is released. If the brake binds then an internal fault in the servo is indicated.
9 With the engine running, apply the brake pedal several times. If the pedal is slow to return, check for damaged hoses or a clogged servo air filter, see next Section.
10 Allow the engine to idle for a few minutes to build up vacuum. Switch off the engine and apply the brake pedal two or three times. The vacuum 'hiss' should be heard on each application. If not, a faulty non-return valve or a leak in the system is indicated.
11 With the engine switched off, apply the footbrake pedal several times to destroy the vacuum in the system. Apply light foot pressure to the brake pedal and start the engine. If the servo is operating correctly, the foot pedal will move nearer the floor. If it does not move then the system is leaking.

## 27 Vacuum servo unit – maintenance

1 Occasionally check the security and condition of the vacuum hose to the inlet manifold.
2 At specified intervals (see Routine Maintenance) or when the foot brake pedal seems to be sluggish in operation, renew the air filter in the following way.
3 Remove the brake vacuum servo unit, as described in Section 24 or 25.
4 Remove the dust cover, detach the end cap and withdraw the filter and filter felt rings. Cut the filter rings to permit them to pass over the clevis fork.
5 Fit the new filter felts by cutting them cleanly so that they will pass over the clevis fork. Ensure that the cuts in the various filter rings are not in line, but stagger their position.
6 Refit the end cap and dust cover.
7 Refit the brake vacuum servo unit.

## 28 Vacuum servo unit – removal and refitting

1 The vacuum servo unit is removed and refitted in conjunction with the pedal box as described in Section 24 or 25.

## 29 Vacuum servo non-return valve – removal and refitting

1 Disconnect the vacuum flexible hose from the non-return valve on the intake manifold. After 1983, the non-return valve is located in the servo vacuum hose.
2 Unscrew and remove the non-return valve and its copper washer (if applicable).
3 The valve can be tested by blowing through it, first in one direction and then in the other. Air should only pass one way.
4 Refit by reversing the removal operations, but use a new copper washer (if applicable).

## 30 Vacuum reserve tank – removal and refitting

1 Jack up the front of the car and remove the right-hand front roadwheel.

### *XJ12 and Double Six*

2 Remove the horn relay.
3 Disconnect the hose from the vacuum tank.

### *XJS*

4 Extract the screws which hold the lower edge of the diaphragm panel to the front skirt panel.
5 Prise out the plastic studs which hold the top of the diaphragm panel to the inner wing. Remove the diaphragm panel.

### *All models*

6 Disconnect the tank mounting clamp or straps and withdraw the tank from the car. On XJS models the vacuum pipe must be disconnected from the tank before it can be completely withdrawn.
7 Refitting is a reversal of removal.

## 31 Fault diagnosis – braking system

| Symptom | Reason(s) |
|---|---|
| Pedal travels almost to floor before brakes operate | Brake fluid level too low<br>Caliper leaking<br>Master cylinder leaking (bubbles in master cylinder fluid)<br>Brake flexible hose leaking<br>Brake line fractured<br>Brake system unions loose<br>Pad linings over 75% worn |
| Brake pedal feels springy | New pads not yet bedded-in<br>Brake discs badly worn or cracked<br>Master cylinder securing nuts loose |
| Brake pedal feels spongy and soggy | Caliper leaking<br>Master cylinder leaking (bubbles in master cylinder reservoir)<br>Brake pipe line or flexible hose leaking<br>Unions in brake system loose |
| Excessive effort required to brake car | Pad linings badly worn<br>New pads recently fitted – not yet bedded-in<br>Harder pads fitted than standard causing increase in pedal pressure<br>Pads or discs contaminated with oil, grease or hydraulic fluid<br>Servo unit inoperative or faulty |
| Brakes uneven and pulling to one side | Pads or discs contaminated with oil, grease or hydraulic fluid<br>Tyre pressures unequal<br>Brake caliper loose<br>Brake pads fitted incorrectly<br>Different type of pads fitted at each wheel<br>Anchorages for front suspension or rear suspension loose<br>Brake discs badly worn, cracked or distorted |
| Brakes tend to bind, drag or lock-on | Air in hydraulic system<br>Caliper pistons seized<br>Handbrake cables too tight<br>Fault in servo unit |

# Chapter 10 Electrical system

*For modifications, and information applicable to later models, see Supplement at end of manual*

**Contents**

Specifications

## System type

| | |
|---|---|
| System type | 12 volt, negative earth |

## Battery capacity

| | |
|---|---|
| XJ12 and Double Six | 70 Ah at 20-hour rate |
| XJS | 68 Ah at 20-hour rate |

## Alternator

| | |
|---|---|
| Make and type | Lucas 20 ACR or 25 ACR, or Motorola 9AR 2512P |
| Cut-in voltage | 13.5V |
| Cut-in speed | 950 to 1500 (alternator) rpm |
| Maximum output | 66A |
| Maximum operating speed | 15 000 (alternator) rpm |

## Starter motor

| | |
|---|---|
| Make and type | Lucas M45G pre-engaged |

## Windscreen wiper motor

| | |
|---|---|
| Make and type | Lucas 16W, two-speed |

## Lamp bulbs

*The bulbs listed below are typical, but precise details may vary according to model year and operating territory. For exact specification consult the operator's handbook supplied with the vehicle.*

| | Bulb No | Wattage |
|---|---|---|
| Headlamp: | | |
| Main and dip | 411 | 60/45 |
| Main beam only | 411 | 50 |
| Halogen | H1 | 55 |
| N America | 15602 | 37.5/50 |
| Front flasher and parking (N. America) | GLB 380 | 21/6 |
| Front flasher | GLB 382 | 21 |
| Front parking | GLB 207 | 5 |
| | or GLB 989 | 6 |
| Reversing lamp | GLB 273 | 21 |
| Rear number plate | GLB 989 | 6 |
| | or GLB 254 | |
| Rear flasher | GLB 382 | 21 |
| Tail | GLB 207 | 5 |
| Stop/tail | GLB 380 | 21/6 |
| Map reading | GLB 254 | 6 |
| Interior and pillar | GLB 272 | 10 |
| Luggage boot | GLB 989 | 6 |
| Clock | GLB 987 | 2.2 |
| Warning lamps | Capless | 1.2 |
| Opticell | GLB 989 | 6 |
| Speedometer | GLB 981 | 2.2 |
| Tachometer | GLB 987 | 2.2 |
| Choke warning | GLB 987 | 2.2 |
| Choke handle | GLB 281 | 2 |
| Main beam warning | GLB 987 | 2.2 |
| Safety belt warning | GLB 987 | 2.2 |
| Heater control panel | GLB 280 | 1.5 |
| Automatic transmission indicator | GLB 281 | 2 |
| Foglamp or spotlamp (Cibie) | H2 | 55 |
| Cigar lighter | G70112 | 2.2 |
| Warning lamp (catalytic converter) | GLB 281 | 2 |

## 1 General description

1 All models have a 12 volt negative earth system.
2 The major components of the system comprise a battery, a belt-driven alternator and a pre-engaged type starter motor.
3 On cars equipped with an air-conditioning system, a heavy duty alternator is fitted.
4 The battery supplies a steady current for the ignition, lighting and other electrical circuits and provides a reserve of electricity when the current consumed by the electrical equipment exceeds that being produced by the charging system.
5 Although full instructions for the periodic overhaul and minor servicing of the various electrical components are given in this Chapter it must be appreciated that rectification of major faults will require specialised knowledge and equipment and therefore, where such faults arise, the defective item should be removed and replaced with a serviceable item which can usually be obtained on an exchange basis.
6 Wiring diagrams covering the various models will be found at the end of the Chapter.

## 2 Battery – maintenance and inspection

1 On XJ12 and Double Six models, the battery is located within the engine compartment against the rear bulkhead (photo).
2 On XJS models, the battery is located in the luggage compartment

under a cover held in place by two screws.

3 Keep the top of the battery clean by wiping away dirt and moisture.

4 Remove the plugs or lid from the cells and check that the electrolyte level is just above the separator plates. If the level has fallen, add only distilled water until the electrolyte level is just above the separator plates. Where a Lucas Pacemaker battery is fitted, lift the vent cover and check that electrolyte is visible in all the filling tubes. If it is, do not add any more. If any tube is empty, add distilled water into the filler trough to the indicated level, then refit the vent cover.

5 As well as keeping the terminals clean and covered with petroleum jelly, the top of the battery, and especially the top of the cells, should be kept clean and dry. This helps prevent corrosion and ensures that the battery does not become partially discharged by leakage through dampness and dirt.

6 If topping up the battery becomes excessive and the case has been inspected for cracks that could cause leakage, but none are found, the battery is being over-charged and the voltage regulator within the alternator will have to be checked.

7 At three-monthly intervals, measure the electrolyte specific gravity with a hydrometer to determine the state of charge and condition of the battery. There should be very little variation between the different cells and if a variation in excess of 0.25 is present it will be due to either:

*(a) Loss of electrolyte from the battery at some time caused by spillage or a leak, resulting in a drop in the specific gravity of electrolyte when the deficiency was replaced with distilled water instead of fresh electrolyte*

*(b) An internal short circuit caused by buckling of the plates or a similar malady pointing to the likelihood of total battery failure in the near future*

8 The specific gravity of the electrolyte for fully charged conditions at the electrolyte temperature indicated, is listed in Table A. The specific gravity of a fully discharged battery at different temperatures of the electrolyte is given in Table B.

**Table A**

Specific Gravity – Battery Fully Charged

| | |
|---|---|
| *1.268 at* | *100°F or 38°C electrolyte temperature* |
| *1.272 at* | *90°F or 32°C electrolyte temperature* |
| *1.276 at* | *80°F or 27°C electrolyte temperature* |
| *1.280 at* | *70°F or 21°C electrolyte temperature* |
| *1.284 at* | *60°F or 16°C electrolyte temperature* |
| *1.288 at* | *50°F or 10°C electrolyte temperature* |
| *1.292 at* | *40°F or 4°C electrolyte temperature* |
| *1.296 at* | *30°F or-1.5°C electrolyte temperature* |

**Table B**

Specific Gravity – Battery Fully Discharged

| | |
|---|---|
| *1.098 at* | *100°F or 38°C electrolyte temperature* |
| *1.102 at* | *90°F or 32°C electrolyte temperature* |
| *1.106 at* | *80°F or 27°C electrolyte temperature* |
| *1.110 at* | *70°F or 21°C electrolyte temperature* |
| *1.114 at* | *60°F or 16°C electrolyte temperature* |
| *1.118 at* | *50°F or 10°C electrolyte temperature* |
| *1.122 at* | *40°F or 4°C electrolyte temperature* |
| *1.126 at* | *30°F or-1.5°C electrolyte temperature* |

## 3 Battery – removal and refitting

### *XJ12 and Double Six*

1 The battery incorporates a cooling fan. Remove the battery in the following way. Open the bonnet.

2 Peel back the flexible covers from the battery terminals, release the pinch-bolts and disconnect the leads from the battery terminals. Always disconnect the earth lead first and reconnect last.

3 Disconnect the leads to the battery cooling fan by detaching them at the snap connectors.

4 Slacken the battery holding down bolts.

5 Prise the flexible outlet pipe from the cooling jacket grommet.

6 Detach the battery positive lead from the clip on the cooling jacket.

7 Ease the battery and its cooling jacket forward until the jacket can be withdrawn from the battery (photo).

8 Lift the battery from the car.

9 The cooling fan can be removed from the cooling jacket after withdrawing the seven securing screws. The nylon impeller can be levered from the motor shaft (photo).

10 Reassembly and refitting are reversals of removal and dismantling.

### *XJS*

11 Release the two screws and lift the cover from the battery.

12 Peel back the battery terminal covers, release the clamp bolts and disconnect the leads. Always disconnect the earth lead first and reconnect last.

13 Release the battery filler cover securing strap and remove the filler cover.

14 Unscrew the battery clamp nuts and remove the clamp.

15 Keeping the battery level, lift it from the luggage compartment.

## 4 Electrolyte replenishment (battery)

1 If the battery is in a fully charged state and one of the cells maintains a specific gravity reading which is 0.25 or more lower than the others, then it is likely that electrolyte has been lost from the cell with the low reading at some time.

2 Top up the cell with a solution of 1 part sulphuric acid to 2.5 parts of water. If the cell is already fully topped up draw some electrolyte out of it with a hydrometer. Do not mix the electrolyte yourself, but obtain it from your dealer or service station ready mixed. Recharge the battery and check the hydrometer readings.

3 If the specific gravity reading is still not satisfactory a new battery will have to be obtained, as the design of the intercell connectors prevents any further tests with, for example, a high rate discharge meter.

2.1 Battery (XJ12, Double Six) in cooling jacket

3.7 Battery with cooling jacket removed

3.9 Interior of battery cooling jacket

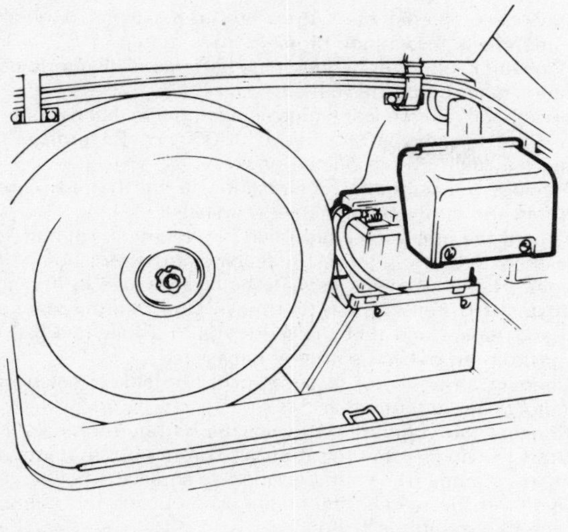

Fig. 10.1 Battery and cover in the luggage compartment (XJS) (Sec 2)

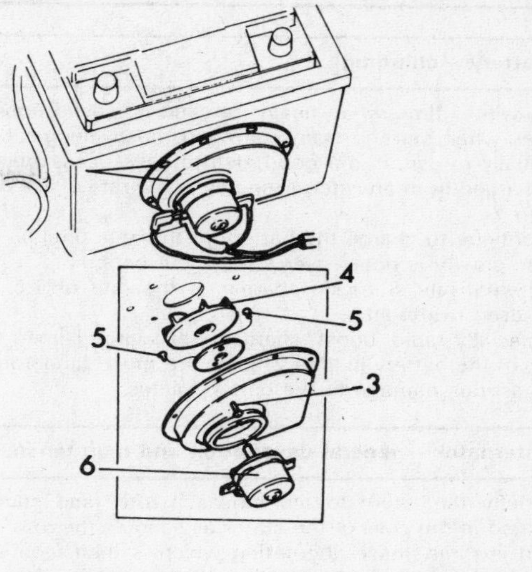


Fig. 10.2 Battery and cooling fan (XJ12, Double Six) (Sec 3)

3 *Fan securing screw*
4 *Fan*
5 *Keeper plate screws*
6 *Fan motor*

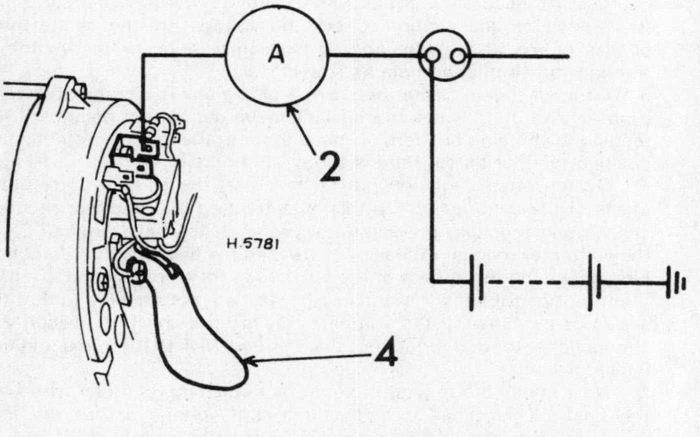


Fig. 10.3 Alternator output test (Lucas type) (Sec 8)

2 *Ammeter*
4 *Jump lead*

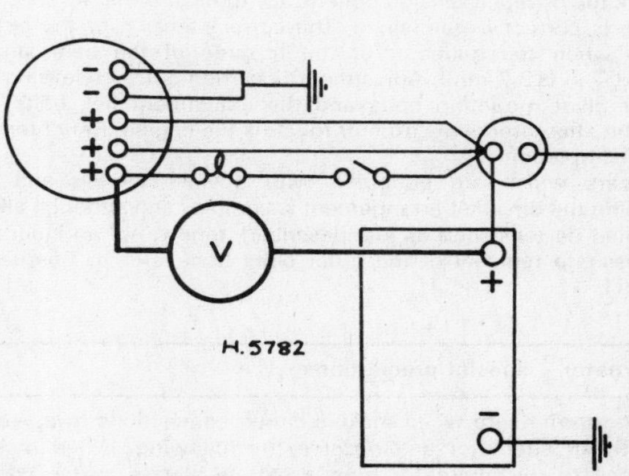


Fig. 10.4 Voltage drop test – positive side (Lucas alternator) (Sec 8)

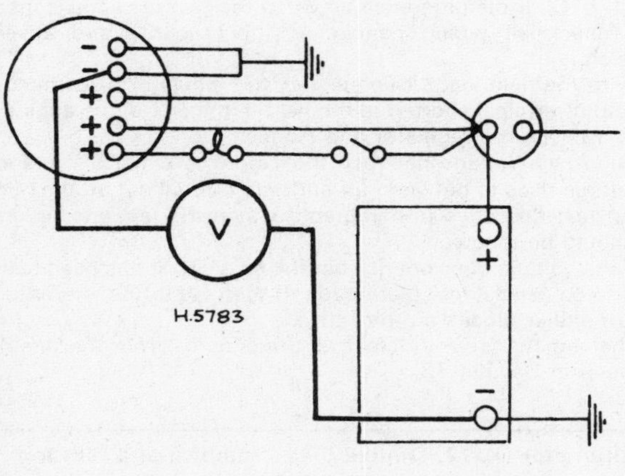


Fig. 10.5 Voltage drop test – negative side (Lucas alternator) (Sec 8)

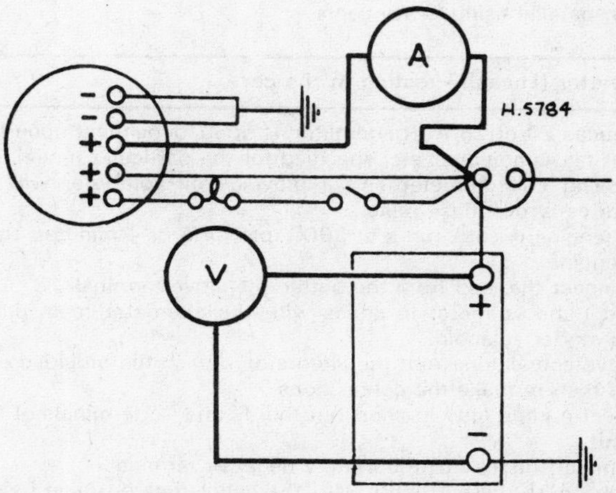


Fig. 10.6 Control unit test (Lucas alternator) (Sec 8)

## 5 Battery – charging

1 In winter time when heavy demand is placed upon the battery, such as when starting from cold, and much electrical equipment is continually in use, it is a good idea to have occasionally the battery fully charged from an external source at the rate of 3.5 or 4 amps (see Section 7).
2 Continue to charge the battery at this rate until no further rise in specific gravity is noted over a four hour period.
3 Alternatively, a trickle charger at the rate of 1.5 amps can be safely used overnight.
4 Specially rapid 'boost' charges which are claimed to restore the power of the battery in 1 to 2 hours are most dangerous as they can cause serious damage to the battery plates.

## 6 Alternator – general description and maintenance

1 Briefly the alternator comprises a rotor and stator. Current is generated in the coils of the stator as soon as the rotor revolves. This current is three-phase alternating which is then rectified by positive and negative silicon diodes and the level of voltage required to maintain the battery charge is controlled by a regulator within the alternator.
2 Maintenance consists of occasionally wiping away any oil or dirt which may have accumulated on the outside of the unit.
3 No lubrication is required as the bearings are grease sealed for life.
4 Check the drivebelt tension periodically to ensure that its specified deflection is correctly maintained. The correct tension of the belt is indicated when the midpoint of the top run of the belt can be depressed ½ in (12.7 mm). Adjustment is carried out by releasing the alternator pivot mounting bolts and the adjustment link bolts and moving the alternator away from or towards the engine. Retighten the bolts on completion.
5 On cars which are equipped with power steering and air-conditioning the drivebelt arrangement is complex and although all the belts should be tensioned as just described, renewal of an inner belt will necessitate removal of the outer belts first; refer to Chapter 1, Section 51.

## 7 Alternator – special precautions

Take extreme care when making circuit connections to a vehicle fitted with an alternator and observe the following. When making connections to the alternator from a battery always match correct polarity. Before using electric-arc welding equipment to repair any part of the vehicle, disconnect the connector from the alternator and disconnect the negative battery terminal. Never start the car with a battery charger connected. Always disconnect both battery leads before using a mains charger. If boosting from another battery, always connect in parallel using heavy cable.

## 8 Alternator (Lucas) – testing in the car

1 The Lucas 20 or 25 ACR alternator, is fitted, dependant upon the equipment (air-conditioner etc) specified for the particular model.
2 A moving coil ammeter and a moving coil voltmeter will be required to carry out these tests.
3 If the engine is cold, run it at 3000 rpm for 3 or 4 minutes, then stop the engine.
4 Disconnect the lead from the battery negative terminal.
5 Connect the ammeter in series with the alternator main outut cable and starter solenoid.
6 Remove connectors from the alternator, detach the moulded end cover and then re-make the connections.
7 Connect a jump lead to short out the 'F' and '–' terminals of the control unit.
8 Reconnect the lead to the battery negative terminal.
9 Switch on all the car lights with the headlamps on main beam. Switch on the ignition and check that the warning lamp is on.
10 Start the engine, slowly increase its speed to 3000 rpm. The reading on the ammeter should be equivalent to the alternator maximum rated output which is 66 amps. If it is not, the alternator requires overhaul and reconditioning.
11 Having completed the output test, remake the original connections and check for voltage drop.
12 Connect a voltmeter between the battery positive terminal and the alternator main output terminal.
13 Switch on all the car lights including the headlamps on main beam. Start the engine and run at 3000 rpm. Record the voltmeter reading and then switch off the engine.
14 Transfer the voltmeter connections to the battery negative terminal and the alternator negative terminal.
15 Repeat the operations described in paragraph 13, and again note the reading on the voltmeter. The readings recorded should not exceed 0.5 volts. Higher readings indicate high resistance in the circuit.
16 To test the control unit, first make sure that all connections are clean and secure and that the battery is in a fully charged condition (charge from an outside source if necessary).
17 Connect an ammeter in series with the starter solenoid and the alternator main output cable.
18 Connect the voltmeter between the battery terminals.
19 Start the engine and run it at 3000 rpm until the ammeter reads less than 10 amps. The voltmeter reading should be between 13.6 and 14.4 volts. If the reading fluctuates or is outside the range specified then the control unit is faulty.

## 9 Alternator (Motorola) – testing in the car

1 Before carrying out the tests, make sure that the battery is fully charged. An accurate voltmeter and ammeter will be required.
2 Switch off the ignition. Check the voltage on one of the three phases of the stator windings by passing a probe of the voltmeter through the ventilation hole as shown.
3 Connect the voltmeter between a phase and earth, then between a phase and the positive terminal. Observe the correct polarity. If the reading is anything but zero on the voltmeter then there is a defective positive rectifier diode. Renew the diode bridges.
4 Switch on the ignition but do not start the engine. Carry out a check of the field circuit. Do this by extracting the regulator securing screws and touching the voltmeter probe on the field terminal EX. If the voltmeter reading exceeds 2 volts then the field circuit is defective. First check the movement of the brushes in their holders and examine them for wear. Check that the brush leads are not frayed and that the slip rings are clean. If the voltmeter reads zero, check the security of connections to the regulator, the ignition switch and the ignition indicator lamp.
5 Now check the regulator circuit by detaching its green wire from the field EX terminal and measuring the voltage across the field windings. This should not exceed 2 volts. If it is between 8 and 12 volts then the alternator is faulty. If the voltage is correct, switch on the ignition and start the engine. Have the engine speed faster than the normal idle. Check the output voltage at the alternator B+ terminal and then at the battery positive terminal. The correct reading at both checking points should be 14.2V ± 0.5V at an ambient temperature of 77°F (25°C). If the difference between the two readings is more than 0.3V, check all wiring connections for security and absence of corrosion.
6 With the field lead disconnected, the regulator disconnected and the output terminal shorted to the field terminal, run the engine at fast idle and check the regulator and diodes.
7 Check the voltage between the output terminal B+ and earth. If the voltage rises to between 14 and 16V but did not attain 14V in the second test described in paragraph 5 then the regulator is defective and should be renewed.
8 If the voltage does not rise but the field circuit has been tested and found to be satisfactory (paragraph 4) then either the alternator stator or the rectifier diodes are defective.
9 The removal of any defective components from the alternator is described in Section 13.

## 10 Alternator (XJ12, Double Six) – removal and refitting

1 Disconnect the battery.
2 Remove the right-hand air cleaner (Chapter 3).
3 Where fitted, remove the air pump (Chapter 3).
4 Release the alternator mounting bolt and the adjuster link nut.
5 Slacken the adjuster trunnion block to bracket bolt.

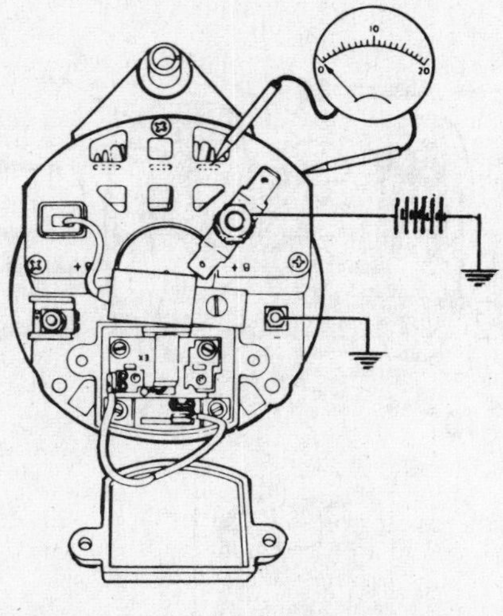

Fig. 10.7 Test circuit (phase to earth) – Motorola alternator (Sec 9)

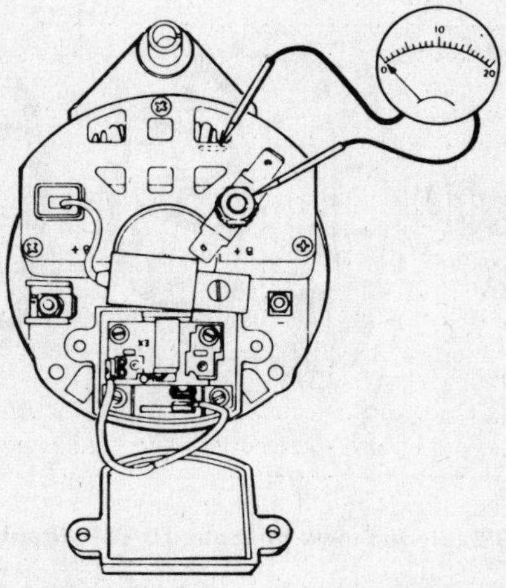

Fig. 10.8 Test circuit (winding to positive terminal) – Motorola alternator (Sec 9)

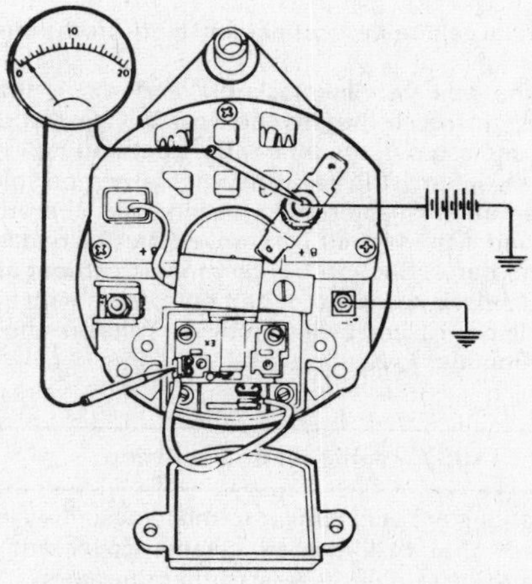

Fig.10.9 Test circuit (field winding check) – Motorola alternator (Sec 9)

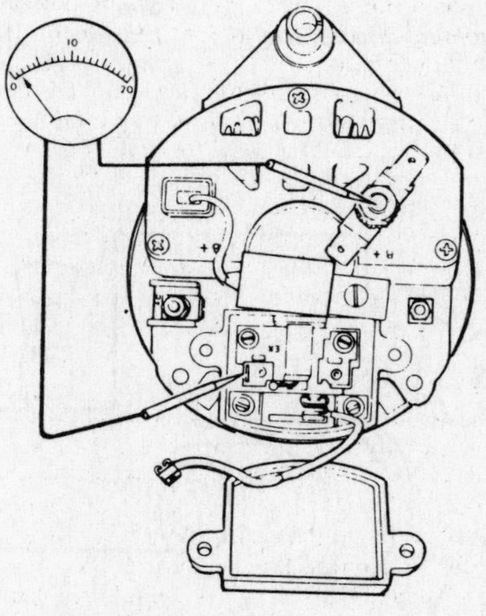

Fig. 10.10 Test circuit (regulator) – Motorola alternator (Sec 9)

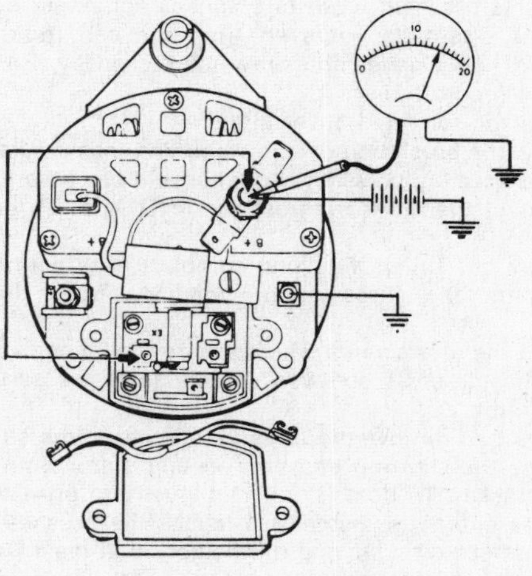

Fig. 10.11 Test circuit (diode) – Motorola alternator (Sec 9)

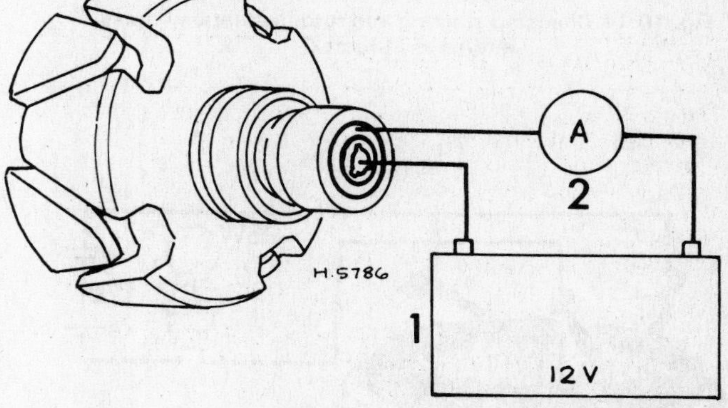


Fig. 10.12 Checking slip ring resistance (Lucas alternator) (Sec 12)

1 Battery
2 Ammeter

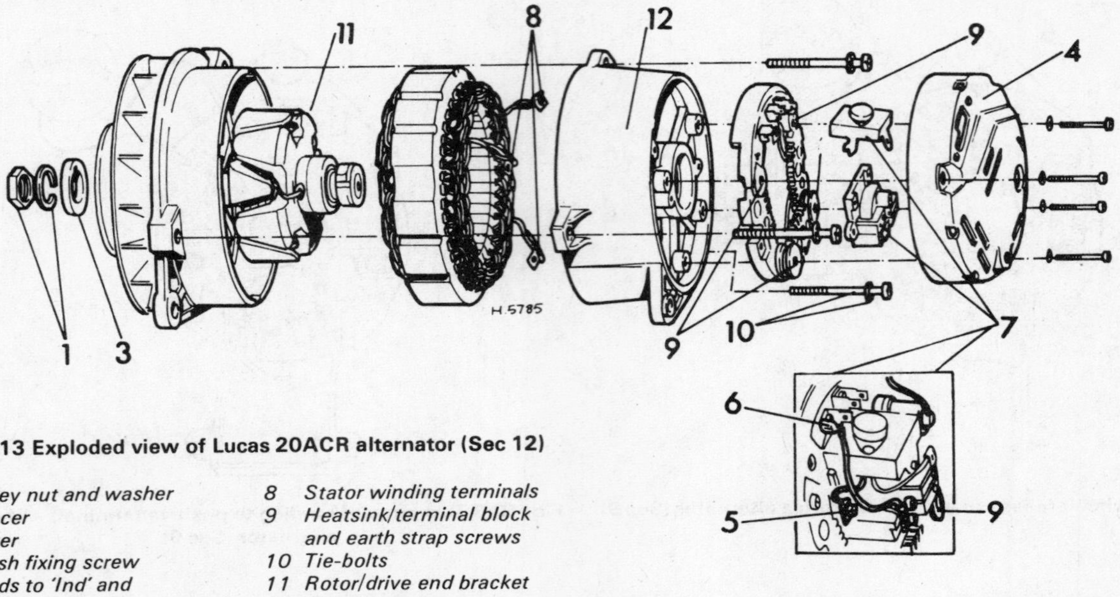


**Fig. 10.13 Exploded view of Lucas 20ACR alternator (Sec 12)**

*1 Pulley nut and washer*
*3 Spacer*
*4 Cover*
*5 Brush fixing screw*
*6 Leads to 'Ind' and '+' terminals*
*7 Brush moulding and control box*
*8 Stator winding terminals*
*9 Heatsink/terminal block and earth strap screws*
*10 Tie-bolts*
*11 Rotor/drive end bracket*
*12 Slip ring end bracket*

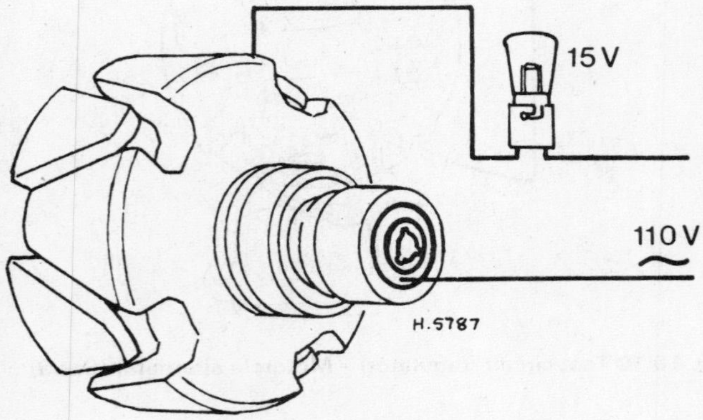


**Fig. 10.14 Checking slip ring and rotor insulation (Lucas alternator) (Sec 12)**

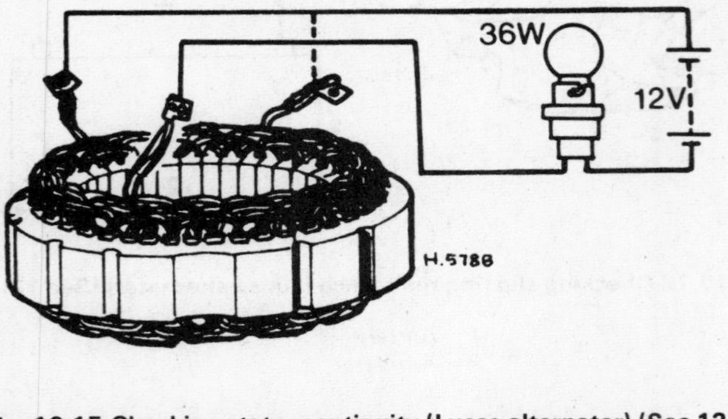


**Fig. 10.15 Checking stator continuity (Lucas alternator) (Sec 12)**

6 Pull out the electrical connector plug from the back of the alternator.
7 Release the adjuster link locknuts and move the alternator in towards the engine until the drivebelt can be slipped off the pulley.
8 Unscrew and remove the alternator front and rear mounting pivot bolts and lift the alternator from the engine compartment.
9 If the alternator drivebelt must be renewed, then the old belt can only be removed if the fanbelt is removed first by releasing the jockey pulley (see Chapter 1, Section 51) on models without air conditioning, or the fanbelt and the compressor belt on models with air conditioning.
10 Refitting is a reversal of removal. Tension the drivebelts as described in Chapter 1, Section 51.

## 11 Alternator (XJS) – removal and refitting

1 The operations are very similar to those described in the preceding Section, except that only the air cleaner cover and filter element should be removed to gain access to the alternator.

## 12 Alternator (Lucas) – overhaul

1 There are detail differences between the 20 and 25 ACR alternators but this overhaul procedure applies equally to both types.
2 With the alternator removed from the car, remove the pulley retaining nut and washer and draw off the pulley. Remove the fan, spacer and Woodruff key.
3 Remove the moulded cover plate.
4 Unscrew the brush holder screws, noting that they also secure the radio interference suppression capacitor and black earth cable.
5 Disconnect the red leads from the 'IND' and '+' terminals of the alternator.
6 Withdraw the brush moulding complete with control box.
7 Disconnect the three stator windings from their respective heatsinks.
8 Remove the four screws which secure the heatsink/terminal block assembly and the small screw which connects the earth strap to the alternator frame.
9 Unscrew and remove the three tie bolts from the alternator frame.
10 Separate the slip ring end bracket and stator from the rotor and drive end bracket. To do this, insert a lever and prise them apart.
11 With the alternator dismantled, check the brushes for wear. The brushes must protrude beyond the holder by at least 0.32 in (8 mm), otherwise renew them, noting the location of the leaf spring at the side of the inner brush.
12 The slip rings should normally only require cleaning with a fuel soaked cloth but if essential, they can be burnished with finest grade glasspaper (not emery).

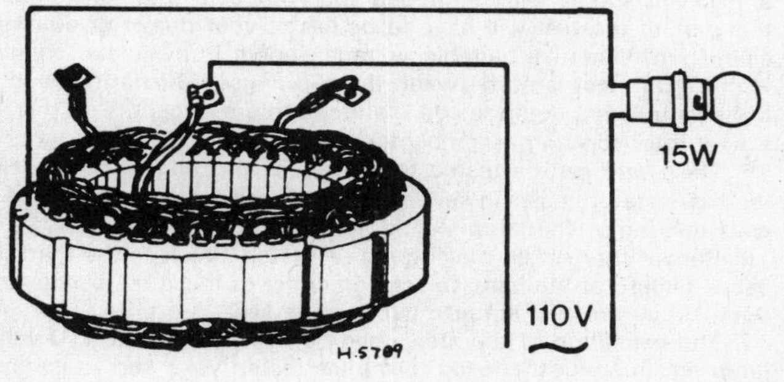


Fig. 10.16 Checking stator insulation (Lucas alternator) (Sec 12)

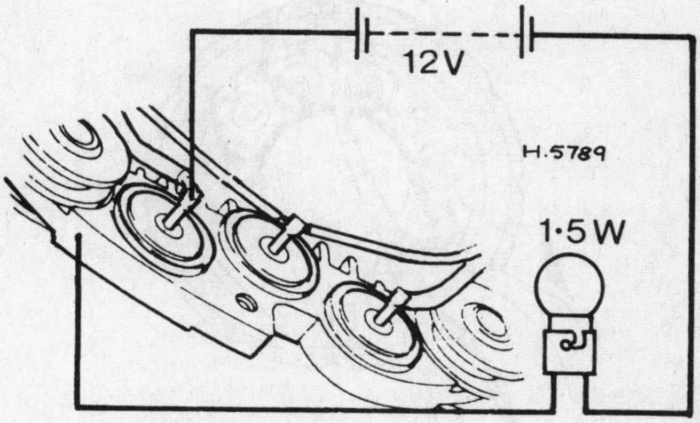


Fig. 10.17 Testing diodes (Lucas alternator) (Sec 12)

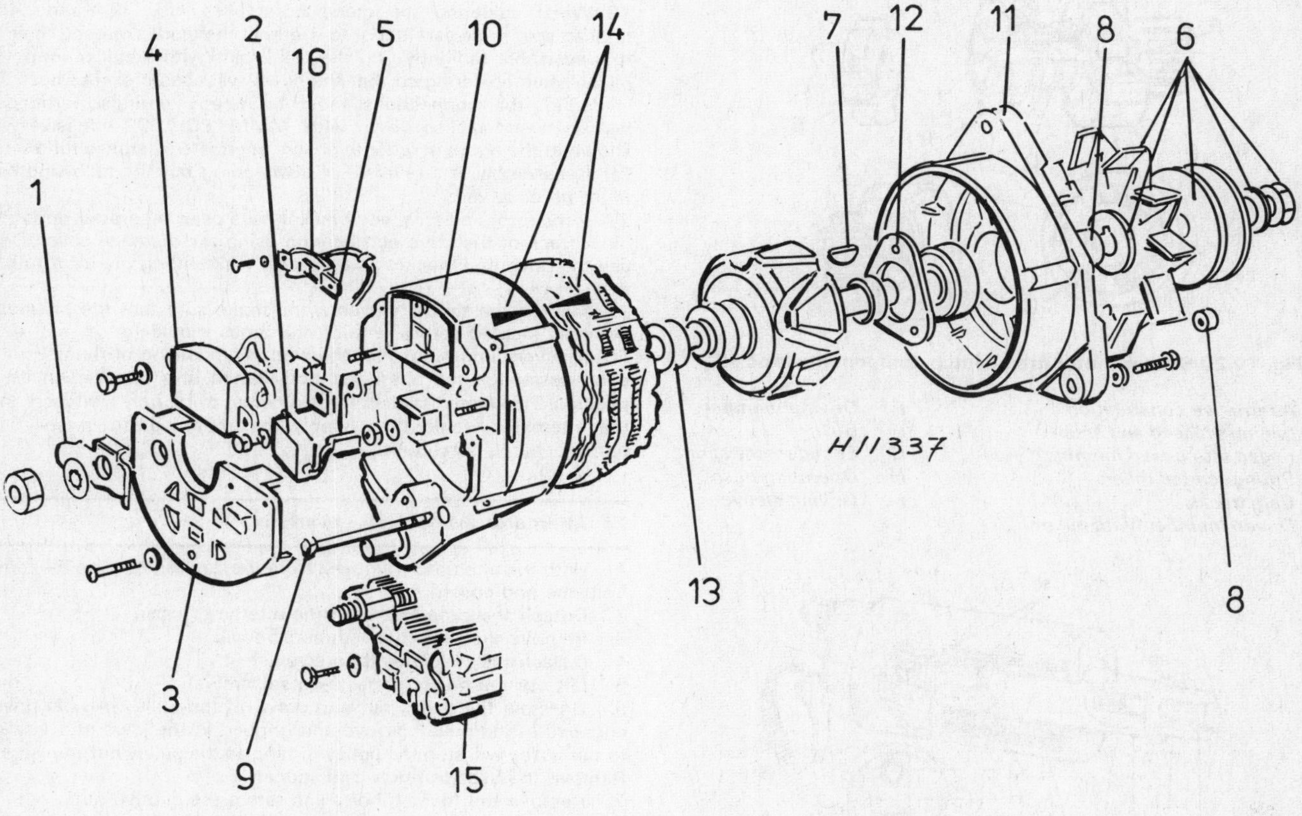


Fig. 10.18 Exploded view of Motorola alternator (Sec 13)

| | | | | | | | |
|---|---|---|---|---|---|---|---|
| *1* | *B+ terminal* | *5* | *Brush holder* | *9* | *Tie-bolt* | *13* | *Rear bearing* |
| *2* | *Capacitor* | *6* | *Pulley/fan components* | *10* | *Rear housing* | *14* | *Stator and alignment marks* |
| *3* | *Moulded rear cover* | *7* | *Woodruff key* | *11* | *Front housing* | *15* | *Diode bridge* |
| *4* | *Regulator* | *8* | *Spacer* | *12* | *Front bearing retainer* | *16* | *D+ lead assembly* |

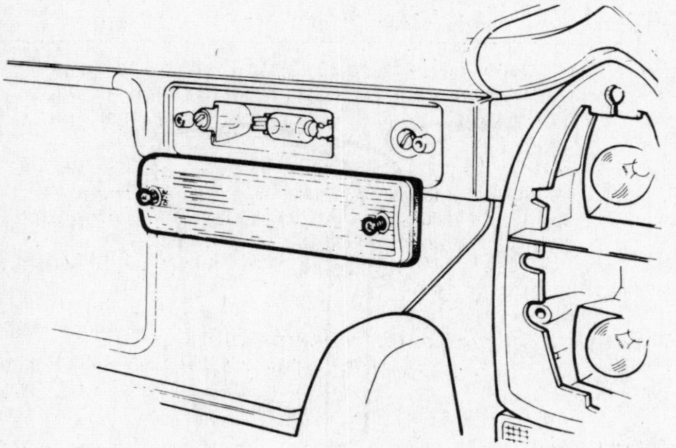

Fig. 10.56 Reversing lamp (XJ12 and Double Six, Series 1) (Sec 34)

Fig. 10.57 Interior pillar lamp (XJ12 and Double Six, Series 1) (Sec 34)

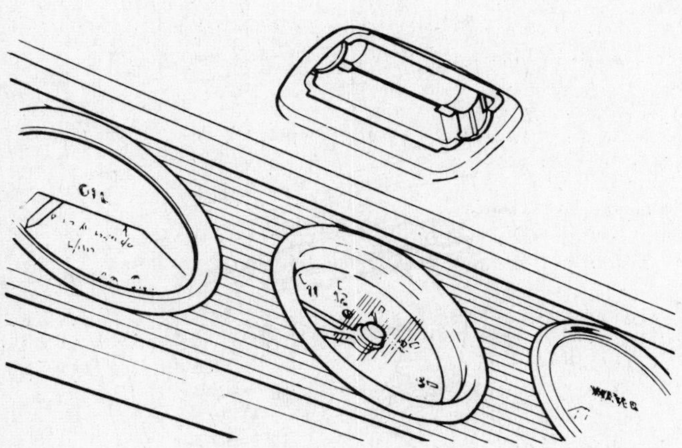

Fig. 10.58 Map reading lamp (XJ12 and Double Six, Series 1) (Sec 34)

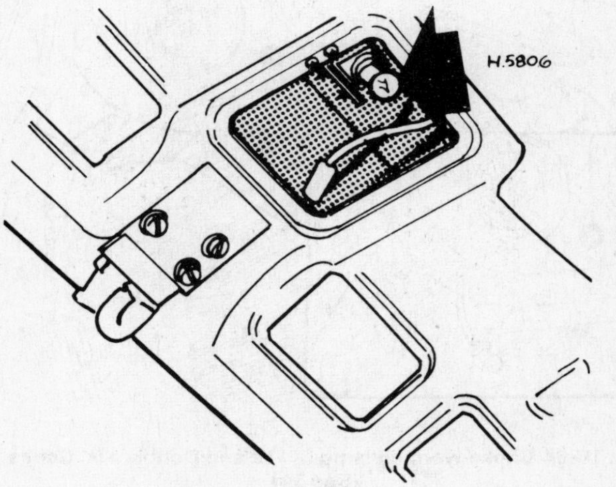


Fig. 10.59 Luggage boot lamp (XJ12 and Double Six, Series 1) (Sec 34)

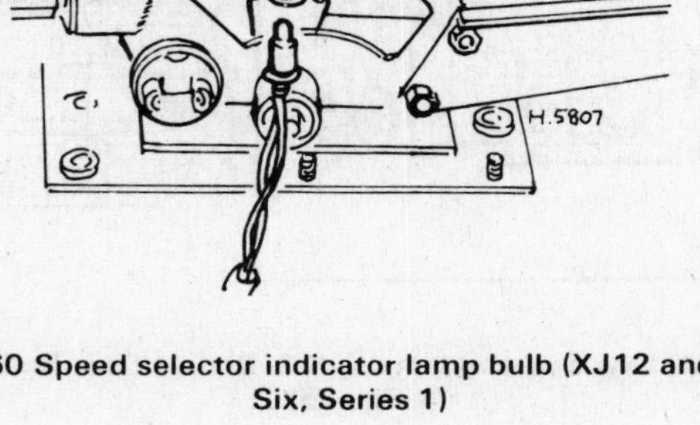

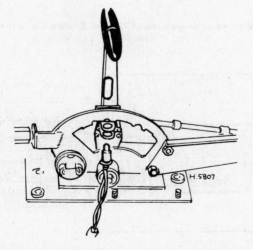

Fig. 10.60 Speed selector indicator lamp bulb (XJ12 and Double Six, Series 1)

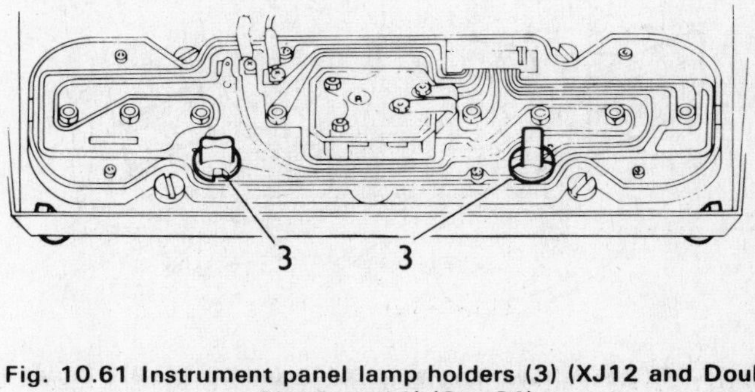


Fig. 10.61 Instrument panel lamp holders (3) (XJ12 and Double Six, Series 1) (Sec 34)

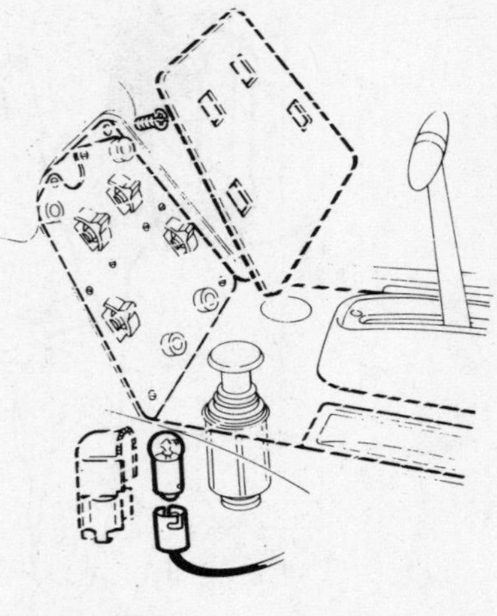

Fig. 10.62 Cigar lighter bulb renewal (XJ12 and Double Six, Series 1) (Sec 34)

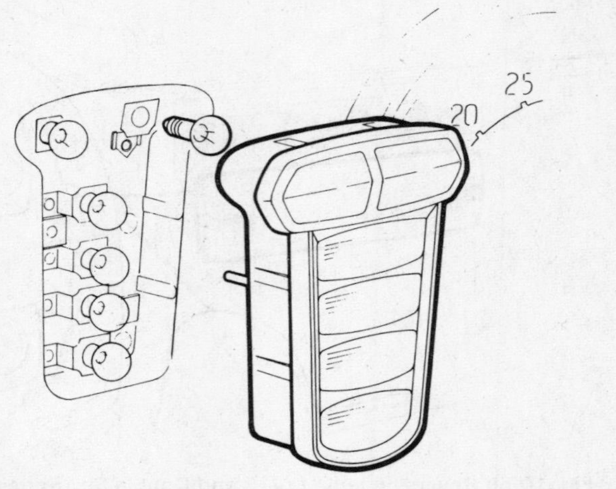


Fig. 10.63 Instrument panel warning lamp cluster (XJ12 and Double Six, Series 1) (Sec 34)

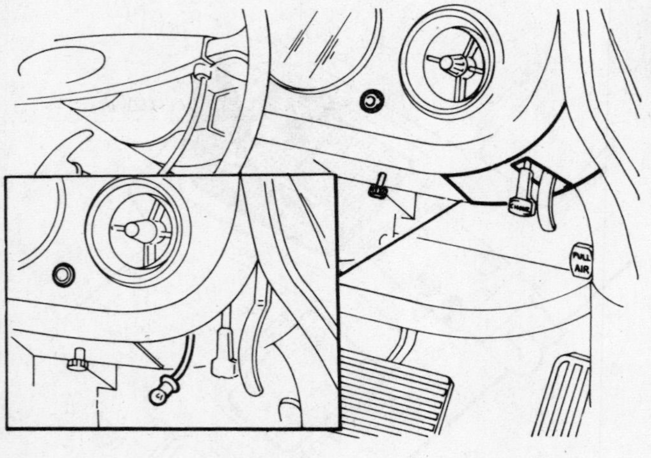


Fig. 10.64 Choke warning lamp (XJ12 and Double Six, Series 1) (Sec 34)

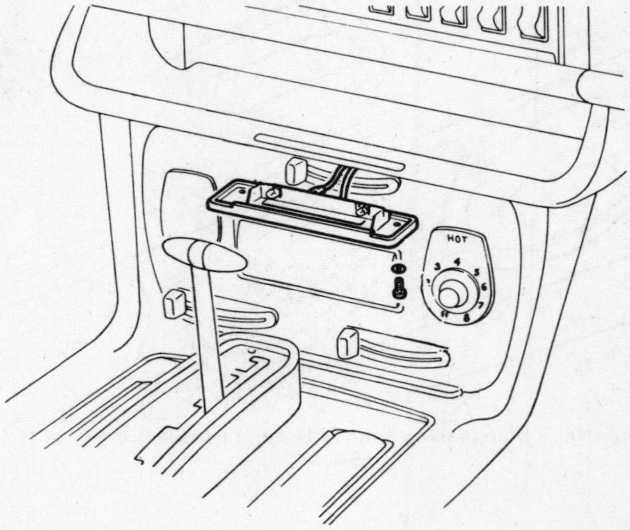


Fig. 10.65 Heater panel lamp (XJ12 and Double Six, Series 1) (Sec 34)

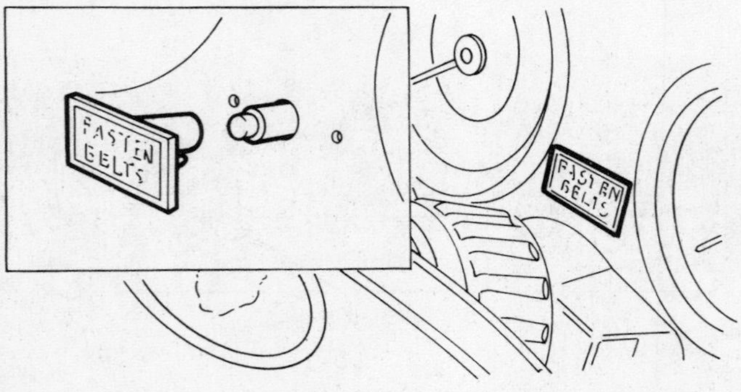


Fig. 10.66 Seat belt warning lamp (XJ12 and Double Six, Series 1) (Sec 34)

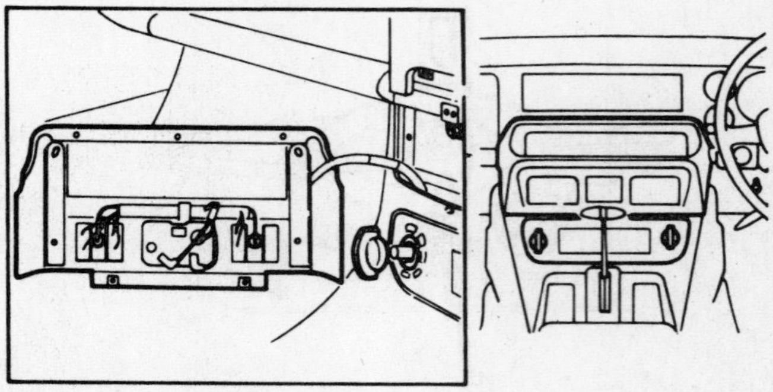

Fig. 10.67 Switch panel lamp (XJ12, Double Six – Series 2 on) (Sec 35)

29.2 Removing headlamp (outer)

29.5 Inner headlamp rim retaining screw (arrowed)

30.1 Bulb type headlamp unit

30.2 Outer headlamp unit showing parking lamp bulb

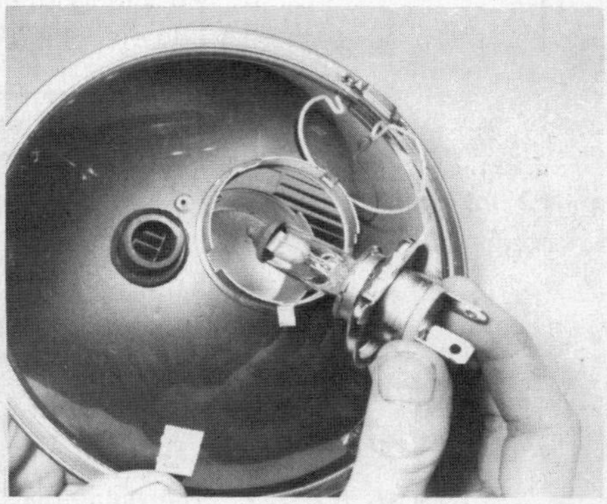

30.3 Headlamp bulb holder and retaining clip

35.1A Front parking/flasher lamp

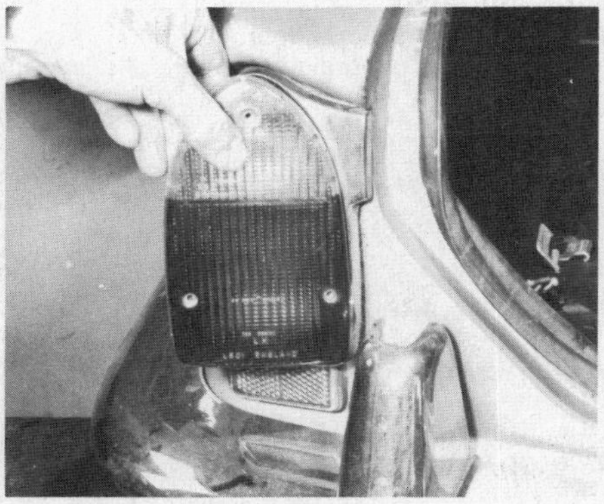

35.1B Rear lamp cluster

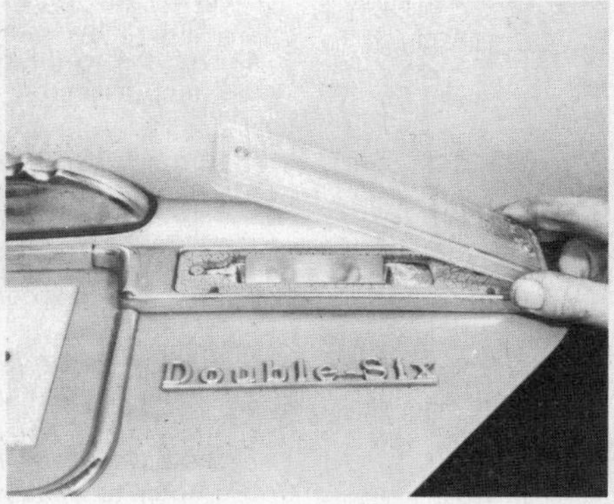


35.1C Reversing lamp

35.1D Rear number plate lamp

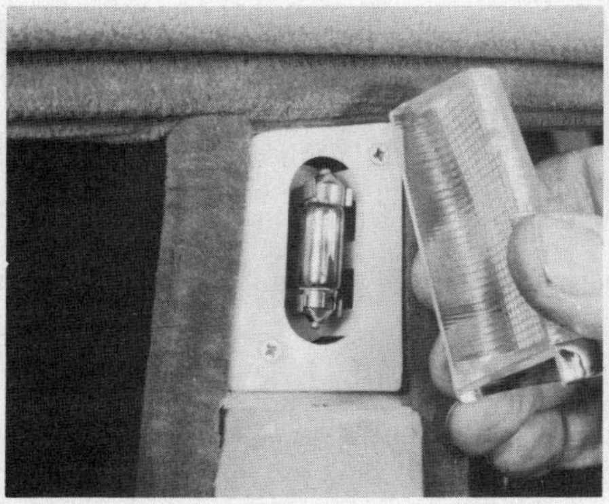

35.5 Interior pillar lamp

35.13 Clock bulb holder

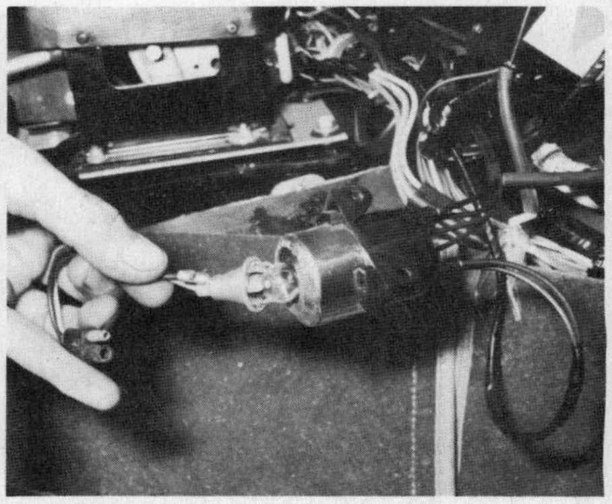

38.6 Opticell unit

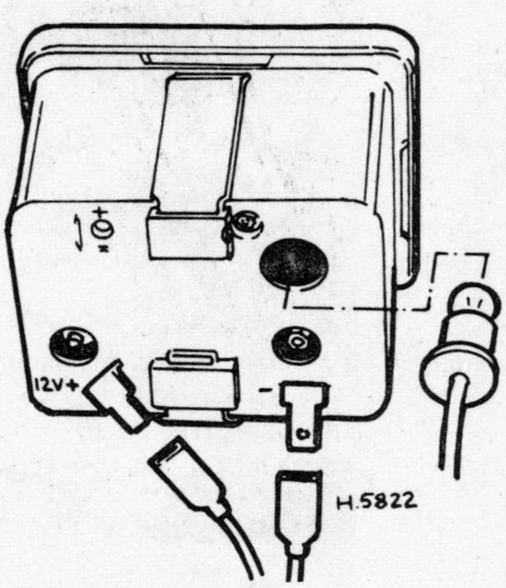


Fig. 10.68 Clock bulb (XJ12, Double Six – Series 2 on) (Sec 35)

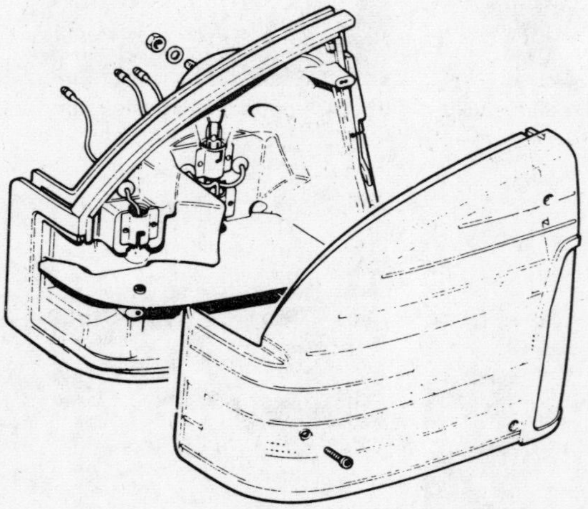

Fig. 10.69 Tail lamp lens and bulbs (XJS) (Sec 36)

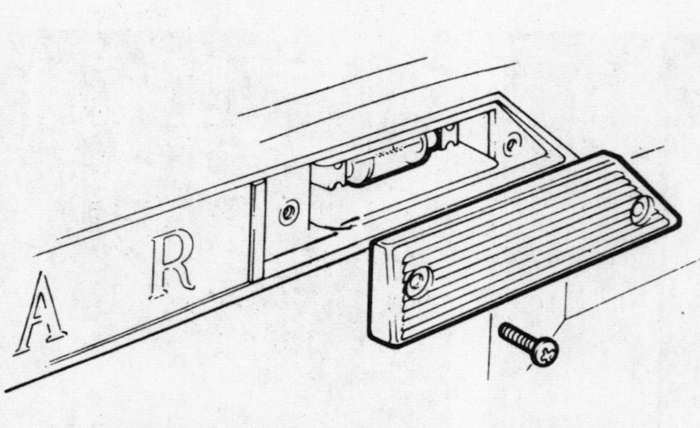

Fig. 10.70 Reversing lamp lens and bulb (XJS) (Sec 36)

*Warning lamp cluster*

30 Using two thin screwdriver blades, carefully lever the cover from the bulb holder casing.

31 Individual screw-in type bulbs can be renewed as necessary.

*Choke warning lamp*

32 Disconnect the battery and remove the under scuttle casing (two screws) as described in Chapter 12.

33 Pull the bulb holder from the lens carrier.

*Heater panel bulb*

34 Unscrew the two screws and withdraw the escutcheon.

35 Remove the two screws inside the escutcheon to expose the bulb.

*Seat belt warning lamp*

36 Prise the indicator plate from the facia. The plate is held in position by two friction nylon bushes.

37 Pull the bulb holder from the lamp unit and remove the bulb.

**35 Bulbs (XJ12 and Double Six, Series 2 on) – renewal**

1 Access to the bulbs in all the following lamps is obtained by extracting the lens securing screws and removing the lens (photos):

*Front flasher/parking lamp*
*Front flasher repeater lamp*
*Side marker lamp*
*Rear lamp cluster*
*Reversing lamps*
*Rear number plate lamp*
*Foglamp (bulbs not to be handled with the fingers).*

2 The bulbs may be of conventional bayonet fitting, capless or of festoon type. This can be determined by inspection or by reference to the Specifications at the beginning of this Chapter.

*Interior lamps (2-door models)*

3 One of these lamps is fitted above each door.

4 Access to the festoon type bulb is obtained by carefully levering the lamp assembly from its recess.

*Interior lamp (4-door models)*

5 Refer to Section 34 (photo).

*Map reading lamp*

6 Refer to Section 34.

*Luggage boot lamp*

7 Refer to Section 34.

*Speed selector indicator lamp*

8 Refer to Section 34.

*Switch panel lamp*

9 Pull off the control knobs from the heater/air conditioner. Remove the radio aperture escutcheon.

10 Extract the four screws which hold the centre oddments tray and lift the tray forward.

11 Pull the bulb holder from the diffuser assembly.

12 A miniature bayonet fitting type bulb is used at this position.

*Clock bulb*

13 Pull the centre oddments tray forward as described in paragraphs 9 and 10 (photo).

14 The bulb holder can now be pulled directly from the rear of the clock case.

*Warning lamp cluster*

15 Carefully lever off the cover plate.

16 The individual capless type bulbs can be removed by giving them a straight pull, do not twist.

*Direction indicator warning lamp*

17 The lamps are incorporated in the speedometer and tachometer.

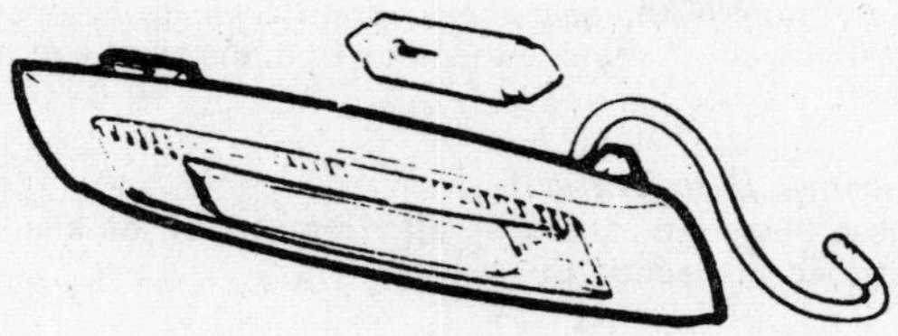

Fig. 10.71 Roof interior lamp (XJS) (Sec 36)

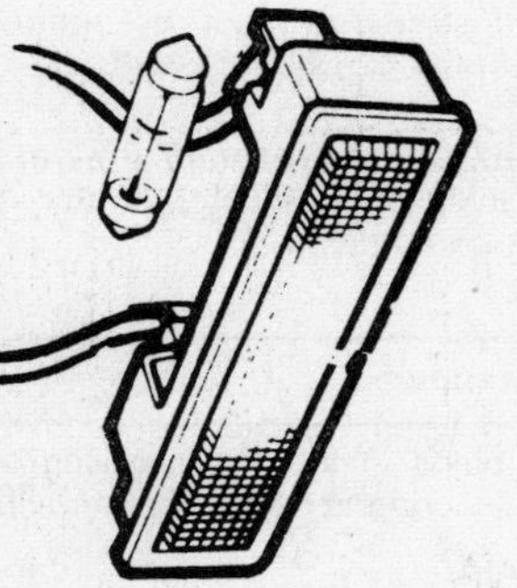

Fig. 10.72 Map reading lamp (XJS) (Sec 36)

*Also luggage boot lamp type on late XJS models*

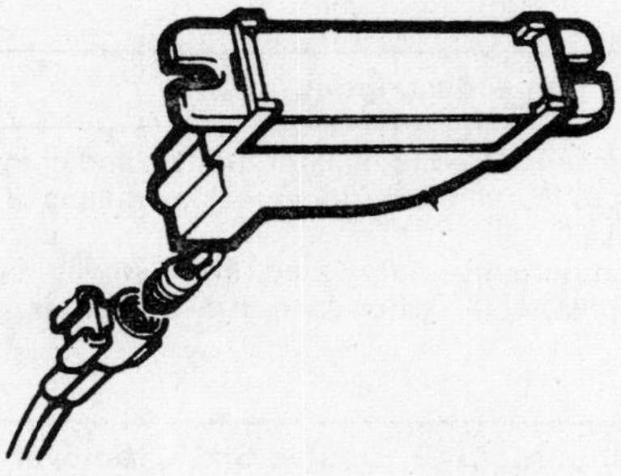

Fig. 10.73 Switch panel bulb (XJS) (Sec 36)

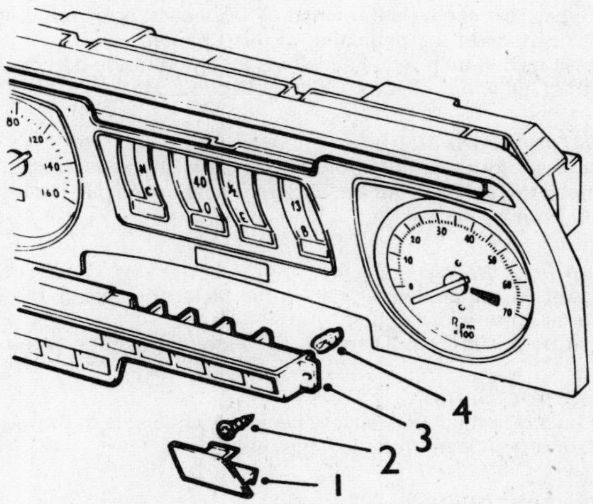


Fig. 10.74 Warning lamp bulb (XJS) (Sec 36)

1 *End cover*
2 *Screw*
3 *Warning lamp strip*
4 *Bulb*

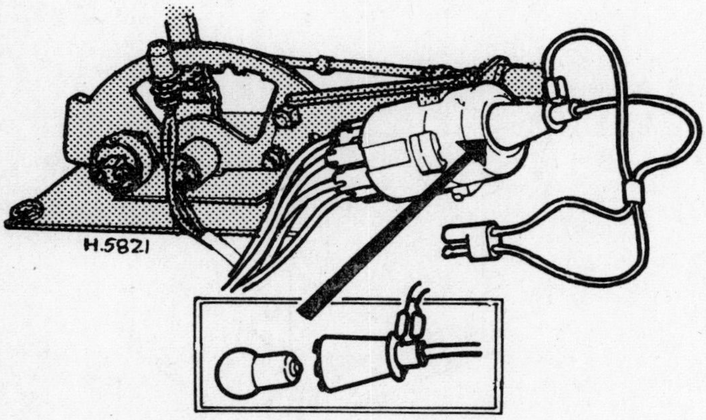


Fig. 10.75 Opticell unit (XJ12, Double Six) (Sec 38)

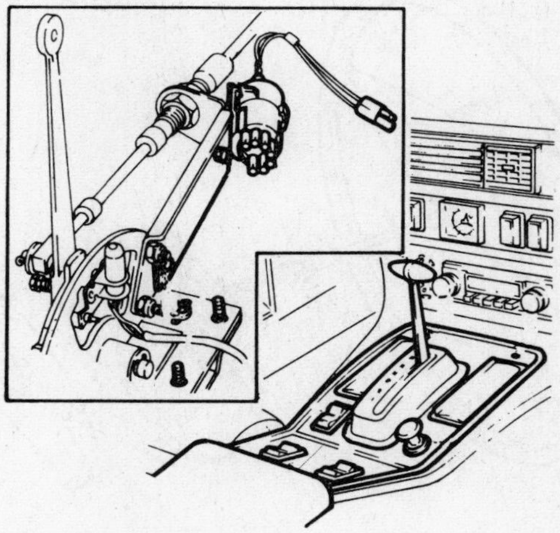

Fig. 10.76 Opticell unit (XJS) (Sec 39)

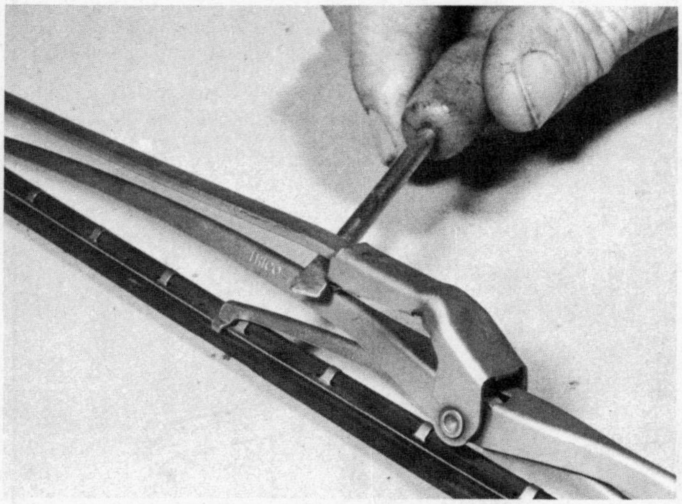

54.1 Depressing a wiper blade securing tag

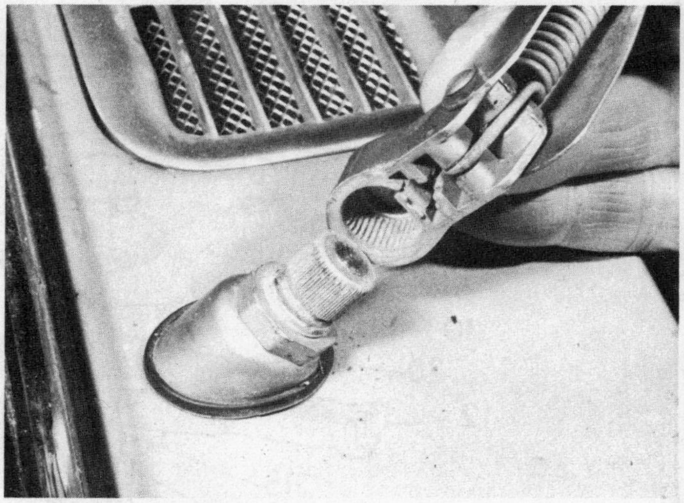

54.2 Wiper arm removed from its spindle

56.2 Windscreen wiper motor is located next to the battery

59.3 Windscreen washer pump

and then unscrew it one quarter of a turn and tighten the locknut.

## 59 Windscreen washer (XJ12, Double Six) – description and jet adjustment

1 The windscreen washer reservoir is located towards the front of the engine compartment on the left-hand valance.
2 Use washer fluid additive, particularly in cold weather, which will prevent the fluid freezing. Never add engine anti-freeze to the reservoir, but in an emergency or in severe weather, methylated spirit (denatured alcohol) may be added to the fluid.
3 The washer pump is located on the engine compartment rear bulkhead (Series 1) or on the bumper support strut on later models (photo).
4 The washer jets are located on the air intake grille at the base of the windscreen. They can be cleaned with thin wire, removed by unscrewing them with a screwdriver or adjusted to provide the best wash pattern by moving them with a screwdriver blade inserted into their slots.

## 60 Windscreen washer (XJS) – description and jet adjustment

1 On this model, the washer reservoir is located at the left rear corner of the engine compartment.
2 The electric washer pump is attached to the reservoir mounting clamp band.
3 The jets are located in the air intake grille and can be removed after detaching the grille and raising it slightly. Jet adjustment is similar to that described in the preceding Section.

## 61 Headlamp wash/wipe mechanism

1 This equipment, fitted to later models (optional extra on some), comprises the following main assemblies:

### *Washer reservoir and pump*

2 This is located under the front left-hand wheel arch and supplies both the windscreen and headlamp washer systems.
3 To remove the reservoir, jack up the front of the car and take off the left hand roadwheel.
4 The washer pump is mounted close to the reservoir on the bumper support strut.

### *Washer jets and supply tubes*

5 The headlamp washer jets and supply tubes can be removed in the

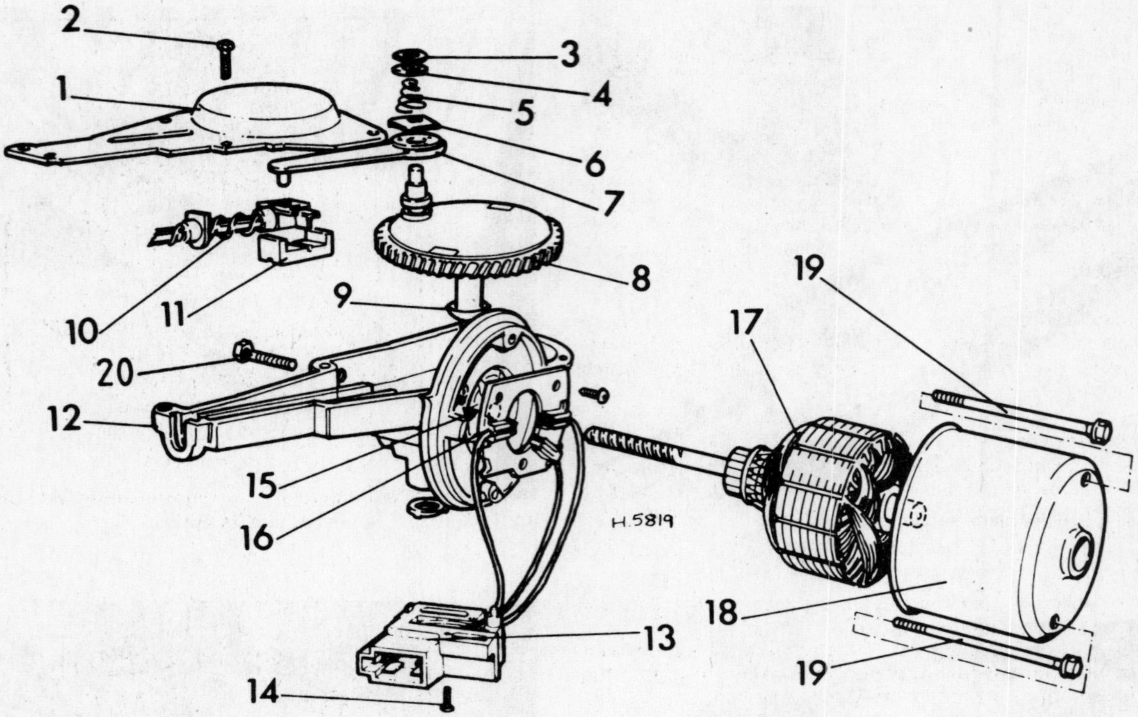


**Fig. 10.101 Exploded view of typical windscreen wiper motor (Sec 58)**

| | | | |
|---|---|---|---|
| *1* | *Gearbox cover* | *11* | *Slider block* |
| *2* | *Screw* | *12* | *Gearbox* |
| *3* | *Circlip* | *13* | *Limit switch* |
| *4* | *Washer* | *14* | *Screws* |
| *5* | *Spring* | *15* | *Bush* |
| *6* | *Friction plate* | *16* | *Brush gear* |
| *7* | *Crankarm* | *17* | *Armature* |
| *8* | *Gear* | *18* | *Yoke* |
| *9* | *Dished washer* | *19* | *Tie-bolts* |
| *10* | *Cable rack* | *20* | *Armature endfloat adjuster screw and locknut* |

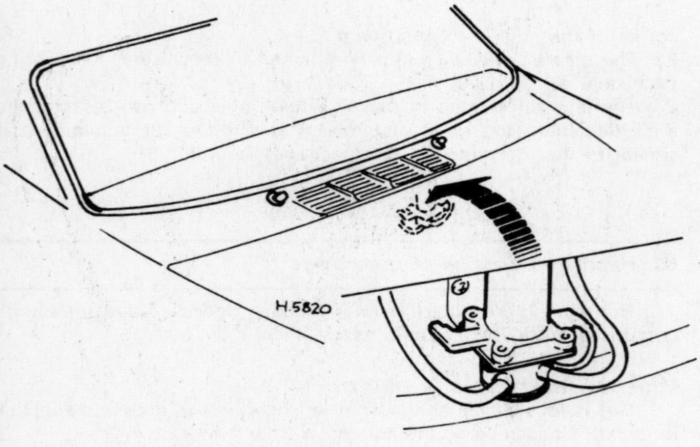


**Fig. 10.102 Windscreen washer pump location (XJ12 and Double Six, Series) (Sec 59)**

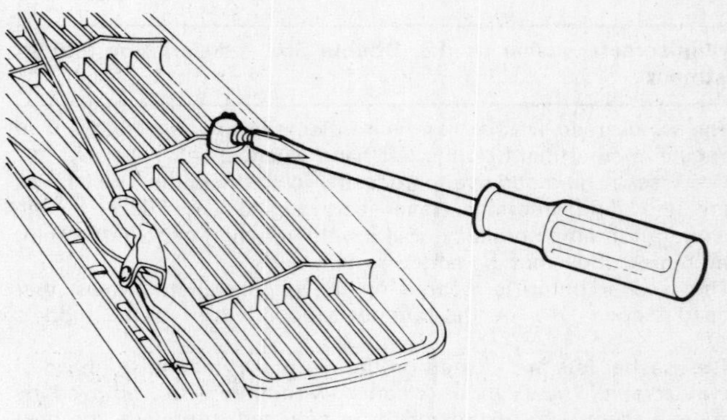

**Fig. 10.103 Adjusting a washer jet (Sec 59)**

following way.
6 Lift the bonnet and carefully pull the supply tubes from the jets. Hold the jets outside the car with the hand and unscrew the nuts which secure the jet assemblies to the headlamp panel.
7 The fluid supply tubes are secured in spring clips to the flange below the lower grille.

## *Wiper arm*

*See also Chapter 13, Section 11, paragraph 83*

8 The headlamp wiper arm is removable after unscrewing the pivot screw. Press the wiper arm towards the headlamp glass and remove it together with the spacer cup.

## *Washer/wiper switch*

9 The headlamp washer/wiper switch is mounted in the centre console top panel. The panel can be removed for access to the switch after extracting the screws.

## *Wiper motor and rack*

10 The headlamp wiper motor is located within the engine compartment. To remove the motor, first disconnect the battery and then remove the cover plate from the rack drive section of the motor (four self-tapping screws).
11 Remove the nylon channel and lift the rack drive peg from its recess.
12 Unbolt the motor from its mounting plate, disconnect the electrical leads and withdraw the motor.
13 The motor gear can be withdrawn if the two screws are removed from the cover plate on the gear housing. Detach the circlip from the spindle, remove the gear and plain and conical washers.
14 The rack drive cables are simply removed by withdrawing them from their conduits.
15 The wiper wheel boxes and rack tubes can be removed if the headlamp outer rim finisher is first withdrawn. Extract the three screws which hold the headlamp rim and rack tube. Ease the rim and tube forward and slacken the collet nut. Draw the rim away and let the wiper blade rotate as the rack is withdrawn.
16 Refitting of all the headlamp wash/wipe components is a reversal of removal, but when fitting the wiper arm, turn the blade to the parked position (in alignment with the drive tube) and hold it from moving with the hand while tightening the pivot screw.

## 62 Speedometer (XJ12 and Double Six, Series 1) – removal and refitting

1 Disconnect the battery.
2 Remove the under scuttle casing (two screws).
3 Reach up behind the speedometer and disconnect the drive cable by unscrewing the knurled retaining ring.
4 Disconnect the trip reset cable by unscrewing the knurled ring.
5 Apply hand pressure to the speedometer bezel and turn the instrument in an anti-clockwise direction until it is felt to release from its bayonet fixing.
6 From the speedometer casing, pull out the bulb holders for the illumination of the instrument and the warning lamp(headlamp main beam).
7 Disconnect the earth lead and remove the speedometer from the instrument panel.
8 Wear in the right-angled gearbox at the rear of the speedometer can only be rectified by fitting a new unit. The unit can be detached by unscrewing its knurled retaining ring.
9 Refitting is a reversal of removal.

## 63 Speedometer inner cable (XJ12 and Double Six, Series 1) – renewal

1 Remove the speedometer as described in the preceding Section.
2 It is now possible to grip the end of the inner cable with a pair of pliers and pull it from the cable conduit.
3 If the cable has broken, then the assembly will have to be disconnected at the transmission end to extract the lower section.
4 Lubricate the lower two thirds of the cable with thin grease, sparingly, before inserting it from the speedometer end of the conduit.

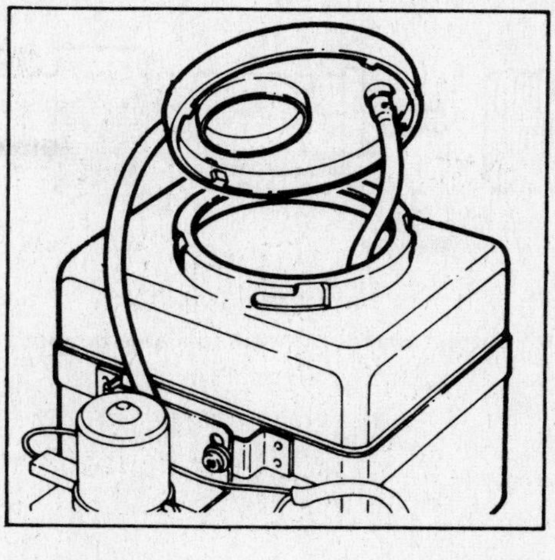

Fig. 10.104 Windscreen washer reservoir and pump (XJS) (Sec 60)

Fig. 10.105 Headlamp wash/wipe arrangement (typical) (Sec 61)

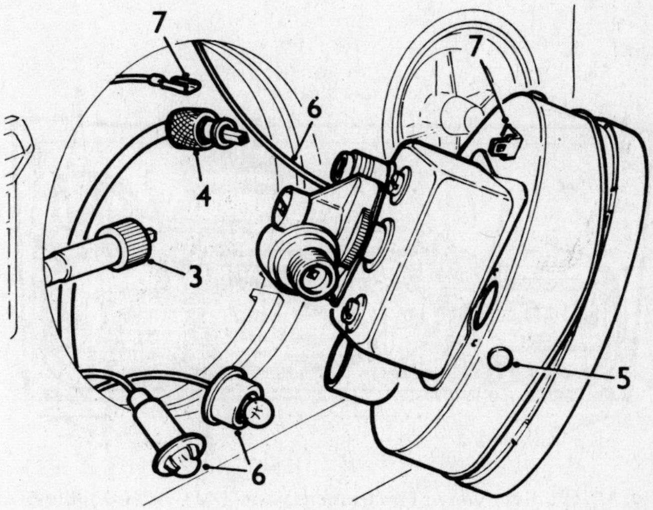


Fig. 10.106 Speedometer cable connections (XJ12 and Double Six, Series 1) (Sec 62)

*3 Drive cable*
*4 Trip reset cable*
*5 Bayonet fitting pin*
*6 Warning lamp leads and bulb holders*
*7 Earth lead and terminal*

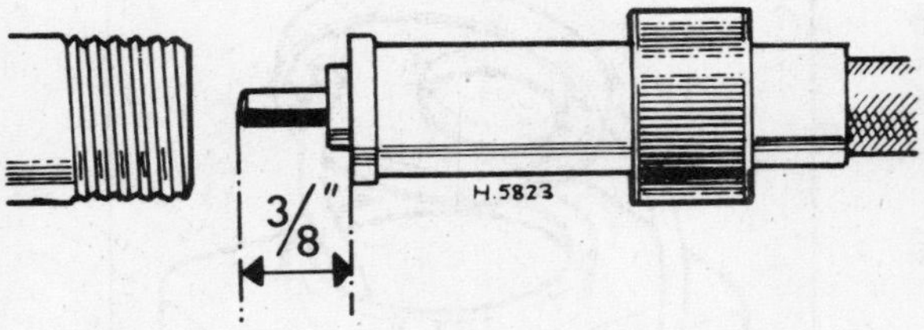


Fig. 10.107 Correct speedometer inner cable projection (Sec 63)

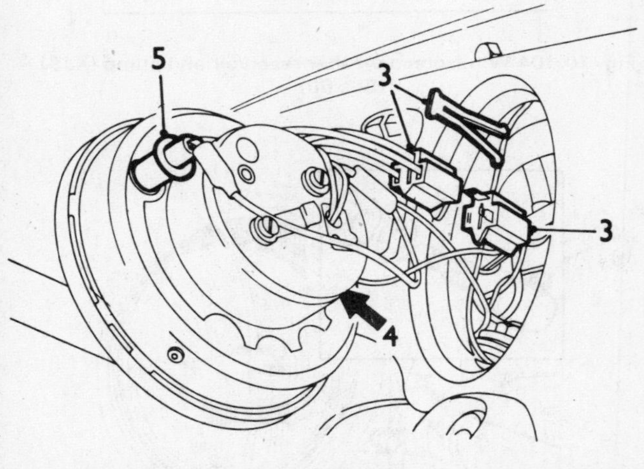


Fig. 10.108 Tachometer removal (XJ12 and Double Six, Series 1) (Sec 64)

3 *Plug and socket*
4 *Earth connection*
5 *Tachometer illumination bulb*

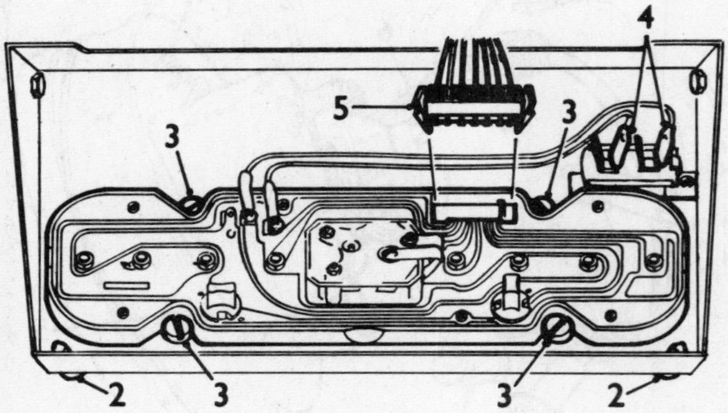


Fig. 10.109 Rear view of instrument panel (XJ12 and Double Six, Series 1) (Sec 64)

2 *Knurled retaining screws*
3 *Cheese-headed screws*
4 *Voltage stabiliser*
5 *Multi-pin harness connector*

The upper end of the inner cable should project by $\frac{3}{8}$ in (9.52 mm) to ensure correct engagement.

## 64 Tachometer (XJ12 and Double Six, Series 1) – removal and refitting

1 Disconnect the battery.
2 Apply hand pressure to the front of the instrument and turn it anti-clockwise until its bayonet fixing is released.
3 Withdraw the tachometer until the bulb holder for instrument illumination can be pulled from the casing. Disconnect the multi-pin plug and socket and the earth lead.
4 Refitting is the reverse of removal.

## 65 Supplementary instruments (XJ12 and Double Six, Series 1) – removal and refitting

1 The following instruments can be removed as a complete sub panel:

*Battery condition indicator*
*Clock*
*Oil gauge*
*Coolant temperature gauge*

2 Disconnect the battery.
3 Remove the two knurled retaining screws and lower the instrument panel.
4 Pull the leads from the instrument voltage stabiliser and withdraw the wiring harness connector plug from its socket.
5 Unscrew and remove the four setscrews and lift the sub panel away.
6 Extract the six screws which hold the back panel to the sub panel. Disconnect the clock leads and withdraw the back panel complete with instruments.
7 The individual instruments can be removed from the back panel if the two securing nuts are unscrewed.
8 The printed circuit board is removable once the instruments have been withdrawn.
9 A faulty instrument voltage stabiliser can give rise to incorrect readings on the instruments, and should be suspected if the fuel contents and coolant temperature gauges malfunction at the same time.
10 Refitting is a reversal of removal. Take care not to damage the gauge needles as the gauges are pushed into the housing, and do not scratch the printed circuit.
11 Do not reverse the leads to the electric clock. The clock must be re-started as soon as the battery is re-connected otherwise it may be damaged. To start the clock and reset the time, pull out the knob on the front of the clock, turn to the correct time and release it. Fast or slow correction is made by turning the small slotted screw on the back of the clock.

## 66 Speedometer, inner cable and tachometer (XJ12 and Double Six, Series 2 on) – removal and refitting

1 The operations are as described for earlier models in Sections 62, 63 and 64.

## 67 Supplementary instruments (XJ12 and Double Six, Series 2 on) – removal and refitting

1 The following instruments can all be removed individually from the facia panel using the same method:

*Battery condition indicator*
*Oil pressure gauge*
*Coolant temperature gauge*
*Fuel gauge*

2 Disconnect the battery.
3 Remove the speedometer or tachometer as necessary to gain access to the instrument holding strap and knurled nut. Remove the nut and strap.

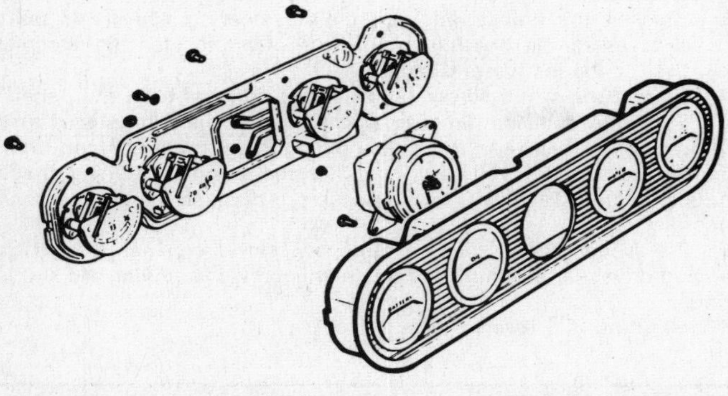

Fig. 10.110 Instrument housing (XJ12 and Double Six, Series 1) (Sec 65)

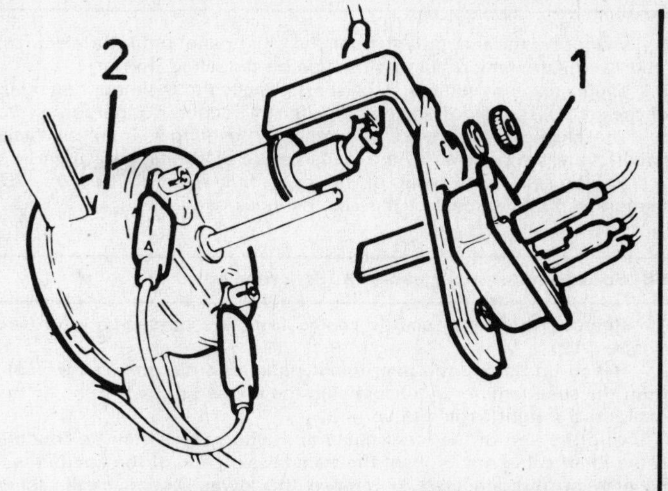


Fig. 10.111 Voltage stabiliser (1) attached to battery condition indicator (2) (XJ12 and Double Six, Series 2) (Sec 67)

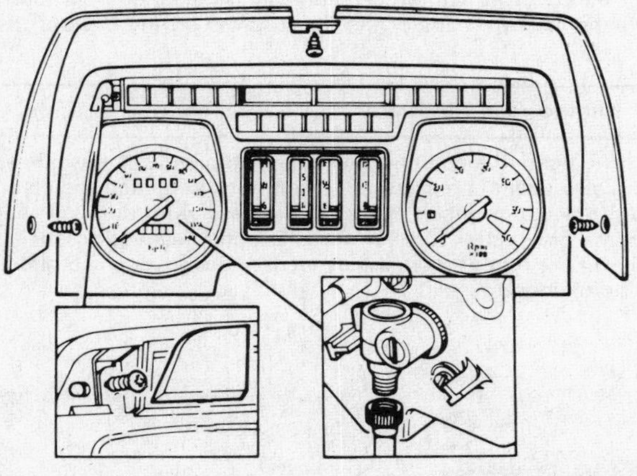

Fig. 10.112 Instrument panel and gauges (XJS) (Sec 69)

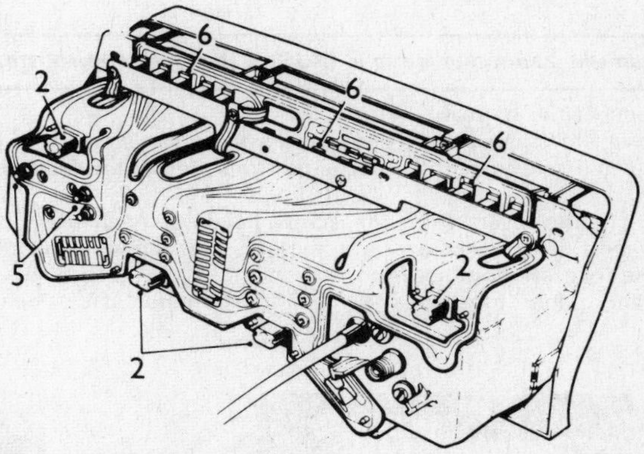


Fig. 10.113 Rear view of instrument panel (XJS) (Sec 69)

*2 Illumination bulb holders*
*5 Printed circuit-to-tachometer fixing nuts*
*6 Warning lamp bulb holders*

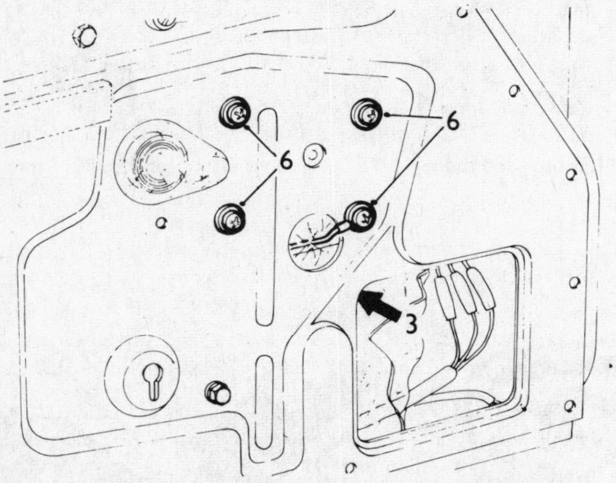


Fig. 10.114 Front window lift motors (XJ12 and Double Six, 4-door) (Sec 72)

*3 Harness plug and socket*
*6 Regulator mounting screws*

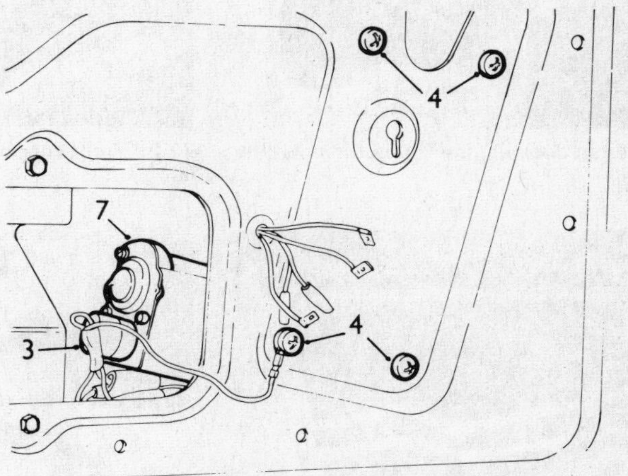


Fig. 10.115 Rear window lift motors (XJ12 and Double Six, 4-door) (Sec 72)

*3 Harness plug*
*4 Regulator mounting screws*
*7 Motor*

4 Withdraw the instrument from the facia panel until the electrical leads and illumination bulb holder can be detached from it.
5 The instrument voltage stabiliser is attached to the mounting strap of the battery condition indicator. Refer to Section 65, paragraph 9.
6 The clock can be removed simply by levering it from the facia panel. Note the position of the leads before disconnectimg them.
7 Refitting is a reversal of removal, but refer to Section 65, paragraph 11 in respect of the electric clock.

## 68 Speedometer inner cable (XJS) – renewal

1 Remove the under scuttle casing from the passenger side (see Chapter 12).
2 Reach up behind the instrument panel and disconnect the cable from the speedometer by unscrewing the knurled nut which holds the cable to the right-angled drive unit.
3 Grip the end of the inner cable and withdraw it from its conduit. If the inner cable has broken, the transmission end of the conduit will have to be disconnected to retrieve the lower section of the inner cable.
4 Insert the new cable from the speedometer end, having applied thin grease sparingly to the lower two thirds of its length.

## 69 Instrument panel and gauges (XJS) – removal and refitting

1 Disconnect the battery.
2 Remove the under scuttle casing from the driver's side.
3 Extract the screws and the surround from around the instrument panel.
4 Prise off the covers from the screw heads at each end of the warning lamp strip. Unscrew and remove the screws which will release the instrument panel from the facia.
5 Pull the panel forward until the speedometer cable can be disconnected from the rear of the speedometer and the wiring harness disconnected.
6 Slacken the adjustment ring on the steering wheel and pull it upwards as far as possible to provide clearance for the complete removal of the instrument panel.
7 Extract the seven screws and remove the lens from the panel.
8 The individual instruments (excluding the speedometer) can be removed if the screws or nuts holding the printed circuit to the instrument are first withdrawn and then the mounting screws or spire nuts extracted. Take care not to scratch or damage the printed circuit board.
9 The speedometer can be removed from the panel if the right-angled drivegear assembly is first detached by unscrewing the knurled ring.
10 Refitting is a reversal of removal.

## 70 Clock (XJS) – removal and refitting

1 Disconnect the battery and prise the clock out of the switch panel.
2 Pull the bulb holder from the rear of the clock casing and disconnect the electrical leads.
3 The hands of the clock are set by depressing the reset knob at the right-hand lower corner of the face. Adjustment for fast or slow correction is by means of the small screw on the back of the casing.

## 71 Heated rear window

1 The heating element on all cars is applied to the inside surface of the glass. Great care must be taken not to damage the element with sharp objects or, when cleaning the glass, with rings on the fingers.
2 Use only water to clean the glass and never stick labels onto the inside of the rear window if they are likely to cover any of the fine wires of the element.

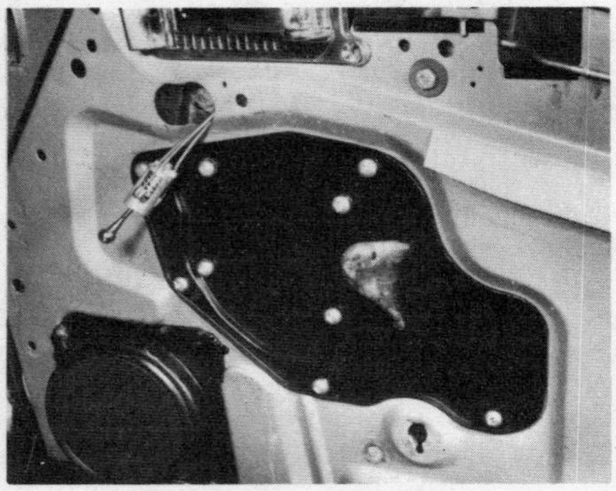
72.5A Front door window lift motor mounting plate

72.5B Front door window lift motor and regulator

72.7 Window lift motor/regulator removed

75.3A Door lock solenoid attached to pushrod

75.3B Removing door lock solenoid from a front door

78.2 Power operated aerial motor and relay within luggage boot (XJ12, Double Six – Series 3)

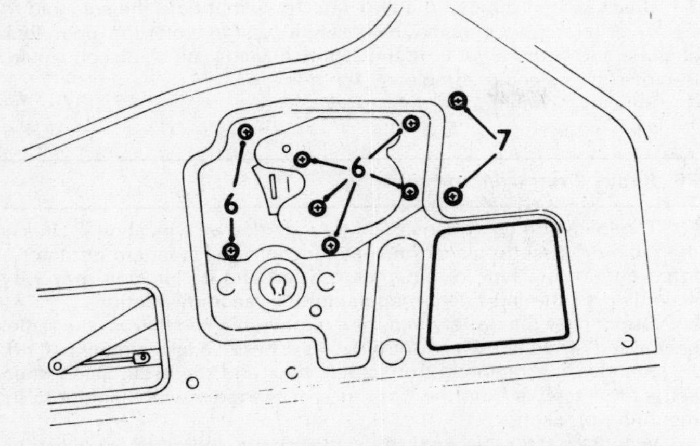


Fig. 10.116 Window lift motors (XJ12 and Double Six, 2-door) (Sec 73)

*6 Regulator mounting plate screws*
*7 Motor mounting bracket*

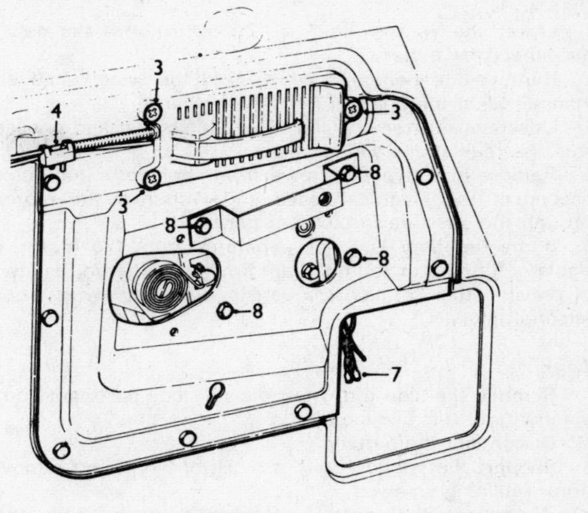


Fig. 10.117 Window lift motor (XJS) (Sec 74)

*3 Door inner handle screws*
*4 Control lever to handle connection*
*7 Motor electrical harness*
*8 Motor mounting screws*

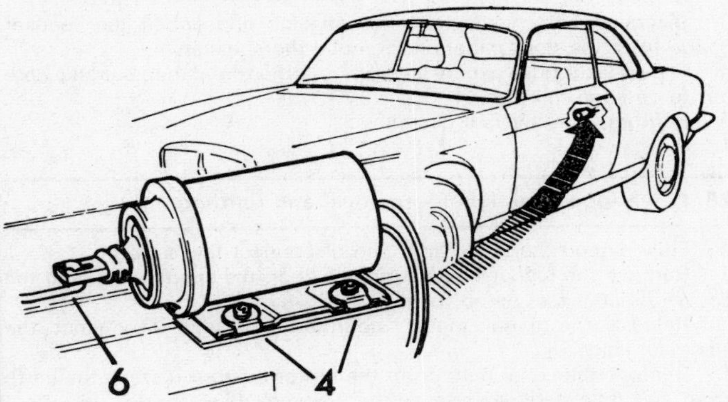


Fig. 10.118 Typical door lock solenoid (Sec 75)

*4 Mounting screws*
*6 Piston/rod connection*

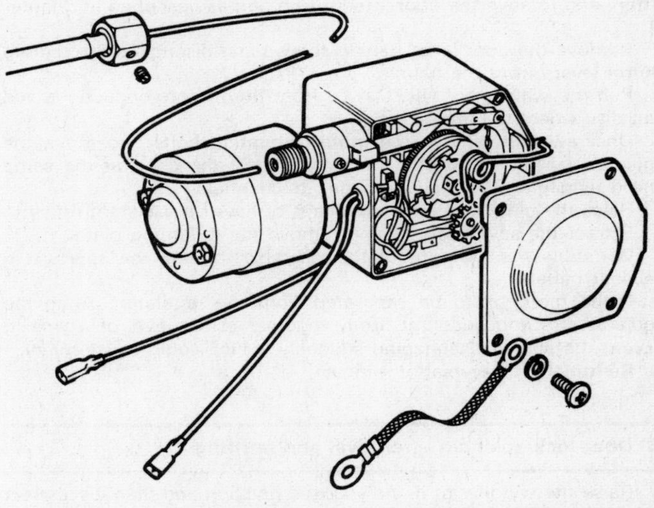

Fig. 10.119 Typical power-operated radio aerial (Sec 78)

## 72 Window lift motors (XJ12 and Double Six, 4-door models) – removal and refitting

### *Front*

1 Disconnect the battery.
2 Remove the door interior trim panel and armrest as described in Chapter 12.
3 Disconnect the motor wiring harness by separating the multi-pin plug from the socket.
4 Remove the upper bolt which holds the glass channel to the door inner panel.
5 Extract the outer ring of pan-headed screws to release the window regulator mounting panel from the door panel (photos).
6 Slide the regulator towards the hinge side of the door until the arm roller clears its channel.
7 Raise the regulator arm so that it passes over the outer side of the glass channel and then remove the regulator through the aperture in the door inner panel (photo).
8 The electric motor can now be separated from the regulator mechanism after withdrawing the three setscrews.

### *Rear*

9 Disconnect the battery.
10 Remove the door interior trim panel and armrest as described in Chapter 12.
11 Remove the four pan-headed setscrews and detach the regulator/motor from the door inner panel. Move the assembly until the regulator arm can be slipped out of its channel.
12 Withdraw the assembly through the aperture in the door inner panel, raising the glass if necessary to enable it to pass.
13 Separate the motor from the regulator mechanism by extracting the three setscrews.
14 If the motor is faulty, it must be renewed complete as it is a sealed unit.
15 Refitting is a reversal of removal.

## 73 Window lift motor (XJ12 and Double Six, 2-door models) – removal and refitting

### *Front*

1 Remove the door interior trim panel and armrest as described in

Chapter 12.
2 Lower the window to 1 in (25 mm) above the door and then disconnect the battery.
3 Remove the two nuts which hold the window lift arm bobbin channel. Slide the channel from the bobbin.
4 Unscrew and remove the seven setscrews and one drive screw from the regulator mounting plate.
5 Remove the two setscrews from the motor mounting bracket, disconnect the electrical leads and withdraw the motor/regulator through the aperture in the door panel.
6 If the regulator is to be separated from the motor, clamp the regulator lifting arm and quadrant firmly together in the jaws of a vice to prevent the spring disengaging suddenly, which could cause personal injury.

*Rear*

7 Remove the side trim from the rear compartment and lower the window until it is horizontal.
8 Disconnect the battery.
9 Support the window with a block of wood and remove the four motor retaining screws.
10 Disconnect the wiring, detach the motor from the window channel, and withdraw the assembly through the aperture.
11 Observe the warning given in paragraph 6.

## 74 Window lift motor (XJS) – removal and refitting

1 Lower the window glass to its lowest position and disconnect the battery and remove the door interior trim pad as described in Chapter 12.
2 Remove the door inner handle screws and disengage the remote control levers from the handle.
3 Pull the waterproof sheet away from the motor connections and then disconnect the leads.
4 Unscrew and remove the motor mounting bolts and move the regulator assembly towards the rear edge of the door, at the same time disengaging the regulator from its channel.
5 Raise the glass and either wedge it or have an assistant retain it.
6 Extract the seven screws and remove the mounting plate.
7 Withdraw the motor/regulator assembly through the aperture in the door panel.
8 If the motor is to be separated from the regulator, clamp the regulator arm and quadrant firmly together in the jaws of a vice to prevent the spring disengaging suddenly, which could cause injury.
9 Refitting is a reversal of removal.

## 75 Door lock solenoid – removal and refitting

1 Raise the window to its fully closed position and then disconnect the battery.
2 Remove the door interior trim panel and armrest as described in Chapter 12.
3 Unscrew and remove the two setscrews that hold the solenoid to the door stretcher, unhook the solenoid piston from the door lock pushrod and withdraw it until the electrical leads can be disconnected. Remove the solenoid completely (photos).
4 Refit by reversing the removal operations.

## 76 Radio – removal and refitting

1 The following operations must be regarded as typical only. Unless the radio or cassette player has been installed as standard or factory-fitted option, the type of equipment fitted and its location may vary according to the individual manufacturer's recommendations.
2 Disconnect the battery and then remove the knobs from the radio, heater and air conditioner control levers. These usually simply pull off.
3 Remove the radio control spindle nuts and the escutcheon, then extract the screws from the front face of the radio which hold it to its mounting bracket.
4 Withdraw the radio until the aerial, power and earth leads can be disconnected from it, then lift it away.
5 Refitting is a reversal of removal.

## 77 Speaker – removal and refitting

1 Disconnect the battery.
2 Remove the door interior trim panel, armrest and casing.
3 Disconnect the leads from the speaker and unbolt the speaker flange from the door panel and remove the speaker.
4 The speaker grille can be levered from the trim panel, but take care not to damage the trim.
5 Refitting is a reversal of removal.

## 78 Power-operated aerial – removal and refitting

1 Fully extend the aerial and then disconnect the battery.
2 Remove the luggage compartment floor, the spare wheel and the cover from the fuel pump (photo).
3 Release the aerial motor mounting clip and disconnect the electrical leads.
4 Remove the cover plate from the motor gearbox, detach the earth strap and then carefully release the pressure roller spring.
5 Release the grub screw and nut which secure the flexible drive and then pull the nylon drive from the motor gearbox.
6 Retract the aerial by hand and unscrew the aerial retaining nut. Remove the curved adaptor plate and the weather seal.
7 The rear lamp cluster may have to be removed before the aerial can be withdrawn from inside the rear wing.
8 Refitting is a reversal of removal.

## 79 Fault diagnosis – electrical system

| Symptom | Reason(s) |
|---|---|
| Starter fails to turn engine | Battery discharged<br>Battery defective internally<br>Battery terminal leads loose or earth lead not securely attached to body<br>Loose or broken connections in starter motor circuit<br>Starter motor switch or solenoid faulty<br>Starter brushes badly worn, sticking, or brush wires loose<br>Commutator dirty, worn or burnt<br>Starter motor armature faulty<br>Field coils earthed |
| Starter turns engine very slowly | Battery in discharged condition<br>Starter brushes badly worn, sticking or brush wires loose<br>Loose wires in starter motor circuit |
| Starter spins but does not turn engine | Pinion or flywheel gear teeth broken or worn<br>Battery discharged |

| Symptom | Reason/s |
|---|---|
| Starter motor noisy or excessively rough engagement | Pinion or flywheel gear teeth broken or worn<br>Starter motor retaining bolts loose |
| Battery will not hold charge for more than a few days | Battery defective internally<br>Electrolyte level too low or electrolyte too weak due to leakage<br>Plate separators no longer fully effective<br>Battery plates severely sulphated<br>Alternator drivebelt slipping<br>Battery terminal connections loose or corroded<br>Alternator not charging<br>Short in lighting circuit causing continual battery drain<br>Alternator internal regulator unit not working correctly |
| Ignition light fails to go out, battery runs flat in a few days | Alternator drivebelt loose and slipping or broken<br>Alternator brushes worn, sticking, broken or dirty<br>Alternator brush springs weak or broken<br>Internal fault in alternator |

***Failure of individual electrical equipment to function correctly is dealt with alphabetically, item by item, under the headings listed below***

| Symptom | Reason/s |
|---|---|
| **Electrically-operated windows** | |
| Complete system failure | Faulty control box<br>Blown fuse<br>Overloaded circuit breaker |
| Driver's window normal, remainder inoperative | Sticking switch<br>Circuit earthed |
| Failure of one window only | Faulty switch<br>Poor electrical connection<br>Stiff mechanism or sticking window |
| **Horn** | |
| Horn emits intermittent or unsatisfactory noise | Cable connections loose<br>Horn incorrectly adjusted |
| Horn fails to operate | Blown fuse<br>Cable or cable connection loose, broken or disconnected<br>Horn has an internal fault |
| Horn operates all the time | Horn push either earthed or stuck down<br>Horn cable to horn push earthed |
| **Lights** | |
| Lights come on but fade out | If engine not running battery discharged<br>Wire connections loose, disconnected or broken<br>Light switch shorting, disconnected or broken<br>Light switch shorting or otherwise faulty |
| Lights do not come on | If engine not running, battery discharged<br>Wire connections loose, disconnected or broken<br>Light switch shorting or otherwise faulty |
| Lights give very poor illumination | Lamp glasses dirty<br>Lamps badly out of adjustment |
| Lights work erratically – flashing on and off, especially over bumps | Battery terminals or earth connection loose<br>Lights not earthing properly<br>Contacts in light switch faulty |
| **Wipers** | |
| Wiper motor fails to work | Blown fuse<br>Wire connections loose, disconnected or broken<br>Brushes badly worn<br>Armature worn or faulty<br>Field coils faulty |
| Wiper motor works but wiper blades remain static | Wiper motor gearbox parts badly worn<br>Stripped splines on wheelbox spindles |

| Symptom | Reason/s |
| --- | --- |
| Wiper motor works slowly and takes little current | Brushes badly worn<br>Commutator dirty, greasy or burnt<br>Armature badly worn or faulty |
| Wiper motor works very slowly and takes excessive current | Commutator dirty, greasy or burnt<br>Armature bearings dirty or unaligned<br>Armature badly worn or faulty |

## Fig. 10.120 Wiring diagram for XJ12 and Double Six, Series 1

1 Alternator
3 Battery (12V)
4 Starter solenoid
5 Starter motor
6 Lighting switch
7 Headlamp dipswitch
8 RH headlamp
9 LH headlamp
10 Main beam warning lamp
11 RH sidelamp
12 LH sidelamp
13 Panel lamps switch
14 Panel lamps
15 Number plate illumination lamps
16 RH stop & tail lamp
17 LH stop & tail lamp
18 Stop lamp switch
20 Interior lights
21 RH door switch
22 LH door switch
23 Horns
24 Horn push
25 Flasher unit
26 Direction indicator switch
27 Direction indicator warning lamp
28 RH front flasher lamp
29 LH front flasher lamp
30 RH rear flasher lamp
31 LH rear flasher lamp
32 Heater or fresh air motor switch
33 Heater or fresh air motors
34 Fuel gauge
35 Fuel gauge tank unit
36 Windscreen wiper switch
37 Windscreen wiper motor
38 Ignition switch
39 Ignition coil
40 Distributor
41 Fuel pumps
42 Oil pressure switch
43 Oil pressure warning lamp or gauge
44 Ignition or no charge warning lamp
46 Water temperature gauge
47 Water temperature transmitter
49 Reversing lamp switch
50 Reversing lamps
53 Fog lamp switch
54 RH fog lamp
55 LH fog lamp
56 Clock
57 Cigar lighter
59 Interior light switch
61 Horn relay
64 Bi-metal instrument voltage stabiliser
65 Boot light switch
66 Boot light
67 Line fuse
75 Automatic gearbox safety switch
76 Automatic gearbox selector indicator lamp
77 Electric windscreen washer
78 Electric windscreen washer switch
82 Switch illumination lamps
95 Tachometer
101 Map light switch
102 Map light
113 RH headlamp inner (4 headlamps)
114 LH headlamp inner (4 headlamps)
115 Rear window demist switch
116 Rear window demist unit
140 Fuel tank changeover switch
146 Battery condition indicator
147 Oil pressure transmitter
152 Hazard warning lamp
153 Hazard warning switch
154 Hazard warning flasher unit
158 Printed circuit instrument panel
160 Split brake differential switch
164 Ballast resistor
165 Handbrake switch
166 Handbrake warning lamp
168 Ignition key warning buzzer
169 Buzzer door switch
177 Radiator cooling fan relay
178 Radiator cooling fan thermostat
179 Radiator cooling fan motor
180 Auto transmission kickdown switch
181 Auto transmission kickdown solenoid
182 Brake fluid level switch
183 Opus ignition amplifier
184 Panel light resistor
187 Air conditioning relay
188 Air conditioning resistor
190 Air conditioning compressor
191 Air conditioning thermostat switch
192 Air conditioning control switch
194 Starter solenoid/ballast coil relay
198 Driver's seat belt switch
199 Passenger's seat belt switch
200 Passenger's seat switch
201 Seat belt warning gearbox switch
202 Seat belt warning lamp
203 Blocking diode-seat belt warning
204 Ignition protection relay
205 Fuel solenoid valves
206 Battery cooling fan motor
207 Battery cooling thermostat
208 Cigar lighter illumination
209 Left-right hand dipped beam
210 Panel light rheostat
211 Heater panel illumination
212 Choke warning light switch
213 Choke warning light
214 Choke control illumination
215 Window lift master switch
216 Window lift switch (front) RH
217 Window lift switch (rear) RH
218 Window lift switch (front) LH
219 Window lift switch (rear) LH
220 Window lift motor
221 Window lift safety relay
222 Window lift circuit breaker

### Colour code for wiring diagrams

| | | | |
|---|---|---|---|
| N | Brown | B | Black |
| U | Blue | O | Orange |
| R | Red | P | Purple |
| K | Pink | G | Green |
| W | White | L | Light |
| Y | Yellow | S | Slate |

*When a cable has two colour code letters, the first denotes the main colour and the second the tracer colour*

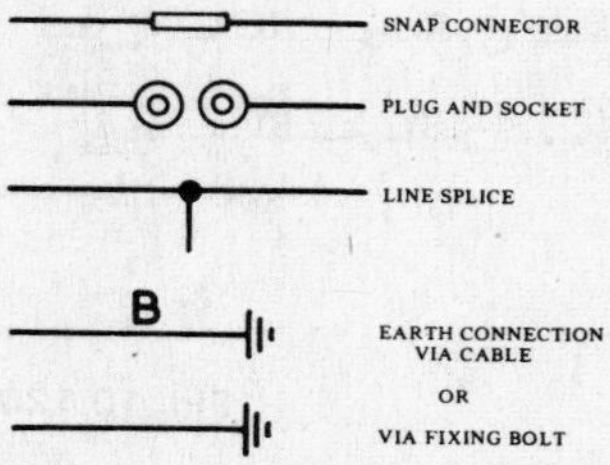

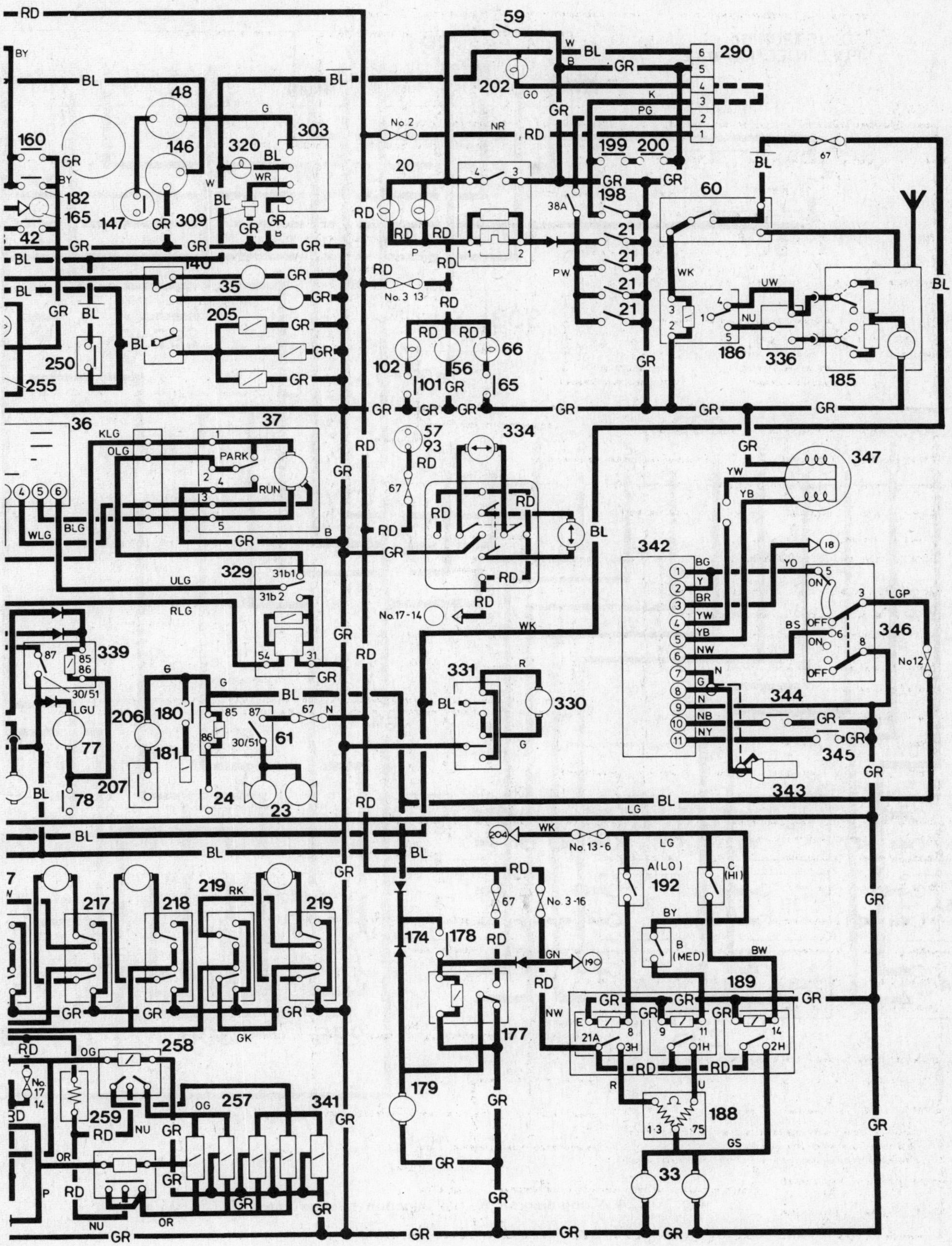


Fig. 10.123 Wiring diagram for XJ12 and Double Six, Series 3 - continued

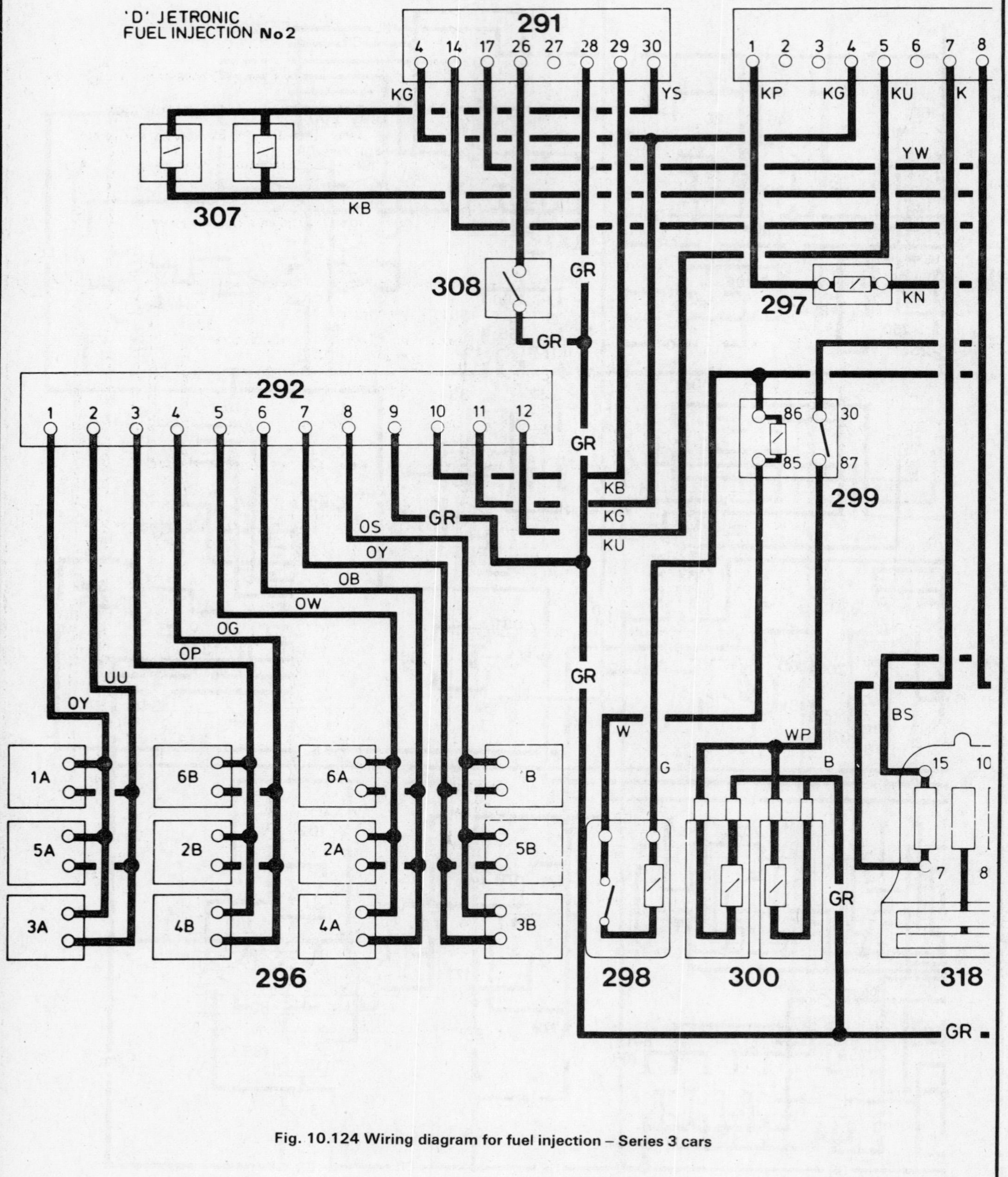


Fig. 10.124 Wiring diagram for fuel injection – Series 3 cars

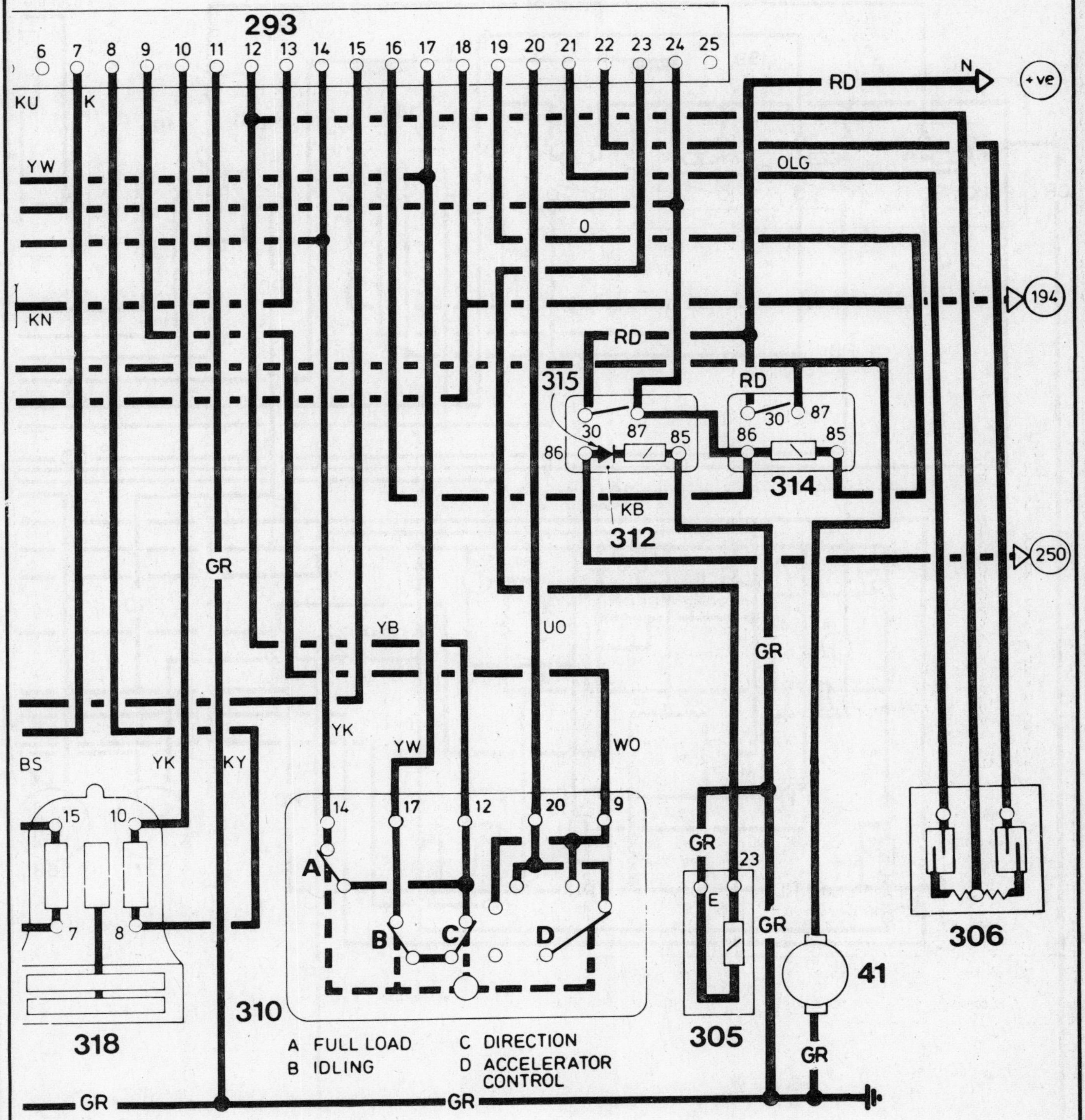


Fig. 10.124 Wiring diagram for fuel injection – Series 3 cars – continued

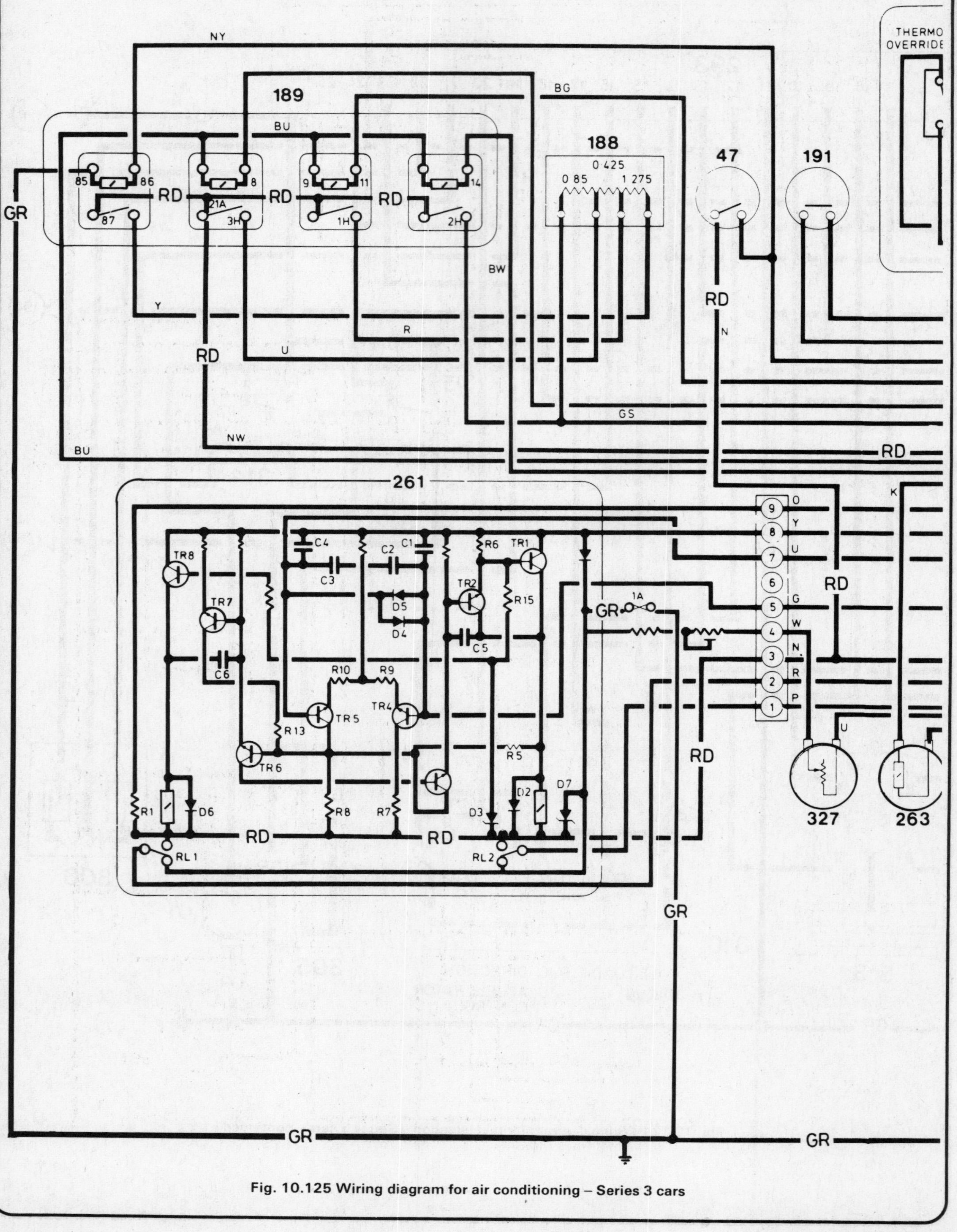


Fig. 10.125 Wiring diagram for air conditioning – Series 3 cars

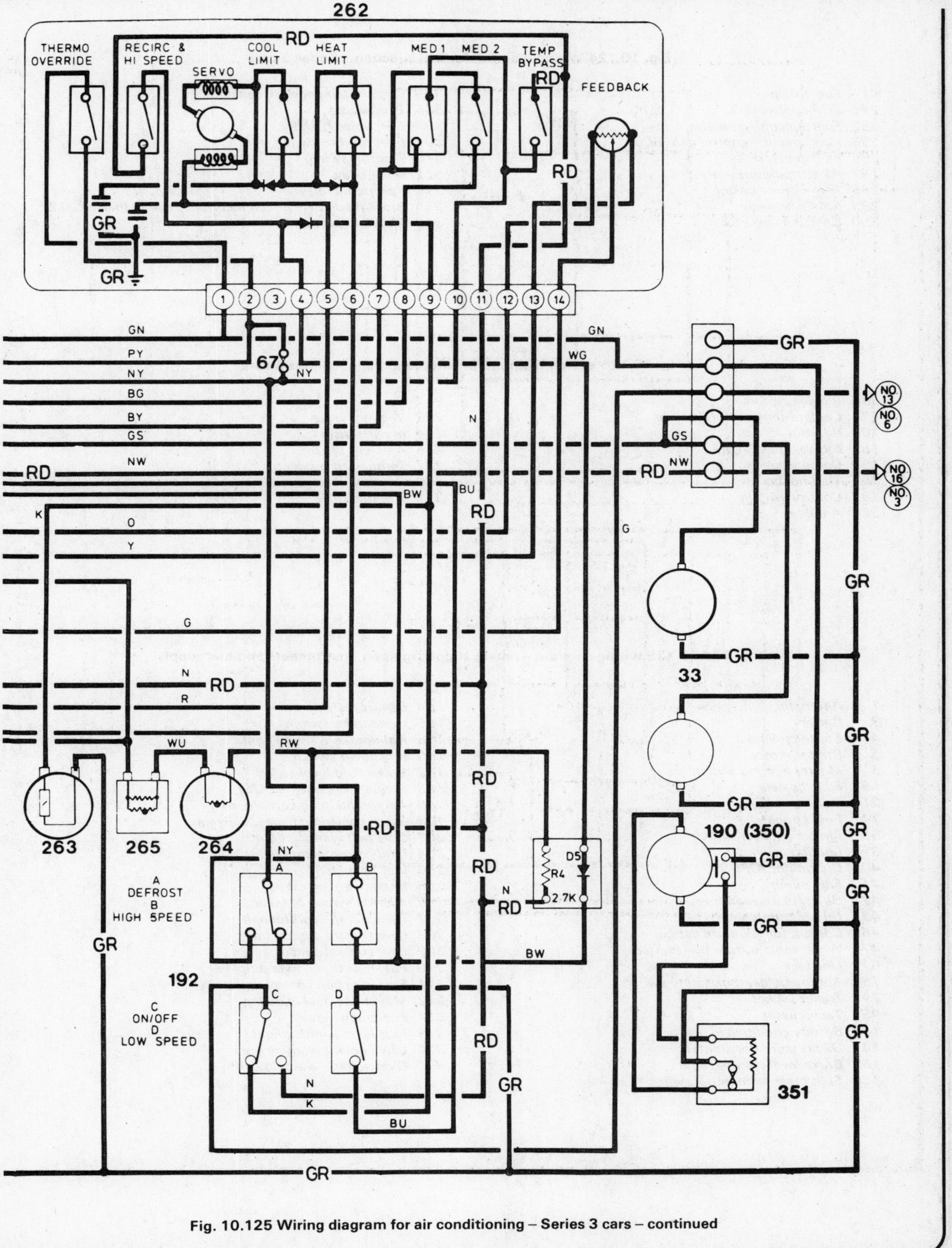


Fig. 10.125 Wiring diagram for air conditioning – Series 3 cars – continued

## Fig. 10.124 Wiring diagram for fuel injection – Series 3 cars

*41 Fuel pump*
*291 EGR control unit*
*292 Fuel injection amplifier*
*293 Fuel injection control unit (ECU)*
*296 Fuel injectors*
*297 Air temperature sensor*
*298 Thermotime switch*
*299 Cold start relay*
*300 Cold start injector*
*305 Coolant temperature sensor*
*306 Trigger unit*
*307 EGR valve*
*308 EGR thermo switch*
*310 Throttle switch*
*312 Main relay*
*314 Fuel pump relay*
*315 Blocking diode – inhibit incorrect polarity (part of 312)*
*318 Manifold pressure sensor*

## Fig. 10.125 Wiring diagram for air conditioning – Series 3 cars

*33 Blower motors*
*47 Coolant temperature sensor*
*188 Resistor*
*189 Blower speed relay*
*190 Compressor clutch*
*191 Thermostat*
*192 Control switch*
*261 Amplifier*
*262 Servo*
*263 Vacuum valve*
*264 In car sensor*
*265 Ambient sensor*
*327 Temperature selector*
*350 Overtemperature switch*
*351 Thermal fuse*

## Fig. 10.126 XJS wiring diagram – power supply, ignition, instruments and fuel supply

*1 Alternator*
*3 Battery*
*4 Starter solenoid*
*5 Starter motor*
*6 Master lighting switch*
*19 Fuse box(es)*
*21 Door switch*
*34 Fuel gauge*
*38 Ignition/Starter switch*
*39 Ignition coil*
*40 Distributor (OPUS)*
*41 Fuel pump*
*42 Oil pressure switch*
*43 Oil pressure gauge*
*46 Coolant temperature gauge*
*47 Water temperature transmitter*
*67 Line fuse*
*75 Automatic gearbox safety switch*
*79 Trailer socket*
*95 Tachometer*
*146 Battery condition indicator*
*147 Oil pressure transmitter*
*159 Brake level warning light*
*160 Split brake differential switch*
*164 Ballast resistor*
*165 Handbrake switch*
*166 Handbrake warning light*
*180 Kickdown switch*
*182 Brake fluid level switch*
*183 Ignition amplifier (OPUS)*
*190 Air conditioning compressor*
*194 Starter solenoid ballast coil relay*
*202 Seat belt warning light*
*204 Ignition protection relay*
*250 Inertia switch*
*256 Brake warning diode*
*259 Thermal circuit breaker*
*302 Over voltage control unit*
*303 Low coolant control unit*
*309 Low coolant sensor*
*310 Fuel injection power amplifier*
*311 Fuel injection control unit*
*312 Main relay, fuel injection*
*314 Fuel pump relay*
*319 Fuel level warning light*
*320 Low coolant warning light*
*321 Over voltage warning light*

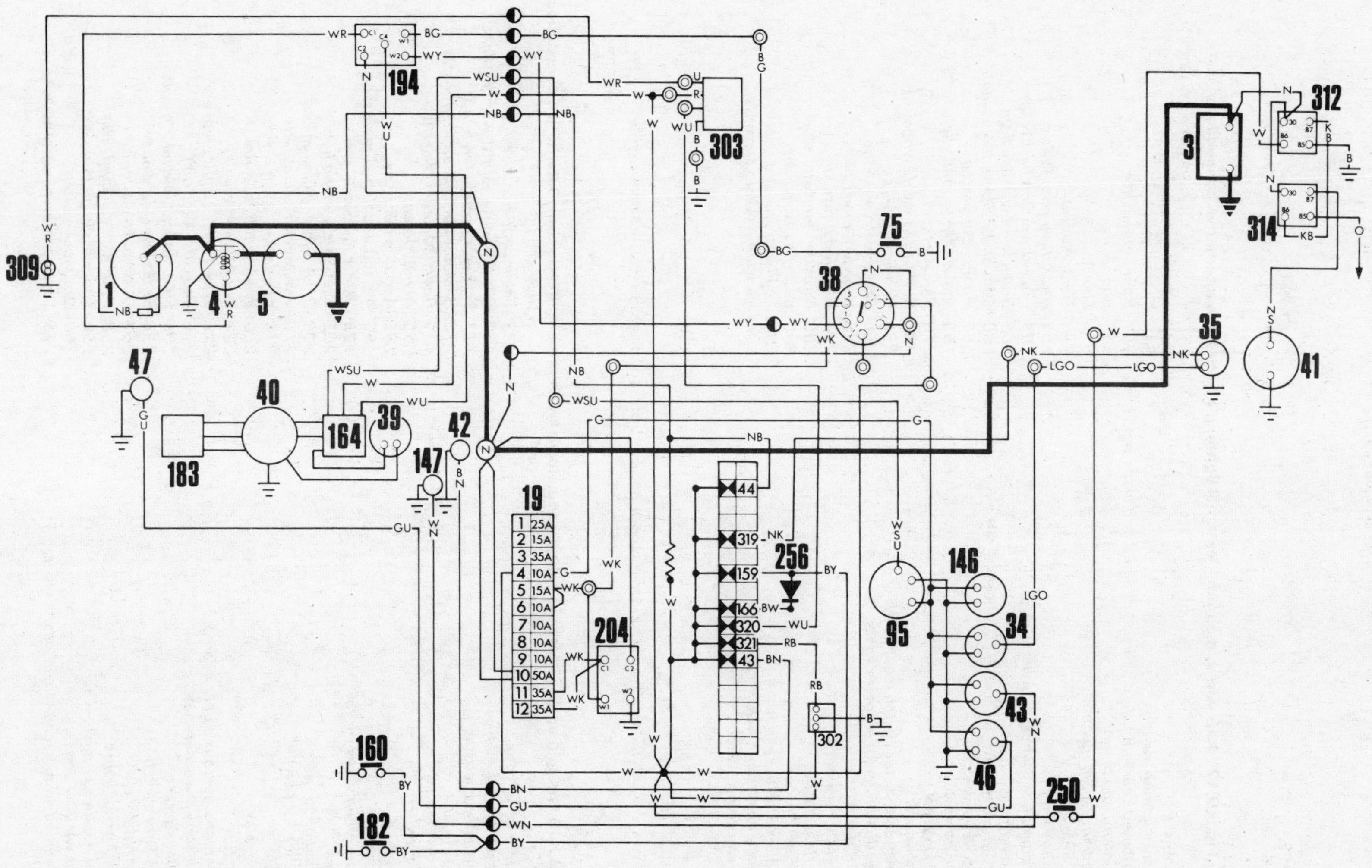


Fig. 10.126 Wiring diagram – power supply, ignition, instruments and fuel supply – XJS

**Fig. 10.127 XJS wiring diagram – external lighting. Insets show alternative connections**

| | |
|---|---|
| 3 | *Battery* |
| 6 | *Master lighting switch* |
| 7 | *Combined headlamp/dip/flash and direction indicator switch* |
| 8 | *Headlamp dip beam* |
| 9 | *Headlamp main beam* |
| 11 | *RH Side lamp* |
| 12 | *LH Side lamp* |
| 15 | *Number plate illumination lamp(s)* |
| 16 | *Stop lamp(s)* |
| 17 | *Tail lamp RH* |
| 18 | *Stop lamp switch* |
| 19 | *Fuse box(es)* |
| 22 | *Tail lamp LH* |
| 25 | *Flasher unit* |
| 26 | *Direction indictor switch (see No 7)* |
| 27 | *Direction indicator warning lights* |
| 28 | *RH Front flasher* |
| 29 | *LH Front flasher* |
| 30 | *RH Rear flasher* |
| 31 | *LH Rear flasher* |
| 38 | *Ignition/Starter switch* |
| 45 | *Headlamp flasher switch (see No 7)* |
| 49 | *Reverse lamp switch* |
| 50 | *Reverse lamp(s)* |
| 54 | *Fog lamps* |
| 65 | *Boot light switch* |
| 66 | *Boot light* |
| 67 | *Line fuse* |
| 79 | *Trailer socket* |
| 153 | *Hazard warning switch* |
| 154 | *Hazard warning flasher unit* |
| 159 | *Brake level warning light* |
| 160 | *Split brake differential switch* |
| 165 | *Handbrake switch* |
| 166 | *Handbrake warning light* |
| 170 | *Side markers* |
| 182 | *Brake fluid level switch* |
| 231 | *Headlamp relay* |
| 256 | *Brake warning diode* |
| 286 | *Rear fog guard switch* |
| 288 | *Rear fog guard lamp* |
| 289 | *Direction indicator diode* |
| 291 | *Brake warning relay* |
| 293 | *Fog lamp warning light* |
| 304 | *Park lamp failure sensor(s)* |

**Fig. 10.128 XJS wiring diagram – interior lighting and auxiliary equipment. Insets show alternative connections**

| | |
|---|---|
| 3 | *Battery* |
| 6 | *Master lighting switch* |
| 13 | *Panel lamp rheostat* |
| 14 | *Panel lamps* |
| 20 | *Interior light(s)* |
| 21 | *Door switch* |
| 23 | *Horn(s)* |
| 24 | *Horn push* |
| 37 | *Windscreen wiper motor* |
| 56 | *Clock* |
| 57 | *Cigar lighter* |
| 59 | *Interior light switch* |
| 60 | *Radio* |
| 61 | *Horn relay* |
| 67 | *Line fuse* |
| 76 | *Automatic gearbox selector lamp* |
| 77 | *Windscreen washer motor* |
| 79 | *Trailer socket* |
| 101 | *Map light switch* |
| 102 | *Map light* |
| 105 | *Rear interior lights* |
| 115 | *Rear window demist switch* |
| 116 | *Rear window demist unit* |
| 118 | *Combined windscreen wiper/washer switch* |
| 139 | *To air conditioning circuit* |
| 150 | *Rear window demist warning light* |
| 177 | *Radiator cooling fan relay* |
| 178 | *Radiator cooling fan thermostat* |
| 179 | *Radiator cooling fan motor* |
| 185 | *Aerial motor* |
| 186 | *Aerial motor relay* |
| 190 | *Air conditioning compressor* |
| 198 | *Seat belt switch, driver* |
| 202 | *Seat belt warning light* |
| 208 | *Cigar lighter illumination* |
| 216 | *Window lift switch, RH* |
| 218 | *Window lift switch, LH* |
| 220 | *Window lift motor(s)* |
| 221 | *Window lift relay* |
| 222 | *Window lift circuit breaker* |
| 245 | *Seat belt logic unit* |
| 255 | *Fibre optics illumination bulb* |
| 256 | *Brake warning diode* |
| 257 | *Door lock solenoid* |
| 258 | *Door lock solenoid relay* |
| 259 | *Thermal circuit breaker* |
| 260 | *Door lock switch* |
| 278 | *Service interval warning light* |

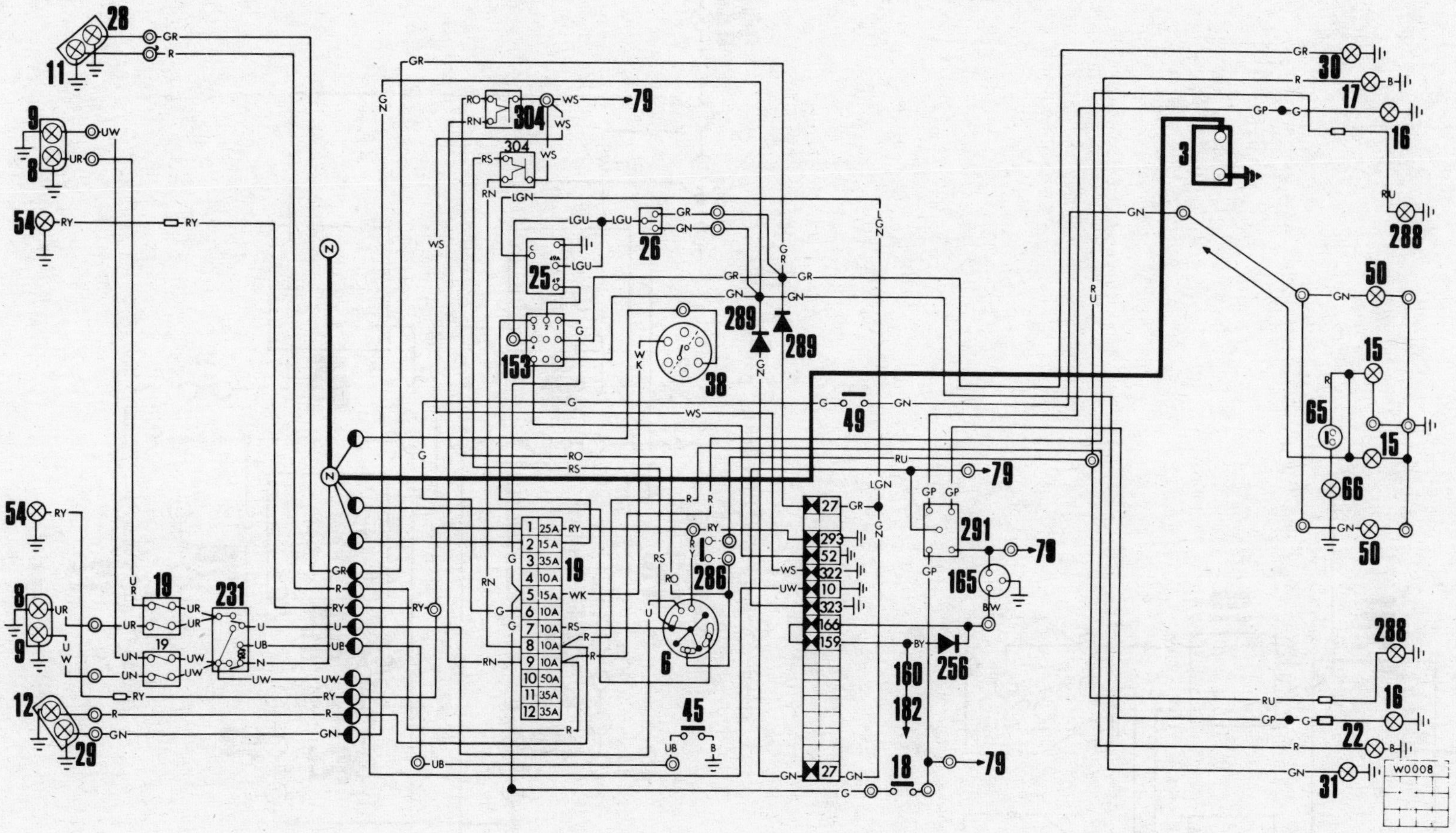

Fig. 10.127 Wiring diagram – external lighting. Insets show alternative connections – XJS

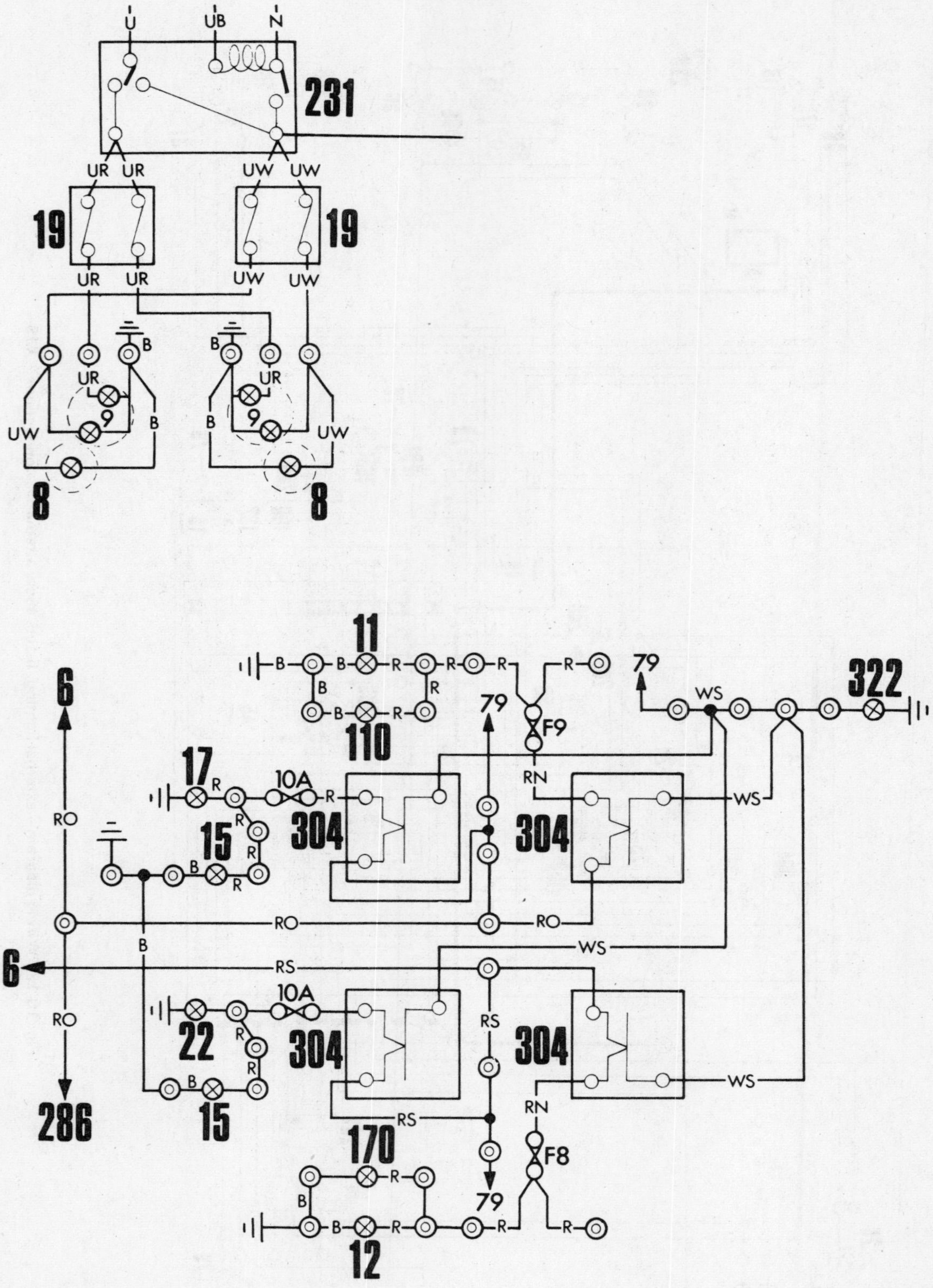


Fig. 10.127 Wiring diagram – external lighting. Insets show alternative connections – XJS continued

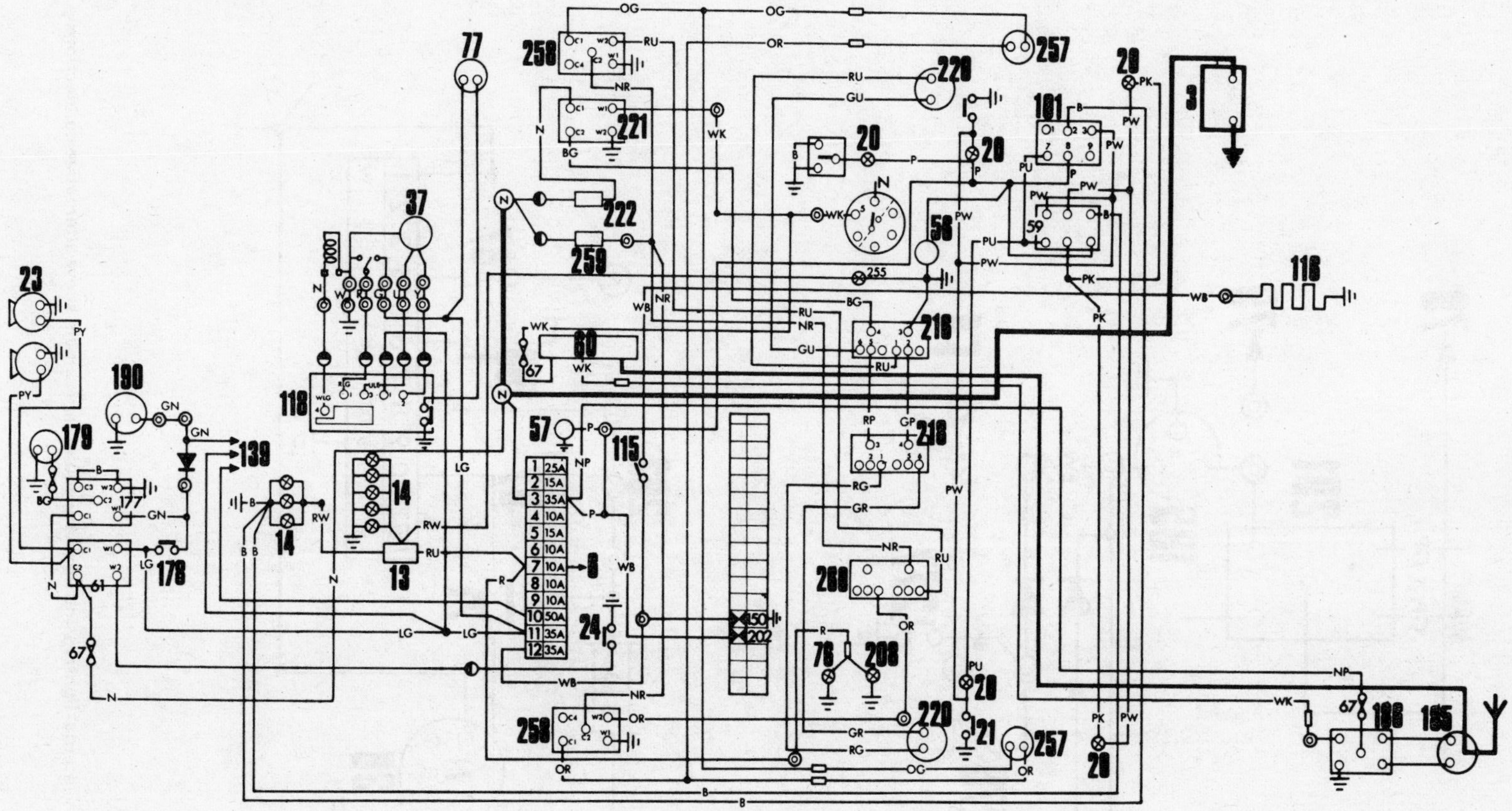

Fig. 10.128 Wiring diagram – interior lighting and auxiliary equipment. Insets show alternative connections – XJS

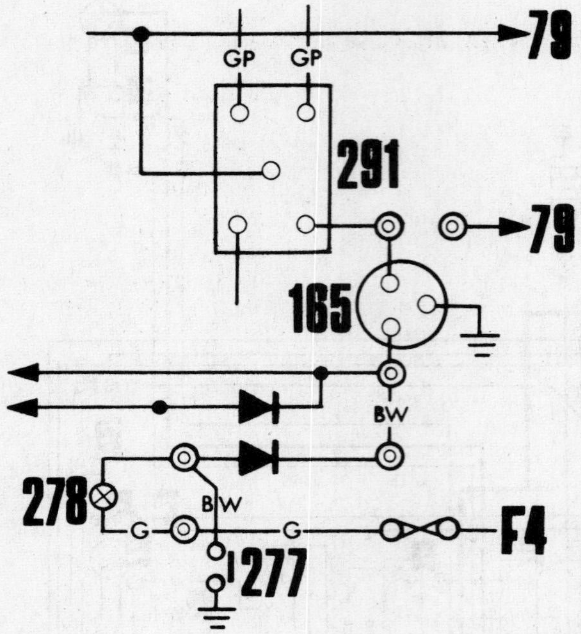


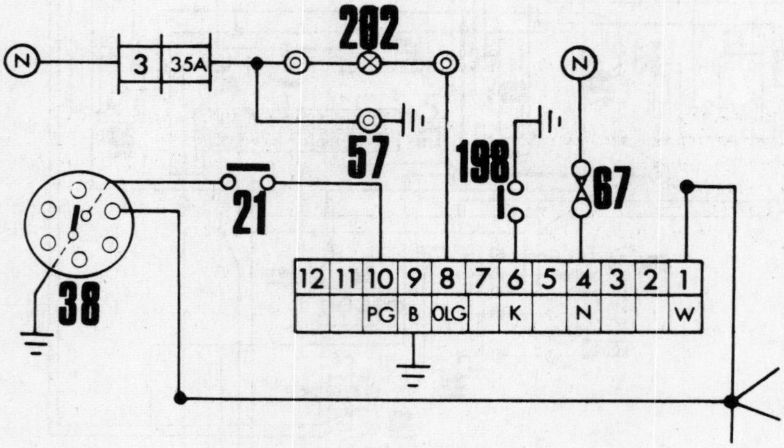


Fig. 10.128 Wiring diagram – internal lighting and auxiliary equipment. Insets show alternative connections – XJS – continued

**Fig. 10.129 XJS wiring diagram – fuel injection**

1 *Pressure sensor*
2 *Power amplifier*
3 *Air temperature sensor*
4 *Coolant temperature sensor*
5 *Thermotime switch*
6 *EGR thermo switch (if fitted)*
7 *Cold start valve*
8 *Cold start valve*
9 *EGR valve*
10 *EGR valve*
11 *Trigger unit*
12 *Throttle switch*
13 *Cold start relay*
14 *Electronic control unit*
15 *Battery*
16 *Main relay*
17 *Pump relay*
18 *Fuel pump*
19 *EGR control unit*
20 *Axle solenoid*
194 *Starter solenoid ballast resistor relay*
250 *Fuel cut-off inertia switch*
1A to 6B *Fuel injectors*

**Fig. 10.130 XJS wiring diagram – air conditioning**

33 *Blower motors*
47 *Water temperature transmitter*
187 *Air conditioning relays*
188 *Air conditioning resistors*
190 *Air conditioning compressor*
191 *Air conditioning thermostat*
192 *Air conditioning control switches*
261 *Air conditioning amplifier unit*
262 *Air conditioning servo control unit*
263 *Vacuum solenoid valve*
264 *In car temperature sensor*
265 *Ambient temperature sensor*

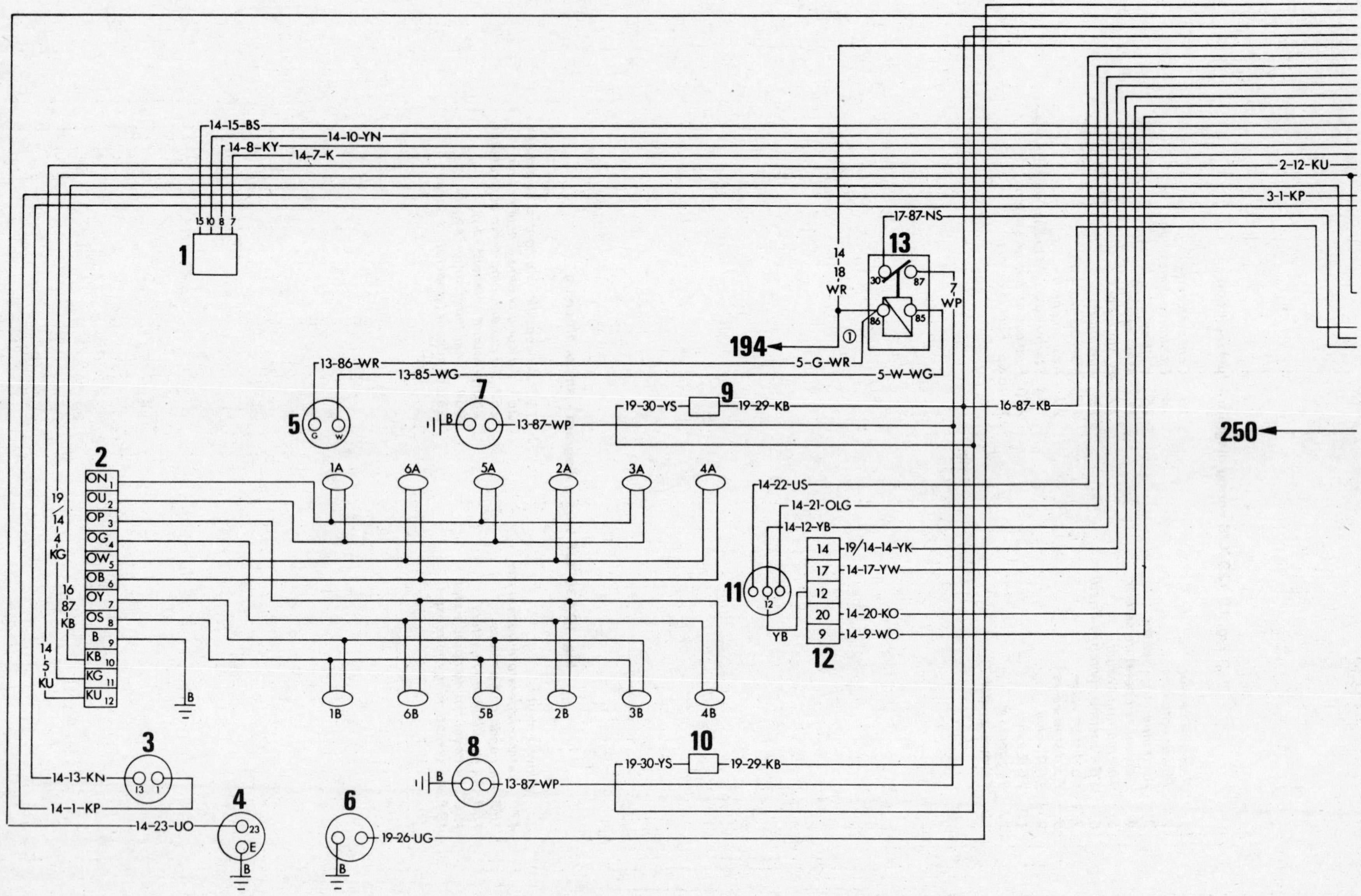


Fig. 10.129 Wiring diagram – fuel injection XJS

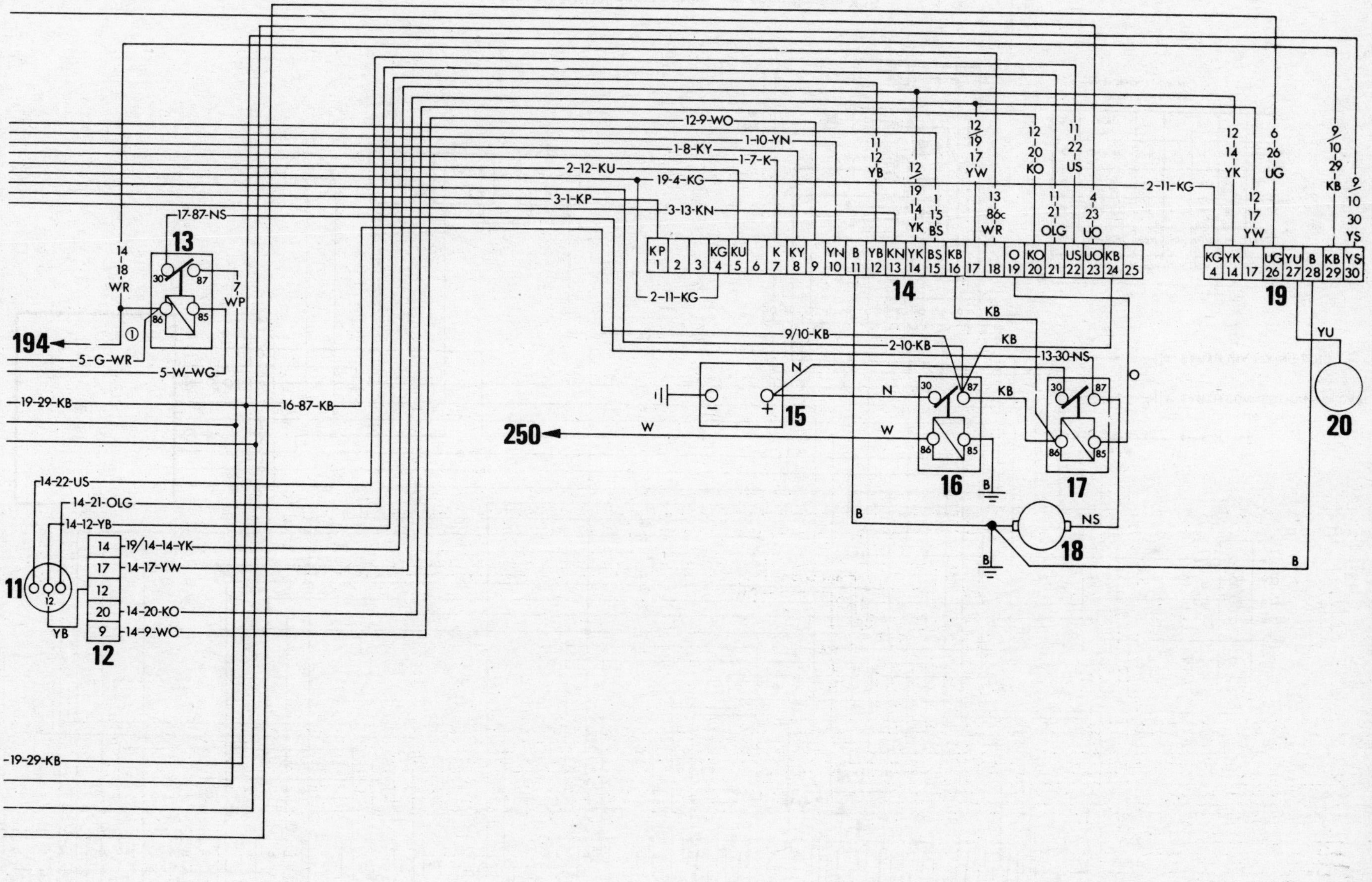


Fig. 10.129 Wiring diagram – fuel injection XJS – continued

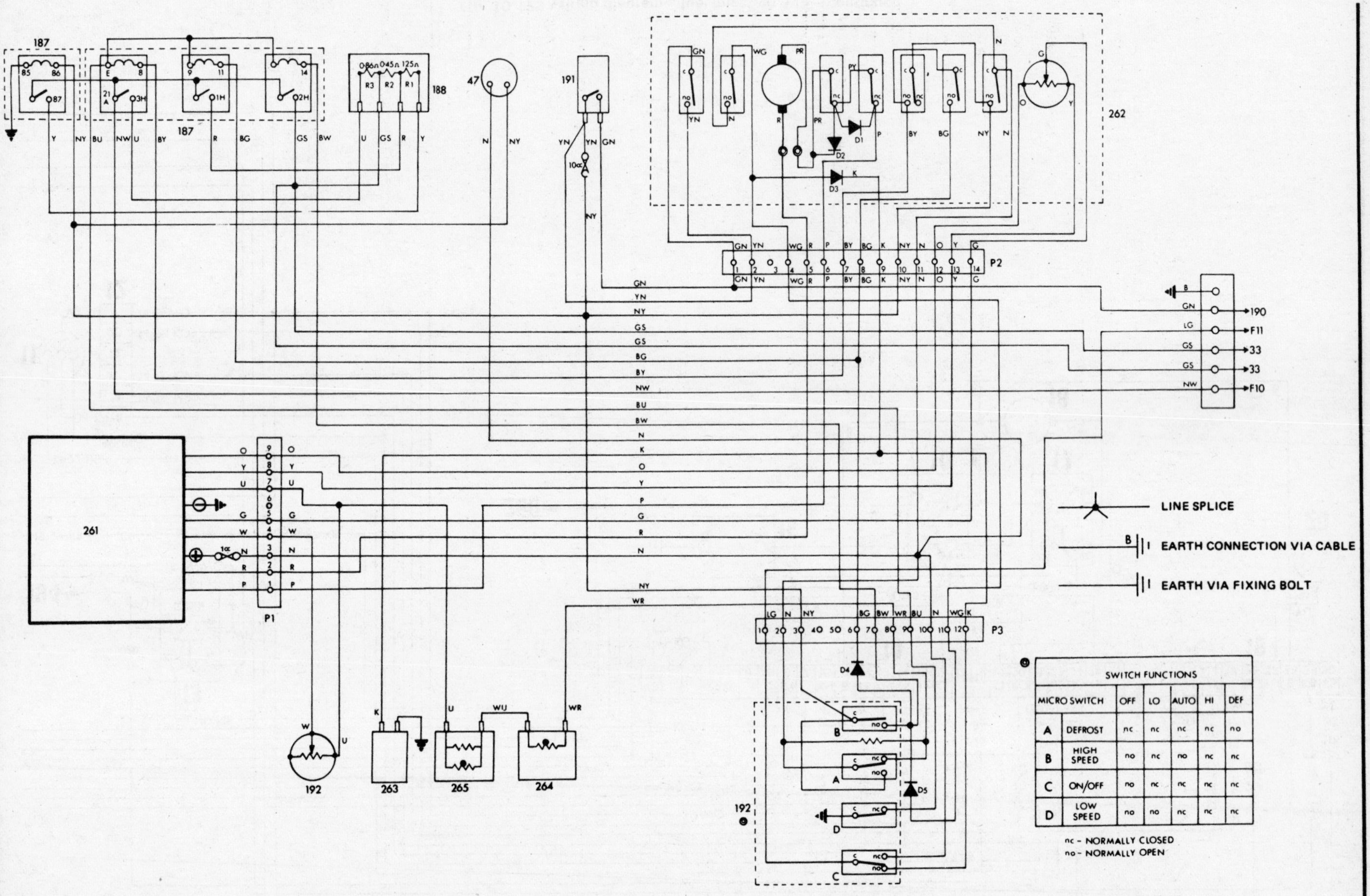


SWITCH FUNCTIONS

| MICRO SWITCH | | OFF | LO | AUTO | HI | DEF |
|---|---|---|---|---|---|---|
| A | DEFROST | nc | nc | nc | nc | no |
| B | HIGH SPEED | no | nc | no | nc | nc |
| C | ON/OFF | no | nc | nc | nc | nc |
| D | LOW SPEED | no | no | nc | nc | nc |

Fig. 10.130 Wiring diagram – air conditioning XJS

# Chapter 11 Suspension and steering

*For modifications, and information applicable to later models, see Supplement at end of manual*

**Contents**



**Specifications**

## Front suspension

| | |
|---|---|
| Type | Independent with wishbones, coil springs, telescopic shock absorbers and anti-roll bar |

## Front hubs

| | |
|---|---|
| Lubricant type/specification | Multi-purpose lithium-based grease, to NLGI No 2 (Duckhams LB 10) |

## Steering angles

| | |
|---|---|
| Castor: | |
| XJ12 and Double Six, Series 1 | $2°$ to $2\frac{1}{2}°$ positive |
| All other models | $3\frac{1}{4}°$ to $3\frac{3}{4}°$ positive |
| Camber (all models) | $\frac{1}{4}°$ to $\frac{3}{4}°$ positive |
| Front wheel alignment (toe): | |
| XJ12 and Double Six, Series 1 and Series 2 with carburettors, and XJS | $\frac{1}{16}$ to $\frac{1}{8}$ in (1.6 to 3.2 mm) toe-in |
| XJ12 and Double Six with fuel injection | 0 to $\frac{1}{16}$ in (0 to 1.6 mm) toe-out |

## Steering system

| | |
|---|---|
| Type | Rack-and-pinion, power-assisted with safety column |
| Number of turns lock to lock: | |
| XJ12 and Double Six | 3.15 |
| XJS | 2.9 |

| | |
|---|---|
| Turning circle: | |
| XJ12 and Double Six, Series 1 | 39 ft (11.9 m) |
| XJ12 and Double Six, Series 2 on: | |
| Standard wheelbase | 38 ft 8 in (11.79 m) |
| Long wheelbase | 40 ft (12.2 m) |
| XJS | 36 ft 3 in (11.05 m) |
| Fluid type/specification | ATF type F (to M2C 33F), type G (to M2C 33G), or Dexron IID (Duckhams D-Matic or Q-Matic) |

## Rear suspension

| | |
|---|---|
| Type | Independent, with coil springs and telescopic shock absorbers. Anti-roll bar on XJS models |
| Camber (all models) | $\frac{1}{2}$° to 1° negative |
| Roadwheel alignment (all models) | $\frac{1}{32}$ in (0.8 mm) toe-in to $\frac{1}{32}$ in (0.8 mm) toe-out |

## Roadwheels

| | |
|---|---|
| Type and size | Pressed steel or alloy $6^1/_2$ x 15 in |

## Tyres

| | | |
|---|---|---|
| Size (all models) | 205/70VR15 | |
| Pressures in $lbf/in^2$ ($kgf/cm^2$)*: | **Normal conditions** | **High speed/full load** |
| XJ 12 and Double Six: | | |
| Series 1, front and rear | 26 (1.83) | 34 (2.4) |
| Series 2 on, front | 28 (1.97) | 36 (2.5) |
| Series 2 on, rear | 26 (1.83) | 36 (2.5) |
| XJS: | | |
| Front | 26 (1.83) | 32 (2.2) |
| Rear | 24 (1.69) | 30 (2.1) |

***Refer also to individual vehicle tyre pressure label**

## Torque wrench settings

| | lbf ft | Nm |
|---|---|---|
| *Front suspension* | | |
| Stub axle to stub axle carrier | 85 | 115 |
| Steering arm to stub axle carrier | 50 | 68 |
| Disc to hub | 35 | 48 |
| Caliper to stub axle carrier | 55 | 75 |
| Upper swivel balljoint to stub axle carrier | 50 | 68 |
| Lower swivel balljoint to lower wishbone | 55 | 75 |
| Upper wishbone pivot shaft nuts | 50 | 68 |
| Lower wishbone pivot shaft nuts | 45 | 61 |
| Upper swivel balljoint to wishbone | 30 | 41 |
| Upper pivot shaft to crossmember | 50 | 68 |
| Spring pan bolts | 30 | 41 |
| Shock absorber mounting bracket | 30 | 41 |
| Shock absorber upper mounting | 30 | 41 |
| Shock absorber lower mounting | 50 | 68 |
| Buffers to spring pan | 10 | 14 |
| Upper wishbone rebound rubbers | 10 | 14 |
| Anti-roll bar bracket to body | 30 | 41 |
| Anti-roll bar to link and link to wishbone | 18 | 25 |
| Suspension crossmember clamp bolt | 30 | 41 |
| Suspension crossmember front mounting bolt | 100 | 136 |
| Vee mounting to body | 25 | 34 |
| Vee mounting to crossmember | 25 | 34 |
| *Rear suspension* | | |
| Tie-plate to crossmember | 18 | 25 |
| Inner pivot bracket to final drive unit | 60 | 82 |
| Final drive to crossmember | 75 | 102 |
| Caliper mounting bolts | 55 | 75 |
| Wishbone inner pivot shaft nuts | 50 | 68 |
| Wishbone outer pivot shaft nuts | 100 | 136 |
| Driveshaft inner flange bolts | 50 | 68 |
| Driveshaft to hub carrier | 100 | 136 |
| Radius rods to wishbone | 65 | 88 |
| Radius rods to body | 40 | 54 |
| Radius rod safety strap bolts | 40 | 54 |
| Radius rod safety strap to floor panel | 30 | 41 |
| Shock absorber upper mounting | 35 | 48 |
| Shock absorber lower mounting | 35 | 48 |
| Vee mounting to body | 30 | 41 |
| Vee mounting to crossmember | 18 | 25 |
| Bump stop rubber to body | 18 | 25 |
| Anti-roll bar bracket to body (XJS only) | 18 | 25 |
| *Steering* | | |
| Pinion housing cover plate | 18 | 25 |
| Rack balljoints | 50 | 68 |

| | lbf ft | Nm |
|---|---|---|
| Tie-rod end locknuts | 140 | 190 |
| Tie-rod end balljoint to steering arm | 45 | 61 |
| Steering gear mounting bolts | 18 | 25 |
| Universal joint pinch-bolts | 18 | 25 |
| Steering wheel to shaft | 28 | 38 |
| Steering column to lower bracket | 18 | 25 |
| Lower column to body | 18 | 25 |
| Column to upper bracket | 18 | 25 |
| Fluid pipe adaptor on rack housing | 50 | 68 |
| *Wheels* | | |
| Roadwheel nuts | 45 | 61 |

## 1 General description

*The front suspension* assembly comprises a pressed steel crossmember to which is attached the steering mechanism and the upper and lower suspension wishbones.

The front suspension incorporates coil springs, hydraulic telescopic (gas-pressurised) shock absorbers (photo) and an anti-roll bar fitted between the two lower wishbones.

*The rear suspension* assembly also comprises a pressed steel crossmember, rubber mounted to the body and located by radius arms. The open driveshafts are located in the transverse plane by two links. The suspension incorporates four coil springs which enclose hydraulic telescopic shock absorbers, which are gas pressurised.

On XJS models, an anti-roll bar is fitted at the rear as well as to the front of the car.

*The steering gear* is of rack and pinion type with power assistance on all models. The steering column is of collapsible type incorporating shear plugs and two universal joints.

There are differences in detail between many of the components used on XJ12, Double Six and XJS models.

## 2 Maintenance and inspection

1 At the intervals specified in Routine Maintenance, apply grease to the four top and bottom swivel balljoints of the front suspension.
2 Remove the hub caps from the front roadwheels and apply the grease gun to the exposed nipple. A bleed hole is provided to indicate when sufficient grease has been injected.
3 Check and adjust the front hub bearings (Section 5) and the front wheel alignment (Section 49).
4 Grease the inner and outer pivot bearings of the rear suspension. Remove the rear hub grease plug and fill (but do not pressurise) with grease.
5 Check the reservoir oil level in the steering pump and lubricate sparingly the rack and pinion assembly using the nipple provided.
6 Give four or five strokes of the grease gun to the track rod end grease nipples. A bleed hole is provided, covered with a nylon disc which will lift when sufficient grease has been injected.
7 Check the security of all suspension and steering nuts and bolts, examine rubber dust excluders and gaiters for splits or cuts and renew as necessary. Check steering linkage and balljoints for wear and adjust or renew as described in this Chapter.

## 3 Front shock absorbers – removal, testing and refitting

1 The shock absorbers should be removed and tested whenever the cornering or roadholding characteristics of the car appear to have deteriorated, if there is evidence of oil on the shock absorber casing, or at 30 000 mile (48 000 km) intervals.
2 To remove a shock absorber, disconnect the upper mounting nuts and cushions which are accessible within the engine compartment. Jack up the front of the car and remove the roadwheel.
3 Unscrew and remove the self-locking nut from the lower mounting and withdraw the bolt.
4 Compress the shock absorber and remove it from the car.
5 Grip the shock absorber lower mounting in the jaws of a vice so that the shock absorber is held vertically. Now fully extend and contract the unit ten or twelve times. If there is any lack of resistance in either direction or seizure, then the unit (which is sealed) must be renewed. Never attempt to dismantle a shock absorber, particularly the gas-pressurised type.
6 Refitting the shock absorber is a reversal of removal but if the original unit is being refitted, check the rubber bushes and cushions for deterioration and renew, if necessary.

## 4 Front anti-roll bar – removal and refitting

### *XJ12, Double Six*

1 Place the car over a pit or raise and support it securely on stands placed under its front end. Remove both front roadwheels.
2 Remove the two self-locking nuts which secure the anti-roll bar link to the bracket on the front suspension lower wishbone.
3 Remove the four setscrews which secure the keeper plates to the front crossmember. Lift the anti-roll bar away.
4 The link arm bush can be renewed by pressing it out of the link arm eye. The rubber support bushes are split to enable them to be removed easily. Their splits should face the rear of the car.
5 Refitting is a reversal of removal, but do not fully tighten the nuts and setscrews until the weight of the car has been lowered onto the roadwheels.

### *XJS*

6 Jack up the front of the car and support the side members on stands. Remove both front roadwheels and place a jack under the centre of the front crossmember.
7 Prise out the plastic fasteners which secure the stoneguards under the wheel arches.
8 Remove the two screws and thirteen plastic fasteners which hold the spoiler undertray to the body and the spoiler proper.
9 Using a balljoint separator, disconnect the left-hand tie-rod from the steering arm.
10 Remove the self-locking nuts and disconnect the links from the anti-roll bar on both sides of the car.
11 Unscrew and remove the mounting bolts from the front suspension assembly. Lower the jack until the spacers, bushes and sleeves can be removed.
12 Unbolt the anti-roll bar clamp plates from the bodyframe and detach the rubber insulators.
13 Withdraw the anti-roll bar past the left-hand front hub.
14 Refitting is a reversal of removal, but observe the following points.
15 Locate the rubber insulators so that their splits are towards the rear of the car.
16 Do not fully tighten connecting nuts and bolts until the weight of the car has been lowered onto its roadwheels.
17 When refitting the spoiler undertray and the stoneguards, use new plastic fasteners.
18 Tighten all bolts and nuts to the specified torque.
19 The anti-roll bar mounting clamp rubber insulators and link cushions can be renewed without having to withdraw the anti-roll bar from the car if the securing nuts are released and the bar prised away. Use rubber lubricant or soapy water to ease refitting.

## 5 Front hub – overhaul and adjustment

1 Apply the handbrake fully, jack up the front of the car and remove

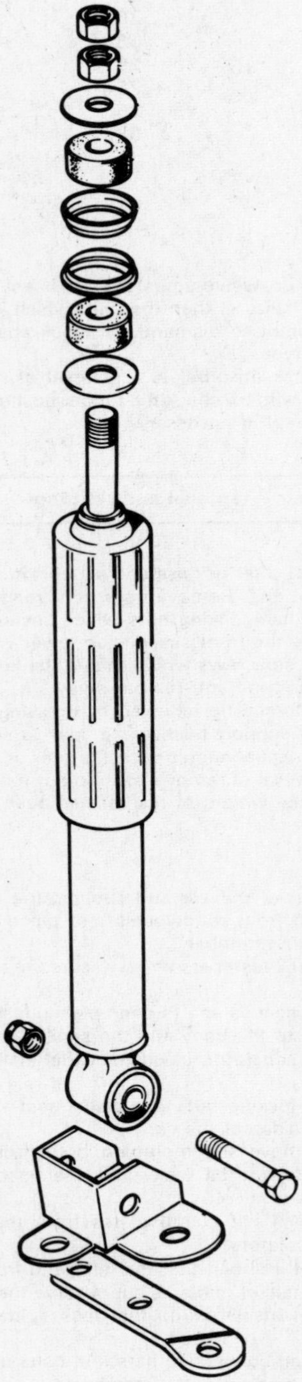

Fig. 11.1 Typical front shock absorber (Sec 3)

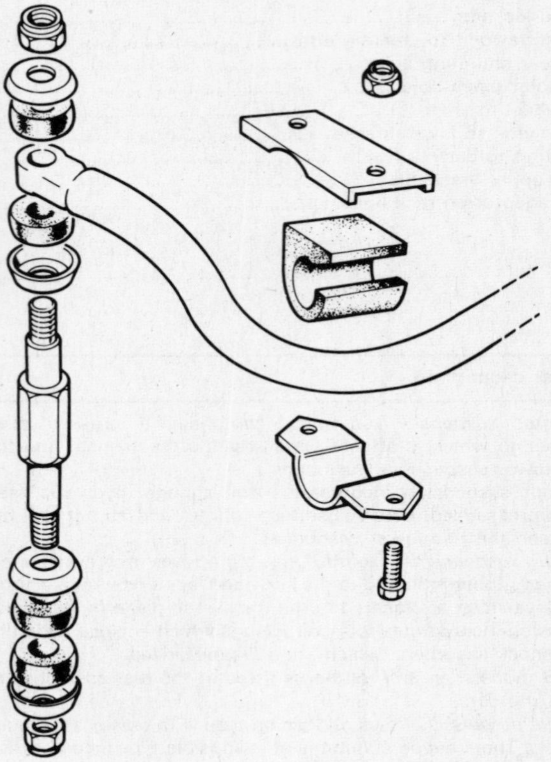

Fig. 11.2 Front anti-roll bar end link and clamp (Sec 4)

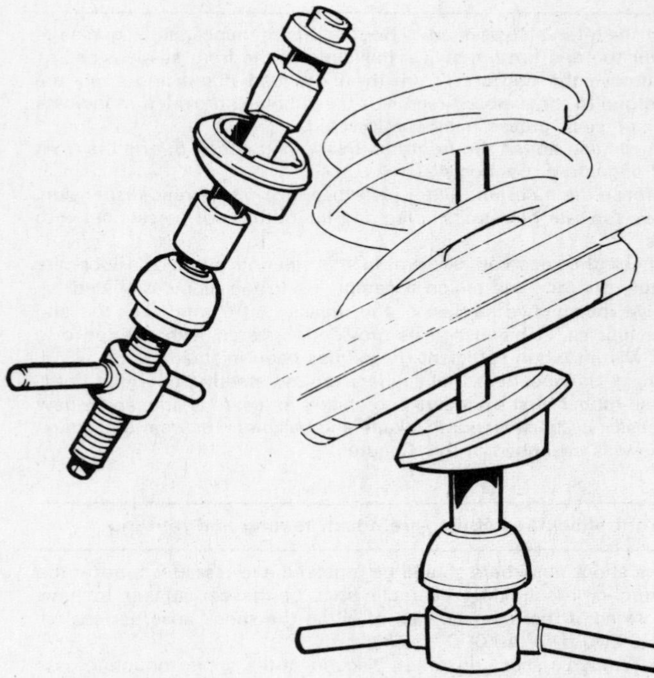

Fig. 11.3 Typical coil spring, compressor (Sec 6)

**Fig. 11.4 Front hub components (Sec 5)**

1. *End cap*
2. *Split pin*
3. *Castellated nut*
4. *Thrust washer*
5. *Outer bearing*
6. *Hub*
7. *Inner bearing*
8. *Oil seal*
9. *Spacer*
10. *Dust excluder*
11. *Stub axle carrier*
12. *Steering arm*
13. *Stub axle*
14. *Bolt*

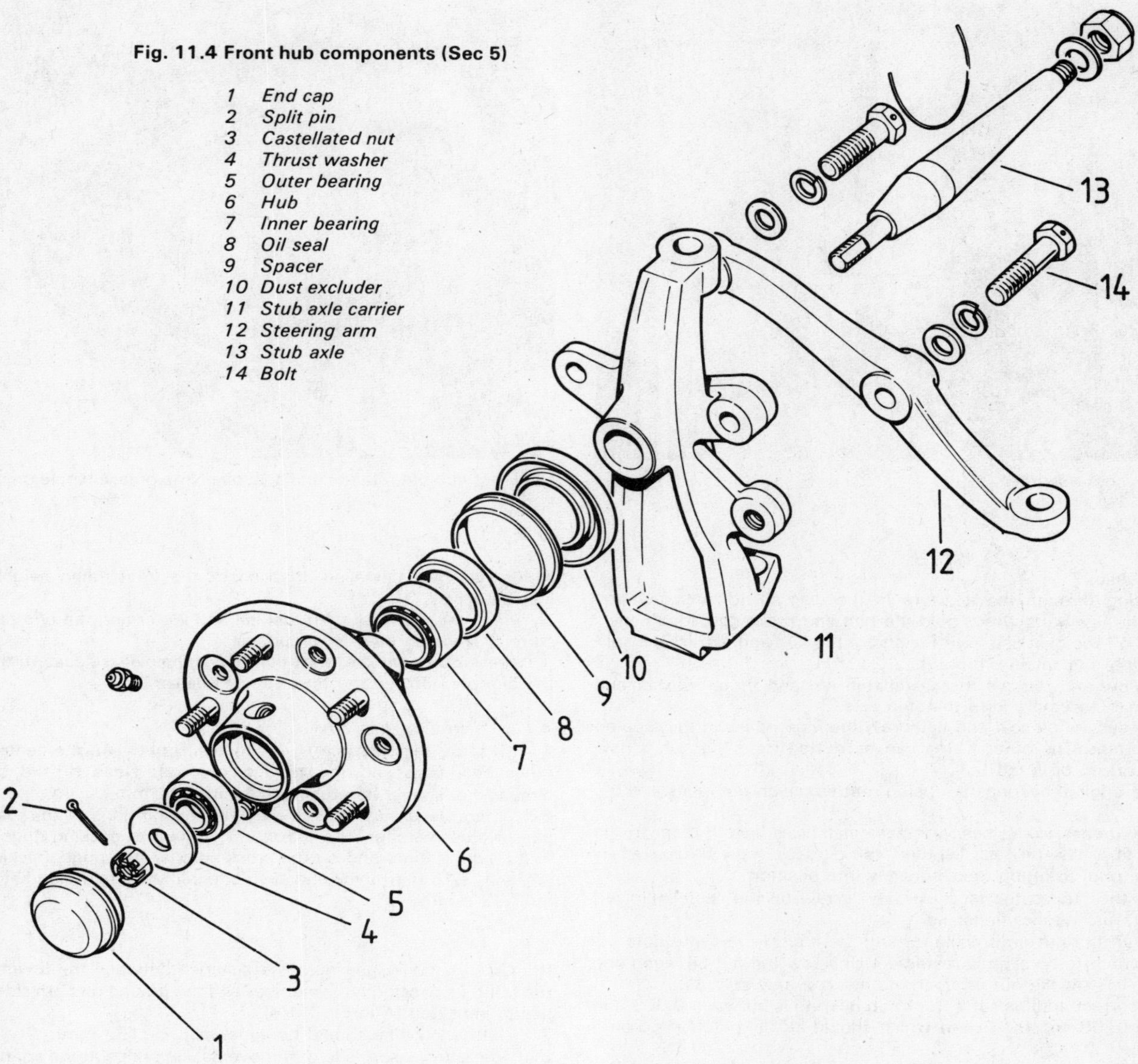

**Fig. 11.5 Front riding height adjustment diagram (XJ12, Double Six) (Sec 7)**

*A = 24$\frac{5}{8}$ in (611 mm)*

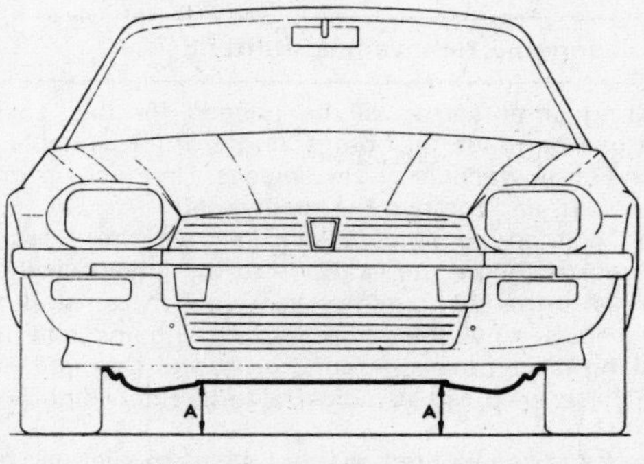


**Fig. 11.6 Front riding height adjustment diagram (XJS) (Sec 7)**

*A = 6 in (152 mm)*

1.1 Front shock absorber

5.3 Front hub nut retainer and split pin. Note grease nipple on hub

the roadwheel.
2 Working through the aperture in the disc shield, unscrew and remove the five bolts which hold the hub and brake disc together.
3 Prise off the dust cap from the end of the hub and extract the split pin from the nut retainer (photo).
4 Unscrew and remove the castellated nut and thrust washer and pull the hub assembly from the stub axle.
5 Prise out the oil seal and withdraw the inner races of the tapered roller bearings. The outer tracks can be drifted from the hub if new bearings are to be fitted.
6 If the original bearings are being refitted, clean the races and dry them.
7 Apply grease to the bearing tracks and races, install them to the hub and fit a new oil seal. Leather type oil seals must be soaked in engine oil prior to fitting them squarely into position.
8 Refit the hub to the stub axle and screw on the castellated nut with its thrust washer finger-tight.
9 Tighten the nut until while turning the hub at the same time, its rotation is felt to be slightly restricted. Unscrew the nut between one and two flats, fit the nut retainer and insert a new split pin.
10 The correct endfloat of a front hub bearing is between 0.003 and 0.005 in (0.08 and 0.13 mm) which should ideally be checked on a dial gauge.
11 Fit the grease cap and bolt the disc to the hub, tightening to the specified torque.
12 Fit the roadwheel and lower the car to the ground.

## 6 Front coil spring – removal and refitting

1 A coil spring compressor will be needed for this operation. A suitable tool can be made up from a length of rod suitably threaded using nuts and large washers or crosspieces. First jack up the front of the car, support it, and remove the roadwheel.
2 With the coil spring compressed, remove the setscrews and lockwashers which secure the seat pan to the lower wishbone.
3 Slowly release the spring compressor until the tension of the coil spring is relieved. Remove the compressor, spring and seat pan. On all models, packing pieces may be found on top of the spring or in the spring pan. These are used to adjust side-to-side riding height (see next Section).
4 Refitting is a reversal of removal but align the seat pan holes with the tapped holes in the lower wishbone by using pilot studs. Withdraw these once the spring is installed.

## 7 Front riding height – adjustment

1 If the original roadsprings have been refitted, together with the packing pieces, the riding height should not have altered. Where a new spring has been installed, then check the front riding height in the following way.
2 Have the car filled with fuel, oil and water and the tyre pressures correct, standing on a level surface.
3 Press down on the front bumper and slowly release it, then grip the bumper, lift out and then slowly release it.

### *XJ12 and Double Six*

4 Measure the distance (A in Fig. 11.5) between the centre of the outer headlamp and the ground on both sides of the car. The dimensions should be equal at 24$\frac{5}{8}$ in (611 mm).
5 Where necessary, add or remove packing rings at the roadspring pan or crossmember. The maximum number of packing rings located in the pan is three and on the crossmember two rings. Packing rings are $\frac{1}{8}$ in (3.18 mm) thick and each one will vary the riding height by $\frac{5}{16}$ in (7.93 mm).

### *XJS*

6 On this model, measure the distance between the lower face of the front suspension crossmember and the ground on both sides at the points indicated (A in Fig. 11.6).
7 The dimensions should be equal at 6 in (152 mm).
8 Where necessary add or remove packing rings at the spring turret, limiting their number to two.
9 The thickness and effect of the spring packing rings is as described in paragraph 5.

## 8 Front stub axle carrier – removal and refitting

1 Raise the front of the car by placing a jack under the lower wishbone. Remove the roadwheel.
2 Remove the brake caliper (Chapter 9).
3 Remove the hub/disc assembly (Section 5).
4 Remove the self-locking nut which secures the upper balljoint to the stub axle carrier.
5 Remove the nut which secures the lower balljoint to the lower wishbone.
6 Using a suitable extractor, separate the upper and lower balljoints from the stub axle carrier and remove the carrier.
7 The stub axle can be removed from the carrier and the disc shield unbolted and detached if necessary.
8 Refitting is a reversal of removal. Bleed the front brake hydraulic system and tighten all bolts to the specified torque.

## 9 Front suspension upper swivel balljoint – removal and refitting

1 The front suspension upper wishbone balljoint is a sealed unit and

if worn must be renewed as a unit.
2 To remove the balljoint, jack-up the car under the lower wishbone and remove the roadwheel.
3 Remove the bolts which secure the balljoint to the upper wishbone. Take great care to retain the packing pieces and shims and to record their locations precisely as they control the castor angle.
4 Remove the self-locking nut which secures the balljoint to the stub axle carrier. Use a suitable balljoint separator to disconnect the balljoint from the stub axle carrier.
5 During the foregoing operation, restrict the movement of the stub axle carrier by tying it with a piece of wire to prevent strain on the brake flexible hose.
6 Refitting is a reversal of removal, but make sure that the shims are returned to their original positions and that the balljoint securing bolts have their heads nearer the front of the car.

## 10 Front suspension lower swivel balljoint – overhaul and adjustment

1 Remove the stub axle carrier complete with balljoint as described in Section 8.
2 Remove the retaining ring and withdraw the flexible gaiter from the balljoint.
3 Extract the insert from around the taper pin.
4 Flatten the tab washers and remove the four setscrews which secure the ball pin cap to the stub axle carrier.
5 Remove the cap, shims, ball pin socket and the ball pin.
6 Renew any worn components and reassemble and re-shim in the following way.
7 The correct clearance of the ball pin in its socket is very important. Select shims which are available in two thicknesses until with the ball cap fully tightened, the ball pin can be moved stiffly by hand pressure.
8 Refit the stub axle carrier complete with the balljoint, as described in Section 8, and then grease the joint as described in Section 2.
9 Do not confuse this ball pin pre-load with removal of shims to try and compensate for wear. This must never be resorted to, always renew a worn ball pin or socket.

## 11 Front suspension lower wishbone – removal and refitting

1 Remove the front suspension unit as described in Section 14 or 15.
2 Using a suitable extractor, separate the tie-rod balljoint from the steering arm.
3 Unscrew the three bolts which hold the steering rack to the front crossmember.
4 Remove the roadspring as described in Section 6.
5 Unbolt the suspension upper balljoint from the wishbone levers, noting carefully which way the bolt heads are fitted (nearer rear of car) and the location of the castor control shims.
6 Unscrew the self-locking nut and using an extractor, separate the lower balljoint from the wishbone. Take off the anti-roll bar support bracket and the shock absorber lower mounting.
7 Extract the split pin from the wishbone pivot shaft nut and then drive the pivot shaft from the crossmember, recovering the plain washers.
8 Refitting is a reversal of removal. Do not fully tighten the pivot shaft nut until the weight of the car is on the roadwheels.
9 Check the front wheel alignment, castor and camber angles as described in Section 49.

## 12 Front suspension upper wishbone – removal, dismantling and refitting

1 Raise the car by placing a jack under the lower wishbone and remove the front roadwheel.
2 Remove the bolts from the upper wishbone arms and separate the balljoint. Note the castor control shims.
3 Tie the stub axle carrier to the suspension crossmember to prevent strain on the flexible brake hose.
4 Remove the two bolts which secure the upper wishbone pivot shaft to the crossmember. Take great care to retain and identify the locations of the shims as these control the camber angle and they

**Fig. 11.7 Front road spring (Sec 6)**

*1 Ride height control packing piece*
*2 Coil spring*
*3 Bump stop*
*4 Spacers (XJS only)*
*5 Spring pan*
*6 Pan securing bolts*

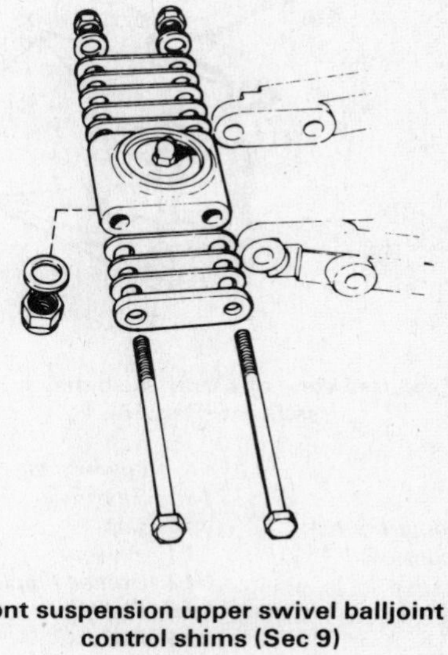

**Fig. 11.8 Front suspension upper swivel balljoint and castor control shims (Sec 9)**

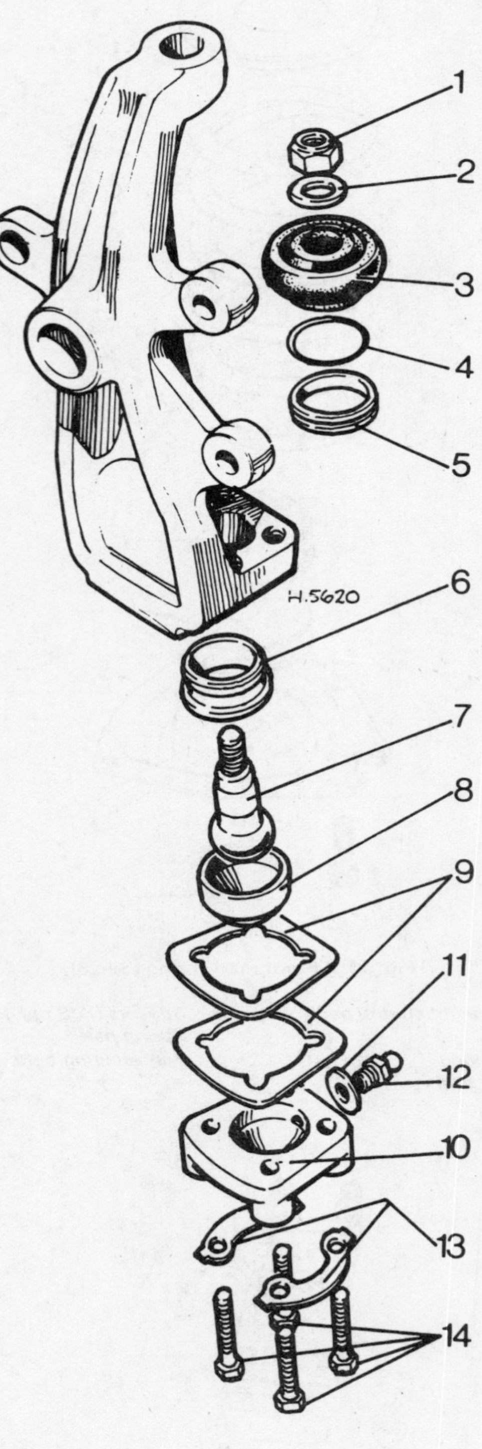


**Fig. 11.9 Exploded view of a front suspension lower swivel balljoint (Sec 10)**

*1 Nut*
*2 Washer*
*3 Dust-excluding boot*
*4 Boot-retaining clip*
*5 Insert*
*6 Upper seat*
*7 Ballpin*
*8 Lower seat*
*9 Shims*
*10 Cap*
*11 Washer*
*12 Grease nipple*
*13 Lockplate*
*14 Bolts*

must be returned to their original positions.
5 Withdraw the upper wishbone assembly so that the outboard ends pass either side of the shock absorber.
6 Remove the self-lockin nuts and their plain washers and withdraw the wishbone arms from the pivot shaft.
7 Release the locknuts and unscrew the rebound buffers from the wishbone.
8 The flexible bushes can be renewed after pressing them from the wishbone eyes. Use soapy water or a smear of hydraulic brake fluid to facilitate pressing in the new ones.
9 Reassembly and refitting are reversal of removal and dismantling. Make sure that the bolts which secure the balljoint to the wishbone arms have their heads towards the rear of the car.
10 Tighten all bolts to the specified torque, but do not tighten the castellated nuts which hold the wishbone arms to the pivot shaft until the weight of the car has once again been lowered onto the roadwheels.
11 Check the front steering angles on completion (see Section 49).

## 13 Front suspension bump and rebound stops – removal and refitting

### *Bump stop*

1 Jack up the front of the car and remove the roadwheel.
2 Unscrew and remove the nuts from the bump stop. Withdraw the stop through the spring coils, which may require prising slightly apart.
3 On XJS models, two spacers are located under the bump stop.

### *Rebound stop*

4 Only renew rebound stops in pairs.
5 Raise the front of the car and support the spring pan with a stand or second jack.
6 Remove the roadwheel.
7 Unscrew and remove the rebound stops from the upper wishbone.
8 Refitting is a reversal of removal.

## 14 Front suspension assembly (XJ12 and Double Six) – removal and refitting

1 If major operations are to be carried out to the front suspension, it may be advantageous to remove the suspension assembly complete.
2 Disconnect the battery.
3 Remove the air cleaners.
4 Working within the engine compartment, disconnect the shock absorber upper mountings.
5 With a syringe, drain the fluid from the power steering pump. Unless the fluid is absolutely clean, discard it.
6 Disconnect the hoses from the power steering pump and plug or cap the openings to prevent the entry of dirt.
7 Unscrew and remove the nuts which hold the engine front mountings to their brackets.
8 Unscrew and remove the nuts which secure the crossmember rear mountings.
9 Disconnect the links from the ends of the anti-roll bar.
10 Turn the steering wheel until the column lower universal joint pinch-bolt is accessible, then remove the bolt.
11 Turn the steering wheel until the front roadwheels are in the straight-ahead position.
12 Disconnect the wiring harness from the horns including the earth strap.
13 Remove the self-locking nuts from the pivot bolts at the crossmember front mountings. Do not attempt to drive out the pivot bolts at this stage.
14 Working within the car in the driver's footwell, slacken both pinch-bolts on the column upper universal joint. Do not turn the steering wheel from this point on.
15 Slide the steering lower universal joint off the splines of the steering gear pinion shaft.
16 Slacken the nuts on the front roadwheels.
17 An adjustable engine support crossbeam will now be required as described in Chapter 1, Section 3. Adjust the hooks until the weight of the engine is just taken.

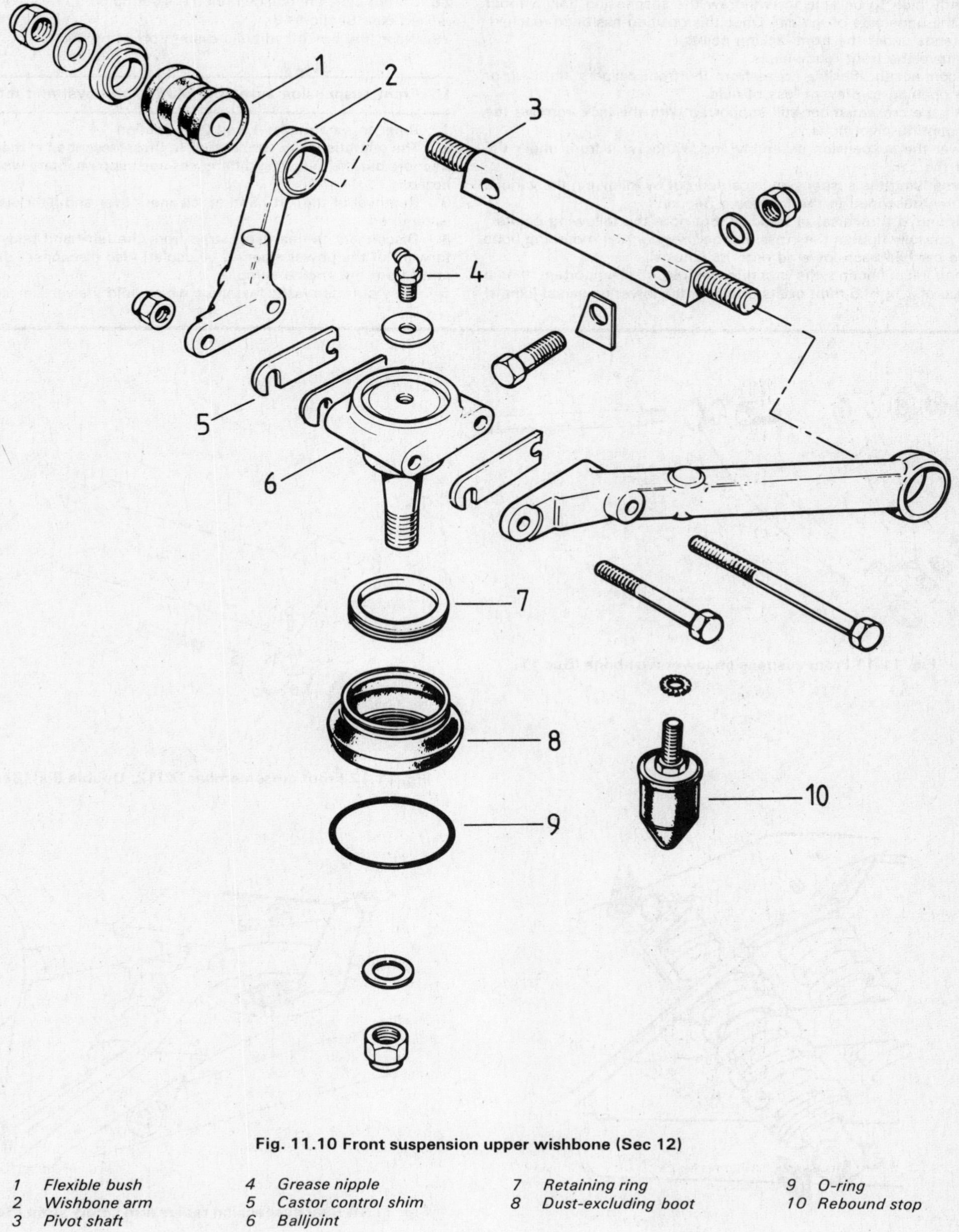


**Fig. 11.10 Front suspension upper wishbone (Sec 12)**

1 *Flexible bush*
2 *Wishbone arm*
3 *Pivot shaft*
4 *Grease nipple*
5 *Castor control shim*
6 *Balljoint*
7 *Retaining ring*
8 *Dust-excluding boot*
9 *O-ring*
10 *Rebound stop*

18 Set the speed selector lever to 'P' and apply the handbrake fully.
19 Place a trolley jack under the front crossmember and raise the car sufficiently high to be able to withdraw the suspension unit without fouling the underside of the car. Once this position has been reached, place stands under the front jacking points.
20 Remove the front roadwheels.
21 Disconnect the flexible hoses from the front calipers and plug or cap the opening to prevent loss of fluid.
22 With the crossmember still supported with the jack, remove the front mounting pivot bolts.
23 Lower the suspension assembly and withdraw it from under the front of the car.
24 Dismantling the suspension is carried out by following the various procedures described in the foregoing Sections.
25 Refitting is a reversal of removal, but note the following points.
26 Do not fully tighten the crossmember front or rear mounting bolts until the car has been lowered onto its wheels.
27 When reconnecting the steering column, it is important that a clearance of $\frac{3}{8}$ in (9.5 mm) exists axially in the lower universal joint. If not, move the upper joint further along the lower column to adjust the clearance.
28 Do not start the engine until the steering pump reservoir has been refilled (see Section 48).
29 Bleed the brake hydraulic system on completion.

## 15 Front suspension assembly (XJS) – removal and refitting

1 Refer to paragraphs 1 and 2 of Section 14.
2 The operations are very similar to those described in the preceding Section, but the following differences and suppementary work must be noted.
3 Removal of the left-hand air cleaner cover and filter element only is required.
4 Disconnect the earthing strap from the left-hand bodyframe just forward of the power steering oil cooler. Also disconnect the earthing strap from the engine sump.
5 Prise out the plastic fasteners which hold the vertical stoneguards

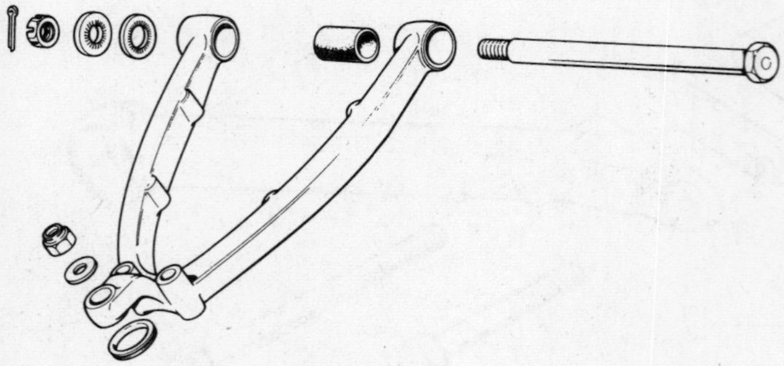

Fig. 11.11 Front suspension lower wishbone (Sec 11)

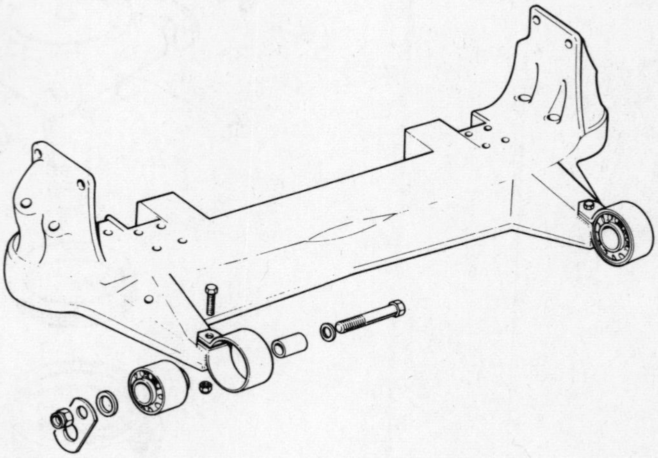

Fig. 11.12 Front crossmember (XJ12, Double Six) (Sec 14)

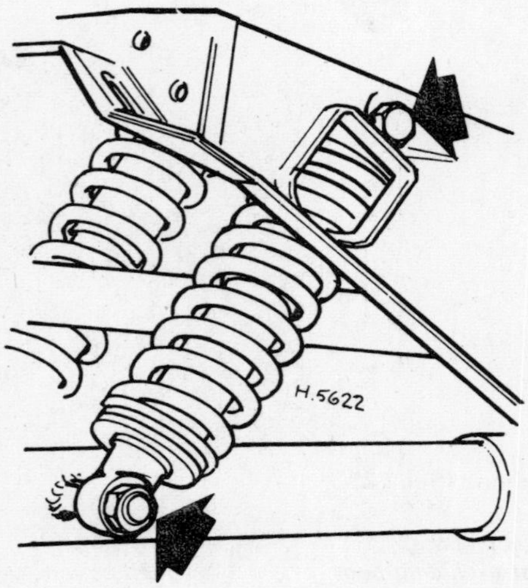


Fig. 11.13 Rear spring/shock absorber mountings (arrowed) (Sec 16)

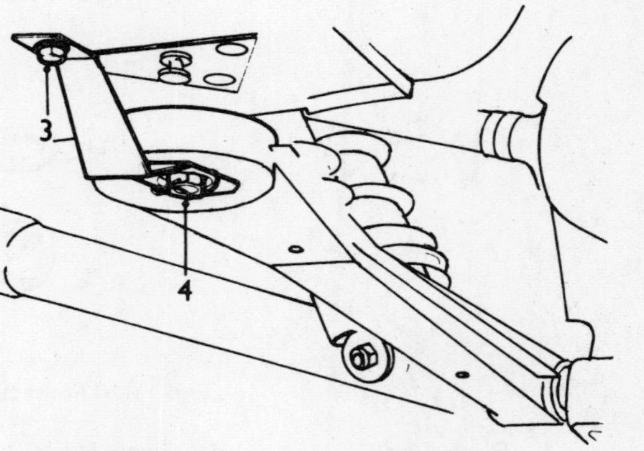


Fig. 11.14 Rear suspension radius arm safety strap (Sec 18)

*3 Bolt to body floor*
*4 Safety strap attachment to radius arm*

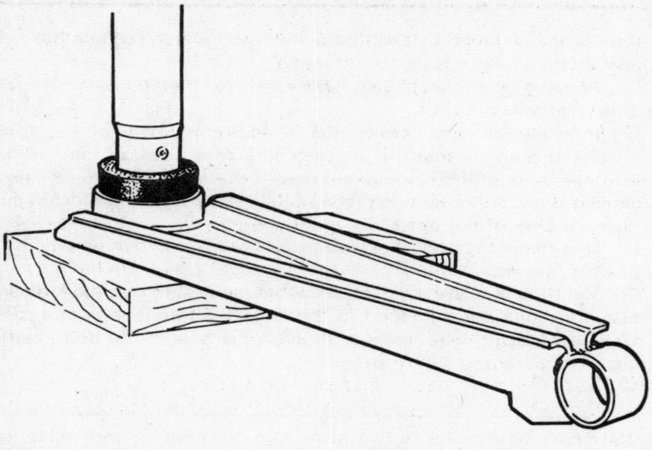

Fig. 11.15 Removing a rear suspension radius arm bush (Sec 18)

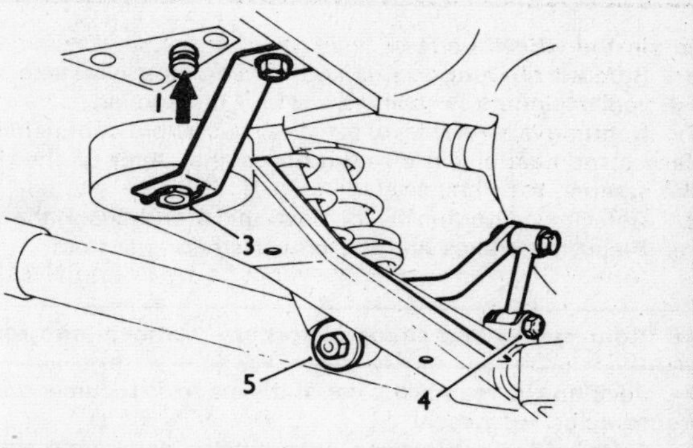


**Fig. 11.16 Rear suspension radius arm showing anti-roll bar attachment on XJS models only (Sec 19)**

*1 Radius arm anchor point*
*3 Radius arm to body bolt*
*4 Anti-roll bar attachment*
*5 Spring/shock absorber lower mounting*

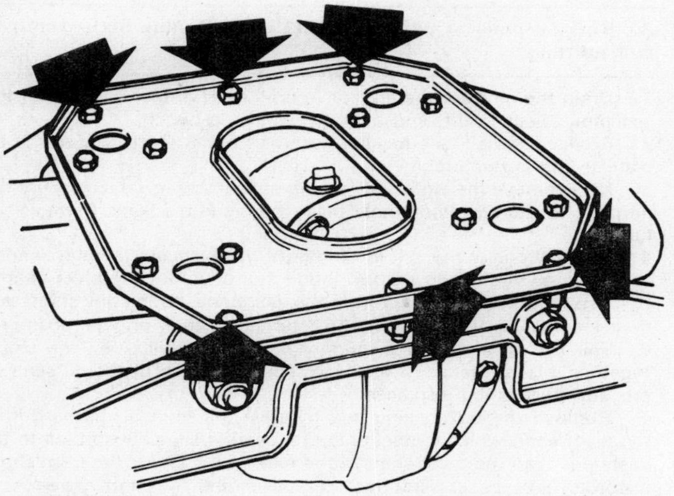

**Fig. 11.17 Tie plate to crossmember securing bolts (arrowed) (Sec 20)**

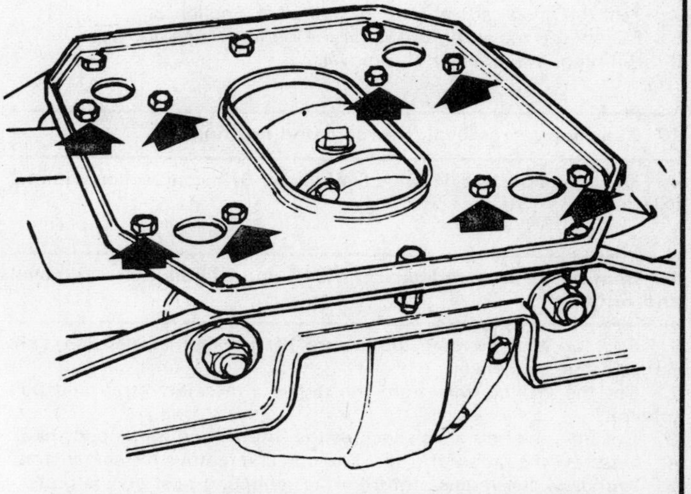

**Fig. 11.18 Tie plate to inner pivot mounting bracket bolts (arrowed) (Sec 20)**

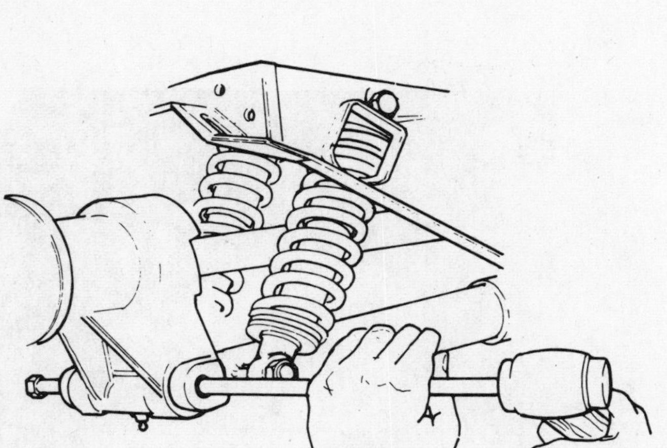

**Fig. 11.19 Driving out a rear suspension wishbone outer pivot shaft (Sec 20)**

**Fig. 11.20 Installing rear suspension wishbone inner pivot shaft (propeller shaft removed for clarity) (Sec 20)**

within the wheel arches.
6 Remove the two screws and thirteen plastic fasteners which hold the spoiler undertray to the body and the spoiler.
7 Refitting is a reversal of removal, but before commencing the work detach the heat shield which protects the gaiter on the pinion end of the steering rack housing.
8 Refer to paragraph 27 of Section 14 and check the clearance.
9 Bleed the brakes and the power steering system.

## 16 Rear spring and shock absorber – removal and refitting

1 Jack up the rear of the car and support it securely on axle stands. Remove the roadwheel.
2 Remove the self-locking nut from the end of the shock absorber lower mounting pivot pin (photo).
3 Support the suspension wishbone with a jack and drive out the pivot pin.
4 Remove the spacer from the front shock absorber.
5 Disconnect the shock absorber upper mounting from the rear crossmember and withdraw the shock absorber/coil spring.
6 The coil spring must now be compressed so that the lower split type retainer can be removed and the spring removed in a downward direction.
7 Test the shock absorber as described in Section 3.
8 Renew the mounting bushes if the original ones are worn.
9 Refitting is a reversal of removal.

## 17 Rear hubs – removal, overhaul and refitting

1 The operations are described in Chapter 8, in conjunction with the axleshafts.

## 18 Rear suspension radius arm (XJ12 and Double Six) – removal and refitting

1 Jack up and support the centre of the rear suspension unit. Remove the roadwheel.
2 Cut the locking wire from the radius arm safety strap and bolt (photo).
3 Unscrew the bolt which secures the safety strap to the body floor.
4 Unscrew the radius arm securing bolt and remove the safety strap.
5 Withdraw the radius arm from the mounting post on the body.
6 Unscrew the self-locking nut which is nearest the front of the shock absorber lower pivot pin. Drive the pin far enough to clear the forward shock absorber and spacer. Extract the spacer, bend back the tabs of the lockwasher and remove the bolt which secures the radius arm to the lower wishbone mounting.
7 Remove the radius arm and examine the flexible bushes for deterioration.
8 If inspection has proved the need for renewal of the flexible bushes, make sure that the larger bush is fitted so that the two holes in it are in longtitudinal alignment with the arm. When installing the smaller bush, make sure that the metal centre sleeve projects equally on each side of the bush.
9 It is recommended that a press is used to remove and install the flexible bushes.
10 Refitting is a reversal of removal but make sure that the radius arm securing bolts are tightened to the specified torque wrench settings. Use new locking wire inserted through the hole in the bolt head and secured round the safety strap.

## 19 Rear suspension radius arm (XJS) – removal and refitting

1 The operations are similar to those described in the preceding Section, but the anti-roll bar link must also be disconnected from the radius arm.

## 20 Rear suspension wishbone (XJ12 and Double Six) – removal and refitting

1 Drain the oil from the final drive unit, remove the rear suspension assembly (Section 27) and then invert it on a bench.
2 Remove the six self-locking nuts and bolts which secure the tie plate to the crossmember.
3 Now remove the eight self-locking nuts and bolts which secure the tie plate to the wishbone inner pivot mounting brackets. Remove the tie plate.
4 Remove one of the self-locking nuts which secure the hub bearing assembly pivot shaft to the wishbone and drive out the pivot shaft.
5 Separate the hub carrier from the wishbone, noting any shims and their location so that they will be returned to their original positions.
6 The use of a rod as a dummy pivot shaft will keep the shims together. Place a piece of masking tape over each of the oil seals to prevent them being displaced.
7 Remove the self-locking nut, (nearest the front of the car), from the pivot shaft which connects the roadspring/shock absorbers to the wishbone. Tap the pivot shaft to the rear until it clears the front shock absorber and spacer. Retrieve the spacer and then move the shock absorber towards the centre of the suspension assembly.
8 Turn down the locking tab and remove the special bolt which holds the radius arm to the wishbone. Remove the radius arm.

16.2 Rear spring/shock absorber lower mounting

18.2 Radius arm safety strap

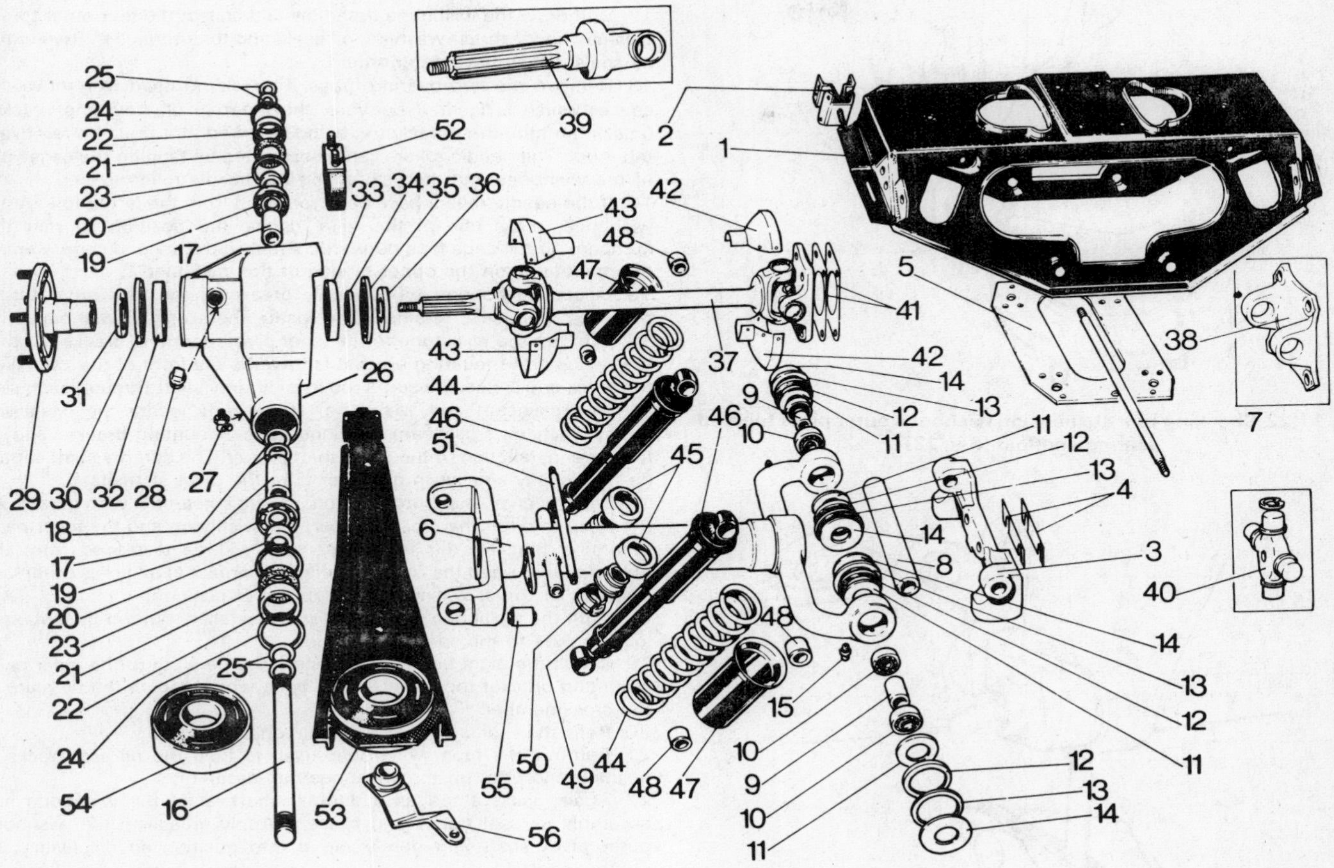

**Fig. 11.21 Exploded view of the rear suspension (Sec 20)**

1 Crossmember
2 Flexible mounting
3 Inner pivot mounting
4 Shims
5 Bracing plate
6 Wishbone
7 Inner pivot shaft
8 Spacer tube
9 Spacer tube
10 Needle bearing
11 Thrust washer
12 Seal
13 Retainer
14 Thrust washer
15 Grease nipple
16 Outer pivot shaft
17 Sleeve
18 Shim
19 Bearing
20 Ring
21 Oil seal
22 Oil seal retainer
23 Spacer
24 Washer
25 Shim
26 Hub carrier
27 Grease nipple
28 Grease retaining cap
29 Hub
30 Outer oil seal
31 Ring
32 Outer bearing
33 Inner bearing
34 Spacer
35 Oil seal
36 Ring
37 Driveshaft
38 Driveshaft flange
39 Splined yoke
40 Universal joint
41 Shim (camber control)
42 Joint cover (inner)
43 Joint cover (outer)
44 Coil spring
45 Packing ring
46 Shock absorber
47 Dust shield
48 Flexible bush
49 Seat
50 Retainer
51 Shock absorber lower mounting shaft
52 Bump stop
53 Radius arm
54 Flexible bush
55 Flexible bush
56 Safety strap

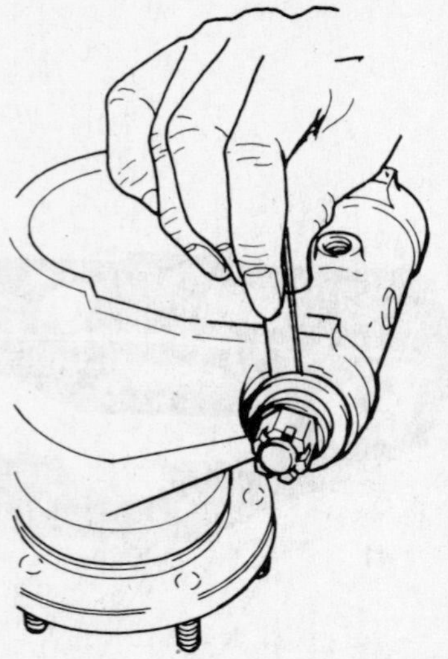

Fig. 11.22 Checking rear suspension wishbone outer pivot tapered bearing endfloat (Sec 22)

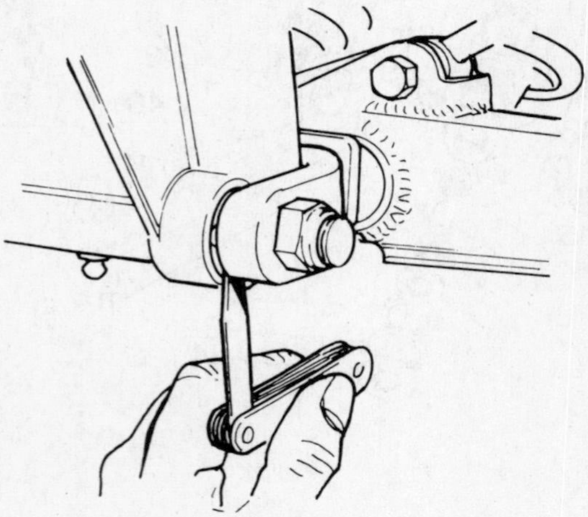

Fig. 11.23 Checking clearance between hub carrier oil seal retainer and wishbone of rear suspension (Sec 22)

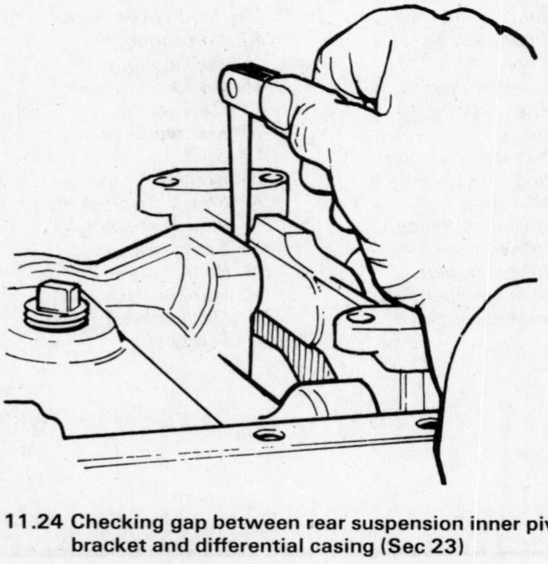

Fig. 11.24 Checking gap between rear suspension inner pivot bracket and differential casing (Sec 23)

9 Remove the pivot shaft which secures the lower ends of the roadspring/shock absorbers.

10 Remove the self-locking nut which secures the wishbone pivot shaft to the crossmember.

11 Drive the inner pivot shaft out of the wishbone and inner pivot mounting bracket.

12 Withdraw the wishbone assembly and collect the four outer thrust washers, inner thrust washers, oil seals and their retainers. Renew the oil seals if they have deteriorated.

13 Remove the two bearing tubes. There is no need to remove the spacer which is located between the inner pivot mounting bracket unless the mounting bracket is being renewed. If it must be removed, tap it out. The needle rollers can be extracted by tapping the cages out of the wishbone and then extracting the needle roller spacer.

14 If the needle rollers have been removed from the larger fork of the wishbone, press one of the roller cages into position so that the numbers on the cage face outwards. Press in the second cage. Repeat the operations on the opposite side of the wishbone.

15 Insert the bearing tubes, apply grease to the four outer thrust washers, oil seals, retainers and locate them on the wishbone.

16 Offer up the wishbone to the inner pivot mounting bracket so that the radius arm mounting bracket is towards the front of the car. Align the holes and spacers. Insert a rod as a dummy shaft through each side of the crossbeam and wishbone. These rods locate the wishbone thrust washers, crossbeam and inner pivot mounting bracket and so facilitate installation of the pivot shaft proper. The dummy shaft should be fractionally smaller in diameter than the pivot shaft itself.

17 Tap the pivot shaft into position, having smeared it with grease. As it passes through the crossmember, the wishbone and the inner pivot mounting bracket, the temporary rods will be displaced from the opposite end. Keep the rods and shaft in contact at all times otherwise a spacer or thrust washer may drop out of position.

18 With the wishbone inner pivot shaft installed, tighten the two self-locking nuts to the specified torque.

19 Install the eight bolts which secure the tie plate to the inner pivot mounting bracket then refit the six bolts which secure the tie plate to the crossmember.

20 Refit the radius arm to the wishbone.

21 Remove the tape which was used to hold the oil seal tracks in position and offer up the wishbone/hub assembly.

22 Again using a rod as a dummy shaft, align the wishbone hub assembly oil seal tracks and spacers. Apply grease to the wishbone outer pivot shaft and gently tap it into position so displacing the dummy shaft.

23 Slide the pivot shaft through the wishbone and hub carrier. Using feeler blades, check the clearance between the hub carrier and the wishbone. Where necessary, install shims between the hub carrier and the wishbone to centralise the hub carrier. Tighten the nuts on the pivot shaft to the specified torque.

24 Refit the rear suspension assembly.

25 The rear suspension camber angle should be checked after a major overhaul (see Section 49).

26 Refill the final drive unit with specified oil.

27 Lubricate the wishbone grease nipples.

## 21 Rear suspension wishbone (XJS) – removal and refitting

1 The operations are very similar to those described in the preceding Section, except that the anti-roll bar link must also be disconnected from the radius arm.

## 22 Rear suspension wishbone outer pivot – dismantling, re-assembly and bearing adjustment

1 Support the hub carrier and wishbone securely.

2 Remove one of the self-locking nuts which secure the outer pivot shaft.

3 Drive out the pivot shaft and retain any shims which may be located between the hub carrier and the wishbone.

4 Separate the hub carrier and the wishbone.

5 Remove the oil seal retainer and prise out the oil seals.

6 Remove the inner races of the tapered roller bearings by tapping them out with a drift.

7 Remove the spacers and shims.

8 If new tapered roller bearings have been fitted, it will be necessary

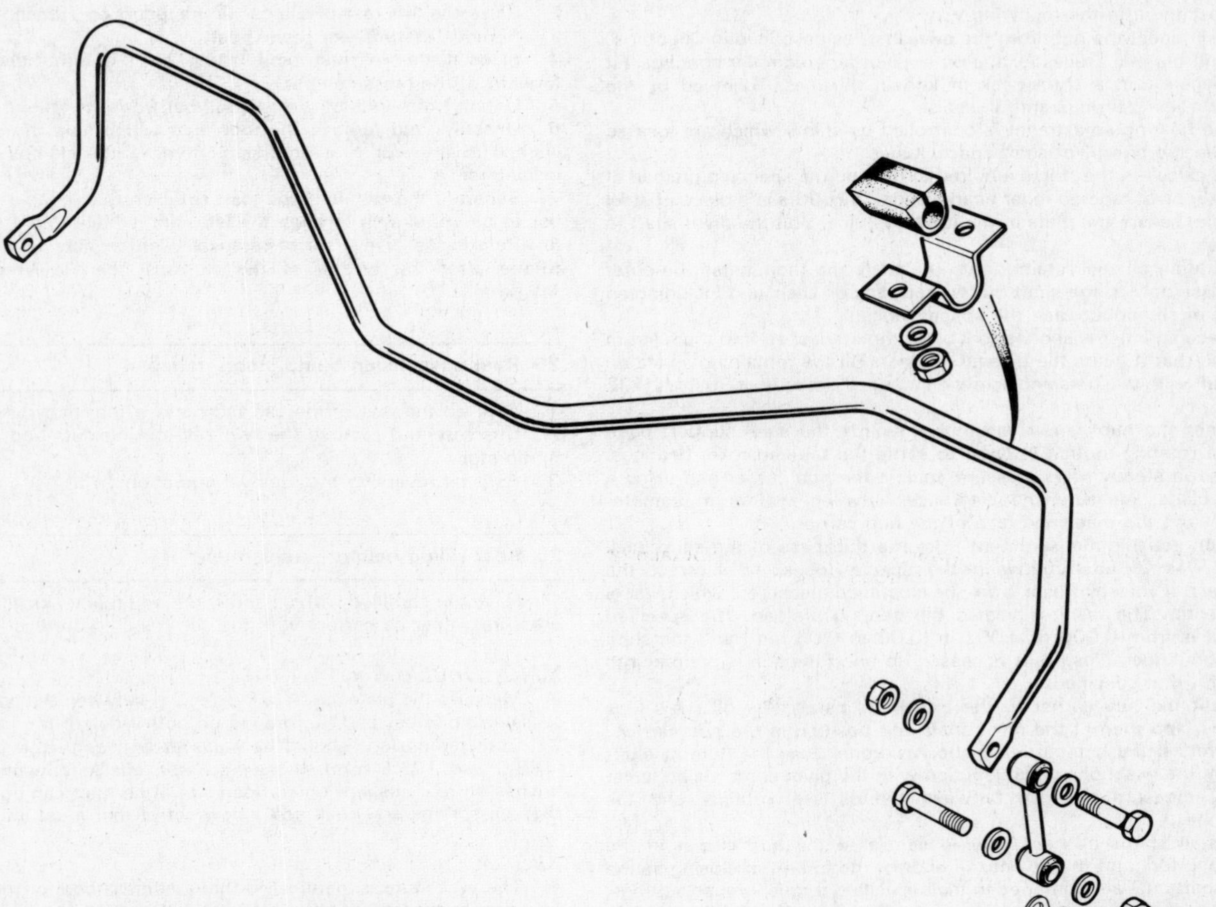

Fig. 11.25 Rear anti-roll bar (XJS) (Sec 24)

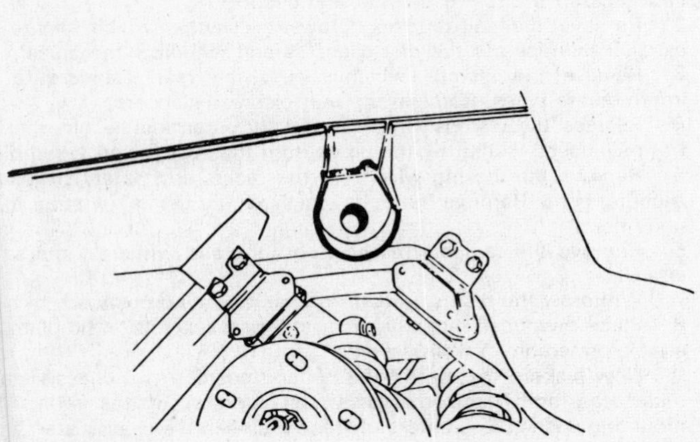

Fig. 11.26 Rear suspension bump stop (Sec 25)

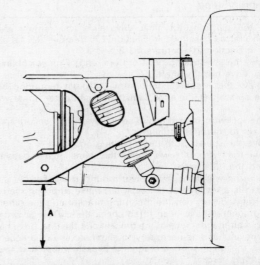

Fig. 11.27 Rear riding height adjustment diagrams (Sec 26)

*A See text*

to adjust them in the following way.
9 Disconnect the hub from the driveshaft as described in Chapter 8.
10 Refit the inner races for the outer pivot tapered roller bearings. Fit the spacers and a shim pack of known thickness followed by the tapered roller bearings and oil seals.
11 The bearing adjustment is controlled by shims which are located between the two pivot shaft spacer tubes.
12 To calculate the shims required to provide the specified preload of the outer pivot tapered roller bearings, drill a ho00le in a piece of steel plate and secure the plate in the jaws of a vice. Bolt the pivot shaft to the plate.
13 Slide an oil seal retainer onto the shaft and then install the outer pivot assembly to the shaft but without any oil seals and including an excess of shims between the spacer tubes.
14 Place an inner wishbone fork outer thrust washer onto the fulcrum shaft so that it abuts the oil seal retainer. Fill the remaining space on the shaft with washers and screw on a nut to a torque of 95 lbf ft (132 Nm).
15 Press the hub carrier assembly towards the steel support plate using a rotating motion in order to settle the tapered roller bearings. Maintain a steady hand pressure against the hub carrier and using a feeler blade, measure the clearance between the large diameter washer and the machined face of the hub carrier.
16 Subtract this measurement from the thickness of the shim pack which was included between the spacer tubes, or subtract the thickness of the shim pack from the clearance measured, whichever is the greater. The result indicates the bearing preload. The specified preload is from 0.000 to 0.002 in (0.00 to 0.05 mm) and the shim pack should be adjusted as necessary to bring the actual preload into line with that specified.
17 Refit the hub carrier to the axleshaft, install new oil seals (lips inwards) and then fit the pivot shaft into position in the hub carrier.
18 Offer up the hub carrier to the wishbone. Ease the dummy shaft through the wishbone in conjunction with the pivot shaft. Using feeler blades, measure the gap between the oil seal retainer and the wishbone.
19 Install shims as necessary to centralise the hub carrier in the wishbone fork and to prevent the ends of the fork from closing as the pivot shaft nuts are tightened to their specified torque wrench settings.
20 It will be found easier to install the wishbone if a dummy shaft is passed through the hub carrier before offering the wishbone to the carrier.
21 Refitting is otherwise a reversal of removal. Apply grease to the lubrication nipples on completion.

### 23 Rear suspension wishbone inner pivot mounting bracket – removal and refitting

1 Drain the oil from the final drive unit and remove the rear suspension unit as described in Section 27. Remove the tie plate as described in Section 20, paragraphs 2 and 3.
2 Remove the self-locking nut from one end of the wishbone inner pivot shaft, drive out the shaft.
3 Withdraw the wishbone fork from the pivot mounting bracket. Collect the oil seal retainers, oil seals, inner and outer thrust washers and tubes.
4 Cut the lockwire from the two setscrews which secure the inner pivot bracket to the differential unit.
5 Remove the spacer from the mounting bracket.
6 Remove the two setscrews, noting the shims located between the bracket and the differential unit.
7 Remove the wishbone inner pivot mounting bracket.
8 Refitting is a reversal of removal, but make sure that the original shims are refitted between the mounting bracket and the differential. If new components have been fitted check the clearance with feeler blades between the rear face of the bracket and the final drive housing. Add or remove shims as necessary to eliminate any clearance at this point. Pass the pivot shaft through the crossmember and the inner pivot mounting bracket.
9 Tighten the pivot bolt nut to the specified torque.
10 Refill the final drive unit.

### 24 Rear anti-roll bar (XJS) – removal and refitting

1 Position the car on ramps or over an inspection pit.
2 Raise the left rear of the car and support on stands.
3 Remove the left rear roadwheel.
4 Slacken the exhaust pipe clamp on the right-hand pipe just forward of the crossmember.
5 Unbolt both ends of the anti-roll bar from the links.
6 Unscrew and remove the four nuts which hold the anti-roll bar clamps to the rear seat underpan. Remove the clamps and rubber insulators.
7 Separate the exhaust pipe joint sufficiently to enable the anti-roll bar to be withdrawn through the left-hand wheel arch.
8 Refitting is a reversal of removal. Tighten nuts to the specified torque after the weight of the car has been lowered onto the roadwheels.

### 25 Rear suspension bump stop – renewal

1 Jack up the rear of the car and remove the roadwheel.
2 Unscrew and remove the two self-locking nuts and remove the bump stop.
3 Refit by reversing the removal operations.

### 26 Rear riding height – adjustment

1 Have the car filled with oil and water and fuel tanks filled. The tyre pressures must be correct with the car standing on level ground.

*XJ12, Double Six*

2 Measure the distance (A in Fig. 11.27) between the bottom of the rear crossmember and the ground on both sides of the car.
3 Both dimensions should be equal at between 7.20 and 7.70 in (183.0 and 195.5 mm). If they are not, check for worn mounting bushes on rear suspension components. If no fault can be found then the coil springs are weak and a new set of four must be fitted.

*XJS*

4 The procedure is identical to that just described for the XJ12 and Double Six models, but the measured clearance should be between 7.30 and 7.80 in (185.4 and 198.1 mm).

### 27 Rear suspension assembly (XJ12 and Double Six) – removal and refitting

1 If major operations are to be carried out to the rear suspension, it may be advantageous to remove the suspension assembly complete. First jack up the rear of the car and support it.
2 Remove the self-tapping screws or clamps which secure the exhaust tail pipes to the rear silencers and withdraw the pipes.
3 Release the clamps which secure the rear silencers to the intermediate pipes. Remove the rear exhaust silencers.
4 Release the clamps which secure the intermediate pipes to the front silencers. Withdraw the pipes from the suspension assembly.
5 Remove the locking wire from the radius arm safety straps and securing bolts. Remove the bolts which secure the safety strap to the body floor.
6 Remove the radius arm securing bolts and withdraw the safety straps.
7 Withdraw the radius arms from their mounting posts on the body.
8 Place a wooden block between the rear suspension tie plate and a jack, preferably of trolley type.
9 Now jack-up the rear of the car and position two chassis stands under the bodyframe members just forward of the radius arm mounting posts. Place blocks of wood between the chassis stands and the bodyframe to avoid damage.
10 Remove the rear roadwheels.
11 Disconnect the flexible brake pipe at the support bracket on the body.
12 Disconnect the handbrake cable from the caliper actuating lever which is mounted on the suspension crossbeam. Withdraw the outer cable from the trunnion on the opposite lever.
13 Remove the four bolts which secure the mounting rubbers at the front of the crossmember to the bodyframe.
14 Remove the nuts and bolts which secure the rear mounting

rubbers to the crossmember.
15 Disconnect the propeller shaft from the differential pinion flange.
16 Lower the rear suspension assembly on the jack and withdraw it from under the car.
17 Refitting is a reversal of removal, but note the following points:

*(a) Renew any mounting rubbers which have deteriorated*
*(b) Tighten the radius arm to wishbone bolts after the weight of the car has been lowered onto the roadwheels*
*(c) Bleed the brake hydraulic circuit*
*(d) Adjust the handbrake*

## 28 Rear suspension assembly (XJS) – removal and refitting

1 The operations are similar to those described in the preceding Section for XJ12 and Double Six models except that an additional operation must be carried out, to unbolt the anti-roll bar links from the radius arms.

## 29 Tie-rod outer balljoints – renewal

1 If wear is found in the tie-rod end balljoints then they must be renewed as sealed assemblies.
2 Unscrew and remove the ball pin nut and separate the balljoint from the steering arm using a suitable extractor or forked wedges.
3 Hold the tie-rod end quite still with an open-ended spanner applied to its flats and unscrew the locknut one quarter of a turn. Hold the tie-rod quite still and unscrew the tie-rod end from it. If the bellows are perforated, release their clips and withdraw them.
4 Screw on the new tie-rod end until it almost touches the locknut and then tighten the locknut, making sure that the tie-rod end is again supported in an open-ended spanner.
5 Reconnect the tie-rod end to the steering arm.
6 The front wheel alignment must be checked and adjusted, as described in Section 49.
7 It is important that the lengths of the tie-rods are equal. If for any reason thay have become unequal, set the tie-rod ends on the rods so that the distance between the centre of the tie-rod end balljoint and the face of the inner balljoint is equal to the corresponding dimension on the opposite tie-rod. Release the inner clips on the flexible bellows to measure.
8 When measuring, the front roadwheels and the steering wheel must be in the straight-ahead attitude. If there is any doubt about the steering wheel position, centre the steering rack and check the position of the steering wheel spokes.
9 To centre the steering rack, remove the grease nipple on the steering rack housing and insert a thin rod. Maintain pressure on the rod while slowly turning the steering wheel until the rod is felt to drop into an indentation on the rack. The rack is now centred. Remove the rod and screw the grease nipple back into place. If the steering wheel is not in the straight-ahead attitude, it will have to be removed and re-positioned as described in Section 32 or 33.
10 Ball pin knock which may be heard when turning right or left may be due to wear in the tie-rod inner balljoints. No adjustment can be carried out and new tie-rod/ball pin assemblies must be fitted. This work can be carried out without removing the rack from the car as described in the next Section.

## 30 Tie-rod inner balljoints – renewal

1 Disconnect the tie-rod outer balljoint from the steering arm.
2 Remove the bellows retaining clip from the rack housing.
3 Peel the bellows back until the inner balljoint is exposed and then flatten the tabs of the lockwasher which secures the balljoint assembly to the rack.
4 Remove the inner balljoint and tie-rod and extract the spring and spacer.
5 Remove the outer tie-rod end and then discard the worn inner balljoint/tie-rod assembly.
6 Fit the tie-rod end to the new rod/inner balljoint assembly, setting the components as described in the preceding Section.
7 Refit the inner balljoint to the rack, using a new lockwasher, and smear the joint with 2 oz (57 g) of grease.

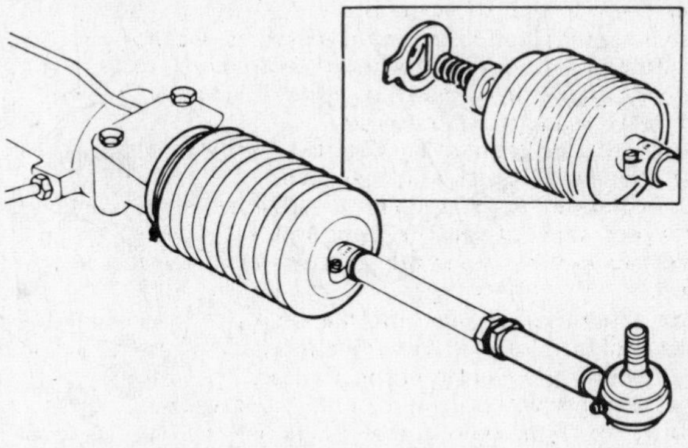

**Fig. 11.28 Steering tie-rod and outer balljoint. Inset shows fixing details of inner balljoint (Sec 29)**

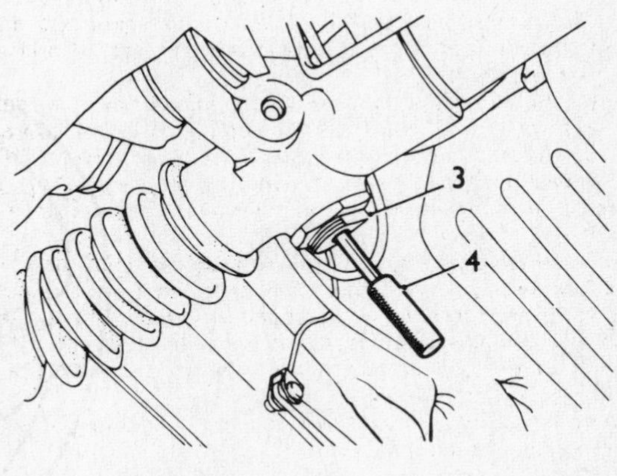


**Fig. 11.29 Centering the steering rack (Sec 29)**

*3 Damper adjusting plug*
*4 Rod*

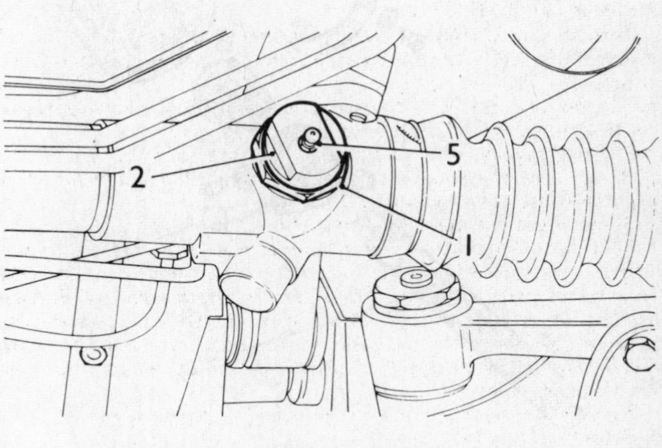


**Fig. 11.30 Rack damper on steering housing (Sec 31)**

*1 Locknut*
*2 Adjuster plug*
*5 Grease nipple*

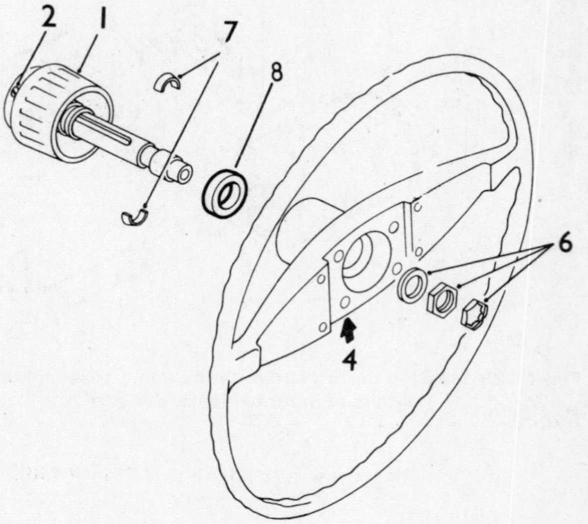


**Fig. 11.31 Steering wheel details (Series 1) (Sec 32)**

1 *Height adjuster*
2 *Safety screw*
4 *Steering wheel*
6 *Nut, locknut and washer*
7 *Cone halves*
8 *Impact rubber*

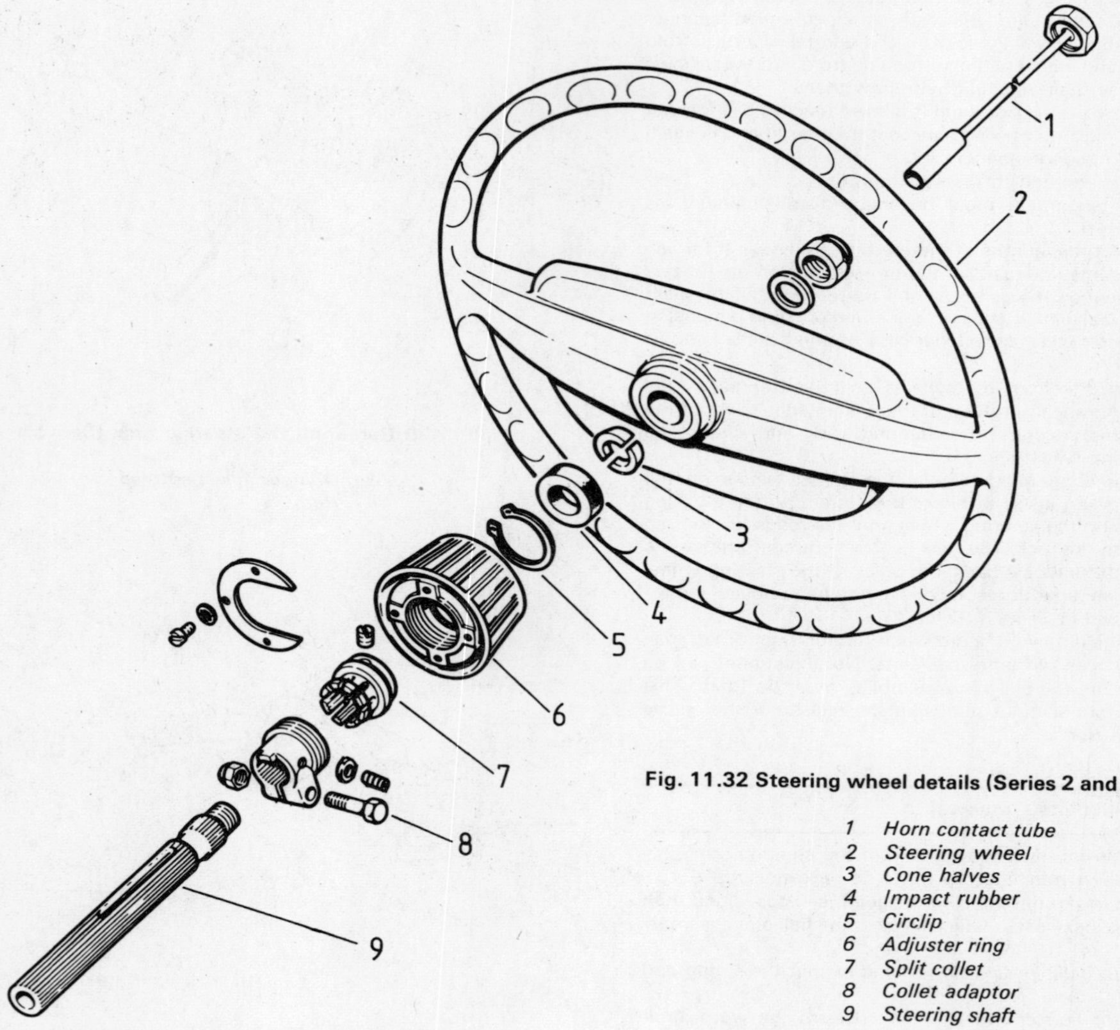


**Fig. 11.32 Steering wheel details (Series 2 and XJS) (Sec 33)**

1 *Horn contact tube*
2 *Steering wheel*
3 *Cone halves*
4 *Impact rubber*
5 *Circlip*
6 *Adjuster ring*
7 *Split collet*
8 *Collet adaptor*
9 *Steering shaft*

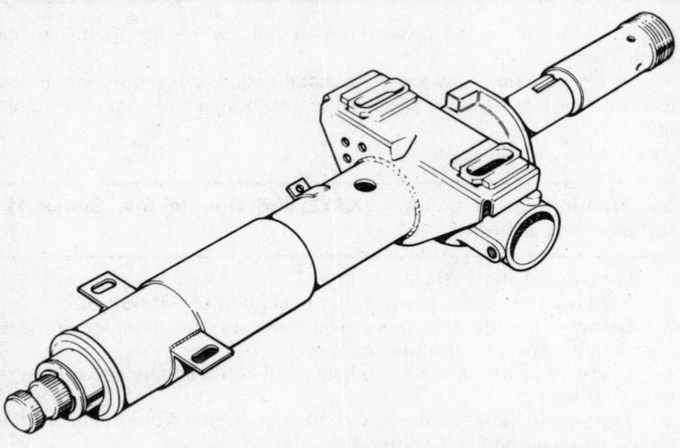

Fig. 11.33 Steering upper column (XJ12 and Double Six, Series 2 onwards) (Sec 35)

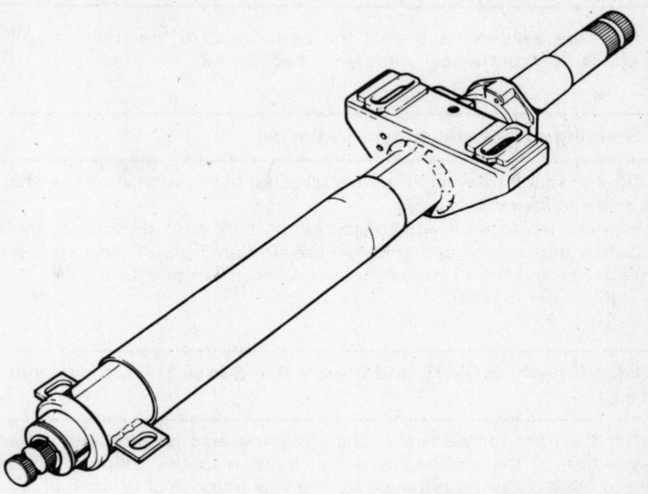

Fig. 11.34 Steering upper column (XJS) (Sec 36)

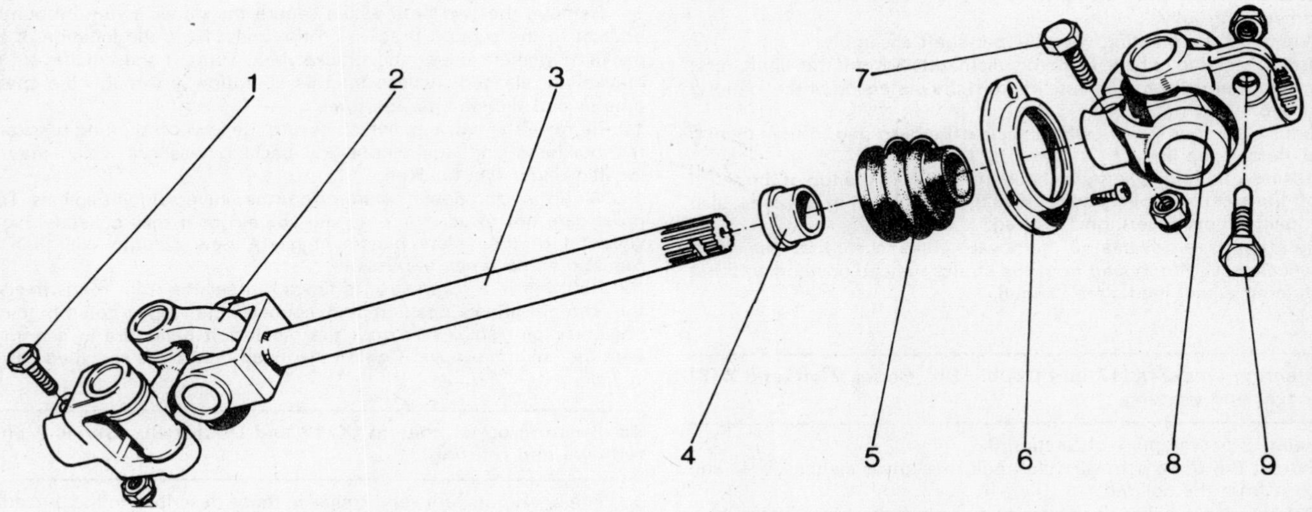


Fig. 11.35 Steering lower column (XJ12, Double Six) (Sec 37)

*1 Pinch-bolt*
*2 Bottom universal joint*
*3 Lower column*
*4 Bush*
*5 Gaiter*
*6 Retaining plate*
*7 Pinch-bolt*
*8 Top universal joint*
*9 Pinch-bolt*

Fig. 11.36 Steering lower column (XJS) (Sec 38)

8 Refit the bellows, reconnect the tie-rod end to the steering arm and check the front wheel alignment (Section 49).

## 31 Steering rack – adjustment in the car

1 Should rack rattle occur when travelling over rough surfaces, the rack pad requires adjustment.
2 Release the locknut which secures the rack pad adjusting screw.
3 Screw the rack adjusting screw inwards until a stiff resistance is encountered and then release the screw one sixth of a turn.
4 Tighten the locknut.

## 32 Steering wheel (XJ12 and Double Six, Series 1) – removal and refitting

1 Set the front roadwheels in the straight-ahead position and mark the position of the steering wheel in relation to the column. If the steering wheel is being removed for the sole purpose of re-positioning it, then the steering rack and front roadwheels should be centred as described in Section 29. Disconnect the battery.
2 Unscrew the knurled height adjustment ring until the safety screw is exposed. Slacken the screw two turns and then unscrew the knurled adjustment ring fully.
3 Withdraw the steering wheel/upper shaft assembly.
4 If the steering wheel is to be dismantled from the shaft, first extract the four self-tapping screws from the underside of the steering wheel hub.
5 Extract the four screws which secure the horn ring to the steering wheel, detach the ring.
6 Unscrew and remove the locknut and nut from the top of the shaft. Pull off the steering wheel and retrieve the two halves of the cone, also the impact rubber where one is fitted.
7 Refitting is a reversal of removal. Make sure that the front roadwheels have not moved from the straight-ahead position and that the steering wheel marks are aligned.

## 33 Steering wheel (XJ12 and Double Six, Series 2 on, and XJS) – removal and refitting

1 Refer to paragraph 1 of Section 32.
2 Extract the three screws which hold the lower switch cover and detach it from the column.
3 Working from below, unscrew and remove the pinch-bolt which holds the collet adaptor to the steering column (photo).
4 Slacken the locknut of the grub screw in the collet adaptor and unscrew the grub screw two turns. On later models, a second pinch-bolt is fitted instead of the grub screw.
5 Withdraw the steering wheel complete with knurled height adjusting ring, impact rubber, collet adaptor and upper shaft (photo).
6 To remove the steering wheel from the shaft, extract the two screws from the rear face of the steering wheel boss and lift off the padded horn contact (photo).
7 Unscrew and remove the nylon nut from the top of the shaft, withdrawing the horn contact tube with it.
8 Unscrew and remove the nut which holds the steering wheel to the shaft, withdraw the wheel and retrieve the two halves of the cone.
9 Refitting is a reversal of removal, but smear all the internal friction surfaces with engine oil.
10 An alternative method of removing the steering wheel/upper shaft assembly can be carried out as follows.
11 Release the knurled steering wheel adjuster ring and pull the wheel up to its fullest extent.
12 Working from below the steering wheel, extract the three screws which hold the horseshoe-shaped retaining plate to the underside of the adjuster ring (photo).
13 Remove the plate and pull off the steering wheel with upper splined shaft.
14 The collet adaptor (some later versions incorporate two pinch-bolts) can then be removed, followed by the steering column switches and the upper cowl (photos).
15 Refitting is a reversal of removal. If the method described in paragraphs 10 to 14 was employed, make sure that the horn contact probe is central in the lower column hole when fitting the splined upper shaft.
16 Fit the column switches in conjunction with the upper cowl followed by the adaptor, pinch-bolts and horseshoe-shaped retaining plate.

## 34 Steering upper column (XJ12 and Double Six, Series 1) – removal and refitting

1 Disconnect the battery.
2 Remove the steering wheel, as described in Section 32.
3 Remove the three screws which secure the direction indicator switch and cowl to the outer column.
4 Disconnect the direction indicator switch leads by separating the plug and socket.
5 Remove the speedometer and the tachometer from the instrument panel, as described in Chapter 10.
6 Disconnect the horn switch lead from the contact on the steering column.
7 Disconnect the ignition switch leads at the plug and socket connector.
8 Remove the pinch-bolt which secures the upper universal joint to the steering column.
9 Remove the two nuts which secure the upper column mounting bracket to the support bracket on the body. Note the location of any packing washers under the bracket, and support the column as the bracket is released. Access for this operation is through the speedometer and tachometer apertures.
10 Remove the two nuts which secure the lower mounting bracket to the bulkhead and again note any packing washers which may be located under this bracket.
11 Withdraw the upper column from the universal joint splines. Take great care not to use force on the column or it may collapse due to shearing of the safety plastic plugs. A new column will then be required as no repair is possible.
12 Refitting is a reversal of removal but set the front roadwheels in the straight-ahead position and connect the upper column to the universal joint splines so that the pinch-bolt holes are in alignment with the column groove. Tighten the pinch-bolt to the specified torque.

## 35 Steering upper column (XJ12 and Double Six, Series 2 on) – removal and refitting

1 The operations are very similar to those described in the preceding Section, but additionally the under scuttle casing must be removed (see Chapter 12).
2 The electrical harness to the steering column switches is disconnected by uncoupling the three multi-pin plugs.
3 When refitting, make sure that a $\frac{3}{8}$ in (9.5 mm) clearance exists axially in the lower universal joint. If less, move the upper joint along the column to increase the clearance.
4 Once everything is refitted, check that the direction indicators self-cancel correctly. If not, remove the lower switch cover (three screws) and check that the lower dogs on the fixed section of the switch engage correctly with the cutaways on the outer (fixed) column and that a dog on the split collet enters a slot in the moveable section of the switch.
5 Turn the steering wheel until the clamp bolt of the collet adaptor is in a horizontal attitude underneath the column.
6 Remove the steering wheel again (Section 33) and turn the steering wheel to the straight-ahead position while holding the collet adaptor in its previously set position. Refit the wheel, in this attitude, to the column.

## 36 Steering upper column (XJS) – removal and refitting

1 Remove the instrument module as described in Chapter 10.
2 Remove the steering column lower shroud (one screw).
3 Set the front roadwheels and the steering wheel in the straight-ahead position.
4 Remove the steering wheel complete with shaft and height adjuster as described in Section 33.

33.3 Removing the collet adaptor pinch-bolt

33.5 Removing the steering wheel/upper shaft

33.6 Extracting the steering wheel boss screws

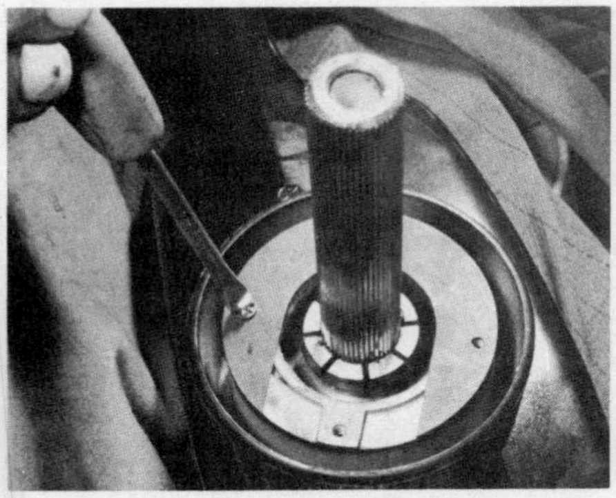

33.12 Extracting the retainer plate screws

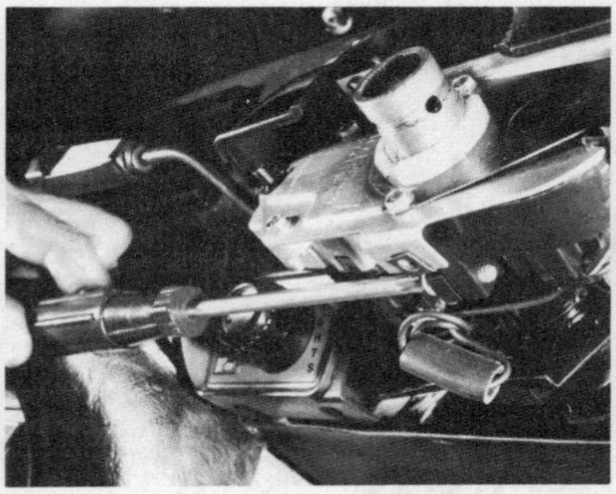

33.14A Slackening the steering column switch clamp screw

33.14B Withdrawing the steering column switches

33.14C Steering column switches removed

37.1 Steering lower shaft universal joint

45.5 Steering pump mounting (lower)

5 Remove the upper and lower shrouds from the ignition switch and disconnect the switch wiring harness at the connector plug.
6 Unscrew and remove the pinch-bolt which holds the universal joint to the upper column.
7 Remove the column lower mounting bolts.
8 Disconnect the horn lead from the steering column.
9 Remove the bolts from the column upper mounting. Retrieve the distance pieces and washers.
10 Remove the column from the car.
11 Remove the switches and lock if necessary as described in Chapter 10.
12 Refitting is a reversal of removal, but screw in the mounting bolts only finger-tight until the column has been positioned centrally in its housing in the facia. Make sure that the distance pieces and washers are returned to their locations at the upper mounting and then tighten the upper and lower bolts to the specified torque.

## 37 Steering lower column (XJ12 and Double Six) – removal and refitting

1 Raise the front of the car and remove the pinch-bolt which secures the steering column lower universal joint to the pinion shaft on the rack housing (photo).
2 Lower the car and set the roadwheels and the steering wheel in the straight-ahead position.
3 Remove the parcels shelf and extract both pinch-bolts from the universal joint which joins the upper and lower columns.
4 Release the two mounting bolts from the bottom end of the upper column.
5 Pull the lower column from the upper universal joint.
6 Pull the lower universal joint from the steering pinion shaft and withdraw the lower column.
7 Refitting is a reversal of removal, but make sure that the steering

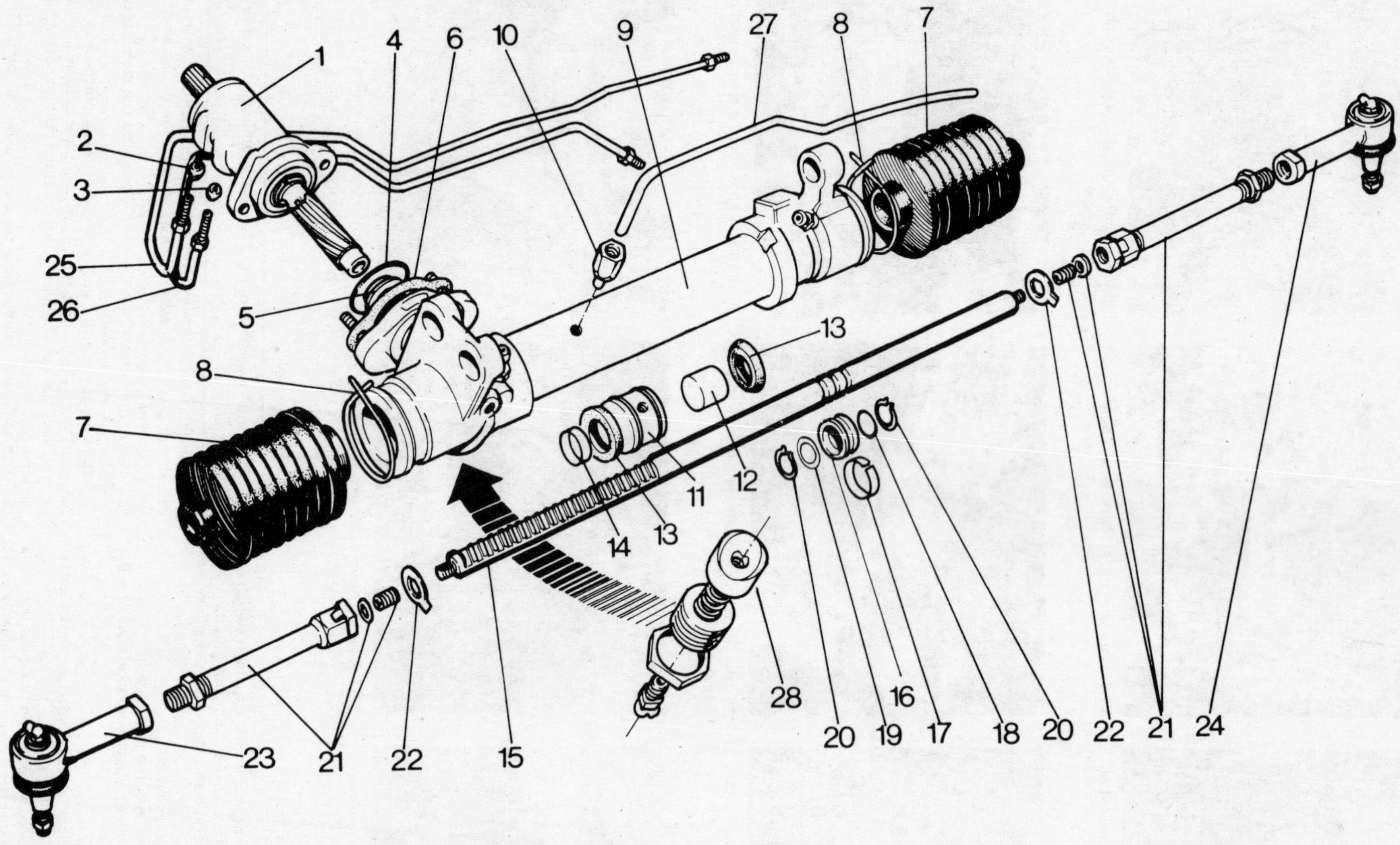

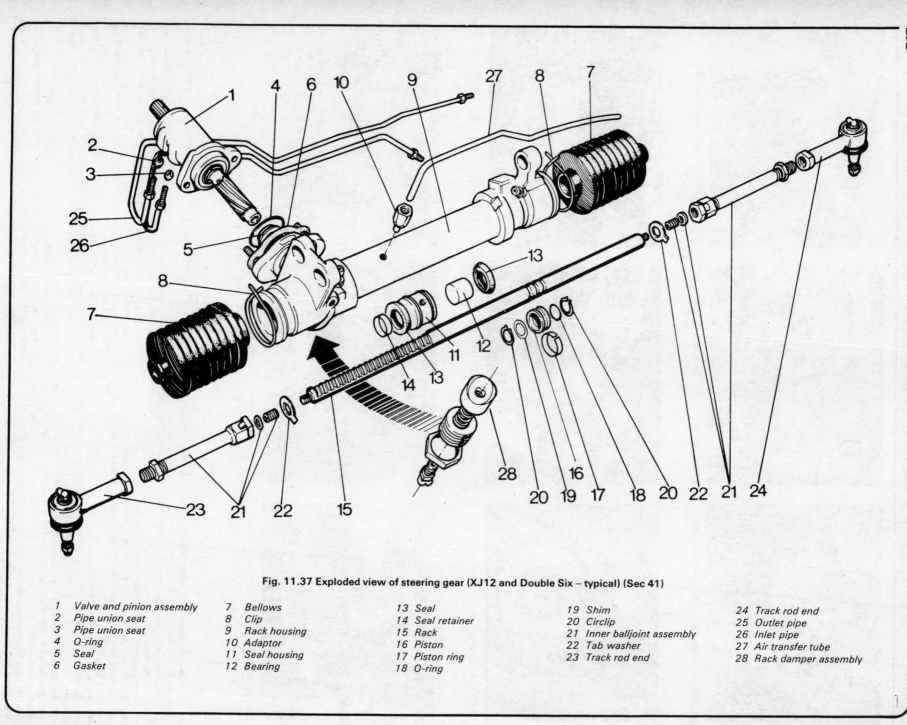

**Fig. 11.37 Exploded view of steering gear (XJ12 and Double Six – typical) (Sec 41)**

*1 Valve and pinion assembly*
*2 Pipe union seat*
*3 Pipe union seat*
*4 O-ring*
*5 Seal*
*6 Gasket*
*7 Bellows*
*8 Clip*
*9 Rack housing*
*10 Adaptor*
*11 Seal housing*
*12 Bearing*
*13 Seal*
*14 Seal retainer*
*15 Rack*
*16 Piston*
*17 Piston ring*
*18 O-ring*
*19 Shim*
*20 Circlip*
*21 Inner balljoint assembly*
*22 Tab washer*
*23 Track rod end*
*24 Track rod end*
*25 Outlet pipe*
*26 Inlet pipe*
*27 Air transfer tube*
*28 Rack damper assembly*

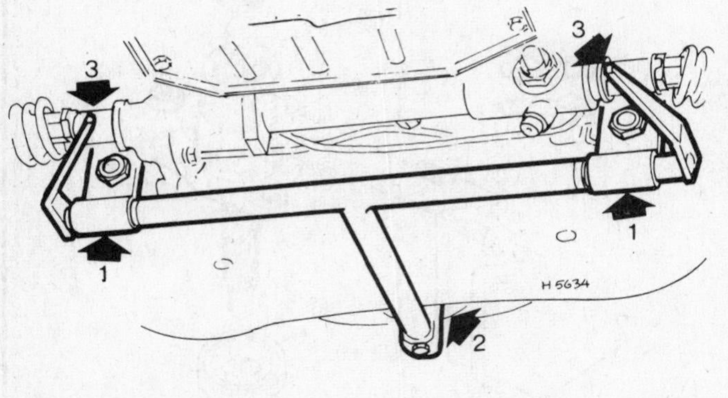


Fig. 11.38 Special tool being used to align steering gear (Sec 40)

1 *Attachment brackets* 3 *Checking levers*
2 *Sliding section*

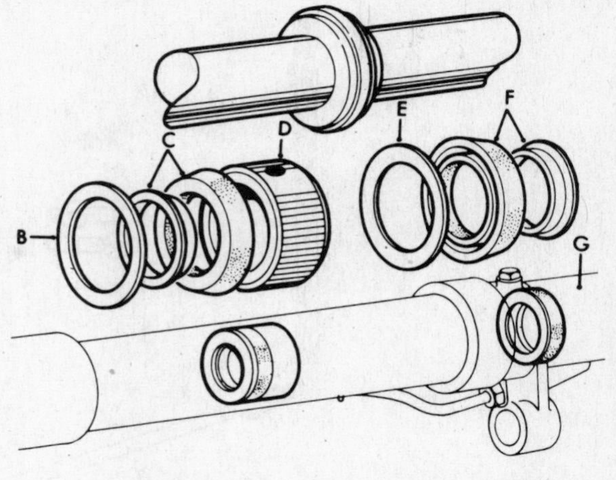


Fig. 11.39 Power steering seal arrangement (Sec 41)

*For key see text*

wheel and the front roadwheels are in the straight-ahead position. Make sure also that a gap of $\frac{3}{8}$ in (10.0 mm) exists between the two moving sections of the lower universal joint.

## 38 Steering lower column (XJS) – removal and refitting

1 Set the front roadwheels in the straight-ahead position.
2 Extract the screws which hold the right-hand heat shield adjacent to the exhaust downpipe and remove the shield.
3 Unbolt and remove the steering rack right-hand heat shield.
4 Remove the pinch-bolt which holds the lower universal joint to the pinion shaft on the rack housing.
5 Working inside the car, remove the pinch-bolts which hold the universal joint to the upper and lower columns.
6 Slide the joint from the upper column and then pull the same joint from the top of the lower column.
7 Slacken the draught-excluder clip on the lower column and working under the car, push the lower column through the bulkhead $\frac{1}{4}$until the lower universal joint disengages from the rack pinion cshaft.
8 Withdraw the lower column assembly from the draught-excluder.
9 Refitting is a reversal of removal. Make sure that the front roadwheels and the steering wheel are in the straight-ahead position before connecting the lower column joints, and adjust the position of the lower joint to provide a clearance between the moving sections of the lower joint of $\frac{3}{8}c$ in (10.0 mm).

## 39 Steering column lock – removal and refitting

1 Refer to Chapter 10, Section 43 or 44.

## 40 Steering gear – removal and refitting

1 Disconnect the fluid hoses from the pinion housing and cdrain the fluid into a container.
2 Plug or cap the openings to prevent the entry of dirt.
3 On right-hand drive cars only, disconnect the hose retaining clip from the rack housing.
4 Using a suitable extractor, disconnect the tie-rod ends from the steering arms.
5 Unscrew and remove the pinch-bolt which holds the lower universal joint to the steering gear pinion shaft.
6 Unscrew the three self-locking nuts from the steering gear mounting bolts.
7 Withdraw the steering gear downwards, retrieving the rubber bonded steel washers and shims which are located between the lugs and brackets.
8 Installation of the steering gear will require the use of a special alignment tool (JD 36) and if this cannot be borrowed, then the steering gear should be refitted and the car driven to your dealer's to have it aligned at the earliest opportunity.
9 Commence refitting by offering the steering rack to its mounting brackets.
10 Select shims so that the single lug at the end of the rack housing opposite to the pinion end is positioned midway between the lugs of the bracket on the suspension crossmember.
11 With the help of an assistant, add further shims as necessary until a gap of between 0.10 and 0.12 in (2.54 and 3.05 mm) exists between the rubber faces of the thrust washers and the inner faces of the lugs on the crossmember.
12 Check that the universal joint is engaged on the pinion shaft and tighten the steering gear mounting bolts finger-tight.
13 Pull both bellows from the rack housing having first cut the securing wire.
14 The two attachment brackets of the special alignment tool must now be located on the large hexagonal heads of the lower wishbone pivot shafts.
15 Release the locking screw and move the sliding section of the tool (2 in Fig. 11.37) until the slot registers with the weld flange at the front of the suspension member. Lock the tool in this position.
16 Lift the two checking levers (3) until contact is made with one or both rack shafts. Move the position of the steering gear if necessary until both levers make contact. Tighten the three securing bolts fully and remove the tool.
17 Reconnect the flexible bellows and fit new locking wire.
18 Reconnect the fluid lines to the steering housing, refit the upper and lower steering columns.
19 Refill the steering pump reservoir to the 'FULL' mark with clean automatic transmission fluid. Bleed the system, as described in Section 48.
20 Reconnect the tie-rod ends and check the front wheel alignment, as described in Section 49.

## 41 Steering gear (XJ12 and Double Six) – overhaul

1 With the steering gear removed from the car, clean away external dirt and remove the fluid pipes.
2 Mark the position of the valve/pinion housing relative to the rack housing and unbolt and remove it.
3 Cut the locking wires and fold back the flexible bellows to expose the inner balljoints.
4 Flatten the tab washers, release the locknuts and unscrew the tie-rods from the ends of the rack. Retrieve the springs and packing washers.

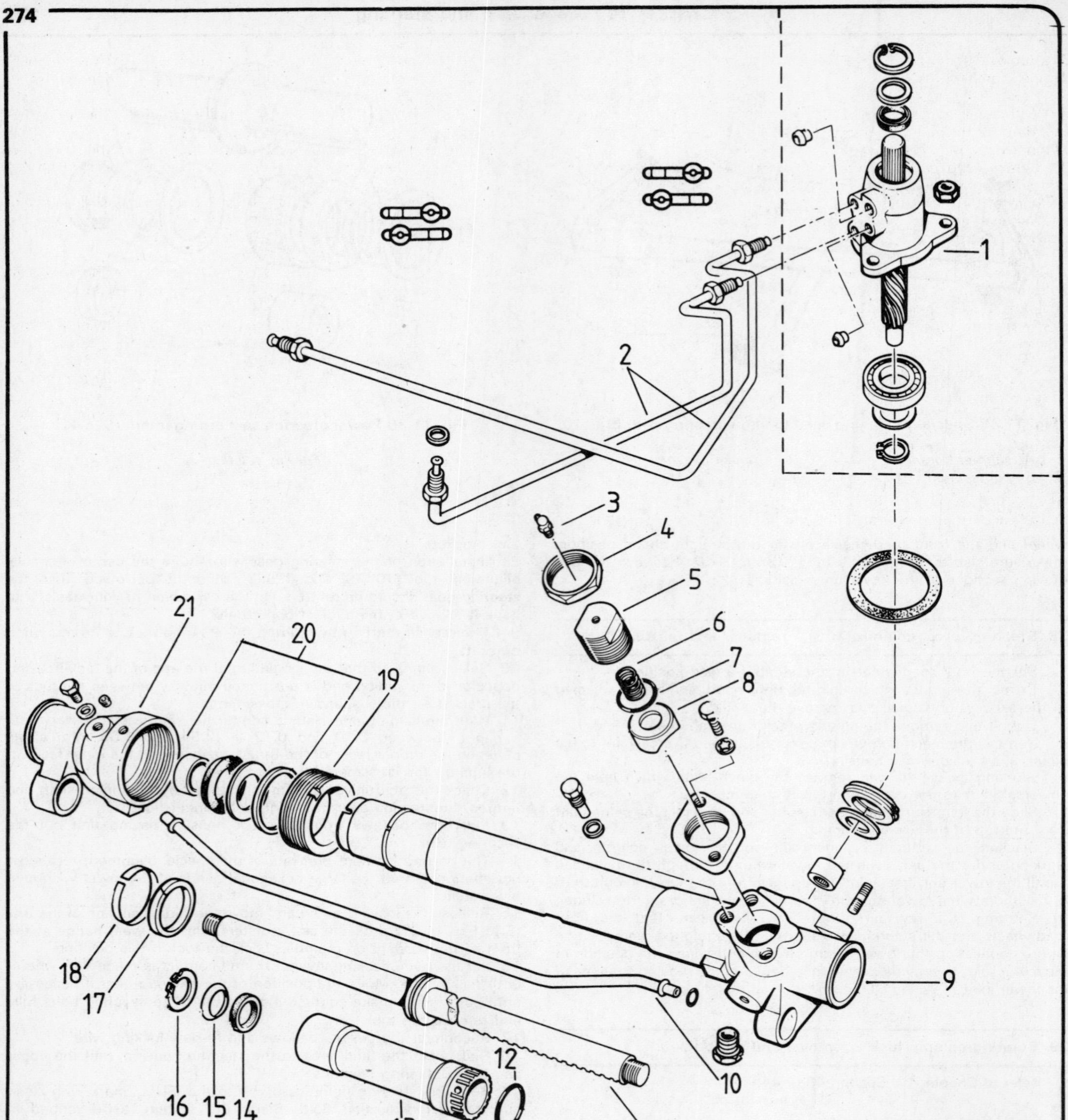


**Fig. 11.40 Exploded view of steering gear (XJS – typical) (Sec 42)**

1 *Pinion housing*
2 *Fluid pipes*
3 *Grease nipple*
4 *Locknut*
5 *Adjuster plug*
6 *Spring*
7 *O-ring*
8 *Damper shoe*
9 *Rack housing*
10 *Air transfer pipe*
11 *Rack*
12 *O-ring*
13 *Inner sleeve*
14 *Seal*
15 *Nylon washer*
16 *Circlip*
17 *Seal*
18 *Clip*
19 *Locking ring*
20 *End cap seal assembly*
21 *End cap*

5 Remove the rack damper locknut and unscrew and remove the damper components.
6 Remove the air transfer pipe from both rack housing end caps.
7 With a C-spanner, unscrew the ring nut from the rack housing end cap. Remove the end cap with bush, seal, retaining washer and O-ring. Withdraw the rack and piston.
8 Remove the union adaptor and bonded seal washer from the centre of the rack housing and then extract the centre pipe fitting from the bore of the rack housing.
9 Remove the seal and washer from behind the centre fitting. Discard the seal.
10 Early models are fitted with a rack from which the piston is detachable. Such racks are identified by not having a suffix W to the code number on the rack housing. To remove the piston, extract the circlips and draw out the piston, noting any shims fitted.
11 Renew any worn or damaged components and obtain a repair kit of seals.
12 Commence reassembly by taping the rack teeth or sliding a plastic tube over them to prevent damage to the seal lips as they are installed.
13 Slide the centre pipe fitting (D in Fig. 11.39), a new seal (C) and the retaining washer (B) over the protected rack teeth and onto the plain section of the rack. Make sure that the seal lips face the centre pipe fitting. Remove the protective tape or sleeve.
14 Enter the rack into the housing so that the toothed end enters first. Align the threaded hole in the centre pipe fitting so that it registers with the hole in the rack housing.
15 Screw in the centre pipe fitting and adaptor with bonded seal washer. Tighten fully.
16 Over the plain end of the rack, fit the cap seal retaining washer (E) and then the seal (F), lips towards washer.
17 Slide the housing (G) onto the rack so that it pushes the seal into position. Secure with the ring nut.
18 Fit the air transfer pipe and the rack damper components, but do not adjust at this stage.
19 Refit the valve/pinion assembly using a new gasket.
20 Reconnect the inner balljoints to the rack using new lockwashers. Apply 2 oz (57 g) of grease to each balljoint assembly.
21 Adjust the rack damper as described in Section 31.
22 Using a grease gun apply 1 oz (28 g) of grease to the nipple on the rack housing. Too much grease will distend the flexible bellows.
23 Fit the fluid pipes.

## 42 Steering gear (XJS) – overhaul

1 Carry out the operations described in paragraphs 1, 3 and 4 of Section 41.
2 Remove the external fluid pipes.
3 Mark the relative position of the pinion housing to the rack housing, unscrew the nuts and remove it.
4 Discard the pinion seals in the housing recess and retrieve the metal washer.
5 Unscrew and remove the bolts which hold the rack housing to the end cap and the inner sleeve.
6 Using an Allen key, extract the socket screw from the end cap.
7 Using a C-spanner, or a hammer and a drift, unscrew the locking ring from the end cap. Remove the end cap.
8 Remove the air transfer pipe.
9 Remove the end cap O-ring seal, washer, nylon spacer, seal and seal seat.
10 Remove the bolts which hold the rack damper plate. Remove the plate, seal and spring followed by the damper.
11 Withdraw the rack from the housing.
12 Using an angled drift, drive the inner sleeve from the rack housing.
13 Extract the circlip from the end of the inner sleeve and remove the nylon washer, seal and seal seat.
14 Extract the O-ring seal from the periphery of the inner sleeve.
15 Remove the seal from the seal carrier on the rack.
16 Inspect all components for wear or damage. Obtain a seal repair kit and new gaskets.
17 Commence reassembly by lubricating the new seal for the inner sleeve.
18 Fit the seal seat, seal and nylon washer to the inner sleeve and secure with the circlip.
19 Lubricate and fit the new O-ring seal to the periphery of the inner sleeve.
20 Push the inner sleeve into the rack housing so that the notched end enters first and the hole for the locating peg is aligned with the hole in the rack end casing. Insert the locating bolt.
21 Tape over the teeth of the rack to prevent damage to the lips of the seals.
22 Fit the new nylon seal to the carrier on the rack and then push the rack into the rack housing and inner sleeve. Locate the rack centrally in the rack housing.
23 Lubricate the new seals and fit them to the rack housing end cap. These include the seal seat, seal, nylon washer, metal washer and O-ring.
24 Fit new O-rings to the air transfer pipe.
25 Fit the end cap to the end of the rack housing, making sure that the cut-out in the housing aligns with the bolt hole. Fit the bolt.
26 Fit the air transfer pipe.
27 Secure the end cap to the rack housing by screwing up the threaded sleeve. Lock the sleeve with the socket-headed screw.
28 Remove the tape from the teeth of the rack.
29 Lubricate the new seal and fit it with the metal washer and O-ring to the pinion housing.
30 Fit the pinion housing, using a new gasket and tighten the securing nuts.
31 Fit the rack damper and the fluid pipes.
32 Reconnect the inner balljoints using new lockplates. Smear each balljoint with 2 oz (57 g) of grease.
33 Adjust the damper as described in Section 31 and then inject 1 oz (28 g) of grease into the rack damper grease nipple.
34 Reconnect the bellows with wire or a clip.

## 43 Steering rack bellows – renewal in car

1 A split or perished bellows can be renewed without having to remove the rack assembly from the car.
2 Using a suitable extractor, separate the outer tie-rod balljoint from the steering arm.
3 Unscrew the tie-rod end locknut one quarter of a turn and then unscrew and remove the tie-rod end balljoint assembly.
4 Release the bellows clips and slide the bellows off the tie-rod.
5 If dirt has entered the split in the bellows, wipe the grease from the inner balljoints and apply 2 oz (57 g) of fresh lubricant.
6 Fit the new bellows and the clips or locking wire.
7 Screw on the tie-rod balljoint until it resumes its original position, when the locknut will only require one quarter of a turn to lock the balljoint.
8 Reconnect the balljoint to the steering arm.
9 Check the front wheel alignment as described in Section 49.

## 44 Steering oil cooler – removal and refitting

1 Remove the filler cap from the power steering pump reservoir and syphon out the fluid with a syringe or other suitable device.
2 Disconnect the hoses from the cooler, expect some loss of fluid.
3 Unbolt the cooler from the suspension and lift it from the car.
4 Refitting is a reversal of removal. Bleed the power steering system as described in Section 48.

## 45 Steering pump (XJ12 and Double Six) – removal and refitting

1 Remove the left-hand air cleaner.
2 Disconnect the hose from the outlet at the rear of the pump reservoir. Allow the fluid to drain into a suitable container and then plug the openings.
3 Disconnect the second (high pressure) hose frcom the reservoir.
4 Disconnect the pump adjusting link. Press the pump inwards, and slip the drivebelt from the pump pulley.
5 Pull the pump outwards and disconnect the bottom pivot mounting bolt (photo). Lift the pump and its mounting bracket from the engine compartment.
6 Refit the pump by reversing the removal operations. The pump drivebelt is tensioned by pulling the pump away from the engine and then tightening the adjuster link bolt. Refer to Chapter 1, Section 51.
7 Reconnect the fluid hoses, and fill the reservoir to the full mark on the dipstick with the specified fluid. Turn the pump pulley anti-

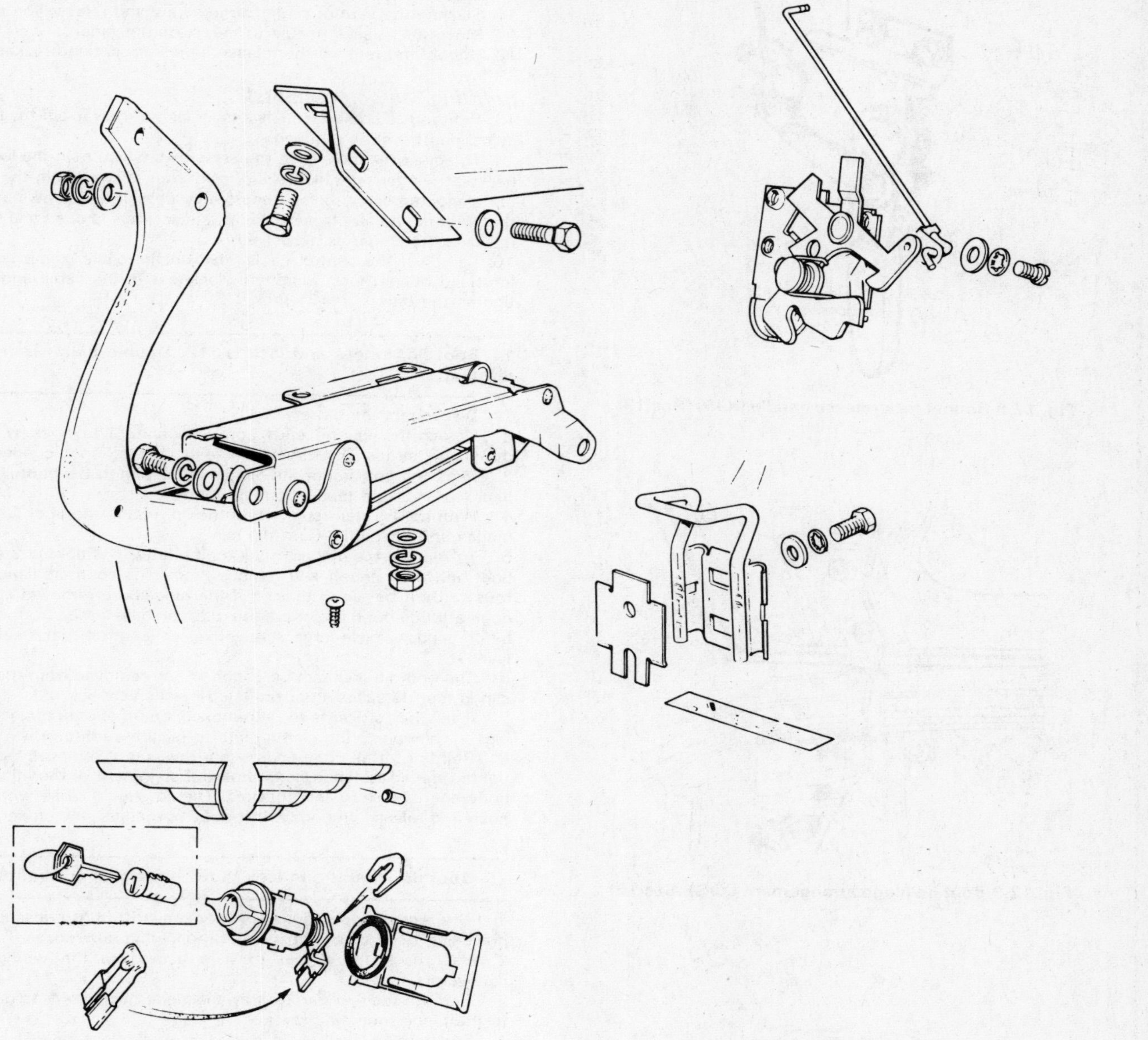

Fig. 12.7 Boot lid hinge and lock components (XJ12, Double Six) (Sec 14)

screws from both ends of the stay and remove the stay.
2 Extract the screws which hold the radiator grille to the bonnet and remove the grille.
3 Mark the position of the hinges in relation to the bonnet using a pencil or masking tape.
4 Unscrew and remove the bonnet-to-hinge bolts and with the help of an assistant, lift the bonnet from the car.
5 If the hinges must now be removed, mark their position in relation to the crossmember, extract their bolts and remove them.
6 Refitting is a reversal of removal, but do not fully tighten the bonnet-to-hinge bolts until the alignment of the bonnet has been checked.

## 13 Bonnet lock/cable (XJS) – removal, refitting and adjustment

1 Removal operations for the bonnet lock vary according to whether it is a left-hand or right-hand unit.

### *Left-hand lock removal*

2 Release the control cable from the release handle and from the lock pivot.
3 Unbolt the lock from the bulkhead and remove it complete with control cable. Unbolt the lock from its mounting plate.

### *Right-hand lock removal*

4 Extract the two screws which hold the cold start relay cover to the valance and remove the cover.
5 Unbolt the bonnet lock from the bulkhead.
6 Release the cable from the left-hand bonnet lock pivot. Remove the lock complete with cable.
7 Unbolt the lock from the backplate.

### *Lock trigger/release handle removal*

8 Remove the side trim panel from the driver's footwell. To do this, unclip the crash roll adjacent to the pillar trim pad. Extract the screws and remove the pillar trim pad.

Fig. 12.8 Bonnet lock release handle (XJS) (Sec 13)

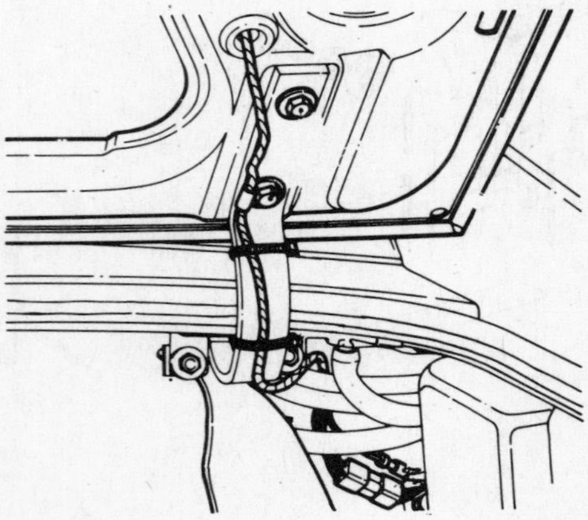

Fig. 12.9 Boot lid hinge arrangement (XJS) (Sec 15)

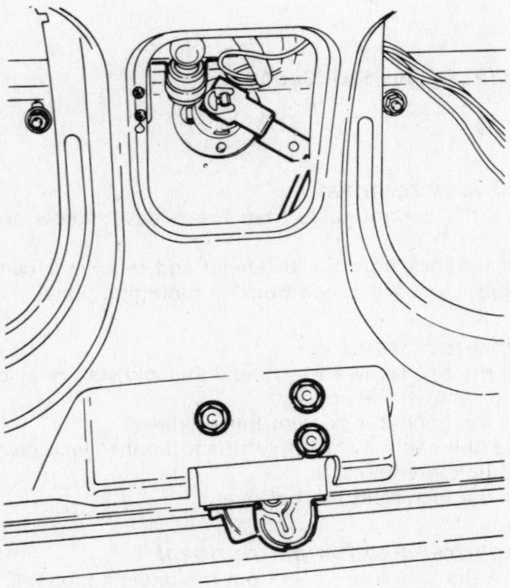

Fig. 12.10 Boot lid lock (XJS) (Sec 15)

9 Move the bonnet release handle to the 'open' position.
10 Slacken the control cable clamp screw and release the cable.
11 Move the release handle to the 'closed' position.
12 Unbolt and remove the release handle mounting bracket.

### *Refitting (all components)*

13 Refitting all components is a reversal of removal, but the following adjustments will be required.
14 To adjust the lock, have the setscrews which hold the lock to the backplate finger-tight. Move the lock up or down within the limits of the elongated screw holes, temporarily tighten the screws and check that with the bonnet closed, the lock is securely latched and smoothly released. Re-adjust as necessary.
15 To adjust the control cable, slacken the cable clamp bolt at the left-hand bonnet lock. Eliminate slackness in the cable and then re-tighten the bolt.

## 14 Boot lid, hinges and lock (XJ12, Double Six) – removal and refitting

1 Disconnect the battery.
2 Detach the electric leads from the bonnet lid hinges by releasing the plastic straps. Disconnect the leads at their snap connectors.
3 Mark the position of the hinges in relation to the boot lid, using a pencil or masking tape to outline them.
4 With an assistant supporting the lid, unbolt the boot lid from the hinges and lift the lid from the car.
5 To remove the hinges, mark their relative position on the luggage boot and then unbolt and remove them. The counterbalance torsion rods will not be under tension if the hinges are removed in the fully open attitude but if preferred, the rods can be released from the hinges beforehand, using a large screwdriver or length of flat steel bar as a lever.
6 The boot lid lock can be unbolted and removed from the lid if the clip is first detached from the latch mechanism link rod.
7 If the lock striker is to be removed, first mark the projection of its legs in relation to the clamp plate to facilitate refitting.
8 Refitting of all components is a reversal of removal. Do not fully tighten the lid-to-hinge bolts until the alignment of the lid within the body aperture has been checked. The lid should close with a gentle push and release smoothly. If it does not, adjust the striker.

## 15 Boot lid, hinges and lock (XJS) – removal and refitting

1 The removal operations are very similar to those described in the preceding Section, but observe the following differences.
2 Peel back the carpet to gain access to the wiring harness connectors.
3 Remove the rear parcels tray shelf (see Section 44) to gain access to the hinge mounting bolts.
4 The boot lid lock handle is sited remotely from the lock and can be removed after first withdrawing the rear number plate and reversing lamp assemblies.
5 Extract the spring clip and disconnect the lock operating rod from the handle lever. Extract the handle securing screws and manoeuvre the assembly out of the aperture in the boot lid.
6 Refitting is a reversal of removal.

## 16 Front underrider and rear overrider (XJ12, Double Six) – removal and refitting

1 These components are simply removed from the front and rear bumpers by extracting the securing bolts.
2 If both rear overriders are being removed, note that once they are withdrawn, the bumper centre section becomes free.
3 When refitting the front underriders, make sure that their top mounting brackets are located under the rubber mounting pad.

## 17 Bumper blades (XJ12, Double Six) – removal and refitting

### *Front*

1 Working within the front wheel arches, remove the bolts that hold

Fig. 12.11 Front underrider (XJ12, Double Six) (Sec 16)

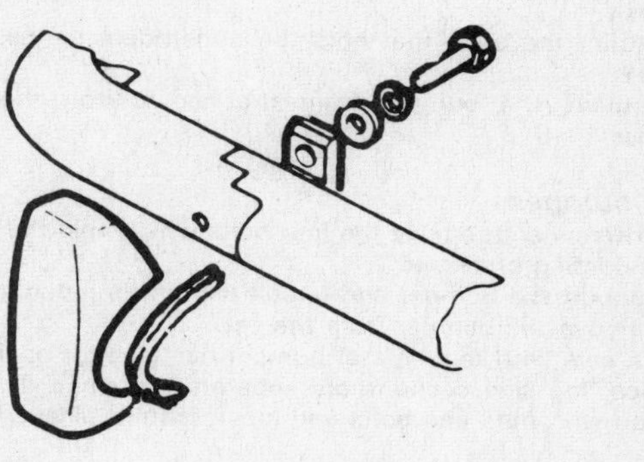

Fig. 12.12 Rear overrider (XJ12, Double Six) (Sec 16)

Fig. 12.13 Front bumper end fixings (XJ12, Double Six) (Sec 17)

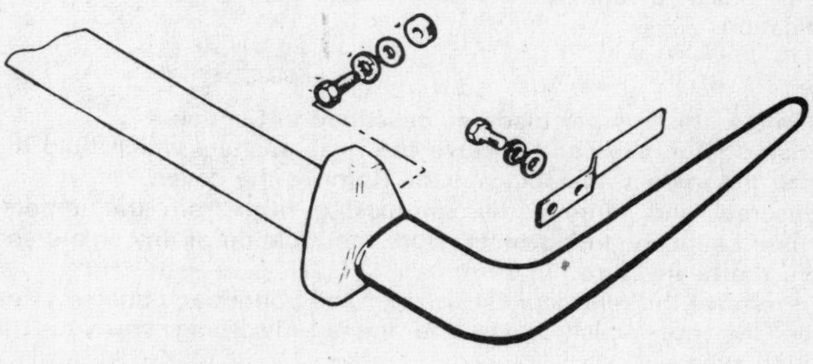

Fig. 12.14 Rear bumper end fixings (XJ12, Double Six) (Sec 17)

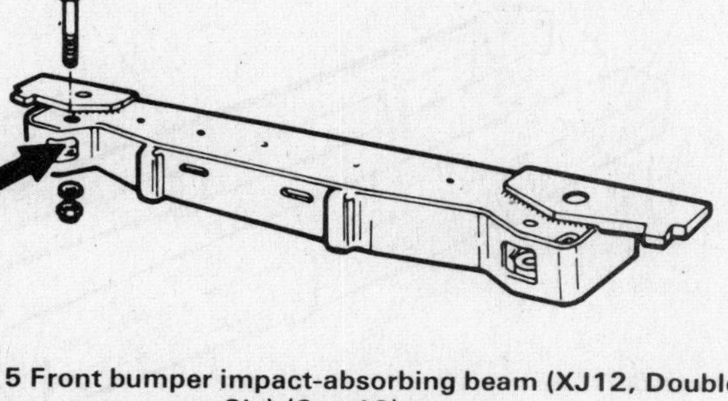

Fig. 12.15 Front bumper impact-absorbing beam (XJ12, Double Six) (Sec 18)

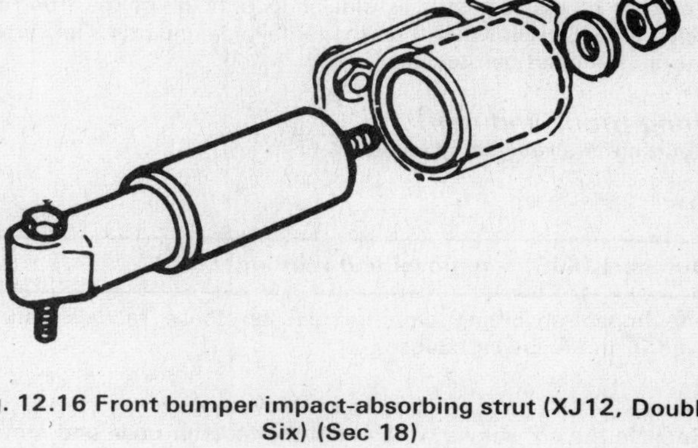

Fig. 12.16 Front bumper impact-absorbing strut (XJ12, Double Six) (Sec 18)

the sides of the bumper to the front wing support stays. Retrieve the washers, spacers and nuts.
2 Unbolt the front of the bumper from the bonnet hinge brackets (photos).
3 Extract the bolts that hold the underriders to the bonnet hinge brackets.
4 Remove the bumper from the car. Unbolt the overriders if necessary.

*Rear bumper*
5 Unscrew and remove the four bolts which hold the bumper to the side mounting brackets.
6 Support the bumper and unbolt it from its mountings.
7 Remove the bumper from the car.
8 On cars with this type of bumper destined for operation in North America, the side sections are separate pressings. They are held in position with nuts and bolts and incorporate a plastic beading at the joint.

*Refitting (front and rear)*
9 Refitting of the front and rear bumpers is a reversal of removal.

## 18 Bumpers (impact-absorbing type – XJ12, Double Six) – removal and refitting

1 This design of bumper is fitted to cars built to North American specification.

*Front*
2 Remove the bumper blade as described in Section 17.
3 Prise off the clips and remove the oval washers which hold the cover to the impact-absorbing beam. Remove the cover.
4 Unscrew and remove the self-locking nuts from the impact-absorbing beam mounting bolts. Note the location of any shims and remove the beam from the struts.
5 To remove the telescopic strut, open the bonnet and unscrew and remove the nut which holds the impact-absorbing strut to the mounting tube.
6 Using a plastic-faced hammer, tap the end of the strut stud, so driving the strut out of the mounting tube.

*Rear*
7 Remove the bumper blade as described in Section 17, noting particularly paragraph 8.
8 Unscrew and remove the six bolts which hold the underside of the cover to the impact-absorbing beam, release the cover clips and pull the cover from the beam.
9 Unscrew and remove the self-locking nuts from the impact-absorbing beam mounting bolts. Note the position of the shims and guide tubes and then withdraw the bolts. Lift the beam from the car.
10 Removal of the rear strut is similar to removal of the front one described above, except that the exhaust tailpipe and rear silencer will have to be removed beforehand.

*Refitting (front and rear)*
11 Refitting is a reversal of removal.

## 19 Bumpers (XJS) – removal and refitting

1 The impact-absorbing type bumper on these models can be removed in the following stages.

*Front*
2 Remove the six screws which hold the radiator grille and remove the grille.
3 Remove the nuts, bolts and washers which hold the centre section of the bumper blade to the impact-absorbing beam. Remove the section.
4 Remove the front flasher lamp assemblies and then extract the five screws which secure the cover to the impact-absorbing beam.
5 Disengage the cover clips and pull the cover from the beam.
6 Unbolt the impact-absorbing beam from the struts and lift the beam from the car, noting the location of the spacers.
7 The telescopic struts can be removed once the single fixing nut is unscrewed and the strut stud tapped with a plastic-faced hammer.

*Rear*
8 Removal is similar to that described earlier for the front assembly. Withdraw the centre section of the bumper blade, the cover from the impact-absorbing beam and then the beam itself.
9 Access to the struts can be obtained after peeling back the carpet in the luggage compartment.

*Refitting (front and rear)*
10 Refitting all components is a reversal of removal.

## 20 Radiator grille (XJ12, Double Six) – removal and refitting

1 Unscrew and remove the nuts and cross-head screws which hold the grille to the bonnet. Retrieve the washers.
2 Withdraw the grille evenly from the bonnet.
3 The lower grille can be removed if the two screws which hold the lower grille to the apron and which are located behind the spotlamps are removed.
4 The centre bar is removable independently if the two nuts which hold the upper section of the bar to the retaining plate are unscrewed, followed by the single nut which holds the lower section of the bar to the radiator grille.
5 Refitting is a reversal of removal.
6 On Series 1 models, the horn grilles are simply pulled from their locations. Do this using a piece of cord and give an even straight pull.

## 21 Radiator grilles and spoiler (XJS) – removal and refitting

1 The main grille can be removed from the bonnet once the securing screws have been extracted.
2 The lower grille is detachable if the screws which hold it to the wings are first extracted.
3 If the spoiler is to be removed, the front of the car should be raised or the car placed over an inspection pit.
4 Remove the two securing screws and withdraw the oil cooler grille.
5 Prise out the plastic fasteners which hold the spoiler undertray to the body and the spoiler.
6 Unscrew and remove the screws and detach the spoiler undertray.
7 Unscrew and remove the spoiler securing screws.
8 Refitting is a reversal of removal, but use new plastic fasteners on the spoiler undertray.

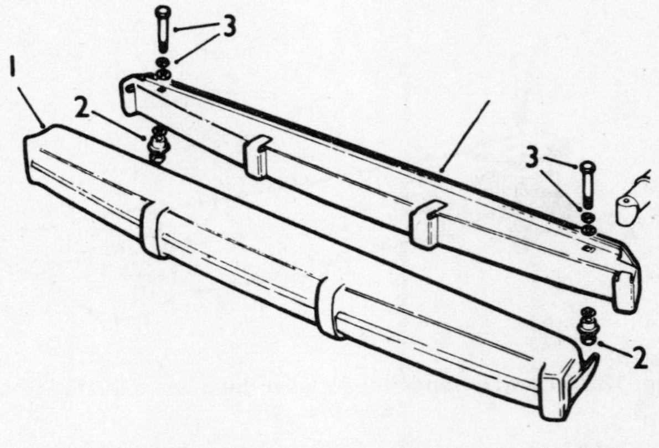


**Fig. 12.17 Rear impact-absorbing bumper (XJ12, Double Six) (Sec 18)**

*1 Cover*
*2 Mounting nuts and washers*
*3 Mounting bolts and washers*

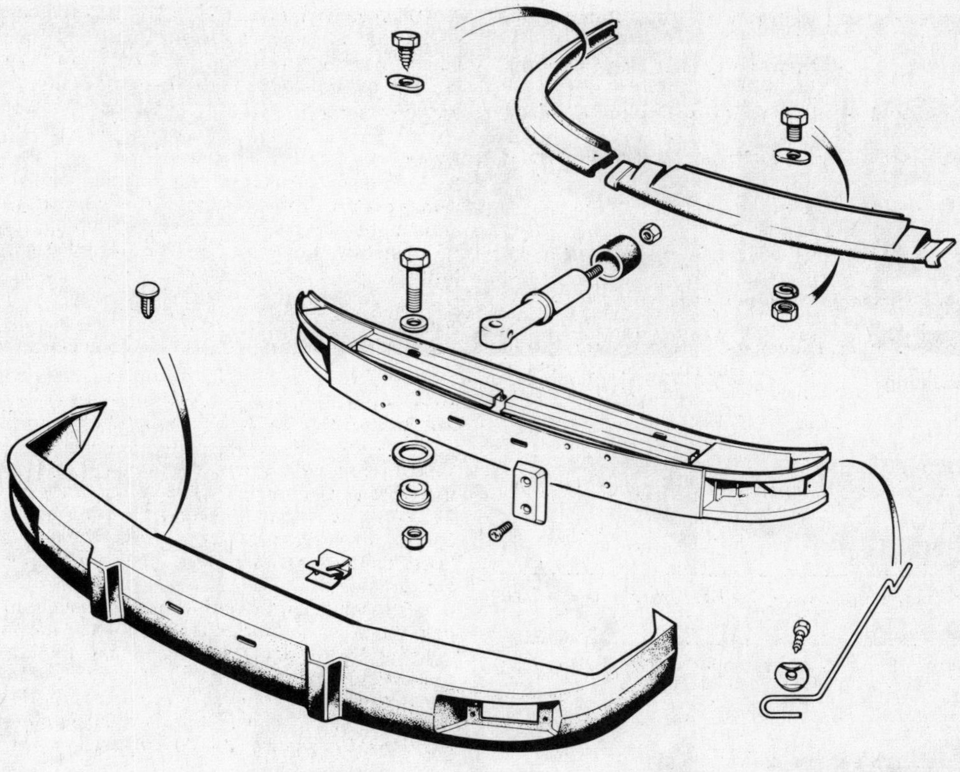

Fig. 12.18 Front bumper components (XJS) (Sec 19)

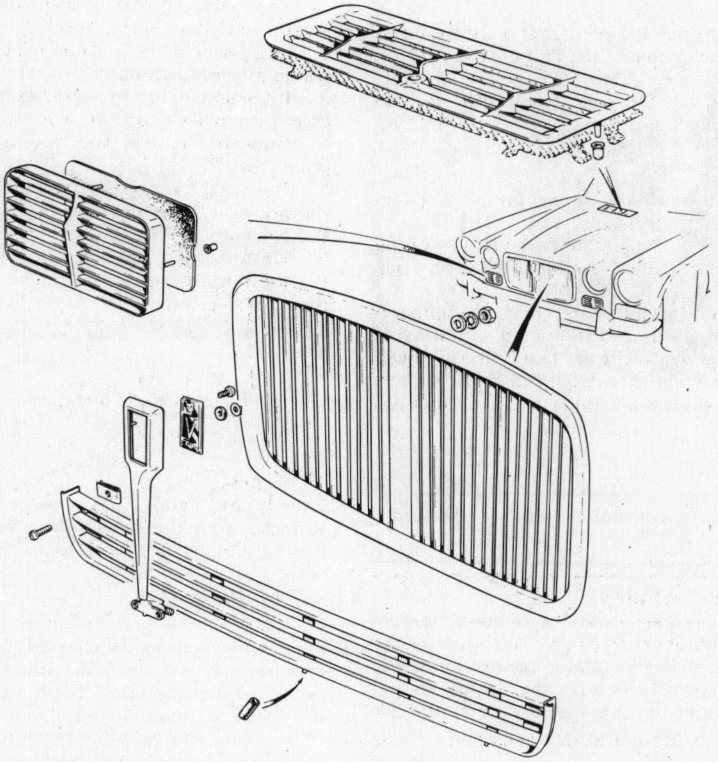

Fig. 12.19 Grilles (XJ12, Double Six) (Sec 20)

17.2A Front bumper mounting

17.2B Front bumper under-rider

22.4 Armrest screw cover plate

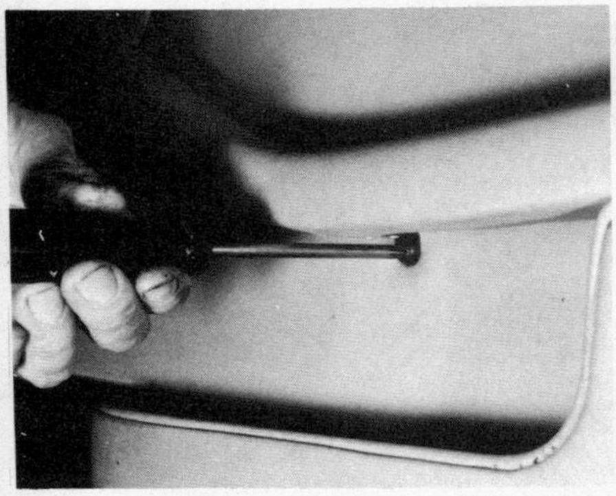
22.6A Armrest lower screw

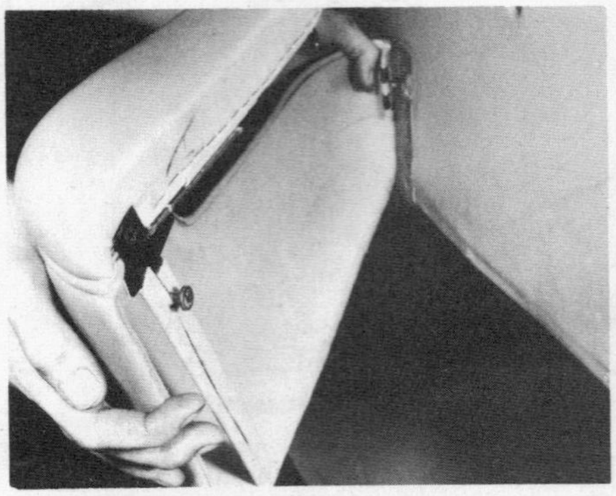
22.6B Removing door armrest

22.8 Front door inner panel

22.14 Door latch

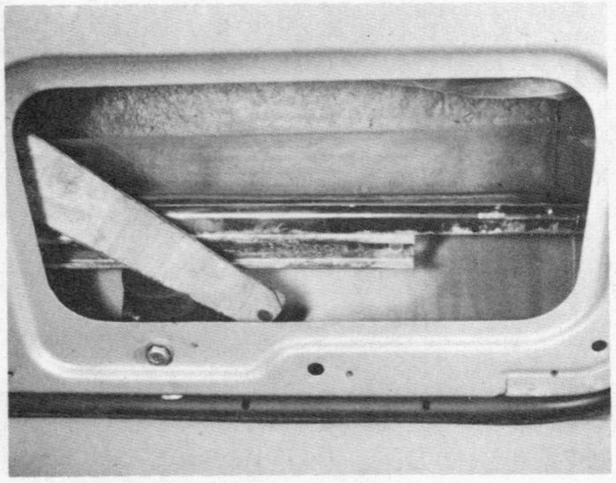
22.19 Window lift arm and guide channel

## 22 Front door (XJ12 and Double Six, 4-door models) – dismantling and reassembly

### *Series 1*

1 On Series 1 models with a swivelling ventilator, remove the door capping (six screws).

2 Prise out the centre bezel from the ventilator control knob and then unscrew the bolt which is exposed. Remove the control knob.

3 Extract the securing screws and remove the crash roll and the armrest.

### *Series 2 onwards*

4 On Series 2 and later models, pull the chrome cover from the forward end of the armrest (photo).

5 Unscrew and remove the screw which is now exposed.

6 Unscrew and remove the four screws from the underside of the armrest and remove the armrest from the door. If manually-operated window regulators are fitted, extract the single screw and pull off the handle and escutcheon (photos).

### *All models*

7 On all models, if a remotely controlled exterior mirror is fitted, extract the screws which hold the adjuster control lever escutcheon and partially withdraw the escutcheon until the grub screw can be extracted and the escutcheon removed from the lever.

8 Insert a broad blade between the trim panel of the door and the door casing and twist the blade to release the first retaining clip. Now insert the fingers and working round the trim panel, release the remaining retaining clips. Withdraw the panel. Self-tapping screws are sometimes used at the bottom edge (photo).

9 If the door lock is to be removed, first make sure that the window is wound fully up by actuating the lift button or temporarily refitting the regulator handle.

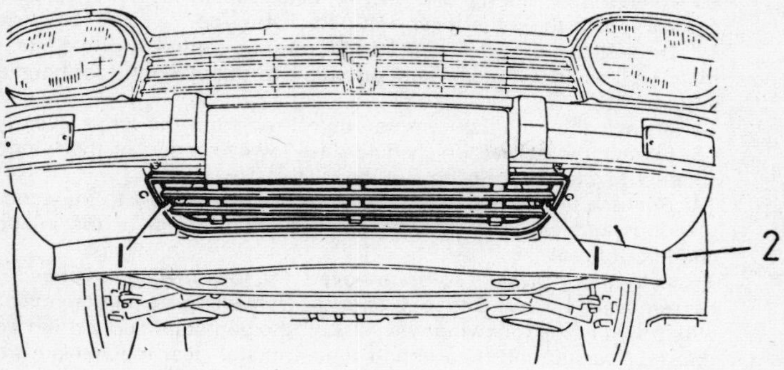


**Fig. 12.20 Radiator lower grille (XJS) (Sec 21)**

*1 Securing screws*  *2 Spoiler*

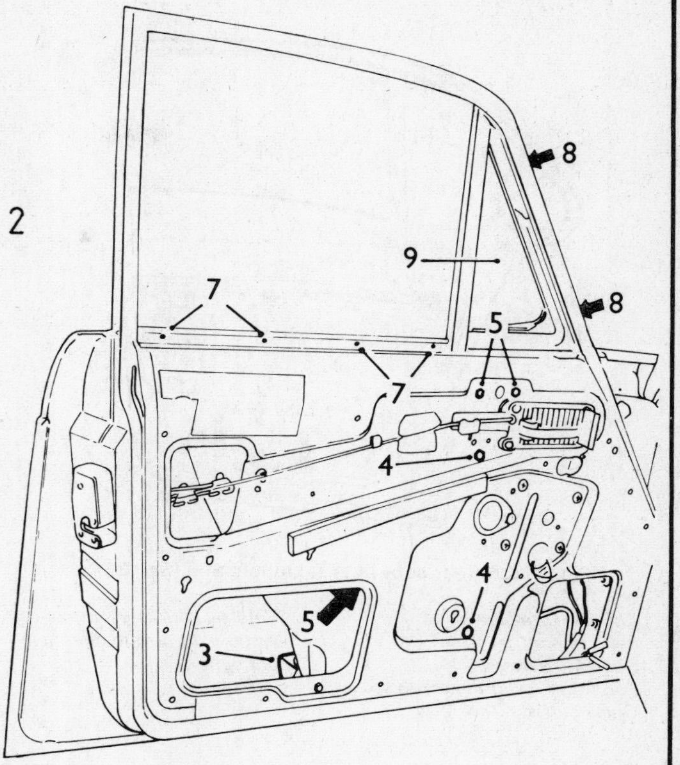


**Fig. 12.21 Front door (XJ12 and Double Six, Series 1) (Sec 22)**

*3 Glass buffer*
*4 Ventilator support bolts*
*5 Ventilator gear fixing bolts*
*7 Weatherstrip screws*
*8 Ventilator fixing screws*
*9 Ventilator*

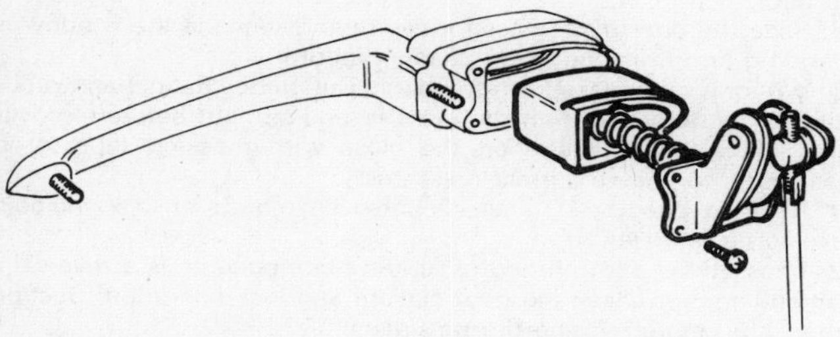

**Fig. 12.22 Exterior door handle (XJ12, Double Six) (Sec 22)**

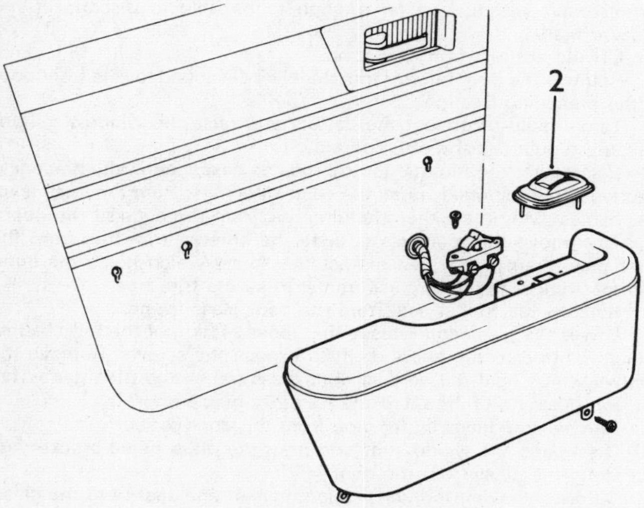


**Fig. 12.23 Typical XJ12, Double Six Series 1 rear door armrest (Sec 23)**

*2 Window lift switch*

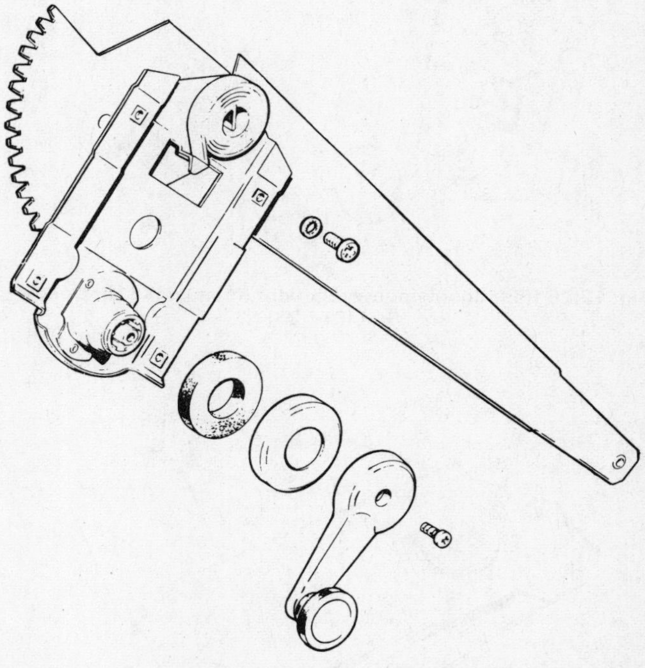

**Fig 12.24 Window regulator (manually operated) (XJ12, Double Six) (Sec 22)**

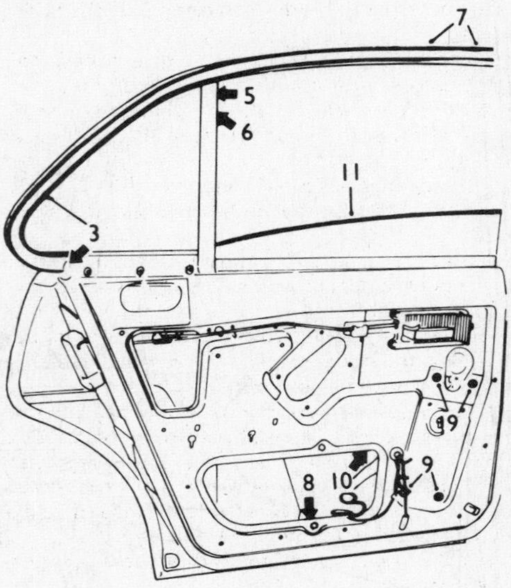


Fig. 12.25 Rear door (XJ12, Double Six) (Sec 23)

3 *Chrome trim screw*
5 *Felt channel*
6 *Securing screws*
7 *Top frame securing screws*
8 *Glass buffer screw*
9 *Window lift fixing screws*
10 *Window lift arm to channel connection*
11 *Glass*

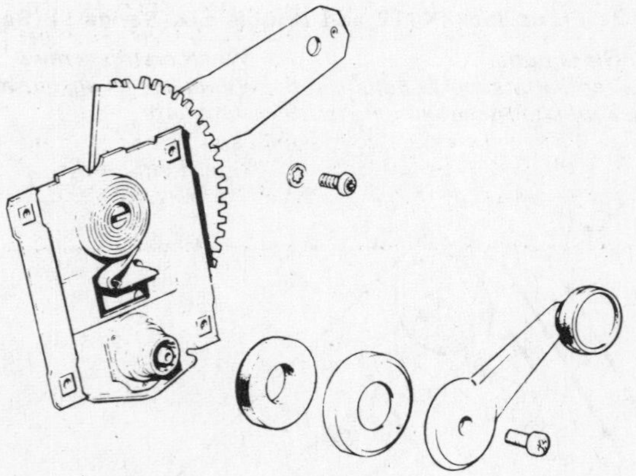

Fig. 12.26 Rear door window regulator (manual (XJ12, Double Six) (Sec 23)

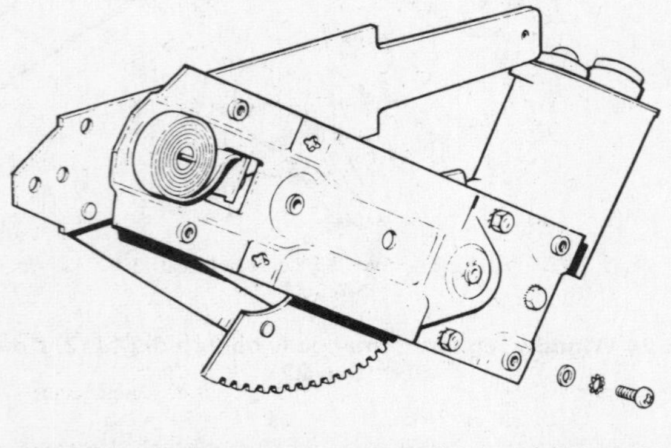

Fig. 12.27 Rear door window regulator (electric) (XJ12, Double Six) (Sec 23)

10 Release the spring clip which holds the inside handle remote control rod to the latch lever and detach the rod.
11 Detach the exterior door handle remote control rod in a similar manner. Unscrew the two nuts and remove the exterior door handle if required.
12 Detach the key lock remote control rod from the latch lever.
13 Extract the screw which holds the lower section of the window channel to the door casing.
14 Remove the screws which hold the latch assembly to the edge of the door and withdraw the assembly from the rear of the window channel (photo).
15 If the door glass is to be removed, the lock mechanism need not be removed, but on Series 1 cars the swivelling ventilator must be withdrawn in the following way. Unbolt the ventilator support leg from the door casing and then unbolt the ventilator gear mechanism from the door. Lower the main window glass to its fullest extent. Extract the weatherstrip screws and the screws which hold the ventilator to the door. Withdraw the ventilator assembly.
16 On Series 2 and later models, lower the door glass to its fullest extent and prise off the chrome beading from the base of the fixed quarterlight.
17 Remove the two bolts which hold the quarterlight support leg to the door panel and then extract the screws which hold the glass weatherstrip to the door. Remove the weatherstrip.
18 Remove the two screws which hold the quarterlight to the angular section of the door glass frame and carefully pull the quarterlight from the door.
19 Slide the door main glass forward and disengage the window lift operating arm from the guide channel (photo).
20 Withdraw the glass from the door. The guide channel and rubber seal can be detached from the glass if required, but before removing them mark their position on the glass with masking tape, or by measuring, to ensure correct reassembly.
21 Refer to Chapter 10 if the window lift motors or lock solenoids have to be removed.
22 Reassembly and refitting of all door components is a reversal of dismantling, but check the door closure and lock operation (Sections 7 and 25) before refitting the trim panel.
23 Seal the gap between the quarterlight and the chrome beading with suitable sealant.

## 23 Rear door (XJ12 and Double Six, 4-door models) – dismantling and reassembly

1 If the armrests incorporate the radio speakers, disconnect the battery, extract the securing screws from the lower edge of the armrest and withdraw it far enough to be able to disconnect the speaker leads.
2 Lift the armrest from the door.
3 Remove the door interior trim panel as described for the front door in the preceding Section.
4 Temporarily reconnect the battery and raise the window fully or refit the regulator handle temporarily.
5 Disconnect the remote control rods as described in the preceding Section and additionally prise the child safety link from the latch lever mechanism. Withdraw the operating link from the edge of the door.
6 To remove the main glass, prise the chrome trim free from the door glass frame and then extract the screw which holds the inner chrome trim to the door glass frame. Prise the trim free.
7 Release the rubber seal from the door glass frame.
8 Lower the glass and release the upper section of the felt channel which is fitted to the quarterlight to expose the screws. Remove the screws which hold the vertical door glass frame and then gently tap the top glass frame free. Lift the frame from the door.
9 Remove the glass buffer stop from the door panel.
10 Disengage the window lift arm from the glass guide bracket and withdraw the glass from the door.
11 Before removing the glass guide bracket and seal from the glass, mark their position with masking tape or by measuring.
12 The quarterlight can be removed independently of the main door glass. Commence by prising the chrome trim free from the quarterlight frame.
13 Prise the chrome beading from the base of the quarterlight and remove the screw from the inner chrome trim which is attached to the door glass frame. Prise off the trim.

14 Release the door seal from the quarterlight frame and extract the three screws which hold the base of the quarterlight to the door.
15 Lower the door glass to its fullest extent by temporarily reconnecting the battery and operating the control button.
16 Release the upper section of the felt channel from the quarterlight and extract the exposed screws.
17 Prise the chrome trim from the quarterlight vertical post and lift the quarterlight from the door.
18 Refitting is a reversal of removal, but check the lock adjustment as described in Section 28 before refitting the interior panel to the door.
19 Seal the gap between the base of the quarterlight and the chrome beading.

## 24 Door (XJ12 and Double Six, 2-door models) – dismantling and reassembly

1 The operations are similar to those described in Section 22, except that a separate quarterlight is not fitted and manually-operated windows are used on earlier models.
2 To remove the door glass, take off the trim panel and crash roll from the inside of the door. The window regulator handle will first have to be detached by extracting the screw from the chrome bezel.
3 Remove the securing screws and lift the glass bezel/guide from the front of the door.
4 Remove the securing screws from the crash roll retaining plate and withdraw the plate.
5 Prise off the glass anti-rattle pads.
6 Detach the lower portion of the polythene sheet from the door.
7 Lower the window sufficiently to gain access to the window mounting plate screws. Slacken the screws.
8 Release the two nuts which hold the window lift quadrant guide channel to the glass mounting.
9 Raise the window to its fullest extent and then remove the two screws which hold the glass to the mounting plate.
10 Remove the glass sealing rubber and carefully withdraw the glass from the door.
11 Once the glass has been withdrawn, the winder mechanism can be removed.
12 Commence by extracting the screws which hold the chrome beading and the weatherstrip to the door. Remove the weatherstrip.
13 Raise the glass carrier fully and then disengage the spring from the glass carrier plate.
14 Lower the carrier plate sufficiently to give access to the guide channel which engages with the lift motor quadrant.
15 Remove the two nuts which hold the guide channel to the glass carrier. Slide the channel from the window lift quadrant and lift the guide from the door.
16 Disengage the spring assembly and remove it.
17 Remove the nylon anti-rattle pads from the top corners of the pulley frame.
18 Move the glass carrier to give access to the four setscrews which hold the carrier plates and remove the setscrews. Remove the outer plates from the door.
19 Remove the four setscrews which hold the corners of the pulley mechanism frame to the door. Retrieve the washers which are located between the frame and the door panel.
20 Withdraw the glass carrier/pulley assembly from the door.
21 Refitting is a reversal of removal, but observe the following points.
22 When refitting the glass, have the mounting plate screws slackened and adjust the glass to obtain a $\frac{9}{32}$ in (7.0 mm) clearance between the drip rail and the glass edge. Once this clearance is obtained, fully tighten the mounting plate screws.
23 Check the door lock operation and adjust if necessary after reference to Section 28.

## 25 Front door (XJ12 and Double Six, 4-door models) – removal and refitting

1 Disconnect the battery and remove the door interior trim panel as described previously.
2 If speakers are fitted, remove the securing screws and pull the speakers forward until the leads can be disconnected.
3 Identify all other leads and disconnect them at their snap connectors. Withdraw the wiring loom through the hole in the leading edge of the door.
4 Support the door under its lower edge on jacks or a block in its fully open position.
5 Unscrew and remove the bolts which hold the door to the hinges. Lift the door from the car and recover the packing pieces.
6 If the hinges must be removed, jack up the front of the car and turn

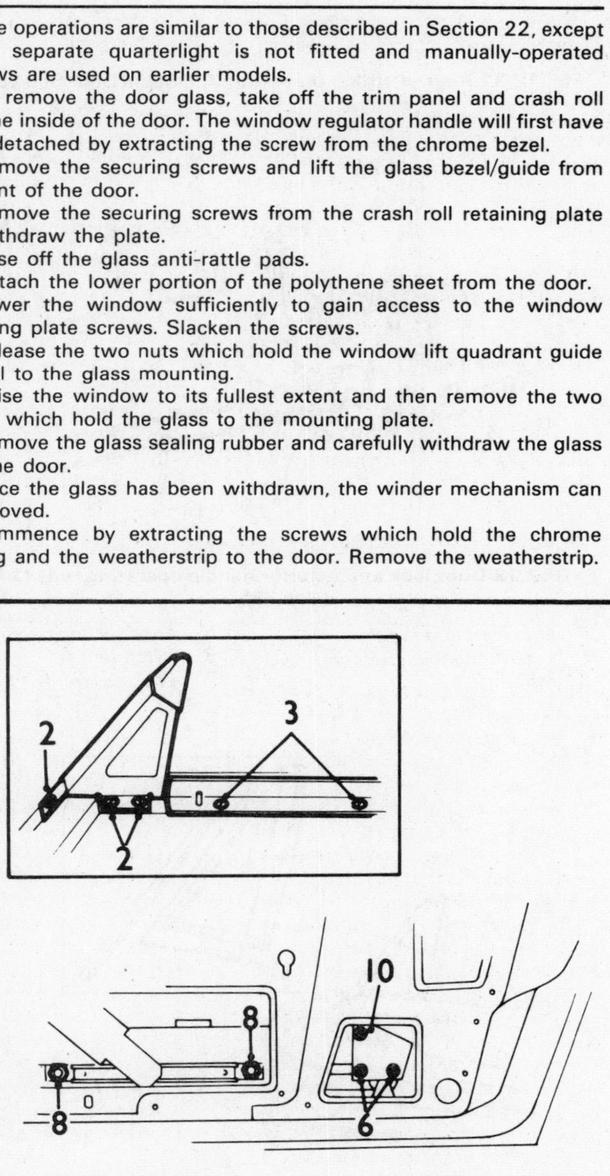


**Fig. 12.28 Door components (XJ12 and Double Six, 2-door) (Sec 24)**

- *2 Glass bezel guide screws*
- *3 Door crash roll plate screws*
- *6 Window mounting plate screws*
- *8 Window lift guide channel screws*
- *10 Screws (glass to mounting plate)*

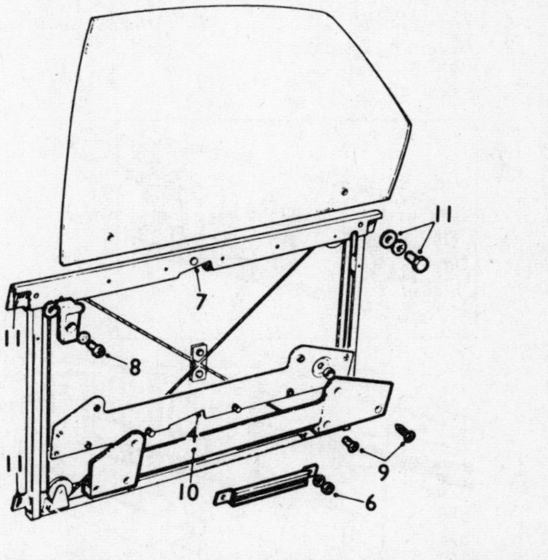


**Fig. 12.29 Window winder (XJ12 and Double Six, 2-door) (Sec 24)**

- *4 Glass carrier plate*
- *6 Guide channel to glass carrier nuts*
- *7 Spring to spigot fixing*
- *8 Nylon anti-rattle pads and screws*
- *9 Carrier plate screws*
- *10 Carrier plate*
- *11 Pulley pivot screws*

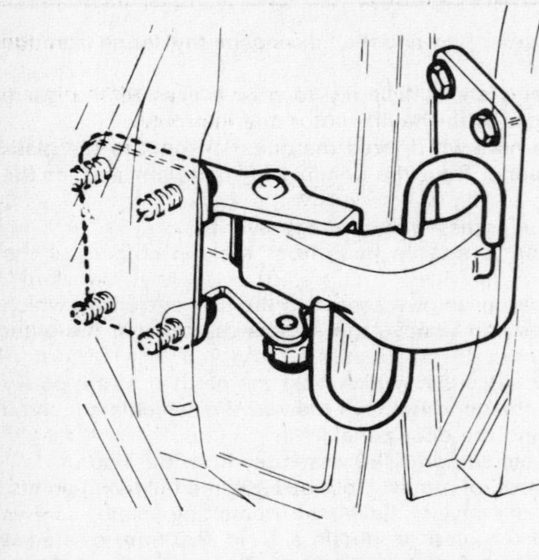

**Fig. 12.30 Door hinge (XJ12, Double Six) on front doors of 4-door models and both doors on 2-door models (Sec 25)**

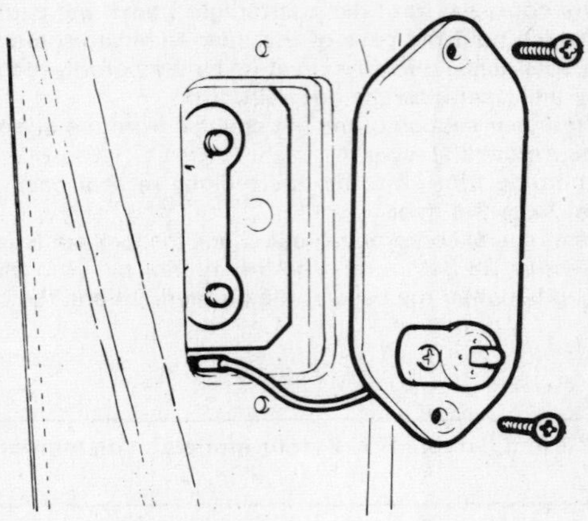

**Fig. 12.31 Rear of striker plate (XJ12, Double Six) (Sec 28)**

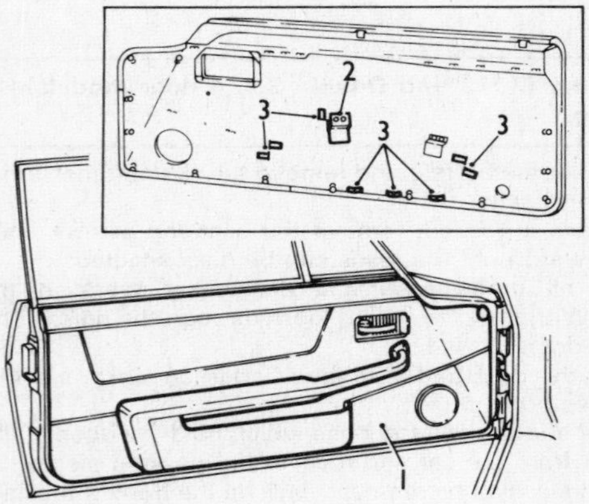


**Fig. 12.32 Door trim panel (XJS) (Sec 29)**

*1 Trim panel*
*2 Retaining bracket*
*3 Armrest securing lugs*

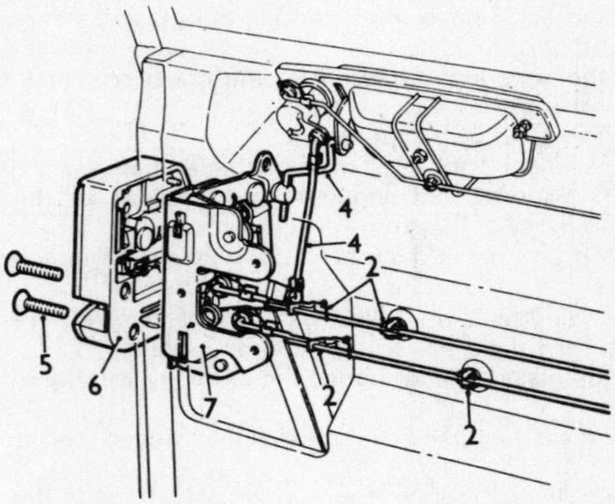


**Fig. 12.33 Door lock and exterior handle operating rods (XJS) (Sec 29)**

*2 Lock operating rods*
*4 Exterior handle operating rod*
*5 Lock securing screws*
*6 Latch unit*
*7 Lock assembly*

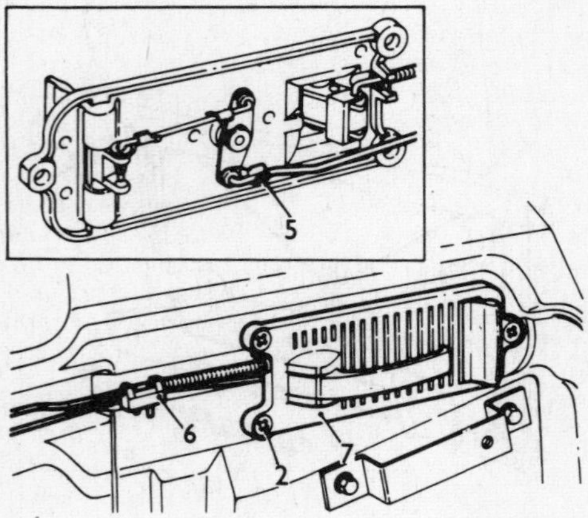


**Fig. 12.34 Door lock interior handle (XJS) (Sec 29)**

*2 Securing screws*
*5 Lock control rod and clip*
*6 Handle control rod and plastic clip*
*7 Interior handle*

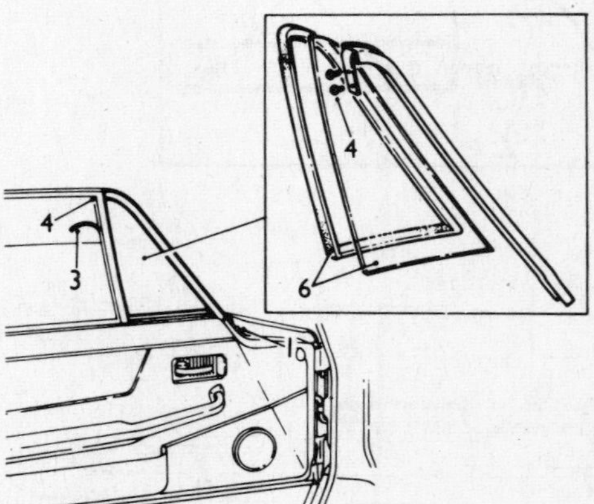


**Fig. 12.35 Front fixed quarterlight (XJS) (Sec 29)**

*1 Quarterlight fixing screws*
*3 Door glass rubber*
*4 Quarterlight fixing screws*
*6 Quarterlight glass and rubber surround*

the steering to full lock.
7 Working under the front wing, unbolt and remove the panel from the wheel arch. Remove the two bolts inside the wheel arch which hold the lower part of the wing to the sill.
8 Remove the two bolts located between the door hinges which hold the wing to the body pillar. Note the earth strap fitted under the top bolt.
9 Remove the bolts and washers which hold the top edge of the wing to the valance. Using a wedge, separate the lower part of the wing from the body.
10 The front door hinges can now be unbolted and removed from the body pillar.
11 To refit the hinges, reverse the removal operations. Seal the wheel arch panel with underseal on completion.
12 To refit the door, make sure that the earth strap is located behind one hinge bolt.
13 Do not fully tighten the hinge bolts until the door has been closed and has been set so that it is flush with adjacent body panels and the gap all around its edge is even. Open the door gently and fully tighten the bolts.
14 Reconnect all leads and refit the door trim panel.
15 Reconnect the battery.

## 26 Door (XJ12 and Double Six, 2-door models) – removal and refitting

1 The operations are identical to those described in Section 25.

## 27 Rear door (XJ12 and Double Six, 4-door models) – removal and refitting

1 Remove the door interior trim panel.
2 Disconnect the battery, identify the wiring inside the door and separate the leads at the snap connectors. Withdraw the wiring harness through the hole in the leading edge of the door.
3 Support the door in the fully open position on jacks or blocks padded with rag.
4 Unscrew and remove the bolts which hold the door to the hinges. Lift the door from the car.
5 If the hinges must be removed, simply unbolt them from the body pillar (photo).
6 When refitting the hinges, note the earth lead located under the hinge top bolt.
7 When refitting the door, do not fully tighten the hinge bolts until the door has been closed and adjusted to be flush with the adjacent body panels.

## 28 Door lock and striker (XJ12, Double Six) – adjustment

1 If the door does not open or close correctly, fails to lock when the inside handle is operated, or opens immediately the inside handle is moved, the remote control rods or their spring connections will require adjustment. Remove the door interior panel for access to the rods.
2 The door should close with little effort and close securely.
3 If necessary, release the setscrews on the striker plate and move the striker. Re-tighten the striker plate screws on completion (photo).
4 The front door striker plate can be removed completely in the following way.
5 Disconnect the battery and then remove the courtesy light switch mounting plate. Disconnect the lead at the snap connector.
6 Extract the striker plate screws and withdraw the striker assembly from the interior of the body pillar.
7 The rear door striker plate can be removed if the rear seat squab is first withdrawn (see Section 49).
8 Peel back the trim and adhesive tape which covers the striker plate access hole.
9 Unscrew and remove the striker plate screws and withdraw the striker assembly from the interior of the body pillar.
10 Refitting both striker assemblies is a reversal of removal. After adjustment, seal the edges of the striker mounting plate with suitable body sealer.

## 29 Door (XJS) – dismantling and reassembly

1 Release the armrest finisher from its spring clip.
2 Undo and remove the screw which holds the armrest to the door interior trim panel.
3 Release the two screws which hold the courtesy switch plate to the door. Pull the trim panel away from the striker plate.
4 Extract the screw which holds the bottom edge of the trim panel to the door.
5 Insert a broad blade between the trim panel and the door casing, twist the blade and release the first of the trim panel clips. Now use the fingers to release the remaining clips.
6 Pull the trim panel far enough from the door to be able to disconnect the radio speaker leads.
7 Extract the screws from the armrest retaining bracket and straighten the lugs if the armrest/pocket assembly is to be removed from the trim panel.
8 Disconnect the rods from the door lock interior handle.
9 Carefully move the waterproof sheeting to one side and disconnect the operating rods from the exterior door handle.
10 Extract the four screws which hold the outer lock unit to the door.
11 Remove the outer lock unit, followed by the inner unit.
12 The interior lock handle can be removed by extracting the three securing screws and disconnecting the control rods.
13 To remove the quarterlight, first withdraw the two screws which hold the bottom of the quarterlight front frame to the door casing.
14 Lower the door glass completely by operating the control button.
15 Ease the door glass rubber aside and remove the two screws which hold the quarterlight to the frame.
16 Withdraw the quarterlight.
17 To remove the main glass from the door, fully raise the window and extract the two screws which hold the window channel to the door.
18 Ease the rubber clear of the channel and then remove the channel.
19 Unbolt the glass stop from the base of the door.
20 Lower the glass, guiding it with the hand, and then tilt the glass foward so that the lift arm can be disconnected from it.
21 Holding the glass in the tilted position, lift it from the door.
22 Once the glass has been withdrawn, the door exterior handle can be removed. First detach the control rods and then unscrew the retaining nuts and withdraw the mounting plate.
23 Refitting of all components is a reversal of removal but on completion, adjust the lock and striker as described in Section 28.

## 30 Door (XJS) – removal and refitting

1 Open the door to the half open position and support it on jacks or blocks covered with pads of rag.
2 Remove the cover from the fuel cut-off inertia switch on the driver's door only if this door is to be removed. Release the switch from its spring clips and swing it aside.
3 Extract the two screws which hold the footwell side trim pad.
4 Remove the under scuttle casing (see Section 40).
5 Unbolt the door lock solenoid relay and ease the relay aside.
6 Disconnect the door harness electrical lead connectors, including the radio cable connector.
7 Unbolt the hinge plates from the body. With the help of an assistant, life the door from the car.
8 If the hinges must be removed, they can be unbolted from the door, but note the rubber plug on the access hole for the upper hinge.
9 Refitting is a reversal of removal, but only screw on one nut to each hinge finger-tight until the door has been closed and set so that it is flush with adjacent body panels and the gap all around its edge is of even width. Open the door gently, screw on the remaining nuts and tighten them fully.
10 Adjust the striker and lock if necessary as described in Section 28.

## 31 Rear quarterlight (XJ12 and Double Six, 2-door models) – removal and refitting

1 Remove the rear quarter trim casing and crash roll.
2 Extract the securing screws and remove the crash roll mounting from the quarter panel.
3 Peel away the waterproof sheeting.
4 Unbolt and remove the glass buffer from the quarter panel.
5 Lower the glass to the half open position and support it in this position.

4 Remove the four self-tapping screws which secure the air outlet duct in the right-hand footwell.
5 Remove the three self-tapping screws which secure the duct assembly in the right-hand footwell and at the rear outlet. One of these screws is located behind the control mounting panel and needs the use of a right-angled crosshead screwdriver.
6 Set the temperature control knob in the vent position, loosen the flap link operating rod locknut on the main drive wheel. Remove the nut and washer from the pivot of the main drive wheel.
7 Lift the jockey pulleys against the tension of the springs and withdraw the main drive wheel from its pivot.
8 Ease the radio/heater control panel and the right-hand footwell outlet assembly away from the heater.
9 Disconnect the control cable.
10 When refitting the cable, wind it round the main drive wheel $2\frac{1}{2}$ times. Make sure that the cable can be locked to the bollard on the wheel by the washer under the locking screw, but do not tighten it at this stage.
11 Set the temperature control at the 10 o'clock position and locate the cable round the jockey pulleys in such a way that the upper strand of the cable leaves the bollard and passes round the forward pulley. Pull the ends of the cable as far as possible horizontally and then adjust the cable until the nipples are level with each other.
12 Tighten the bollard locking screw and fit the cable end nipples into the main driving wheel, making sure that the ends of the cable do not cross.
13 Refit the radio/heater control panel and the footwell outlet assembly.
14 Keeping the cable taut, refit the main driving wheel to the pivot and screw on the nut and washer.
15 The flap linkage should be adjusted as described in the next Section.
16 Complete the refitting by reversing the rest of the removal operations.

## 59 Heater flap linkage (XJ12 and Double Six, Series 2 on) – adjustment

1 Turn the temperature control knob to vent.
2 Refer to Fig. 12.64 and slacken the locking screws 'A', 'B' and 'C'.
3 Turn the lever 'R' to a fully clockwise position and hold in this position using firm finger-pressure. Tighten locking screw 'A'.
4 Press flap 'N' to a fully clockwise position and tighten locking screw 'C'.
5 Turn the temperature control knob to defrost. Using a screwdriver engaged in the slotted end of the adjusting link, push the operating flap 'Q' fully clockwise and tighten lockscrew 'B'.
6 The eccentric pivot 'T' on the upper flap actuating cam is adjustable through 180° to vary the level of face level air temperature.

## 60 Heater air grilles (XJ12 and Double Six, Series 2) – removal and refitting

### *Demister duct outlets*

1 These can be removed by levering them from their surround.
2 Refit by pressing firmly into place.

### *Demister flap and actuator*

3 Remove the crash roll from the facia (Section 38).
4 Remove the two nuts which secure the flap assembly to the screen rail.
5 Disconnect the plastic ducting and the vacuum tube and lift the flap/actuator assembly from the screen rail.
6 Refitting is a reversal of removal.

### *Ventilator facia outlets*

7 Disconnect the battery.
8 Remove the facia (Section 38).
9 Unclip the side outlets at the rear of the facia or remove the four securing screws from the centre outlet.
10 Refitting is a reversal of removal.

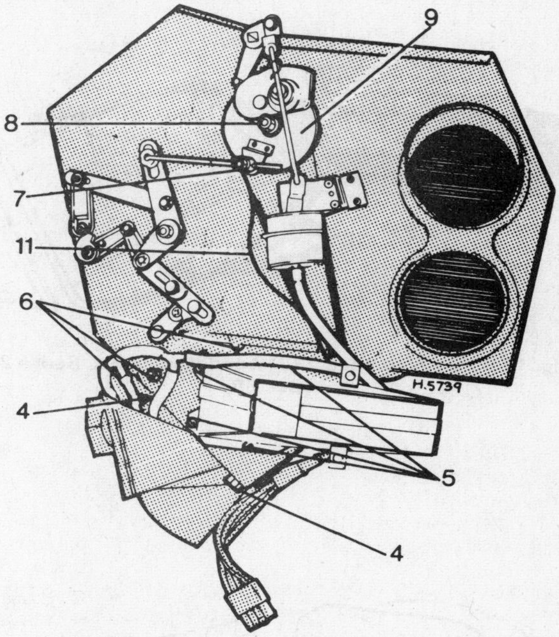


**Fig. 12.63 Heater temperature control cable assembly (XJ12 and Double Six, Series 2 on) (Sec 58)**

*4 Control panel to heater securing unit*
*5 Footwell air outlet duct screws*
*6 Rear air outlet screws*
*7 Flap link rod nut*
*8 Drive wheel pivot nut*
*9 Main drive wheel*
*11 Temperature control cable*

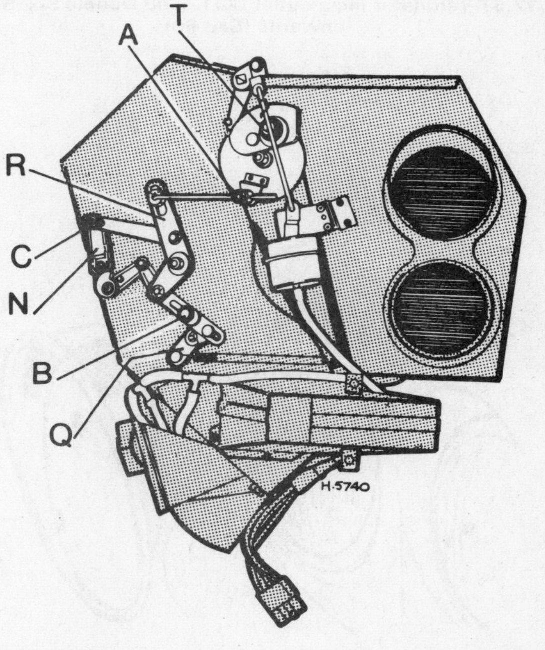


**Fig. 12.64 Heater flap linkage (XJ12 and Double Six, Series 2 on) (Sec 59)**

*A Locking screw*
*B Locking screw*
*C Locking screw*
*N Lever operating flap*
*Q Lever operating flap*
*R Lever*
*T Eccentric pivot*

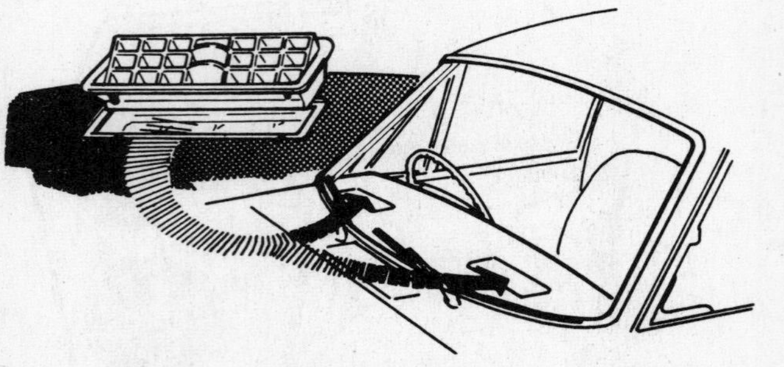

Fig. 12.65 Demister duct (XJ12 and Double Six, Series 2 on) (Sec 60)

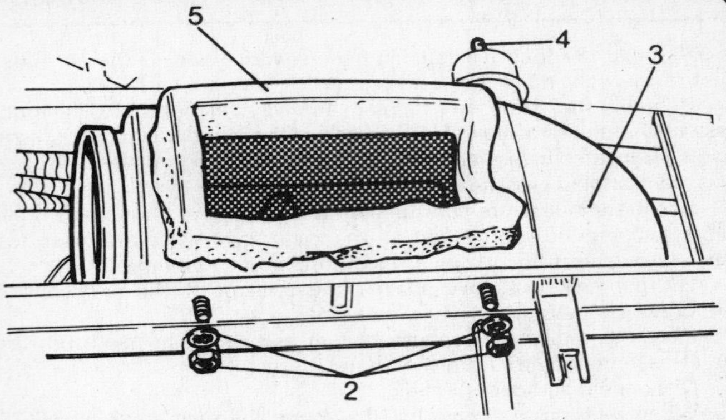


Fig. 12.66 Demister flap and actuator (XJ12 and Double Six, Series 2 on) (Sec 60)

*2 • Securing nuts to screen rail*
*3 Plastic ducting*
*4 Vacuum tube connection on actuator*
*5 Flap assembly*

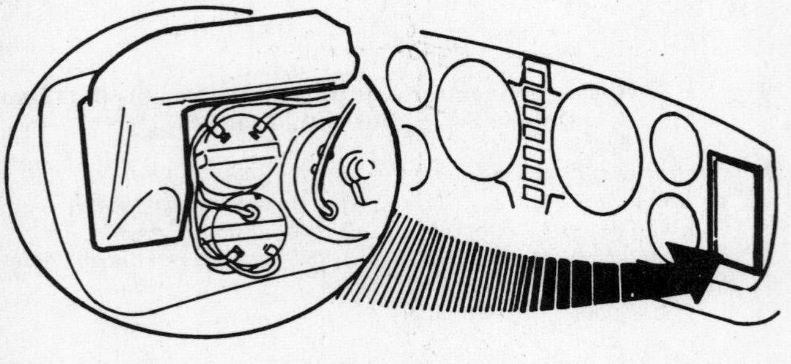

Fig. 12.67 Ventilator facia outlet (XJ12 and Double Six, Series 2 onwards (Sec 60)

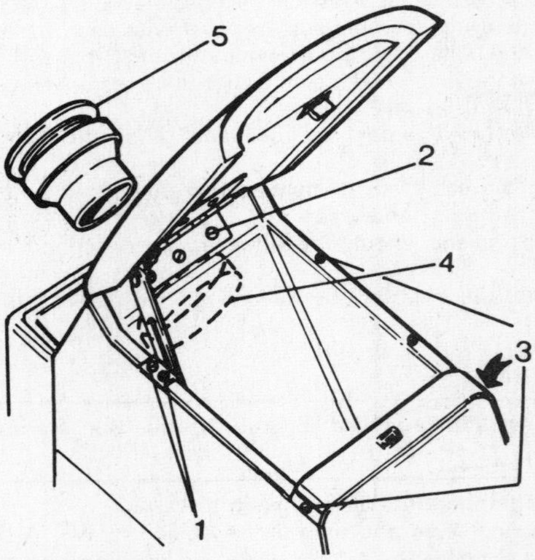


Fig. 12.68 Rear ventilator (XJ12 and Double Six, Series 2 on) (Sec 60)

*1 Lid retaining bar screws*
*2 Hinge plate screws*
*3 Liner screws*
*4 Air vent locking ring*
*5 Air vent assembly*

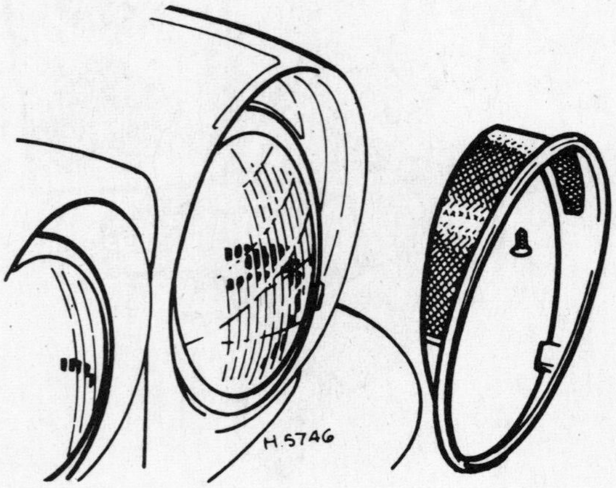


Fig. 12.69 Fresh air intake on outer headlamp (Sec 60)

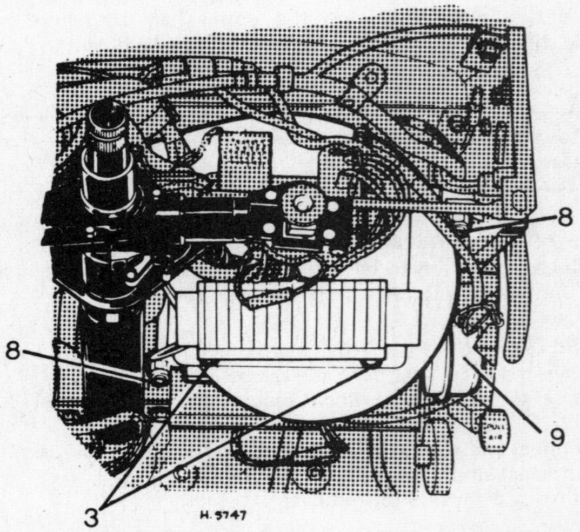


Fig. 12.70 Heater motor mounting (XJ12 and Double Six, Series 2 on) (Sec 61)

*3 Fuse block mounting nuts*
*8 Heater motor assembly mounting nuts*
*9 Vacuum actuator*

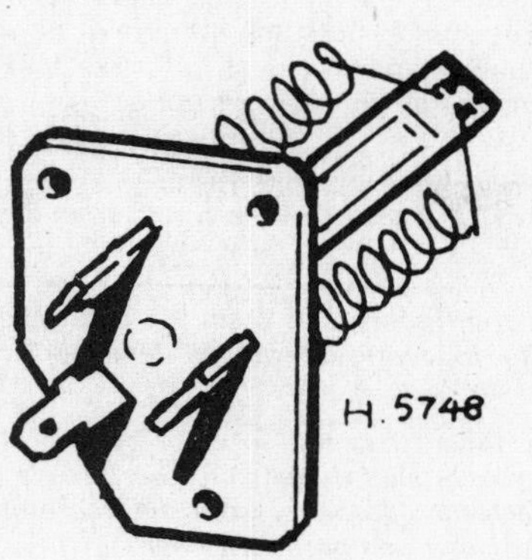


**Fig. 12.71 Heater motor resistor (XJ12 and Double Six, Series 2 on) (Sec 62)**

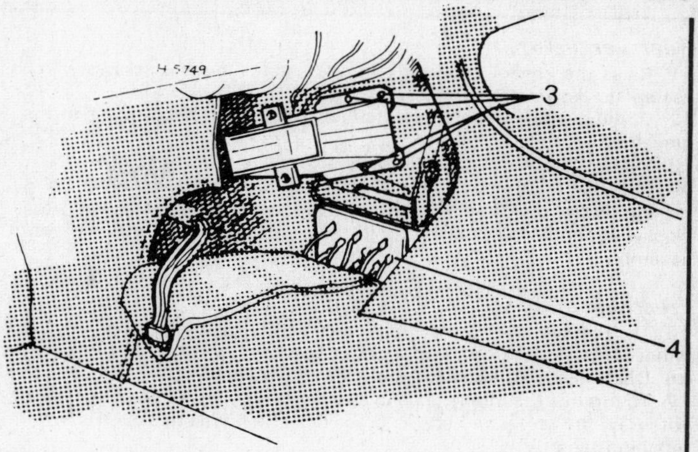


**Fig. 12.72 Location of heater motor relays (XJ12 and Double Six, Series 2 on) (Sec 63)**

*3 Footwell air outlet* *4 Heater relay*

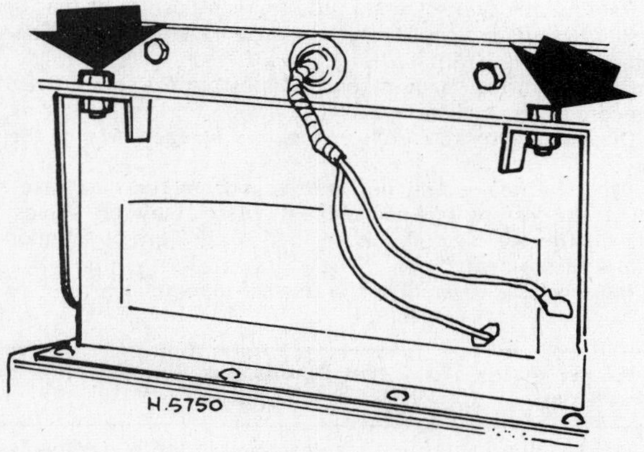


**Fig. 12.73 Heater securing nuts on bulkhead (arrowed) (Sec 64)**

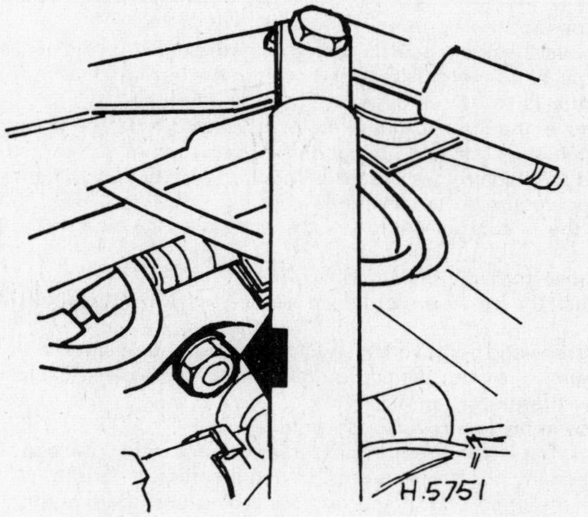


**Fig. 12.74 Heater securing nuts on top rail (XJ12 and Double Six, Series 2 on) (Sec 64)**

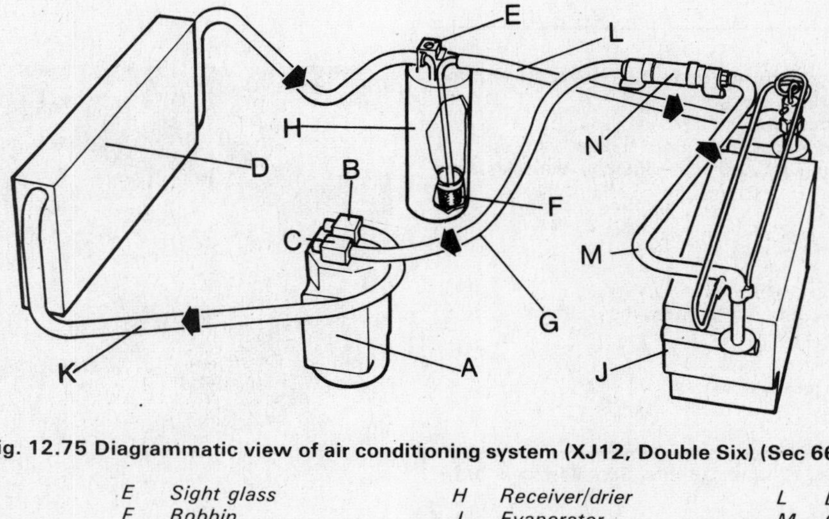


**Fig. 12.75 Diagrammatic view of air conditioning system (XJ12, Double Six) (Sec 66)**

*A Compressor*
*B Discharge valve*
*C Suction valve*
*D Condensor*
*E Sight glass*
*F Bobbin*
*G Dessicant*
*H Receiver/drier*
*J Evaporator*
*K Hot vapour line*
*L Liquid*
*M Cold vapour line*
*N Heat exchanger (fuel)*

*Rear ventilator*

11 Raise the console glovebox lid and extract the two screws which secure the lid retaining bar.
12 Withdraw the three screws which secure the hinge plate to the glovebox.
13 Extract the three screws which secure the glovebox liner.
14 Pass the hand under the glovebox liner and grip the bayonet type locking ring of the air vent assembly. Press in and rotate the vent anticlockwise until the locking ring releases. Withdraw the air vent assembly.

*Fresh air intakes*

15 To remove the grille from the scuttle just in front of the windscreen, prise it out with a sharp screwdriver.
16 Disconnect the washer tube from the washer jet.
17 To remove the intake grille located above the outer headlamp lens, withdraw the screw and lift the embellisher upwards to clear the lower retaining tags.
18 Refitting is a reversal of removal.

## 61 Heater motor/fan unit (XJ12 and Double Six, Series 2 on) – removal and refitting

1 Disconnect the battery.
2 Remove the under scuttle casing from the right-hand side if access to the right-hand motor is required or from the left-hand side if the left-hand motor is to be removed.
3 Remove the fusebox and move it to one side, or alternatively remove the glovebox liner, dependent upon whether the car is LHD or RHD and to which motor access is required. Inspection will enable the correct procedure to be adopted.
4 Pull the pliable air duct from the outlets at the side of the heater unit.
5 Remove the side facia panels.
6 Extract the two screws which secure the fresh air outlet control bracket.
7 Unscrew and remove the two motor mounting nuts, disconnect the vacuum tube from the actuator, disconnect the electrical leads and withdraw the motor/fan assembly.
8 Reassembly is a reversal of removal but the top air flap should be closed so that it can enter into its aperture and seal. To close the flap apply vacuum to the actuator by connecting a length of tubing between the open end of the original tubing and the actuator.

## 62 Heater motor resistance unit (XJ12 and Double Six, Series 2 on) – removal and refitting

*Left-hand drive cars*

1 Disconnect the battery and remove the facia under scuttle casing from the driver's side.
2 Remove the side panel from the centre console.
3 Mark the cables and disconnect them from the resistance unit.
4 Remove the three securing screws and withdraw the resistance unit from the heater casing.

*Right-hand drive cars*

5 Disconnect the battery.
6 Remove the glove compartment liner.
7 Repeat the operations described in paragraphs 3 and 4.

*All cars*

8 Refitting is a reversal of removal.

## 63 Heater motor relays (XJ12 and Double Six, Series 2 on) – removal and refitting

1 Disconnect the battery.
2 Remove the left-hand side casing from the centre console.
3 Remove the left-hand air outlet duct (four screws) from the footwell.
4 Mark the electrical leads and disconnect them.
5 Remove the securing nuts and withdraw the relay unit.
6 Refitting is a reversal of removal, but make sure that the earth lead is secured under one of the relay securing nuts.

## 64 Heater unit (XJ12 and Double Six, Series 2 on) – removal and refitting

1 Disconnect the battery and drain the cooling system.
2 Carry out the following operations described in other Sections of this Chapter:

*Remove the facia crash roll.*
*Remove the facia side panel from the driver's side.*
*Remove the facia side panel from the passenger's side.*
*Remove the glove compartment liner.*
*Remove the centre parcels shelf.*
*Remove the centre console.*
*Remove the facia panel.*

3 Disconnect the heater hoses from the nozzles on the engine compartment rear bulkhead.
4 Remove the two large nuts from the centre of the bulkhead within the engine compartment.
5 Remove the two retaining nuts from the centre of the top rail.
6 Remove the bayonet fixing type stub pipes from the sides of the heater unit.
7 Disconnect the vacuum control tubes but first mark them clearly for reconnection (photo).
8 Disconnect the multi-pin connectors at each side of the heater unit.
9 Ease the heater unit out and lift it from the car. Take care to protect the carpet against coolant which may be spilled during removal. The gearlever should be in '1' to prevent obstruction during removal of the heater.
10 Refitting is a reversal of the removal operations.

## 65 Heater matrix (XJ12 and Double Six, Series 2 on) – removal and refitting

1 Remove the heater unit, as described in the preceding Section.
2 Using a quick drying paint, mark the relative positions of all the heater control rods, knobs and cams.
3 Disconnect the tensioning springs from the heater matrix control flap operating arms.
4 Disconnect the operating rods.
5 Disconnect the inlet and outlet pipes from the heater casing.
6 Remove the heater matrix cover plate (six screws).

64.7 Heater vacuum control valve on engine compartment rear bulkhead

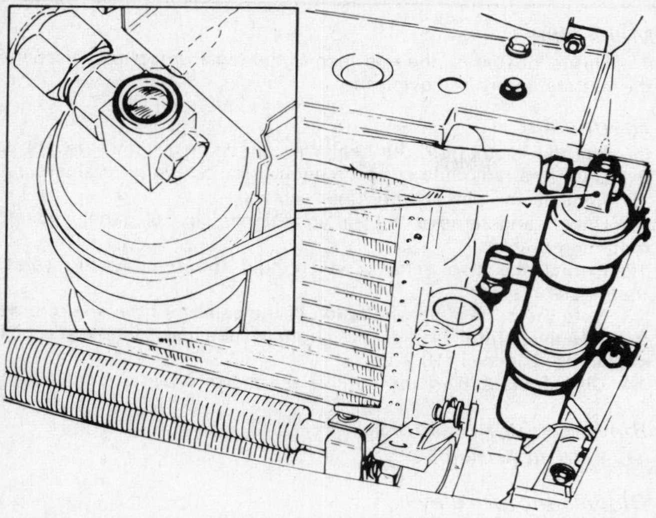

**Fig. 12.76 Receiver/dryer unit (XJ12 and Double Six, Sereis 1) (Sec 67)**

**Fig. 12.77 Blower motor power relay (XJ12 and Double Six, Series 1) (Sec 67)**

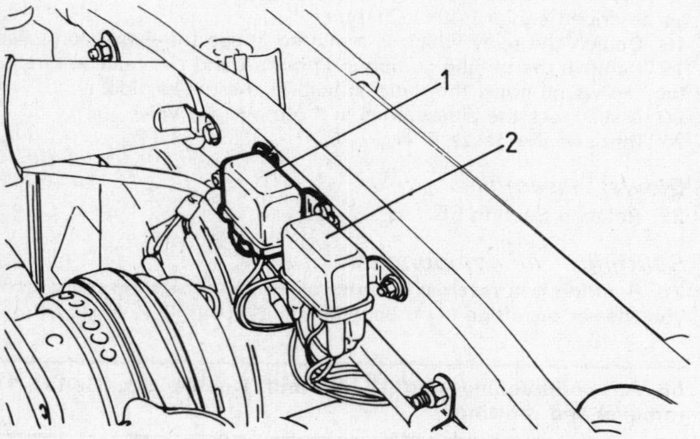


**Fig. 12.78 Air conditioner main relay (XJ12 and Double Six, Series 1) (Sec 67)**

1 *Air conditioner relay* 2 *Headlamp relay*

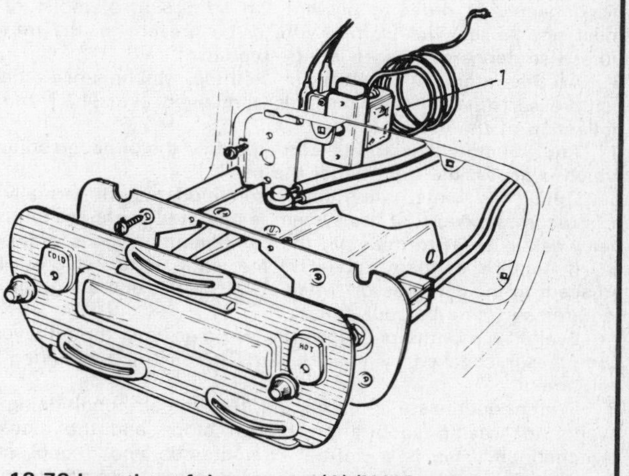


**Fig. 12.79 Location of thermostat (1) (XJ12 and Double Six, Series 1) (Sec 67)**

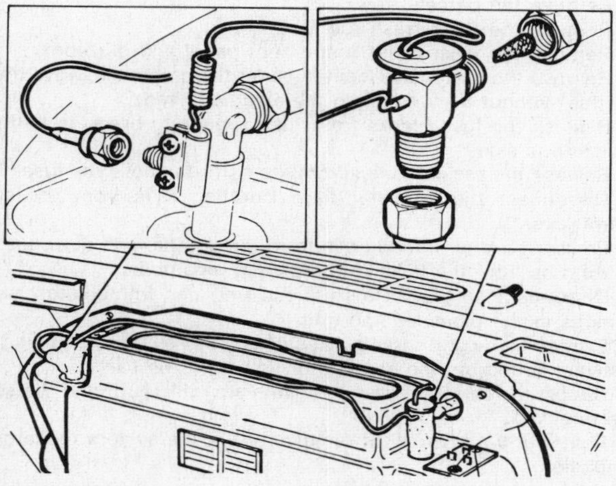

**Fig. 12.80 Location of expansion valve (XJ12 and Double six, Series 1) (Sec 67)**

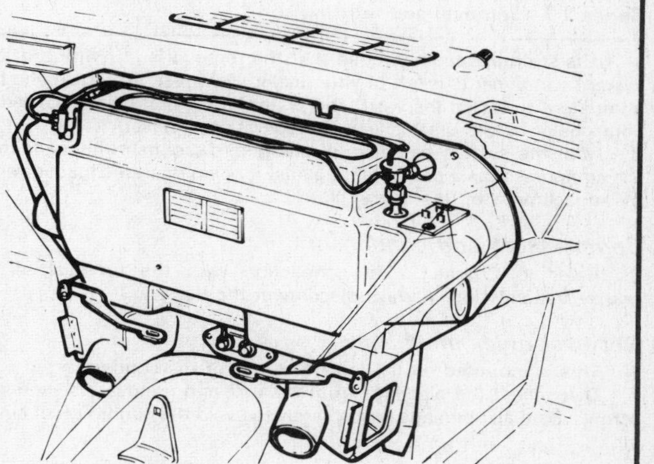

**Fig. 12.81 Air conditioner (XJ12 and Double Six, Series 1) (Sec 68)**

7 Remove the single screw which secures the cam and the operating arm to the footwell outlet flap shaft and remove the arm.
8 Withdraw the heater matrix from the side of the heater casing using a steady pull.
9 If the matrix has been leaking, do not waste your time trying to solder it as the heat must be localised otherwise more damage will be caused. It is better to renew the matrix on an exchange basis. If the matrix is blocked, try reverse flushing with a cold water hose. In extreme cases use a proprietary descaler and cleanser. If this fails, renew the matrix.
10 Refitting is a reversal of removal, but make sure that the shock absorbing pads are correctly positioned and that the control rods are connected with their paint marks in alignment.

## 66 Air conditioning system (XJ12, Double Six) – maintenance

1 This is a factory-fitted option and operations must be restricted to those described in the following Sections. On no account disconnect any part of the system as the gases and chemicals contained in the circuit can cause injury if released. If it is essential to remove one of the system components in order to gain access to other parts or assemblies always have the air conditioning system discharged and later recharged by your Jaguar/Daimler dealer or a professional refrigeration engineer.
2 Always seal pipes and components immediately the joints are disconnected in order to prevent the admission of moisture which must not be allowed to mix with, or be present in, the refrigerant, otherwise dangerous gases will be produced.
3 At the intervals specified in Routine Maintenance check the compressor drivebelt tension. This should be $\frac{1}{2}$ in (12.7 mm) total deflection at the centre of the belt.
4 Any adjustment should be carried out on the threaded adjuster rod which is accessible from under the car.
5 During the winter when the air conditioner is not normally in use, it is recommended that the system is operated for about ten minutes per week in order to maintain the components in good order.
6 If bubbles or foam appear in the sight glass (which is located adjacent to the compressor) when the system is operating, the system requires servicing by your dealer.
7 Every 12 months or before the summer have the oil level in the compressor checked by your dealer. This is a job requiring special equipment.
8 Water condensate is discharged from the air-conditioning system evaporator casing soon after the car stops and the blowers are switched off. This is a normal characterstic and a pool of water observed under cars fitted with these systems need cause no alarm.

## 67 Air conditioning system components (XJ12 and Double Six, Series 1 ) – removal and refitting

1 It is strongly recommended that the removal and refitting of any system components is left to your dealer. However, for those who feel competent to tackle the work, the system must first be discharged by your dealer before undertaking the operations marked *.
2 After the system has been discharged, disconnect the leads from the compressor as a precaution against it being operated inadvertently by engagement of its integral clutch.

### *Compressor* and condensor**

3 Refer to Chapter 1 in connection with the removal of the engine/transmission. Always disconnect the battery.

### *Receiver/dryer unit**

4 This is mounted on the left-hand side of the condensor.
5 Disconnect the pipelines from the unit and remove the mounting screws. Seal all openings immediately to avoid the admission of humid air.

### *Blower motor power relay*

6 The location of the relay is as shown. Disconnect the battery before removing it. Remove the facia crash roll and the centre instrument panel when removing the override relay.

### *Main relay*

7 This is located on the rear face of the radiator top rail. Disconnect the battery before removing it.

### *Thermostat*

8 Pull the knobs from the heater/air conditioner control levers.
9 Lever the radio/heater escutcheon from its spring retainers.
10 Remove the parcels tray (four screws).
11 Unbolt and remove the air conditioner control panel and radio mounting bracket.
12 Extract the two screws which hold the temperature selector thermostatic switch.
13 Note the pattern of installation of the capillary tube and remove it from the evaporator casing. The length of tube inserted into the casing should be 4 inches (10.2 cm).
14 Disconnect cables and remove the thermostat.

### *Blower motor resistors*

15 Refer to Section 55.

### *Blower motor relays*

16 These are located adjacent to the power relay described in paragraph 6.

### *Expansion valve**

17 Remove the facia crash roll, the facia side panel and the glovebox as described earlier in this Chapter.
18 Detach the relay which is mounted above the expansion valve.
19 Remove the sealing compound from around the valve and release the clip which holds the thermal bulb to the outlet pipe.
20 Disconnect the pipe unions and remove the valve.
21 Retrieve the gauze filter.

### *Blower assemblies*

22 Refer to Section 55.

### *Refitting – all components*

23 Refitting is a reversal of removal. Have the system recharged by your dealer or refrigeration engineer.

## 68 Air conditioning unit (XJ12 and Double Six, Series 1) – removal and refitting

1 Have the system discharged by your dealer or a refrigeration engineer.
2 Disconnect the battery.
3 Remove the front seats.
4 Remove the radio/heater control knobs and the escutcheon panel.
5 Remove the centre console.
6 Remove the parcels tray.
7 Remove the facia crash roll.
8 Remove the facia panel, instrument panel and glovebox.
9 Remove the two relays located under the crash roll. Move them to one side without disconnecting the electrical leads.
10 Release the fuse blocks from their mounting brackets and move them to one side.
11 Release the securing clips from the harness above the fuse blocks.
12 Disconnect the demister flap operating rods from the central control lever.
13 Prise out the air intake grille from the scuttle, and disconnect the control rods from the lever in the plenum chamber.
14 Disconnect all pipelines from the unit and immediately seal all openings in the pipelines and unit.
15 Extract the eight screws which hold the evaporator unit to the bulkhead. Withdraw the evaporator unit from the car.
16 Ducts may be removed if the rivets are drilled out and the sealing tape removed.
17 Refitting is a reversal of removal. Have the system recharged on completion.

## 69 Air conditioning system components (XJ12 and Double Six, Series 2 on) – removal and refitting

1 Refer to paragraph 1 of Section 67. If you are determined to work

on the air conditioning system, it must be discharged by your dealer or by a qualified refrigeration engineer before removing any component below marked*. Disconnect the leads from the compressor after discharging the system to prevent inadvertent operation.

### *Compressor* and condensor**

2 Refer to Chapter 1 in connection with the removal of the engine/transmission. Always disconnect the battery.

### *Receiver/drier unit**

3 The unit is located in front of the radiator top rail.
4 Disconnect the pipelines from the unit and remove the mounting screws. Seal the openings in the unit and the pipelines immediately.

### *Blower assembly*

5 Refer to Section 61 and carry out the operations described. Additionally disconnect the electrical leads from the ambient temperature sensor.

### *In-car temperature sensor*

6 Remove the centre parcels tray.
7 Disconnect the leads and air tube and extract the two sensor mounting screws.

### *Ambient temperature sensor*

8 Remove the right-hand blower motor assembly (Section 61) and remove the sensor from the blower motor.

### *Blower motor power relay and relay box*

9 Remove the left-hand front side panel from the centre console by removing the footwell air outlet grille (two screws).
10 Pull the relay directly downward from its mounting block.
11 The adjacent relay box can be unbolted and removed after extracting the connecting leads. Note the earth strap under one of the mounting nuts.
12 On later models, a four-way relay unit is fitted.

### *Temperature and mode selectors*

13 Pull the knobs from the levers and remove the radio escutcheon panel.
14 Remove the centre console (Section 46).
15 Unbolt the selector mounting bracket from the heater/cooler unit. Identify and disconnect the vacuum pipes when removing the mode selector.
16 Disconnect the electrical leads. Note the location of the nylon limit stop and remove it from the operating shank.
17 Unbolt and remove the selector from its mounting when removing the temperature selector. Remove the switches in pairs.

### *Thermostat*

18 Remove the right-hand front side panel from the centre console.
19 Remove the right-hand underscuttle casing.
20 Unbolt the thermostat from its bracket on the heater/cooler unit. Identify and disconnect the electrical leads.
21 Remove the thermostat by gently pulling the capillary tube.

### *Blower motor resistor units*

22 Refer to Section 62.

### *Water valve temperature switch*

23 Remove the under scuttle casing from the left-hand side of the car, also the glovebox liner from right-hand drive cars.
24 Identify and disconnect the electrical leads from the switch and then extract the switch mounting screws.

### *Water valve*

25 Refer to Section 54 of this Chapter.

### *Expansion valve*

26 Working within the engine compartment release the clip which holds the thermal bulb to the outlet pipe.
27 Disconnect the hose unions and seal the openings.
28 Remove the valve by unscrewing the union nut. Renew the mesh filter.

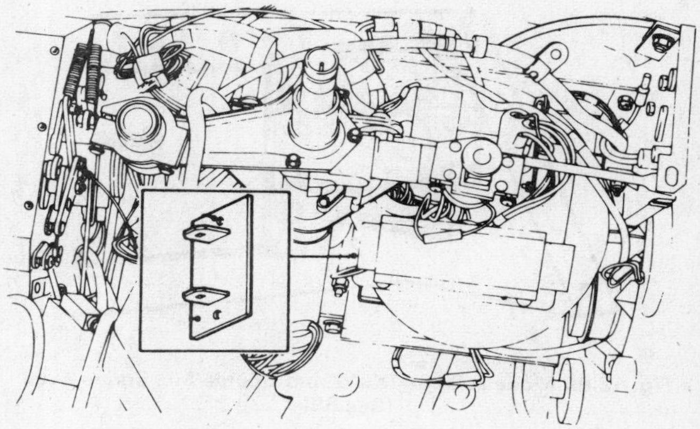

**Fig. 12.82 In-car temperature sensor (XJ12 and Double Six, Series 2 on) (Sec 69)**

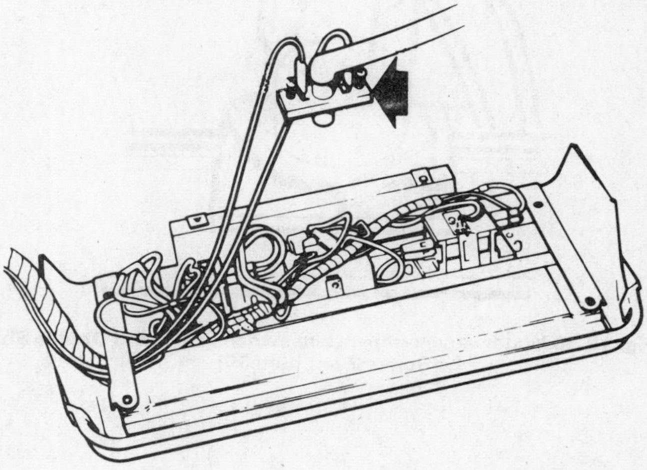

**Fig. 12.83 Ambient temperature sensor (arrowed) (XJ12 and Double Six, Series 2 on) (Sec 69)**

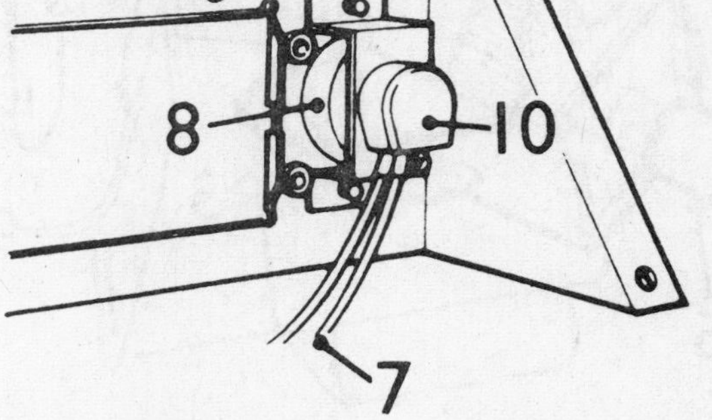


**Fig. 12.84 Temperature selector (XJ12 and Double Six, Series 2 onwards) (Sec 69)**

*7 Leads*
*8 Nylon limit stop*
*10 Temperature selector*

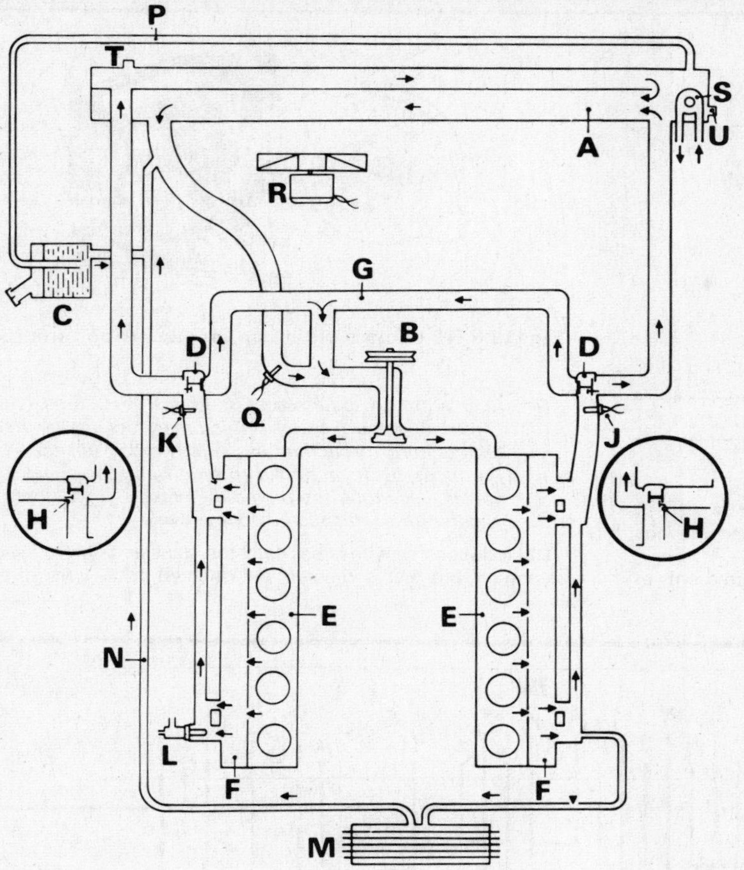


**Fig. 13.5 Cooling system, 1980 on (not HE) (Sec 4)**

- *A* *Radiator*
- *B* *Coolant pump*
- *C* *Remote type expansion tank*
- *D* *Thermostats*
- *E* *Cylinder block*
- *F* *Cylinder head*
- *G* *Coolant crosspipe*
- *H* *Jiggle pins*
- *J* *Thermotime switch*
- *K* *Coolant temperature sensor*
- *L* *Auxiliary air valve*
- *M* *Heater matrix*
- *N* *Coolant pipe*
- *P* *Coolant pipe*
- *Q* *Thermostatic switch and*
- *R* *Radiator cooling fan (electric)*
- *S* *Transmission fluid cooler*
- *T* *Bleed screw*
- *U* *Drain top*

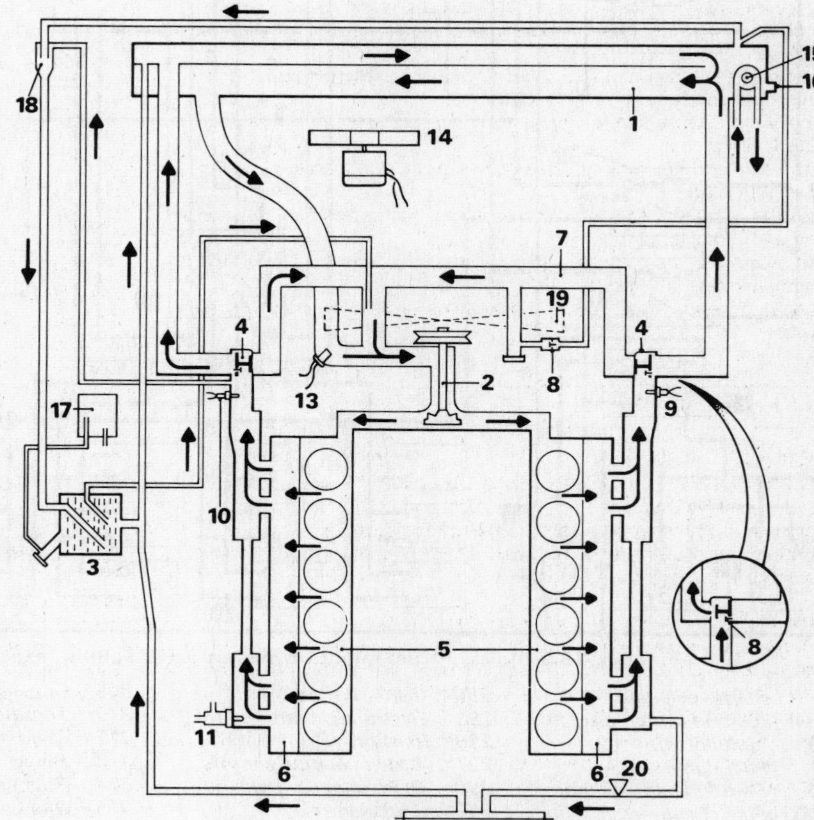


**Fig. 13.6 Cooling system – HE engine (Sec 4)**

1. *Radiator*
2. *Coolant pump*
3. *Remote type expansion tank*
4. *Thermostat*
5. *Cylinder block*
6. *Cylinder head*
7. *Coolant crosspipe*
8. *Jiggle pins*
9. *Thermotime switch*
10. *Coolant temperature sensor*
11. *Auxiliary air valve*
12. *Heater matrix*
13. *Thermostatic fan switch*
14. *Radiator cooling fan (electric)*
15. *Transmission fluid cooler*
16. *Radiator drain tap*
17. *Atmospheric catchment tank*
18. *Venting jet*
19. *Belt driven fan*
20. *Heater coolant control valve*

**Fig. 13.7 HE coolant filler cap on engine (Sec 4)**

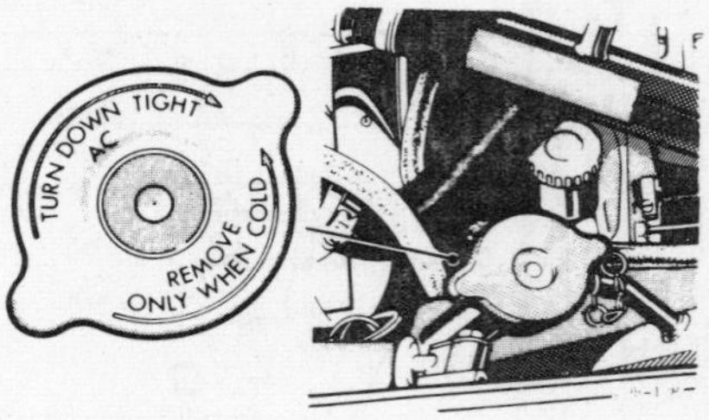


**Fig. 13.8 HE coolant filler cap on expansion tank (Sec 4)**

## 5 Fuel injection

### *Fuel injection system (1981 on) – description*

1 From 1981, the fuel injection system fitted to all models, except those marketed in Australia, Japan and some North American versions is of electronic, Digital P pressure-sensing type.

2 The system is divided into two sub-systems interconnected only at the injectors. They are:

*(i) Fuel supply, pressurised at 36.25 lbf/in² (2.5 bar)*

*(ii) Electronic control system which monitors engine load, speed, temperature, induction air and throttle position and then produces electrical pulses to hold open the injector solenoid valves just enough to permit the precise quantity of fuel to be ejected for each specific engine cycle.*

3 The induction system is basically the same as fitted to a carburettor type engine, but fuel is injected and directed at the back of each inlet valve.

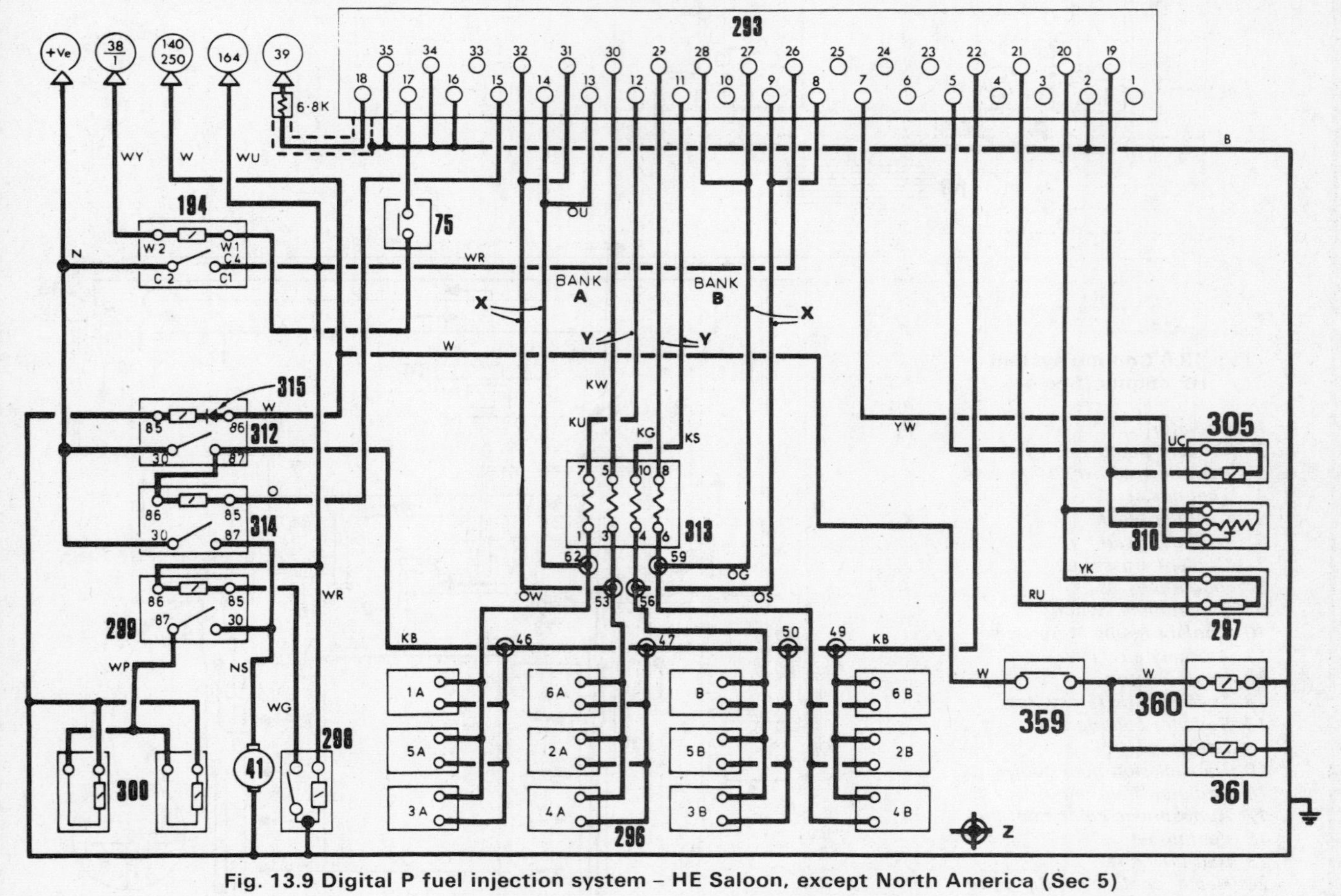


**Fig. 13.9 Digital P fuel injection system – HE Saloon, except North America (Sec 5)**

| | | | | | | | |
|---|---|---|---|---|---|---|---|
| *4* | *Starter solenoid* | *250* | *Inertia switch* | *305* | *Coolant sensor* | *360* | *Vacuum changeover switch* |
| *38/1* | *Ignition switch pin (1)* | *293* | *Electronic control unit (ECU)* | *310* | *Throttle potentiometer* | *361* | *Supplemetary air valve* |
| *39* | *Ignition coil* | *296* | *Injectors* | *312* | *Main relay* | *X* | *Turn on* |
| *41* | *Fuel pump* | *297* | *Air temperature sensors* | *313* | *Power resistors* | *Y* | *Hold on* |
| *75* | *Start inhibitor switch* | *298* | *Thermotime switch* | *314* | *Pump relay* | *Z* | *Part of ten-way engine harness* |
| *140* | *Fuel change-over switch* | *299* | *Cold start relay* | *315* | *Block diode* | | |
| *164* | *Ballast resistor* | *300* | *Cold start injectors* | *359* | *Oil temperature switch* | | |
| *194* | *Starter relay* | | | | | | |

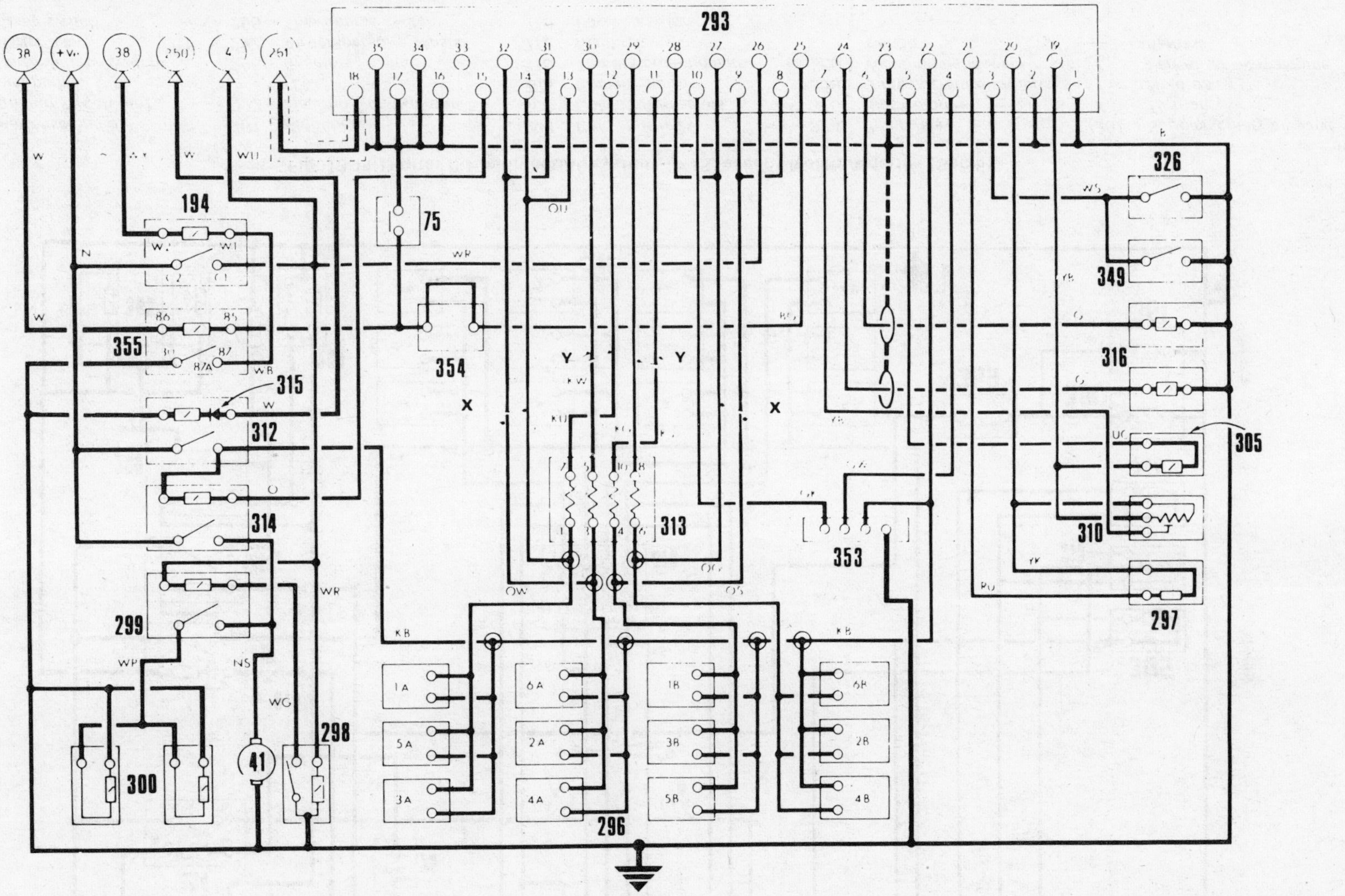

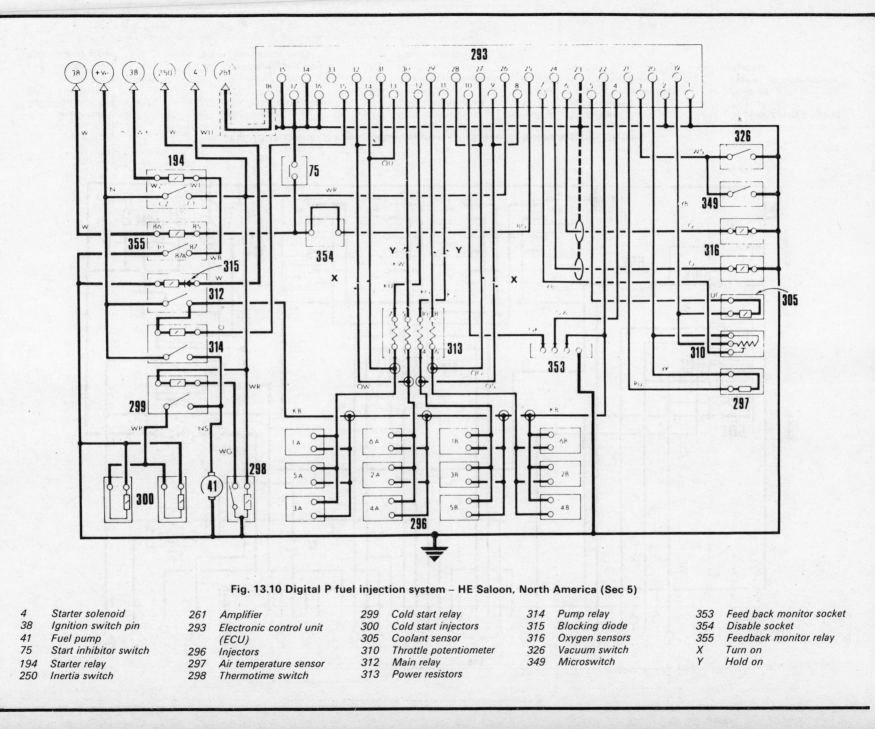

**Fig. 13.10 Digital P fuel injection system – HE Saloon, North America (Sec 5)**

| | |
|---|---|
| 4 | Starter solenoid |
| 38 | Ignition switch pin |
| 41 | Fuel pump |
| 75 | Start inhibitor switch |
| 194 | Starter relay |
| 250 | Inertia switch |
| 261 | Amplifier |
| 293 | Electronic control unit (ECU) |
| 296 | Injectors |
| 297 | Air temperature sensor |
| 298 | Thermotime switch |
| 299 | Cold start relay |
| 300 | Cold start injectors |
| 305 | Coolant sensor |
| 310 | Throttle potentiometer |
| 312 | Main relay |
| 313 | Power resistors |
| 314 | Pump relay |
| 315 | Blocking diode |
| 316 | Oxygen sensors |
| 326 | Vacuum switch |
| 349 | Microswitch |
| 353 | Feed back monitor socket |
| 354 | Disable socket |
| 355 | Feedback monitor relay |
| X | Turn on |
| Y | Hold on |

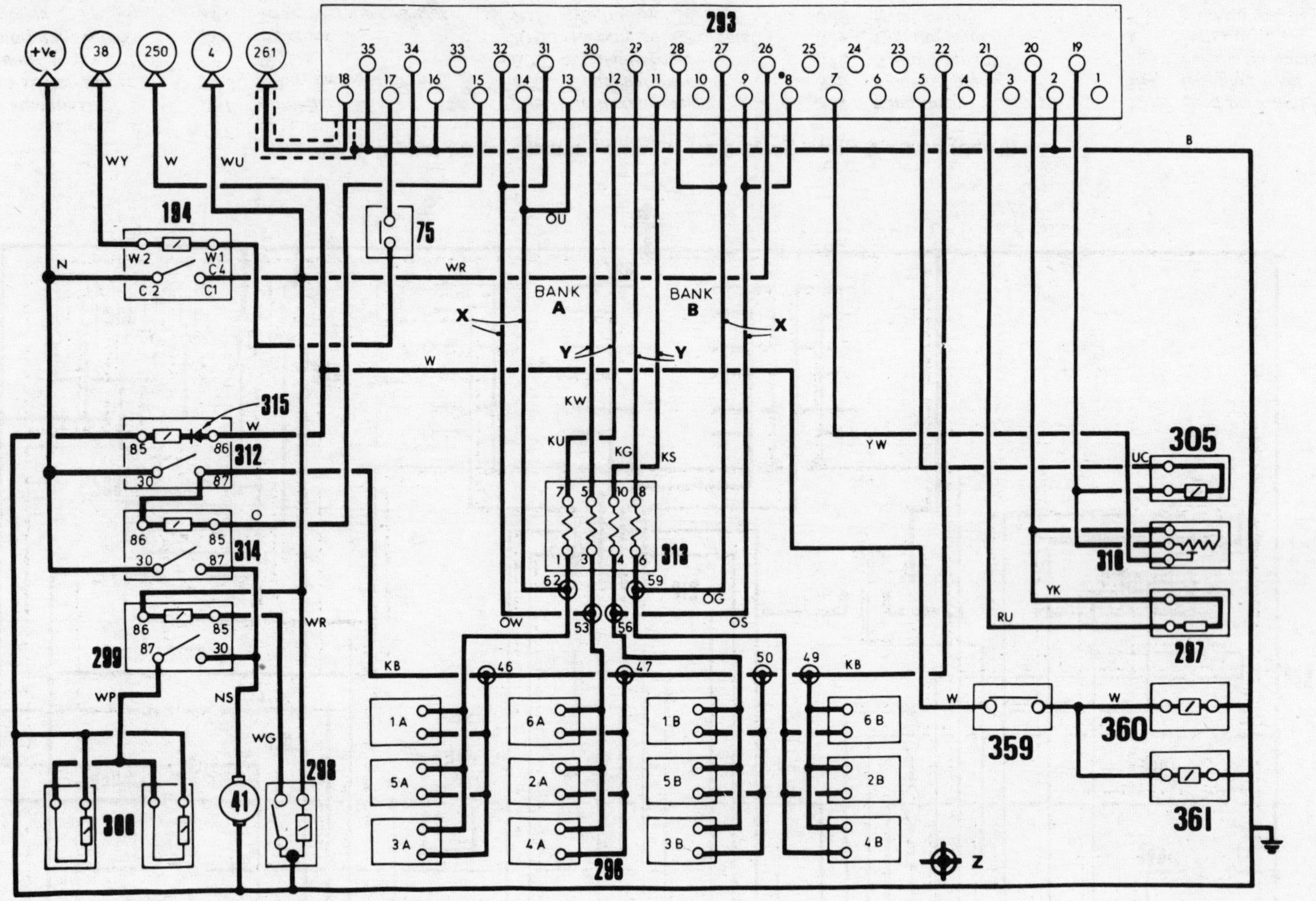


Fig. 13.11 Digital P fuel injection system – XJS, except North America (Sec 5)

| | | | | | | | | | |
|---|---|---|---|---|---|---|---|---|---|
| 4 | Starter solenoid | 261 | Amplifier | 299 | Cold start relay | 314 | Pump relay | 361 | Supplementary air valve |
| 38 | Ignition switch pin | 293 | Electronic control unit (ECU) | 300 | Cold start injectors | 315 | Block diode | X | Turn on |
| 41 | Fuel pump | 296 | Injectors | 305 | Coolant sensor | 359 | Oil temperature switch | Y | Hold on |
| 75 | Start inhibitor switch | 297 | Air temperature sensor | 310 | Throttle potentiometer | 360 | Vacuum changeover switch | Z | Part of ten-way engine harness |
| 194 | Starter relay | 298 | Thermotime switch | 312 | Main relay | | | | |
| 250 | Inertia switch | | | 313 | Power resistors | | | | |

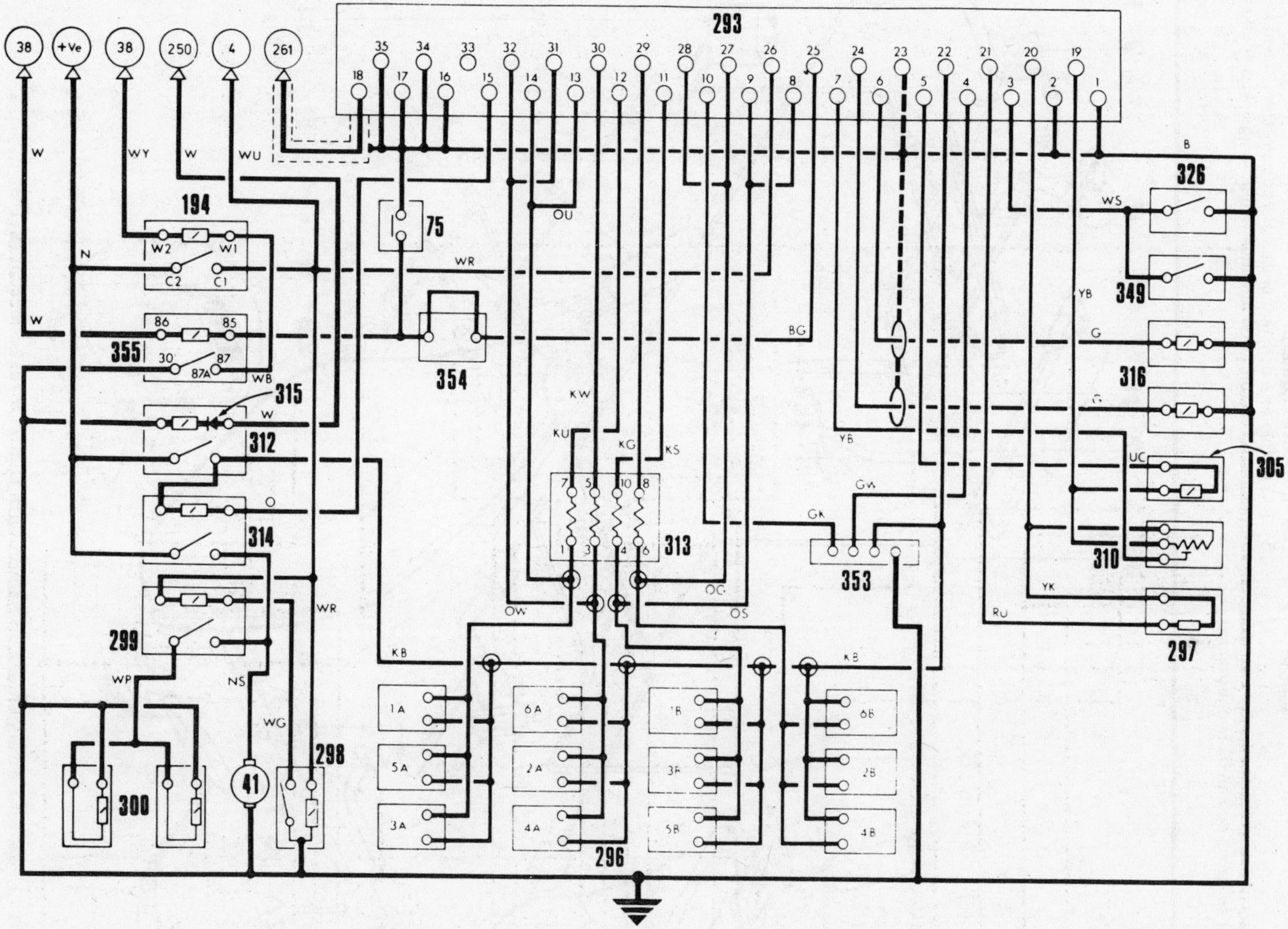

Fig. 13.12 Digital P fuel injection system – XJS, North America (Sec 5)

| | | | | | | | | | |
|---|---|---|---|---|---|---|---|---|---|
| 4 | Starter solenoid | 261 | Amplifier | 298 | Thermotime switch | 312 | Main relay | 326 | Vacuum switch |
| 38 | Ignition switch pin | 293 | Electronic control unit (ECU) | 299 | Cold start relay | 313 | Power resistors | 349 | Microswitch |
| 41 | Fuel pump | 296 | Injectors | 300 | Cold start injectors | 314 | Pump relay | 353 | Feed back monitor socket |
| 75 | Start inhibitor switch | 297 | Air temperature sensor | 305 | Coolant sensor | 315 | Block diode | 354 | Disable socket |
| 194 | Starter relay | | | 310 | Throttle potentiometer | 316 | Oxygen sensors | 355 | Feedback monitor relay |
| 250 | Inertia switch | | | | | | | | |

4 System components differ slightly between Saloon, and XJS Coupe and Cabriolet models, but a brief description of their function is given in the following paragraphs.

### *Fuel injection system components (Saloon) – purpose and function*

**Fuel supply**

5 Fuel is drawn from the rear-mounted fuel tanks by an electric pump. The fuel passes through a solenoid-operated changeover valve, an in-line fuel filter and pressure regulator to a fuel rail. Excess fuel is returned, through a fuel cooler, to the tank.

6 Fuel is also supplied to two cold start injectors which only operate when starting a cold engine.

7 An air bleed valve allows the fuel supply line to purge itself of vapour when changing over fuel tanks.

**Fuel pressure regulator**

8 This maintains a constant pressure drop across the injector nozzles. It operates by vacuum from the inlet manifold against a spring-loaded diaphragm.

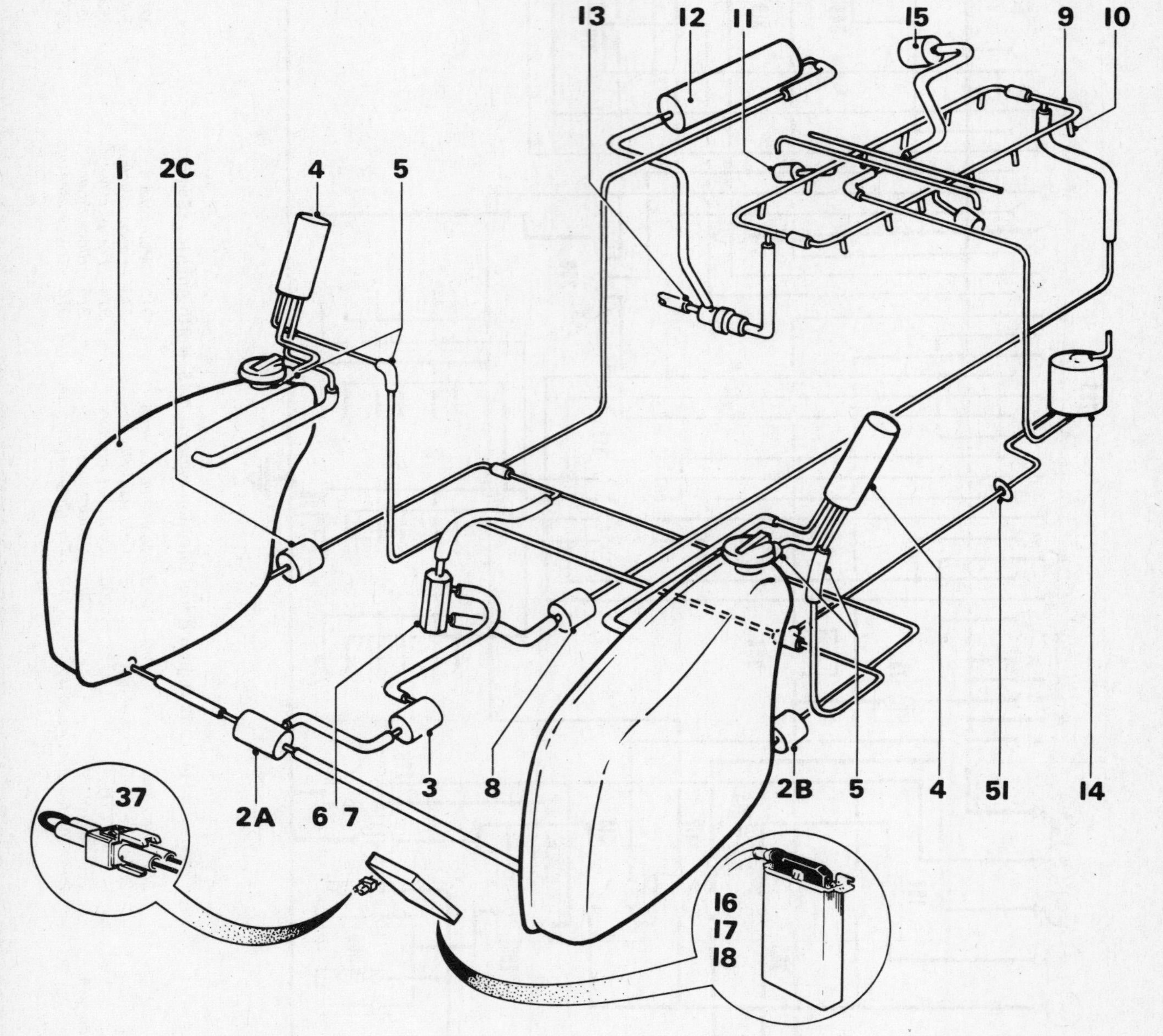


**Fig. 13.13 Fuel tank arrangement on Saloon with Digital P fuel injection (Sec 5)**

*1 Fuel tank*
*2A Changeover valve*
*2B Changeover valve*
*2C Changeover valve*
*3 Fuel pump*
*4 Vapour separators*
*5 Restrictors*
*6 Air bleed valve*
*7 Non-return valve*
*8 Fuel filter (in boot)*
*9 Fuel rail*
*10 Fuel injectors*
*11 Cold start injectors*
*12 Fuel cooler*
*13 Fuel pressure regulators*
*14 Charcoal canister*
*15 Positive crankcase ventilation (PCV) valve*
*16 Electronic control unit (ECU)*
*17 Manifold pressure sensor (in ECU)*
*18 Idle setting screw (in ECU)*
*37 Feedback disable socket*
*51 Pressure relief valve*

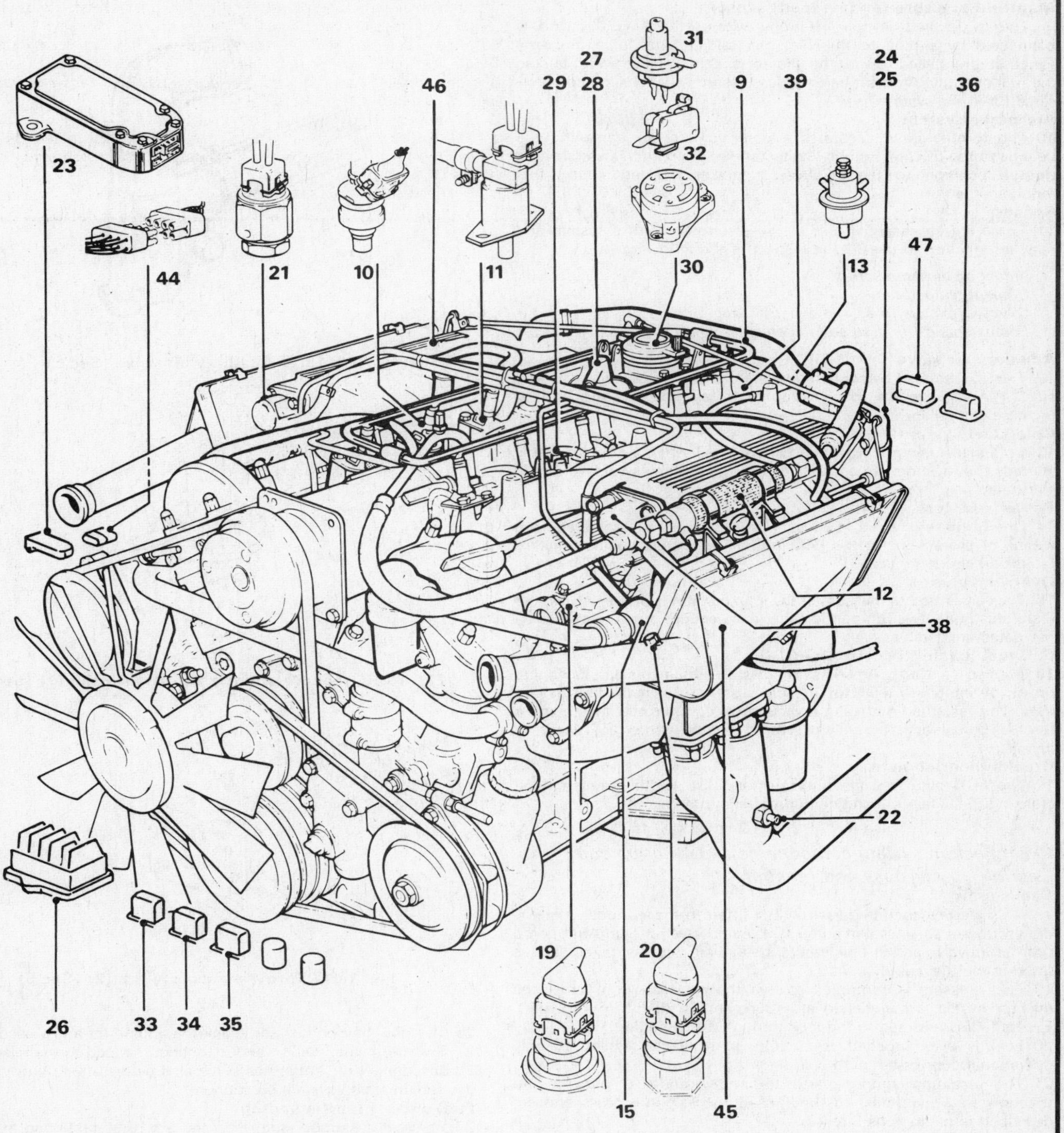


**Fig. 13.14 Digital P fuel system components on Saloon (Sec 5)**

*9 Fuel rail*
*10 Fuel injectors*
*11 Cold start injectors*
*12 Fuel cooler*
*13 Fuel pressure regulators*
*15 PCV valve*
*19 Coolant temperature sensor*
*20 Air temperature sensor*
*21 Thermotime switch*
*22 Oxygen sensor*
*23 Power resistors*
*24 Auxiliary air valve*
*25 Idle speed screw*
*26 Ignition amplifier*
*27 Ignition coil (speed sensor)*
*28 Ballast resistor*
*29 Distributor and vacuum capsule*
*31 Throttle vacuum switch (full loading)*
*33 Main relay*
*34 Pump relay*
*35 Cold start relay*
*36 Feedback monitor relay*
*38 Overrun valve*
*44 Four-way sockets*
*45 Air cleaner*
*46 Inlet manifolds*
*47 Start relay*

**Manifold pressure (engine load) sensor**

9 This is located in the Electronic Control Unit (ECU) and is connected by a pipe to the inlet manifold balance pipe. Pressure variation is signalled to vary the injector operating pulse width and so the fuel quantity. Ambient barometric pressure variations are compensated for in the system.

**Air intake system**

10 The throttle pulley actuates a potentiometer so transmitting a voltage to the ECU. A vacuum switch and micro-switch also relay the throttle position to the ECU as a means of determining fuel requirements.

**Sensors**

11 These are an essential part of the electronic control system and relay information to the ECU in respect of the following:

*Induction air temperature*
*Coolant temperature*
*Oxygen (exhaust gas) – in exhaust downpipe*
*Engine speed (ignition coil negative terminal)*

**Auxiliary air valve**

12 This is controlled by coolant temperature to prevent stalling at cold start. The valve opens to allow air to bypass the throttles and so increase engine speed.

**Cold start system**

13 Cold start injectors provide additional fuel when a cold engine is started. The injectors are controlled by a thermotime switch and cold start relay.

**Power resistors**

14 One of these is wired in series with each three fuel injectors as a means of protection for the ECU output transistors against injector faults and short circuits.

**Overrun valve**

15 The valve fitted to the front of the inlet manifolds bleeds air into the manifolds under overrun conditions when vacuum pressure exceeds a pre-determined value.

**Full fuel loading (North America)**

16 Applied to North American models to obtain maximum engine power by inhibiting the 'closed loop' system to increase the fuelling level. This is carried out using a vacuum/electric throttle switch and a throttle pulley actuated micro-switch. The switches are wired in parallel.

**Cranking enrichment**

17 The ECU increases the fuel injector pulse width during engine cranking to sustain the engine during initial running.

## *Fuel injection system components (XJS Coupe and Cabriolet) – purpose and function*

**Fuel supply**

18 A single rear-mounted fuel tank is fitted to these models. Fuel is drawn from a small sealed sump tank by an electric pump through a non-return valve and in-line filter to the fuel rail. A pressure regulator is fitted in the fuel supply circuit.

19 Fuel pressure is controlled so that the pressure drop across the injector nozzle is maintained at a constant 36.25 lbf/in² (2.5 bar). Excess fuel is returned to the tank through a fuel cooler.

20 Fuel is also supplied to a cold start injector which is only operational during starting a cold engine.

21 The remaining components of the system and their purpose and function are very similar to those used for Saloon models and are described in paragraphs 8 to 17.

## *Fuel injection system (Digital P) – idle speed adjustment*

22 Have the engine at normal operating temperature.

23 Remove the air cleaners and balance the throttles, as described in Chapter 3, Section 47.

24 Now adjust the idle speed screw, as described in Chapter 3, Section 46.

## *Fuel injection system (Digital P) components – removal and refitting*

25 Before any fuel carrying components are uncoupled or removed, the system must be depressurised. To do this, pull the lead from terminal 85 of the fuel pump relay which is mounted on the radiator top rail.

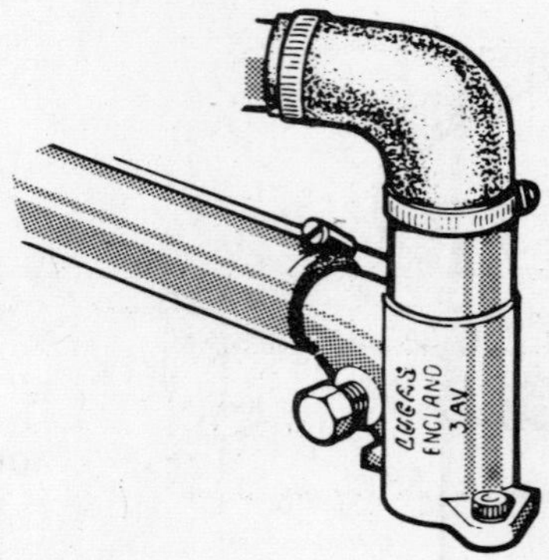


**Fig. 13.15 Auxiliary air valve (Sec 5)**

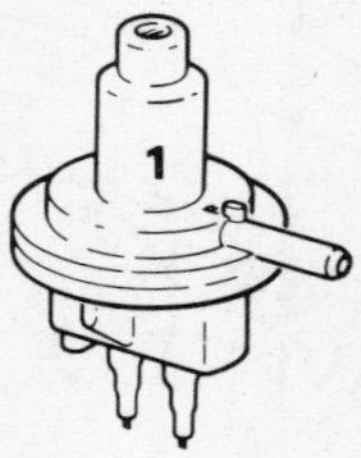


**Fig. 13.16 Vacuum/electric throttle switch (1) (Sec 5)**

**Fig. 13.17 Throttle microswitch (2) (Sec 5)**

26 Turn the ignition key and crank the engine for a few seconds.

27 Switch off the ignition and reconnect the lead to the relay.

28 Disconnect the battery negative lead before attempting to remove any fuel injection system component.

**Fuel cut-off inertia switch**

29 Remove the rubber knob fom the trip reset cable and extract the trim panel fixing screws from the side of the driver's footwell. Disconnect the trip reset cable from its bracket and withdraw the trim panel.

30 Remove the switch cover and disconnect the multi-plug. Extract the switch mounting screws and remove the switch.

31 Refitting is a reversal of removal. The switch is reset by depressing the knob.

**Power resistor**

32 Disconnect the power resistor multi-plug. Extract the fixing screws and remove the power resistor block from the wing valance.

**Fuel main filter**

33 Depressurise the fuel system, as described in paragraphs 25 to 27.

34 Remove the spare wheel cover and spare wheel.

35 Clamp the fuel hoses on each side of the fuel filter. Self-locking grips are useful for this purpose.

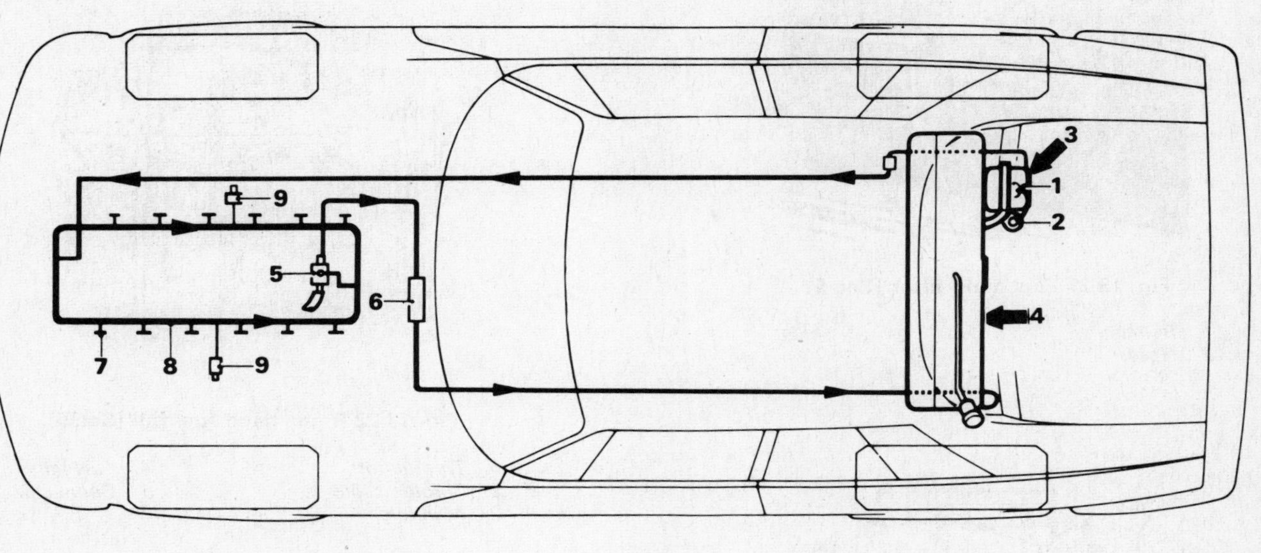


Fig. 13.18 Fuel supply system – XJS Coupe and Cabriolet (Sec 5)

1 *Sump fuel pump*
2 *Fuel pump*
3 *Non-return valve*
4 *Fuel filter*
5 *Pressure regulator*
6 *Fuel cooler*
7 *Injectors*
8 *Fuel rail*
9 *Cold start injectors*

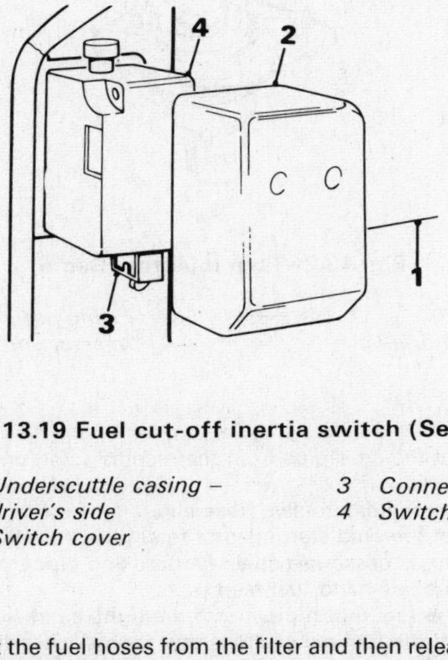


Fig. 13.19 Fuel cut-off inertia switch (Sec 5)

1 *Underscuttle casing – driver's side*
2 *Switch cover*
3 *Connector*
4 *Switch*

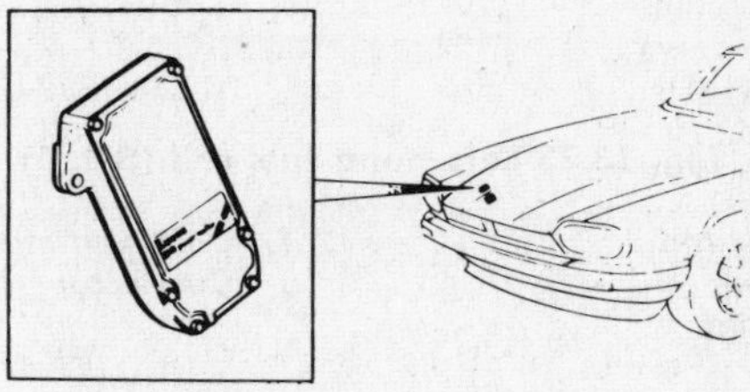

Fig. 13.20 Power resistor (Sec 5)

36 Disconnect the fuel hoses from the filter and then release the clamp and remove the filter.
37 Refit the new filter by reversing the removal operations.

**Fuel cooler**

38 The operations are similar to those described in Chapter 3, Section 58.

**Pressure regulator**

39 Depressurise the fuel system as previously described.
40 Disconnect the hose that runs betweeen the fuel cooler and the pressure regulator, from the regulator. Plug the hose and the regulator.
41 Unscrew the nut which fixes the regulator to its bracket.
42 Disconnect the hose that runs between the regulator and the fuel rail from the fuel rail. Plug the hose and the rail.
43 Withdraw the regulator and disconnect the vacuum hose.
44 Refitting is a reversal of removal.

**Fuel rail (right-hand side)**

45 Depressurise the fuel system as previously described (paragraphs 25 to 27).
46 Disconnect the right-hand throttle rod from the throttle pedestal.
47 Disconnect the manifold cross pipe from the right-hand manifold.
48 Disconnect the cold start injector hose from the fuel rail. Plug the hose and rail.
49 Release the hose clips and disconnect the two halves of the fuel rail.
50 Slacken the injector hose clips and remove the fuel rail.
51 Refitting is a reversal of removal.

**Fuel rail (left-hand side)**

52 Depressurise the fuel system as previously described (paragraphs 25 to 27).
53 The remaining operations are as for the right-hand rail just described, but disconnect the right-hand components.

**Fuel injectors**

54 Depressurise the fuel system as previously described (paragraphs 25 to 27).
55 Remove the appropriate fuel rail.
56 Disconnect the injector wiring plug.
57 Unscrew the injector clamp plate nuts and remove the plate.
58 Pull out the injector.
59 Refitting is a reversal of removal.

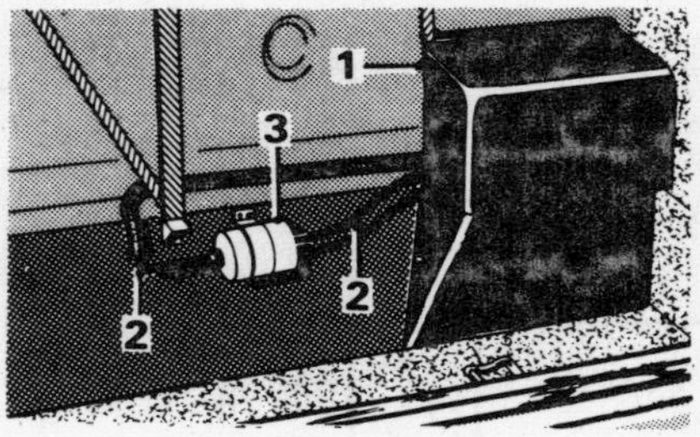


**Fig. 13.21 Fuel main filter (Sec 5)**

*1 Battery*
*2 Hoses*
*3 Filter*

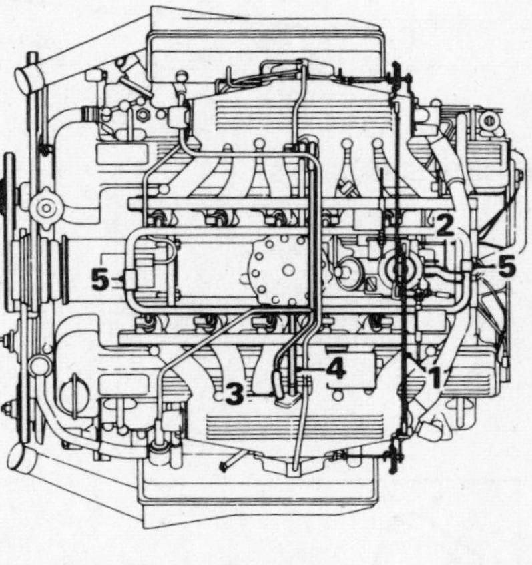


**Fig. 13.23 Left-hand fuel rail (Sec 5)**

*1 Throttle rod*
*2 Fuel rail*
*3 Manifold*
*4 Cold start injector hose*
*5 Connector*

## *Fuel injection system (D type) – modifications*

60 Later models equipped with this system may incorporate certain modifications depending upon operating territory. These include an ignition amplifier, EGR control unit and valve.

**Throttle switch**

61 On later models the switch is of potentiometer type and can only be adjusted using a special Lucas setting gauge.

**Fuel main filter**

62 This is located within the luggage compartment and is accessible after removal of the spare wheel.

63 Depressurise the fuel system (Chapter 3, Section 48) and disconnect and plug the filter hoses. Release the filter clamp, discard the filter and fit the new one.

**Fuel pressure regulator**

64 The removal and refitting procedure is as described in paragraphs 39 to 44 of this Section.

**Fuel injectors**

65 Removal and refitting of injectors is as described in paragraphs 54 to 59 of this Section.

**Fuel rail**

66 Depressurise the system (Chapter 3, Section 38) and disconnect the battery.

67 Disconnect the throttle rod (on the side from which the rail is being removed) from the throttle pedestal.

68 Disconnect the throttle kickdown switch.

69 Disconnect the throttle control cable from the throttle pedestal and move the cable aside.

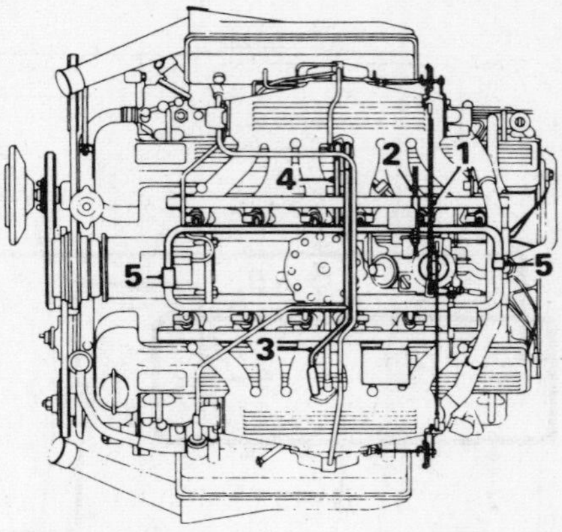


**Fig. 13.22 Right-hand fuel rail (Sec 5)**

*1 Throttle rod*
*2 Throttle cable*
*3 Manifold*
*4 Fuel rail*
*5 Connector*

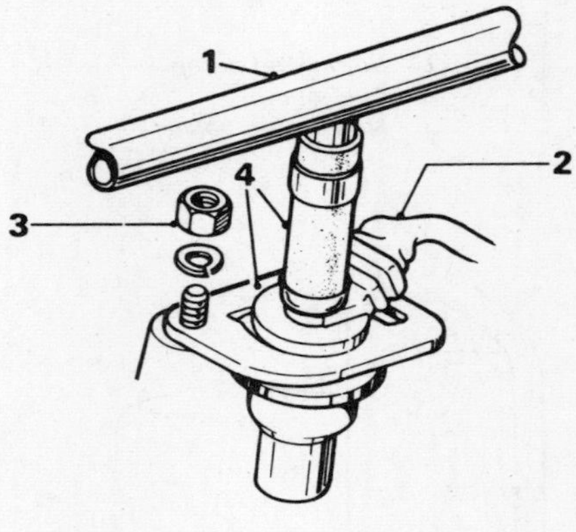


**Fig. 13.24 Fuel injector (Sec 5)**

*1 Fuel rail*
*2 Connector plug*
*3 Fixing nut*
*4 Injector and clamp plate*

70 Disconnect the crosspipe from the manifold and unclip it from the fuel rail.

71 Slacken the regulator valve hose clip.

72 Disconnect the cold start injector feed pipe from the fuel rail.

73 Remove the Econocruise cable harness and pipe from the fuel rail.

74 Remove the left-hand fuel feed pipe.

75 Remove the fuel return pipe from the right-hand side.

76 Disconnect the fuel rail sections and then slacken the fuel injector clips and withdraw the fuel rail from the injectors.

77 Refitting is a reversal of removal.

## *Fuel injection system (Digital P) – cold start problem*

78 A problem can occur on 1980 models causing stalling immediately after cold start. This can be overcome by removing the cold start relay, located as shown in Fig. 13.28.

## *Fuel injection system (Digital P) – vacuum reservoir*

79 Commencing with the following vehicle identification numbers – Saloon 343234 and XJS 107102, a vacuum reservoir has been located adjacent to the ECU to eliminate resonance from the inlet manifold vacuum sensor pipe.

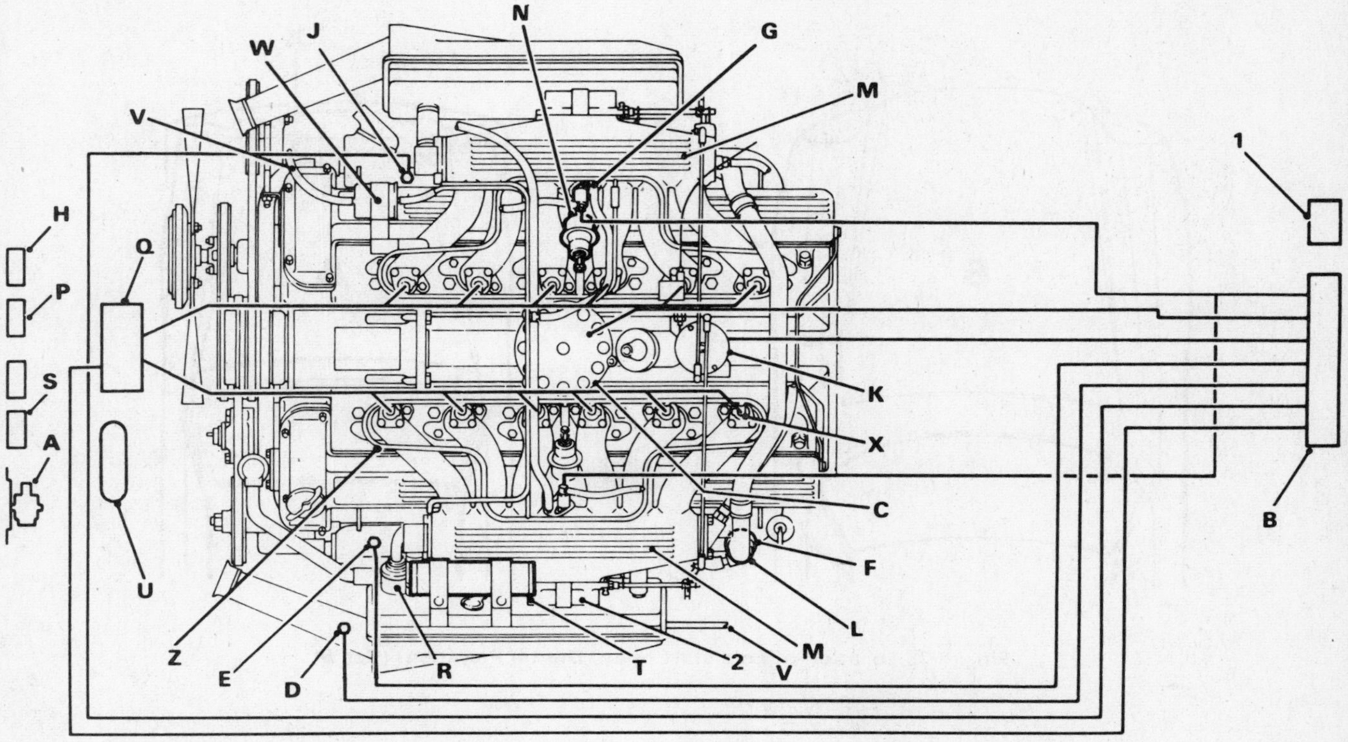


**Fig. 13.25 Modified D type fuel injection system (Sec 5)**

*A* *Manifold pressure sensor*
*B* *Electronic control unit (ECU)*
*C* *Trigger unit (distributor)*
*D* *Air temperature sensor*
*E* *Coolant temperature sensor*
*F* *Auxiliary air valve*
*G* *Cold start injector*
*H* *Cold start relay*
*J* *Thermotime switch*
*K* *Throttle switch*
*L* *Idle speed screw*
*M* *Inlet manifolds*
*N* *Fuel pressure regulator*
*P* *Fuel pump relay*
*Q* *Power amp*
*R* *Overrun valve*
*S* *Main relay*
*T* *Fuel cooler*
*U* *Ignition amplifier*
*V* *Fuel feed and return*
*W* *Fuel filter*
*X* *Injector*
*Z* *Fuel rail*
*1* *EGR control unit*
*2* *EGR valve*

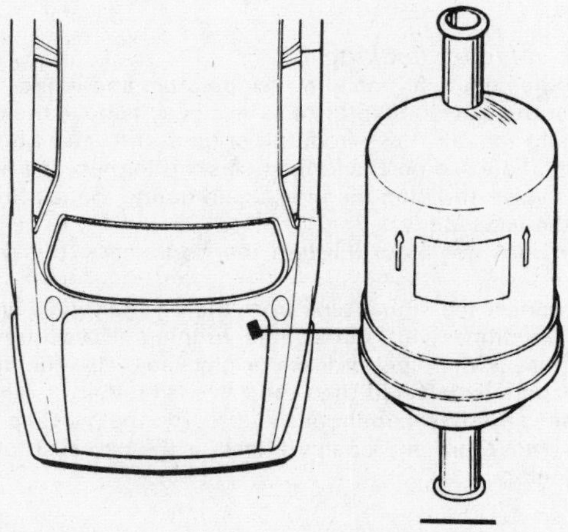

**Fig. 13.26 Fuel main filter in boot (Sec 5)**

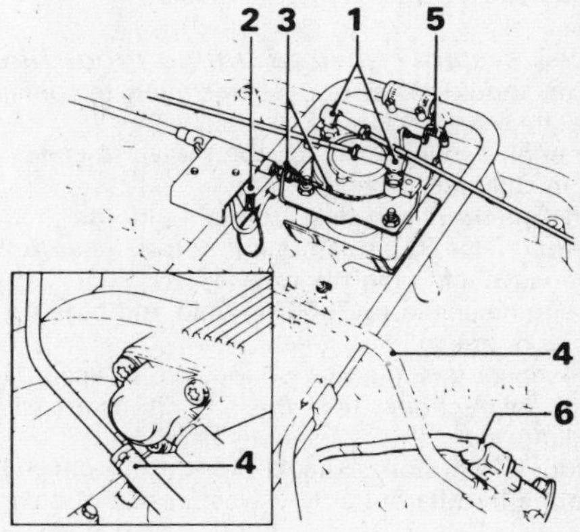


**Fig. 13.27 D type fuel injection system fuel rail on later cars (Sec 5)**

*1* *Throttle rod*
*2* *Throttle kick-down switch*
*3* *Throttle control cable*
*4* *Cross pipe*
*5* *Regulator hose clip*
*6* *Cold start injector*

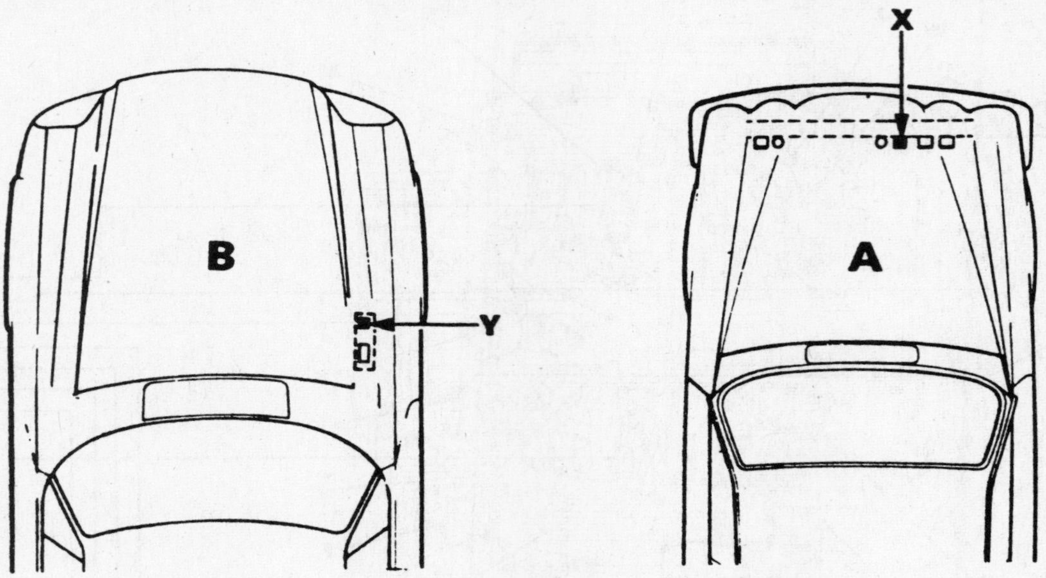


**Fig. 13.28 Location of cold start relay (Digital P system) (Sec 5)**

*A Saloon*
*B XJS*
*X Relay*
*Y Relay*

### *Fuel injection system – difficult hot starting*

80 Should this occur after the engine has been switched off for a period of between 25 and 45 minutes, it is probably due to fuel vaporisation.
81 This is overcome from the following Vehicle Identification Numbers by fitting a temperature-sensitive switch in the fuel rail and connected into the air temperature sensor circuit.

| | |
|---|---|
| *Saloon* | *365261* |
| *XJS* | *111980* |

82 Earlier models can be modified.

### *Fuel solenoid valves*

83 The valves referred to in Chapter 3, Section 8 are located at the rear of the rear roadwheel arches on later models.

### *Fuel injection system – revised tuning procedure*

84 The engine should be at normal operating temperature with the ignition correctly set.
85 Have the engine idling with the throttle valve plates correctly set, as described in Chapter 3, Section 47.
86 On North American vehicles, except California, remove the cap from the diverter valve. On Californian models, release the tube from the top of the valve and plug the tube.
87 Increase engine speed to 2000 rev/min and hold for ten seconds then allow it to return to idle.
88 With an exhaust gas analyser connected, in accordance with the manufacturer's instructions, take the CO emission reading after 15 seconds of idling.
89 Take readings from both exhaust pipes in turn. If the readings are unequal then the throttle butterfly valves are out of balance and must be adjusted.
90 If the emission level is outside the specified percentage range then the idle potentiometer knob on the ECU will have to be adjusted and both exhaust pipe emissions rechecked.
91 On completion, refit the diverter valve cap or pipe and check and adjust the idle speed if necessary.

### *Exhaust gas recirculation (EGR) valve – checking*

92 Switch on the ignition and then open the throttle at the pedestal by 0.125 in (3.0 mm). Within two seconds, the EGR valve should be heard to open. If the same check is carried out with the engine running then a slight roar will be heard in the air cleaner pipes on both cylinder banks.
93 If the EGR valve does not perform as described, check that the throttle switch is correctly adjusted and all switch and valve wires are secure.
94 Disconnect the leads from each EGR valve in turn and connect a 12V 6W test bulb between them. Switch on the ignition and the bulb should glow with the throttle in the idle position.
95 Open the throttle at the pedestal through 0.125 in (3.0 mm). The light should go out after two seconds but come on again when the throttle is fully open.
96 If the test lamp check proves satisfactory, then the EGR valve is faulty. If the test does not prove satisfactory, then the EGR control unit is faulty.

### *Diverter valve – checking*

97 Have the engine at operating temperature and idling.
98 To test the valve on North American cars, remove the cap from the valve noting that air flows from the ports in the valve body.
99 To test the valve on Californian cars, disconnect the pipe from the top of the valve and plug the pipe, again noting that air flows from the ports in the valve body.
100 If air does not blow through the ports, carry out the following tests.
101 Disconnect the signal pipe from the diverter valve and check for vacuum (suction) with the engine running. If vacuum cannot be detected, check the pipe for leaks or blockage, also the manifold.
102 If vacuum is detected then the valve is faulty.
103 If the air flows continuously through the valve ports without diverting then there is probably a leak at the cap seal, otherwise the valve is faulty.

### *Emission control systems – modifications*

**Ignition vacuum advance system**

104 The ignition vacuum advance system described in Chapter 3, Section 75 has been modified on later models as shown in the illustrations according to operating territory (Figs. 13.29 to 13.34).
105 The dump valve is used to modify the signal applied to the ignition vacuum advance capsule.
106 The vacuum delay valve is fitted in the distributor vacuum advance

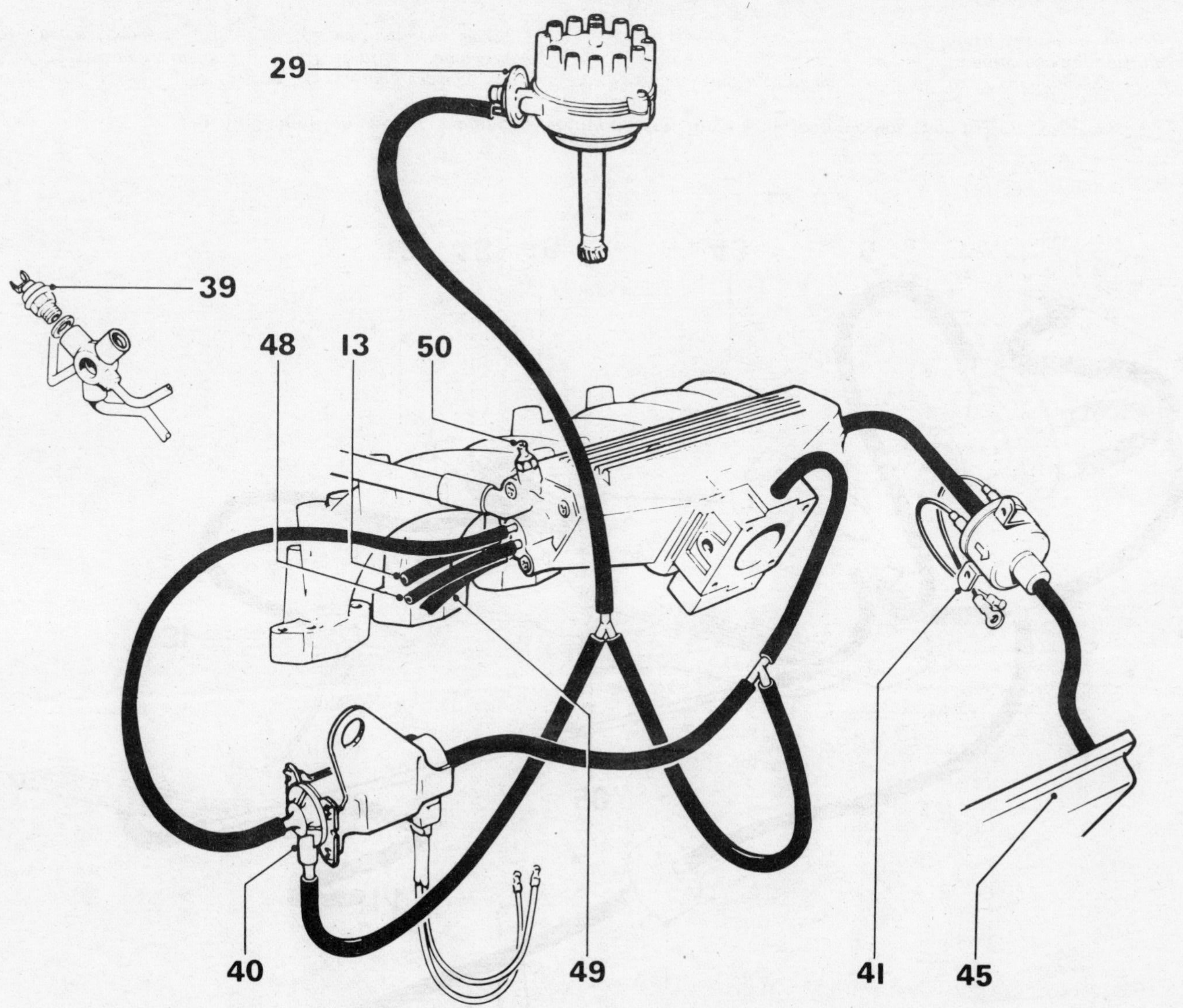


Fig. 13.29 Ignition vacuum advance system on later models, except North America (Sec 5)

13 *Fuel pressure regulator*
29 *Vacuum capsule*
39 *Oil temperature switch*
40 *Three-way changeover valve*
41 *Supplementary air valve*
45 *Air cleaner*
48 *To air conditioner*
49 *To automatic transmission*
50 *Servo non-return valve*

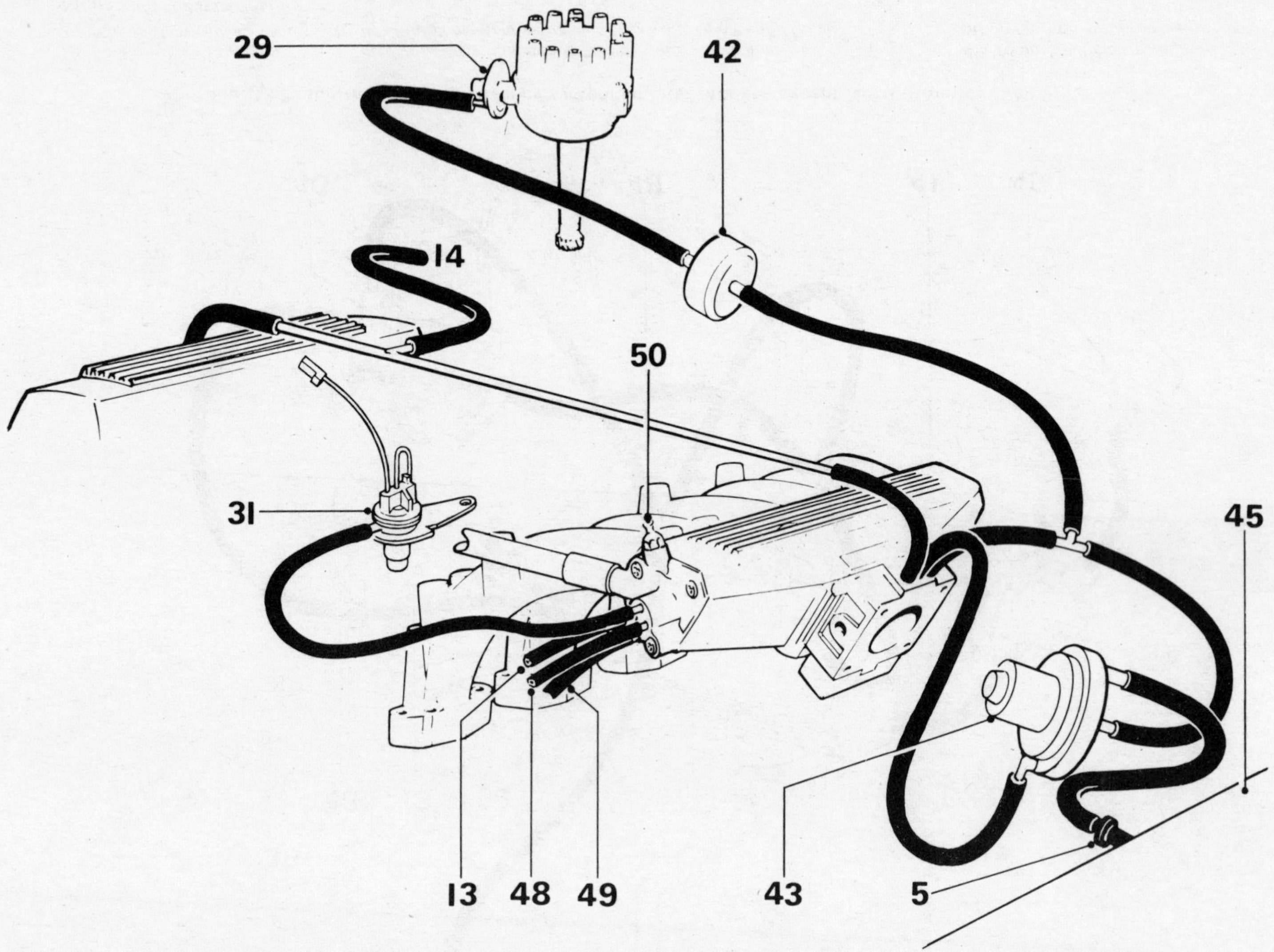


Fig. 13.30 Ignition vacuum advance system on later North American models (Sec 5)

*5 Restrictors*
*13 Fuel pressure regulator*
*14 Charcoal canister*
*29 Vacuum capsule*
*31 Throttle vacuum switch*
*42 Vacuum delay valve*
*43 Vacuum advance dump valve*
*45 Air cleaner*
*48 To air conditioner*
*49 To automatic transmission*
*50 Servo non-return valve*

Fig. 13.31 Ignition vacuum advance system on North American models – pre 1983 (Sec 5)

*E* Dump valve
*H* Solenoid air switch
*J* Vacuum capsule
*P* Timer/relay
*Q* Solenoid vacuum valve
*R* Delay valve
*S* Thermal valve
*T* Air switching valve
*V* Purge control valve

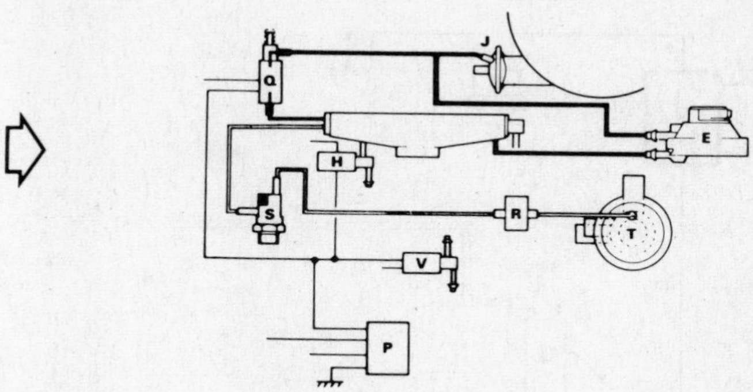


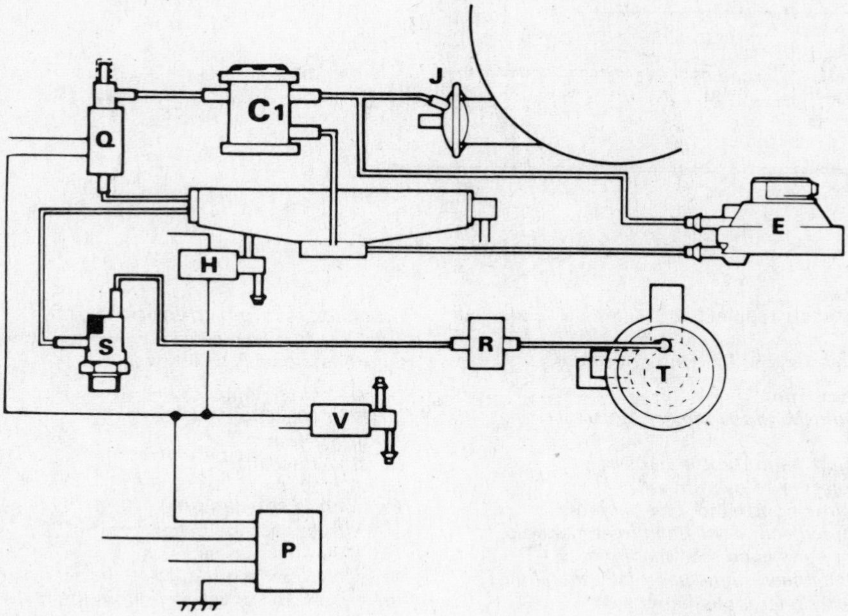


Fig. 13.32 Ignition vacuum advance system on North American models – post 1983 (Sec 5)

*E* Dump valve
*H* Solenoid air switch
*J* Vacuum capsule
*P* Timer relay
*Q* Solenoid vacuum valve
*R* Delay unit
*S* Thermal valve
*T* Air switching valve
*V* Purge control valve
*C1* Vacuum regulator

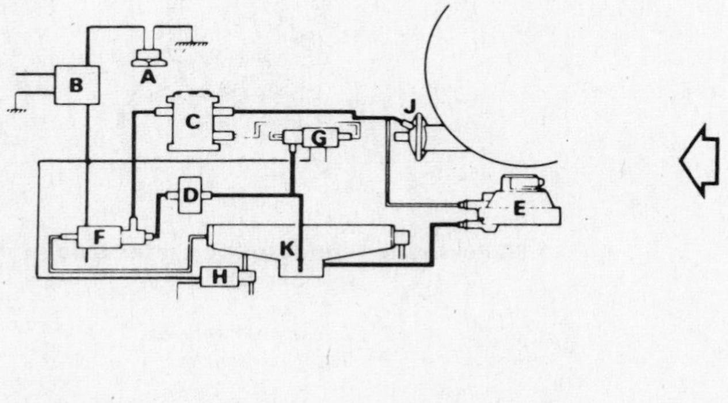


Fig. 13.33 Ignition vacuum advance system on UK and European models (Sec 5)

*A* Coolant temperature switch
*B* Time delay module
*C* Vacuum regulator
*D* Vacuum delay valve
*E* Vacuum dump valve
*F* Three-way solenoid valve
*G* Two-way solenoid valve
*H* Solenoid air switch
*J* Distributor advance capsule
*K* Throttle edge tapping

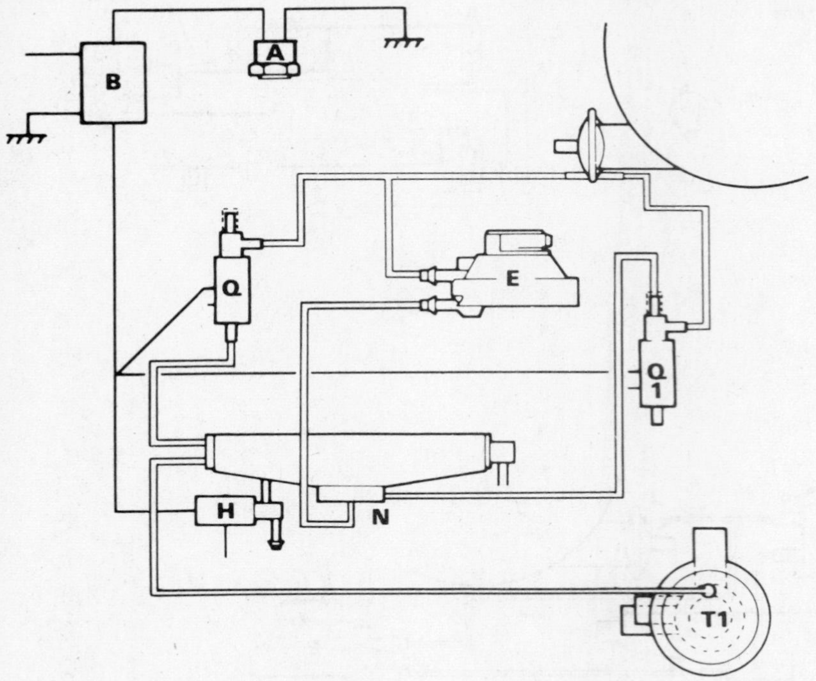


**Fig. 13.34 Ignition vacuum advance system on Australian models (Sec 5)**

*A* *Coolant temperature switch*
*B* *Time delay module*
*E* *Vacuum dump valve*
*H* *Solenoid air switch*
*N* *Throttle body*
*Q* *Two-way solenoid valve*
*Q1* *Two-way solenoid valve*
*T1* *Diverter valve*

line to ensure that vacuum is not applied too suddenly when the throttle is opened.

107 The components are located in the following positions.

| **Component** | **Location** |
|---|---|
| *Dump valve* | *Right-hand thermostat housing* |
| *Two-way solenoid valve* | *Right-hand throttle housing* |
| *Three-way solenoid valve* | *Adjacent to overrun valve below right-hand inlet manifold* |
| *Delay valve* | *Underneath right-hand inlet manifold* |
| *Solenoid air switch* | *On right-hand inlet manifold* |
| *Vacuum regulator* | *Underneath right-hand inlet manifold* |
| *Time delay unit* | *Relay board, passenger side* |
| *Coolant temperature switch* | *Right-hand rear coolant rail* |

## *Emission system identification*

108 The significance of the code letters for the various emission control systems is as follows:

*A* *North America*
*B* *UK, Europe*
*C* *Japan*
*D* *Australia*

## *Fuel tank sender unit (Saloon) – removal and refitting*

109 Disconnect the battery.

110 Drain the fuel tanks.

111 On earlier models, raise the rear of the car and remove the rear roadwheel and cover plate from the rear of the wheel arch.

112 On later models, remove the rear lamp assembly for access to the sender unit through the luggage compartment.

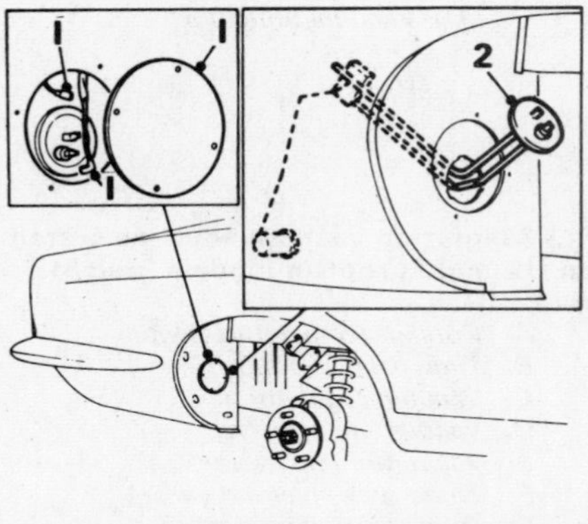


**Fig. 13.35 Fuel tank sender unit on earlier Saloon models (Sec 5)**

*1* *Cover plate and Lucar connections*
*2* *Tank sender unit*

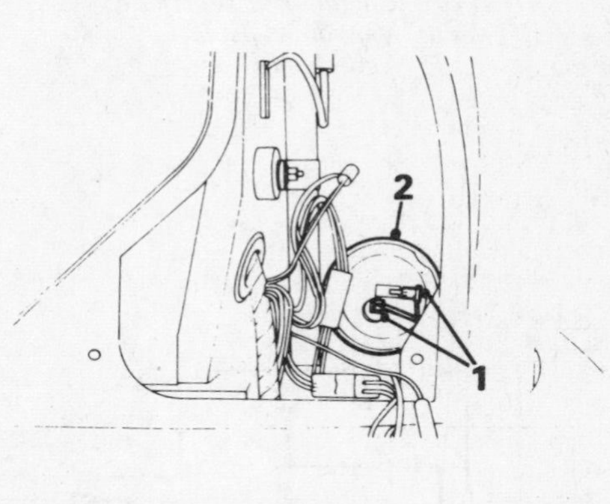


**Fig. 13.36 Fuel tank sender unit on later Saloon models (Sec 5)**

*1* *Lucar connections*
*2* *Tank sender unit*

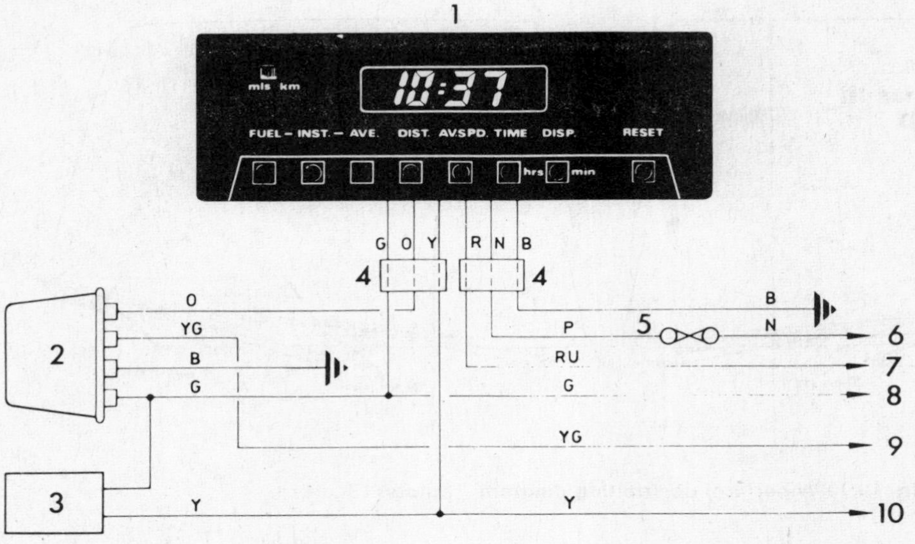


**Wiring colour code**

| | |
|---|---|
| B | Black |
| G | Green |
| N | Brown |
| O | Orange |
| P | Purple |
| R | Red |
| RU | Red/blue |
| Y | Yellow |
| YG | Yellow/green |

**Fig. 13.78 Trip computer connections (Sec 11)**

*1 Computer*
*2 Interface unit*
*3 Speed transducer*
*4 Connectors*
*5 Fuse No 16 (2A)*
*6 Full-time power supply*
*7 'Lights on' power supply*
*8 'Ignition on' power supply (Fuse No 4)*
*9 To ECU (fuel injection)*
*10 To speedometer*

average and instantaneous fuel consumption, and total fuel used. A digital clock display is also available.

116 This type of computer is relatively simple to understand and to operate. The speed information is derived from the electronic speedometer transducer. Fuel consumption information comes from the fuel injection ECU. Time measuring equipment is built in.

117 Reference to Fig. 13.78 will show that there are three separate power supplies to the computer. The full-time supply enables the clock and the memory to function continuously. The ignition-controlled supply energises the display and the control functions; the supply from the sidelights dims the display and illuminates the control legend strip.

118 No repair is possible in the event of computer malfunction. Assuming the wiring to be sound and all fuses intact, faults can be due to only three items:

(a) *Defective speedometer transducer (speedometer will also malfunction)*
(b) *Defective interface unit (fuel data will be inaccurate, speed/time data will be OK)*
(c) *Defective computer*

119 A defective ECU could be the cause of inaccurate fuel data displays, but other effects on the fuel injection system would make this obvious.

## *Trailer socket wiring (Series 3)*

120 If it is wished to connect a socket for trailer lighting and signalling, it is important that the auxiliary harness provided by the makers be used. Attempts to connect the socket wiring directly to the rear lamp clusters may result in damage to the bulb failure indicator units.

121 The auxiliary wiring harness is accessible after removing the spare wheel and the fuel pump cover panel (fuel injection models). The wiring colour code is as follows.

| | | |
|---|---|---|
| *Green/red* | – | *Left-hand indicator* |
| *Green/white* | – | *Right-hand indicator* |
| *Red/slate* | – | *Left-hand tail lamp* |
| *Red/orange* | – | *Right-hand tail lamp* |
| *Green/purple* | – | *Stop-lamps* |
| *Black* | – | *Earth* |

122 For other electrical connections (eg rear foglamps) and details of the latest regulations and standards relating to trailer lighting, consult an authorised dealer or other specialist.

## *Windscreen wiper arm positioning*

123 It is important that the windscreen wiper arms are positioned exactly as shown in the diagrams when in the parked position (Figs. 13.79 and 13.80).

124 Failure to locate the arms correctly on the splined driveshafts can cause the blades to lock together when the wipers are working.

## *Fuses and bulbs (1984 and later)*

125 Later models have revised fuse and bulb ratings; refer to the Specifications Section.

126 The main fuse block is located under the facia panel on the driver's side, with the auxiliary fusebox under the glovebox on the passenger side.

127 The headlamp fusebox is located within the engine compartment on the left-hand wing valance.

## *Cruise control system (1981 on) – description*

128 This is fitted as standard equipment on some models and optionally available on others. Its purpose is to maintain a set roadspeed with the foot released from the accelerator pedal. This is a most useful facility for long distance travel.

129 Immediate reversion to normal control is obtained once the brake pedal is operated.

130 An inhibitor switch is incorporated to prevent the engine over-revving should the speed selector lever be moved to neutral whilst the cruise control system is in operation.

131 The main components of the system include the following:

**Throttle actuator**

132 This is vacuum-operated and located near the distributor.

133 The device incorporates solenoid valves which are triggered by a speed control unit and in turn cause the unit bellows to open the throttle.

**Speed control unit**

134 This is located behind the underscuttle casing on the passenger side near the blower motor.

135 The unit receives signals from the speed transducer and then signals the throttle actuator solenoids to open or close the throttle.

136 The control unit is engaged and the memory recorded when the 'set' button is pressed. After an override, the memorised speed may be recalled by operation of the 'resume' switch. The memory is cancelled when the control switch is moved to the 'off' position.

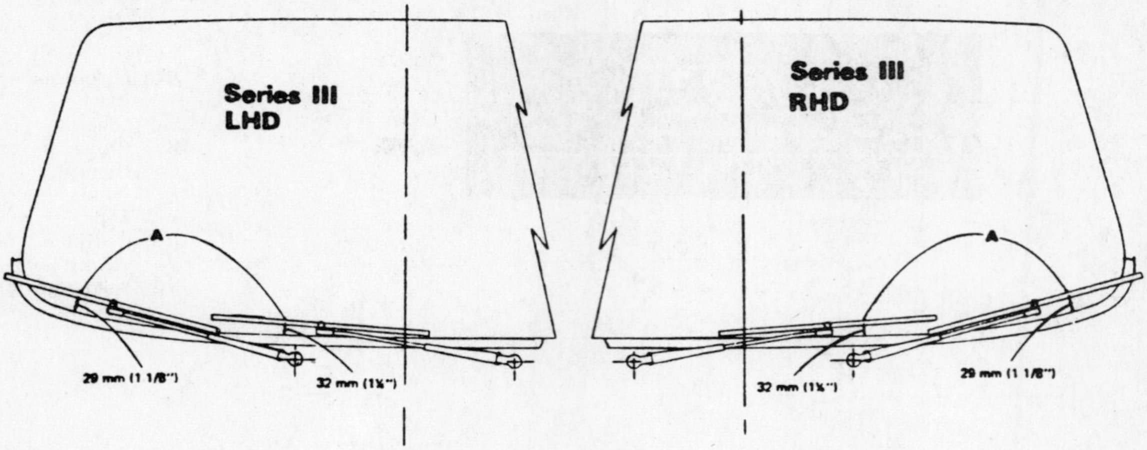


Fig. 13.79 Wiper arm positioning diagram – Saloon (Sec 11)

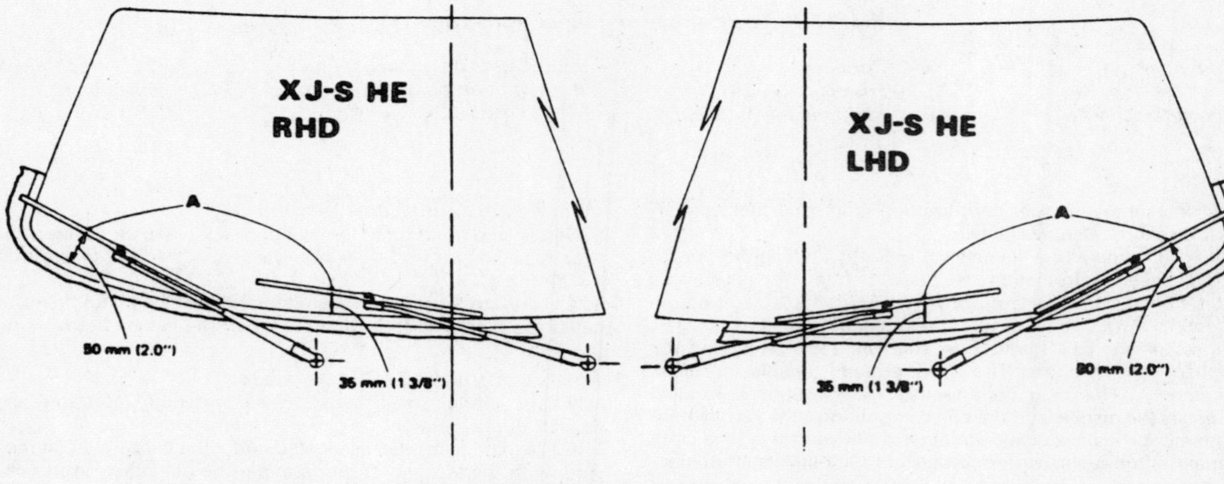


Fig. 13.80 Wiper arm positioning diagram – XJS (Sec 11)

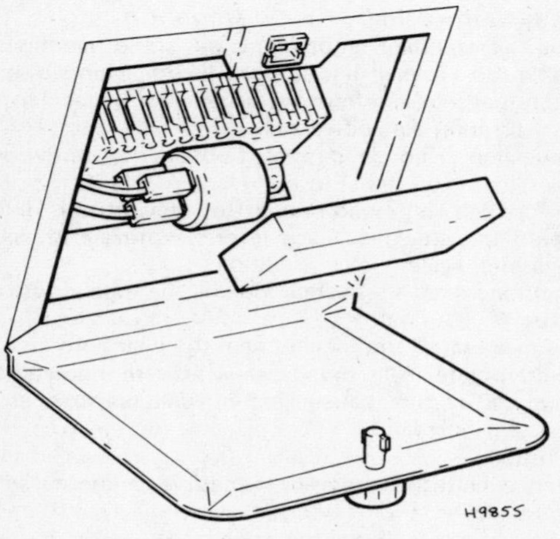


Fig. 13.81 Main fusebox (Sec 11)

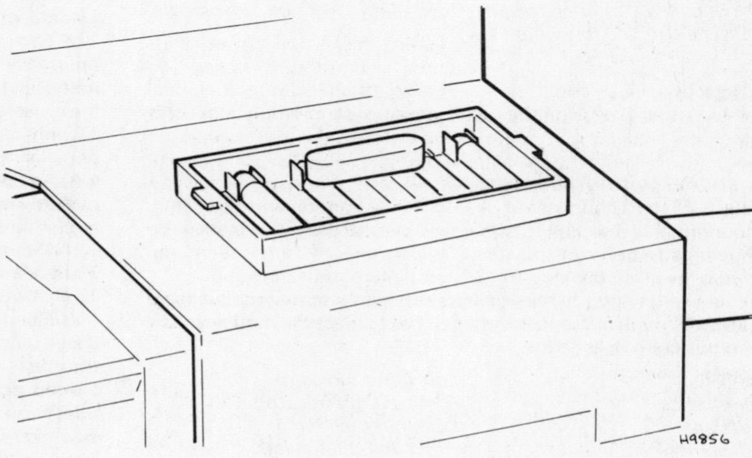


Fig. 13.82 Underbonnet fusebox (Sec 11)

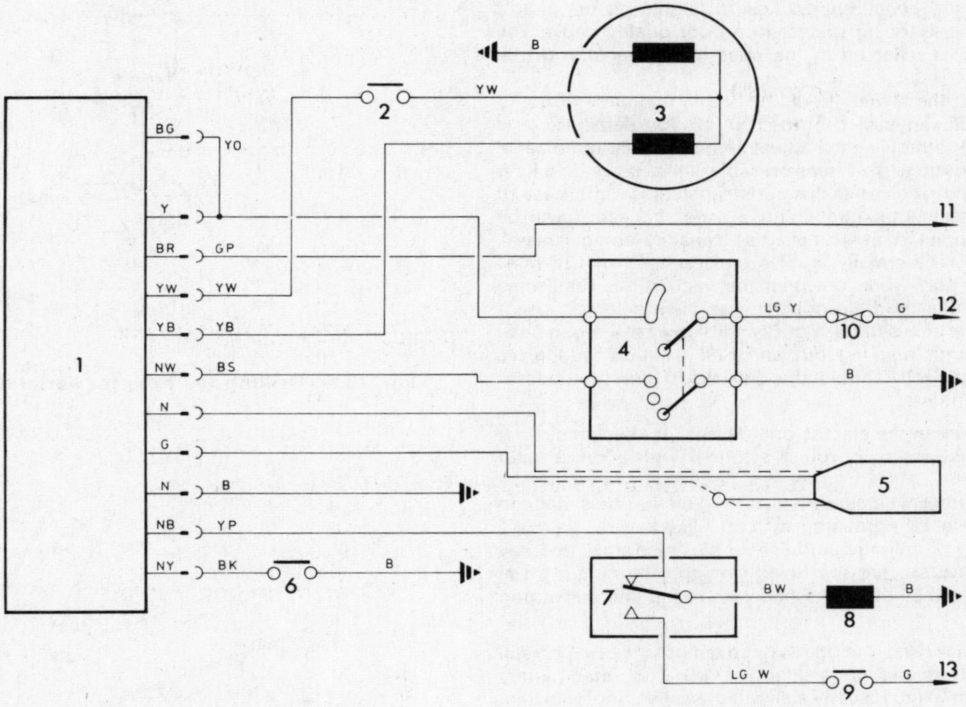


Fig. 13.83 Circuit and components of cruise control system (Sec 11)

| | | | | | | | |
|---|---|---|---|---|---|---|---|
| *1* | *Control unit* | *5* | *Magnetic pick-up* | *8* | *Kick-down solenoid* | *11* | *To stop-lamp switch* |
| *2* | *Brake operated switch* | *6* | *Set switch* | *9* | *Kick-down switch* | *12* | *Hazard switch* |
| *3* | *Throttle actuator* | *7* | *Inhibitor switch* | *10* | *Fuse No 17* | *13* | *To fuse No 5* |
| *4* | *Control switch* | | | | | | |

137 When the brake pedal is touched, the unit signals the throttle actuator to dump its vacuum, causing the throttle to close.

138 Adjustment of the 'set speed' is possible through an access hole in the speed control unit.

**Speed sensor (transducer)**

139 The magnetic speed transducer is mounted on the rear suspension cradle. Its sensor transmits a signal to the control unit indicating the roadspeed of the vehicle.

**Three position master switch**

140 Located at the rear of the automatic transmission speed shift control lever, the switch has three positions – off, on and resume.

**Set switch**

141 This switch is located on the end of the direction indicator stalk and triggers the speed control unit to bring the system into operation. By depressing the switch button once, the car will cruise within one mile per hour of the indicated roadspeed at the moment of depressing the switch.

142 If the button is constantly depressed, the car will accelerate until the button is released.

**Inhibit switch**

143 This is mounted on the transmission speed selector mechanism and prevents the cruise control system from operating in any selector position other than 'D'.

**Brake pedal switches**

144 The existing stop-lamp switch is used for cancelling the cruise mode while an additional safety switch is used to make and break the signal circuit between the control unit and throttle actuator.

## *Cruise control system – checking*

145 The system cannot be thoroughly tested without the use of special equipment, but the following elementary checks may be carried out in an endeavour to trace a fault.

146 Check all system wiring and vacuum connections for security.

147 Adjust the throttle actuator free play so that it does not exceed 0.040 in (1.0 mm).

148 Check that the air gap at the speed transducer is maintained between 0.235 in (6.0 mm) and 0.315 in (8.0 mm).

149 Check that the stop-lamp fuse and the main fuse have not blown.

## *Mobile radio equipment – interference-free installation*

**Aerials – selection and fitting**

The choice of aerials is now very wide. It should be realised that the quality has a profound effect on radio performance, and a poor, inefficient aerial can make suppression difficult.

A wing-mounted aerial is regarded as probably the most efficient for signal collection, but a roof aerial is usually better for suppression purposes because it is away from most interference fields. Stick-on wire aerials are available for attachment to the inside of the windscreen, but are not always free from the interference field of the engine and some accessories.

Motorised automatic aerials rise when the equipment is switched on and retract at switch-off. They require more fitting space and supply leads, and can be a source of trouble.

There is no merit in choosing a very long aerial as, for example, the type about three metres in length which hooks or clips on to the rear of the car, since part of this aerial will inevitably be located in an interference field. For VHF/FM radios the best length of aerial is about one metre. Active aerials have a transistor amplifier mounted at the base and this serves to boost the received signal. The aerial rod is sometimes rather shorter than normal passive types.

A large loss of signal can occur in the aerial feeder cable, especially over the Very High Frequency (VHF) bands. The design of feeder cable is invariably in the co-axial form, ie a centre conductor surrounded by a flexible copper braid forming the outer (earth) conductor. Between the inner and outer conductors is an insulator material which can be in solid or stranded form. Apart from insulation, its purpose is to maintain the correct spacing and concentricity. Loss of signal occurs in this insulator, the loss usually being greater in a poor quality cable. The quality of cable used is reflected in the price of the aerial with the attached feeder cable.

The capacitance of the feeder should be within the range 65 to 75 picofarads (pF) approximately (95 to 100 pF for Japanese and American equipment), otherwise the adjustment of the car radio aerial trimmer may not be possible. An extension cable is necessary for a long run between aerial and receiver. If this adds capacitance in excess of the above limits, a connector containing a series capacitor will be required, or an extension which is labelled as 'capacity-compensated'.

Fitting the aerial will normally involve making a 7/8 in (22 mm) diameter hole in the bodywork, but read the instructions that come with the aerial kit. Once the hole position has been selected, use a centre punch to guide the drill. Use sticky masking tape around the area for this helps with marking out and drill location, and gives protection to the paintwork should the drill slip. Three methods of making the hole are in use:

(a) Use a hole saw in the electric drill. This is, in effect, a circular hacksaw blade wrapped round a former with a centre pilot drill.
(b) Use a tank cutter which also has cutting teeth, but is made to shear the metal by tightening with an Allen key.
(c) The hard way of drilling out the circle is using a small drill, say 1/8 in (3 mm), so that the holes overlap. The centre metal drops out and the hole is finished with round and half-round files.

Whichever method is used, the burr is removed from the body metal and paint removed from the underside. The aerial is fitted tightly ensuring that the earth fixing, usually a serrated washer, ring or clamp, is making a solid connection. *This earth connection is important in reducing interference.* Cover any bare metal with primer paint and topcoat, and follow by underseal if desired.

Aerial feeder cable routing should avoid the engine compartment and areas where stress might occur, eg under the carpet where feet will be located. Roof aerials require that the headlining be pulled back and that a path is available down the door pillar. It is wise to check with the vehicle dealer whether roof aerial fitting is recommended.

**Loudspeakers**

Speakers should be matched to the output stage of the equipment, particularly as regards the recommended impedance. Power transistors used for driving speakers are sensitive to the loading placed on them.

Before choosing a mounting position for speakers, check whether the vehicle manufacturer has provided a location for them. Generally door-mounted speakers give good stereophonic reproduction, but not all doors are able to accept them. The next best position is the rear parcel shelf, and in this case speaker apertures can be cut into the shelf, or pod units may be mounted.

For door mounting, first remove the trim, which is often held on by 'poppers' or press studs, and then select a suitable gap in the inside door assembly. Check that the speaker would not obstruct glass or winder mechanism by winding the window up and down. A template is often provided for marking out the trim panel hole, and then the four fixing holes must be drilled through. Mark out with chalk and cut cleanly with a sharp knife or keyhole saw. Speaker leads are then threaded through the door and door pillar, if necessary drilling 10 mm diameter holes. Fit grommets in the holes and connect to the radio or tape unit correctly. Do not omit a waterproofing cover, usually supplied with door speakers. If the speaker has to be fixed into the metal of the door itself, use self-tapping screws, and if the fixing is to the door trim use self-tapping screws and flat spire nuts.

Rear shelf mounting is somewhat simpler but it is necessary to find gaps in the metalwork underneath the parcel shelf. However, remember that the speakers should be as far apart as possible to give a good stereo effect. Pod-mounted speakers can be screwed into position through the parcel shelf material, but it is worth testing for the best position. Sometimes good results are found by reflecting sound off the rear window.

**Unit installation**

Many vehicles have a dash panel aperture to take a radio/audio unit, a recognised international standard being 189.5 mm x 60 mm. Alternatively a console may be a feature of the car interior design and this, mounted below the dashboard, gives more room. If neither facility is available a unit may be mounted on the underside of the parcel shelf; these are frequently non-metallic and an earth wire from the case to a good earth point is necessary. A three-sided cover in the form of a cradle is obtainable from car radio dealers and this gives a professional appearance to the installation; in this case choose a position where the controls can be reached by a driver with his seat belt on.

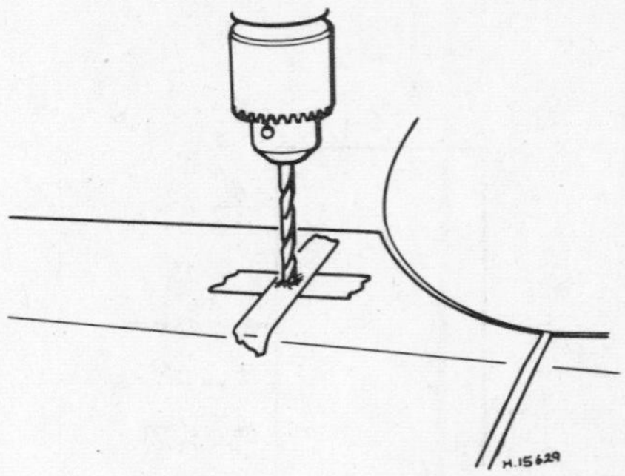


**Fig. 13.84 Drilling the hole for aerial mounting (Sec 11)**

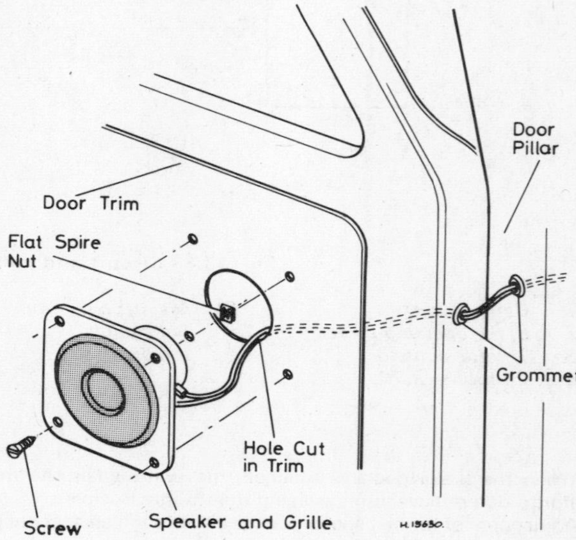


**Fig. 13.85 Door mounted speaker installation (Sec 11)**

Installation of the radio/audio unit is basically the same in all cases, and consists of offering it into the aperture after removal of the knobs (*not* push buttons) and the trim plate. In some cases a special mounting plate is required to which the unit is attached. It is worthwhile supporting the rear end in cases where sag or strain may occur, and it is usually possible to use a length of perforated metal strip attached between the unit and a good support point nearby. In general it is recommended that tape equipment should be installed at or nearly horizontal.

Connections to the aerial socket are simply by the standard plug terminating the aerial downlead or its extension cable. Speakers for a stereo system must be matched and correctly connected, as outlined previously.

**Note:** *While all work is carried out on the power side, it is wise to disconnect the battery earth lead.* Before connection is made to the vehicle electrical system, check that the polarity of the unit is correct. Most vehicles use a negative earth system, but radio/audio units often have a reversible plug to convert the set to either + or – earth. *Incorrect connection may cause serious damage.*

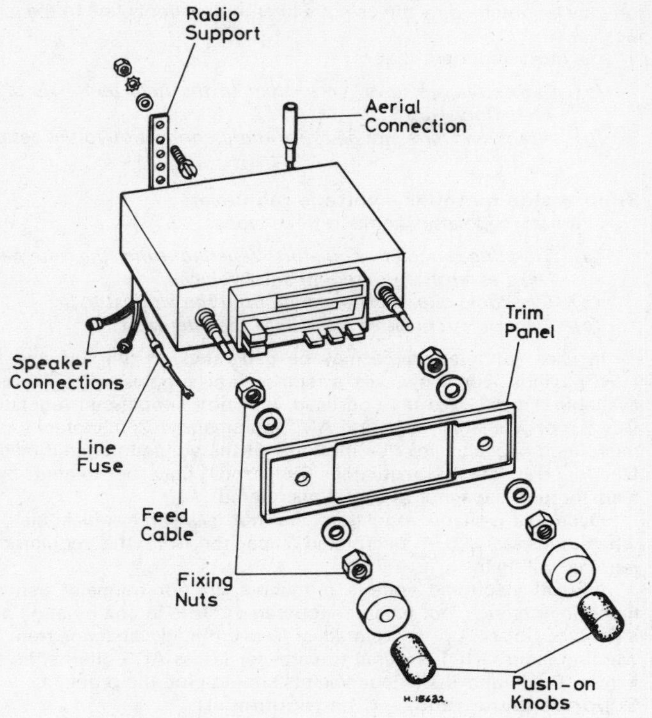


**Fig. 13.86 Mounting components for radio/cassette (Sec 11)**

The power lead is often permanently connected inside the unit and terminates with one half of an in-line fuse carrier. The other half is fitted with a suitable fuse (3 or 5 amperes) and a wire which should go to a power point in the electrical system. This may be the accessory terminal on the ignition switch, giving the advantage of power feed with ignition or with the ignition key at the 'accessory' position. Power to the unit stops when the ignition key is removed. Alternatively, the lead may be taken to a live point at the fusebox with the consequence of having to remember to switch off at the unit before leaving the vehicle.

Before switching on for initial test, be sure that the speaker connections have been made, for running without load can damage the output transistors. Switch on next and tune through the bands to ensure that all sections are working, and check the tape unit if applicable. The aerial trimmer should be adjusted to give the strongest reception on a weak signal in the medium wave band, at say 200 metres.

**Interference**

In general, when electric current changes abruptly, unwanted electrical noise is produced. The motor vehicle is filled with electrical devices which change electric current rapidly, the most obvious being the contact breaker.

When the spark plugs operate, the sudden pulse of spark current causes the associated wiring to radiate. Since early radio transmitters used sparks as a basis of operation, it is not surprising that the car radio will pick up ignition spark noise unless steps are taken to reduce it to acceptable levels.

Interference reaches the car radio in two ways:

(a) by conduction through the wiring.
(b) by radiation to the receiving aerial.

Initial checks presuppose that the bonnet is down and fastened, the radio unit has a good earth connection *(not* through the aerial downlead outer), no fluorescent tubes are working near the car, the aerial trimmer has been adjusted, and the vehicle is in a position to receive radio signals, ie not in a metal-clad building.

Switch on the radio and tune it to the middle of the medium wave (MW) band off-station with the volume (gain) control set fairly high. Switch on the ignition (but do not start the engine) and wait to see if irregular clicks or hash noise occurs. Tapping the facia panel may also produce the effects. If so, this will be due to the voltage stabiliser, which is an on-off thermal switch to control instrument voltage. It is located usually on the back of the instrument panel, often attached to the speedometer. Correction is by attachment of a capacitor and, if still troublesome, chokes in the supply wires.

Switch on the engine and listen for interference on the MW band. Depending on the type of interference, the indications are as follows.

A harsh crackle that drops out abruptly at low engine speed or when the headlights are switched on is probably due to a voltage regulator.

A whine varying with engine speed is due to the dynamo or alternator. Try temporarily taking off the fan belt – if the noise goes this is confirmation.

Regular ticking or crackle that varies in rate with the engine speed is due to the ignition system. With this trouble in particular and others in general, check to see if the noise is entering the receiver from the wiring or by radiation. To do this, pull out the aerial plug, (preferably shorting out the input socket or connecting a 62 pF capacitor across it). If the noise disappears it is coming in through the aerial and is *radiation noise.* If the noise persists it is reaching the receiver through the wiring and is said to be *line-borne.*

Interference from wipers, washers, heater blowers, turn-indicators, stop lamps, etc is usually taken to the receiver by wiring, and simple treatment using capacitors and possibly chokes will solve the problem. Switch on each one in turn (wet the screen first for running wipers!) and listen for possible interference with the aerial plug in place and again when removed.

Electric petrol pumps are now finding application again and give rise to an irregular clicking, often giving a burst of clicks when the ignition is on but the engine has not yet been started. It is also possible to receive whining or crackling from the pump.

Note that if most of the vehicle accessories are found to be creating interference all together, the probability is that poor aerial earthing is to blame.

**Component terminal markings**

Throughout the following sub-sections reference will be found to various terminal markings. These will vary depending on the manufacturer of the relevant component. If terminal markings differ from those mentioned, reference should be made to the following table, where the most commonly encountered variations are listed.

| **Alternator** | *Alternator terminal (thick lead)* | *Exciting winding terminal* |
|---|---|---|
| DIN/Bosch | B+ | DF |
| Delco Remy | + | EXC |
| Ducellier | + | EXC |
| Ford (US) | + | DF |
| Lucas | + | F |
| Marelli | +B | F |
| **Ignition coil** | *Ignition switch terminal* | *Contact breaker terminal* |
| DIN/Bosch | 15 | 1 |
| Delco Remy | + | – |
| Ducellier | BAT | RUP |
| Ford (US) | B/+ | CB/– |
| Lucas | SW/+ | – |
| Marelli | BAT/+B | D |
| **Voltage regulator** | *Voltage input terminal* | *Exciting winding terminal* |
| DIN/Bosch | B+/D+ | DF |
| Delco Remy | BAT/+ | EXC |
| Ducellier | BOB/BAT | EXC |
| Ford (US) | BAT | DF |
| Lucas | +/A | F |
| Marelli | | F |

**Suppression methods – ignition**

Suppressed HT cables are supplied as original equipment by manufacturers and will meet regulations as far as interference to neighbouring equipment is concerned. It is illegal to remove such suppression unless an alternative is provided, and this may take the form of resistive spark plug caps in conjunction with plain copper HT cable. For VHF purposes, these and 'in-line' resistors may not be effective, and resistive HT cable is preferred. Check that suppressed cables are actually fitted by observing cable identity lettering, or measuring with an ohmmeter – the value of each plug lead should be 5000 to 10 000 ohms.

A 1 microfarad capacitor connected from the LT supply side of the ignition coil to a good nearby earth point will complete basic ignition interference treatment. *NEVER fit a capacitor to the coil terminal to the contact breaker – the result would be burnt out points in a short time.*

If ignition noise persists despite the treatment above, the following sequence should be followed:

(a) Check the earthing of the ignition coil; remove paint from fixing clamp.
(b) If this does not work, lift the bonnet. Should there be no change in interference level, this may indicate that the bonnet is not electrically connected to the car body. Use a proprietary braided strap across a bonnet hinge ensuring a first class electrical connection. If, however, lifting the bonnet increases the interference, then fit resistive HT cables of a higher ohms-per-metre value.
(c) If all these measures fail, it is probable that re-radiation from metallic components is taking place. Using a braided strap between metallic points, go round the vehicle systematically – try the following: engine to body, exhaust system to body, front suspension to engine and to body, steering column to body (especially French and Italian cars), gear lever to engine and to body (again especially French and Italian cars), Bowden cable to body, metal parcel shelf to body. When an offending component is located it should be bonded with the strap permanently.
(d) As a next step, the fitting of distributor suppressors to each lead at the distributor end may help.
(e) Beyond this point is involved the possible screening of the distributor and fitting resistive spark plugs, but such advanced treatment is not usually required for vehicles with entertainment equipment.

Electronic ignition systems have built-in suppression components, but this does not relieve the need for using suppressed HT leads. In some cases it is permitted to connect a capacitor on the low tension supply side of the ignition coil, but not in every case. Makers' instructions should be followed carefully, otherwise damage to the ignition semiconductors may result.

**Suppression methods – generators**

Alternators should be fitted with a 3 microfarad capacitor from the B+ main output terminal (thick cable) to earth. Additional suppression may be obtained by the use of a filter in the supply line to the radio receiver.

It is most important that:

*(a) Capacitors are never connected to the field terminals of an alternator.*
*(b) Alternators must not be run without connection to the battery.*

**Suppression methods – voltage regulators**

Alternator regulators come in three types:

*(a) Vibrating contact regulators separate from the alternator. Used extensively on continental vehicles.*
*(b) Electronic regulators separate from the alternator.*
*(c) Electronic regulators built-in to the alternator.*

In case (a) interference may be generated on the AM and FM (VHF) bands. For some cars a replacement suppressed regulator is available. Filter boxes may be used with non-suppressed regulators. But if not available, then for AM equipment a 2 microfarad or 3 microfarad capacitor may be mounted at the voltage terminal marked D+ or B+ of the regulator. FM bands may be treated by a feed-through capacitor of 2 or 3 microfarad.

Electronic voltage regulators are not always troublesome, but where necessary, a 1 microfarad capacitor from the regulator + terminal will help.

Integral electronic voltage regulators do not normally generate much interference, but when encountered this is in combination with alternator noise. A 1 microfarad or 2 microfarad capacitor from the warning lamp (IND) terminal to earth for Lucas ACR alternators and Femsa, Delco and Bosch equivalents should cure the problem.

**Suppression methods – other equipment**

**Wiper motors** – Connect the wiper body to earth with a bonding strap. For all motors use a 7 ampere choke assembly inserted in the leads to the motor.

**Heater motors** – Fit 7 ampere line chokes in both leads, assisted if necessary by a 1 microfarad capacitor to earth from both leads.

**Electronic tachometer** – The tachometer is a possible source of ignition noise – check by disconnecting at the ignition coil CB terminal. It usually feeds from ignition coil LT pulses at the contact breaker terminal. A 3 ampere line choke should be fitted in the tachometer lead at the coil CB terminal.

**Horn** – A capacitor and choke combination is effective if the horn is directly connected to the 12 volt supply. The use of a relay is an

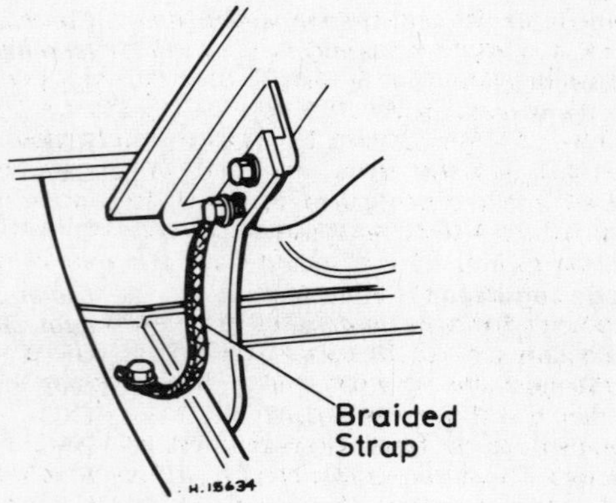


Fig. 13.87 Bonnet-to-body earth strap (Sec 11)

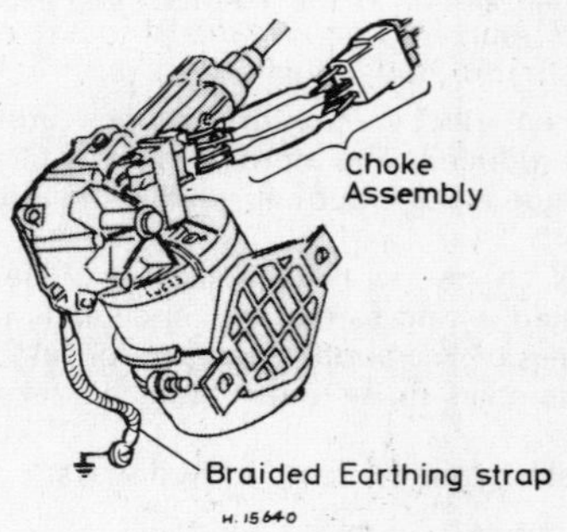


Fig. 13.88 Wiper motor suppressor (Sec 11)

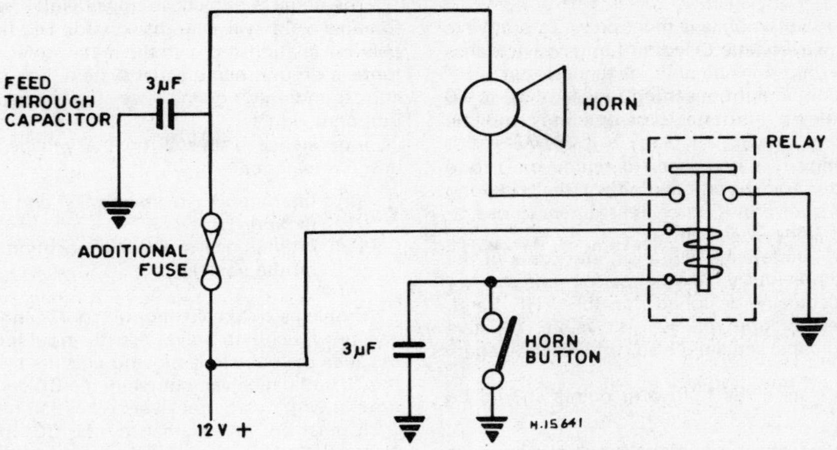


Fig. 13.89 Horn relay used to reduce interference (Sec 11)

alternative remedy, as this will reduce the length of the interference-carrying leads.

**Electrostatic noise** – Characteristics are erratic crackling at the receiver, with disappearance of symptoms in wet weather. Often shocks may be given when touching bodywork. Part of the problem is the build-up of static electricity in non-driven wheels and the acquisition of charge on the body shell. It is possible to fit spring-loaded contacts at the wheels to give good conduction between the rotary wheel parts and the vehicle frame. Changing a tyre sometimes helps – because of tyres' varying resistances. In difficult cases a trailing flex which touches the ground will cure the problem. If this is not acceptable it is worth trying conductive paint on the tyre walls.

**Fuel pump** – Suppression requires a 1 microfarad capacitor between the supply wire to the pump and a nearby earth point. If this is insufficient a 7 ampere line choke connected in the supply wire near the pump is required.

**Fluorescent tubes** – Vehicles used for camping/caravanning frequently have fluorescent tube lighting. These tubes require a relatively high voltage for operation and this is provided by an inverter (a form of oscillator) which steps up the vehicle supply voltage. This can give rise to serious interference to radio reception, and the tubes themselves can contribute to this interference by the pulsating nature of the lamp discharge. In such situations it is important to mount the aerial as far away from a fluorescent tube as possible. The interference problem may be alleviated by screening the tube with fine wire turns spaced an inch (25 mm) apart and earthed to the chassis. Suitable chokes should be fitted in both supply wires close to the inverter.

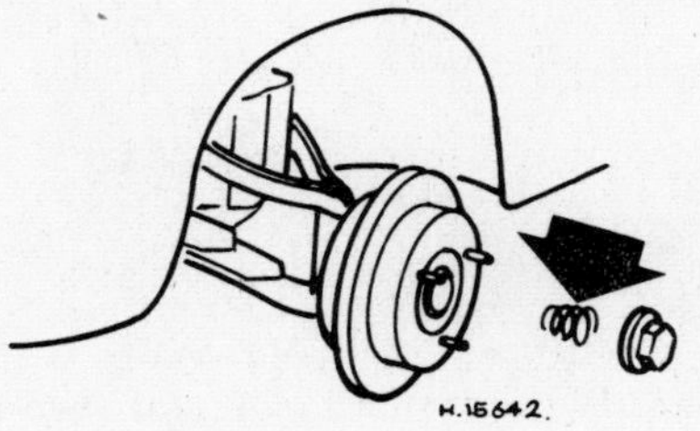


Fig. 13.90 Roadwheel spring contacts (Sec 11)

**Radio/cassette case breakthrough**

Magnetic radiation from dashboard wiring may be sufficiently intense to break through the metal case of the radio/cassette player. Often this is due to a particular cable routed too close and shows up as ignition interference on AM and cassette play and/or alternator whine on cassette play.

The first point to check is that the clips and/or screws are fixing all parts of the radio/cassette case together properly. Assuming good earthing of the case, see if it is possible to re-route the offending cable – the chances of this are not good, however, in most cars.

Next release the radio/cassette player and locate it in different positions with temporary leads. If a point of low interference is found, then if possible fix the equipment in that area. This also confirms that local radiation is causing the trouble. If re-location is not feasible, fit the radio/cassette player back in the original position.

Alternator interference on cassette play is now caused by radiation from the main charging cable which goes from the battery to the output terminal of the alternator, usually via the + terminal of the starter motor relay. In some vehicles this cable is routed under the dashboard, so the solution is to provide a direct cable route. Detach the original cable from the alternator output terminal and make up a new cable of at least 6 mm² cross-sectional area to go from alternator to battery with the shortest possible route. *Remember – do not run the engine with the alternator disconnected from the battery.*

Ignition breakthrough on AM and/or cassette play can be a difficult problem. It is worth wrapping earthed foil round the offending cable run near the equipment, or making up a deflector plate well screwed down to a good earth. Another possibility is the use of a suitable relay to switch on the ignition coil. The relay should be mounted close to the ignition coil; with this arrangement the ignition coil primary current is not taken into the dashboard area and does not flow through the ignition switch. A suitable diode should be used since it is possible that at ignition switch-off the output from the warning lamp alternator terminal could hold the relay on.

**Connectors for suppression components**

Capacitors are usually supplied with tags on the end of the lead, while the capacitor body has a flange with a slot or hole to fit under a nut or screw with washer.

Connections to feed wires are best achieved by self-stripping connectors. These connectors employ a blade which, when squeezed down by pliers, cuts through cable insulation and makes connection to the copper conductors beneath.

Chokes sometimes come with bullet snap-in connectors fitted to the wires, and also with just bare copper wire. With connectors, suitable female cable connectors may be purchased from an auto-accessory shop together with any extra connectors required for the cable ends after being cut for the choke insertion. For chokes with bare wires, similar connectors may be employed together with insulation sleeving as required.

### VHF/FM broadcasts

Reception of VHF/FM in an automobile is more prone to problems than the medium and long wavebands. Medium/long wave transmitters are capable of covering considerable distances, but VHF transmitters are restricted to line of sight, meaning ranges of 10 to 50 miles, depending upon the terrain, the effects of buildings and the transmitter power.

Because of the limited range it is necessary to retune on a long journey, and it may be better for those habitually travelling long distances or living in areas of poor provision of transmitters to use an AM radio working on medium/long wavebands.

When conditions are poor, interference can arise, and some of the suppression devices described previously fall off in performance at very high frequencies unless specifically designed for the VHF band. Available suppression devices include reactive HT cable, resistive distributor caps, screened plug caps, screened leads and resistive spark plugs.

For VHF/FM receiver installation the following points should be particularly noted:

(a) Earthing of the receiver chassis and the aerial mounting is important. Use a separate earthing wire at the radio, and scrape paint away at the aerial mounting.
(b) If possible, use a good quality roof aerial to obtain maximum height and distance from interference generating devices on the vehicle.
(c) Use of a high quality aerial downlead is important, since losses in cheap cable can be significant.
(d) The polarisation of FM transmissions may be horizontal, vertical, circular or slanted. Because of this the optimum mounting angle is at 45° to the vehicle roof.

### Citizens' Band radio (CB)

In the UK, CB transmitter/receivers work within the 27 MHz and 934 MHz bands, using the FM mode. At present interest is concentrated on 27 MHz where the design and manufacture of equipment is less difficult. Maximum transmitted power is 4 watts, and 40 channels spaced 10 kHz apart within the range 27.60125 to 27.99125 MHz are available.

Aerials are the key to effective transmission and reception. Regulations limit the aerial length to 1.65 metres including the loading coil and any associated circuitry, so tuning the aerial is necessary to obtain optimum results. The choice of a CB aerial is dependent on whether it is to be permanently installed or removable, and the performance will hinge on correct tuning and the location point on the vehicle. Common practice is to clip the aerial to the roof gutter or to employ wing mounting where the aerial can be rapidly unscrewed. An alternative is to use the boot rim to render the aerial theftproof, but a popular solution is to use the 'magmount' – a type of mounting having a strong magnetic base clamping to the vehicle at any point, usually the roof.

Aerial location determines the signal distribution for both transmission and reception, but it is wise to choose a point away from the engine compartment to minimise interference from vehicle electrical equipment.

The aerial is subject to considerable wind and acceleration forces. Cheaper units will whip backwards and forwards and in so doing will alter the relationship with the metal surface of the vehicle with which it forms a ground plane aerial system. The radiation pattern will change correspondingly, giving rise to break-up of both incoming and outgoing signals.

Interference problems on the vehicle carrying CB equipment fall into two categories:

(a) Interference to nearby TV and radio receivers when transmitting.
(b) Interference to CB set reception due to electrical equipment on the vehicle.

Problems of break-through to TV and radio are not frequent, but can be difficult to solve. Mostly trouble is not detected or reported because the vehicle is moving and the symptoms rapidly disappear at the TV/radio receiver, but when the CB set is used as a base station any trouble with nearby receivers will soon result in a complaint.

It must not be assumed by the CB operator that his equipment is faultless, for much depends upon the design. Harmonics (that is, multiples) of 27 MHz may be transmitted unknowingly and these can fall into other user's bands. Where trouble of this nature occurs, low pass filters in the aerial or supply leads can help, and should be fitted in base station aerials as a matter of course. In stubborn cases it may be necessary to call for assistance from the licensing authority, or, if possible, to have the equipment checked by the manufacturers.

Interference received on the CB set from the vehicle equipment is, fortunately, not usually a severe problem. The precautions outlined previously for radio/cassette units apply, but there are some extra points worth noting.

It is common practice to use a slide-mount on CB equipment enabling the set to be easily removed for use as a base station, for example. Care must be taken that the slide mount fittings are properly earthed and that first class connection occurs between the set and slide-mount.

Vehicle manufacturers in the UK are required to provide suppression of electrical equipment to cover 40 to 250 MHz to protect TV and VHF radio bands. Such suppression appears to be adequately effective at 27 MHz, but suppression of individual items such as alternators/dynamos, clocks, stabilisers, flashers, wiper motors, etc, may still be necessary. The suppression capacitors and chokes available from auto-electrical suppliers for entertainment receivers will usually give the required results with CB equipment.

### Other vehicle radio transmitters

Besides CB radio already mentioned, a considerable increase in the use of transceivers (ie combined transmitter and receiver units) has taken place in the last decade. Previously this type of equipment was fitted mainly to military, fire, ambulance and police vehicles, but a large business radio and radio telephone usage has developed.

Generally the suppression techniques described previously will suffice, with only a few difficult cases arising. Suppression is carried out to satisfy the 'receive mode', but care must be taken to use heavy duty chokes in the equipment supply cables since the loading on 'transmit' is relatively high.

**Wiring diagrams overleaf**

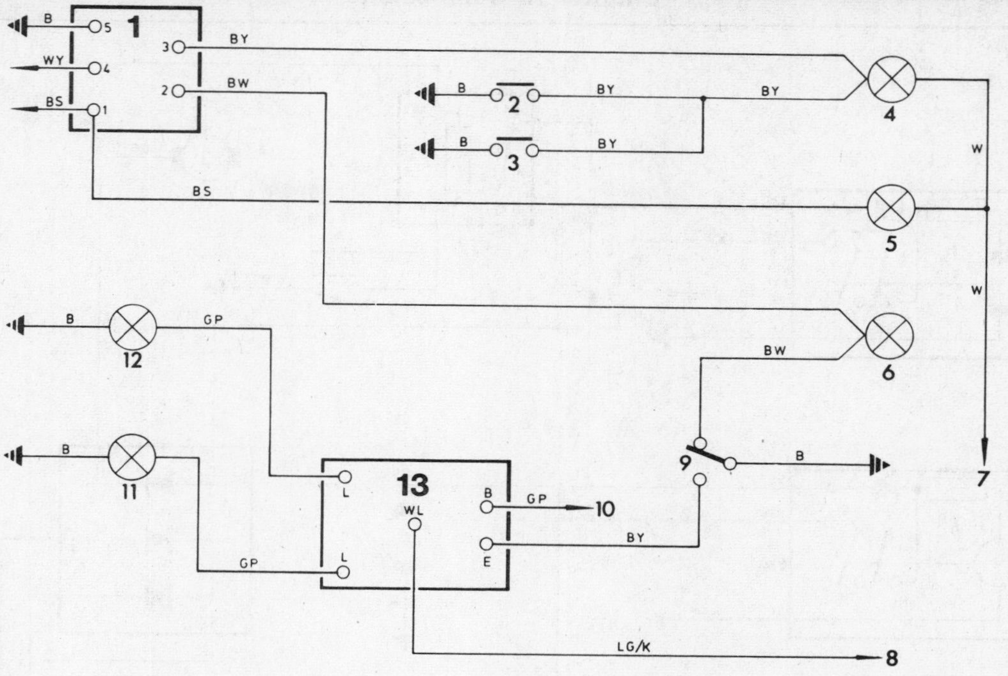


**Fig. 13.99 Bulb failure unit wiring diagram**

1 Failure unit
2 Brake fluid level switch
3 Brake pressure differential valve
4 Brake stop-lamp
5 Oxygen sensor warning lamp
6 Handbrake 'ON' warning lamp
7 To ignition switch
8 To bulb failure warning lamp via blocking diode
9 Handbrake switch
10 To footbrake switch
11 LH stop-lamp
12 RH stop-lamp
13 Stop-lamp bulb failure unit

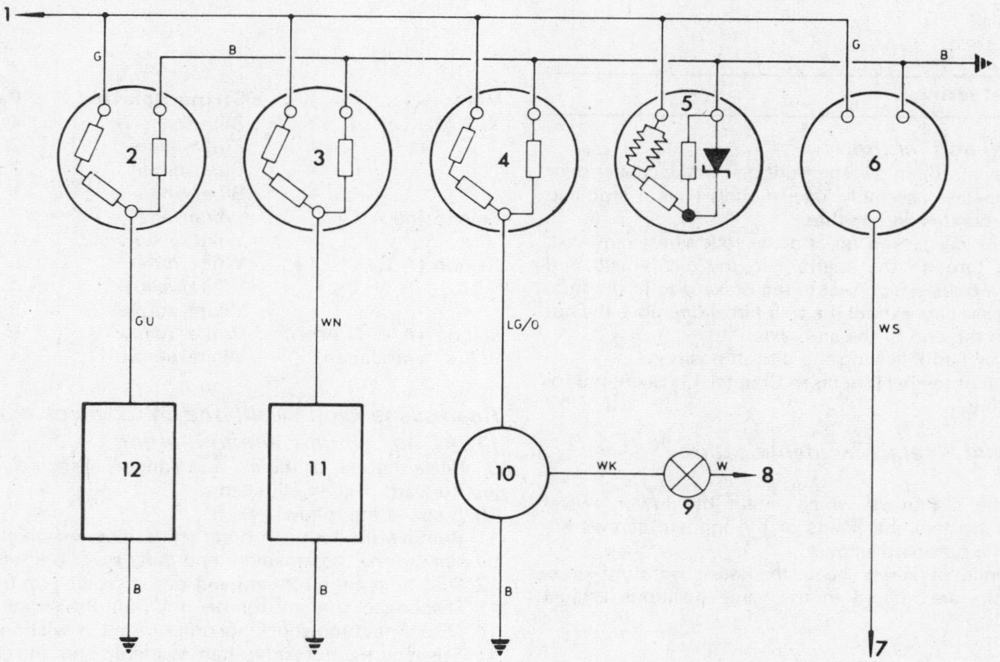


**Fig. 13.100 Instrument panel wiring diagram**

1 To fuse No 4
2 Coolant temperature gauge
3 Oil pressure gauge
4 Fuel contents gauge
5 Battery condition gauge
6 Tachometer
7 To amplifier
8 To ignition switch
9 Low fuel level warning lamp
10 Fuel tank sender unit
11 Oil pressure sender switch
12 Coolant temperature sender switch

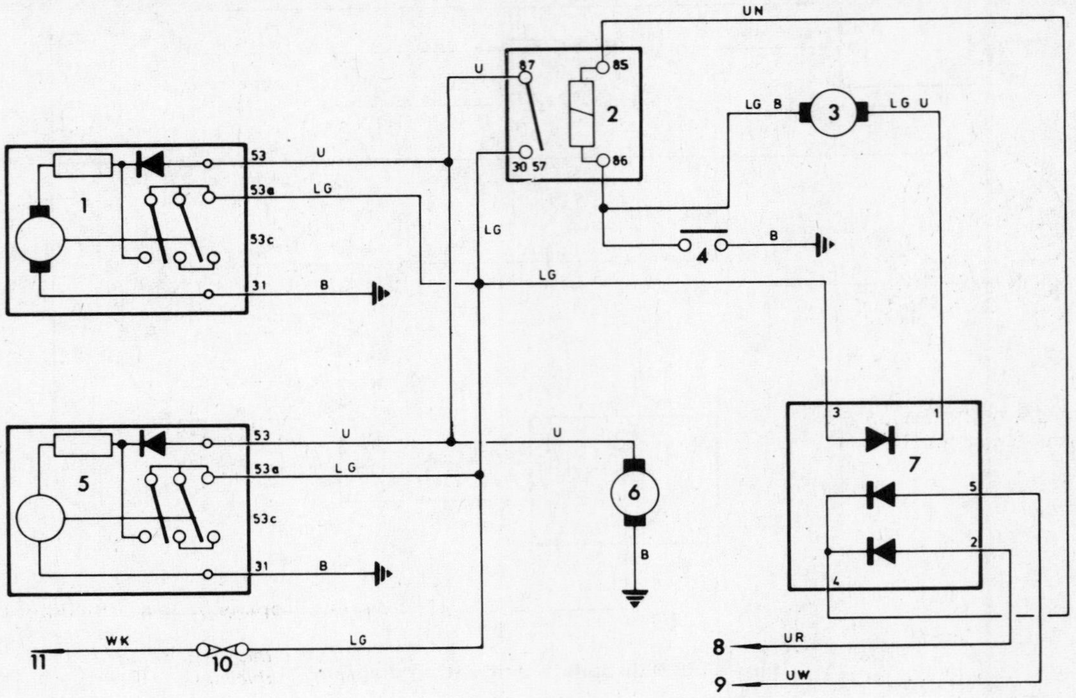


Fig. 13.101 Headlamp wash/wipe wiring diagram

1 RH headlamp wiper motor
2 Wash/wipe relay
3 Windscreen washer pump
4 Windscreen washer switch
5 LH headlamp wiper motor
6 Headlamp washer pump
7 Diode pack
8 To headlamp dipped beam
9 To headlamp main beam
10 Fuse No 11
11 To ignition protection relay

## 12 Suspension and steering

### *Front hub – removal and refitting*

1 In order to avoid having to remove the front disc brake caliper prior to withdrawing the hub/disc assembly, later models have a modified disc shield which incorporates an aperture.

2 With the front of the car jacked up and the roadwheel removed, pass a socket wrench through the aperture in the disc shield and unscrew in turn the five bolts which secure the brake disc to the hub.

3 Take off the hub grease cap, extract the split pin and remove the nut and thrust washer from the end of the stub axle.

4 Withdraw the hub by hand, leaving the disc in position.

5 Refitting is a reversal of removal. Refer to Chapter 11, Section 5 for the adjustment procedure.

### *Lower swivel balljoint – setscrew identification (all models)*

6 When removing the setscrews which retain the lower swivel balljoint, it may be found that the heads of the inboard screws are thicker than those of the outboard screws.

7 Where this difference in screw head thickness is found, it is important that the bolts are refitted in the same positions as just described.

### *Front roadsprings – colour coding*

8 Front roadsprings are identified by a coloured stripe running the length of the spring and a splash of coloured paint on the spring centre coil. The following table indicates spring application. The number of spring packing pieces used with a particular spring is indicated by the coloured splash.

| Vehicle | Stripe/Splash | Packing pieces |
|---|---|---|
| XJS Auto | Blue/yellow | 4 |
| | Blue/purple | 3 |
| | Blue/white | 2 |
| XJS Manual | Blue/red | 4 |
| | Blue/yellow | 3 |
| | Blue/purple | 2 |
| | Blue/white | 1 |
| Saloon (no A/C) | White/red | 2 |
| | White/yellow | 1 |
| Saloon (A/C) | White/red | 5 |
| | White/yellow | 4 |
| | White/purple | 3 |
| Saloon (A/C, N America and Japan) | White/Yellow | 5 |
| | White/purple | 4 |

### *Rear suspension wishbone inner pivot mounting bracket (1981 on) – removal and refitting*

9 Raise the rear of the car and support it securely on stands placed just forward of the radius arms.

10 Remove the roadwheels.

11 Remove the fourteen bolts and setscrews which hold the bottom tie plate to the crossmember and inner pivot brackets.

12 Disconnect the forward end of the radius arm from the body.

13 Disconnect the anti-roll bar link from the radius arm.

14 Disconnect the shock absorber from the wishbone.

15 Suspend the hub/driveshaft assembly from the crossmember using wire or string. Remove the rear nut from the inner pivot shaft, then tap the shaft forward to free the wishbone from the inner pivot. Tap the spacer tube from between the lugs of the pivot bracket.

16 Cut the locking wire from the two setscrews which hold the pivot bracket to the final drive unit. Unscrew and remove the securing setscrews and lift away the pivot bracket. Note carefully the location and number of shims.

17 Refitting is a reversal of removal, but make sure that all shims are replaced exactly as originally fitted.

18 The use of two dummy shafts when offering up the wishbone to

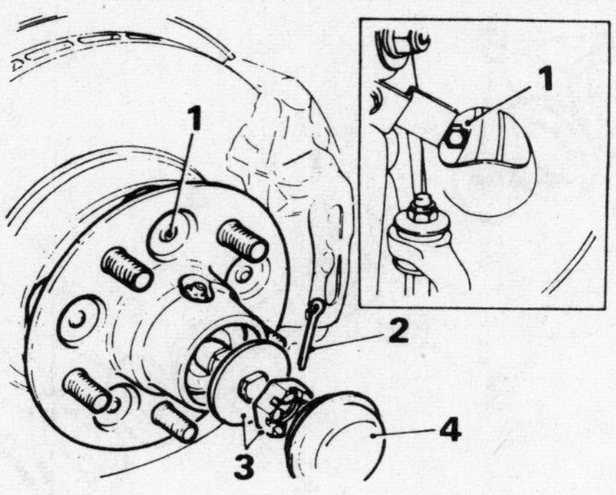


**Fig. 13.102 Front hub showing access to hub/disc bolts through disc shield aperture (Sec 12)**

*1 Bolt*
*2 Split pin*
*3 Nut and thrust washer*
*4 Grease cap*

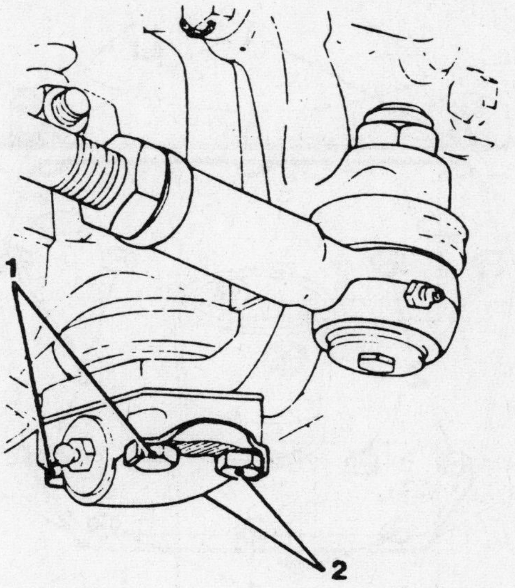


**Fig. 13.103 Front suspension lower balljoint bolts (Sec 12)**

*1 Bolt head thickness = 0.3125 in (7.94 mm)*
*2 Bolt head thickness = 0.1875 in (4.76 mm)*

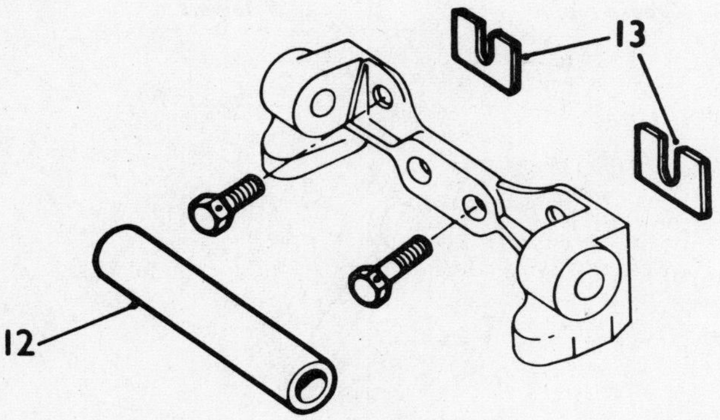


**Fig. 13.104 Rear suspension inner pivot bracket (Sec 12)**

*12 Spacer tube*
*13 Shims*

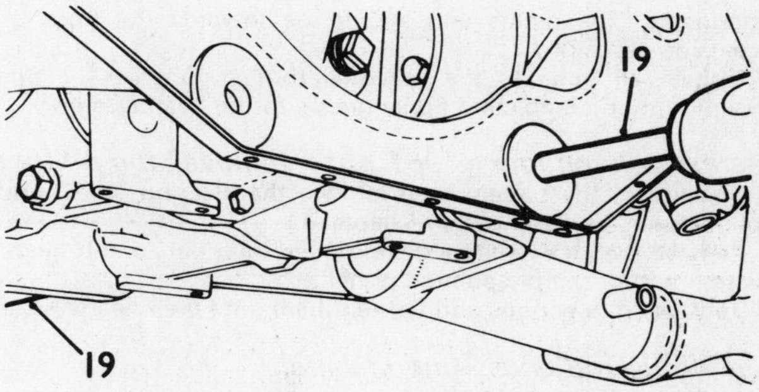


**Fig. 13.105 Using dummy shafts (19) to position rear suspension wishbone on pivot bracket (Sec 12)**

the pivot bracket lugs will greatly facilitate installation and prevent displacement of the various components.

### *Rear suspension wishbone (1981 on) – removal and refitting*

19 Raise the rear of the car and support it on axle stands placed just forward of the radius arms.
20 Remove the roadwheel.
21 Remove the self-locking nut from the outer pivot shaft and drive out the shaft.
22 Fit a suitable rod to the hub carrier in place of the shaft and use adhesive tape to retain the shims and oil seal washers.
23 Raise the hub/driveshaft and tie it to the crossmember with string or wire.
24 Unbolt the tie plate from the crossmember (six bolts).
25 Cut the locking wire and unbolt the radius arm from the body.
26 Unbolt the tie plate from the inner pivot brackets.
27 Disconnect the shock absorbers from the wishbone.
28 Unscrew the rear nut from the inner pivot shaft, and then drive the shaft forward to free the wishbone from the inner pivot.
29 Remove the wishbone and the radius arm.
30 Refitting is a reversal of removal, but apply grease to the needle bearing cages. The wishbone inner pivot boss must have its engraved face pointing outwards.
31 Use the dummy shafts when offering up the wishbone to the inner pivot mounting bracket to prevent displacement of the pivot bearing

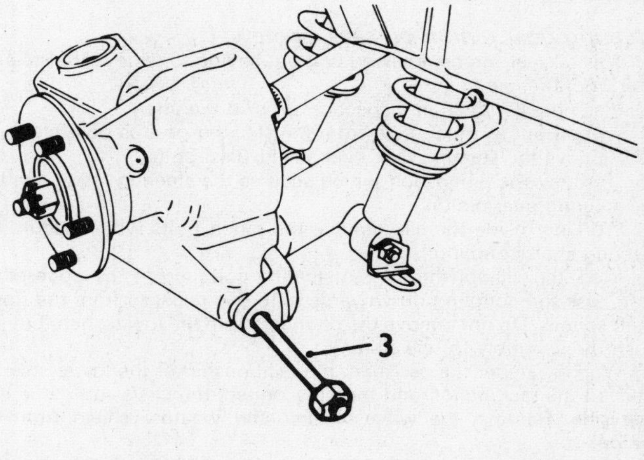


**Fig. 13.106 Rear suspension outer pivot shaft (3) (Sec 12)**

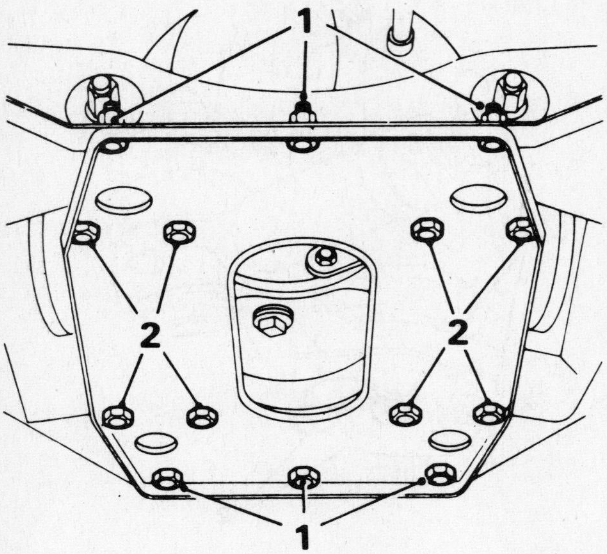


Fig. 13.107 Rear suspension tie plate nuts and bolts (Sec 12)

*1 To crossmember* *2 To inner pivot bracket*

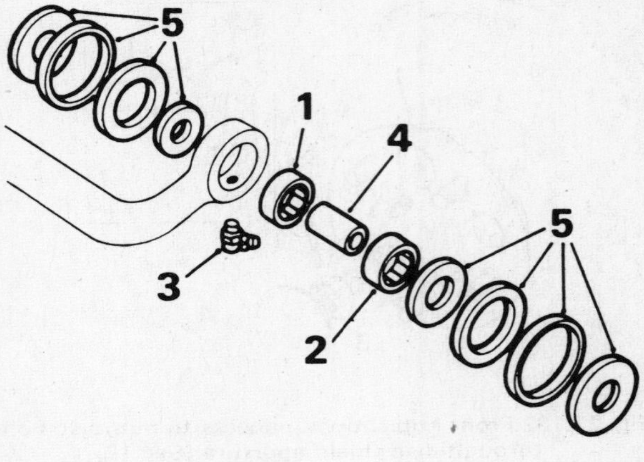


Fig. 13.108 Rear suspension wishbone pivot bearing components (Sec 12)

*1 Cage*
*2 Cage*
*3 Grease nipple*
*4 Tube*
*5 Thrust washers, seals and retainers*

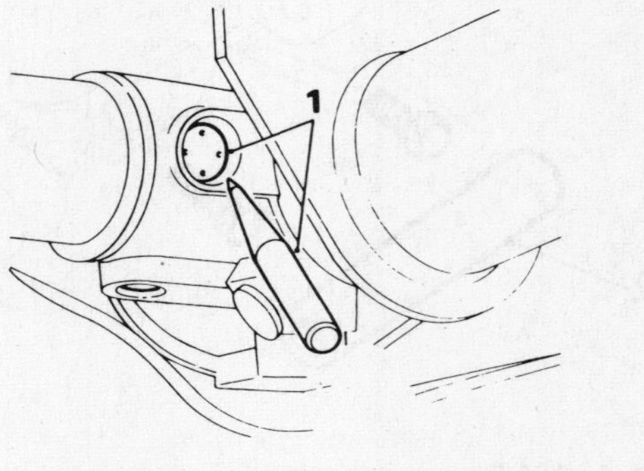


Fig. 13.109 Removing steering lock shear bolts with a punch (1) (Sec 12)

components. The radius arm should be towards the front of the suspension assembly.
32 Tighten all bolts to the specified torque (Chapter 11 Specifications) and on completion apply grease to the bearing nipples.

*Steering column lock (1981 on) – removal and refitting*
33 Disconnect the battery then remove the steering wheel and the upper column, as described in Chapter 11.
34 Remove the lock bolts by driving them round in an anti-clockwise direction with a sharply pointed punch.
35 Refit using new bolts and tighten them until their heads break off.

*Steering tie-rod ends – modification*
36 As from 1983, sealed type tie-rod end balljoints are fitted which require no lubrication.

*Steering column upper bearing – modification*
37 A redesigned upper steering column, incorporating a spring-loaded top bearing, was introduced during the 1982 model year. The new column is less likely to rattle or to transmit noise from elsewhere.
38 The new type upper column is interchangeable, as a complete unit, with the old type.

*Steering gear pinion oil seal – renewal*
39 This oil seal can be renewed without having to remove the steering gear from the car.
40 Place the car over an inspection pit or on ramps.
41 Syphon out as much fluid from the steering gear as possible.
42 Remove the steering rack heat shield (two bolts).
43 Unscrew the pinch-bolt which secures the steering lower shaft to the steering gear pinion.
44 Working inside the car, remove the pinch-bolts which secure the steering shaft coupling.
45 Mark the relationship of the steering coupling to the upper shaft then ease the coupling downwards until it is released from the upper shaft splines. Do not remove the coupling from the lower shaft, but just push the assembly to one side.
46 Working under the car, mark the relationship of the lower steering shaft to the rack pinion and then disconnect the shaft and move it to one side. Remove the wave washer and weather shield from the pinion.
47 Mark the relationship of the steering rack to the suspension crossmember.
48 Remove the steering rack upper mounting nut and bolt.
49 Remove the steering rack right hand lower mounting nut, leaving the bolt in place.
50 Remove the rack heat shield mounting bracket.
51 Slacken the remaining rack mounting nut and pivot the rack downwards to give access to the pinion oil seal.
52 Place a drain tray under the rack assembly and extract the pinion oil seal circlip and washer.
53 Using a thin screwdriver blade or similar, prise out the oil seal and clean the oil seal recess.
54 Wrap PVC tape around the pinion shaft splines and smear the oil seal lips with petroleum jelly. Tap the new seal into position and then remove the tape.
55 Refit the washer and circlip. Reassemble the rack and shaft by reversing the dismantling operations. Make sure that the marks made before dismantling are in alignment, and tighten nuts and bolts to the specified torque (see Specifications, Chapter 11).
56 Fill the steering system with fluid and bleed it, as described in Chapter 11, Section 48.

*Rear anti-roll bar (XJS-HE)*
57 This suspension component is not fitted to XJS-HE models.

*Alloy roadwheels – precautions*
58 When cast alloy roadwheels are fitted, they must be inspected regularly for freedom from cracks and corrosion. The protective coating on the alloy, which prevents corrosion, must be undamaged.

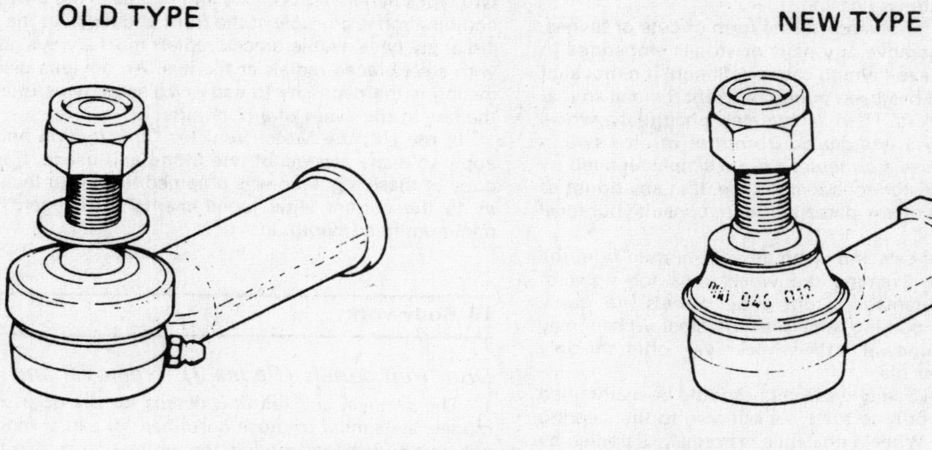


Fig. 13.110 Old and new type tie-rod end balljoints (Sec 12)

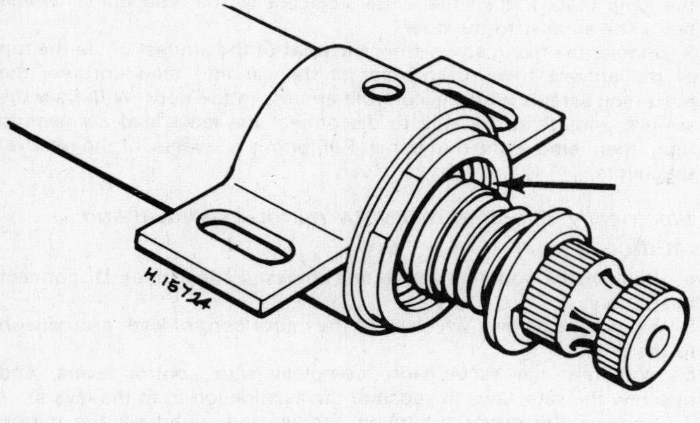


Fig. 13.111 Steering shaft spring-loaded top bearing (arrowed) (Sec 12)

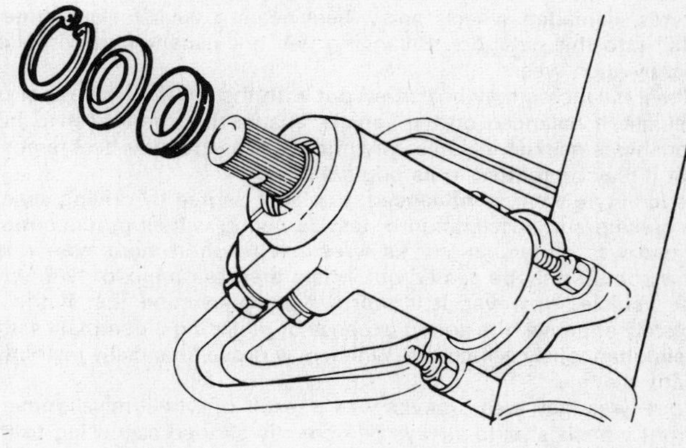

Fig. 13.112 Steering gear pinion oil seal, circlip and washer (Sec 12)

59 Tyre removal and refitting must **not** be performed using tyre levers or any form of leverage on the wheel. Only entrust such work to experts.

60 When refitting a wheel, always tighten the wheel nuts evenly and in sequence, making sure that they are properly seated. Do not exceed the specified tightening torque.

### *Power-assisted steering system – fluid level checking*

61 Have the engine at normal operating temperature.

62 Unscrew and remove the filler cap/dipstick from the fluid reservoir.

63 The oil level on the dipstick should be up to the FULL-HOT mark.

64 Turn the steering from lock to lock several times and recheck the level. Top up if necessary only with clean specified fluid.

### *Wheels and tyres – general care and maintenance*

Wheels and tyres should give no real problems in use provided that a close eye is kept on them with regard to excessive wear or damage. To this end, the following points should be noted.

Ensure that tyre pressures are checked regularly and maintained correctly. Checking should be carried out with the tyres cold and not immediately after the vehicle has been in use. If the pressures are checked with the tyres hot, an apparently high reading will be obtained owing to heat expansion. Under no circumstances should an attempt be made to reduce the pressures to the quoted cold reading in this instance, or effective underinflation will result.

Underinflation will cause overheating of the tyre owing to excessive flexing of the casing, and the tread will not sit correctly on the road surface. This will cause a consequent loss of adhesion and excessive wear, not to mention the danger of sudden tyre failure due to heat build-up.

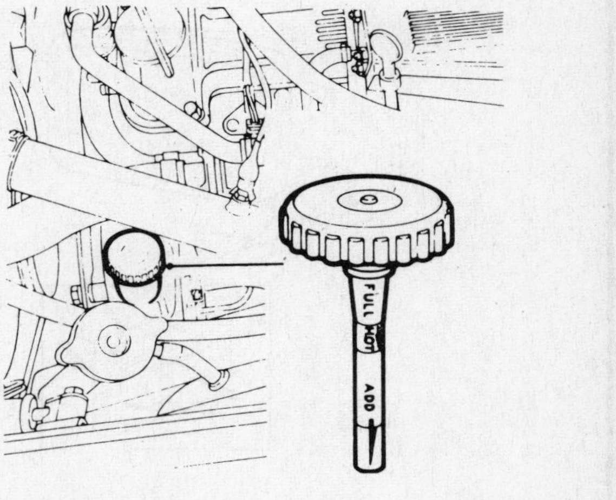


Fig. 13.113 Power steering fluid dipstick (Sec 12)

Overinflation will cause rapid wear of the centre part of the tyre tread coupled with reduced adhesion, harsher ride, and the danger of shock damage occurring in the tyre casing.

Regularly check the tyres for damage in the form of cuts or bulges, especially in the sidewalls. Remove any nails or stones embedded in the tread before they penetrate the tyre to cause deflation. If removal of a nail *does* reveal that the tyre has been punctured, refit the nail so that its point of penetration is marked. Then immediately change the wheel and have the tyre repaired by a tyre dealer. Do *not* drive on a tyre in such a condition. In many cases a puncture can be simply repaired by the use of an inner tube of the correct size and type. If in any doubt as to the possible consequences of any damage found, consult your local tyre dealer for advice.

Periodically remove the wheels and clean any dirt or mud from the inside and outside surfaces. Examine the wheel rims for signs of rusting, corrosion or other damage. Light alloy wheels are easily damaged by 'kerbing' whilst parking, and similarly steel wheels may become dented or buckled. Renewal of the wheel is very often the only course of remedial action possible.

The balance of each wheel and tyre assembly should be maintained to avoid excessive wear, not only to the tyres but also to the steering and suspension components. Wheel imbalance is normally signified by vibration through the vehicle's bodyshell, although in many cases it is particularly noticeable through the steering wheel. Conversely, it should be noted that wear or damage in suspension or steering components may cause excessive tyre wear. Out-of-round or out-of-true tyres, damaged wheels and wheel bearing wear/maladjustment also fall into this category. Balancing will not usually cure vibration caused by such wear.

Wheel balancing may be carried out with the wheel either on or off the vehicle. If balanced on the vehicle, ensure that the wheel-to-hub relationship is marked in some way prior to subsequent wheel removal so that it may be refitted in its original position.

General tyre wear is influenced to a large degree by driving style – harsh braking and acceleration or fast cornering will all produce more rapid tyre wear. Interchanging of tyres may result in more even wear, but this should only be carried out where there is no mix of tyre types on the vehicle. However, it is worth bearing in mind that if this is completely effective, the added expense of replacing a complete set of tyres simultaneously is incurred, which may prove financially restrictive for many owners.

Front tyres may wear unevenly as a result of wheel misalignment. The front wheels should always be correctly aligned according to the settings specified by the vehicle manufacturer.

Legal restrictions apply to the mixing of tyre types on a vehicle. Basically this means that a vehicle must not have tyres of differing construction on the same axle. Although it is not recommended to mix tyre types between front axle and rear axle, the only legally permissible combination is crossply at the front and radial at the rear. When mixing radial ply tyres, textile braced radials must always go on the front axle, with steel braced radials at the rear. An obvious disadvantage of such mixing is the necessity to carry two spare tyres to avoid contravening the law in the event of a puncture.

In the UK, the Motor Vehicles Construction and Use Regulations apply to many aspects of tyre fitting and usage. It is suggested that a copy of these regulations is obtained from your local police if in doubt as to the current legal requirements with regard to tyre condition, minimum tread depth, etc.

## 13 Bodywork

### *Door trim panels (Series 3) – removal and refitting*

1 The removal and refitting details for the door trim panels on later models are similar to those described for earlier models in Chapter 12, but on Vanden Plas models the armrest must also be removed. To do this proceed as follows.

2 Disconnect the battery and then extract the screw which holds the lamp lens to the armrest. Slide the lens towards the rear and take out the lamp bulb. Extract the screw adjacent to the bulb holder which holds the armrest to the door.

3 Extract the fixing screw from the front of the armrest. Slide the top of the armrest towards the rear of the car and then unscrew the remaining screws which secure the armrest to the door. Withdraw the armrest enough to be able to disconnect the lamp lead connecting plug, then remove the trim panel. Refitting is a reversal of the removal procedure.

### *Electrically-operated rear view mirror – removal and refitting*

4 Remove the door trim panel (and armrest if applicable). Disconnect the battery.

5 Extract the screws which hold the mirror control lever escutcheon to the door.

6 Withdraw the escutcheon, complete with control levers, and unscrew the setscrews to separate the escutcheon from the levers.

7 Remove the mirror mounting screws and withdraw the mirror, mounting pad, wiring harness and lever assembly.

8 Refitting is a reversal of removal.

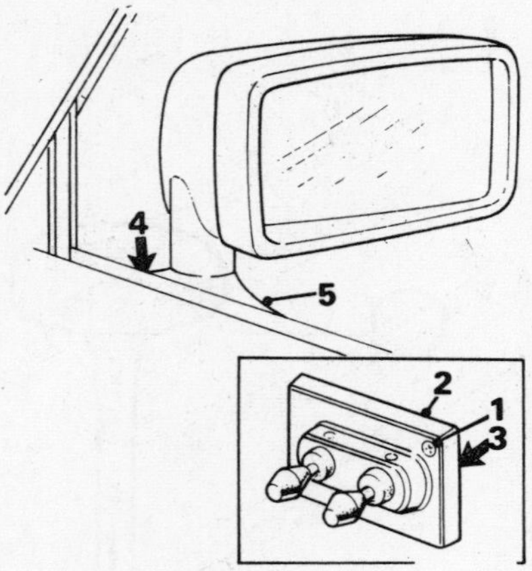


**Fig. 13.114 Electrically-operated mirror (Sec 13)**

*1 Screw*
*2 Escutcheon*
*3 Setscrews*
*4 Mirror fixing screws*
*5 Mirror mounting*

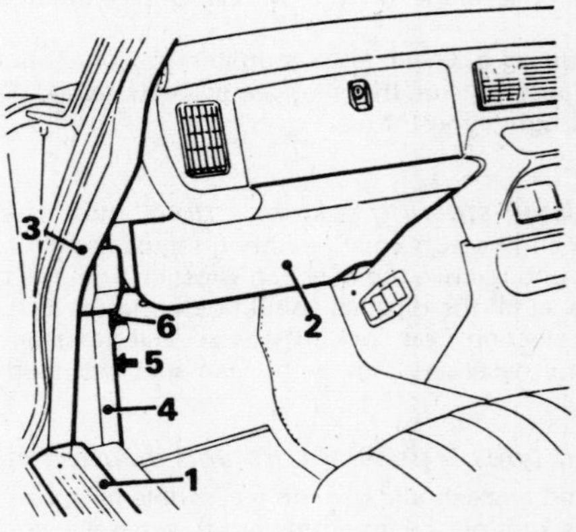


**Fig. 13.115 Front trim casing and underscuttle casing (Sec 13)**

*1 Door tread plate*
*2 Underscuttle casing*
*3 Draught weatherseal*
*4 Trim casing*
*5 Trim casing screws*
*6 Air vent control*

### *Front trim casing – removal and refitting*

9 Remove the door tread plate (1) – Fig. 13.115.
10 Remove the underscuttle casing (2), as described in Chapter 12, Section 40.
11 Prise off the draught excluder from the body flange adjacent to the trim casing.
12 Peel the edge of the trim from the edge of the door aperture.
13 Extract the two screws which hold the trim casing to the side of the footwell.
14 Disengage the trim casing from the air vent regulator control and remove the casing.
15 Refitting is a reversal of removal.

### *Centre pillar (B-post) trim – removal and refitting*

**Upper panel**

16 Prise off the seat belt mounting plastic cover.
17 Disconnect the seat belt mounting.
18 Prise off the pillar lamp lens.
19 Working from the bottom, prise off the trim casing from the pillar.

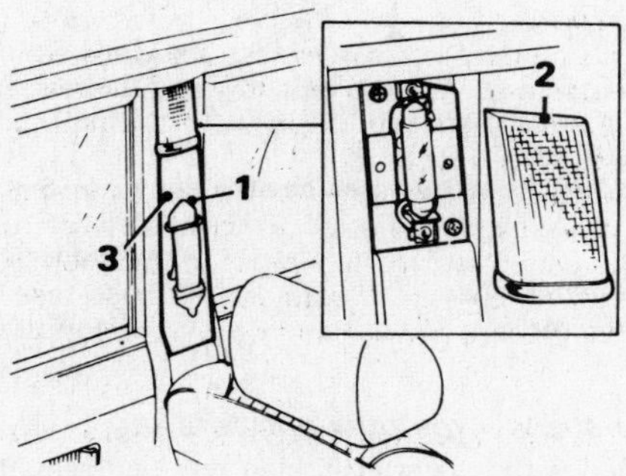


**Fig. 13.116 Centre pillar upper trim (3), lens (2) and belt mounting cover (1) (Sec 13)**

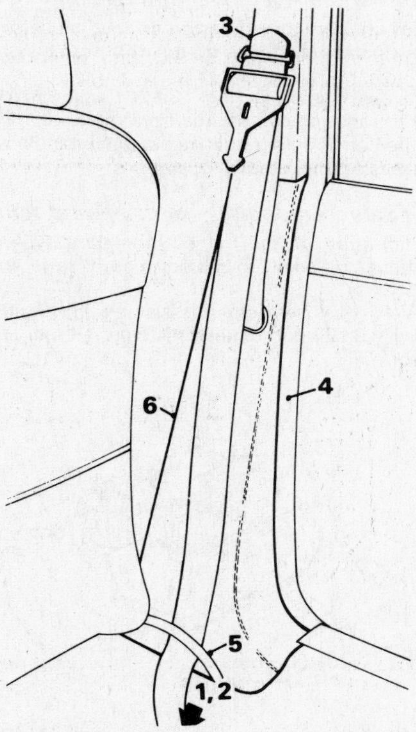


**Fig. 13.117 Centre pillar lower trim (6), seat belt retaining strap (5), draught weatherseal (4), seat belt mounting cover (3), belt anchorage components (2) and plastic cover (1) (Sec 13)**

**Lower panel**

20 Prise off the plastic covers from both the seat belt pillar mountings.
21 Disconnect the seat belt mountings from the pillar.
22 Prise off the draught excluder from the body flange and remove the seat belt safety strap.
23 Working from the bottom, prise the trim casing from the body pillar. Feed the seat belt through the slot provided and remove the trim casing.

### *Bonnet retaining struts (XJS)*

24 Later models have gas-filled struts to support the bonnet in the open position instead of the previous mechanical stay.

### *Front bumper (non-impact absorbing type, Saloon 1981 on) – removal and refitting*

25 Disconnect the battery. Unbolt the chrome finishers from the side mounting brackets.
26 Prise up the plastic covers located beneath each inner headlamp and unbolt the finishers from the inner mounting brackets. Remove the finisher and the upper apron.
27 Unclip and remove the rubber finishers from the bumper beam.
28 Disconnect the lamp units by rotating the wiring connector in an anti-clockwise direction.
29 Unbolt and remove the bumper beam.
30 Refitting is a reversal of removal.

### *Front bumper (impact absorbing type, Saloon 1981 on) – removal and refitting*

31 The operations are similar to those described in paragraphs 25 to 30, but the bumper beam is bolted to two energy absorbing struts.
32 The struts can be removed from their mounting tubes by unscrewing the fixing nut from the tube which is accessible from within the engine compartment. Tap the strut stud to expel the strut from its mounting tube.

### *Rear bumper (Saloon 1981 on) – removal and refitting*

**Centre section**

33 If rear fog warning lamps are fitted, disconnect the battery and lamp leads.
34 Remove the clips (1) (Fig. 13.120) and remove the rubber finisher (2).
35 Unscrew the nuts (3) which secure the bumper beam and remove the beam.
36 Remove the nuts (5) which hold the bumper side blade. Remove the side blade and the sealing strips.

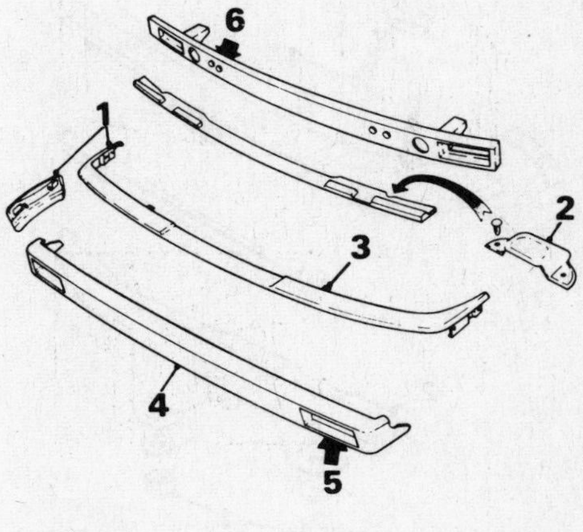


**Fig. 13.118 Front bumper components – non-impact absorbing type (Sec 13)**

| | |
|---|---|
| *1 Chrome finisher* | *4 Rubber finisher* |
| *2 Plastic covers* | *5 Lamp units* |
| *3 Finisher* | *6 Bumper beam* |

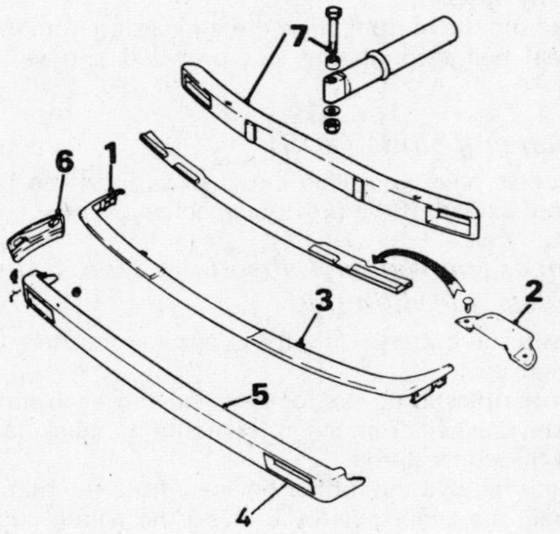


**Fig. 13.119 Front bumper components – impact absorbing type (Sec 13)**

1 *Chrome finisher*
2 *Plastic covers*
3 *Finisher*
4 *Lamp unit*
5 *Rubber finisher*
6 *Side finisher*
7 *Bumper beam*

**Side section**

37 This can be removed after first having taken off the centre section.

38 Refer to Fig. 13.121 and remove the nuts (1) and take off the rubber finisher (2) from the quarter blade (3).

39 Unbolt and remove the quarter blade (3).

**All sections**

40 Refitting is a reversal of removal.

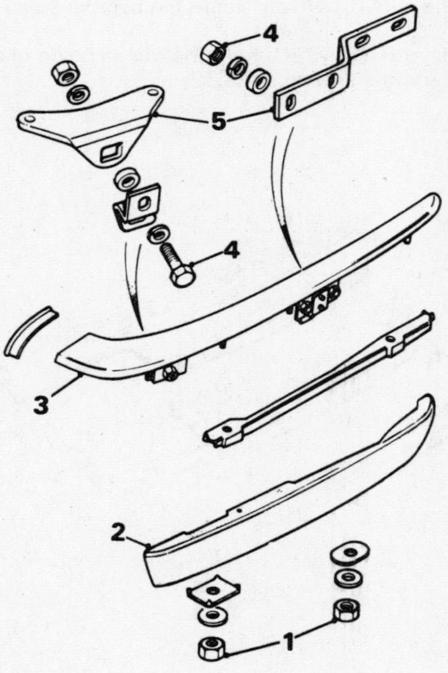


**Fig. 13.121 Rear bumper side section (Sec 13)**

1 *Nuts*
2 *Rubber finisher*
3 *Quarter blade*
4 *Bolt*
5 *Body mounting brackets*

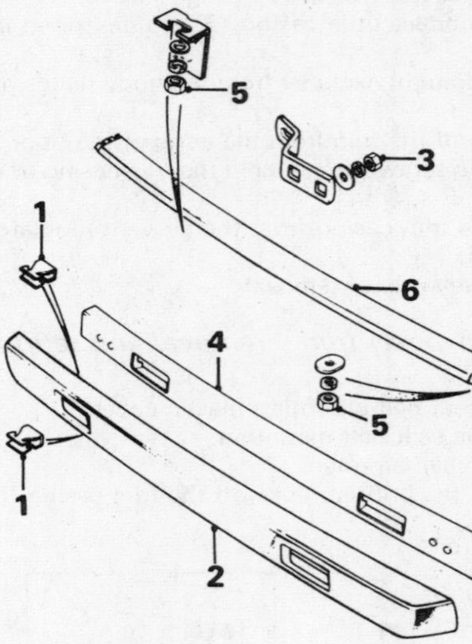


**Fig. 13.120 Rear bumper centre section (Sec 13)**

1 *Clip*
2 *Rubber finisher*
3 *Fixing nuts*
4 *Bumper beam*
5 *Nut*
6 *Blade*

## *Rear bumper struts – removal and refitting*

41 On cars fitted with impact absorbing rear bumpers, the struts are accessible for removal after having taken off the bumper beam, exhaust tail pipe and rear silencer.

42 Remove the struts, as described in paragraph 32.

## *Door exterior handle – removal and refitting*

43 The handles are of modified design on later models.

44 To remove a handle, first take off the door trim panel and raise the glass fully.

45 Release the spring clip (1) (Fig. 13.122) which holds the link rod to the latch lever, and remove the rod from the lever.

46 Unscrew the handle fixing nuts, remove the handle and its gasket.

47 Refit by reversing the removal operations.

## *Headlining (Saloon models) – removal and refitting*

48 The headlining is of pre-formed fibreglass type and suitable precautions should be taken to protect mouth, nose and eyes when handling it.

49 A strip of Velcro will be useful to assist in removing the headlining.

50 Refer to Fig. 13.123 and remove the cant rail trim and the interior rear view mirror.

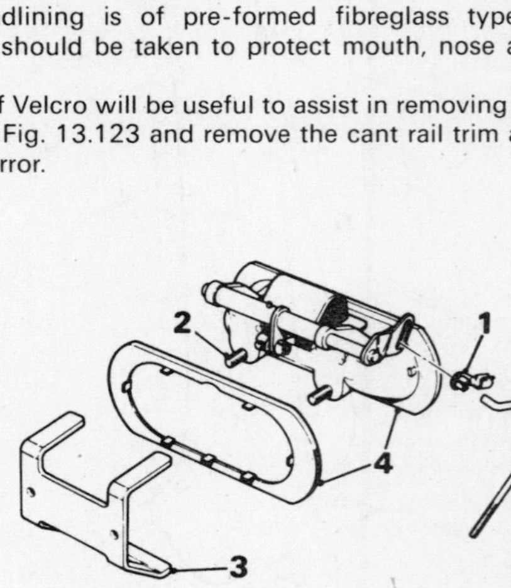


**Fig. 13.122 Later model door exterior handle (Sec 13)**

1 *Spring clip*
2 *Mounting stud*
3 *Retaining bracket*
4 *Handle assembly*

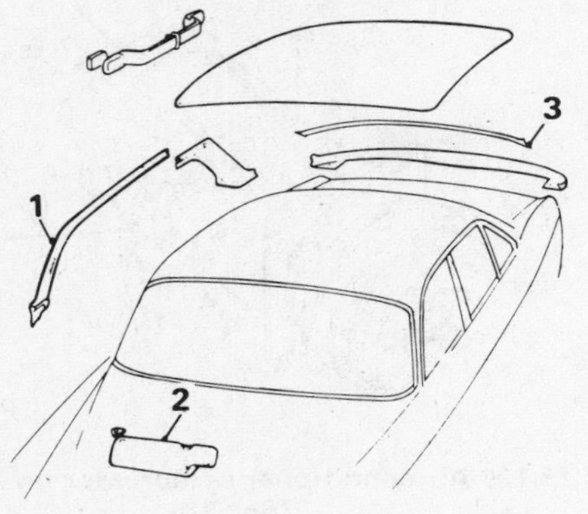


Fig. 13.123 Headlining – Saloon (Sec 13)

1 *Cant rail trim*
2 *Sun visor*
3 *Upper trim panel*

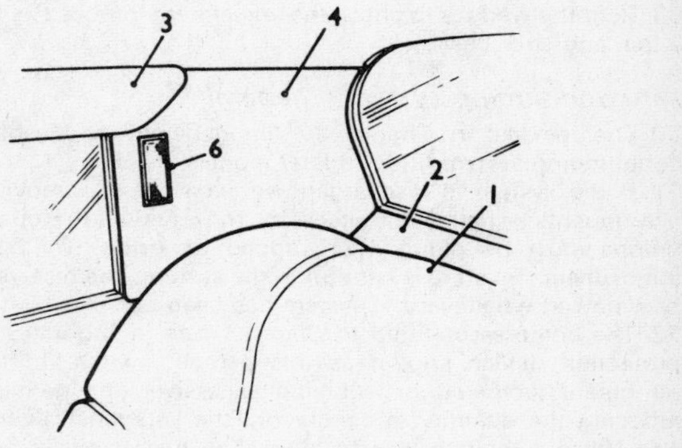


Fig. 13.124 XJS rear quarter trim (Sec 13)

1 *Seat back*
2 *Rear shelf*
3 *Cant rail crash roll*
4 *Quarter trim pad*
6 *Interior lamp*

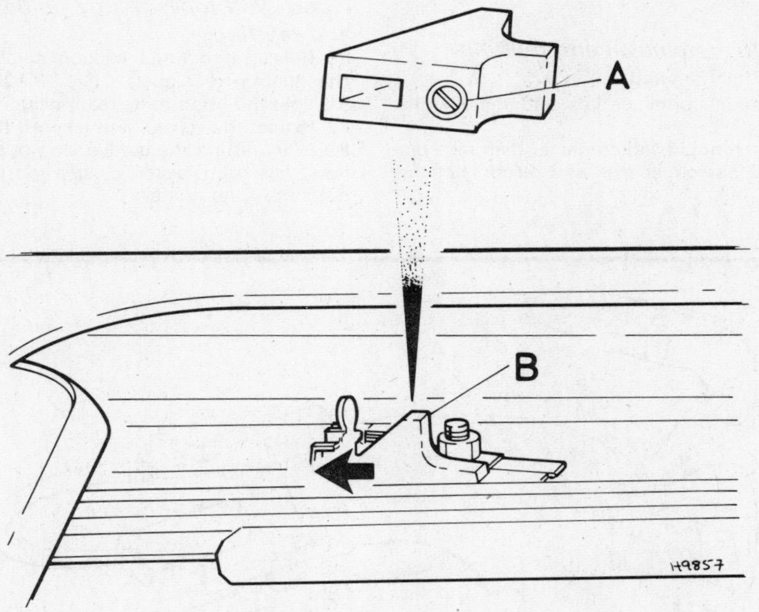


Fig. 13.125 Sliding roof adjustment (Sec 13)

A *Wedge screw* B *Wedge unclipping direction (arrowed)*

51 Extract the hinge screws and remove the sun visors.
52 Prise the windscreen and rear window upper trim panels free from the roof rail.
53 Attach the Velcro strip to the headlining and pull the headlining forward until its rear edge can be released from its locating recess.
54 Move the headlining to the right so that the left-hand edge can be disengaged, then move it to the left to disengage the right-hand edge.
55 Move the headlining to the rear and withdraw it from the car.
56 Refitting is a reversal of removal.

## *Headlining (XJS) – removal and refitting*

57 Remove the sunvisors and their brackets.
58 Remove the interior rear view mirror.
59 Remove the front interior lamp.
60 Remove the cant rail crash rolls.
61 Remove the rear parcel shelf and quarter trim pads (Chapter 12, Section 44) and interior lamp.
62 Bend back the six tabs which hold the headlining. Withdraw the headlining through the passenger's door.
63 Refitting is a reversal of removal.

## *Rear headrests*

64 These are fitted as standard to later Daimler models. Remove them before taking out the rear seat squab.

## *Sliding roof – adjustment*

65 Should wind noise or other misalignment be a problem, proceed as follows.
66 Open the sliding roof as far as possible.
67 Remove the black nylon wedges, one on each side of the roof opening, by sliding them rearwards.
68 On the underside of each wedge is a screw. Turn the screw anti-clockwise to raise the rear of the roof, or clockwise to lower it.

Beware of excessive upward adjustment, which may cause the roof to jam.
69 Refit the wedges to check the adjustment; proceed as necessary on a trial and error basis.

### *Air conditioning system – general*

70 The remarks in Chapter 12 are generally applicable to the air conditioning system fitted to later models.
71 If the system is discharged with a view to removing particular components, whether for access or for renewal, the open refrigerant unions must be plugged or capped **at once**. The absorption of atmospheric moisture is harmful to the system. The receiver/dryer must be renewed whenever the system has been opened.
72 The compressor fitted to Series 3 cars incorporates an overload protection device known as a superheat switch. In the event of refrigerant temperature becoming excessive, due perhaps to a leak reducing the quantity in circulation, the superheat switch will close and cause a thermal fuse to blow. The fuse is easily renewed (Fig. 13.126), but this should **not** be done until the reason for the superheat switch operation has been established and corrected.
73 Repair of the automatic temperature regulation system should be left to a specialist.

### *Air conditioning system – hoses and unions*

74 It is recommended that hose and pipe unions are tightened in accordance with the settings given in Fig. 13.127 whenever new components are fitted.

### *Concealed storage box (XJS) – removal and refitting*

75 Tilt and push the front seats fully forward.
76 Unlock and open both storage container lids and remove the interior mats from them.
77 Unscrew the five screws which hold each container then take out the rear courtesy lamp from the passenger side and disconnect the leads.

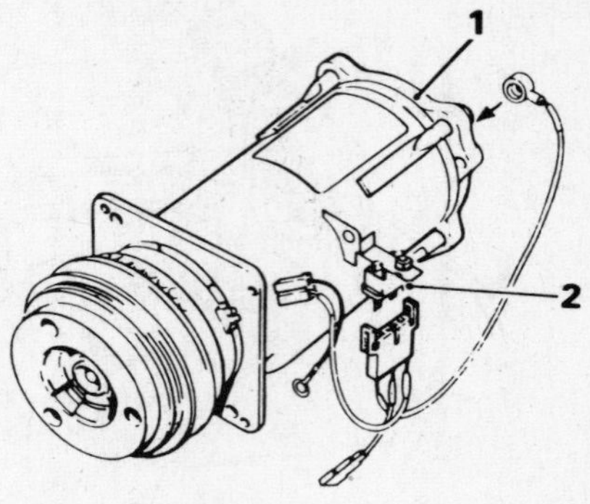


**Fig. 13.126 Air conditioner compressor on later models (Sec 13)**

*1 Compressor* *2 Thermal fuse*

78 Tilt and remove the storage container through the passenger door opening. The seat belt will have to be extended to provide clearance.
79 Refitting is a reversal of removal.

### *Hood (soft top) canopy guides (XJS Cabriolet) – removal and refitting*

80 Release the hood locking catch and then the Velcro fastening (headlining-to-D-post) – Fig. 13.128.
81 Fold the hood to its rear position.
82 Extract the screws and take off the canopy guides (2).
83 When fitting the guides, do not tighten their screws fully until the hood has been locked closed and the guide pins are located in the notches of the guides.

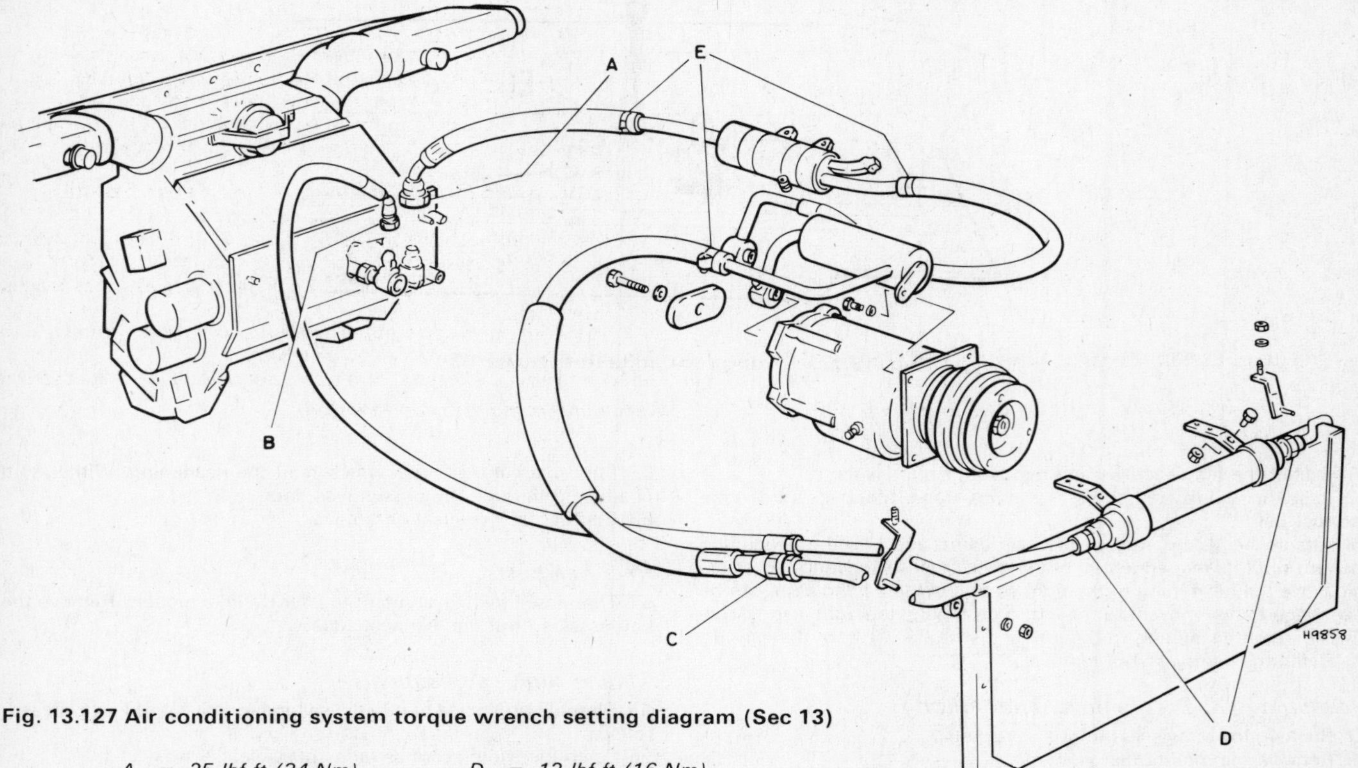


**Fig. 13.127 Air conditioning system torque wrench setting diagram (Sec 13)**

*A = 25 lbf ft (34 Nm)*
*B = 12 lbf ft (16 Nm)*
*C = 25 lbf ft (34 Nm)*
*D = 12 lbf ft (16 Nm)*
*E = 4 lbf ft (6 Nm)*

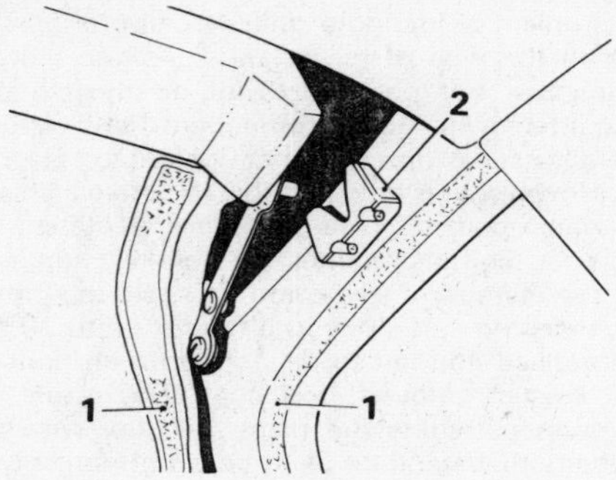


Fig. 13.128 Canopy guide (2) and Velcro fastening (1) (Sec 13)

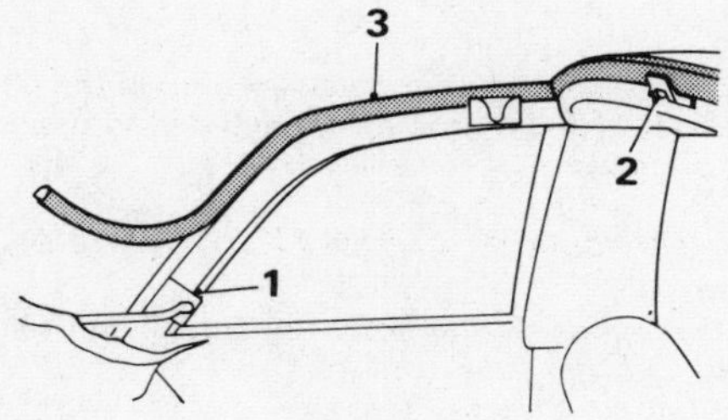


Fig. 13.129 Canopy seal (Sec 13)

*1 Velcro fastening*
*2 Latch*
*3 Seal*

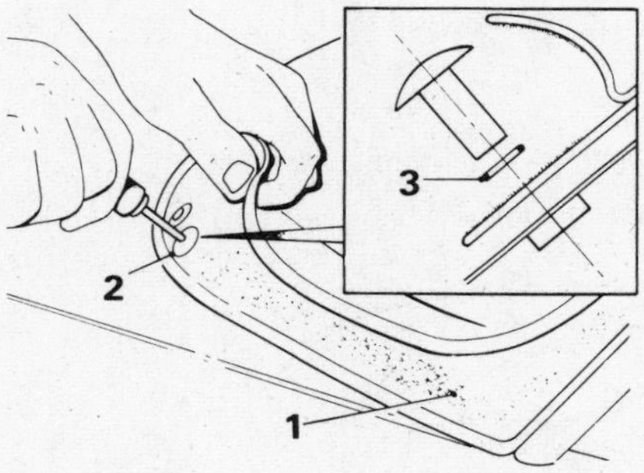


Fig. 13.130 Hood-to-body screws (1) (Sec 13)

*2 Screw*
*3 O-ring seal*

### *Hood canopy latches (XJS Cabriolet) – removal and refitting*

84 Release the hood locking catch and the Velcro (headlining-to-D-post).
85 Fold the hood to the rear.
86 Extract the canopy latch screws and remove the latches from the roll bar.
87 When fitting the latches, do not fully tighten their screws until the hood has been raised and locked in position.

### *Hood canopy seal (XJS Cabriolet) – renewal*

88 Release the hood and lower it to its rearward position.
89 Release the hood outer Velcro fastening.
90 Extract the three hood fixing screws from each side also remove the hood latches.
91 Remove the seal (3) – Fig. 13.129.
92 Fit the new seal; taking great care not to split it, especially at the corners of the roll bar and side panels.
93 Fit the clamps and new O-rings to the hood screws.

### *Targa top seal (XJS Cabriolet) – renewal*

94 Unlock and remove the targa panels.
95 Extract the screws and remove the panel latches.
96 Remove the seal.
97 When fitting the new seal, make sure that the red alignment mark is in the front and centred.
98 When refitting the latches, do not fully tighten the screws until the large panels are in position and the latches correctly aligned.

### *Front headlining (XJS Cabriolet) – renewal*

99 Remove the targa panels.
100 Extract the screws and remove the windscreen pillar (A-post) trim panels.
101 Remove the sun visors and interior rear view mirror.
102 Disconnect and remove the interior lamp.
103 Disconnect the front edge of the targa panel top seal.
104 Extract the front screws from the cant rails and release the trim.
105 Remove the remaining screws and take off the headlining.
106 Refitting is a reversal of removal.

### *Rollover bar trim (XJS Cabriolet) – renewal*

107 Fold back the hood canopy and take off the targa panels.
108 Remove the targa panel and the hood canopy catches.
109 Remove the B-post trim and seat belt anchorage.
110 Remove the seal from the rollover bar and then remove the trim.
111 Refit the new trim by reversing the removal procedure.

### *Hood canopy (XJS Cabriolet) – removal and refitting*

112 Lower the hood canopy to its rear position.
113 Release the outer cover Velcro fastening and, using an Allen key, unscrew the hood fixing screws.
114 Push the rear of the hood upwards to release the headlining fasteners (1) – Fig. 13.131.
115 Manoeuvre the hood until the hinge plate fixing screws can be extracted and the hood canopy removed.
116 Refitting is a reversal of removal but use new O-rings and rubber spacers.

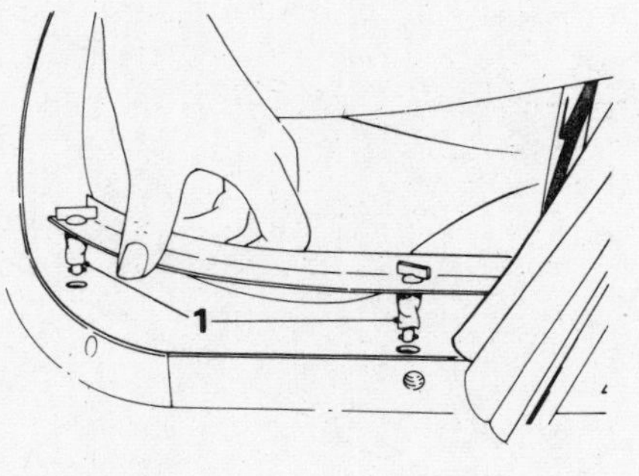


Fig. 13.131 Hood headlining fasteners (1) (Sec 13)

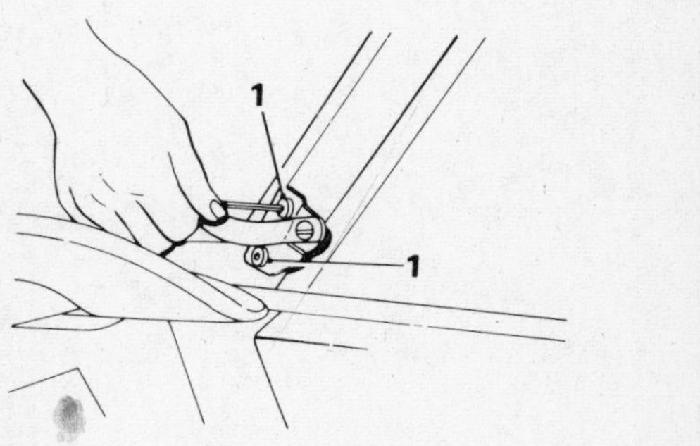


Fig. 13.132 Hood hinge plate screws (1) (Sec 13)

*Plastic components*

With the use of more and more plastic body components by the vehicle manufacturers (eg bumpers, spoilers, and in some cases major body panels), rectification of damage to such items has become a matter of either entrusting repair work to a specialist in this field, or renewing complete components. Repair by the DIY owner is not really feasible owing to the cose of the equipment and materials required for effecting such repairs. The basic technique involves making a groove along the line of the crack in the plastic using a rotary burr in a power drill. The damaged part is then welded back together by using a hot air gun to heat up and fuse a plastic filler rod into the groove. Any excess plastic is then removed and the area rubbed down to a smooth finish. It is important that a filler rod of the correct plastic is used, as body components can be made of a variery of different types (eg polycarbonate, ABS, polypropylene).

If the owner is renewing a complete component himself, he will be left with the problem of finding a suitable paint for finishing which is compatible with the type of plastic used. At one time the use of a universal paint was not possible owing to the complex range of plastics encountered in body component applications. Standard paints, generally speaking, will not bond to plastic or rubber satisfactorily. However, it is now possible to obtain a plastic body parts finishing kit which consists of a pre-primer treatment, a primer and coloured top coat. Full instructions are normally supplied with a kit, but basically the method of use is to first apply the pre-primer to the component concerned and allow it to dry for up to 30 minutes. Then the primer is applied and left to dry for about an hour before finally applying the special coloured top coat. The result is a correctly coloured component where the paint will flex with the plastic or rubber, a property that standard paint does not normally possess.

# Routine maintenance – late models

On later models the weekly service checks remain the same as those given for earlier models at the start of the manual. The longer term maintenance and service schedules are revised as follows.

## ALL VEHICLES (EXCLUDING NORTH AMERICAN VERSIONS) FROM VIN 322374

**Every 7500 miles (12 000 km) or at six monthly intervals, whichever comes first**

Check tyre tread wear (Chapter 11)
Check disc pads for wear and discs for condition (Chapter 9)
Check handbrake adjustment (Chapter 9)
Check condition of all steering and suspension gaiters, flexible bushes and balljoints (Chapter 11)
Renew engine oil and filter (Chapter 1 or Section 3, Chapter 13)
Check transmission fluid level (Chapter 6 or Section 8, Chapter 13)
Apply grease gun to all lubrication points (except hubs)
Check rear axle oil level (Section 9, Chapter 13)
Check condition of all hydraulic hoses/pipelines (Chapters 9 and 11)
Check exhaust system for corrosion (Chapter 3)
Lubricate handbrake linkage (Chapter 9)
Clean and regap spark plugs (Chapter 4)
Check battery terminals for corrosion, clean and apply petroleum jelly (Chapter 10)
Check brake fluid reservoir level (Section 10, Chapter 13)
Check coolant level (Chapter 2)
Check power steering fluid level (Chapter 11)
Lubricate controls, hinges and locks

**Every 15 000 miles (24 000 km) or annually, whichever comes first**

Check condition and operation of safety belts (Chapter 12)
Move roadwheels front to rear (same side of car and only if balanced off car) to even out tyre wear (Chapter 11)
Adjust front hub bearings (Chapter 11)
Grease front suspension and rear hubs (Chapter 11)
Inspect handbrake pads for wear (Chapter 9)
Check torque of propeller shaft coupling bolts (Chapter 7)
Renew air cleaner elements (Chapter 3)
Check drivebelt tension, renew if cut or frayed (Chapter 1)
Renew spark plugs (Chapter 4)
Renew fuel filter (Chapter 3)
Clean engine breather filter (Chapter 3)
Check and adjust engine idle speed and mixture (CO) settings (Chapter 3)
Check headlamp beam alignment (Chapter 10)
Check front wheel alignment (Chapter 11)
Check wiper blade condition (Chapter 10)
Check battery electrolyte level (Chapter 10)

**Every 30 000 miles (48 000 km) or at two yearly intervals, whichever comes first**

Renew rear axle oil (Section 9, Chapter 13)
Renew brake hydraulic fluid by bleeding (Chapter 9)
Renew engine coolant (antifreeze) (Chapter 2)
Renew automatic transmission fluid and filter (Chapter 6)

**Every 60 000 miles (96 000 km) or every four years, whichever comes first**

Check all brake hydraulic hoses for condition and components for leakage. Ideally, all seals should be renewed (Chapter 9)

## NORTH AMERICAN VEHICLES – 1981 AND LATER

**Every 7500 miles (12 000 km) or at six monthly intervals, whichever comes first**

Lubricate all grease points
Renew engine oil and filter (Section 3, Chapter 13)
Check transmission fluid level (Chapter 6 or Section 8, Chapter 13)
Check coolant level (Chapter 2)
Check rear axle oil level (Section 9, Chapter 13)
Check power steering fluid level (Section 12, Chapter 13)
Lubricate all locks, controls, hinges
Check drivebelt tension and condition (Chapter 1)
Check condition of all fuel system hoses and connections (Chapter 3)
Check all steering and suspension gaiters, bushes and balljoints (Chapter 11)
Check disc pads for wear and discs for scoring (Chapter 9)
Check tyres for wear and damage (Chapter 11)

**Every 15 000 miles (24 000 km) or annually, whichever comes first**

Clean and regap spark plugs (Chapter 4)
Check front wheel alignment (Chapter 11)
Check headlamp beam alignment (Chapter 10)
Adjust front hub bearings (Chapter 11)
Check torque of propeller shaft flange bolts (Chapter 7)
Check condition of wiper blades (Chapter 10)
Grease front suspension and rear hubs (Chapter 11)
Check condition and operation of safety belts (Chapter 12)

**Every 30 000 miles (48 000 km) or at two yearly intervals, whichever comes first**

Renew catalytic converter (Chapter 3)
Renew automatic transmission fluid and filter (Chapter 6)
Renew air cleaner elements (Chapter 3)
Check crankcase ventilation system and fuel evaporative control system hoses and connections (Chapter 3)
Renew spark plugs (Chapter 4)
Renew oxygen sensors (Lambda) (Section 5, Chapter 13)
Renew fuel filter (Chapter 3)
Renew charcoal canister (Chapter 3)
Renew rear axle oil (Section 9, Chapter 13)
Renew brake hydraulic fluid by bleeding (Chapter 8)
Renew engine coolant (antifreeze) (Chapter 2)

**Every 50 000 miles (80 000 km) or every three years, whichever comes first**

Check idle speed and mixture (CO) (Chapter 3)
Renew EGR valve (Chapter 3)
Check all brake hydraulic hoses for condition and components for leakage. Ideally, all seals should be renewed (Chapter 9)

# General repair procedures

Whenever servicing, repair or overhaul work is carried out on the car or its components, it is necessary to observe the following procedures and instructions. This will assist in carrying out the operation efficiently and to a professional standard of workmanship.

### *Joint mating faces and gaskets*

Where a gasket is used between the mating faces of two components, ensure that it is renewed on reassembly, and fit it dry unless otherwise stated in the repair procedure. Make sure that the mating faces are clean and dry with all traces of old gasket removed. When cleaning a joint face, use a tool which is not likely to score or damage the face, and remove any burrs or nicks with an oilstone or fine file.

Make sure that tapped holes are cleaned with a pipe cleaner, and keep them free of jointing compound if this is being used unless specifically instructed otherwise.

Ensure that all orifices, channels or pipes are clear and blow through them, preferably using compressed air.

### *Oil seals*

Whenever an oil seal is removed from its working location, either individually or as part of an assembly, it should be renewed.

The very fine sealing lip of the seal is easily damaged and will not seal if the surface it contacts is not completely clean and free from scratches, nicks or grooves. If the original sealing surface of the component cannot be restored, the component should be renewed.

Protect the lips of the seal from any surface which may damage them in the course of fitting. Use tape or a conical sleeve where possible. Lubricate the seal lips with oil before fitting and, on dual lipped seals, fill the space between the lips with grease.

Unless otherwise stated, oil seals must be fitted with their sealing lips toward the lubricant to be sealed.

Use a tubular drift or block of wood of the appropriate size to install the seal and, if the seal housing is shouldered, drive the seal down to the shoulder. If the seal housing is unshouldered, the seal should be fitted with its face flush with the housing top face.

### *Screw threads and fastenings*

Always ensure that a blind tapped hole is completely free from oil, grease, water or other fluid before installing the bolt or stud. Failure to do this could cause the housing to crack due to the hydraulic action of the bolt or stud as it is screwed in.

When tightening a castellated nut to accept a split pin, tighten the nut to the specified torque, where applicable, and then tighten further to the next split pin hole. Never slacken the nut to align a split pin hole unless stated in the repair procedure.

When checking or retightening a nut or bolt to a specified torque setting, slacken the nut or bolt by a quarter of a turn, and then retighten to the specified setting.

### *Locknuts, locktabs and washers*

Any fastening which will rotate against a component or housing in the course of tightening should always have a washer between it and the relevant component or housing.

Spring or split washers should always be renewed when they are used to lock a critical component such as a big-end bearing retaining nut or bolt.

Locktabs which are folded over to retain a nut or bolt should always be renewed.

Self-locking nuts can be reused in non-critical areas, providing resistance can be felt when the locking portion passes over the bolt or stud thread.

Split pins must always be replaced with new ones of the correct size for the hole.

### *Special tools*

Some repair procedures in this manual entail the use of special tools such as a press, two or three-legged pullers, spring compressors etc. Wherever possible, suitable readily available alternatives to the manufacturer's special tools are described, and are shown in use. In some instances, where no alternative is possible, it has been necessary to resort to the use of a manufacturer's tool and this has been done for reasons of safety as well as the efficient completion of the repair operation. Unless you are highly skilled and have a thorough understanding of the procedure described, never attempt to bypass the use of any special tool when the procedure described specifies its use. Not only is there a very great risk of personal injury, but expensive damage could be caused to the components involved.

# Fault diagnosis

*Introduction*

The vehicle owner who does his or her own maintenance according to the recommended schedules should not have to use this section of the manual very often. Modern component reliability is such that, provided those items subject to wear or deterioration are inspected or renewed at the specified intervals, sudden failure is comparatively rare. Faults do not usually just happen as a result of sudden failure, but develop over a period of time. Major mechanical failures in particular are usually preceded by characteristic symptoms over hundreds or even thousands of miles. Those components which do occasionally fail without warning are often small and easily carried in the vehicle.

With any fault finding, the first step is to decide where to begin investigations. Sometimes this is obvious, but on other occasions a little detective work will be necessary. The owner who makes half a dozen haphazard adjustments or replacements may be successful in curing a fault (or its symptoms), but he will be none the wiser if the fault recurs and he may well have spent more time and money than was necessary. A calm and logical approach will be found to be more satisfactory in the long run. Always take into account any warning signs or abnormalities that may have been noticed in the period preceding the fault – power loss, high or low gauge readings, unusual noises or smells, etc – and remember that failure of components such as fuses or spark plugs may only be pointers to some underlying fault.

The pages which follow here are intended to help in cases of failure to start or breakdown on the road. There is also a Fault Diagnosis Section at the end of each Chapter which should be consulted if the preliminary checks prove unfruitful. Whatever the fault, certain basic principles apply. These are as follows:

**Verify the fault.** This is simply a matter of being sure that you know what the symptoms are before starting work. This is particularly important if you are investigating a fault for someone else who may not have described it very accurately.

**Don't overlook the obvious.** For example, if the vehicle won't start, is there petrol in the tank? (Don't take anyone else's word on this particular point, and don't trust the fuel gauge either!) If an electrical fault is indicated, look for loose or broken wires before digging out the test gear.

**Cure the disease, not the symptom.** Substituting a flat battery with a fully charged one will get you off the hard shoulder, but if the underlying cause is not attended to, the new battery will go the same way. Similarly, changing oil-fouled spark plugs for a new set will get you moving again, but remember that the reason for the fouling (if it wasn't simply an incorrect grade of plug) will have to be established and corrected.

**Don't take anything for granted.** Particularly, don't forget that a 'new' component may itself be defective (especially if it's been rattling round in the boot for months), and don't leave components out of a fault diagnosis sequence just because they are new or recently fitted. When you do finally diagnose a difficult fault, you'll probably realise that all the evidence was there from the start.

*Electrical faults*

Electrical faults can be more puzzling than straightforward mechanical failures, but they are no less susceptible to logical analysis if the basic principles of operation are understood. Vehicle electrical wiring exists in extremely unfavourable conditions – heat, vibration and chemical attack – and the first things to look for are loose or corroded connections and broken or chafed wires, especially where the wires pass through holes in the bodywork or are subject to vibration.

All metal-bodied vehicles in current production have one pole of the battery 'earthed', ie connected to the vehicle bodywork, and in nearly all modern vehicles it is the negative (–) terminal. The various electrical components – motors, bulb holders etc – are also connected to earth, either by means of a lead or directly by their mountings. Electric current flows through the component and then back to the battery via the bodywork. If the component mounting is loose or corroded, or if a good path back to the battery is not available, the circuit will be incomplete and malfunction will result. The engine and/or gearbox are also earthed by means of flexible metal straps to the body or subframe; if these straps are loose or missing, starter motor, generator and ignition trouble may result.

Assuming the earth return to be satisfactory, electrical faults will be due either to component malfunction or to defects in the current supply. Individual components are dealt with in Chapter 10. If supply wires are broken or cracked internally this results in an open-circuit, and the easiest way to check for this is to bypass the suspect wire temporarily with a length of wire having a crocodile clip or suitable connector at each end. Alternatively, a 12V test lamp can be used to verify the presence of supply voltage at various points along the wire and the break can be thus isolated.

If a bare portion of a live wire touches the bodywork or other earthed metal part, the electricity will take the low-resistance path thus formed back to the battery: this is known as a short-circuit. Hopefully a short-circuit will blow a fuse, but otherwise it may cause burning of the insulation (and possibly further short-circuits) or even a fire. This is why it is inadvisable to bypass persistently blowing fuses with silver foil or wire.

*Spares and tool kit*

Most vehicles are supplied only with sufficient tools for wheel

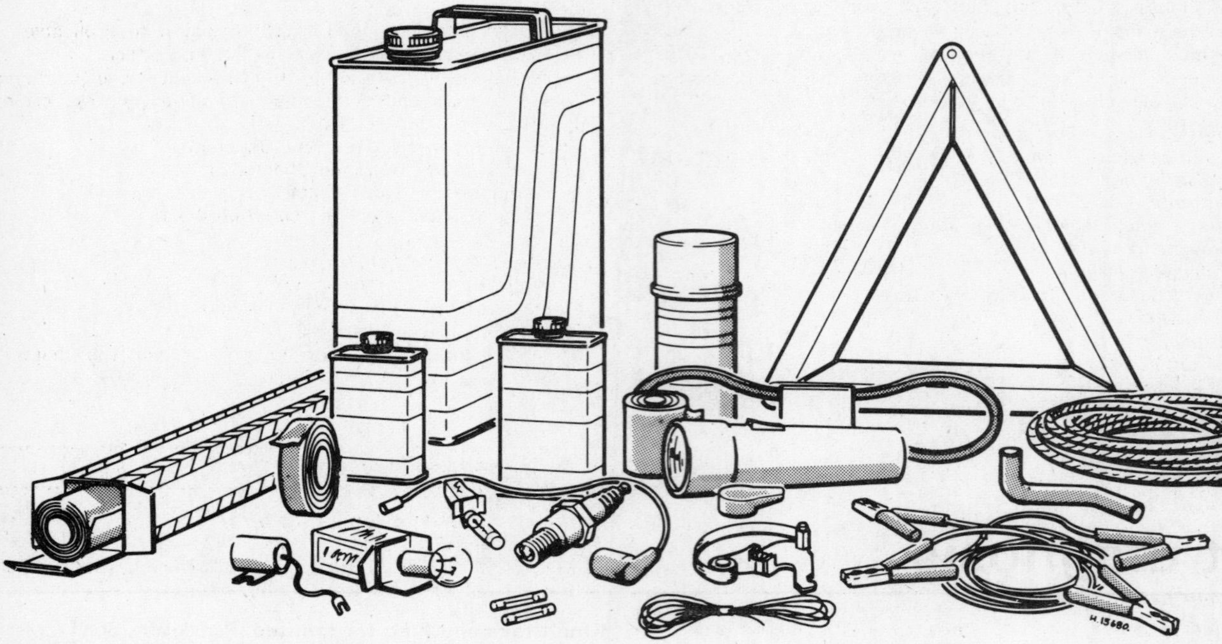


Carrying a few spares can save you a long walk

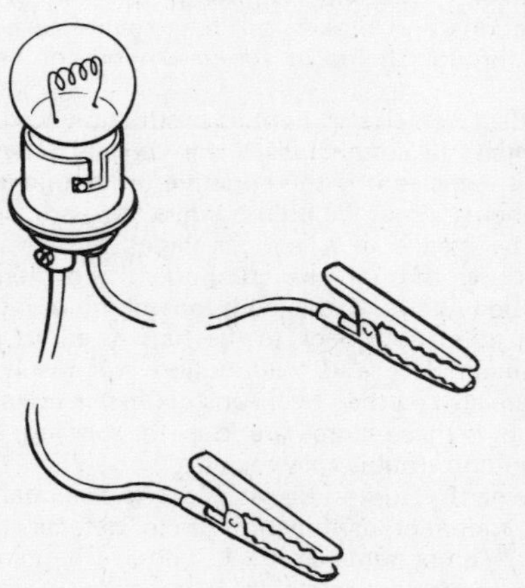

A simple test lamp is useful for tracing electrical faults

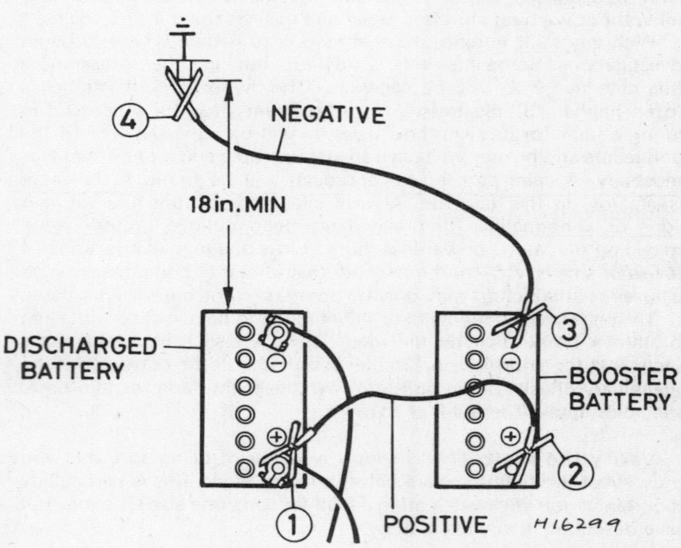


Jump start connections for negative earth vehicles – connect leads in order shown

changing; the *Maintenance and minor repair* tool kit detailed in *Tools and working facilities,* with the addition of a hammer, is probably sufficient for those repairs that most motorists would consider attempting at the roadside. In addition a few items which can be fitted without too much trouble in the event of a breakdown should be carried. Experience and available space will modify the list below, but the following may save having to call on professional assistance:

*Spark plugs, clean and correctly gapped*
*HT lead and plug cap – long enough to reach the plug furthest from the distributor*
*Distributor rotor*
*Drivebelt(s) – emergency type may suffice*
*Spare fuses*
*Set of principal light bulbs*
*Tin of radiator sealer and hose bandage*
*Exhaust bandage*
*Roll of insulating tape*
*Length of soft iron wire*
*Length of electrical flex*
*Torch or inspection lamp (can double as test lamp)*
*Battery jump leads*
*Tow-rope*
*Ignition waterproofing aerosol*
*Litre of engine oil*
*Sealed can of hydraulic fluid*
*Emergency windscreen*
*Worm drive clips*
*Tube of filler paste*

If spare fuel is carried, a can designed for the purpose should be used to minimise risks of leakage and collision damage. A first aid kit and a warning triangle, whilst not at present compulsory in the UK, are obviously sensible items to carry in addition to the above.

When touring abroad it may be advisable to carry additional spares which, even if you cannot fit them yourself, could save having to wait while parts are obtained. The items below may be worth considering:

*Clutch and throttle cables*
*Cylinder head gasket*
*Alternator brushes*
*Fuel pump repair kit*
*Tyre valve core*

One of the motoring organisations will be able to advise on availability of fuel etc in foreign countries.

## Engine will not start

### *Engine fails to turn when starter operated*

Flat battery (recharge, use jump leads, or push start)
Battery terminals loose or corroded
Battery earth to body defective
Engine earth strap loose or broken
Starter motor (or solenoid) wiring loose or broken
Automatic transmission selector in wrong position, or inhibitor switch faulty
Ignition/starter switch faulty
Major mechanical failure (seizure)
Starter or solenoid internal fault (see Chapter 10)

### *Starter motor turns engine slowly*

Partially discharged battery (recharge, use jump leads, or push start)
Battery terminals loose or corroded
Battery earth to body defective
Engine earth strap loose
Starter motor (or solenoid) wiring loose
Starter motor internal fault (see Chapter 10)

### *Starter motor spins without turning engine*

Flat battery
Starter motor pinion sticking on sleeve
Flywheel gear teeth damaged or worn
Starter motor mounting bolts loose

### *Engine turns normally but fails to start*

Damp or dirty HT leads and distributor cap (crank engine and check for spark)
Dirty or incorrectly gapped distributor points (if applicable)
No fuel in tank (check for delivery at carburettor)
Excessive choke (hot engine) or insufficient choke (cold engine)
Fouled or incorrectly gapped spark plugs (remove, clean and regap)
Other ignition system fault (see Chapter 4)
Other fuel system fault (see Chapter 3)
Poor compression (see Chapter 1)
Major mechanical failure (eg camshaft drive)

### *Engine fires but will not run*

Insufficient choke (cold engine)
Air leaks at carburettor or inlet manifold
Fuel starvation (see Chapter 3)
Ballast resistor defective, or other ignition fault (see Chapter 4)

## Engine cuts out and will not restart

### *Engine cuts out suddenly – ignition fault*

Loose or disconnected LT wires
Wet HT leads or distributor cap (after traversing water splash)
Coil or condenser failure (check for spark)
Other ignition fault (see Chapter 4)

### *Engine misfires before cutting out – fuel fault*

Fuel tank empty
Fuel pump defective or filter blocked (check for delivery)
Fuel tank filler vent blocked (suction will be evident on releasing cap)
Carburettor needle valve sticking
Carburettor jets blocked (fuel contaminated)
Other fuel system fault (see Chapter 3)

### *Engine cuts out – other causes*

Serious overheating
Major mechanical failure (eg camshaft drive)

## Engine overheats

### *Ignition (no-charge) warning light illuminated*

Slack or broken drivebelt – retension or renew (Chapter 1)

### *Ignition warning light not illuminated*

Coolant loss due to internal or external leakage (see Chapter 2)
Thermostat defective
Low oil level
Brakes binding
Radiator clogged externally or internally
Electric cooling fan not operating correctly
Engine waterways clogged
Ignition timing incorrect or automatic advance malfunctioning
Mixture too weak

**Note:** *Do not add cold water to an overheated engine or damage may result*

## Low engine oil pressure

### *Gauge reads low or warning light illuminated with engine running*

Oil level low or incorrect grade
Defective gauge or sender unit
Wire to sender unit earthed

- Engine overheating
- Oil filter clogged or bypass valve defective
- Oil pressure relief valve defective
- Oil pick-up strainer clogged
- Oil pump worn or mountings loose
- Worn main or big-end bearings

**Note:** *Low oil pressure in a high-mileage engine at tickover is not necessarily a cause for concern. Sudden pressure loss at speed is far more significant. In any event, check the gauge or warning light sender before condemning the engine.*

**Engine noises**

*Pre-ignition (pinking) on acceleration*

- Incorrect grade of fuel
- Ignition timing incorrect
- Distributor faulty or worn
- Worn or maladjusted carburettor
- Excessive carbon build-up in engine

*Whistling or wheezing noises*

- Leaking vacuum hose
- Leaking carburettor or manifold gasket
- Blowing head gasket

*Tapping or rattling*

- Incorrect valve clearances
- Worn valve gear
- Worn timing chain
- Broken piston ring (ticking noise)

*Knocking or thumping*

- Unintentional mechanical contact (eg fan blades)
- Worn drivebelt
- Peripheral component fault (generator, water pump etc)
- Worn big-end bearings (regular heavy knocking, perhaps less under load)
- Worn main bearings (rumbling and knocking, perhaps worsening under load)
- Piston slap (most noticeable when cold)

# Conversion factors

| | | | | | |
|---|---|---|---|---|---|
| ***Length (distance)*** | | | | | |
| Inches (in) | X 25.4 | = Millimetres (mm) | X 0.0394 | = Inches (in) |
| Feet (ft) | X 0.305 | = Metres (m) | X 3.281 | = Feet (ft) |
| Miles | X 1.609 | = Kilometres (km) | X 0.621 | = Miles |
| ***Volume (capacity)*** | | | | |
| Cubic inches (cu in; in³) | X 16.387 | = Cubic centimetres (cc; cm³) | X 0.061 | = Cubic inches (cu in; in³) |
| Imperial pints (Imp pt) | X 0.568 | = Litres (l) | X 1.76 | = Imperial pints (Imp pt) |
| Imperial quarts (Imp qt) | X 1.137 | = Litres (l) | X 0.88 | = Imperial quarts (Imp qt) |
| Imperial quarts (Imp qt) | X 1.201 | = US quarts (US qt) | X 0.833 | = Imperial quarts (Imp qt) |
| US quarts (US qt) | X 0.946 | = Litres (l) | X 1.057 | = US quarts (US qt) |
| Imperial gallons (Imp gal) | X 4.546 | = Litres (l) | X 0.22 | = Imperial gallons (Imp gal) |
| Imperial gallons (Imp gal) | X 1.201 | = US gallons (US gal) | X 0.833 | = Imperial gallons (Imp gal) |
| US gallons (US gal) | X 3.785 | = Litres (l) | X 0.264 | = US gallons (US gal) |
| ***Mass (weight)*** | | | | |
| Ounces (oz) | X 28.35 | = Grams (g) | X 0.035 | = Ounces (oz) |
| Pounds (lb) | X 0.454 | = Kilograms (kg) | X 2.205 | = Pounds (lb) |
| ***Force*** | | | | |
| Ounces-force (ozf; oz) | X 0.278 | = Newtons (N) | X 3.6 | = Ounces-force (ozf; oz) |
| Pounds-force (lbf; lb) | X 4.448 | = Newtons (N) | X 0.225 | = Pounds-force (lbf; lb) |
| Newtons (N) | X 0.1 | = Kilograms-force (kgf; kg) | X 9.81 | = Newtons (N) |
| ***Pressure*** | | | | |
| Pounds-force per square inch (psi; lbf/in²; lb/in²) | X 0.070 | = Kilograms-force per square centimetre (kgf/cm²; kg/cm²) | X 14.223 | = Pounds-force per square inch (psi; lbf/in²; lb/in²) |
| Pounds-force per square inch (psi; lbf/in²; lb/in²) | X 0.068 | = Atmospheres (atm) | X 14.696 | = Pounds-force per square inch (psi; lbf/in²; lb/in²) |
| Pounds-force per square inch (psi; lbf/in²; lb/in²) | X 0.069 | = Bars | X 14.5 | = Pounds-force per square inch (psi; lbf/in²; lb/in²) |
| Pounds-force per square inch (psi; lbf/in²; lb/in²) | X 6.895 | = Kilopascals (kPa) | X 0.145 | = Pounds-force per square inch (psi; lbf/in²; lb/in²) |
| Kilopascals (kPa) | X 0.01 | = Kilograms-force per square centimetre (kgf/cm²; kg/cm²) | X 98.1 | = Kilopascals (kPa) |
| Millibar (mbar) | X 100 | = Pascals (Pa) | X 0.01 | = Millibar (mbar) |
| Millibar (mbar) | X 0.0145 | = Pounds-force per square inch (psi; lbf/in²; lb/in²) | X 68.947 | = Millibar (mbar) |
| Millibar (mbar) | X 0.75 | = Millimetres of mercury (mmHg) | X 1.333 | = Millibar (mbar) |
| Millibar (mbar) | X 0.401 | = Inches of water ($inH_2O$) | X 2.491 | = Millibar (mbar) |
| Millimetres of mercury (mmHg) | X 0.535 | = Inches of water ($inH_2O$) | X 1.868 | = Millimetres of mercury (mmHg) |
| Inches of water ($inH_2O$) | X 0.036 | = Pounds-force per square inch (psi; lbf/in²; lb/in²) | X 27.68 | = Inches of water ($inH_2O$) |
| ***Torque (moment of force)*** | | | | |
| Pounds-force inches (lbf in; lb in) | X 1.152 | = Kilograms-force centimetre (kgf cm; kg cm) | X 0.868 | = Pounds-force inches (lbf in; lb in) |
| Pounds-force inches (lbf in; lb in) | X 0.113 | = Newton metres (Nm) | X 8.85 | = Pounds-force inches (lbf in; lb in) |
| Pounds-force inches (lbf in; lb in) | X 0.083 | = Pounds-force feet (lbf ft; lb ft) | X 12 | = Pounds-force inches (lbf in; lb in) |
| Pounds-force feet (lbf ft; lb ft) | X 0.138 | = Kilograms-force metres (kgf m; kg m) | X 7.233 | = Pounds-force feet (lbf ft; lb ft) |
| Pounds-force feet (lbf ft; lb ft) | X 1.356 | = Newton metres (Nm) | X 0.738 | = Pounds-force feet (lbf ft; lb ft) |
| Newton metres (Nm) | X 0.102 | = Kilograms-force metres (kgf m; kg m) | X 9.804 | = Newton metres (Nm) |
| ***Power*** | | | | |
| Horsepower (hp) | X 745.7 | = Watts (W) | X 0.0013 | = Horsepower (hp) |
| ***Velocity (speed)*** | | | | |
| Miles per hour (miles/hr; mph) | X 1.609 | = Kilometres per hour (km/hr; kph) | X 0.621 | = Miles per hour (miles/hr; mph) |
| ***Fuel consumption**** | | | | |
| Miles per gallon, Imperial (mpg) | X 0.354 | = Kilometres per litre (km/l) | X 2.825 | = Miles per gallon, Imperial (mpg) |
| Miles per gallon, US (mpg) | X 0.425 | = Kilometres per litre (km/l) | X 2.352 | = Miles per gallon, US (mpg) |

***Temperature***

Degrees Fahrenheit = (°C x 1.8) + 32

Degrees Celsius (Degrees Centigrade; °C) = (°F - 32) x 0.56

**It is common practice to convert from miles per gallon (mpg) to litres/100 kilometres (l/100km), where mpg (Imperial) x l/100 km = 282 and mpg (US) x l/100 km = 235*

# Index